BENEDICT XVI: A LIFE

BENEDICT XVI: A LIFE

Volume II
Professor and Prefect
to Pope and Pope Emeritus
1966–The Present

Peter Seewald

Translated by Dinah Livingstone

BLOOMSBURY CONTINUUM
LONDON · OXFORD · NEW YORK · NEW DELHI · SYDNEY

BLOOMSBURY CONTINUUM
Bloomsbury Publishing Plc
50 Bedford Square, London, WC1B 3DP, UK
29 Earlsfort Terrace, Dublin 2, Ireland

BLOOMSBURY, BLOOMSBURY CONTINUUM and the Diana logo are trademarks
of Bloomsbury Publishing Plc

First published in 2020 in Germany as *Benedikt XVI: Ein Leben* by Droemer Verlag, an imprint
of Verlagsgruppe Droemer Knaur GmbH & Co.KG, Munich

First published in Great Britain 2021

A catalogue record for this book is available from the British Library
Library of Congress Cataloguing-in-Publication data has been applied for

ISBN: HB: 978-1-4729-7921-6; eBook: 978-1-4729-7925-4; ePDF: 978-1-4729-7923-0

2 4 6 8 10 9 7 5 3 1

Typeset by Deanta Global Publishing Services, Chennai, India
Printed and bound in Great Britain by CPI Group (UK) Ltd, Croydon CR0 4YY

To find out more about our authors and books visit www.bloomsbury.com
and sign up for our newsletters

Contents

List of Illustrations   vii

PART ONE PROFESSOR

1 Tübingen   3
2 Deeply Afraid   13
3 1968 and the Myth of the Change   23
4 The Catholic Crisis   35
5 A Fresh Start   47
6 Tensions   56
7 The Vision of the Church of the Future   66
8 Reconquest   77
9 The Doctrine of Eternal Life   88
10 Archbishop   100
11 The Year of Three Popes   112
12 The Küng Case   123
13 The Legacy of Munich   134

PART TWO PREFECT

14 The Prefect   149
15 Ratzinger's Report   161
16 The Fight over Liberation Theology   174
17 Teamwork   185
18 The Collapse   196
19 The Long Suffering of Karol Wojtyła   212
20 Millennium   225
21 Agony   240
22 Conclave   257
23 *Habemus Papam*   272

PART THREE POPE

24 The First Pope of the Third Millennium   287
25 In the Shoes of the Fisherman   300
26 Benedetto Mania   315
27 The Regensburg Speech   328
28 *Deus caritas est*   345
29 Salt of the Earth, Light of the World   356
30 The Rupture   373
31 The Condom Crisis   399
32 The Abuse Scandal   414
33 The Shepherd   433
34 Human Ecology   445
35 Desecularization   456
36 The Betrayal   470
37 The Resignation   487
38 The Beginning of a New Era   503

Afterword: Final Questions to Benedict XVI   533

Notes   540
Index   558

List of Illustrations

1. Archbishop Joseph Ratzinger greets Roger Schutz, the founder of the Taizé community, at the ecumenical prayer night in the Cathedral of Our Lady in Munich, 1978. (© KNA-Bild)
2. Joseph Ratzinger prays at the Auschwitz concentration camp with Polish and German bishops, 13 September 1980. (© KNA-Bild)
3. Pope John Paul II and Joseph Ratzinger during John Paul II's visit to Germany, November 1980. (© INTERFOTO/amw)
4. Ratzinger gives communion to the severely ill Pope John Paul II. (© picture alliance/dpa/EPA/Maurizio Brambatti)
5. As dean of the College of Cardinals, Ratzinger celebrates John Paul II's funeral mass in Rome on 8 April 2005. (© Getty Images/Peter Macdiarmid)
6. Joseph Ratzinger steps out onto the balcony of St Peter's as Pope Benedict XVI, 19 April 2009. (© Getty Images/WireImage/Daniele Venturelli)
7. Benedict XVI and his private secretary, Georg Gänswein. (© picture alliance/Stefano Spaziani)
8. Benedict XVI at his summer residence in Castel Gandolfo. (© Getty Images/Mondadori Portfolio/Archivio Grzegorz Galazka)
9. Students welcome Benedict XVI to the Cologne World Youth Day, 18 August 2005. (© Getty Images/Pool Bassignac/Vandeville/Gamma-Rapho)
10. The pope gives communion to a nun. (© Getty Images/AFP/Patrick Hertzog)
11. An aerial picture of the mass celebrated on 20 August 2005 in Marienfeld, near Cologne, on the twentieth World Youth Day. (© imago/Ulmer)

12. Benedict XVI meets with former concentration camp prisoners at Auschwitz–Birkenau, 28 May 2005. (© picture-alliance/dpa/EPA/Radek Pietruszka)
13. Benedict XVI visits the Wailing Wall on his 2009 trip to Jerusalem. (© Getty Images/Menahem Kahana-Pool)
14. Benedict XVI prays at Ground Zero in New York with relatives of the victims of the 2001 9/11 attacks. (© picture-alliance/dpa/EPA/Max Rossi)
15. Benedict XVI visits Benin on his second trip to Africa. (© Getty Images/AFP/Alessandro Bianchi)
16. To the shock of the cardinals assembled in the Sala del Concistoro, Benedict XVI announces his resignation on 11 February 2013. (© picture alliance/AP Photo/*L'Osservatore Romano*)
17. The helicopter carrying Pope Benedict XVI on the last day of his papacy flies over the dome of St Peter's on its way to Castel Gandolfo, 28 February 2013. (© Getty Images/Giorgio Cosulich)
18. Pope Benedict XVI and Pope Francis, pictured during the visit of Pope Francis to his predecessor in the Vatican. (© KNA/ Servizio Fotografico Vaticano)

PART ONE

Professor

I

Tübingen

Nineteen sixty-six was a year of geopolitical, social and socio-cultural change that gave the world a hefty shove. The uncrewed Soviet spacecraft Luna 9 made a soft landing on the moon and sent television pictures back to Earth for the first time. There was a military coup in Argentina. African countries such as Botswana and Lesotho declared independence. In China the beginning of the 'Great Proletarian Cultural Revolution' was announced on 18 August. The waves of purges carried out by Mao Zedong's 'Red Guards' would cost millions of human lives.

The USA began their air attacks on North Vietnam. In Los Angeles the so-called race riots (the Watts riots) were brutally suppressed by the National Guard. Thirty-four African Americans were killed and 800 were severely injured. In Barcelona the first student riots forced the university management to suspend teaching. Rome University was also closed, after 1,500 students occupied the campus and forced the rector to resign.

Young people went their own way. That was expressed in colourful hippie gear, mini-skirts and long hair. Performers such as Bob Dylan, John Lee Hooker, The Animals, The Doors, Procol Harum and the Rolling Stones created the rhythm for the new way of life. The year's top 100 songs included 'Summer in the City', 'My Generation' and 'Good Vibrations'. Most popular of all were The Beatles who, as John Lennon casually remarked, were 'now more popular than Jesus'.

In German universities the Socialist German Students' Society (Sozialistische Deutsche Studentenbund, or SDS) appeared, and became increasingly radicalized. The Frankfurt School provided the theoretical basis for the fermentation with newly brushed-up ideas from Hegel and Marx. Their gurus included Theodor W. Adorno, Herbert Marcuse and Max Horkheimer. Adorno's *Dialektik der Aufklärung* (*Dialectic of Enlightenment*) put the capitalist 'culture industry' on trial. According to the book, its control methods were subtler than those of authoritarian regimes but no less effective. The masses were indoctrinated through the media, intellectually lulled and groomed to adapt.

The theology professor Joseph Ratzinger, who was now 39, was at the height of his career. He had achieved everything that an academic could: attention, recognition, influence. His mop of hair had now turned a distinguished grey, belying his otherwise youthful appearance. But everyone took the theological rising star for what he was, and still greater things were expected of him. He had worked in Rome together with the greatest theologians of the time – and that was where he found his final master. The Cologner Gottlieb Söhngen had developed Ratzinger into a brilliant theologian in Munich. Another Cologner, Cardinal Joseph Frings, gave him what he still lacked, such as the art of dealing with the high-ranking Curia monsignori or the courage to correct himself if necessary, and really to assimilate new insights.

Frings was a practical man, a people's priest, who had worked for a quarter of a century as a simple pastor. Then through his experience, steadiness and unobtrusive, almost aristocratic manner he had risen at the Second Vatican Council to become one of the most important figures in the universal church. Ratzinger was the better theologian, but he profited from Frings's diplomacy and composure. Whereas his contemporaries, like Küng, often shot from the hip, in the cardinal's school Ratzinger always remained cautious, in order then to hit exactly the right spot. He took Frings as his model, thinking of him 'as a father'. He was grateful and perhaps even guessed that one day he would have to shoulder great burdens himself. Perhaps the secret of their synergy could best be described in the words Ratzinger spoke in December 1978 at Frings's funeral. His master, he said, 'regarded people and the world from God's viewpoint and God and heaven from the human viewpoint'.

Ratzinger's move from Münster to the Protestant university city of Tübingen was one of the most puzzling decisions in the life of the future pope. All the later forks in his road followed an inner logic and were generally not chosen by himself. Ratzinger was a fighter, but then again he let personal things run their course and often chose according to how he felt, without displaying a particular goal or ambition. However, his farewell to Münster, in Westphalia, did not just come out of the blue. His brother Georg had moved from Traunstein to the Danube and was now leading the world-famous Regensburg Domspatzen ('Cathedral Sparrows') boys' choir. In Münster his sister Maria missed her friends and felt lonely. Recently she had also become afraid of one of the students in the house, who suffered from a psychosis. She never tired of saying that her favourite place in Münster was the city's railway station, from which trains departed to Bavaria.

Ratzinger would happily have moved to Munich. The chair of dogmatics was vacant at the Ludwig Maximilian University, but he was not on the list of professors wished for by the faculty. Indeed, Söhngen and a few others had voted for Ratzinger. '[Cardinal Julius] Döpfner was also for me,' Ratzinger reported in our conversation. 'But the whole Munich situation would have been difficult for me.' In a telephone conversation he told Karl Rahner, who was involved in the selection process, that they should on no account fall back on him, but should choose the dogmatic theologian Leo Scheffczyk. And, following a decision by the Bavarian state parliament, a new university was being built in Regensburg. That enabled the brother and sister to dream of reuniting the family in one place.

Ratzinger was still hoping to be able to teach in peace, do his research and get on with the great work that he had in mind. He was finding the situation in Münster 'tricky', despite the comfortable provision for his chair as professor, the esteem of his colleagues and the crowd of students at his feet. But now he was not only troubled by the distance from home. ('I am such a Bavarian patriot that for me to live permanently in Münster was simply too far away'.) He was also bothered by the fundamental theologian Johann Baptist Metz, one year his junior. Ratzinger had helped this student of Rahner's to get the teaching chair. The two of them had got on well. However, since Metz had propagated his 'political theology', the relationship had become difficult. He had the growing impression, said Ratzinger, 'that Metz's political theology had taken a wrong direction, trying to bring politics into theology. It was not my thing to be constantly having rows in my own faculty, although I got on well with Metz personally.'[1] He wanted to avoid an open break. So it had 'seemed better to go to Tübingen and enter into the Tübingen tradition'. As well as that, he 'felt closer at that time to Küng's work than to Metz's'.

Tübingen could be an interim solution. During the Council, in July 1964 Hans Küng had already invited him to give a guest lecture there. Küng dreamed of making his faculty the centre of modern theology. But in order to do so, he needed the most capable and popular theologians of the new generation there with him. He also found Ratzinger 'humanly congenial' and praised his 'high standing' and 'great openness to current questions'.[2]

On 2 May 1965 Küng visited Ratzinger in Münster, where they discussed the details of a possible move. Küng promised that the appointment would be treated as *unico loco*, an application with no competition. Nine days later he wrote a letter stressing the joys of Tübingen again, such as 'the academic collaboration with Catholic and Evangelical colleagues in a place with a great free tradition', the 'excellent working conditions' and, with Maria in mind, 'the closeness to your home'. If necessary, they could wait till Easter 1966. In the meantime, they would find a pleasant place for him and Maria to live. 'But in that case we would have to be sure that you were coming, so that we were not left without a dove on the roof or a spade in hand.' (A play on the German proverb: 'The spade in hand is better than the dove on the roof'.) On 15 May 1965 Ratzinger replied that on the given conditions, 'I will gladly offer myself as a spade in hand to the Tübingen faculty'.[3]

Küng himself had taken up his chair in the summer semester of 1960. In part 1 of his three-volume memoirs he reported that Hans Urs von Balthasar had been invited before him. After Balthasar declined the post, two more candidates had also dropped out before his name came up.[4] What Küng did not mention was that at the beginning there had been a clear favourite, Ratzinger. But he had already been appointed to Bonn. It was only after Ratzinger, as well as the other candidates, turned down the Tübingen post that the ministry was prepared to appoint a theologian such as Küng, who had no *habilitation* (the post-doctoral qualification for a full professorship at a German university). It was a way to solve the problem, although contrary to Rome's stipulations. As Daniel Deckers related in his biography of Karl Lehmann, it was also despite the misgivings of Hermann Volk (Küng's professor in Münster), Michael Keller (the bishop in charge of the Münster faculty) and Franziskus von Streng of Basel (Küng's home bishop).[5]

Independently from each other, Volk, Keller and von Streng had advised the bishop of Rottenburg, Carl Josef Leiprecht, who was in charge of the Tübingen faculty, to defer Küng's appointment. Certainly, the young man was highly gifted but also very self-absorbed. The prelate Josef Höfer, theological adviser to the German embassy to the Holy See, warned Küng that his 'book about the Council, in my opinion, had better not be published. You must definitely keep it quiet.'[6] Küng obeyed and begged Verlag Herder to delay publication of his book, *The Council and Reunion*, until he was sure of his professorial chair.

In the mid-1960s Tübingen was a small town with 40,000 inhabitants. For any self-respecting theologian it was the Promised Land, organically developed in the rarefied world of an inter-denominational intellectual elite. The Evangelical faculty had been founded in the late Middle Ages, and a Catholic faculty had been added to it at the beginning of the nineteenth century. In the summer semester of 1966 the university had 7,467 students, with 547 in the Evangelical faculty and 315 in the Catholic faculty. On the Olympus of German theology Ratzinger looked forward to 'interesting meetings with important Evangelical theologians'. In the cosy little Swabian town of Hegel, Schelling and Hölderlin they saw themselves as an emphatically critical vanguard.

Ratzinger's new home, a plain end-of-terrace house, was at 22 Friedrich-Dannemann Street, a peaceful situation on the edge of the town with a view of the Wurmlinger Kapelle. He enjoyed the 'magic of the little Swabian town' with its Alemannic half-timbered houses, the sleepy squares in the old town and the quiet water meadows on the banks of the Neckar. His sister Maria took charge of the housekeeping. There was also a neighbour's black cat called Panther, who accompanied him every morning on his way to celebrate Mass. His assistant was Peter Kuhn, who drove him through the town in a rusty Citroën 2CV. Occasionally Esther Betz came to visit, and 'Uncle Ratzinger', as her nephew called him, hurried to meet her at the station to carry her suitcase and amble together through the town.

At first, Ratzinger commuted by train to give the main lecture on dogmatics at his new workplace and also still hold seminars and examinations in Münster. Together with a Lebanese student in Tübingen he visited Ernst Bloch and was amused that the celebrated left-wing philosopher awkwardly held a hookah in his hand, although he insisted that he smoked it regularly. There was no return invitation. It is a myth that he met Küng for dinner every week on Thursdays, but it is true that they got on well.

'I completely agree with my colleague Ratzinger,' the students heard in Küng's lecture. The reverse was also true: 'I agree with Küng.' However, when they both parked in front of the university, observers noticed a marked difference. The extrovert Swiss Küng drove a smart white Alfa Romeo and was tastefully and elegantly dressed. The reserved Bavarian Ratzinger wore a beret and bent over his old bicycle in the corner. Their appearance acted 'as a symbol of two theological worlds', was how Küng's biographer described the scene. It was an image contrasting 'a speedy with a dogged, and a worldly with a modest' theology. 'Even when Küng flashed past, Ratzinger always sat a bit higher. One was fast and the other had more of an overview.'

The two professors had equally large audiences, of 400. Both of them were editors of the *Ökumenische Forschungen* (*Ecumenical Investigations*) series, in which Küng's work on *The Church* was published that later caused his conflict with Rome. Their collaboration went very well, perhaps, as the assistant Siegfried Wiedenhofer observed, because at first neither of them formulated their 'important theological differences'.[7] Even when Ratzinger refused to give a reference for Josef Nolte, a doctoral student of Küng's, he explained that he did not want to prevent Nolte getting his doctorate with a thesis that adopted Küng's theology in its purest form. Nolte later distanced himself from Küng. Who but his former teacher could 'package his dogmas so that the mind perceives almost nothing?' he argued in his *Spiegel* article. 'Only Küng can do that. With quick tricks and James Bond mannerisms he tells us even Catholics could drop all their clothing and get to heaven blown on the wind of the world.'[8]

As in Bonn and Münster before, the Tübingen students also found Ratzinger helpful and friendly but also, according to his assistant Peter Kuhn, occasionally 'a bit odd'. Ratzinger 'never reprimanded anyone' but also did nearly everything by himself. Faced with Ratzinger's 'singular personality', Kuhn felt it was his job to 'break down the barrier, smash the glass container in which he got no air. For when you got through he was glad.' 'Every person is a riddle,' Kuhn mused, 'and Ratzinger is a particularly difficult riddle. I know him and yet at the same time I don't know him.'[9]

With his doctoral students Ratzinger visited Hans Urs von Balthasar in Basel, as well as the Protestant theologian Karl Barth, one of his 'theological fathers, with whom I grew up under Gottlieb Söhngen's auspices'. Ratzinger's habit of beginning his seminars with a Mass seemed rather exotic in Tübingen. 'The meaning was: first talk with God and then about God,' said Ratzinger's Italian student Cornelio del Zotto. Ratzinger had 'a harmonious vision of humanity and the world, an unbelievable ability to get to the heart of things and the truth of everything. Personally, I can say that he revealed to me the wonderful elaboration of God's word, thereby showing us the meaning of humanity, the world and history.' Ratzinger's motto 'co-operatores veritatis: fellow-workers for the truth' did not mean working individually but working together. 'It is not about something external but an inner development. A development of the spirit is a new dimension of being.'[10]

One day in the lecture hall there was an open debate on the primacy of the pope. Küng discussed with several other professors and declared that the true model of a pope was embodied in John XXIII, whose primacy had not had a legal but a pastoral character. Ratzinger was sitting in the audience when the students began chanting his name: 'Rat-zing-er! Rat-zing-er!' They wanted to know what *he* thought about it. Calmly he explained that Küng's description ought to be corrected, because every aspect of the papacy should be taken into account. If only the pastoral aspect was kept in mind, then the risk would arise that the pope was not presented as the shepherd of the universal church but perhaps as a universal puppet, who could be manipulated at will.

A common denominator between Küng and Ratzinger was freedom as the prerequisite for ecumenical dialogue. Küng sent his colleague his

Theologische Meditation (*Theological Meditation*), and Ratzinger replied that he did not need to say 'how much I agree with you on this matter'. In January 1967, in their joint series, they both called for the 'jettisoning of theological deadweight' and the solution to 'problems separating the churches'. 'And then that stroke of luck!' Walter Jens, the professor of rhetoric, rejoiced in the university magazine *Attempto!* over both the champion theologians: 'A fundamental article from Ratzinger's pen, the basis for ongoing reflections, rising boldly into the sky like a rocket, launched in Swiss colours.'[11]

Küng was regarded as the leader of a new church, open to the world. He was able to express Christian faith in a language that had an aura of freedom and independence. 'He looked forward with Ratzinger to leading the Council theology to new heights,' Kuhn reported. 'Of course, Ratzinger embodied an aspect of the church that Küng hated, but at the same time Küng respected him.'[12] In Küng's vision, together with Ratzinger, Johann Baptist Metz and second-rank professors such as Hermann Häring, Küng's assistant Walter Kasper and Rahner's assistant Karl Lehmann, he could create a bastion of German theology in Tübingen. They had the journal *Concilium* at their disposal as a forum.

The plan was good. However, it depended on a serious misjudgement. Karl Rahner, for example, had long since turned away from Küng. Their brotherhood in arms had become a mutual aversion. Progressive allies such as Henri de Lubac had also withdrawn and were wary of Küng's ecumenical ideas. De Lubac thought it would not help understanding between the denominations if, without due care, theologians on the Catholic side reached a premature consensus where none existed.

Above all, Küng disregarded and wanted to disregard the fact that his colleague Ratzinger, one year his senior, had long since warned against precisely those developments that Küng had in mind as the follow-up to the Council. 'I wish for you the gift of discernment of spirits,' Ratzinger had said at his farewell lecture in Münster on 25 May 1966: 'It will be necessary for the future of the church!' That was not just talk. During the Council debates he told his Münster colleagues, whom he had taken out once more to dinner, 'I became aware that tradition – persisting and remaining – are also key words in the New Testament.'[13]

Ratzinger still saw himself as belonging to the progressive forces. Unlike Küng, he never split from his travelling companions of Council days. He sympathized with all the theologians who were known and persecuted in Rome as dissidents. One was the Belgian Dominican Marie-Dominique Chenu, whose *Manifesto* was put on the Index by decree of the Holy Office. Another was the Frenchman Yves Congar, who was 'one of the people I respect most'.[14] Ratzinger also said that he owed 'great new insights' to reading the works of Henri de Lubac. And Jean Daniélou supplied him with the historical material on which he based the thesis that Christianity was 'essentially faith in an event' – God's entry into human history and being with us – and not a cosmic or mystical religion like others.

'Certainly I was progressive,' he said in our conversation. 'At that time "progressive" did not yet mean that you broke away from the faith, but that you learned from its origins to understand it better and live it better.' Translating the faith into the present, the search for up-to-date forms in teaching and liturgy, was the first requirement for any advance towards being a missionary church. His difference from other theologians was that Ratzinger argued *with* the church's faith and never *against* it. In a contribution to the journal *Wort und Wahrheit* in 1960 he wrote: 'The point is to rescue the faith from the rigidity of the system and reawaken its original vital power, without giving up what is really valid in it.' He said in a lecture for Frings that the aim was the one 'that the pope set for this Council, namely to renew Christian life and to adapt church discipline to the demands of the time, so that witness to the faith can shine with a new brightness in the darkness of this world'.[15]

Rebellion against obsolete ideas and opposition to a fossilized authority were not only key points in his *Sturm und Drang* period. Ratzinger was disgusted by a conventional, all too conformist, Christianity lulled by its cosiness. He had grown up with a theology of renewal, which sought to reclaim the whole deposit of faith and at the same time to deal constructively with contemporary life, thought and knowledge. He understood the word 'awakening' as 'revitalizing'. It was not primarily about reorganization but about inward, spiritual reforms. The church could not win people over by inappropriate adaptation to the world. It would just lose itself.

The German input was what had made the Second Vatican Council become open and forward-looking. At the beginning of the 1960s, no one else could express the agenda of the Catholic Church more accurately and in such inspired words as Ratzinger. But neither did anyone else grasp so early on that, instead of the desired 'leap forward', it might all turn into a 'process of decline and fall'.

He reported later: 'An important difference had arisen between what the Council fathers wanted and what was communicated to the public and became the general awareness.'[16] 'The fathers wanted to bring the faith up to date – but express it in its full force.' Instead, an impression had arisen that '"reform" simply meant discarding dead weight; making it easier for ourselves, so that now reform was not seen as a radicalization of the faith but as a kind of watering down of the faith'.[17]

2

Deeply Afraid

The post-conciliar debate had not only triggered discussions about the historical Jesus, the interpretation of Scripture and questions about virgin birth and infallibility. Suddenly the debate began to see-saw awkwardly between church reform and church crisis, between happy creativity and loss of identity.

To many it seemed as if a dark cloud had appeared, obscuring the understanding of faith and church. Priests claiming to be emancipated invented their own private Masses; others took to the pulpit and preached to the faithful like soapbox orators. Baptisms, weddings and church attendance declined dramatically, and confession became an exception. Even in strictly Catholic families, the parish priests complained, life became ever more secular. The Tübingen student Helmut Moll reported:

> In lectures the professors seemed to have lost the consensus about what was essential to the faith. A position had to be taken towards things that had previously been beyond question: does the devil exist or not? Are there seven sacraments or only two? Is there a primacy of the bishop of Rome, or is the papacy merely a despotic regime that should be abolished?[1]

Ratzinger was 'deeply disturbed by the change in the church climate, that was becoming increasingly evident'. He saw ever more clearly the danger of a falsification of the Council. There was 'no reason for scepticism and despair', was still his judgement on its third session: There 'was every reason for hope, confidence and patience'. But even before the beginning of the fourth session his tone changed. He expressed a first clear warning in a lecture to the Catholic university community in Münster on 18 June 1965. His subject was 'true and false renewal in the church'. He tried to illustrate the dangers with two examples from history. The first was Gnosticism in Corinth in the apostle Paul's time, when 'Christian freedom' changed into 'unauthorized reforming zeal'. His other example was the 'chaotic fanaticism' in Martin Luther's time. Even in such a sensible town as Münster there had been a fanatical movement, against hierarchy and for a renewal of society by a transformation of values. Finally, a reign of dread developed from this zealotry. He was referring to the radical sect of Anabaptists, who in 1533, after the Reformation, set up a kind of early Christian community. The results of this 'theocracy' were terror and famine, until the prince-bishop's mercenaries, together with others, put an end to the commune.

For Ratzinger these two historical events were examples of two different kinds of false renewal. The first was an obstinate pursuit of an individual course, the second a rejection of tradition in order to adapt to the world. In contrast to these, true Christian renewal, he stressed, led to a new 'simplicity'. For the Council the opposite to conservative was not progressive but missionary. That antithesis expressed what the Council meant and what it did not mean by opening up to the world. It was not to make Christians more comfortable by releasing them to conform with a worldly or fashionable mass culture, but demanded the nonconformity of the Bible: 'Do not be conformed to this world.'[2] One particular statement by their professor in June 1965 made his listeners prick up their ears: many of those who in the first three Council sessions had 'struggled and suffered together to bring about renewal', said Ratzinger, had felt since then almost as if they were being crushed between two millstones.

A year before that Ratzinger had already attracted attention by his critical remarks. He complained that in their Council reporting some journalists tended to reduce complex matters to slogans and so give a false impression to the public. That tendency was reinforced by individual Council theologians who expressed their own interests and demands in the press as the views and aims of the Council fathers.[3] Later Ratzinger also added a criticism of his own fellow workers: 'The part that theologians played at the Council increasingly created a new self-awareness among scholars who saw themselves as the true custodians of knowledge, which meant that they could no longer be subordinate to church leaders.' In his analysis he pointed out the consequences of that revision: 'Behind this tendency towards the dominance of specialists, another could also be felt, the idea of a people's sovereignty over the church, whereby the people themselves decided what they wanted church to mean.'[4]

Indeed, long before his move to Tübingen, no one could fail to see what was disturbing the celebrated young star theologian. From the beginning of 1966 he used every opportunity to make clear his concern. For example, from 13 January until 24 February he gave a series of one-hour lectures on the right interpretation and implementation of the Council's resolutions. The Council fathers' basic intention was expressed particularly in the pastoral constitution *Gaudium et spes* (*Joy and Hope*): to bring Christ closer to the world of today. There is a draft prologue to that document in Joseph Ratzinger's handwriting in the archive of Benedict XVI in Regensburg. It sounds a disillusioned note: 'The church has indeed tried to open its doors to the world, but the world has not streamed into the church's open house. It gives us an even harder time.'[5]

The Italian writer Gianni Valente reported that the advances that so enthused Ratzinger during the Council – biblical renewal, opening up to the world, the question of unity with other Christians, freeing the church from illusions that hindered its mission – 'had nothing in common with the destructive, almost iconoclastic progressivism, with which many of his colleagues seemed to be obsessed'.[6] In a lecture series during the 1966 summer semester Ratzinger recalled earlier councils which saw themselves as reforming councils but had always come out 'against the secularization of the church'. They were 'inspired by the desire for holiness, for a Christian radicalism, purified from worldliness and standing firm in its unconditional claim and message, against what Christ is not'. However, the Second Vatican Council was 'apparently' seen quite differently by the public. Its goal was 'not seen as desecularization but as opening up to the world'. Among other things this 'resulted in a shifting of the battle front': 'The approval came first from the outside, from those who did not share the church's faith and life, whereas those who truly did share in the church's life might feel they were being condemned.'[7]

As a theologian who learned from Augustine, Newman and Guardini and was inspired by the 'Nouvelle Théologie', Ratzinger made no secret of the fact that he could not go along with the new 'progressivist' triumphalism. Through his studies of Bonaventure he had become immune to blind faith in the future or hopes for the uninterrupted progress of humanity. In his 1966 lecture series he saw Christianity in Europe as heading towards 'a radical minority situation'. He used the 1966 Catholics' Conference in Bamberg to speak to a large audience on 'the shadow side of "Catholicism after the Council"':

> Let us say it openly. There exists a certain dismay, a feeling of disillusionment and disappointment [...] For some the Council still did too little. But for others it is a scandal, a surrender of the church to the evil spirit of the time, whose eclipse of God results from its wrongheaded obsession with earthly things. They see with alarm how what was holiest for them is faltering. So they turn sadly away from a renewal that seems to degrade and dissolve Christianity, when what is needed is more faith, hope and love.[8]

Ratzinger spoke with hindsight of that 'first warning signal' he had tried to give in Bamberg. However, the warning had been 'hardly noticed'. The Bamberg Catholics' Conference went down in history as the 'turbulent conference'. *Der Spiegel* reported on 18 July 1966: 'The discord – which had previously been between Evangelicals – also spread among the Catholics at the Catholics' Conference.' The magazine quoted Bishop Franz Hengsbach of Essen: 'It is a stormy time for the church.'

As the fundamental theologian Siegfried Wiedenhofer reported, Ratzinger's criticism was that in the prevalent progressivist mentality church reform 'leads to a mere adaptation to a plausible modern culture and society'. A false modernization threatened the identity of faith, church and theology. Ratzinger's recommended cure was to 'take the measure of the church's faith as it is expressed in the testimonies of Scripture, the church fathers, dogma, liturgy and the saints. The church should be redirected towards the core and essence of the faith.'[9] However, the Catholic establishment was affronted by Ratzinger's remarks. The first sign of the changed attitude to him was the public disapproval expressed by Julius Döpfner, who had become chairman of the Bishops' Conference. Döpfner spoke of a 'conservative streak' which he thought he discerned in Ratzinger, the still celebrated *peritus*. That was the beginning of the latent uneasiness felt by some of the German bishops about this uncomfortable admonisher, which lasted throughout his career, up to his papacy and beyond.

Others felt differently about Ratzinger's approach. For example, the Jesuit Henri de Lubac, who had participated in the Council, wrote to the editor of the French Catholic newspaper *La Croix*: 'I have just read in *La Croix* about Dr Joseph Ratzinger's speech at the Catholics' Conference, and if you will allow me, I should like to add: this text by Dr Ratzinger contains the model for a strong course correction, which is urgently needed in the genuine spirit of the Council and true *aggiornamento*.' De Lubac regarded Ratzinger's view as salvation 'from the muddy holes of a "progressivism" which leads us to spiritual corruption', and also as the answer to 'many people's longing for genuine renewal'. He appealed to the editor of *La Croix* 'firmly to follow the course indicated by this speech of Dr Ratzinger's. The Holy Father and our bishops will surely be grateful to you for that.' It would help all Christians 'who are unsettled by the current confusion faithfully to follow the true way of the gospel'.[10]

Ratzinger remained firmly convinced that the Council texts were in total continuity with the faith. A clear interpretation of them really opened 'a way forward which offers a long future'. He also had no doubt that the great church assembly had been necessary. 'So was it a mistake to call the Second Vatican Council?' I asked Benedict XVI in our conversations. 'No, it was definitely right,' was his answer. It had been 'a moment in the church when something new was expected, a renewal by the whole church, not just by Rome. It was simply the right time.'

In February 1968 Ratzinger insisted in an essay that 'the upheaval in theology begun in Rome' was 'one of the most important requirements for the future renewal of the church'. Theology 'of course always remained bound to the faith, but within that bond freedom was necessary. And that freedom in theology is one of he most important things to happen at the Second Vatican Council.'[11] However, he remarked critically: 'A non-specialist will not be able to recognize what was decisively new in the Council documents. That could hardly be doubted.'[12] Increasingly often people now spoke about 'the spirit of the Council' but no longer referred to its actual statements, only to what it might have meant.

Ratzinger was a reformer who wanted to regain the treasure, rather than to plunder it. He and Cardinal Frings had been firmly convinced that at the Council they would 'make a big contribution to the church of today and tomorrow', he said in his interview in 1988. They had returned from Rome 'full of hope'. But when he became a professor in Tübingen he realized 'how differently they interpreted the Council'. In his faculty one of the theologians – 'who I knew had fallen away from the faith, because he had told me so, who did not believe in anything – began to teach that his opinion was true Catholicism'. That 'demolition of what the Council had been' gave Ratzinger 'great pain'.[13]

Ratzinger was not alone in his feelings. Many progressive voices that had significantly influenced the Council shared in his criticism. De Lubac and Congar warned of betrayal and excesses. Important academics, artists and writers – such as Julien Green, Salvador Dalí and Georges Brassens – signed a petition to the Vatican to stop the distortions. Hans Urs von Balthasar praised the high quality of the texts adopted by the Council but criticized the fact that small-minded folk had homed in on them. These people wanted to make themselves cheaply interesting by selling old liberal stocks as new Catholic theology.

In 1965 during the Council's last session De Lubac had already resigned from the editorial board of Küng's journal *Concilium*. He said he had realised how far the post-conciliar teaching had begun to move away from what he regarded as Catholic theology. Twenty years later he even spoke of an 'underground council' that had been active since 1962, determined to break away from the Council in progress. Indeed the pastoral constitution *Gaudium et spes* had recommended an 'opening up to the world'. That was intended to overcome an anxious attitude with which the church egocentrically 'withdraws into a kind of quarantine'.

But aren't we now experiencing the opposite? Through a massive illusion doesn't this 'opening' lead to forgetting what is holy, estrangement from the gospel, dismissing Christ's cross? Isn't it a way into secularism, to letting go, abdication, even a loss of identity, that is a betrayal of our duty to the world?[14]

During a visit to the USA Hubert Jedin remarked that 'through their lectures some German theologians have unleashed a revolutionary wave in the church'. Jedin named no names, but clearly he was referring to Hans Küng, who had just finished a lecture tour in the USA. 'When I returned to Germany in June 1966, the surge of "turbulence" was already very strong.' He concluded by saying: 'The Council set the points, but at this historical moment we can't say where the train will get to.'[15]

Many of the radical reformers supported the view that the faithful should 'participate' actively in the Mass and therefore hold a 'dialogue' with the priest. They regarded traditional prayers such as 'perpetual adoration' or the rosary as negligible devout practices. For example, the Catholic theologian Gotthold Hasenhüttl was soon demanding a 'radical openness to the world' whose culmination would be a 'black pregnant woman pope'. Priests declared proudly that they had removed the cross from their altar, because not every day was Good Friday. Even atheists such as the psychoanalyst Alfred Lorenzer were scandalized by the 'loss of meaning'. The restructuring cut deep into the human symbols, myths, rituals and cult objects and led to a new sort of Catholic, who no longer had any internal or external images with which to understand themselves and others. So their religious devotion became a mere technique, abstract rather than vivid, bare speech that was formalistic without vital forms.[16]

Such procedures somewhat resembled those described by the Austrian academic Joseph Schumpeter as 'creative destruction'. Paul Hacker, Ratzinger's Münster colleague, drummed into him that he ought to come out even more strongly against the dangers and beware of the Protestantization of Catholicism. 'The church no longer radiates. That is my greatest concern,' Hacker complained in a letter of 12 July 1966.

It is particularly those who call loudest for 'openness' who do most to darken the church [...] Their idea of 'openness' is just a worldly diplomatic arrangement [...] The worst ideas are those of the religiously active laity today. With them you can see most plainly that progressivism is merely a different form of the old mistakes.[17]

Ida Friederike Görres, who described her own experiences of the Council as 'amazing and way beyond my expectations', was shocked by the interpretation and application of it that followed. She wrote in February 1966 to a friend: 'Now it often seems as if the specifically Catholic elements – such as priesthood, hierarchy, Eucharist, sacraments – are regarded by many as "excrescences".' The *grande dame* of German Catholicism could not refrain from a side-swipe: 'Küng is very much to blame with his eternal carry-on about the Reformation that has finally arrived 400 years late.' Many of the innovators hoped 'to participate in worldly power through unconditional adaptation to it' and 'worship of the *Zeitgeist*'. Görres found 'the church's relativization of nearly everything it teaches, represents and embodies' to be 'so wholesale, so relentless, that the ground in which I am rooted seems to be collapsing'.[18]

Unintentionally, the Council had brought about an unprecedented cultural revolution within itself. 'Among the clergy and, even more so among the Christian "rank and file", the feeling spread that everything said or heard or read about Jesus was at best a half-truth', according to the theologian Hansjürgen Verweyen. 'Now it seemed as if the choice was between silent agnosticism, blind fundamentalist faith or an exodus into spiritually more attractive forms of truth and security.'[19] According to the political scientist Franz Walter's analysis, 'Catholicism's powers of resistance and immunity from secularization seem to be failing.' Among the Catholic faithful 'there was a growing sense of crisis, pessimism, disorientation and unhappiness'.[20] Cardinal Frings said in his memoirs: 'Indeed then there came a time of crisis in the church and many things were done "in the spirit of the Council" that the Council fathers had not dreamed of.'[21]

In the 1950s there had already been a decrease in vocations, confessions and attendances at Mass. But two years after the end of the Council there was a dramatic drop in churchgoing among Catholics. From 1967 to 1973 it sank from 55 to 35 per cent. Every year until 1970 the number of those leaving the Catholic Church in Germany increased from about 25,000 up to 70,000. Frings was 'deeply afraid', as his biographer Norbert Trippen noted. 'When a revolutionary development came about in the church with people referring to the "spirit of the Council" without regard for what the Council had actually decided,' his conscience was very troubled. 'Have we done everything right?' he implored his secretary Hubert Luthe. According to Luthe, Frings was beset by the question of whether he 'was partly responsible for the Council's unforeseen consequences through his own input into it'.[22] Among those close to him he complained that the whole Nazi period had not tormented him as much as the time after the Council. 'Everyone is talking about the Council,' the old cardinal shook his head, 'and they haven't read the texts.' In his pastoral letter of 25 January 1968 Frings complained of 'self-will, idiosyncrasy and a contraction of church life'. But, he recalled, 'The liturgical reform did not do away with the Latin. Side by side with the single-track Latin a second track was laid for services in the mother tongue. We encouraged priests to cultivate silence during services, the treasury of church hymns and church choirs, as well as traditional forms of popular piety.' The archbishop reflected on the spiritual situation in Germany:

> As you know, in recent times bishops have had to stress repeatedly that the tradition of the faith will be fully maintained. The action of God must not be reinterpreted as purely human imaginings; it is wrong to declare that those ideas from times gone by can no longer be accepted by today's thinking and therefore need to be re-expressed.[23]

The Council pope also supported Ratzinger's diagnosis. 'After the Council the church enjoyed a great awakening and is still enjoying it,' Paul VI recapitulated in a general audience of 25 April 1968, 'but the church has also suffered and is still suffering from a turmoil of ideas and events that are certainly not in a good spirit and do not promise that healthy revival the Council promised and promoted.'[24]

On 21 June 1972, in a sermon on the ninth anniversary of his enthronement, Pope Paul spoke with dramatically increased urgency of the 'powerful and complex change, which no one had expected'. That was not quite true. Italian churchmen, in particular, had warned that the Council's unlooked-for liberality would open sluice gates that should have been kept shut. Then the pope uttered his famous words about 'the reek of Satan that has penetrated through some cracks in God's temple'. He went on: 'Doubt has infiltrated our minds and it has infiltrated though the windows which ought to be open to the light.'

After the end of the Second Vatican Council Ratzinger and colleagues such as de Lubac, Frings, Daniélou, Balthasar, Congar and Jedin found that the drive towards reform would only be outwardly accepted and then adapted to a society that had largely become secular. However, very different questions were soon dominating public discussion. Enthusiasm for the Council was succeeded by an enthusiasm for Marxist ideas. Now it was not about liquidating musty church traditions but about abolishing religion and the church altogether.

At the end of this period the political theorist Franz Walter drew a stark conclusion: for a century 'German Catholicism had successfully defended its values and organizational structures'. 'Because of their traditional values' Catholics had resisted 'the crises produced by modernity' far better than other sectors of the population. The long-standing director of the Göttinger Institute for Democratic Research stressed that modern society had 'undermined the values that provided social and cultural guidelines and identity', because liberal societies 'hardly offered these bonding agents'. After the upheavals of the 1960s and 1970s it had to be said: 'The Catholic way of life, as an easily recognizable and distinguishable group culture, no longer exists as a mass phenomenon.'[25]

3

1968 and the Myth of the Change

On 17 February 1968 thousands of young people gathered in the Audimax of the Free University of Berlin for the first 'International Vietnam Congress', a protest against the USA's continual bombing of North Vietnam. The hall was draped in giant flags in the colours of the Vietcong. Portraits of Ho Chi Minh, Rosa Luxemburg, Che Guevara and Mao Zedong hung on the walls.

The Congress had been summoned by the Socialist German Students' Society. A young man stood up at the lectern. It was the 27-year-old Rudolf 'Rudi' Willi Alfred Dutschke, from Luckenwalde in Brandenburg. He was a bright, eloquent and charismatic rebel who had grown up in the Evangelical youth community in his East German home and celebrated Christ as 'the greatest revolutionary in the world'. Dutschke's voice sounded hoarse, as with raised fist he shouted: 'Long live the world revolution! Long live the free society of free individuals!'[1] Two months later Josef Bachmann shot the student leader on the street. Bachmann was a 23-year-old refugee from the GDR, an unskilled worker with neo-Nazi contacts.

Nobody knows when and how the 1968 revolt began. Was it unease about the atom bomb and racism? The Vietnam War? Perhaps just the younger generation's dream of a different, better world, a new lifestyle without alienation, oppression or monotony. However, the Berlin attack was the signal for an uprising that shook Germany.

Dutschke survived the assassination attempt. He was covered in blood and had been shot in the head and chest. After a five-hour operation he lay in a coma. The icon of the revolution never became wholly fit again. He only reappeared in public in 1973. On Christmas

Eve 1979 he drowned in the bath following an epileptic fit, a long-term effect of the attack. He was 39.

In the evening after the attack on Dutschke the students gave vent to their rage by a march on Springer Verlag, the publisher of *Bild* newspaper, which had harried Dutschke as Public Enemy Number One. There followed five days of street battles in Berlin, Frankfurt, Hamburg and other towns: at 27 different places in total. Twenty-one thousand police were deployed. They fired water cannons and set dogs on the demonstrators. Four hundred people were hurt, many of them badly. In Munich on Easter Monday there was a battle in which the 32-year-old Associated Press photographer Klaus Frings and the 27-year-old student Rüdiger Schreck were killed in circumstances that were never made clear.

After the attack on Dutschke the revolt spread to other countries. In May 1968 in Paris the students engaged in fierce battles with the police. Cars were burned. The Latin Quarter became a no-go area. The rioters saw themselves as successors to the 1871 Paris Commune. Daniel Cohn-Bendit, their most prominent spokesman, later explained in an interview: it was 'a sublime feeling, we were making history'.

For much of the media and many politicians the students were fifth columnists working for Moscow; for many others they were just a mob of drop-outs. 'Stop the Youth Red Terror Now!' screamed a headline in *Bild*. A year earlier, on 2 June 1967, there had been a demonstration during a visit by the Shah of Persia, at which the 26-year-old German philology student Benno Ohnesorg was killed. He was shot in the head by Detective Chief Inspector Karl-Heinz Kurras. Kurras's true identity was only revealed in 2009. He was employed by the GDR Ministry for State Security (Stasi). He had been ordered to fight against the class enemy by acting as an *agent provocateur* to escalate the turbulent situation in West Berlin.

Never before in German history had a generation grown up in such material comfort as the post-1945 generation. In 1968 the Economic Miracle was in full bloom. Unemployment was at 0.9 per cent. But the young people's anger was not about jobs. The revolt was more complex than how it was presented afterwards in the iconographic images of figures such as Dutschke and Fritz Teufel or the later Red Army Faction (RAF) leaders Andreas Baader and Ulrike Meinhof.

It was predominantly a generational conflict, a rebellion against conventional gender roles and upbringing. But 1968 was also about fashion, smart cars, sex, drugs and rock and roll. It was a mixture of many things. Disgust at parents' narrow-mindedness. A desire to provoke and make a fuss. A search for the meaning of life. A longing for justice. The students 'nourished an almost religious faith' in what concerned them, the *Süddeutsche Zeitung* declared 50 years later, picking up on an earlier diagnosis by Joseph Ratzinger, for which he was long berated. Their goal was: 'We could create heaven on Earth. And they raged against capitalism for failing to do so.'[2]

At his university Ratzinger sympathized with the youth protest. He saw it as 'anger against welfare pragmatism'. One of the rebels was Karin, a blonde, pretty but demanding girl, who dreamed of a different, happier life. Ratzinger listened to her, gave her his time and discussed things openly with her. In the light of current events he turned in his lectures from Rudolf Bultmann's demythologizing and Heidegger's existential philosophy to the ideas of Marx and Engels. First he formulated what was positive in Marx, his student Irmgard Schmidt-Sommer reported. 'Then he went on to argue that humanity concerned only with the empirical and the material is an abstract humanity, which does not really connect with people and may turn to violence.'[3]

'The Tübingen faculty had always been argumentative, but that was not the problem,' Ratzinger recalled. 'The problem was really the task presented to us by the time and the invasion of Marxism and its promises.'[4] For him the danger was that 'the corruption of theology, which was now going in the direction of Marxist messianism' fascinated people precisely because 'it was based on the biblical hope'. Here indeed 'the religious fervour remained' but 'God was dismissed and replaced by human political action'.[5]

Ratzinger's analysis corresponded with his *habilitation* research on politicized religious movements in the Middle Ages. These had also electrified people with their promises of earthly salvation, like that offered by the founder of scientific communism from Trier. Marx dreamed of radical social change violently brought about through a 'dictatorship of the proletariat'. He replaced individual freedom with collectivism. Private property and family were to be abolished, the education of children taken over by the state. For Marx one of the main enemies was religion, which he saw as a tool for oppression. 'The criticism of religion is the precondition for all criticism,' he wrote in the introduction to his *Critique of Hegel's Philosophy of Right*.

Many things that Marx said in his communist programme about a society increasingly dominated by capitalist interests sounded compelling; his economic analysis was intelligent and reasonable. Atheism was to replace Judaism and Christianity as the true way of life, offering the goal of an earthly paradise. However, as the editor-in-chief of the *Neue Rheinische Zeitung* Marx, the child of a respected rabbinic family, began to develop racial theories. He wrote about the workers' leader Ferdinand Lassalle as 'The Jewish nigger Lassalle, who is fortunately leaving [the newspaper] at the end of this week [...] It is now completely clear to me, as the shape of his head and the way his hair grows proves, that he is descended from Negroes who came out of Egypt with Moses.'

After his exile in the USA, Ernst Bloch had taught in the GDR, then came to Tübingen, where he propagated neo-Marxist ideas and even found arguments to defend Stalin's purges. Ratzinger, on the other hand, never forgot the terror and misery that had come into the world with atheist regimes. In the first two decades of Soviet power in Russia alone, between 30 and 35 million people were victims of the social transformation, as recent research shows. The Bolsheviks themselves boasted that in the years after the Revolution they had liquidated 28 bishops, 1,215 priests, 6,000 monks, 55 officers, 55,000 police officers and officials, 350,000 academically educated people in public life and 50,000 artisans and peasants.[6] It is a fact that from Stalin's gulags to the battlefields of Cambodia and Mao's death camps there has not been a single communist regime that did not persecute Christianity and other religions. According to *Das Schwarzbuch des Kommunismus* (*The Black Book of Communism*), the Marxist-Leninist-inspired regimes are responsible for the death of about a million people.[7]

In Tübingen they thought they had a defence against 'the onslaught of neo-Marxism', at least among theology students. The previous year had been the 150th anniversary of the founding of the Catholic theological faculty. In a festive procession through the town the professors wore velvet robes with purple trim. In front of them marched their assistants, the so-called ushers, with splendid ceremonial staves. It was to be the last academic festival in the old style. For it was the theological faculties themselves that became the ideological centre of the uproar. 'Existentialism collapsed,' Ratzinger recalled, 'and the Marxist revolution ignited the whole university and shook it to the foundations.'[8]

The rebellion began with sit-ins, demonstrations and blockades of lectures. Increasingly, red activists gained the upper hand, preventing professors from entering the lecture halls or forcing them to answer their 'revolutionary' questions. 'The tone was ideologically determined and rancorous,' Ratzinger reported; 'the university of which I had then become dean boiled over to the point of assaults on professors.'[9]

Everything was up for questioning: your consciousness, which side you were on, what car you drove, what you wore, why you should want to marry and have children. Feminist papers gave young women instructions on how to masturbate with spread legs in front of a mirror. One of the slogans was: 'Sleeping with the same one twice is an Establishment device' (or literally, 'Whoever sleeps with the same one twice belongs to the Establishment'). According to the Munich historian Benedikt Sepp, the aim was 'revolution in every area of life, rebellion against all standards, so-called cultural values and sexual abuse'.[10] Young people enthusiastically brandished Mao's 'Little Red Book' and studied the *Peking Rundschau* (*Peking Review*), 'motivated by the certainty of a globally successful theory feared by the Establishment', which bore the character of 'a legitimating rule of action and secret knowledge'. School classes in Berlin presented a sentence from the 'Little Red Book' every morning. Even Christmas trees were decked with it. In retrospect, said Sepp, it seemed as if schoolchildren and students read the 'Little Red Book' with 'the same earnestness as their parents had read Holy Scripture'.[11]

Few of the young idealists guessed that their dreams of the future had little to do with the anticipated paradise of real socialism in far-off Asia. And those who did guess didn't want to know. Even Mao's 'Great Leap Forward', a gigantic modernization project with which China announced in 1957 that it would soon overtake the West, proved a disaster. Most of the livestock were lost. Gigantic construction works became time bombs, so that in 1975 two great dams in Henan province would burst and 230,000 people were drowned. According to *Die Zeit*, recent estimates say that about 2.5 million people were victims of the waves of purges. In the 'Great Leap Forward' at least 45 million died from hunger, poverty and misery.[12]

On 16 May 1966, while Western Maoists began to gather under the portrait of the 'Great Chairman', Mao Zedong ordered the start of the 'Great Proletarian Cultural Revolution', a further 'eruption of idealism and violence, religious zeal and sadism', reported the *Süddeutsche Zeitung*.[13] With the help of the children and youth organized into 'red guards' Mao regained his power after the fiasco of the 'Great Leap Forward'. According to the *Süddeutsche Zeitung*, during this period a group of schoolgirls shot dead their headmistress, students drowned their professors, husbands sent their wives to labour camps and sons sent their mothers to the scaffold. Many class enemies were buried alive, others beheaded or stoned. In the province of Guangzxi the hearts and livers of more than a dozen 'enemies' of Mao Zedong were torn out and consumed. Fifty years later a contemporary witness said that 'our whole immune system is corrupt and we as a society are powerless against any kind of disease'. He meant his society had lost its value system and the capacity to empathize. 'All this has its roots in the catastrophe of that time.'[14]

On the Tübingen campus pamphlets now appeared denouncing the cross as a symbol of the sado-masochistic glorification of pain. Prospective theologians sang along with 'Cursed be Jesus!' According to the contemporary witness Helmut Moll, 'It suddenly became the practice to celebrate Mass in private houses. Everybody held a glass of red wine.'[15]

For Ratzinger that was enough. Years after National Socialist totalitarianism the theologian was reminded of the darkest period in German history. 'I saw the brutal face of that atheistic piety clearly revealed,' as he put it dramatically in his memoirs. 'I saw the psycho-terror, the lack of restraint, with which every moral consideration was dismissed as a bourgeois leftover if it hindered the ideological goal.' He saw what he had already experienced in his youth happening again in another way. He found it particularly intolerable when ideology was 'introduced in the name of faith and the church was used as a tool'. Instead of God 'the Party takes his place and with it a totalitarianism of atheist worship, which is prepared to sacrifice all humanity to its false God.'[16]

Ratzinger was constantly attacked for saying these things. They were said to be exaggerated and also historically false. Since then more research has been published. 'Christians in the neo-Marxist camp wanted to build the messianic kingdom in the here and now,' says the political scientist Wolfgang Kraushaar. The historian Götz Aly was involved in one of the communist splinter groups in 1968 and then penalized by the *Radikalenerlass* (Anti-Radicals Decree) in the 1970s. In his research into leaflets and pamphlets produced by 1968 activists Aly discovered that a considerable part of the movement was openly terrorist, with totalitarian fantasies. They respected mass murderers like Lenin, Stalin, Mao and later Pol Pot, sympathized with the killings by the Red Army Faction, rejected democracy and a state with laws and a constitution, rejected the market economy and masked anti-Semitism by calling it 'Anti-Zionism'. Many of this generation's social ideas partly followed the same basic principles as 'had been aired in the *Reichsapothekerkammer* [Reich's Association of Pharmacists], the *NS-Kraftfahrerkorps* [National Socialist Motor Corps], the *Reichsfrauenschaft* [Reich's Women's Association] or the *Reichsnährstand* [Reich's Food Supply Organization]'.[17]

The students' revolt is commonly regarded as a turning point in the thought and action of the future pope. So it is constantly repeated in books and portrayals of him that there were two Ratzingers, one before Tübingen and one after Tübingen – a progressive theological teenager and a resigned conservative with occasional apocalyptic impulses. In particular, there is a widespread theory that Ratzinger had a 'trauma' in Tübingen, that he experienced a kind of personality-splitting Waterloo. From then he regarded anything with a whiff of progress as simply dangerous.

That theory sounded plausible, especially for contemporaries who knew neither Ratzinger's life story nor his battle against the reinterpretation of the Council, which he began at the latest in 1964. The theory goes on being repeated, as in an example from the *Lausitzer Rundschau* newspaper, dated 29 April 2018: as in so many reports, the title is 'The Students' Revolt – His Traumatic Experience'. The text reproduces what many generations of journalists copied from one another: 'The revolt at the University of Tübingen changed the Council theologian. For Küng the protests were a motivation and a stimulus, but for Ratzinger they were a trauma.' It continued: 'With his dislike of conflicts and quiet voice he had nothing with which to counter "the revolutionary spirit"'. So 'all he could do was retreat to tranquil Regensburg. The Tübingen experience continued to have an effect and turned the Council theologian into a staunch conservative.'[18]

The legend was further perpetuated by Hans Küng: 'We were the two who faced the most problems. I defended myself strongly and did not put up with anything. He was really shocked. And I think that is a vital factor in understanding him.' It should 'not be forgotten that at the time you had physically to defend your microphone in the lecture room. Of course that was not his thing [...] For me there was no question about it that you just stuck it out. So he withdrew to Regensburg, because he thought it would be peaceful there.' If you want to analyse 'how his change came about, his U-turn, then that was the point'.[19]

No journalist has taken the trouble to verify the story. Or at least subject it to a plausibility check. That was partly because fellow campaigners were happy to repeat Küng's theory. For example, there was Horst Herrmann. In 1975 Herrmann had lost his ecclesiastical permission to teach as a professor of church law. When he was officially condemned for unorthodoxy, he left the church in 1981. In a monograph on 'Joseph Ratzinger's career' published in 2005 the 'critical theologian' wrote: 'Then came the break [...] the shy theologian was shouted down. In the middle of the students' revolt the reforming theologian became a conservative, turned from being an optimist into a pessimist.'[20]

Hermann Häring, a theologian and collaborator in Küng's 'world ethos project', reported in a polemical paper: 'He braced himself against the disturbances in his lecture with the pugnacity of a bullfighter.' He was referring to Küng, whose assistant Häring was in Tübingen. On the other hand, the very different Joseph Ratzinger

> did not enjoy a battle: he stood helplessly before a riotous auditorium like the shy schoolboy he had once been [...] The gentle and rather timid professor suffered grievously from the unrest, and was unable to defend himself against it. Occasionally, we felt sorry for him but

more often *Schadenfreude*. The result was clear: since then he has been suspicious of everything that comes from below.[21]

The Regensburg writer Christian Feldmann also played the same record in a 'critical biography' of Ratzinger.[22] One chapter was called 'The Tübingen Trauma and the Change into a Faith Controller'. In a new 2013 edition of his book Feldmann repeated: 'While colleagues like Küng were willing to argue things out, the shy Ratzinger, who disliked conflict, underwent the trauma of his life.'[23] Then the *Vaticanista* Hanspeter Oschwald reported: 'He has never overcome his anxious failure to cope with public criticism. Since then he only fights rearguard actions.'

To end this litany of the legend, we quote the US journalist John Allen with his 'harsh' but 'fair' study of the 'Ratzinger phenomenon', as the publisher's blurb puts it: 'How did Ratzinger, the progressive firebrand, become Ratzinger the grand inquisitor?' Allen asked. His book investigated Ratzinger's change from a prince into a frog. 'Did he sell himself? Did he gain success by betraying his earlier convictions?'[24] The American journalist compared Ratzinger to the young Jedi knight in the blockbuster *Star Wars*, 'who went over to the Dark Side'. At the end of his indictment Allen gave a whole list of reasons why this cardinal would absolutely never become pope. That was written in the year 2000. Soon after Ratzinger's enthronement Allen revoked his objections. He now wrote about the man he had attacked so fiercely not long before:

> His creativity lies in his fresh way of making the core statements of Christian doctrine understandable. Benedict is a pope for the fundamental message and what is fundamental is presented in an intelligent and provocative way, in order to make clear that Christianity is not just a collection of rules but a resounding 'yes' to the dignity of the human person and the embrace of a loving God.[25]

So how does it stand now with the alleged 'trauma'? Ratzinger was not someone about whom anyone could say 'under the gowns [was] the fug of 1,000 years' ('*unter den Talaren den Muff von tausend Jahren*', the slogan on a Hamburg University students' banner at a demonstration against university traditionalism). The paper-tiger antics of the 'revolutionaries' could hardly have been traumatic for him. He had experienced the terror of the war. At the age of 25 he had already stood up before his first audience and radiated a natural authority. He had proved himself to be a fearless campaigner at the Council. The fact is that, contrary to the legend, Ratzinger did not suffer from personal attacks by students. He was not howled down by them at the University of Tübingen, and he did not retreat in fear. 'Let Ratzinger speak! Let Ratzinger speak!' was the cry when the professor at first said nothing in a podium discussion with Küng and the Belgian theologian Edward Schillebeeckx. 'I never heard of Ratzinger being hustled away from the lectern and never saw it happen,' said the then student Helmut Moll. His fellow student Imgard Schmidt-Sommer agreed that Ratzinger 'always got on well with his students'.

Rudi Dutschke's friend Ben van Onna attended Ratzinger's seminar for doctoral students, where there were no problems between the students and their professor. In 1969 van Onna published his book *Kritischer Katholizismus* (*Critical Catholicism*) and produced a monthly paper with the same title, together with Werner Böckenförde, Ratzinger's former assistant. Even Küng's then assistant Gotthold Hasenhüttl confirmed that it was not possible to speak about a 'trauma' suffered by Ratzinger: 'Ratzinger was not in the firing line during the student disturbances. That should be stressed.' The relationship between Küng and Ratzinger had cooled for theological reasons: 'Küng became ever more progressive, Ratzinger became more cautious and critical.'[26] Hasenhüttl, who was later suspended from his ministry as a priest by Bishop Reinhard Marx, remained grateful to Ratzinger, who 'had seen to it when he was dean that, despite my statements criticizing the church, I immediately got a lectureship'.[27]

Furthermore: 'it is completely without foundation that Ratzinger left Tübingen in flight, a typical invention of Küng's,' said Michael Johannes Marmann, who was a doctoral student in Tübingen in 1967.[28] Another contemporary witness, Josef Wohlmuth, professor of dogmatics at Bonn until 2003, stated: 'Ratzinger certainly did not take fright from discussion with students. But Küng withdrew and wrote his book *Unfehlbar?* [*Infallible?*]'[29] The then student Martin Trimpe reported: 'Other lecturers tried to ingratiate themselves with the protesters. Ratzinger, on the other hand, always answered with the logical, factual arguments that were typical of him.'[30] Ratzinger was more concerned about his students than about himself. 'What bothers me [about the crisis]', he wrote to the philosopher Josef Pieper in Münster, 'is the fact that in the current climate here quite a few good-hearted beginners lose their faith. Since many people think my presence in Tübingen has contributed to this, I have to feel partly responsible.'

Ratzinger himself declared that he had never had 'difficulties' with his students. 'It was something very good in itself,' he said in an interview with the Bayerischer Rundfunk radio station, that he had experienced the social changes of 1968 in 'such an intellectually turbulent place as Tübingen'. And with a very varied student body, 'so that you really stood on the front line of the contemporary situation and had to fight that battle'.[31] 'Was the student rebellion a trauma for you?' I asked the pope emeritus again in our final conversations. His answer: 'Absolutely not.'

Ratzinger said that, as dean, he was particularly concerned and really experienced the revolt 'at close quarters'. There he had been able to observe 'the devastation of theology', whose 'politicization now went in the direction of Marxist messianism'. Ratzinger was disgusted at 'the hypocrisy with which people continued to claim to be believers – when it was expedient – in order not to risk losing the means to achieve their own goals'.[32] It became clear to him: 'Not everything could or should be belittled or treated as just an academic argument.' Küng, however, had to admit that he himself had been the target of left-wing students, who stormed his seminars and occupied the lectern. Of course, the actions had 'only temporarily annoyed' him. According to Küng's biographer Freddy Derwahl, it was true that 'at the end of the summer 1968 semester of the "disturbances", Küng was so exhausted that he simply dropped his lectures or sent his assistant to take over for him'.[33] The professor of Jewish studies Peter Kuhn, a Tübingen contemporary, reported: 'Küng politely withdrew and waited until the storm was over. The students wanted to take their exam with him but Küng was not there. He was basking in the Florida sun with some women teachers.'[34]

Contrary to Küng's report that 'he was really shocked and withdrew', Ratzinger organized an action group, together with some Evangelical theologians. The group was called the 'Ecumenical Assembly'. Its permanent members included Peter Beyerhaus, professor of mission studies and ecumenical theology, the Evangelical theologian Ulrich Wickert and the Benedictine priest Beda Müller, from Neresheim. They met at the home of a US free church, the 'Disciples of Christ', at 100 Wilhelmstrasse in Tübingen. Ratzinger was a member of the Academic Freedom Association (*Bund Freiheit der Wissenschaft*), and in a plenary assembly he called upon students to distance themselves from blasphemous propaganda.

He went against the majority opinion when he was the only professor to refuse to sign a resolution in support of the religion teacher and priest Hubert Halbfas. Halbfas had demanded that the church should not proselytize for Christ but simply promote Hindus becoming better Hindus and Muslims better Muslims. In his later books he declared that Jesus 'had not seen himself either as "messiah" or as the "Son of God"'.[35] He doubted the doctrine of the resurrection, and as founder member of the 'Society for Faith Reform' he argued for the reconstruction of Christianity as a mixture with non-Christian religions. The result was the 'fall of Halbfas', as it was widely publicized in the media. The theologian gave up his priesthood, choosing instead the safe harbour of marriage.

4

The Catholic Crisis

As if yet another spark was needed in the charged atmosphere of 1968, on 25 July the Vatican published Paul VI's seventh and last encyclical, *Humanae vitae*. In response to the 'sexual revolution' the pope stressed the dignity of married love. Sexuality, love and parenthood, he said, could not be separated; according to Catholic doctrine they should be understood as a unity.

In paragraph 17 Pope Paul listed the grave consequences of weakened sexual morality: high divorce rates, destabilized families, the suffering of children of divorced parents, dying nations. He had been especially impressed by a plea of the young archbishop of Kraków, Karol Wojtyła, who argued that the contraceptive pill was also to be condemned because it made women sexually available to men at all times. As the encyclical put it, many men could reduce women 'to mere instruments to satisfy their lust with no regard for their bodily or spiritual well-being. They would no longer be seen as partners to be respected and loved.'

Humanae vitae struck like a bomb. This was especially because the media focused on the ban on artificial contraception, which was difficult to defend. Hudson Hoagland, the joint inventor of the pill, spoke of a 'medieval concept whose perpetuation is a moral crime against humanity'. The Swedish Lutheran Church expressed 'sadness and disappointment'. About this 'worst Catholic misjudgement so far this century', *Der Spiegel* wrote that a world 'in which people lived and loved as the pope wants them to' would 'within a short time become a world of horror and death'. It would become 'so overpopulated that every year more people would die of hunger than in all humanity's wars put together'.[1] To calm the storm, the German Catholic Bishops' Conference published a compromise statement, the so-called Königstein Declaration. It fundamentally accepted *Humanae vitae* but said that 'the conscientious and responsible decision of the faithful' was to be respected on the question of birth control, which in the end was up to the individual. Ratzinger criticized the encyclical. 'There are some lights in it. But the way it was presented was on a different wavelength from my own.'[2] It 'should have been written differently', the natural-law justification not so static, narrow and unhistorical.

Until then German Catholics' Conferences had been demonstrations of unity. The laity gave the bishops and pope unconditional loyalty. But everything changed at the Essen Catholics' Conference, from 4 to 8 September 1968. 'Temporary Big Building Site' was the title of the magazine that the German Catholics' central committee gave out at the meeting. Referring to the host bishop, young visitors chanted: '*Hengsbach wir kommen, wir sind die linken Frommen!*' ('Hengsbach we're coming, we're the Catholic left wing!'). One of the new groups called itself 'Kapo' (Katholische Außerparlamentarische Opposition): the 'Catholic Extra-Parliamentary Opposition'; another was called the 'Critical Catholics' Action Committee'. There were sit-ins, banners and chanted slogans such as 'They all talk about the pill, we take it'. Students of Catholic theology demanded the pope's resignation. In a crammed meeting of 5,000 people about the 'pill encyclical', the participants decisively dismissed obedience to the Holy Father.

Ratzinger had not taken part in the conference. But he began quietly to set himself against the general trend. At the invitation of the Augustinian father Johannes Lehmann-Dronke he taught young men and women at a summer school in Bierbronnen on Lake Constance. Lehmann-Dronke and the philosopher Alma von Stockhausen had acquired an old farmhouse there. As a young professor at the Freiburg Teacher Training College, Alma von Stockhausen had experienced the student unrest. She was seeking an answer to Marxism. She thought the errors in theology were often caused by a false philosophy. She led the discussion on Hegel, Fichte and the Frankfurt School and invited Marxist students to debate with her until they gave up their Marxism. Later in Bierbronnen the Gustav Siewerth Academy was founded, the smallest Catholic faculty in Germany.

At the summer school Heinrich Schlier, a colleague from Bonn days, covered the New Testament, while Ratzinger taught dogmatics. After their daily walk they ate in the Kranz Gasthaus. Mass was celebrated in the next village. One of the participants was the nun and former cabaret artist Isa Vermehren. She had converted to the Catholic Church in 1938. During the Nazi period she had belonged to a resistance group. After her arrest she had been interned in Ravensbrück, Buchenwald and Dachau concentration camps.

Ratzinger also joined Josef Pieper and Karl Rahner in the Johann-Adam-Möhler Institute for Ecumenism, a research establishment to promote the reunion of separated Christians. He also developed his relationship with one of the most important thinkers in Germany, the philosopher Robert Spaemann, who was the same age as himself and later became one of his close advisers. Spaemann's parents had converted to Catholicism during the 1930s. After his mother died, his widowed father, Heinrich, was ordained as a priest in 1942 by the bishop of Münster, Count von Galen. Robert Spaemann dodged Nazi war service, married a Jew and took as his motto a saying by the French philosopher Jean-Jacques Rousseau: 'I would not presume to want to teach other people, if I had not seen how others lead them astray.'

The warning calls became louder about a wrong post-conciliar development. In particular, Hubert Jedin, the acknowledged expert on church history and Ratzinger's friend, had become very clear. 'At first I thought I should reject talk of a "crisis in the church",' Jedin wrote in his memoirs. But 'two years later there could be no more doubt about it.' It had arisen because 'people were no longer content just to carry out what had been decided by the Council, but saw it as a spark that would ignite radical reforms that went far beyond the actual Council decrees'.[3]

Two weeks after the Essen Catholics' Conference, in September 1968 Jedin presented Cardinal Julius Döpfner, the new chairman of the German Bishops' Conference, with a comprehensive memorandum. The position paper called upon the bishops resolutely to proclaim Catholic doctrine and to stop the propagation of errors. 'A church that no longer dares to point out heresies' was 'no longer a church. Pluralism in theology, which there has always been, should not be confused with falsifying the truth of the faith.' Today no one 'can still deny that many Catholic Christians' knowledge of the faith is dim and foggy, because the church's doctrine is not being proclaimed in sermons and even less in religious instruction. Instead, theologians who are often poorly educated, express their "opinions"'.[4]

As a historian, Jedin drew parallels with the events of the sixteenth century, which had led to the schism in the Western church. At the time the bishops had dismissed the 'Luther conflict' as a quarrel among theologians and had not realized 'that the Reformation was not a reform of the church but the formation of a new church on a different basis'. Intellectuals also came forward as 'champions of the movement'. In their eyes the previous theology had been an obstacle to progress. 'Then countless priests, monks and nuns, fascinated by the catchword "gospel freedom" threw off the bonds, the vows they had taken.' Finally the total success of Lutheranism was made possible by mastery of the new means of communication via the printing press. Luther's writings spoke the language of the people and were eagerly devoured. The few warning voices had been intelligent Catholics but bad propagandists and were dismissed as 'reactionaries'. 'The church magisterium, pope and bishops were silent.' Jedin concluded: by being so passive, the German bishops had 'aided the almost unrestrained progress of the Lutheran movement. Indeed they had enabled it.'

Jedin's memorandum warned that after the Council much of the press would try to 'manipulate' public opinion. The media was 'almost exclusively dominated by intellectuals who often, even if – especially if – they were Catholics, promoted and spread what was "new" as "progressive" for its own sake, with no regard for whether it was true'. That 'constant stream pouring out on the faithful from the left-wing-dominated media was bound to change their relationship with the church and has already changed it'. Jedin warned urgently of the 'danger of a church schism or – what would be even worse – a total alienation from the church'.

Ratzinger was not involved in the memorandum, but the analysis could just as well have been written by him. In his summing up Jedin enumerated the central points of the crisis:

1. the increasing uncertainty about faith, caused by the unchecked spread of theological errors in lectures, books and articles;
2. the attempt to transfer parliamentary democracy to the church;
3. the de-sacralization of the priesthood;
4. the free 'shaping' of the liturgy instead of following the *Opus Dei*;
5. ecumenism as protestantization.

It had to be urgently inculcated into all the clergy 'that the liturgy was not the free shaping of a community gathering, but a service of God ordained by the church'. In conclusion the position paper said:

We are convinced what was good and true that came about through the church's new awakening at the Council can only really be fruitful if it is kept free from error. The longer the painful operation is delayed, the greater will be the danger that valuable forces will be lost, because they have become mixed up with error and then not only lead to a schism in the church but to a falling away from Christianity.

It was only a couple of years since Jedin, the now 68-year-old professor of church history (who had honorary doctorates from the universities of Louvain, Cologne, Vienna and Milan), had been treated with hostility in conservative circles for being too progressive. From then on, 'instead of being a "progressive" as I was during the Council, in the eyes of certain theologians and their followers I had become a "conservative"'. The former Council adviser shook his head: 'For those who regard what is "new", "modern" and "young" as automatically of value, "conservative" is an insult. In fact the conservatives differ from the traditionalists and reactionaries because they know that preserving must also always mean developing.'

Jedin's position paper did not have a notable effect. 'Several bishops agreed with us and confirmed us in the view that we had not described an imaginary danger,' he noted in his memoirs. However, Cardinal Döpfner 'contented himself with the remark: we receive a lot of that sort of advice.' In the end the German Bishops' Conference had not managed to 'take a clear position towards obviously destructive doctrines. They nearly always came up with compromises that did not overcome the evil but allowed it to grow.'[5]

Ratzinger was disappointed by the post-conciliar tendencies. He was not resigned. Neither did he want to turn back the clock. He insisted there was no point in 'longing for a yesterday that cannot be brought back'. Those who later reproached Benedict XVI for having shrunk from the battle in Tübingen miss one of Ratzinger's main ways of joining in the dispute. The foreword to his *Introduction to Christianity*, published in 1968, stressed that the book was decidedly written in order not to stand idly by and let the 'besetting power of unbelief' take over. Indeed, his *Introduction to Christianity* must be seen as a polemical as well as a rational defence of the Christian faith in the church crisis. He stressed that the church 'was today surrounded by a fog of uncertainty as hardly ever before in its history'. The book begins with a surprising parable. In a few sentences it made clear what was at stake:

Anyone observing the theological movement of the last decade might feel reminded of the old story of *Hans in Luck*. He exchanged the lump of gold, which he found too heavy and exhausting, at first for a horse, then a cow, then a goose, then a grindstone, which he finally threw into the water, without losing anything much. On the contrary, he thought what he got for it instead was the precious gift of perfect freedom. Over the last few years hasn't our theology often done the same? Hasn't it reinterpreted the demands of faith, which were felt to be too burdensome, step by step, always just such a little that nothing important seemed to have been lost, so that soon it was felt possible to take the next one? And won't poor Hans, the Christian, who was led trustingly from one exchange to another – from one reinterpretation to the next – soon find himself without the gold, with which he began, but just with a grindstone, which he can be confidently advised to throw away?[6]

Ratzinger denied that his 'Hans in Luck' was a brazen comparison with his colleague in Switzerland. However, Hans Küng might have recognized himself in it. In his *Introduction to Christianity* Ratzinger described a 'modern theology', which often undeniably 'supported a trend that in fact led from gold to a grindstone'. Of course, he said, that trend 'could not be countered merely by sticking to the precious metal of past firm formulae'. He himself wanted 'to help understand the faith anew as a way of making true humanity possible in our world of today, without converting it into a discourse that merely covers a spiritual void'.[7]

According to the cultural critic Alexander Kissler, the future pope's *Introduction to Christianity*, published in the 1968 'year of revolution', was no less militant that Johann Baptist Metz's *Theologie der Welt* (*Theology of the World*), also published in 1968. Ratzinger also stressed that Christians should not stand aside when it was a question of poverty or injustice. But the use of church and faith for political ends was not in accordance with the gospel. Whereas Metz's theology sought a consensus with the world, according to Kissler, Ratzinger wanted 'to draw Christians more fully and passionately back into the world of Christianity. His aim was not adaptability but an inner revitalizing of faith.'[8]

After a few months Ratzinger's first best-seller had reached its tenth reprint. The author himself could hardly believe it. It was not true, as was often said, that the book arose from transcripts of his lectures made by his students. When he was still in Bonn, the Kösel-Verlag publisher, Dr Heinrich Wild, had suggested he should write a book on the 'Nature of Christianity'. In Tübingen, Ratzinger saw the need for it had come. And it was Hans Küng who helped him to do it. In the winter semester of 1967 his colleague had taken over the main lecture course. Ratzinger used the time to write the manuscript by hand, then dictate it to a secretary and finally edit the typescript. He had produced a classic, which was read by millions of people all over the world in seemingly unending editions. It influenced generations of theologians and stimulated countless vocations and religious lives.

Contrary to the legend of his great change in 1968, Ratzinger's *Introduction to Christianity* shows that his theology and way of thinking were no different before or after 1968, before the Council or after the Council, before his time in Rome or after his time in Rome – apart from nuances and expansions. In his essay *The New Heathens in the Church*, published in 1958, he had already spoken about the urgently necessary 'desecularization' of the church. His basic faith persisted. Genuine renewal was to re-present the truth and convincing power of the Christian faith through the *Logos* and the mystery of Christ. And without using *aggiornamento*, in the way many understood it, to mean adapting to the secular world's ways of speaking, thinking and living. It would be naïve to think that you just needed to change clothes and speak the same way as everyone else and suddenly everything would be all right. The Council had not given the starting signal for a race to question the foundations of the faith or for theologians to seize power. It had awoken enthusiasm for a new language of faith, worship liberated from everything that covered up the nature, the mystery and mission of Christianity, particularly in the liturgy, so that the meaning of the Mass could reappear more clearly.

In his 'Hans in Luck' parable Ratzinger had described the current situation in theology as a development that kept exchanging the content of faith for a so-called improvement, in order to make Christianity easier. In the end the gullible Hans, who had given away all the dogmas, moral principles, tradition and his faith itself, was left empty-handed. As opposed to this goal of a reform process that he saw coming in Tübingen, Ratzinger presented *his* idea: a simple church for simple people. In his introduction he says:

> True believers do not attach great importance to the reorganization of church forms. They live by what the church always is; if we want to know what it really is, we must go to them. For the church is not mainly where it is organized, reformed and ruled, but among those who simply believe and receive the gift of faith in the church that becomes their life.[9]

Of course the book caused controversy. Walter Kasper mocked the lack of a 're-investigation' into the historical Jesus. Kasper belonged to a prominent group of Catholic theologians who followed the 'new quest for the historical Jesus', led by the Protestant Rudolf Bultmann and Ernst Käsemann. According to Kasper, Christian truth 'could only be grasped by means of a historical model subject to constant revision'.[10] Ratzinger answered briskly: 'We have known since Albert Schweitzer that the historical Jesus of the liberals was not real. I believe we will soon also officially know that the same goes for the historical Jesus of Bultmann.'[11]

Ida Friederike Görres showed how differently the Ratzinger message could be read. After the book came out, she wrote enthusiastically to her close friend Father Paulus on 28 November 1968: 'This is exactly what was wanted: genuine fullness of knowledge, unerringly sharp thinking, purest truthfulness.' Ratzinger was 'one of the young theologians who is sympathetically aware of all the new trends, considers them thoroughly and unerringly but lovingly sees through and rejects what is amiss'.[12]

Everything has its time, and Ratzinger's time in Tübingen came to an end. In the turmoil of rebellion academic work could barely continue. The success of his *Introduction* had renewed his awareness of his mission. At a time of upheaval it was necessary to lead new thinking in the right direction and filter out what was mistaken. A mammoth task. But who else should undertake it but a Council theologian who, unlike others, had remained a church theologian in his progressive thinking? He needed space. He needed a different environment, as his assistant Siegfried Wiedenhofer observed, to 'reflect, write, teach'.

But there was no question of a hasty departure or 'flight' from Tübingen, even though Hans Urs von Balthasar described it as a retreat. 'Küng is a rascal. I know him well,' he wrote to de Lubac on 9 December 1967. 'In Tübingen he is so unbearable that his colleague J. Ratzinger, who is a hundred times more important than him, has retreated in flight to the small faculty in Regensburg.'[13] In fact, two years before that Ratzinger had already been offered the chair of dogmatics at the new Bavarian university. He had turned it down for the sake of his friend Johann Baptist Auer, professor of dogmatics in Bonn, who urgently wanted to go back to his home town. When Ratzinger was invited for the second time he accepted, 'because I wanted to develop my theology in a less heady context and not be drawn into constant battle'. Something else became clear to him in Tübingen: 'Anyone who wanted to remain a progressivist here had to sell his soul.'[14] Before he left, Hans

Küng had again confronted him. It was about his free semester, for which Küng now had no one to stand in for him. 'Küng shouted at Ratzinger so loudly that he could be heard in the corridors,' their colleague Max Seckler recalled. 'That was the sad climax of a separation that had long been coming.'[15]

Ratzinger himself stressed that he had not changed course: 'I think anyone who reads my work can verify that.'[16] Perhaps he could be charged with not having defended the 'real Council' in the post-conciliar period more aggressively against a 'virtual council', as he called it. The church historian Vinzenz Pfnür confirmed that his teacher 'had maintained his continuity. I see no difference in his theological thought.' The fact that he recognized shocks to the cultural and spiritual climate, coming from the 1968 revolt, that others only became aware of decades later was not evidence of a 'falling away', but a sign that he observed the events of the time as critically as he had previously criticized an ossified church leadership.

Indeed, if we wanted to talk about changing sides, shouldn't we mention that Küng broke with all the comrades who had worked as the actual Council reformers and defended its documents? Including de Lubac and Congar, and even Rahner. And of course Ratzinger, with whom he would quarrel ever more furiously as Ratzinger advanced in his career. Küng distanced himself from the popes and from Catholic theology – even though he claimed that the true church was as he described it in his books.

As for many other enthusiastic protagonists of the Council, for Ratzinger the joyful expectation of seeing their work come to fruition changed into disappointment about a party that did not take place. They still opposed obsolete forms from past centuries but now suddenly had to resist centrifugal forces dragging the church astray. However, the Italian historian Roberto de Mattei was convinced that Ratzinger's later diagnosis contrasting the 'hermeneutics of break' with the 'hermeneutics of continuity', a virtual council with a real Council, was not conclusive. De Mattei thought the former *peritus* was treating the Council from beginning to end as a single hermeneutic block. But in fact, the post-conciliar developments should be seen as a real part of what happened with the Council: its practical implementation was even more real than all its decrees and carefully negotiated constitutions put together.

The so-called Bologna School, led by Giuseppe Alberigo, gave a similar interpretation. Henceforth the Second Vatican Council should been seen as going beyond its documents, above all, as a historical 'happening'. It had raised hopes and triggered a radical break with the past, ushering in a new age. Wasn't Ratzinger oversimplifying when he maintained that you had to stick just with the texts, as the Council fathers wanted? That sounded rather like saying the gospel texts were absolutely settled and definitive, even though there were constant attempts to interpret them differently, summarize or even paraphrase them.

Nevertheless, Tübingen was a clarification and a parting of the ways. The breach between the two camps had become impossible to ignore. You had to decide which side you were on: history's joke was that those who had stamped the Council as progressive would soon be branded as 'betrayers of the Council'. In fact, Ratzinger held fast to the Council's achievements and tried to straighten things out. 'Even if what is stressed in my thinking has changed and developed according to the settings in which I was placed – and of course my age and its different attitudes – nevertheless my basic impulse, particularly at the Council, was always to release the core of the faith from encrustations and to liberate its power and dynamism. That impulse has been the constant of my life,' he explained. 'It is important for me that I have never deviated from that constant, which has stamped my life from childhood on, and all through my life I have remained faithful to that course.'[17]

He did not look back in anger when after the 1969 summer semester he packed his cases, together with his sister Maria. Not even at his Swiss colleague. He stressed: 'I had a very positive relationship with Küng and I parted from him in peace.'[18] Küng also confirmed: 'The three years in Tübingen did not cast any shadow over our work together. I really got on very well with him.'[19] There was not yet any mention of a 'trauma' or a 'change'. The myth only developed in the course of the following years. Then Ratzinger came to be labelled a renegade in order to eliminate the main opponent of the post-conciliar distortions. The procedure disquietingly recalls George Orwell's classic *Animal Farm*. After the death of 'Old Major', the animals' leader who had wanted to introduce a new beginning with new relationships, two younger protagonists, Napoleon and

Snowball, come into play. Napoleon brings in new words, a new interpretation of the programme, and creates bogeymen, one arch-enemy in particular, who is to blame for everything, including the fact that things do not go well with the necessary improvements. Bit by bit the historical events are falsified. Later his adversary Snowball is even accused of having been a reactionary in disguise from the start. Napoleon builds a world of false information and rules with the support of trained dogs, who bark loudly whenever he is contradicted in any way. Then there are also the sheep, who end any discussion by bleating. In Orwell they bleat: 'Four legs good, two legs bad!' Their slogan could be translated: 'Küng good, Ratzinger bad!'

In his proposed preface to *Animal Farm*, entitled 'The Freedom of the Press', Orwell wrote that there were 'things which on their own merits would get the big headlines being kept right out of the British press, not because the Government intervened but because of a general tacit agreement that "it wouldn't do" to mention that particular fact'. It was 'an orthodoxy, a body of ideas which it is assumed that all right-thinking people will accept without question'. Then: 'Anyone who challenges the prevailing orthodoxy finds himself silenced with surprising effectiveness.'[20]

So what had drawn him to Tübingen, I asked Benedict XVI in our conversations. A town with an Evangelical tradition, colleagues who would not exactly offer him a bed of roses. And there was Hans Küng: he must have realized that the two of them were not on the same wavelength. These were not exactly ideal conditions for productive work. 'I am surprised myself by my naïvety,' the pope emeritus said. 'I had very good relations with many professors in the Evangelical theological faculty. So I had the naïve idea that Küng indeed had a big mouth and said audacious things, but basically wanted to be a Catholic theologian. There were indications of that. But I did not foresee that he would then keep erupting.'[21]

5

A Fresh Start

The autumn leaves shone red, ochre and gold, and the morning sun bathed the winding country road in a soft October light. The old Volkswagen was packed with bags and provisions. There were cases and boxes on the roof, tied with cord. From a distance the two men who could be seen sitting behind the windscreen looked like tourists, making for the south.

Father Lehmann-Dronke, from Bierbronnen, steered his 'beetle', after a fashion, while his travelling companion gazed out over the landscape. Wasn't his situation rather like this October day? Hadn't his own hopes and dreams dissolved like the mist in the autumn sunshine? Yes, he had won with the Council. But now he was about to lose with the post-Council.

Ten whole years had passed on Joseph Ratzinger's wanderings. But after Bonn, Münster and Tübingen this new move would 'definitely be the last'. Maria had booked rooms for the night in the Hotel Karmeliten. After that the brother and sister could stay temporarily with their brother Georg. Regensburg was Bavarian. Regensburg was home. Joseph would be able to work peacefully at his theology. He would build a house for himself and his sister. The family was together again. After five difficult years as the musical director of the Domspatzen (the Regensburg 'Cathedral Sparrows', the cathedral choir), Georg now had them back with him.

The transfer to 'the peaceful province', as Küng later described the move (or 'manoeuvre') to Regensburg on the Danube, was a change from the little Swabian town of Tübingen to a city that was soon to have 100,000 inhabitants. Tübingen had a name, but Regensburg, Germany's best-preserved medieval city, belonged to world culture.

There was the Gothic St Peter's Cathedral, the giant stone blocks of the Porta Pretoria, a gate with which the Romans fortified their city of Castra Regina in AD 179, the base for their Danube settlement. For 150 years, between 1663 and 1806, the city hall had been the seat of the 'Perpetual Assembly' of the Holy Roman Empire of the German Nation. The original 'long benches' and 'green tables' can still be seen there today, for the saying in which 'to put something on the long bench' came to mean 'postpone something', and 'to sit at the green table' to mean 'take decisions'.

In October 1969, when Ratzinger gave his first lecture, the images of the tanks that had recently bulldozed the 'Prague Spring' were still fresh in people's minds. On the night of 21 August 1968, under the code name Operation Danube, 500,000 soldiers from the Soviet Union, Poland, Hungary, Bulgaria and the GDR marched into Czechoslovakia. Tanks rolled in; more than 100 people were killed. The suppression of Alexander Dubček's 'socialism with a human face' put a damper on the Marxist movement among West German students. However, in comparison with the uproar elsewhere, left-wing activity in the Upper Palatinate capital, Regensburg, had been like a storm in a teacup. A poster on the walls of the university canteen still proclaimed 'For the victory of the Vietnamese people', but the red script had long begun to lose its colour. Ratzinger's assistants had renamed the neo-Marxist rector Gustav Obermair's dogs. Now they were no longer called Marx and Lenin but Max and Leni.

The Regensburg university campus on the southern edge of the city was not yet fully built and in the meantime the Catholic faculty was housed in the old Dominican monastery in the Old Town. What luck! The wide corridors, the contemplative cloisters, the Gothic church. 'I really feel at home here,' Ratzinger would soon be saying. Albert the Great, the last medieval polymath and teacher of Thomas Aquinas and Bonaventure, had been one of his predecessors here. That had to be a good omen. 'I rejoiced,' Ratzinger wrote in his memoirs, 'that I could say something of my own, that was new and yet arose wholly from the faith of the church.' He dreamed of a dogmatics, an overall presentation of the Catholic faith, and a 'Christology' that would show the man from Nazareth, who had recently been so badly damaged by theologians, in all his greatness again.

Maria loved now having Sunday lunch with both her brothers in the Bischofshof restaurant and enjoying coffee and cakes at the Golden Cross café. She took care that Joseph did not order mushrooms (poisonous!) or fish (bones!). Their stay with their brother in the Domspatzen Institute soon came to an end and they moved to a rented flat in the Regensburg suburb of Pentling. When there was time, full of anticipation, the new villager paced the newly acquired plot of land on which their own house, with a garden, would soon be built.

Houses can talk. They give information about their owners. In Tübingen, Hans Küng had had a universally admired villa, built on the Roman model with an atrium and including an indoor swimming-pool. He liked to point out the different standard between him and Ratzinger. 'Of course, a policeman's son growing up in a police station, and in a modest farmhouse after his father's retirement, then as a 12-year-old in a minor seminary, has a different background from a businessman's son growing up in a large, hospitable house in the town hall square.' In the prologue to the second volume of his autobiography he wrote that in his home there had been 'no strict spiritual policing but a lively atmosphere open to the world'.[1] He did not mention that the 'openness to the world' of the 'businessman's son' derived from a shoe business in a small market town with just 4,000 inhabitants in the canton of Lucerne. Or that Ratzinger actually did not come from the 'back woods'. His grandfather on his mother's side had been a successful businessman. On his father's side he came from a family that had produced many priests and members of religious orders. And his great uncle Georg Ratzinger had been a deputy in the German Reichstag in Berlin and had made a name for himself far beyond Germany.

However, Ratzinger's own newly built house was very far from being a villa. He had merely insisted on a balcony, which his architect had tried to dissuade him from. Apart from that, the building was so simple in design and fittings that later visitors suggested donations of furniture. The 'showpieces' were the old walnut desk which had been given to him as a farewell present from Freising and his piano. Maria had contributed a few pictures from her store, simple reprints, and also crochet pieces. There was a guest room the size of a monk's cell for brother Georg. The bookshelves on the walls of the work room were partly new. Plainness and utility predominated.

In his 'beloved Pentling', originally a peasant village of 500, the long-standing old inhabitants were astonished at the professor's love of animals. At the edge of his garden he regularly chatted with Tasso, a neighbour's sheepdog. They were also amazed at the way he managed the electric mower. 'The extraordinary thing was that he always just mowed a bit,' neighbour Rupert Hofbauer observed, 'then he went back to his balcony and read. Next day he would mow a bit more.'[2] Soon, however, the professor with a worldwide reputation became 'our priest'. A priest who consecrated bells, blessed the voluntary fire service's new fire engine and said Mass in the village church on weekdays as well as Sundays.[3]

Ratzinger cultivated many contacts, as can be seen from the 30,000 letters that he wrote to colleagues, friends, schoolfellows and his readers up to the time he became bishop. They are archived in the Pope Benedict XVI Institute. In Regensburg his inner circle consisted of the pastoral theologian Josef Goldbrunner and Johann Baptist Auer, his fatherly friend from Bonn days, who sometimes pointed out his weak points with 'fraternal reproach'. It was a special relationship because Auer, as Ratzinger said, 'knew my theological and human limits very realistically. I mean we were friends but as a friend he could criticize me – I was not perfect and I had problems.'[4] In our conversation Ratzinger did not go into detail about what problems these were.

He had a work friendship with Franz Mussner, the Upper Bavarian New Testament professor. Mussner was one of the creators of modern biblical scholarship. Through his *Traktat über die Juden* (*Treatise on the Jews*), which also influenced John Paul II, he was regarded as a pioneer of Christian-Jewish understanding and was honoured with the Buber-Rosenzweig medal in 1985. Mussner's central message was that Judaism was the root of Christianity. It was the noble olive tree onto which the Gentiles were grafted to become Christians. When he became Pope Benedict, Ratzinger wrote in a letter (mistakenly dated 28 January 2011) that Mussner had 'shown the way to the Bible and even to faith in Christ – God become human – to many people at a difficult time'. He could not imagine his own 'theological course without all that I have received from you'. He signed it 'Your Joseph Ratzinger'.[5] For his part, Mussner valued his colleague's 'clarity of expression, art of formulating and gift of quick understanding'.[6]

Ratzinger's new friends included, among others, the conductor Wolfgang Sawallisch and Reinhardt Richardi and his wife, Margarete. The Berliner Richardi had been professor of labour and social law in Regensburg since 1968 and was regarded as the founder of ecclesiastical labour law. Margarete soon became close pen friends with Maria, who was known as a very modest but also extremely intelligent woman. Ratzinger accompanied his colleague, who had been baptized as an Evangelical, on his way into the Catholic Church, and baptized the couple's children. He went with them, together with his Roman friends, the Crescenti family of teachers, on trips to Weltenburg Monastery. He had met the gymnasium (secondary school) teacher Francesco Crescenti and his wife, Anna Maria, a gymnasium mathematics teacher, during the Council. The meeting had resulted in a lifelong friendship, during which Ratzinger conducted the marriage of their daughter Maria Assunta and baptized their grandchildren Gabriele and Antonella. 'He was simply with us, he was part of our family,' Anna Maria said.

Another companion was Ulrich Hommes, professor of practical philosophy. Hommes had got his doctorate with a work on the French philosopher Maurice Blondel. He also wrote about Hegel, Feuerbach and Karl Jaspers. The two got to know each other on a study tour through Israel and at joint events compared the Marxist doctrine of salvation with the Christian alternative – one from the philosophical viewpoint and the other from the theological, complementing each other. Hommes was impressed by Ratzinger's 'intimate relationship with music', 'his great continuity' and 'convincing straightforwardness'. As a philosopher, he noted Ratzinger's 'method of perception' as 'reason from feeling'. Meeting him was like 'reaching for a star'.[7]

Ratzinger's relationship with Rudolf Graber was regarded as controversial. Left-wingers described Graber, bishop of Regensburg, as 'the far right of the German Bishops' Conference' (Hans Küng), a conservative who was a gifted preacher and exemplary pastor. Graber was rightly condemned for his regime-friendly comments as a gymnasium teacher during the National Socialist period. Ratzinger valued his Marian devotion and his understanding of the role of bishops. Graber was Ratzinger's local bishop. While he was in

Regensburg, Ratzinger dedicated a eulogy to him on his honorary doctorate and wrote a short introduction to one of Graber's books.

In April 1970 Esther Betz knocked at the door. She had a particular reason. On a walk with him she asked her long-term friend an awkward question. It was about whether it was advisable to 'set up house together' with Professor Karl Lehmann, the future chairman of the German Bishops' Conference. By sharing a flat with Lehmann she could look after his library, which was getting out of hand. That was reason enough for Ratzinger to raise no objections. She also asked to interview him for the *Rheinische Post* and questioned him on the widespread 'criticism of the church, pope and bishops, pastoral practice and attempts at reform'. Of course criticism was basically in order, was his reply, but today people 'associated all too willingly with the current bywords, without testing their validity'.[8]

Regensburg is the neglected period in the life of the future pope. It was important because in these years Ratzinger tried to find answers to the cultural and religious crisis of the time. He now wanted to settle down and finish his work. He not only built a house but also moved his parents' grave from Traunstein to Pentling. (During the move the stonemasons chiselled his mother's birth date on the tombstone as '7 January 1884' instead of '8 January 1884'.) Ratzinger had made no mistake. Nowhere else was he able to be so productive. Nowhere else did he educate so many students who became bishops, auxiliary bishops, members of religious orders, priests, noted theologians or even cardinals, including, for example, Christoph Schönborn, who became archbishop of Vienna. The new professor brought international flair to the campus. Whenever a Korean, Japanese, Chilean or African came round the corner, it was obvious whose student they were. Nowhere else was Ratzinger's authority so strongly recognized, his name so widely respected. He became dean of the theological faculty and later vice-president of the university.

'A good tactic' contributed to Ratzinger's high reputation, his colleague Richardi reported. 'When there were great heated discussions,' said the former university president Dieter Henrich, 'Ratzinger hardly said anything. When he finally did speak the whole heated discussion came to an end.'[9] Professor Gerhard Winkler related: 'Everyone then in the faculty was on their knees to

Ratzinger. His lectures were also attended by historians, lawyers and economists.' Johann Baptist Auer told his audience: 'Whoever wants to be a brilliant theologian must go to Ratzinger. Whoever wants to be a village priest can stay with me.'

The student body had also grown. The 30 or so doctoral students met every Saturday fortnight morning in the Regensburg seminary for priests. According to Ratzinger's student Josef Zöhrer, they enjoyed enormous freedom, quite unlike with many doctoral supervisors, regarded as liberal, 'who cut off their students, even penalized them for the smallest sign of dissent'.[10] For example, Küng rejected a Tübingen student's dissertation because the student had criticized him in a section of it. 'The discussion covered everything,' Vincent Twomey recalled. 'The professor carefully weighed up the arguments for any thesis and let everyone express their own opinions and hypotheses, including those who had just joined the group.'

The Irishman Vincent Twomey, a Divine Word missionary, had been sent to Germany by his superiors in September 1970, to sniff the air of higher theology after his ordination. In Münster he had at first sat 'at the feet of Karl Rahner, who was then at the height of his reputation'. During seminars Rahner strode up and down the room, 'obviously impatient until the student's presentation was finished and he could begin. The rest of the meeting was a monologue, despite all our attempts to enter into any kind of discussion with him.'[11] In 1971 Twomey went to Regensburg and met a theologian who was 'young and brilliant, a university teacher who inspired enthusiasm. He always treated us students with great respect and gave us the greatest freedom in our search for the truth. Above all, he was restrained, modest and humorous.' Twomey told a story about the professor's universally well-liked secretary, Elisabeth Anhofer. One day she was asked what had most impressed her about Ratzinger. She thought for a moment and then said: 'The reverence in his voice when he spoke the name of Jesus.' Twomey added: 'Perhaps that is the most important thing we can say about Joseph Ratzinger.'[12]

Ratzinger's academic support staff included Karin Bommes, who created the indexes for his books, and the Salvatorian priest Stephan Horn. The doctoral student Martin Trimpe, born in 1942, had at first belonged to the Socialist German Students' Society in Tübingen. He had doubts about Ratzinger. His thought his theology was 'exegetically untenable'. That changed after he attended Ratzinger's seminar on *Lumen gentium*, the Council document on the church. Trimpe said he realized that, as opposed to Ratzinger's teaching, 'all this modern theology in Tübingen had no stable basis, and that Küng was much more concerned with politics than with the truth and justification of his ideas'.[13]

In his lectures and seminars Ratzinger dealt with ecumenism and the work of currently discussed theologians, such as Rahner, Jürgen Moltmann and Piet Schoonenberg. In his 1976 advanced seminar he addressed the question of a possible recognition of the Protestant confession of faith, the *Confessio Augustana* (*Augsburg Confession*), composed by Philipp Melanchthon. Ratzinger proposed the great thinkers of antiquity, Ignatius of Antioch, Irenaeus of Lyon and Augustine as subjects for seminars and doctoral works. He offered medieval masters, such as Thomas Aquinas and Bonaventure, and also contemporary philosophers and writers such as Karl Jaspers, Ernst Bloch and Albert Camus. Study was rounded off by meetings with modern theologians such as Balthasar, Congar, Rahner or the Evangelical scholar Wolfhart Pannenberg.

The students learned from Ratzinger, and Ratzinger learned from the students. For example, his student Barthélemy Adoukonou's dissertation on the Christian hermeneutic of Voodoo in Benin influenced Ratzinger's theology of religions. In his analysis of neo-Marxism he drew support from Friedrich Hartl's doctoral thesis on Ernst Bloch and Franz von Baader. It is striking that he got three of his doctoral students to work on the theology of the papacy: as an office of humility and martyrdom, as the English cardinal and theologian Reginald Pole had defined it in the sixteenth century or on the acceptance of its primacy by the Orthodox churches.

Of course, Ratzinger was 'in some way more of a keeper of tradition than a champion of revolution,' said Siegfried Wiedenhofer, 'but there is not a single instance of his hanging on to the past for its own sake'. There was no difference in the composition of his circle of students before and after Tübingen. 'All were accepted, even those who differed sharply.' He had never rejected anyone in anger. Actually it is not quite true that he never rejected anyone. Not in anger but because of his sympathy with liberation theology, Ratzinger did send his above-mentioned African student Barthélemy

Adoukonou to Küng in Tübingen, and then to Congar in France. In fact, Congar told the student he could not find a better teacher than Ratzinger. Apologetically, Adoukonou returned to Regensburg. Forty years later his former professor, who had by then become Pope Benedict XVI, appointed him titular bishop of Zama Minor and secretary of the Pontifical Council for Culture. Vincent Twomey reported that Ratzinger's 'gift of creating a space for a free and open exchange of opinions' was not 'just a natural talent'. It arose from a 'theory of education': 'Once Ratzinger said in passing that education should not seek to take anything away from the other; it should have the humility simply to accompany the student's own thinking and help them to mature.'

Was there a shadow side? It depends what is meant by that. Ratzinger's organizational and, above all, his financial support for his students was mainly kept in the dark. In fact he had always supported scholarships and also dipped into his own pocket if the need arose. But some of the theologian's weaknesses were less hidden. Wiedenhofer reported that occasionally Ratzinger had reacted 'fairly sarcastically and violently', especially in arguments with Johann Baptist Metz. Many of Ratzinger's 'shots' had been questionable. They had lacked 'a balanced interpretation'. 'Just a single statement was enough to settle the matter. But later on that stopped.'[14]

For Stephan Horn, his academic assistant at the time, Ratzinger's weakness lay in his inability 'to give direction to anyone. He is too retiring.'[15] He often just let things take their course. Ratzinger had 'an almost girlish softness', said Georg May, who belonged to the generation of 1926 and was emeritus professor of church law:

Anything to do with power, strength, the use of force is completely alien to him. By nature he is a scholar. So his appointments as archbishop and Prefect of the Congregation for the Defence of the Faith were actually against his nature. He carried out the duties of these offices, because in his way he is brilliant, but enforcement is not his thing.[16]

6

Tensions

However well things were going in Regensburg, elsewhere things were difficult. The Second Vatican Council was intended to open up the church and thereby lessen its declining acceptance. But now, according to the political scientist Franz Walter, it appeared that Catholics were increasingly giving up on 'actively practising traditional rituals, like celebrating name days, grace before meals, fasting, auricular confession [and] the cult of Mary'. The result was 'Religious practice and socialization in Catholic families were shrinking fast.'[1]

In Latin America the question of how the church saw itself and its relationship to the world had led to the founding of Christian 'base communities', which promoted 'liberation theology'. The Medellín Bishops' Conference in 1968 spoke of the 'beginning of a new era'. The Chilean movement Priests for Socialism called for the church to opt for the poor and for socialism; otherwise it would remain bound to the bourgeoisie.

In 1966 the German bishops had already warned in a pastoral letter about two dangerous adversaries, namely: 'the uncomprehending ones who cling to the past, and the impatient who fail to recognize that you can't take the second step at the same time as the first'. Both were 'equally far from the spirit of the Council'.[2] At the same time the progressives were trying even harder to promote efforts that had been clearly rejected by the Council. For Ratzinger, the main thrust of these ideas was to make the Catholic Church more Protestant. What particularly alarmed him was that this time the destructive forces, as he saw them, were coming not from outside but from within the ranks of theologians. The church seemed to be 'largely still just occupied with itself', he warned in a 1970 lecture: theology was clearly interested only in the 'battle to create new forms of church structure'.[3]

The break also became apparent in the International Committee of Theologians, a group of 30 academics from different theological schools and countries that Paul VI had set up at the suggestion of the first synod of bishops. In the committee, to which Ratzinger had belonged since it began on 1 May 1969, he sided with Hans Urs von Balthasar, Henri de Lubac, Marie-Joseph Le Guillou, Louis Bouyer and the Chilean Jorge Medina Estévez, among others, who regarded the 'state of perpetual revolution' as (in Gianni Valente's words) 'a caricature of the reform promoted by Vatican II'.[4]

The tensions increased. That appeared in the resignation of Karl Rahner and the Swiss ecumenist Johannes Feiner from the papal committee. They left 'because the majority of its members were not prepared to subscribe to radical theses', as Ratzinger recorded.[5] Ratzinger himself spoke of a feeling of boredom in a 'theologians' club' where he was not altogether needed: 'I can eat ice cream in Germany too, although there is very good ice cream in Rome.'[6]

His relationship with de Lubac deepened. In a note made during a conference session in Rome, de Lubac wrote that he was hurrying to the Domus Mariae 'to hear Dr Joseph Ratzinger, who is speaking on the collegiality of bishops and its pastoral implications'. On 6 October 1965 he noted 'Dr Joseph Ratzinger, a peace-loving and sympathetic theologian, as well as being a competent one'. Before that, Ratzinger had thanked de Lubac for sending two books and assured him that he 'had naturally kept track of your further publications, so that I have listened to you without you being present, so to speak, and thus may regard myself as your student'.[7]

In his memoirs Ratzinger remarked that de Lubac had 'suffered so much under the narrowness of the neo-scholastic regime' that he 'became a decided fighter against the fundamental threat to the faith that was changing all previous front lines'.[8] It had been 'a great encouragement' to see that someone 'judged the present situation and our tasks within it in the same way as I did'. When Ratzinger received the insignia of commander of the French Légion d'Honneur in Paris on 11 May 1998, he used the opportunity to highlight de Lubac's fighting spirit once again:

> During the war Father de Lubac was one of the brave inspirers of the resistance in France. He fought against the ideology of lies and violence, but never against a nation. That resistance carried the true power of reconciliation: Christian humanism, based on the universality and uniting power of truth. Truth is also a sword against lies, and Father de Lubac was not afraid to bear that sword against lies inside and outside the church, before and after the Council. Above all, he was a man of peace and fellowship in the love of Christ.

Working with de Lubac – that perfect 'model of a life in accordance with the gospel' – had been for him 'one of the greatest gifts I have received in my life'.[9]

Many Catholics were deeply unsettled. The reforms had changed the ritual they were used to. They were also reading bad news about the dramatic drop in church attendance and in applications to become priests. An unsuspected problem arose when, on 3 April 1969, Paul VI introduced a new missal for the conduct of liturgical services and at the same time forbade the use of the previous missal (the 1962 *Missale Romanum*, in which the Mass was celebrated in Latin). Horrified at the head of the church, Ratzinger fumed: 'Nothing of the sort had ever happened in the entire history of the liturgy.'

In the Constitution on the Liturgy the Council had already dealt with the celebration of Mass, the liturgy of the hours, the liturgical year, church music, church building and sacred art, which had caused considerable dismay among both priests and laity. But Ratzinger regarded the new missal as an alarm signal. Until then any amendment to the missal had always been based on the old design, using the former materials, he commented, but 'erecting it as a new construction, dismissing and banning what had grown up historically, made the liturgy no longer appear to be a living development but the product of academic work and legal authority. This did great damage. It gave the impression that liturgy was a "construct", not something given in advance.'[10]

In a later talk Ratzinger even called it 'a kind of wildfire'. For if liturgy is 'what the community makes up for itself just to reflect itself in it, then it never goes beyond itself'. Liturgy was 'the encounter with what we ourselves have not created, and thus also entering into the whole great course of history. It must not become rigid or fossilized, but neither can it simply be broken off; it must continue as a living process.'[11]

In the book of interviews *Salz der Erde* (*Salt of the Earth*) he put forward another argument: 'A community that suddenly declares what was formerly regarded as the most exalted and holy to be strictly forbidden, and that it is improper to long for it back, raises doubts about itself. For what should people then actually believe about it? Won't it again forbid something tomorrow that it prescribes today?'[12] He drew a sober conclusion:

> I am convinced that the church crisis we are experiencing today is to a large extent due to the disintegration of the liturgy, which at times has even come to be conceived – *etsi Deus non daretur:* 'as if God did not exist'– so that it does not matter whether or not God exists or whether he speaks to us and listens to us.[13]

His dispute with Hans Küng also sharpened. Ratzinger was too discreet to snub his colleague. Here his Achilles' heel showed in his failure to clarify relations with people around him whom he could not avoid. Now, however, confrontation had become inevitable. 'It will be our task for a long time,' he said in Regensburg, 'to use the Council's own words to combat the undermining of it, especially to combat the famous "spirit" of the Council.'[14] There was also a change from the offensive to the defensive. Küng himself, who had an enormous following, described his theology as the new paradigm full stop. With it he would replace 'the medieval anti-reform, anti-modernist Roman Catholic paradigm with its latent or open distrust of reform and modernization'.[15]

Küng rejected dogma. The authority of scholars and scholarship replaced the confession of faith. At the same time he had made the quest for the historical Jesus the decisive basis for his theology. This went with the demand to subject all the official 'doctrines' officially proclaimed by the church to constant critical review. However, the dogmatic theologian Wiedenhofer did not see the argument between Küng and Ratzinger as a quarrel between two different schools of thought, since both theologians represented not only reforming theologies, concerned with the relevance of the Christian faith, but also traditional theologies, concerned with the continuity of the church's faith. Clearly, the quarrel was reinforced by personal animosity. But, according to Wiedenhofer, the confrontation became so sharp because it was about an epochal turning point in church history, which had hardly ever happened before. It was about nothing less than 'the future way the church and theology would go: what was at stake was the identity of the faith and its relevance and relationship to the modern world'.[16]

So the underlying controversy was not between progressive and conservative but about the view of Christ. Who really was Jesus? This was the actual battleground between Ratzinger and Küng. What was the false image, which led to the shattering of the previous foundations of the faith? And what was the right one, which did not reduce the founder of Christianity to a historical figure, so that historical-critical method could keep questioning the historical Jesus?

Küng's book on the Council's theology had already caused 'a rather more serious controversy' (according to Ratzinger) between the two professors, even though the dispute was then still regarded by both of them as an interesting theological difference within their basic agreement as Catholic theologians.

A decisive moment for Ratzinger, 'when I felt clearly that this could not go on', was the publication in April 1967 of Küng's book *Die Kirche* (*The Church*). His book was 'truly Catholic', Küng declared, and for that very reason it 'diverged from the usual Roman Catholicism'. The Lutheran New Testament scholar Ernst Käsemann was gripped and announced in the great hall of Tübingen University that 'the church split between me and Küng has come to an end'. Rather sarcastically, Hans Urs von Balthasar regarded the book as an ecumenical doctrine of the church 'leading to the elimination of anything Catholic that was annoying to Protestants'.[17]

At the time Ratzinger and Küng were editors of the series in which the book was published. However, Küng's *Die Kirche* became the reason for Ratzinger 'to resign from that editorship'.[18] Three years later Küng published his famous polemical work *Unfehlbar? Eine Anfrage (Infallible? An Inquiry)*, which he linked to Paul VI's disputed encyclical on birth control *Humanae vitae*. According to Hansjürgen Verweyen, 'With this well-considered frontal attack on the institutional church he could count on the thunderous applause of a wide public.'[19] But why did Küng connect a statement by the pope, which was not declared to be infallible, with the dogma of papal infallibility? Verweyen's explanation was that Küng had simply seen that the moment had come, 'no longer to bow devoutly to the "old gents" in the Vatican'. The Tübingen fundamental theologian Max Seckler confirmed this: 'Küng said to me before the publication of *Infallible?*, "I'll blast the whole Roman system sky high". Since then that is basically all he has been doing. He has not developed his own theology, but serves all those who are frustrated.'[20]

In his book Küng argued that the 'infallibility' of the pope was not supported either by the Bible or by tradition. He also pointed out papal rulings in the past that in his opinion were wrong. 'I have it all in my head, I have completely mastered all the material,' Küng boasted in his work. Newspapers and journals outdid each other with positive reviews. However, the Roman Congregation for the Doctrine of the Faith began proceedings. Karl Rahner asked theologians for contributions to a book on the question of whether Küng's view of the papacy and the authority of church councils broke with the whole of Catholic tradition. In January 1971 Küng was invited to appear before a committee of German bishops. A month later the Bishops' Conference passed a motion condemning Küng's book.[21] Küng was happy about it: 'They seem to be afraid of my pen just as the king of France was of Voltaire.'[22]

Ratzinger also felt he had to respond. 'We met in the Anima [the German Pontifical College in Rome, also known as the Collegio Teutonico di Santa Maria dell'Anima]', recalled Walter Brandmüller, who later became a cardinal and head of the papal committee for historical science. 'Ratzinger asked at once: "Have you read Küng's book? We must do something, write something against it".'[23] Brandmüller published something in *Hochland*; Ratzinger published an essay in the volume edited by Rahner that came out in the *Quaestiones Disputatae* series. In his essay Ratzinger criticized 'the militant language, which often sounded more like class war than academic analysis or "feeling with the church"'. He also pointed out the many contradictions in Küng's book, which he dealt with in detail. He stressed that, despite his assurance that he was a 'convinced Catholic theologian', Küng argued outside the framework of Catholicism. The 'essential indispensability' of the foundations of the Catholic faith did not mean that the dogma 'could not be expanded, understood more deeply and so better expressed in words'. However, basically it was unchangeable, because it pointed directly towards Jesus Christ and thereby 'partakes of the persistence of truth'.

In his doctoral thesis Ratzinger had established that previously in the church revelation was not equated with the Bible. That was why Scripture and tradition always had to be looked at together: the church was the authentic interpreter of Scripture. That fact was the basis for the doctrine of infallibility. However, for Küng's liberal Protestant understanding of the church, the 'infallibility' of the magisterium was bound to be objectionable, simply because then the reigning theological opinions were not seen as the proper interpreters. But he had to agree with Küng that it was right to 'get out of the prison of Roman scholasticism'. Nevertheless, the concluding sentence of Ratzinger's criticism was crushing: 'The strong words and combative attitude of Küng's book sound to attentive listeners like thunder whose main strength lies in the fact that it can be heard from far away.'[24]

Two years later, as the co-author of the memorandum *Reform und Anerkennung kirchlicher Ämter* (*Reform and Recognition of Church Offices*), Küng downplayed the office of priest. That provoked another statement by the German Bishops' Conference faith committee. Küng still kept his permission to teach, owing not least to Joseph Ratzinger, who stood up for him behind the scenes.[25] With his next book *Christ sein* (*On Being a Christian*), in 1974, Küng hoped to match the sensationally successful sales of *Infallible?*. He decidedly saw his book as a reply to Ratzinger's *Introduction to Christianity*. He pointed out the difference in his foreword: whereas his competitor 'basically only wants to address Catholic Christians', his book was 'written for everyone who for whatever reason honestly and sincerely wants to be informed about what Christianity and being a Christian actually mean'.

On Being a Christian also provoked heated discussion. Ratzinger stated his position initially in a review. Later he wrote at greater length in a joint work edited by Hans Urs von Balthasar, *Diskussion über Hans Küngs 'Christ sein'* (*Discussion about Hans Küng's 'On Being a Christian'*): with this book the corner had decisively been turned in theological thinking. Everything that had been put forward since Albert Schweitzer against taking the 'historical Jesus' as the subject of theology, had now 'radically disappeared' with Küng. The result:

> Because Küng rejects the principle of 'dogma', he also, of course, has to reject the original model of dogma, namely the canon as canon in the theological sense. That means the scholar takes the place of the priest in determining the content of the faith, and becomes the only check on it. The historical Jesus as a 'reconstruction' becomes the criterion for being Christian; but in that case it is historians (or those who see themselves as historians) who hold the key in their hands.[26]

No longer the church magisterium.

Küng's *On Being a Christian* challenged Jesus' eternal sonship and the binding force of the Christological councils. His talk of Jesus as the 'true human being', who 'appeared to us as God's agent, deputy and representative', abandoned Jesus Christ's uniqueness and thus also the whole doctrine of the Trinity. The effects of this process, Ratzinger thought, could only be disastrous. 'It will fundamentally lead to decay. It must be positively and unconditionally recognized,' he said, that Küng's book rated 'high among much that has proliferated as theological undergrowth, so to speak, in second-order literature.'[27] I asked him in our conversation whether the publication of his criticism didn't tell all those involved that the bond between the two star theologians was finally broken? The pope emeritus's answer was short and unambiguous: 'Yes. Clearly.'

In an 'Answer to my Critics' in the newspaper *Frankfürter Allgemeine* Küng described the argument about his book as a 'party of well-selected professors'.[28] He had long been distanced from Balthasar. In a quarrel with 'Karl Rahner, the great disappointment', he accused the once 'great Council theologian' of lacking historical-critical thinking and exegetical expertise. Rahner's neo-scholasticism had appeared 'early on both to me and to Ratzinger' as 'obsolete'.[29] Rahner's assessment of *Infallible?* had been 'a general attack on my person and theology' in order to 'make it unbelievable in the whole Catholic world'. That was not all. In the Jesuit journal *Stimmen der Zeit* Küng also castigated Rahner's 'lack of precision, inaccuracy and patchiness'. The 'constant weaknesses of Rahner's theology' could now 'no longer be overlooked'. It was to be expected that Rahner would not just let this invective go. At a symposium in Frankfurt he shouted into the microphone: 'You, Mr Küng, may call this [theology] conservative, traditionalist and bourgeois, but I must tell you: I feel mortally threatened in my Catholic faith by your book *Infallible?*'[30]

There was no lack of further jibes. Küng commented on Rahner's support for clerical celibacy by referring to Rahner's own breaking of the rule in his relationship with the writer Luise Rinser: 'In fact over these two decades they have both written hundreds of love letters,' he told the public.[31] He also presented his former idol as a heartless Jacobin. After a failed attack on Paul VI during a visit to Manila in 1970, Rahner had said 'with a malicious smile' that 'he would not have been grieved to death if the attack had succeeded'.[32]

Küng felt persecuted. He complained about a lack of support from German theologians in his dispute with the Roman Curia. They were 'all the same, I realized, literally "creatures" of the Roman system'.[33] Karl Lehmann, Rahner's former assistant, wrote him an admiring letter on 30 October 1969: 'I hope that the battles you have fought with Rome have not exhausted you too much. As a Swiss democrat from childhood, you have the right stuff in your bones, which we lack. So you are the only one in many respects who can carry this through.' Lehmann concluded with the appeal: 'Landgrave, stay firm!'[34] Just a year later Küng was disappointed. 'I fear the worst, when on the day before the Brussels congress an article by Rahner's student Karl Lehmann appears in *Publik*. He focuses not on the response to my "Inquiry" (into the subject of infallibility), but on the questioning of my orthodoxy.' After that he also blamed Lehmann for drafting a critical letter for Cardinal Döpfner and Cardinal Höffner 'which formulates three inquisitorial questions', that later led to his losing his professorship. In 'deplorable complicity' with the

Curia and the bishops Lehmann was also responsible for the 'general attacks' by which 'the media was mobilized on a broad front against me' in Germany.

In his review of *Infallible?* Ratzinger had denied that his former colleague was still operating within a Catholic framework in his arguments. Obviously he felt obliged to make a clean break. Now it was no longer a quarrel between two theologians. It was a proxy war, in which the future pope foresaw two sides confronting one another, a war that could turn the split in the church into a permanent deep grave.

7

The Vision of the Church of the Future

Regensburg seemed to do Ratzinger good. When he got ill, he recovered quickly. And his new job gave him room for inspiration, analysis and innovative impulses, which were not 'in line with the general opinion'.[1]

According to his colleague Max Seckler, Ratzinger was convinced 'that his theology is very important for the church'. He attracted attention not only by his theological approach but also by 'a great sense of mission'. His concern was to hold a mirror up to ruthlessly advancing modernity, against forgetting, and thus to develop a clear-sighted vision of a church of the future capable of surviving.

If there is a date for Ratzinger's entry into battle mode, then it is 14 September 1970. In the liturgical calendar the date was the feast of the Exaltation of the Cross. The word 'exaltation' sees the cross as a sign of victory. By his martyr's death Jesus won back life and changed the sign of evil into a sign of love. On that 14 September Ratzinger was invited to give the ceremonial address for Josef Frings's 60th anniversary as a priest. The Cologne cardinal had retired from chairing the German Bishops' Conference in 1965. In 1969 he retired from his bishopric on grounds of age.

Ratzinger called his talk 'The Situation of the Church Today', with the subtitle 'Hopes and Dangers'.[2] There were about 800 priests in the hall; dignitaries with high positions in church or politics sat in the seats of honour. They included Archbishop Joseph Höffner, Frings's successor in Cologne, and Cardinal Döpfner, the chairman of the German Bishops' Conference. Wasn't it rather like nine years before, in the Thomas More Academy in Bensberg? Then too it was about the Council. But that was before Vatican II. With all its hopes. Now it was *after* Vatican II. With all its worries.

The voice spoke softly but was not afraid to set out a tremendous scenario. Ratzinger began with a description from the year 375. He loved to quote from history, in order to illustrate a modern situation. He began his talk by asking, 'What can we compare the modern condition of the church with?' The question was from Basil the Great, one of the most important figures in church history. The bishop of Caesarea, in Cappadocia, spoke of a mighty sea battle. In the 'confused indistinguishable uproar' that 'reigned over the whole sea' a ship was in danger of sinking. The crew, driven by 'the insuperable disease of ambition, had still not given up their 'battle for precedence'. So, said Basil, the turmoil raging in the church was far 'wilder than the surging sea'. Indeed, 'in the church every line drawn by the Fathers has been moved, every foundation stone, every certainty in doctrine has been shaken. Everything is disintegrating. Anything built on weak foundations totters. Falling over one another, we are pushing each other down.' And as if the carnage was not enough, in this situation 'novelty addicts' scented the 'best opportunity to rebel'.[3]

'This text from the fourth century,' Ratzinger continued, sounded 'surprisingly modern', and actually seemed to 'describe precisely the situation in which the church has unexpectedly found itself after the Second Vatican Council'. Certainly, before that the Catholic Church had often given an 'impression of rigidity and uniformity'. But today even those who 'wanted more diversity and movement' were appalled at the way 'in which their wishes have been fulfilled'.

No senior churchman had yet dared to speak so sharply. Ratzinger continued: 'It can't be denied that the crisis is in some way connected with the experience of the Council, even though today that is often hardly taken seriously.' He spoke of 'intellectual convulsions' and a 'flight into action'. He mentioned the 'bishops' conflict over the central statements of the faith', which had aroused 'a previously unknown feeling of uncertainty, to the point where it was thought that there could not actually be clearly ascertainable criteria'.

The Cologne speech precisely documents the programme Ratzinger followed as a theologian, bishop, prefect and finally as pope over the next four decades. It is worth quoting in detail, because it gives a clear insight into Ratzinger's thinking and shows where he saw the problem for the modern church and the options for renewal he recommended. Here it is:

The formula 'we are the church' coined during the youth movement has got a remarkably sectarian meaning: the radius of this 'we' often only embraces the current small group of like-minded people, who then use 'we' to claim a kind of infallibility. In fact, that statement should rule out group self-righteousness. For it is only true if the 'we' includes the community of all believers, not just those of today but from all through the centuries. In this 'we', the 'I' of Christ is implied, which is what has gathered us together as 'we'.

Humanly speaking, what saves the church today is not the often faltering and uncertain rulers, who either retreat into traditionalism or anxiously look to theologians, afraid that they will be labelled as conservative, when they should be brave enough clearly to assert the Creed. What carries the church through such times of uncertainty is the persistence of the faith of communities, in which the union of past, present and future is demonstrated and endures, beyond traditionalism and progressivism: in the reality of a life today lived by the Creed. Perhaps we have to experience the damage done by atheism in order to rediscover how irrepressibly and vitally the cry for God rises from human beings. Then at last we will realize again that human beings really do not live by bread alone; they are not saved just by having an income allowing them to possess everything they desire and freedom allowing them to do anything they want. Then they will realize that free time on its own does not set us free and that having is only the beginning of the whole problem of being. Human beings need something that Western capitalism as well as Marxism is so little able to give.

As Romano Guardini never tires of saying, the nature of Christianity is not just an idea or a programme – the nature of Christianity is Christ. When we lose him, no longer want to know him, only shadows remain. Shadows are not alive. What remains is a ghostly Christianity without power or reality. Anyone who wants to be a Christian today must have the strength to decide and the courage to be unmodern – like all children of tomorrow and yesterday. In a time that has called God dead, they must dare to set their roots in the eternal. They must have a living bond with God revealed in Christ.[4]

According to Ratzinger's crisis scenario, the post-Council process had become self-propelling, without substance or goal. Many advocates of radical reform saw the church primarily from the viewpoint of change, objectification and function. But that meant its actual spiritual nature was no longer recognizable. A dangerous progressivism determined the church's general climate, though it filled the church's life not with the light of joy but with a murky twilight.

Ratzinger distinguished three main forces between which there was a struggle for the future shape of the Catholic Church and theology:

- post-conciliar progressivism linked to the neo–Marxist or liberal pragmatic tendency and now predominant;
- narrow conservatism that stuck to past forms and by its rejection of the Council threatened to slide into sectarianism;
- the forces that had made possible the Second Vatican Council and carried it through. They had initiated a theology and devotional practice that derived 'essentially from Scripture, the church fathers and the great liturgical legacy of the whole church', but which afterwards had been overtaken by a wave of modernity.[5]

In fact the situation was paradoxical. Greater openness and liberalization were supposed to improve the Catholic Church's public image, but exactly the opposite was happening. The more modernly it behaved, the more people saw it as a stronghold of oppression and the past. Ratzinger also presented his diagnosis in a number of broadcasts. They were intended to speak not only of 'the shaking of faith by the present crisis' but also of 'the lure of the future'. He said he wanted to 'unlock', to show what was 'promising in the faith when it remained true to itself'.

Ratzinger's alternative programme was summarized in an essay on *Die Kirche im Jahr 2000* (*The Church in the Year 2000*). The vision was linked to his first paper from 1958 on *Die neuen Heiden in der Kirche* (*The New Heathens in the Church*). His earlier *Thoughts on the Crisis in Preaching* was also included. In that paper, which he had given as a 30-year-old to the Kolping Society in Regensburg on 9 October 1957, he warned against sacrificing 'the church's spiritual values' to the *Zeitgeist*, just because they were less palatable. Neither Ratzinger's diagnosis nor his ensuing prophecies can have pleased the church establishment, which imagined it was still safely in possession of Catholic Church property. As well as the self-confident verve, the author's power of expression is shown in the verbatim extracts from the essay given here. Looking into the future, he said:

We don't need a church that celebrates the cult of action in political 'prayers'. It is quite superfluous. Therefore it will collapse of its own accord. From today's crisis this time too a church of tomorrow will rise, which will have lost much. It will become small, and to a large extent it will have to start again from the beginning. It will no longer be able to fill many of its buildings that were built in times of prosperity. Because of the number of its adherents it will lose many of its privileges in society. Unlike in the past, it will present itself much more strongly as an optional community, which can only be joined through a decision to do so. It will surely find new forms of office and ordain reliable Christians as priests, who also have other jobs. But, as before, full-time priests will be essential too.

The future of the church will not come from those who just follow recipes. It will not come from those who just want to choose the easy way. Those who avoid the passion of the faith and call anything demanding false and obsolete, tyrannical and legalistic. To put it positively: the future of the church, this time as always, will be shaped anew by the saints. By people who are aware of more than mere phrases, people who are modern but have deep roots and live in the fullness of the faith.

But despite all these changes which we can imagine, the church will again decisively find its essential being in what has always been its heart: faith in the triune God and in Jesus Christ. It will be an inward church, which does not bang on about its political mandate and flirts as little with the left as with the right. It will rediscover its own core in faith and prayer and experience the sacraments again as divine service, not a problem of liturgical design. The church will find it hard-going. For the process of crystallization and clarification will cost it much labour. It will become poor, a church of the little people.

The process will be long and difficult. But after the test of this letting go, great power will stream from a church that has been taken to heart and become simplified. For the people of a wholly planned world will become unutterably lonely. When God has disappeared from them, they will feel all their terrible destitution. And then they will discover the little community of believers as something completely new. As a hope that takes root in them, as an answer, which they have always secretly been seeking – as a home which gives them life and hope beyond death.[6]

Celibacy also came up again. On 9 February 1970, in view of the shortage of priests, nine theologians drew up a memorandum for the German bishops, in which they signalled 'the need for a thorough examination and reconsideration of the Latin church's law of celibacy for Germany and the worldwide church as a whole'. It was an internal document and only published decades later in 2011. Together with Karl Rahner, Otto Semmelroth, Karl Lehmann and Walter Kasper, Ratzinger was one of the signatories. 'It was a typical Rahnerish text with qualifying yes and no clauses, which could be interpreted one way or the other,' Ratzinger said in our interview. On the one hand it was 'a defence of celibacy; on the other it called for the question to be kept open and given further consideration. So I signed in that sense more out of friendship between us all. Of course that was not such a good idea.'[7]

In his vision of *The Church in the Year 2000* Ratzinger himself suggested 'new forms of office', and ordaining 'reliable Christians as priests, who also have other jobs', the so-called *viri probati*. It can be seen how seriously Ratzinger took this supplementary model in his previously unpublished letter of 16 September 1971 to the church historian Raymund Kottje: 'Unfortunately. I hear that the German bishops have decided against the *viri probati*. I thought it was the way to create sensible new possibilities without breaking with tradition.'[8]

Ratzinger was also open to new solutions to the problem of communion for remarried divorced people. In a 1972 paper he argued 'with all due care' in the case of a 'second marriage' that 'has proved to be a moral reality over a longer period and with the spirit of faith, particularly in the upbringing of children' to let 'those living in such a second marriage receive communion'. He regarded such a ruling as 'covered by tradition'. Indeed, the church could not cease 'proclaiming the faith of the new covenant, but it often had to live its actual life a bit short of the threshold of Scripture', at least for 'limited exceptions in order to avoid something worse'. Marriage as a sacrament was 'irrevocable'. Nevertheless, 'that does not exclude the church's community from also encompassing those people who acknowledge this doctrine and principle but are in a particularly difficult situation'.[9]

The excitement was great when the fourth volume of Joseph Ratzinger's *Gesammelte Schriften* (*Collected Works*) was published and attentive readers discovered that the sentence printed above had been 'completely revised' and 'rewritten' (as could be seen from the bibliographical references). In the revised text now there was no direct mention of extending permission to receive communion. Both the 'breadth and the boundary of Jesus' words' always had to be fathomed, and it was right to 'support with loving care' divorced Catholics who were not living 'in a sacramental marriage'. The impression should never arise that they were 'disqualified as Christians' if they could not receive the Eucharist. But his 'concrete recommendation' was different from 40 years before: 'a serious self-examination, which might also lead us not to receive communion, would allow us to realize what a great gift the Eucharist is and also be a sort of solidarity with people who are divorced and remarried.' He also referred to a practice that had become common, 'that people who could not receive communion (e.g., those belonging to a different denomination) could go forward with their hands on their breast to show they were not receiving the sacrament but were asking for a blessing, which is then given to them as a sign of Christ's and the church's love'.[10]

Asked why he had revised the text, the pope emeritus told me on 14 April 2015: 'I have said, as it stands it could be wrongly interpreted. I can't put forward an ambiguous text. It is not a question of a new position, but a clarification. I tried to sum up what I said in the family council – that was after the 1980 family synod at which John Paul II appointed me as relator general.' (The relator general presents a report introducing the theme at the beginning of the synod and presides over the creation of the final report.)

Ratzinger's opinions on church and society were accused of being typically alarmist. For example, in a radio broadcast on 9 December 1973 he warned about 'the accelerating process of change'; the future 'had assumed all-importance' and little weight was given to past experience. The question was 'what space suit we would need to stand this cosmic pace at which we are travelling ever faster away from the gravity of tradition'. At its extreme, 'people were disengaging from the Earth's floor, from the basic conditions that sustain them, towards the idea that they can fully dispose over life and death, as in the dissolution of the difference between men and women that was appearing'.[11]

Although his views about our time seem to be proving true, a latent scepticism in Ratzinger cannot be wholly denied. Since the beginning of his studies he had been concerned not only with the crisis of faith but also with visions of the future, which could be called apocalyptic in the broadest sense. His favourite reading on the subject was George Orwell's *1984* and Aldous Huxley's *Brave New World*, and also Robert Hugh Benson's end-time novel *Lord of the World*, whose protagonist finally sets up a regime of anti-Christian world domination in the name of freedom.

During his time in Tübingen, Ratzinger read Vladimir Soloviev's classic *Short Tale of the Antichrist*, which Wewel, Ratzinger's publisher then, reissued in 1968. In the Russian philosopher's story the Antichrist appears in the year 2077. In Soloviev's version of the end-time, which he drew from the Bible, Europe has just overcome 50 years of Islamic rule when a man arises who claims to be completing Christ's work. He is determined to 'reform' the church; outwardly it would still look like the Catholic Church, but inwardly it would be just a social non-government organization with a pseudo-religious aspect. It was no coincidence that Ratzinger often recalled Soloviev's *Short Tale* in many of his texts: for example, in his *Schriftsauslegung im Widerstreit* (*Biblical Interpretation in Crisis*), where he recalled that the 'Antichrist' in Soloviev's book had an honorary doctorate in theology from the University of Tübingen.

Probably inspired by reading Soloviev, in 1968 Ratzinger published a paper on the return of Christ at the end of time. In this highly complicated essay, published in the journal *Hochland*, he dealt with the 'inner consequence of the biblical view' and the 'merging of anthropology and cosmology in definitive Christology'. In its 'twofold construction of cosmos and humanity' creation was always directed towards 'oneness as its final goal'. Cosmos and humanity would at some point 'become one by being assumed into the greater complex of encompassing love that went beyond the *bios* [the fleeting life of this world]'. That would make clear 'how the eschatological dimension and the breakthrough that occurred with Jesus' resurrection are really one'.

The cosmos was movement, meaning 'that it does not just *have* a history but it is history *itself*'. There was the 'process of material being becoming more complex through spirit, and hence becoming subsumed into a new history'. We could get an impression of that from the 'manipulation of what is real', currently taking place through the blurring of the borders between nature and technology. Therefore 'If it is true that at the end there will be the triumph of spirit, that means the triumph of truth, freedom, love. Then it is not just any power that finally wins the victory, it is a face, which is there at the end. Then the world's Omega is a "You", a person, an individual.'

In his presentation of an 'eternally all-embracing confluence' Ratzinger's philosophy spiralled up to heights to which he presumed only a small number of his readers could follow him.

> If the breakthrough in the final ultra–complexity is based on spirit and freedom, then it is in no way a neutral cosmic drift; it carries a responsibility with it. It does not happen of itself like a physical process but depends upon decisions. Therefore the Lord's return is not only salvation, not only the Omega making everything fall into place, but also judgement.[12]

Actually, it sometimes seemed as if the 43-year-old Ratzinger had internalized some of the rhetoric of 1968. For example, he insisted that 'the church needs a revolution of faith. It must get rid of its goods in order to keep its good.' The problem of people today was 'that they live in a world of hopeless profanity, which implacably programmes them, even in their free time'.[13] And this was also a typical Ratzinger statement: 'Resentment of everyone and everything contaminates the ground of the soul and turns it into a waste land.' In order to find an answer to the church's crisis and not to despair at the current state of affairs, people should identify not with the dominant forces in the church but with its faith and the faithful from every century. The legacy of the saints, the great liturgical traditions – all those gifts from heaven would survive and regain their prestige. They were not simply wiped out, over and done with, because they were not highly valued by a temporary *Zeitgeist*.

Draft programmes were one thing. However, for Ratzinger they were hardly believable if they were not followed up by a personal confession. It was 4 June 1970. The lecture was also heard by thousands of listeners to Bayerischer Rundfunk (Bavarian Radio). In it Ratzinger answered the question '*Warum bin ich noch in der Kirche?*' ('Why am I still in the church?').[14] His address began with the basics: what actually is the church? His theology drew on the symbolic language of the church fathers. They had compared the church to the moon and its significance in the cosmos: 'Moonlight is a strange light. Though it gives light, its light is not its own but another's light. The moon itself is dark, but it gives light from somewhere else, whose light it passes on.' That is why the moon is a metaphor for Christ's church: 'The church is not lit by its own light, by what the people in it do, and are, and accomplish; it receives its light from the real cosmic sun, from Christ.'

Meanwhile, said Ratzinger, it often happened that people spoke less and less of 'God's church': 'Instead of saying *his church* they say *our church* and mean many churches – everyone has their own.' In that way 'many little owners' have arisen with '"our churches", which we create ourselves, which are our own work and property and so we can change it or keep it as we wish'. However, a church that did not want to be '*his church*' 'would be just another sandcastle'. Then Ratzinger gave the answer to his title question: 'I am in the church because I believe that now as ever – and we can't do away with it – *his* church stands behind our church. And the only way I can stand by him is standing with and in his church.' Without the church there was only Jesus as a historical reminiscence. The church, said Ratzinger, also brought Christ alive in the present. Despite all its weaknesses. 'Whatever unfaithfulness there may be and is in the church, however true it is that it must constantly retake its measure from Christ, nevertheless there is no final opposition between Christ and church.' The church gave humanity a light and a standard 'far beyond the limits of its own faithful'.

In his address Ratzinger referred to the faithful as *communio*. The 'I believe' in the Creed was a collective 'I'. The individual believed not singly but together with the church from every century, which regarded all peoples as equal in international solidarity. Despite the church's shadow side, if you kept your eyes open you saw people who were a 'living witness to the liberating power of Christian faith'.

'How could I not love a church,' he cried, 'which gave us the splendid basilicas of Christian antiquity, the Romanesque domes, the Gothic cathedrals, the festive Baroque and the joyful Rococo buildings?' Then there were the works of Palestrina and the Mozart Masses, 'Gregorian chant and the sublime poetry of the great ancient liturgies', and the immortal works of an Augustine. It was also a church 'that makes time become history through the liturgical year, in which today and yesterday, eternity and the present, interpenetrate', a church that produced figures like Francis of Assisi and Pope John XXIII, and indeed the people 'who are closest to us, our own parents. I would have to take leave of myself if I wanted to be without them.' Summing up his confession in the fewest possible words he added: 'To put it bluntly, I'd say I remain in the church because I love it.'

By this point, thousands of radio listeners were enthralled. Of course, 'Love makes you blind,' Ratzinger went on to say, and folk wisdom had something true about it. 'But it is no less true that love enables you to see. In an old wrinkled face, which outwardly has no beauty, it discovers the person whose face it is and who is worth all our love. In the church's face, with all its wrinkles and blemishes, it discovers the Lord's mystery shining through.'

Of course this could be called whitewashing. 'But I believe that is mistaken. True love is not uncritical. And it is not static. On the contrary, it alone has the power to change and build. And so today too we should have the courage to look at the church with the eyes of love, in order to rejuvenate and renew it through love's real reforming power.'[15]

8

Reconquest

According to Ratzinger, the deeper reasons for the post-conciliar crisis sprang from 'the fact that two opposing hermeneutics confronted and fought with each other'. He called one interpretation, which corresponded to what the Council fathers wanted, a 'hermeneutic of reform'. It supported the renewal of the church while maintaining continuity and aligned the events of Vatican II with Pope Leo XIII's formula: '*Vetera novis augere et perficere*: to supplement and perfect the old with the new.'

He called the other interpretation, which followed not the Council texts themselves but their 'spirit', a 'hermeneutic of discontinuity and rupture'. It wanted to see the Council as a break with the past to make possible a radical new beginning for the church. Whereas for the Council fathers the Council had been 'a Council of faith seeking understanding', seeking to understand each other and God's signs for the time, the Council of discontinuity and rupture operated 'within the categories of the contemporary media'.[1]

In fact, 'the real Council', as Ratzinger called it, had not touched the fundamental principles of the Catholic Church: celibacy, papal primacy or the ban on women priests. 'Everything that Küng had been dreaming up for decades,' concluded the journalist and media expert Alexander Kissler, 'had no basis in the magisterium.'[2] Ratzinger summed up in his *Bericht zur Lage des Glaubens* (*Report on the State of the Faith*) of 1985 as follows: 'What the popes and the Council fathers looked forward to was a new Catholic unity. Instead, we have been heading for a disunity which – to use Paul VI's words – seems to be going beyond self-criticism towards self-destruction.' We expected 'a step forward but found we were proceeding towards collapse'.[3]

Self-critically, Ratzinger remarked later that the Council fathers had 'undoubtedly expected too much'. But we couldn't 'just make the church ourselves. We can do our job, but the church's weal or woe does not depend on that alone.' They had failed fully to take into account the dynamic of the 'great historic trends' inexorably 'taking their course'. 'And we partly misread them.'⁴ He himself had always wondered 'whether we did the right thing', the pope emeritus answered to the question whether he, as an important contributor to the Council, had ever been haunted by pangs of conscience, as had Cardinal Frings. 'But I must say I have always realized that what we in fact said and carried through was right and also had to happen. Even though we miscalculated the political consequences and actual outcomes. We had been thinking too theologically and failed to consider how things would turn out.'⁵

At the very beginning of his papacy Ratzinger declared in a speech he gave to the College of Cardinals and members of the Roman Curia that he had tried over the decades to remain faithful to the 'real Council'. In it he recalled the words of John XXIII, that the Council wanted to transmit 'the doctrine purely and fully without attenuating or distorting it', and that it was equally necessary 'to deepen the irrevocable and unchangeable doctrine, which must be faithfully kept, and formulate it in a way that meets the requirements of our time'. So, said Benedict XVI, it was worth always going back to the Council itself, its depths and its essential ideas. He was convinced: 'Wherever the reception of the Council has taken this direction in its interpretation, new life has grown and new fruits have come from it. So our deep gratitude keeps on growing for the work the Council did.'⁶

In Regensburg, Ratzinger found it was time to reconquer those achievements he had fought so hard for as a *peritus*. Time for a *Reconquista* of the Council, which was in danger of being manipulated, if not wholly appropriated, by interlopers. He had 'realized that if you wanted to keep to the will of the Council, you had to defend it against such misuse'.⁷ It was necessary to speak out, develop the church's own media communications, in order to reach people and give a voice to those silent masses who were usually excluded from the mainstream.

Up till then Ratzinger's three-step programme – Analysis, Answer, Action – had not reached the third step of putting theory into practice. For his *Reconquista* project (which of course he did not call that), reconquering the true values of the Council, Ratzinger set out a broad programme. It included developing alternative ways of teaching, gathering like-minded people, supporting charismatic movements and a series of book projects, in particular, the plan for a *Kleine Katholische Dogmatik* (*Short Catholic Dogmatics*), to aid proper religious instruction.

Ratzinger showed his combative verve as co-founder and co-editor of the alternative journal *Communio*, established in 1972. Its aim was to work against the alienation and decline in Catholic theology. For the first time theologians had come together to publish their own bi-monthly journal. Those on board with Ratzinger, von Balthasar and de Lubac included Walter Kasper, Karl Lehmann, the Bavarian education and culture minister Hans Maier, the psychologist Albert Görres and the communications expert Otto Roegele. Von Balthasar, de Lubac and Ratzinger himself had also been among the founding fathers of *Concilium*, which had first appeared in 1965, but they had all abandoned Küng's reforming course. (Only Karl Lehmann continued to write sometimes for one journal and sometimes for the other.) De Lubac had been the first to resign from the board of *Concilium*. At first Ratzinger had stayed on and was even among the 38 theologians who signed the 1968 appeal launched by *Concilium* for 'The Freedom of Theologians and Theology', which demanded a reform of the Congregation for the Doctrine of the Faith. De Lubac criticized the appeal for being imbued not with love of the church but with the spirit of propaganda.

'Now it's here at last, the long heralded and awaited international Catholic journal', Ratzinger's former opponent Professor Schmaus rejoiced in a pre-publication review of *Communio*. Fortunately, the editors were not interested in 'an intellectual battlefield'. They would not simply restrict contributors to a particular group 'in the dispute between theological parties'. The aim was 'to develop the truth rooted in the Catholic tradition'. *Communio* would not offer sensations 'but a serious and generally enlightening development of universal Catholic truth from its foundations'. That in itself was important, given the 'confusion in today's fashionable reinterpretations of Catholic doctrine'.[8]

Ratzinger said 'the decision arose when we saw things getting out of hand'.[9] The beginning of *Communio* can be precisely dated to a dinner in a Roman trattoria, at which Balthasar, de Lubac and Ratzinger met colleagues Marie-Joseph Le Guillou and Jorge Medina Estevez after a session of the International Theological Committee in the autumn of 1971. At that time a rumour was abroad in Rome that the pope would lay down his burden of office when he reached the age of 75. It was said that Paul VI had tasked a secret theological committee with drawing up a report to assess the pros and cons of abdication (which in fact decisively opposed his resignation). In the Benedictine abbey of Montecassino living quarters had already been prepared for the pope emeritus, as well as for a cardinal and a small household.[10]

It was no secret that Pope Paul was becoming increasingly worried about the church. As a memorandum for the pope, Von Balthasar had contemplated a substantial book in which he would detail the post-conciliar developments. Now haste was needed. Instead of a book, the idea arose of putting a different weapon in place, a journal, similar to Küng's *Concilium*. And yet completely different. 'It is not a question of bravura,' said von Balthasar, 'but the Christian courage to explain ourselves.'[11]

The declared aim of *Communio* was 'to overcome the uncertainty, where it has arisen in theology and reflection on the church', announced the German newspaper *Christ und Welt*.[12] The publishing director, Franz Greiner, the former editor-in-chief of *Hochland*, set the scene. 'We realize that the rich, often confusing range of post-conciliar Catholicism has not remedied the distress of convinced Catholics but sharpened it.' Karl Lehmann wanted to follow a line that he had already made clear in *Concilium* in his criticism of fashionable developments. In his eyes these trends were 'pseudo-intellectual ingratiation, romantic "love-and-death" for the separated brethren and busybody ministry to specialists in unbelief. At the moment the only thing to do is to make our own house a bit more attractive and inviting.'[13]

The new journal was a novelty in every respect. *Communio*'s founding body were going to support it not only intellectually but also financially. Instead of a central management there was a series of autonomous editorial teams, consisting of equal numbers of clergy and laity. The national editions would carry both national and international contributions. Germany and France made a start. When members of the Communione e Liberazione movement argued for an Italian edition, von Balthasar advised the initiators to go for Angelo Scola (the future cardinal and archbishop of Milan): 'You must talk to Ratzinger. He is the pivot and hub of the German edition. If he agrees …'. From 1974 the journal was published in English, French, Spanish, Polish and Portuguese (including in Brazil). In Poland Bishop Karol Wojtyła, who had prevented a Polish edition of Küng's *Concilium*, received Ratzinger's alternative journal with open arms.

The bishop of Kraków had been just 47 years old when Paul VI appointed him as the second-youngest member of the College of Cardinals. 'I know that I must prove myself, if I follow my new vocation,' he said of his appointment to four Vatican congregations, 'and I must show my worth anew.'[14] In Poland the post-conciliar rifts were almost over. Wojtyła saw the main job as 'skilfully uniting traditional popular piety with intellectual Catholicism', as it said in a confidential report of the Polish secret police in 1967.[15] In 1971 he convened a diocesan synod which set up 300 working groups with 11,000 participants. The aim was enthusiastically to implement the Council doctrines. In 1976 the *New York Times* put Wojtyła on the list of the ten most often named candidates to succeed the pope, who was becoming ever more pale and ill.

Communio was very influential. In the 1980s and 1990s nearly all the bishops and cardinals appointed by Pope Wojtyła came from the *Communio* contingent. But its founding was also a sign of the further split between two theological and church camps. Both called themselves 'Catholic', but they were as far apart as an Eskimo and an inhabitant of Tierra del Fuego. Whereas Küng's *Concilium* treated topics such as 'Communication in the Church' and 'Women in a Men's Church', Ratzinger's *Communio* referred (to mention two of the editor's contributions) to 'Church Unity and the Unity of Humanity' (1972) and 'What is Changeable and Unchangeable in the Church' (1978). To Küng's strategy of 'Against' – *against* the pope, *against* tradition, *against* dogmas – von Balthasar's response was 'whoever wants more action needs better contemplation, whoever wants to shape more must listen and pray more deeply'. 'Only meditation on what is Christian, purifying, deepening and focusing our ideas enables us to represent them faithfully.'[16]

Whereas *Concilium* claimed to represent the cause of progress, which was now to be promoted indefinitely, *Communio* embodied the ethos of *sentire cum ecclesia*, 'thinking with the church'. It followed a line that remained faithful to tradition and the magisterium, and also entered into open dialogue with the world. Ratzinger was very concerned that the new journal should have a widespread influence. This became clear in a self-critical assessment he made on *Communio*'s 20th anniversary: 'Have we really brought word of the faith to a hungry world in an understandable way that reaches hearts?' he asked at an editorial meeting. 'Have we been brave enough? Or have we perhaps hidden behind academic theological language, in order to prove that we too are keeping up with the times?'[17]

The Würzburg Synod gave further evidence that the difference between the two rival views of reform kept widening. The mammoth event, with 300 delegates, began on 3 January 1971 and lasted for eight sessions until 23 November 1975. As the 'Joint Synod of the Dioceses of the Federal Republic of Germany' its aim was to put the Second Vatican Council into practice and develop co-operation between clergy and laity. The idea for a 'National Council' arose at the 1968 Catholics' Conference in Essen. It was called for by the Young Christian Workers, the Critical Catholicism (Kritischer Katholizismus) action group and the German Catholic Youth Society (Bund Deutscher Katholischer Jugend) and was taken up by Cardinal Julius Döpfner as chairman of the German Bishops' Conference. Of course, it was unclear what the organization that assembled in St Kilian's Cathedral in Würzburg should actually achieve and what authority the participants had according to church law.

However, the discussion about the church and National Socialism demanded by Johann Baptist Metz was important and necessary. The Protestant writer Rolf Hochhuth's play *Der Stellvertreter* (*The Representative*), first performed in 1963, had portrayed the Catholic Church in a bad light by accusing it of looking away from or even chumming up with the Nazis. That put the church on the defensive. According to the historian Karl-Joseph Hummel, 'through the findings of contemporary research on the role of Catholics in the Third Reich' it was possible to see plainly what had happened. Hochhuth had not mentioned Pius XII's initiatives, which saved the lives of thousands of Jews. Scholarly research revealed that the Nazi regime in Germany and German-occupied countries had murdered 4,000 Catholic priests, and 12,500 more in Germany had been subjected to police investigation. Hummel argued that the impassioned debate had constantly escalated the church's share of guilt. From originally being a 'victim', in the new interpretation it had become a 'culprit'. 'At the same time the memory of the exemplary Catholic witnesses to the faith and martyrs had suffered'.[18]

In February 2013, in her book *Gott will Taten Sehen* (*God Wants to See Deeds*), Bishop Margot Kässman, the former chair of the Evangelical Church in Germany, asserted that the Catholic Church had not put up any resistance to National Socialism. Without giving any evidence, she wrote about Pius XII: 'His Catholic anti-Judaism associated him with National Socialist anti-Semitism.'[19] The philosopher Karl Jaspers saw quite different associations. Luther's 'advice against the Jews was taken up by Hitler', he declared in 1962.[20] Jaspers was referring to the extreme anti-Semitism of the founder of Protestantism:

1. Burn their synagogues
2. Destroy their houses
3. Take away their religious books
4. Forbid rabbis to teach
5. Forbid their freedom of movement
6. Compulsory expropriation of their property
7. Compulsory labour.[21]

Luther, he said, had had a strong influence on Hitler, who celebrated him as 'the greatest German genius'.

The playwright Hochhuth was later in the firing line himself, when in an interview he sided with the British holocaust denier David Irving. Ralph Giordano, a Jewish journalist and survivor of Nazi persecution, described Hochhuth's remarks as 'one of the greatest disappointments of the last 60 years'. Ion Mihai Pacepa, the former general of the Romanian secret service Securitate, claimed that for his play he had worked on behalf of Eastern-bloc state secret services and drawn on KGB material. Hochhuth denied this.

The Würzburg synod held debates on celibacy, lay preachers, women deacons, permission for remarried divorcees to receive communion, the role of the laity and ecumenical concessions. Karl Lehmann, in particular, had made these issues his own. Lehmann, the future chairman of the German Bishops' Conference, had been professor of dogmatics at the University of Mainz since 1968. (A positive reference from Ratzinger had helped him get the job, as he had no doctorate.) Lehmann became the leader and epitome of the synod. The word of the 'Lehmann church' stood for a policy of seeking common agreement for new compromise formulae in church, state and society. However, while the champions of the mammoth conference were still talking about the church's 'great moment', millions of Catholics were losing their religious home.

Ratzinger had been sceptical from the beginning. In the run-up to the synod in April 1970, in the Cardinal Wendel House in Munich he made clear his antipathy towards sedulous 'committee Catholicism', self-promotion and exhausting debates about structural questions. Paralysis through zeal for reform was his diagnosis. 'People complain that the great majority of the faithful generally show too little interest in the activities of the synod', he began his lecture. But he confessed that 'to me this caution looks more like a sign of health'. It is not only 'understandable' but also 'right from the viewpoint of the church' that people gradually become indifferent to 'the church apparatus talking about itself'. In the end the faithful 'don't want to go on hearing more about how bishops, priests and high-ranking Catholics do their jobs, but what God wants from them in life and death and what he does not want'.[22]

In the synod's constitutive session from 3 to 5 January 1971 Ratzinger lost the vote for the eight members of the central committee. (Lehmann was voted onto the 'Central Committee of German Catholics'.) So between 1973 and 1974, together with Metz and the philosopher Robert Spaemann, Ratzinger joined a working group – then suddenly disappeared. He excused himself for 'health reasons' and 'pressure of work'. But the real reason for his withdrawal lay elsewhere. In October 1972 he had already complained how quickly 'the actual statements and intentions of

Vatican II had been forgotten'. They were 'displaced, first by the utopia of an imminent Vatican III, and then by synods that respected the "spirit", not the texts, of Vatican II. That meant looking to the future as an array of boundless possibilities.'[23] He could not have distanced himself further from the way the church establishment was going. Indeed the Würzburg synod made clear the discrepancy between Ratzinger's ideas of reform and the ideas of the progressive wing, which increasingly dominated the church. It also marked the break – never to be repaired – between Ratzinger, the once celebrated Council adviser, and some of the German bishops. 'The situation had simply changed,' said Siegfried Wiedenhofer, 'and he reacted to that. However I have not found any about-turn, Ratzinger's so-called great change.'[24]

Instead of in the Würzburg synod, Ratzinger invested his time and energy in projects he thought more important:

– He took part in the Regensburg Ecumenical Symposiums, in which he engaged in conversations with Orthodox bishops and theologians. In August 1971 he was the first Catholic theologian to take part, as a full member, in a session of the Ecumenical Council's Committee for Faith and Church Constitution in Louvain, Belgium. His lecture on the future of ecumenism at the University of Graz in January 1976 became famous. In it he suggested a solution to the dispute between the Eastern and Western church on the papal primacy.
– Following a dramatic drop in vocations, at the request of Bishop Joannes Gijsen, he worked on a programme for the Rolduc seminary for priests in the Netherlands, the largest abbey complex in the Benelux countries. He produced a curriculum for alternative places of learning to build up the study of theology.
– He used lectures in Erfurt to support the faith of East German Christians and came under surveillance by the GDR Ministry of State Security. Because of his increasing importance, the ministry's foreign department had opened a file on Ratzinger and set at least a dozen staff onto him. Two GDR university professors gave reports on him. According to

research by the *Mitteldeutscher Rundfunk,* informers from West
Germany included a Benedictine monk from Trier and several
journalists.[25]

– His relationship with Don Giussani, the founder of
Communione e Liberazione became close and led to
his support for new spiritual movements. Then Giussani
developed a habit of saying, 'I'll have to ask Ratzinger what
he thinks about it first.' In October 1976, for the first time,
Ratzinger visited the centre of the 'Integrated Community'
in Herzog Heinrich Street in Munich. This was a group
devoting themselves to an original gospel lifestyle and links
with Judaism. They had been sending him their writings since
April 1969.

From the end of the 1960s Ratzinger had been holding courses of
spiritual exercises that included people from all over Europe. The
spiritual aspect of the faith was as important to him as the intellectual.
From that he developed an idea that the Passau theologian Manuel
Schlögl called a nonconformist programme 'beyond bourgeois
religion'. He borrowed the name from the title of a book by Johann
Baptist Metz.

In Ratzinger's teaching, faith was always also self-transcendence,
going beyond what you knew and were accustomed to. It was an
entry into the dynamic of love, emanating from Christ as the energy
to change. According to Schögl, Ratzinger 'saw a danger in his
environment of theology becoming too bourgeois, giving up its own
tradition and thereby losing its authority to criticize society and the
church'. So, together with Heinrich Schlier, Ratzinger kept up the
summer seminars in the Gustav Siewerth Academy in Bierbronnen
until 1977. 'All night long I discussed Rahner's theology with
Ratzinger,' the academy's co-founder, philosophy professor Alma
von Stockhausen, recalled. 'If I then asked him "What do you want
to do this evening?" he usually said "folk singing". That was the way
he could relax most easily.'[26]

In the summer school Ratzinger mainly dealt with saints: for
example, Irenaeus of Lyon, one of the most important thinkers of
the second century and Christianity's first systematic theologian.
The project reminded him of the example of Romano Guardini.

During the 1930s, as well as doing his university job, Guardini had run a spiritual centre at Rothenfels Castle in Franconia, to oppose Nazi conformism with a place of learning based on solid Christian faith. The academy was sponsored by the Cologne Cardinal Joseph Höffner. 'The holiday courses were a sort of insiders' briefing', said the Benedictine nun Maria–Gratia Köhler, who later became abbess of the Maria Heimsuchung (Visitation) Abbey in the Eifel region. 'Learning, living and celebrating – these things went together in Bierbronnen.'[27]

A letter he wrote to the abbess dated 13 October 1976 shows how overworked Ratzinger was with all this. He had 'a very bad conscience', the letter began 'that I have now left your friendly letter unanswered for a whole month'. Then he gave the reasons:

First, I had to prepare a long report for the Salzburg debate on humanism. I was the only theologian to be speaking there among political scientists, sociologists and philosophers – many of them atheists. That required a lot of energy. Then came a conference in Munich and a Salzburg week. Then I had to compose two broadcasts, one of 30 and one of 45 minutes, on very different subjects. (More than 28 manuscript pages altogether.) It is a torture for me to force the spirit into a tailor-made talk timed to the minute. I can only bear it with difficulty. The recording was done and took up a whole day. Then so many administrative things lay waiting on the table, which I had to deal with.[28]

On 18 December 1976 he sent a Christmas card to Sister Maria-Gratia with a picture of the ox and ass by the manger in Bethlehem. On it he wrote: 'How comforting it is that the Lord lets himself be carried by us donkeys and the dear creature shows us what we have to do.'

9

The Doctrine of Eternal Life

One of his students once asked Professor Ratzinger what method he used to write his books. That was quite simple was the answer. First he wrote the text on paper. Then he added the footnotes. And finally, he checked that the quotations in the footnotes agreed verbatim with their source.

In other words, because of his photographic memory Ratzinger was able to recall quite lengthy quotations, even in foreign languages and from originals that he had read years or decades earlier. In Regensburg he wrote works such as *Das neue Volk Gottes* (*The New People of God*), on ecclesiology and 'church renewal', and *Dogma und Verkündigung* (*Dogma and Proclamation*), on belief in creation and the theory of evolution. He also wrote countless lectures, meditations and reflections. Above all, he finally found the time to return to one of his main subjects, death and life after death. For 'if belonging to the church has any meaning at all,' he said, 'then it is only because it gives us eternal life and thus real, true life.'[1]

Ratzinger had been interested in the subject of the end time for 20 years. From the beginning it had been part of his lecture programme. Now he was able to write about it in what he afterwards described as his 'best-written book'. It appeared in the *Kleine Katholische Dogmatik*, the new theological series he co-edited with Johann Baptist Metz, published by the Regensburg publisher Pustet. The project nearly involved Ratzinger in a court case, because his earlier publisher Wewel had contracted him to write a book on *Dogmatics*, which he failed to produce for lack of time.

'Eschatology', the 'doctrine of the last things', dealt with the fundamental questions of human existence, our 'whence' and 'whither' – where we come from and where we are going – and thus the central content of Christian hope. 'I am the resurrection and the life' was Jesus' spectacular promise. 'Those who believe in me, even though they die, will live, and everyone who believes in me will not die for eternity' (Jn 11.25). It made a difference whether creation and creatures ended in a merciless Big Bang and it didn't matter how anyone lived and loved. Or whether after the end of time a new form of existence dawned, in which a higher authority exercised compensatory justice – in a dimension of harmony and love in which all injustice, all contradictions, were removed.

In the post-conciliar period professors, bishops and priests had begun to find it embarrassing to speak about heaven and hell, the last judgement or even the return of Christ. And if they did, they spoke as if these ideas were merely metaphors, explanatory models for unresolved longings. When Ratzinger finished his manuscript in the autumn of 1976, he was fully aware that his new book was 'against the reigning opinion'. However, his work was driven not by a 'desire to contradict' but by the 'force of the subject matter'.[2] At the start of his research he 'had begun with those theses that were recognized as valid in contemporary theology'. However, it had proved impossible to persist in 'constructing a de-Platonized eschatology'. For 'the longer I thought about the questions, the more deeply I went into the sources, the more the assembled antitheses collapsed and the inner logic of the church tradition was revealed'.[3] In other words: the unchanged validity of the doctrine that the church fathers and the church's thousand-year-old reflection on death and Apocalypse had propagated.

It was no surprise that Ratzinger's interpretation caused a lively dispute. However, according to Bayerischer Rundfunk, his rigorously scholarly publication could be regarded as 'a standard work on the history of the Western idea of "soul" and "life after death"'. With his 'pioneering book', as the theologian Helmut Hoping called it, Ratzinger had hit home.[4] Now that the devastation of our planet, the finite nature of resources and especially the loss of human identity had created a new awareness of an end to the world, the question Ratzinger had raised was very timely. Ratzinger's 'Big History' of the unity of the cosmos and history not only offered a new understanding for concepts such as 'the soul', 'heaven', 'hell' and 'eternity' but also an 'eschatological realism', as he called it. In contrast to a political utopia, it possessed real power to change. The power was not located in a system but in people themselves and made possible a real maturing of their humanity in the here and now, not tomorrow or the day after tomorrow. And it looked forward to that happy future, which Christians believed was inscribed in the *Logos* of creation. That was in accordance with what Jesus had said: 'Truly, I tell you, anyone who hears my word and believes in him who sent me has eternal life, and does not come under judgement, but has passed from death to life' (Jn 5.24).

Ratzinger pointed out that Catholics still prayed in the Nicene Creed: 'I look forward to the resurrection of the dead and the life of the world to come.' However, nowadays even most Christians regarded 'eternal life' as fairly uncertain – and not particularly worth striving for. The reason was the widespread conviction that God could not really act in the world. He was 'no longer one who acted in history, at best a marginal hypothesis'. The grave consequence of that was the 'paralysis of hope for eternity'.

In March 1992 Ratzinger gave a remarkable summary of the results of his research on this subject in a lecture to the Christian Academy in Prague. He began by saying that a look at the history of religion showed that there had hardly ever been a time when it was thought that everything came to an end with death. 'Some sort of idea of judgement and life after death is to be found almost universally.' Generally, the idea was conceived as 'being in non-being, a shadowy existence, curiously related to the world of the living'. The ancient phenomenon of ancestor worship expressed 'an awareness of human community that was not interrupted by death'. Hence it had been 'relatively simple' to think of heaven 'as a place full of beauty, joy and peace'.

The longing for a super-terrestrial world, the speaker continued, corresponded to an 'ancient expectancy in human beings'. For example, for justice: 'We cannot simply resign ourselves to might always being right and the weak being oppressed. We cannot resign ourselves to the innocent suffering, sometimes in such terrible ways, and [to the idea] that all the luck in the world seems to fall into the lap of the guilty.' But anyone longing for justice was automatically longing for truth:

> We see that lies spread, prevail and it proves impossible to counteract them. We hope that it will not always be so: that truth will prevail. We long for senseless gossip, cruelty and misery to cease; we long for the darkness of misunderstanding to be overcome, for love not to be powerless We long for true love that frees our whole being from the prison of its loneliness, opens us up to others, to the infinite, without destroying us. We can also say we long for true happiness. We all do.[5]

That was exactly what was meant by 'eternal life'. It did not mean a long period of time but a quality of existence. Eternal life was 'not an endless succession of moments, in which we had to try to overcome our boredom and fear of the unending'. It was about that new quality, 'in which everything flows together into the Now of love. It was a new quality of being, in which the bit-by-bit existence in a succession of moments is overcome.' Consequently, eternal life was 'not simply what comes afterwards'. Since it was a quality of existence, 'it may already be present as something new, different and greater in earthly life with its fleeting temporality, even though only in fragments and imperfectly'. It was 'that way of living in the present during our earthly existence which is not affected by death, because it reaches beyond it'.[6]

It was no accident that John the evangelist distinguished between *bios* (the fleeting life of this world) and *zoe* ('contact with true life, in which we meet God from within'). So it was

> where we come face to face with God within time. Gazing at the living God can become something like the firm ground of our soul. Like a great love, which is not altered by life's vicissitudes, but is an unshakeable centre from which we draw the joy and courage to go on, even when outward things are painful and difficult.

Ratzinger summed up: people had long been offered 'utopia, the expectation of a better world, instead of eternal life'. According to atheists, ideas such as 'last judgement' or 'a paradise beyond this world' estranged people from their proper task, the struggle for freedom and equality. But we should turn that round. It was not the eschatological but the political utopia, as a goal towards which everyone could work together, that 'was an illusion' – because 'it led to the destruction of our hopes'. 'For that future world to which the present was sacrificed never comes for us; it is always only for a still unknown future generation.'[7]

That was like the drinking water and the fruits offered to Tantalus in Greek mythology. The water only ever came up to his neck and the fruits never reached his mouth. Seen thus, Tantalus was an image for 'that hubris' which tried to replace 'eschatology with a self-made utopia'. It was a utopia 'seeking to fulfil human hopes through their own efforts without faith in God'. This utopia always seemed quite near. But it was also clear: 'It never comes.' It failed to understand the dynamic of history or human shortcomings. Ultimately, the struggle for life, which was also a struggle against evil, had to be engaged in by each generation.

Ratzinger's *Eschatology* showed that the future pope's teaching was also thoroughly political. When he was still coping with the impact of the anti-authoritarian revolt, he demanded that we should 'dismiss' ideas of an earthly paradise of whatever sort, a future 'ideal society', and 'work instead with full commitment' to strengthen those forces which were really a 'guarantee of the future'. That is just what happened 'when eternal life comes into force within time. Then it means that God's will is being done, "on Earth as it is in heaven". Earth becomes heaven, the reign of God, when God's will is done here as it is in heaven.' Of course, we could not force heaven to come down. But that reign was 'always very close where God's will was carried out. For then there was truth, justice and love.' The 'realism of Christian hope' meant 'Eternal life that begins here and now in God's community opens up that here and now and takes it into the fullness of the eternal, which is no longer divided into passing moments of time.' This also made it clear that Christian faith was not a withdrawal into the purely private. The present and eternity (unlike the present and the future) did not lie along a line apart from one another, 'but they lie within one another. That is the real difference between utopia and eschatology.'

The Prague speech concluded:

Living with God, eternal life in temporal life, is possible because God lives with us: Christ is God with us. He is God's time for us and also the opening up of time onto eternity. God is no longer the distant, indefinable God, to whom there is no access. He is God with us: the body of God the Son is our bridge to God.[8]

In the opinion of the future pope, Purgatory was not 'some kind of concentration camp in the other world', in which people had to suffer punishment, but a purification process, the 'necessary process of inner transformation'.[9] The setting of 'purification' was 'ultimately Christ himself'. The Lord's presence would work like a burning fire on everything in people that was 'involved in wrong, hatred and lies. It will become a cleansing pain, burning everything out of us that is incompatible with eternity, the vital coursing of Christ's love.' Hence we could also understand what 'judgement' meant. 'Christ himself is the judgement, he who is truth and love in person. He came into this world as the inner measure for each individual life.'[10] Likewise, hell was not a red-hot place of torture under the Earth, but 'the zone of unutterable loneliness and love refused'. That is 'what happens when people become locked in themselves'. Heaven was not a timeless place above the clouds but a reality, which arose from close contact between God and humans – 'love fulfilled'.

Ratzinger's friend the eccentric French-American writer Julien Green had the same view: 'The other world is a world of light and love and also of Purgatory,' he said. One of philosophy's greatest errors was about 'the concept of time. Time is nothing. We are meant to live in eternity.' Green and Ratzinger had met in Freiburg. Green was 'a complex man, a believing man,' said Benedict XVI in our conversation. 'I got on well with him.' However, his books were 'a bit bleak. I prefer cheerful Catholicism.'

So we could trust what was promised for eternal life in the final New Testament book: God 'will wipe away every tear from their eyes. Death will be no more; morning and crying and pain will be no more' (Rev. 21.4). Every suffering, said Ratzinger, 'every silent endurance of wrong, every inner overcoming, every impulse of love, every care and every committal to God' would have an effect.

For 'nothing good is in vain'. Moreover, Christ's return had already begun in a certain way: the saying that 'God was all in all' had 'begun with Christ's self-sacrifice on the cross'. 'It will be fulfilled when the Son finally hands over the kingdom, that is all humanity, together with all creation, to the Father.'[11]

People began to forget that Ratzinger, as a theologian who thought in an eminently historical way, now as before still supported reforms. But now they were more clearly linked back to the sources of the faith. He was not only engaged in the rediscovery of the 'old', as Vincent Twomey emphasized, but combined it with discovery of the 'new', like de Lubac, Guardini, Scheler or Peterson: 'He was always up with the times and also the best expert on the Catholic tradition.'[12] Siegfried Wiedenhofer said his teacher had not been original in the sense that he offered a developed system, as Rahner did, for example: 'But when it is a question of integral theology, the connection between intellectual reflection, loyalty to the church [*Kirchlichkeit*: 'churchliness'] and personal confession of faith, then Ratzinger is great.' The increasing separation between scholarship and faith in the modern era and specialization in theology, today was 'the core problem. Seen thus, Ratzinger's theology is very original.'[13]

According to his student Stephan Horn, Ratzinger's approach was 'to deepen the faith and to have an effect on the world through the faith'. So Horn was convinced 'that the heart of his spirituality is mystical.'[14] That came particularly from his closeness to Augustine. According to Augustine's 'theology of the living people of God', the new temple in which God dwelt was the church, not as an institution but as a community of faith and love. The central focus for the people of God was not the buildings and organization but the sacraments. Their unity lay in taking part in the liturgy and especially in Holy Communion.

Ratzinger himself stressed his starting point was the Word: 'That we really believe God's Word, that we try to get to know and understand it.' Hence his theology had 'a somewhat biblical stamp and a patristic stamp, especially Augustine'.[15] So one of Ratzinger's central concepts was the *Logos*, the Word, Reason. He spoke of Christianity as a '*Logos* religion'. *Logos*, God's Word, created the world. And the Word became flesh, in order to recreate the fallen world. All order, all law, was moral reason and permeated with meaning to its utmost ramification, even when people could not always easily understand that. Therefore believing meant seeking understanding: 'As the creation comes from reason and is reasonable, so faith is, as it were, the completion of creation and hence the door to understanding.'[16]

Ratzinger's concern was also 'to defend a certain legacy'. He acknowledged the ecological battle against the extinction of species, the melting of glaciers and the global climate crisis. But the saving of spiritual resources and of the historical religious treasury was no less important than saving flora and fauna. Then it was possible to understand again that the doctrine of the faith was a key to opening hidden mysteries. It followed that it made no sense to change the key. A new key might seem more modern. But it would no longer fit the lock.

The day came when the pope's ambassador came to Regensburg, the nuncio Guido del Mestri, a solemn, almost sombre looking figure, the son of an Italian nobleman and an Austrian countess. He was a priest-diplomat, born in Banja Luka, in what is today Bosnia and Herzegovina, who had served in Asia, Africa and America. He was regarded as a specialist in resolving particularly difficult issues concerning personnel. Eight months before Mestri's appearance the news of the sudden death of Julius Döpfner, the 63-year-old archbishop of Munich, of a heart attack on 24 July 1976, caused a stir well beyond Bavaria. The metropolitan see of Munich was regarded as one of the most influential in the worldwide church. Countless names were suggested as Döpfner's successor, including that of Regensburg's top theologian. One day a cheeky student laid a local paper on the lectern in front of Ratzinger with the headlines: 'Will the cathedral's director of music's brother be the new bishop?' Ratzinger glanced at the paper and then said, 'We don't want to talk about bishops but about Jesus Christ, the eternal high priest.'[17]

At his university Ratzinger had just ended the summer semester with a seminar on the 'general doctrine of creation' and was finishing his manuscript on 'Eschatology'. He had not taken the gossip about his chances of being Döpfner's successor 'very seriously', he remarked in his memoirs. For 'the state of my health was well known', as was 'my unsuitability for leadership and administrative jobs'. Even when the nuncio invited him to the Hotel Münchner Hof in Regensburg, he did not 'fear anything untoward'. Especially as del Mestri only chatted to him about trivial matters. But just as he was leaving, the nuncio pressed a letter into his hand. He was to read it calmly at home and think it over. As soon as he reached Pentling, he opened the envelope – and went rigid with shock. In his memoirs he stated baldly it was 'my appointment as archbishop of Munich and Freising'.

Ratzinger confessed that Pope Paul's letter had really been 'a surprise, yes a shock' for him. Perhaps he would have been less shocked if he had realized before their meeting that del Mestri had already been engaging in discreet consultations. 'Ratzinger definitely never strove to become a bishop,' Archbishop Karl-Josef Rauber reported. At the time Rauber was substitute secretary of state for Giovanni Benelli in the Vatican. His task in the run-up to an appointment was to make inquiries among a few bishops. 'Cardinal Höffner told me, for example, that Ratzinger is very gifted and a very loyal churchman, but when he is attacked he sinks into himself.'[18] In Munich, Rauber learned from auxiliary bishop Ernst Tewes that the cathedral chapter would prefer Karl Lehmann as bishop rather than Ratzinger. Stronger opposition came from Hans Urs von Balthasar, who was also included in the secret inquiry. Ratzinger's appointment had to be stopped It was unacceptable that theology should lose such an important thinker.[19]

What should he do? Ought he to accept the appointment? He could not take advice from his sister Maria. She should not know about the pope's letter; neither should their brother Georg (both were decidedly against the move to Munich, they said later). What had actually led to the pope's decision? Was his appointment as bishop an act of revenge because he had harshly criticized the pope's ban on the old missal? Or was it because he constantly refused to take positions on the theological questions that Pope Paul importunately sent him about his house theologian Father Mario Ciappi? Rauber reported: 'Whereas Balthasar always cordially engaged in this and felt honoured, Ratzinger had once even responded indignantly that he had no time for such things.' And two years earlier hadn't he even turned down an invitation to the Curia's Lent exercises?

Certainly, Ratzinger must have regarded the pope's decision as a demotion. How could he not? Sermon-writing and international congresses – that was all right. But financial planning, endless deanery meetings and clerical council meetings – how could he cope with all that? As well as the sessions of the Standing Council of the German Bishops' Conference! A waste of time! And then there was the press. De Lubac had said that using the media was a tactic of the 'anti-Council'. And who did it better than Hans Küng? No other theologian had used the mainstream and anti-church press more cleverly than him. It was 'You scratch my back, I'll scratch yours'. Küng delivered the statements – and in return he received goodwill that was close to veneration of the saints. How could you fight that, being always on the defensive? The German church was split, and its leaders privately sympathized with Küng's line.

Ratzinger opposed the theological experts who felt they were above bishops and popes and were contemptuous of simple folk and their 'stupid' piety. If he had an ambition, it was to be a theologian who offered his own contribution to the demands of the time. 'From the beginning I felt my vocation was to teach. I believed that by this time – I was 50 years old – I had found my own theological vision and could now create a body of work with which I would contribute something to theology as a whole.'[20] Hadn't the Regensburg years been 'a time of fruitful theological work'? What a blow of fate! And to happen now! He admitted openly: 'I was looking forward to being able to say something of my own that was new and also completely in accordance with the faith of the church.'[21]

The nuncio had advised him to consult his confessor. But he preferred to go to his fatherly friend Johann Baptist Auer. He was sure to get the right advice from him. Hadn't Auer often protested? 'No, you can't!' he would say, if he did not agree with something. 'But the joke was on me,' Ratzinger told me in our conversation. 'I thought he would tell me: "That's not for you!"' But his answer was different: 'To my great surprise he said without a second thought: "You must accept."'[22]

Eventually, his doubts were overcome. As well as his worry about his relative lack of pastoral experience, there had been another worry: 'I knew that my health was weak and this job would be more physically demanding.'[23] In that dreadful night the future pope confessed Psalm 73 had come into his head. In it the psalmist asked why the wicked of this world so often prosper. And why do so many people in the world have such a hard time? But when he went into the Temple, it became clear to him: 'I was stupid and ignorant; I was like a brute beast towards you. Nevertheless I am continually with you; you hold my right hand (vv. 22–3).' St Augustine, Ratzinger said, had been in a similar situation when he was ordained as a priest and bishop. He had 'kept going back to that psalm with love and in the sentence "I was like a brute beast towards you" [*iumentum* in the Latin] he had thought of it as a draft animal'. Then he had recognized himself as God's beast of burden. As one who had to bear the *sarcina episcopalis*, the burden of a bishop's office. Indeed Augustine 'had chosen the life of a scholar', but then he had realized: 'as the draft animal is so near the farmer, and is led by him in its work, so I too am very near God, since I serve him directly to establish his kingdom, build his church.'[24]

The nuncio was still at the Hotel Münchner Hof. All night long Ratzinger had deliberated and prayed. Next morning he signed his agreement, written on the hotel's headed paper in his tiny handwriting, accepting the appointment as archbishop of Munich and Freising. There were situations, he said in retrospect, when you had 'to accept something that did not seem to follow the life course you had seen before you at the start'.[25] Not much later he informed his assistant Siegfried Wiedenhofer: 'I have something dreadful to tell you, something awful has happened. I have been appointed as bishop of Munich. And I have accepted.'[26] The official papal letter of appointment was dated '24 March in the year of salvation 1977' and began as follows: 'Paul, bishop, servant of the servants of God, to beloved son Joseph Ratzinger, of the archdiocese of Munich and Freising, professor of theology at the University of Regensburg, appointed archbishop of the metropolitan see of Munich and Freising, greetings and apostolic blessing.'

Ratzinger could feel flattered: 'Our pastoral care compels us to pay regard to the extensive and important church of Munich and Freising', the papal letter continued. 'We are looking at you in spirit, beloved son: you are endowed with outstanding spiritual gifts; above all you are an important master of theology, which you have imparted as a teacher to your students with zeal and fruitfulness.' Pope Paul did not fail to point out the responsibility involved: 'Finally we heartily exhort you, dear son, in the words of St Augustine: work in God's cornfield. Strive with all your might that all those committed to your care should be living stones to build the church, formed by faith, confirmed by hope and united in love.'[27]

The pope's decision was announced on 25 March. With the Curia's fine instinct for the meaning of a date, a major feast day in the Catholic Church was chosen, which must have acted as a sign: 'the Annunciation of the Lord'. The event was even reported in *Der Spiegel*. With Ratzinger's appointment to 'one of the most important offices the Catholic Church has to offer in Germany' the pope had 'departed from custom', said the magazine. It had hitherto been the practice 'to appoint an experienced bishop' to a metropolitan see. However, Ratzinger had not yet served an apprenticeship in the Roman training school the Germanicum. As a member of the faith committee, he was one of the main critics of the reform theologian Hans Küng. But his criticism only had weight because

Ratzinger opposed his Tübingen colleague without polemics but with well-founded knowledge of the church's doctrinal tradition. Küng's theology, Ratzinger wrote, ended up 'with abstruse notions'. It was 'doomed to non-commitment'. His 'theology without and against dogma' offered no reason to 'join the church – rather the opposite'.[28]

It was no surprise that Hans Küng declared that his former colleague's appointment was a career step he had long been striving for. It was the logical consequence and reward for his conformity. Later Küng added drily: 'It is to be hoped that, despite his lack of *oeuvres*, he will not be forgotten as quickly as someone like Cardinal Ottaviani, whose name, despite his many speeches and statements, even young theologians hardly remember today.'[29]

Ratzinger had built a house. He had a huge audience in the university. He was in demand internationally as a speaker, and his works were best-sellers. Now fate had decided to 'deprivatize his life as a necessary form of his priestly vocation', as Ratzinger once described a clerical career. In our conversations I asked the pope emeritus whether his departure from Regensburg had been the great rupture in his life. Had it been 'the end of your personal happiness and all your dreams?' The pope's voice expressed a melancholy resignation as he answered: 'You could say that. Yes.'

Archbishop

A few days after his appointment as the 71st successor to St Corbinian, Ratzinger paid a visit to Freising, the ancient diocesan capital. He wanted to pray at the shrine of the bishopric's founder in the cathedral crypt and pay his respects to the Bavarian bishops who were holding a meeting on the Domberg then. He spent the time before his ordination doing seven days of spiritual exercises in the Benedictine monastery of Beuron in Baden-Württemberg. 'He slept in the bishop's room, concelebrated Mass in the mornings and breakfasted alone. During the day he meditated and prepared his ordination sermon', reported Father Michael Seemann, one of his Regensburg students. 'Every afternoon we drank coffee together. I noticed how tense he was and needed these relaxed chats; sometimes he even told me jokes!'[1]

Memories were stirred. As if it had been yesterday, he remembered having to defend his doctoral thesis in February 1957. 'Your subjectivist way of interpreting revelation, Mr Ratzinger, is not properly Catholic,' Professor Schmaus had thundered.[2] It was still a bit oppressive now: the great expectations of the 2 million Catholics in the diocese. The unaccustomed black cassock with the scarlet red buttons, which hardly fitted into the buttonholes! During these days he was still 'trembling inside', Ratzinger confessed. Besides, there were still piles of work to sort out in Regensburg, 'so I approached my ordination day with fairly rocky health'.

But his worries were quite unnecessary. His entry into the Bavarian regional capital on 23 May 1977 was like the triumphal procession of a tribune coming home victorious. As soon as he stepped over the boundary of the diocese, Ratzinger was greeted by an enthusiastic delegation. In Moosburg he was cheered by well over a thousand faithful. And on the outskirts of the city, at the Maria Ramersdorf pilgrim church, many thousands had turned up heartily to welcome the still somewhat shy bishop-in-waiting. They included the SPD (Social Democratic Party) mayor of Munich, Georg Kronawitter. The joy was great because it was the first time in 80 years that Rome had appointed an Old Bavarian and priest from their own diocese.

He also received praise in advance. 'Joseph Ratzinger has the merit of all great personalities. They are accountable to nobody. They are themselves', the *Deutsche Zeitung* enthused. Whoever read his books 'feels how here a theologian is wrestling with the future of the faith and the future of the church'.[3] Munich readers could read in the *Süddeutsche Zeitung* that the successor to Cardinal Döpfner was 'of all the conservatives the one with the strongest capacity for dialogue'. Why?' 'Because he unites intelligence and eloquence to a rare degree.' With Ratzinger the people of Munich were getting 'a devout bishop and brilliant preacher, who formulates his sentences beautifully'.[4]

The *Neue Zürcher Zeitung* also portrayed him as a man who was among 'the internationally supreme ornaments of his craft'. 'His broad education, his gift of formulating simply and elegantly and his developed sense of music make him an archbishop of inestimable worth for Munich.' His 'pastoral abilities' were also 'very well spoken of'. It would 'certainly be false' to describe Ratzinger as 'right-wing' or 'conservative'. Fundamentally, the new bishop wanted to 'devote himself to strengthening faith, and transcendental truth'. As to his 'organizational talent, leadership skills and political effectiveness', all that was still an unwritten page. His abilities in those areas 'were still largely unknown'.[5]

It was the eve of Pentecost, 28 May 1977, a bright early summer's day. The bare pillars of the Cathedral of Our Lady in the centre of Munich were decked with sprays of spring flowers. In the front row sat representatives of the state, city and political parties, as well as representatives of scholarship, the arts and from the parishes. The cathedral was packed. So was the nearby St Michael's Church, in which the event could be followed by video and audio. For the first time in the history of the German church, the ordination of a bishop was also broadcast live on television. Officially, Ratzinger had already taken over the leadership of the diocese on the day before, when he had presented the papal letter of appointment to the cathedral chapter. Unlike the general population, the members of the cathedral chapter had not exactly broken out 'in a storm of enthusiasm',[6] as the then vicar-general Gerhard Gruber recalled. That was due to Ratzinger's critical attitude to the liturgical reforms.

However, these 'beloved sons in the Lord' were exhorted by the papal bull to 'accept [him] gladly, not only as their teacher but also as their leader'. They should 'willingly follow [his] orders' and 'vigorously support [his] pastoral undertakings'. And to Ratzinger Pope Paul addressed these words:

We permit you to receive ordination outside Rome by a Catholic bishop, assisted, in accordance with the liturgical rules, by two co-consecrators of the same rank and dignity. Before that you must make a confession of Catholic faith in the presence of a lawful bishop, as well as taking the oath of loyalty to us and our successors.

At the beginning of the ordination service the new bishop had to lie outstretched at the foot of the altar in the so-called *prostratio* position, as a sign of his total prostration before God. During those minutes, Ratzinger said, he felt 'the burning feeling of inadequacy, his own inability to undertake such a great task even more strongly than when he was ordained as a priest'.[7] The main consecrator was the bishop of Würzburg, Josef Stangl. He was accompanied by del Mestri, Rudolf Graber and auxiliary bishop Ernst Tewes, as well as many cardinals and bishops from Germany and abroad. By the bishops' laying on of hands, Professor Ratzinger entered the ranks of shepherds who went back in an unbroken succession to the twelve who were sent out by Jesus himself. In retrospect Ratzinger expressed the significance of the moment: 'With my ordination as bishop the present course of my life began.' For him 'what began when the bishops ordained me by the laying on of hands in Munich Cathedral remains the present condition of my life'.[8]

After the anointing with chrism oil (a sign of the bishop's sharing in Christ's priesthood), he was given the Gospel, ring, mitre and crosier as insignia of his office. Then the nuncio del Mestri led the newly ordained bishop to the *cathedra*, the bishop's throne, where he received the oaths of loyalty from his cathedral chapter, the professors, the representatives of the diocesan administration, the dean, the parish and lay committees. Ratzinger was inwardly overcome as he had seldom been before: 'I experienced what a sacrament is,' he reported, 'that in it something real happens.' It was not a matter of assenting to a particular person, but 'the bishop is greeted as the bearer of Christ's mystery, even if most of them were not aware of that.'[9]

The new archbishop's first sermon was a panegyric to his home. 'Our Munich, our Bavaria' was 'so beautiful because the Christian faith had inspired its best energies'. Christianity had 'taken nothing of its strength' from the land, but made it 'generous and free'. A Bavaria 'in which people did not have the faith would have lost its soul; just preserving the monuments could not obscure that fact'. To the astonishment of his audience he concluded with a sombre vision, which, he said 'is no longer simply unreal'. In times like these he could not 'avoid the question whether the face of our land will still express the faith, when they take me to my final resting place'.

The finale of the ceremony was a procession to the Marienplatz. At the feet of the *patrona Bavariae*, which had officially been the centre of Munich for the last 350 years, the new bishop said a prayer to God's mother:

In the strife between parties may you be reconciliation and peace; when we get lost in our questioning show us the way; quell the quarrelling, revive the weary; give the mistrustful an open heart; give consolation to the embittered, humility to the self-satisfied, confidence to the fearful, prudence to the hasty, courage to the hesitant and to all of us the comforting assurance of your faith.[10]

At his first press conference Ratzinger said the main points of his programme would be close contact with pastors, fostering vocations, renewal of catechesis, ecumenical dialogue and the authentic implementing of the Council's reforms. People waited with suspense to see what coat of arms he would choose. His choice corresponded to the Ratzingerish ideal of combining old and new. From the thousand-year-old tradition of the bishops of Freising he took the Moor and the bear. The Moor – allegedly the head of an Ethiopian, with red lips, red crown, red ear-rings and collar, was a mysterious symbol. 'We don't really know what it means,' said Ratzinger; 'for me it expresses the universality of the church, that knows no difference between races and classes, because we are "all one" in Christ.'[11]

The bear with a pack on its back recalled a scene from the legend of Corbinian, the patron saint of the bishopric. Corbinian's horse was mauled by a bear on a journey to Rome. So as a punishment the saint made the bear carry his pack until they reached Rome, when Corbinian released it. In the story Ratzinger saw a connection to Psalm 73 from the wisdom tradition, which he had already meditated on in the dramatic night of his surrender in Regensburg. The psalm described 'the necessity of faith', and at the end the one left standing was 'whoever is on God's side', not 'on the side of success'. In the draft animal mentioned in the psalm Augustine had seen 'an image of himself under the burden of his bishop's office'. Wholly going along with that, Ratzinger concluded in the words of the psalmist: 'I have become a beast of burden for you and so I am continually with you.'[12]

An innovation was the scallop shell, the sign of continual pilgrimage but also of the search for wisdom. The shell recalled the Augustine legend when he watched a child on the beach trying to put water from the sea into a small hole in the sand. Augustine saw the endless greatness of God's mystery portrayed before his eyes. 'So for me the scallop shell is a pointer to my great master Augustine and to the greatness of a mystery that goes far beyond all our scholarship.'[13]

His bishop's motto – co-operatores veritatis: 'fellow-workers for the truth' – was taken from the third letter of John. It was meant not in a triumphalist way but as a servant, not singly but as one of many. He was one among many in one great whole. He bore the burden together with them, but was also carried himself. Here 'truth' was not meant in an abstract or legalistic way but related to the revelation by Christ, who had presented himself as the highest authority: 'I am the Way, the Truth and the Life. No one comes to the Father except through me' (Jn 14:6). That was the truth, which humanity could not alter. It could not be bent, for then it would no longer be truth and God would not be God.

In a sense, Joseph Ratzinger had to reinvent himself. Theory was one thing; this was practice. 'How often he had protested against all the minutiae.' Ratzinger recalled his alter ego Augustine, 'who was beset in this way, hindering him from pursuing his great intellectual work, which he knew was his most vital vocation'.[14] The great leap Ratzinger had made was most clearly visible in his new residence. Now he was to live in the Holnstein Palace at 7 Cardinal Faulhaber Street in Munich, formerly the town palace of Prince-Elector (*Kurfürst*) Karl Albrecht. However, from 1821 it had been the official residence of the archbishop of Munich and Freising. It was furnished with Baroque statues, Rococo furniture and historic stoves. Fortunately, the bishop's apartment itself, on the second floor, was simply furnished. It had a living room, bedroom, dressing room and bathroom, a study and a library with an impressive ceiling painting. A corner room was the dining room, large enough to entertain six to eight guests. The roof terrace had a fabulous view of the cathedral and enabled the bishop to take a few steps in the fresh air without being importuned with requests or admiration. Ratzinger left the apartment as it was. The only new thing was the teddy bear from his childhood, who sat in his own chair in the bedroom.

It caused some astonishment that the new bishop brought his sister with him to live in the residence. 'But she was a familiar support for him and protected him from loneliness,' said Professor Richardi, his friend from Regensburg. 'When he came home he could chat with her about everything that had happened during the day.' But Maria herself was a bit lonely there. She was accustomed to doing everything for her brother: the cooking, washing, looking after the money, including his personal accounts. She had her own small flat on the second floor, but now there was a secretary for the clerical work, Sister Eufreda Heidner. The Sisters of Mercy took care of the shopping, cooking and housekeeping, as well as looking after the great house. On the first floor two personal secretaries were at his disposal, Monsignor Erwin Obermaier, who had served Cardinal Döpfner, and Gerhard Schäfer, a layman and father of a family. At the gate sat Brother Friedbald, who had been personally appointed by Cardinal Faulhaber as the archbishop's chauffeur in the 1920s. He was a Franciscan from the monastery of St Anna and was content with his gate room and a small alcove where he slept. Together they formed the episcopal household. They prayed together, ate together and if there was time they played *Mensch-ärgere-Dich-nicht* (a board game similar to ludo) together.

Ratzinger had only been in office a few weeks when the nuncio del Mestri surprised him with some news. His Holiness Pope Paul VI intended to appoint the bishop of Munich a cardinal on 27 June 1977 in Rome. The news was a sensation. But somehow it fitted Ratzinger's life course, which was full of unexpected happenings. 'I have never felt the wish for such things,' Ratzinger declared, when a quarter of a century later an Italian journalist questioned him about the background to his unusually early appointment. 'And I don't wish for them now either. I respect Providence and I am not interested in what implements it makes use of.'[15]

Pope Paul appreciated Ratzinger's theology. He read his books in the original German. However, Ratzinger was not being appointed cardinal for his brilliance. It was more to do with a friend of Paul VI, an Italian Curia official, the progressive Giovanni Benelli, archbishop of Florence. The pope wanted to put in him a privileged position to be his successor. But for that Benelli had to be a cardinal. So a mini-consistory was hastily assembled. Besides Benelli and Ratzinger (seen as a makeweight), there were František Tomášek from communist Prague, Bishop Bernardin Gantin from Benin and the Italian Mario Luigi Ciappi. As the chosen ones mustered in St Peter's Basilica, only Ratzinger was accompanied by a considerable number of people. They consisted of his sister and brother, former students, his colleagues and hundreds of his Bavarian fans. As his titular church he received Santa Maria Consolatrice in a working-class parish of 22,000 souls. 'I didn't really know how I ought to behave and felt rather awkward in that situation', he reported about his private audience with Pope Paul: 'I didn't dare speak to the pope, because I felt I was too unimportant. But he was very friendly to me and encouraged me. He simply wanted to get to know me.'[16]

At first at deanery meetings the new archbishop 'had always given a lecture lasting three quarters of an hour,' said Walter Brugger who was a priest then. But that soon stopped. Ratzinger was set on reconciliation and understanding, even though at the beginning of his time as bishop, he admitted, the words of the church fathers rang in his ears. They 'very sharply condemned pastors who were like dumb dogs, allowing the poison to spread in order to avoid conflicts'.[17] He told his colleagues that they should never ask too much of people, but realize how they were in their own situation.

'He came to all the diocesan meetings and joined in everything,' the vicar-general Gerhard Gruber reported. He gladly left administrative matters to others, but he treated all questions to do with doctrine 'as top level', said Grubner, who had been devoted to Döpfner. 'Archbishop,' he said shyly at the beginning, 'I don't know if my way will please you.' Ratzinger's answer was: 'In Catholic matters we shall surely understand one another.'[18]

In his first pastoral letter Ratzinger promised the faithful of his diocese 'to promote peace' in the 'manifold strife that has confused many people in recent years and made them uncertain'. The church was 'a living organism, which needed patience to grow and mature'. Then he asked what would happen if today Jesus 'visibly appeared in our midst in some parish community, just as he came to his disciples'. Probably, he suggested,

> most of us would feel very disturbed by him, because he would meet much indifference and apathy, a comfortable and timid Christianity that cleverly covered its fear of the world under strong and learned words. He would meet a church at loggerheads. On the one hand, he would find an arrogance, which constructed Christianity according to its own taste, and on the other, he would find the rigidity and lovelessness of those who regarded themselves as the only proper Christians and thus set themselves against the unity of his body.

Here the only way was 'praying together and sharing the Eucharist together'. That gave you 'a sense of proportion to distinguish between the wheat and the chaff'. 'This way of being a Christian is open-hearted and free, without narrow-mindedness or aggression. But neither does it lapse into non-commitment or pseudo-Christian ideologies.'[19]

Ratzinger's main concern was the church not as an institution but as the place to consolidate faith. His idea of renewal was a spiritual deepening. The statistics showed how necessary that was. Between 1967 and 1973 the Catholic Church in Germany lost just under a third of its regular Mass-goers. The loss was greatest among the young. In 1963, 52 per cent of Catholics between the ages of 16 and 29 still went regularly to Mass. But ten years later that figure had sunk to

24 per cent.[20] Ratzinger wanted to dismantle the over-bureaucratic church apparatus. One of his first measures was to set children's first confession in Class 3, *before* their first communion rather than after, as it had been in his predecessor's time. Religious education, he said, included 'instruction about confession from the start'. So 'instruction about confession should precede instruction about the Eucharist'. That followed 'from the structure of the Mass itself'.[21]

In one of the polemics that were typical of him Ratzinger remarked that 'for a long while now the relaxation of dogma had not been leading to the promised land of the glorious freedom of the redeemed but to a waterless desert, which became ever more desolate the further you went into it'.[22] Elsewhere he said that Christian open-mindedness, as it was in Bavaria, meant 'loving creation' and therefore also 'serenely entering into creation's beauty'.[23] No one should be surprised that a 'land that was open but also capable of inertia' had things about it that were uncomfortable. From that, it was understood that the bishop was battling against the effects of regional reorganization, which turned living villages into anonymous dormitories. Indeed, he entered into this question of regional politics 'with an asperity that had not yet been shown on the Catholic side', as the *Süddeutsche Zeitung* remarked.[24]

Since his 1958 essay on *The New Heathens in the Church* Ratzinger had concentrated on developments that challenged society and Christian faith. No other German intellectual in the 1970s spoke out more boldly about questions of ethics, respect, humility and morality. He complained of a 'contamination of the spiritual environment', increasingly evident in the growing number of disturbed children. He criticized both 'the fatty degeneration of the heart in possessions and consumption' and the 'capitalist lust for profit'. He warned against the loss of standards, spurious freedom and self-loathing, and 'the brutalization of society through the mass media'. Our time, he said, suffered from its 'inability to be happy' even more than from its 'inability to mourn'. He called for a 'change of course' in order to rediscover the things that were important to humanity. That also meant 'changing our lifestyle to share with the Third World'.

'Get rid of the war toys' was one of his Christmas messages. At Easter he castigated 'the unleashing of violence, the barbarization of humanity, spreading throughout the globe': for example, in Cambodia, 'where a whole population is slowly becoming extinct'. He also condemned 'discrimination against the Sinti', a Romani tribe in Central Europe. He defended them 'because of our commitment to preserving human dignity'. Then he appealed for Germany to accept Vietnamese refugees. For a rich country anything else would be 'a terrible disgrace'. He demanded that his own church should not follow the current opinion but should 'prophetically proclaim the medicine of the gospel for the evil in the world'. 'If we don't rediscover some of our Christian identity, we will not withstand the challenge of this time,' he preached from his pulpit. Humanity that abandoned God was unredeemed 'and therefore not free but enslaved'.

Ratzinger took part so frequently in the public debate that the *Süddeutsche Zeitung* feared that it would be a 'big shock' for millions of Upper Bavarian Catholics if his name did not appear in any edition of the four Munich daily papers. 'They leaf through their newspaper – and what do they find? Nothing about Cardinal Ratzinger!'[25] People felt their bishop was talking to them. The Munich diocesan office received 50,000 orders for his Lent pastoral letter alone. He presented *Wort zum Sonntag* (*Word on Sunday*) on television. His book production increased, with titles such as *Eucharistie – Mitte der Kirche* (*Eucharist – Heart of the Church*), *Christlicher Glaube und Europa* (*Christian Faith and Europe*) and *Umkehr zur Mitte* (*Return to the Centre*). A large work, *Theologische Prinzipienlehre* (*Principles of Catholic Theology*), dealt with the structure and history of the faith and the church. 'In the beginning his sermons were highly theological,' said Sister Agapita, who worked in the bishop's house. 'That was difficult for normal church-goers.' But Ratzinger had also 'attracted many intellectuals again'.[26] In the end he managed to hold on to the old audience and also win new listeners.

The weekly meetings of the diocesan council were an ordeal for Ratzinger. The generation of priests ordained in the 1960s was decidedly rebellious. 'Many Munich professors also had reservations about Ratzinger,' said Gruber, the vicar-general. 'I don't know whether it wasn't my worst decision to become a bishop', the priest Hermann Theissing once heard Ratzinger sigh. 'In Munich he had many disappointments,' said Sister Agapita; 'he often came home very downhearted from the deanery conference.' But 'he did not become hard or bitter about it'. On the other hand, he often sat down at the piano, especially after a sermon that he thought had been particularly successful. 'That is how he rewarded himself.' But according to his secretary, Bruno Fink, it was also true that Ratzinger 'decided quickly and abruptly about many things. He would say, "We don't need to discuss this. There is no point." And that was the end of the matter.'[27]

Father Klaus Günter Stahlschmidt reported that quite a few priests and members of the cathedral chapter had let it be known at the beginning 'that they had wanted a different bishop'. While on holiday in 1978 Stahlschmidt himself had sent Ratzinger a postcard saying: 'I don't agree with everything you are saying and doing as a bishop, but I like you as a person.' He did not expect an answer. However, one day there was a postcard in his letter box, written in tiny handwriting: 'You don't have to agree with everything the bishop does, but you have to deal with his theology. [...] PS: A bishop needs people to like him as a person.' Stahlschmidt said that Ratzinger was someone 'who does not actively seek intimacy, but allows it and likes it'. When he sent Ratzinger good wishes on his election as the 264th successor to Peter, he received a personal reply dated 11 June 2005: 'I have kept you in mind during all these years.'[28]

After Ratzinger appointed Monsignor Erwin Obermaier to become director of the seminary for priests, in the autumn of 1978, Bruno Fink replaced him as private secretary. Fink was the son of a financial official. He had been ordained as a priest in Freising in 1972 and studied in Rome at the elite papal college, the Germanicum. He thought of himself as *theologus simplex*, a plain theologian without profession or title. Ratzinger always addressed him as 'Mr Secretary'. A first 'deep experience' for him was the 85th German Catholics' Conference in Freiburg in September 1978, which included a meeting with Mother Teresa. 'On the evening we arrived the cardinal led the way to the Freiburg stadium to a youth event with the theme of "Don't forget joy!"' The secretary was astonished when after the blessing immediately crowds of young people pushed forward asking for the cardinal's autograph. 'I had to use all my strength to control the onrush.'[29] Even though 'in these years no one could imagine that Joseph Ratzinger would become pope, nevertheless no one could doubt his outstanding stature.'

There were months when everything became a bit too much for the bishop. 'I have to struggle to find time,' he groaned to Fink. Ratzinger was chairman of the Bavarian Bishops' Conference and chairman of the German bishops' faith committee. In Rome he was a member of the international committee of theologians, a member of the Congregation for the Doctrine of the Faith and, from 1980, also a member of the Council of the Synod of Bishops. As a rule he had to keep 20 to 30 days of the working year free to travel to Italy. In addition, there were the plenary assemblies of the German and the Bavarian bishops, the meetings of the Standing Council of the Bishops' Conference, committee meetings, meetings with the diocesan deans, the priests' and diocesan council, the weekly sessions of the ordinariate and meetings with deacons, pastoral and community leaders, with the heads of religious orders and theology students. Then there were lectures at social clubs, academies and anniversary celebrations. He was still co-editor of *Communio* and supervised doctoral and *habilitation* students from Regensburg. It was important to him to meet with his circle of students, set up since his appointment as bishop, which consisted of more than 30 theologians from all parts of the globe.

In the afternoons he would go for a walk to the Englischer Garten. He went past the Feldherrnhalle (Field Marshals' Hall) and the bookshop in which he had browsed as a student. One day his friend the philosopher Ferdinand Ulrich saw him hurrying along, looking preoccupied, with his hands behind his back and his head sunk between his shoulders. Ulrich said he went up to him and grasped his shoulder: 'Joseph, what is the matter?' Then the cardinal 'poured out his heart. And spoke about the hostility in the cathedral chapter.'[30]

Eventually, he was bound to miss a date in the diocese, because his doctor ordered him complete rest due to overwork and a cold. Ratzinger withdrew to his house in Pentling more and more often. The ground floor was let to an old couple. But on the first floor he could work undisturbed at his books, rest and recover, until he was summoned by events that acted as a catalyst in the Catholic Church and set the ship of Peter on a new course, leading no one knew where.

II

The Year of Three Popes

In August 1978 the situation in Rome was tense. A new schism in the church was threatened by the reactionary archbishop and Council opponent Marcel Lefebvre. Documents also emerged from the Curia naming top church officials as members of the notorious secret society P2 (Propaganda Due, a Roman Masonic organization). On top of that, there were indications that the IOR (Istituto per le Opere di Religione, or Institute for the Works of Religion – the Vatican Bank), was involved in crooked financial dealings.

For Pope Paul personally, the death of his close friend Aldo Moro was particularly painful. The Italian prime minister was kidnapped by the Red Brigades terrorist group, and after being held hostage for 55 days, he was murdered. Moro's corpse was found in the boot of a red Renault 4. A year before that, the pope had offered himself as a hostage in exchange for the 86 passengers who had been hijacked by Palestinian terrorists in a Lufthansa plane and abducted to Mogadishu.[1]

The pope seemed paler and more exhausted than ever. Before his journey to his summer residence Castel Gandolfo, he said goodbye to Archbishop Giuseppe Caprio from the papal secretariat of state with the words: 'We are going away but we don't know whether we shall come back or how we shall come back.'[2] The 80-year-old pope had a temperature but still held his midweek audiences in Castel Gandolfo and worked until late into the night. On 5 August he rang for his secretary, Pasquale Macchi, at about 2.30 a.m. Completely exhausted, the pope talked about the death of Pius XII, who had died in the same room almost exactly 20 years before. On 6 August 1978 at 9.40 p.m. Paul VI also gave his soul back to his Creator.

On holiday in Austria, Ratzinger heard about the pope's rapidly failing health on the morning of 6 August. He immediately directed his vicar-general in Munich to ask the whole diocese to pray for the pope.[3] It had been due to Pope Paul that the Second Vatican Council had reached a successful conclusion. He had speedily introduced many reforms within the church: for example, reorganizing the Holy Office as the Congregation for the Doctrine of the Faith, as Frings and Ratzinger had suggested at the Council, and setting up synods of bishops. He increased the number of papal electors to 120 and excluded cardinals aged 80 from future conclaves. In 2014 Pope Francis praised his predecessor and the encyclical *Humanae vitae* as 'prophetic'. Literally Pope Francis meant: 'He had the courage to stand up against the majority, to defend moral discipline, put on the brakes [...] The question is not whether you change the doctrine but whether you go into the depths.'[4] In September 2016 more than 500 scientists and academics also paid tribute to the so-called 'pill encyclical'. In a joint declaration they praised its insight into questions of marriage, family and sexuality. However, the shadow that became visible over the church after the Council soon also began to darken Pope Paul's papacy. His line was not popular either with conservatives or with progressives.

When Ratzinger attended Pope Paul's funeral, he was struck by the plainness of the ceremony. The pope had ordered that even the hearse that took his body from Castel Gandolfo to Rome should not be decorated. However, for fear of a terror attack 5,000 soldiers and police accompanied the journey. At public insistence, his body was put on display before the high altar in St Peter's. People wanted to say goodbye to their pope. Carlo Confalonieri, the 85-year-old cardinal dean of the College of Cardinals, celebrated the funeral Mass. Finally, the coffin was brought to the Vatican grottoes. Here Pope Paul was laid in the customary three nested coffins: one cypress wood, one lead and one elm wood.

According to the regulations, a few weeks later the cardinals gathered from all over the world to elect a new pope in the Sistine Chapel. One of the cardinals, Albino Luciani, the patriarch of Venice, only just managed to get to the conclave on time in his ancient vehicle, which kept stalling. 'We'll be home again by the middle of next week,' he told his secretary. Then he would take the car straight to the garage.

At 51, Joseph Ratzinger was the youngest cardinal in the conclave. But as a diocesan bishop he belonged to the class of cardinal priests, and by protocol he came before most of the Curia cardinals. His status gave him one of the front seats during the voting in the Sistine Chapel. He sat between the *italianissimo* Cardinal Silvio Oddi and his old acquaintance Pericle Felici, who had been the general secretary of the Council. 'No one pushed to get the papacy,' Ratzinger recalled later, 'they are quite happy not to become pope.' Of course, it was true that 'we met a few times with some German-speaking cardinals'. Those attending these informal meetings included Joseph Schröffer, secretary of the Roman Congregation for Catholic Education, Cardinals Joseph Höffner from Cologne, Franz König from Vienna, Alfred Bengsch from Berlin and Paulo Evaristo Arns and Aloísio Lorscheider from Brazil, who were both of German origin. It was usual to exchange opinions in the run-up to a conclave, Ratzinger explained. 'It definitely was not our intention to come to any decisions; we just wanted to chat a little.'[5]

In his first papal vote Ratzinger wanted 'to be led by Providence', and he obviously had the right inspiration. He said afterwards that, as he went through the names of the possible *papabili* in his mind, he could 'see that a consensus was building in favour of the patriarch of Venice'. And indeed it was the patriarch of Venice, Albino Luciani, who appeared on the balcony of St Peter's as the pope to succeed Paul VI on 26 August 1978. 'God forgive you for what you have done,' Luciani had called to his electors in the conclave. But soon he was being given names that had never been heard before for a pope: 'the Smiling Pope', 'the World's Priest' or 'God's Smile'.

Luciani's father was a seasonal worker, a socialist and anticlerical. With the new pope the papacy laid aside old forms. It was a novelty that a pope should have two names: John Paul I, after his two predecessors. The reason he gave for calling himself 'the First', which was not the custom for the first use of a new papal name, was that he felt there would soon be a John Paul II. Luciani declined coronation and enthronement and no longer used the royal 'We' but just spoke as 'I'. He forbade the Swiss Guards to genuflect when they met him and only reluctantly consented to the use of the papal carrying chair (*sedia gestatoria*). 'God is our Father', he called out in his Angelus address on 10 September 1978, 'but even more so, he is our Mother.'

Ratzinger admired John Paul I's 'great simplicity but also his wide-ranging culture'. He had been 'very pleased' with this election. The two had met long before his election as pope, when Luciani had arrived from Venice on a surprise visit to his fellow bishop Ratzinger, who was on holiday in Bressanone in South Tyrol. Ratzinger praised him: 'To have such a kind man with such shining faith as shepherd of the universal church was a guarantee that everything would go well. He was not a careerist, but regarded the office he was appointed to as service and also suffering.'[6]

Thirty-three days later, on 29 September at 7.42 a.m., Radio Vatican announced that the pope, who had barely taken up his office, had died suddenly. Many thought they must have misheard. Was it really true? How could the pope, who was only 65 and clearly in good health, suddenly be dead? A Vatican press release announced that John Paul I had fallen peacefully asleep while reading *The Imitation of Christ*, by the medieval German mystic Thomas à Kempis. His private secretary had found him dead in the morning. Television stations all over the world interrupted their programmes. Newspaper editors brought out extra editions. But why was the Vatican not allowing a post-mortem?

Joseph Ratzinger heard the news of the pope's death in Ecuador. 'And it was in an extraordinary way,' as he remarked. He was the first, and now turned out to be the last, representative of John Paul I at a Marian congress in Guayaquil in Ecuador. He wanted to use his journey to get to know proponents of liberation theology, which was now so often talked about. 'I slept in the bishop of Quito's house,' he said later. 'I had not locked the door because in the bishop's house I felt as safe as in Abraham's bosom.' It had been the middle of the night 'when suddenly there was a light in my room and someone wearing a Carmelite habit came in. I was startled by the light and this figure in dark clothes, who appeared like a messenger of doom.' Eventually he recognized the figure as the auxiliary bishop of Quito, Luis Alberto Luna Tobar, the future archbishop of Cuenca. 'He told me the pope had died. That is how I heard the sad, totally unexpected news.'[7]

After the Mass that Ratzinger celebrated in the morning his agitated secretary came up to him. He still had no idea what had happened. 'Your Excellency must have made a mistake when you prayed "for our dead Pope John Paul I".' The secretary was not the only one who was confused about the news. Many thousand kilometres away, in the city of Kraków, a nun in the kitchen on the ground floor of the archbishop's palace was equally astounded. Józef Mucha, Karol Wojtyła's chauffeur, burst in and urged her to inform the cardinal, who was next door at breakfast, going over the plan for the day with his closest colleagues. 'You must go in and tell him that the pope has died,' he insisted. 'But that was a month a go.' 'No, the new one.'[8] When Karol Wojtyła heard the news, he was said to have dropped the spoon he was about to put sugar into his coffee with. 'No,' he murmured. After that he shut himself in the chapel for several hours.

The event was an ideal breeding ground for speculation. Quickly a report emerged that, at the time of his death, the Holy Father had not been reading *The Imitation of Christ* but texts of his forthcoming speeches. When it became public that on the morning after his death Luciani had not been discovered by his secretary but by a nun, the first talk of murder began. Rumours spread that John Paul I had been done away with, because he had crossed with corrupt networks in the Vatican. The scandal-mongering French work *La vraie mort de Jean Paul I* later accused Cardinal Secretary of State Jean Villot of planning the murder and then having the pope replaced by a double, after Luciani had discovered a nest of freemasons in the Vatican. In his 1984 book *In God's Name* the British writer David Yallop offered his readers the theory that John Paul I had died from poisoned medicine. The Vatican Bank, the Mafia and the secret society P2 were behind it. The Vatican thriller was translated into 40 languages and 6 million copies of it were printed.

Luciani had still not been buried when the medieval prophecy of a certain Malachy began doing the rounds. It purported to predict the succession of popes to come until the end of the world. The code name that went with Luciani's papacy was *medietate lunae*. Commentators suggested that this was short for *media aetate lunae* – halfway through the moon's cycle. 'In fact, John Paul I died exactly at the point between two full moons', declared the English writer John Cornwell.[9] Cornwell had done detailed research into the pope's sudden death. He suggested the same conclusion as the one reached by Stefania Falasca four decades later, in November 2017. She was a lawyer involved in an inquiry set up by the Vatican, to reassess medical files and medical reports, together with internal notes and witness statements. She concluded that the cause of death could be clearly established as a heart attack brought on by arteriosclerosis. That was 'the sad bare truth'.[10] One of Luciani's private secretaries said of the pope of 33 days: 'He broke down under a burden that was too heavy for his slender shoulders – and the load of immense loneliness.'[11]

Ratzinger flew directly from Ecuador to Rome. 'I am not a doctor,' he replied to reporters when he arrived at the airport, 'but he gave me the impression of being someone who, like me, did not have a very strong bodily constitution.' He had esteemed John Paul I for his 'great kindness, simplicity and humility'. And for his great courage. 'He had the courage to call things by their right names, even when that was swimming against the tide.' All the cardinals were 'somewhat depressed' by the pope's early death. 'It was a really heavy blow' that 'Providence had said "No" to our choice'. Nevertheless, this papacy had also had its importance in church history.[12]

The second conclave within two months began with a Mass in St Peter's Basilica on Saturday, 14 October 1978. The cardinals were housed in the Apostolic Palace, where their rooms were often separated just by cardboard walls. The first vote was set for Sunday morning. Ratzinger said in retrospect that the cardinals' mood was still depressed 'even though Luciani's election had been no mistake'. Somehow the feeling arose 'that something quite new was needed'.[13] In the run-up to the vote Ratzinger had caused irritation when he said in an interview that the assembly of 111 cardinals eligible to vote was under heavy pressure from left-wing views. He warned against the election of a pope who 'overestimated' political and social matters. The *Süddeutsche Zeitung* reported that it was unclear in the Vatican what the archbishop had actually meant by 'left-wing pressure'. His remarks were seen as an attempt to influence the outcome of the vote: 'That was especially because the five German cardinals at the conclave were seen as a very influential group. (One reason for that was the financial clout of the Catholic Church in the Federal Republic of Germany.)'[14]

The conclave was the first opportunity for Karol Wojtyła and Joseph Ratzinger to get to know each other personally. Three weeks earlier Wojtyła had been in Munich with a delegation led by Cardinal Primate Stefan Wyszyński, but Ratzinger had already departed for South America. He had left behind a statue of Mary as a present for his guest. It was inscribed 'Queen of Poland and Patron of Bavaria'. Though he had missed Wojtyła's speech in Munich with the prophetic title 'Our Way Together', now in the time before the conclave he listened to what Wojtyła said with great concentration. Later he said he had had the impression 'of a very cultured person, a very thoughtful person' with 'a considerable philosophical education'.[15]

He found that confirmed when he met him. They spoke German together, the foreign language Wojtyła had learned at the gymnasium. Ratzinger was enthusiastic. There was

> his uncomplicated human directness and openness and the cordiality that emanated from him. There was his humour and his piety that had nothing artificial or external about it. You felt he was someone who was not putting on an act. He was really a man of God and a very original person as well. His spiritual wealth, his enjoyment of conversation and exchange, all that was what made me like him immediately.[16]

At the conclave the cardinals prayed for inspiration to find the one from among them who could best steer the ship of Peter through the storms of the time and hold Christ's flock together. Prayers, vows, meditations and ceremonies were for that purpose. Firm agreements to 'push through' a particular candidate were not allowed. However, according to research by the writers Carl Bernstein and Marco Politi, in October 1978 it was not just the Holy Spirit but also the German pope-makers who heavily influenced the vote, especially Cardinal Franz König of Vienna. When an insoluble stalemate was reached between the two favourites from among the Italian bishops, König spoke up for Wojtyła and Ratzinger did likewise.

In our interviews I asked the pope emeritus about it:

Is it true that the German participants had decisively supported the election of Karol Wojtyła?

Supported, yes.

Did you personally play a large part in his election?

No, I don't think so. I was quite a young archbishop. I was one of the youngest cardinals and I did not presume to play any role in that. I am against plotting and so forth, particularly in papal elections. Everyone should vote completely in accordance with his conscience. Yes, we German-speakers did talk to each other but without making any pacts.

But you scarcely held back altogether?

Well, I can only say that outside the conclave König spoke to various cardinals. But what he said remained secret. No, at that time I kept well out of public activities. We German-speaking cardinals did meet and advise. But I myself did not engage in any politics.

Were you shocked when the vote actually did go to Wojtyła?

No. Certainly not. I was for him. Cardinal König had spoken to me. And my own personal knowledge of him, although not long-standing, convinced me that he really was the right man.

According to the liturgical calendar, 16 October is the feast day of St Hedwig, one of the patrons of Poland, born in Andechs, near Munich. After eight rounds of voting over three days, at first black smoke rose from the Sistine Chapel chimney. As well as the ballot papers someone had put the wrong fuel into the stove prepared for the conclave. But shortly afterwards the long-awaited white smoke signal rose into the sky. The public stood in breathless silence. When the tensely expected cardinal proto-deacon appeared on the balcony of St Peter's to announce the Christian name of the new pope, many were left speechless. They had heard the name 'Carolus'. Which Carolus? The Italians in the crowd only knew one Carlo, Carlo Confalonieri, the dean of the College of Cardinals, who was more than 85 years old. '*O Dio mio*, oh my God, they have gone crazy,' someone shouted.

It was a historic vote. For this 'Carolus', who now came onto the balcony himself, was none other than Karol Jósef Wojtyła, the first Polish pope in history, the first non-Italian for half a millennium. He was 58 years young, athletic, strong, charismatic – a winner, who gave the impression he could lift the world. As Wojtyła did not adhere to the ceremonial and spoke to the faithful much too long, attentive listeners could clearly hear through the microphone a distinct '*Basta!*' from the papal master of ceremonies, Virgilio Noè. But Wojtyła would not be interrupted. '*Vi vengo da un paese lontano*' – 'I come to you from a faraway country' – he said in his still clumsy Italian. He asked to be forgiven if he pronounced any words incorrectly. Below in the square Bruno Fink and Wojtyła's long-standing secretary, Stanisław Dziwisz, stood beside one another. Both were still rigid with shock.

The new pope took the name John Paul II. At his Mass to celebrate his election, he laid the foundation for one of those turning points in history that open the way to far-reaching changes. 'Don't be afraid. Open, yes, wrench the gates wide open for Christ!' he cried. 'Open up the frontiers between states, the economic and political systems, the breadth of culture, civilization and progress to his saving power! Don't be afraid,' he repeated. 'Let Christ speak to people. He alone has words of life!'[17]

On the same day in Munich the auxiliary bishop Ernst Tewes gave a first statement, pre-agreed with Ratzinger. He could not have guessed how true what he said would prove to be: 'Perhaps we have witnessed a significant turning point in the church's history, an event whose importance for the present intellectual and political dispute cannot yet be grasped.'[18]

Ratzinger and Wojtyła got on well from the start. Both were excellent theologians and young, highly intelligent reformers, concerned with philosophy, history and the thorny question of modern development. Both had to suspend their academic work. Both were pushing for a renewal of the faith, from its deepest core. However, for the first nine months after Wojtyła's enthronement there was no contact between them. Not even a telephone conversation. Whereas nearly all the other German bishops almost raced to pay their respects to the new pope, in Munich it was 'His Eminence the Cardinal has plenty to do in his own diocese.'[19]

At the beginning of June 1979 John Paul II visited his home in Poland, a journey that was very nervously awaited. Poland's economy was in a disastrous state. The workers' leader Lech Wałęsa was struggling to create an independent trade union. It had become an absurdity for the millions of people who greeted Karol Wojtyła on his tour to speak of the leading role of the Communist Party. 'You must be strong, strong with the power that comes from the faith!' the pope called to his fellow countrymen. In many cities young people brandished small wooden crosses, the new symbol of resistance. Wiktor Kulerski, a member of the Solidarność (Solidarity) trade union described the situation thus: 'Communism no longer has any meaning. The people repeat the pope's words and they know that he is their mainstay.'[20]

Ratzinger himself had given lectures in Poland and was in close contact with Bishop Alfons Nossol in the Polish city of Opole. 'I think it is important that as many bishops as possible attend these events,' he said to Bruno Fink one morning. 'Mr Secretary, we are going to Poland!' Thus he was able to accompany the second stage of the pope's tour. He was to visit Częstochowa, Auschwitz, Nowa Huta and Kraków. Ten to twelve million, mostly young, people, had taken part in the pope's Masses. Thunderous applause broke out on Trinity Sunday at his final Mass in Kraków. But only a few guessed that it was the beginning of the end of the communist regime, when John Paul II asked a telling question: 'As a successor to the apostle Peter, I ask you today: do you confess your faith in Jesus, the Son of God?' The crowd rose from their seats and answered with one strong voice: 'We want God!'

Shortly after the journey to Poland, again it was the nuncio Guido del Mestri who threw Ratzinger into a state of agitation. He telephoned to say the pope wanted to speak to the cardinal as soon as possible, regardless of his duties at home. Hastily, appointments were postponed, meetings were cancelled and Ratzinger was on his way to Rome. But in Rome they knew nothing of an appointment with the Holy Father. A monsignor in the Vatican secretariat of state shrugged his shoulders. '*Un attimo*, I will try to find out.' Half an hour later the order came that a meeting was planned for 1 p.m.

the next day. John Paul II was inviting Ratzinger to come to an audience last in the queue in order to invite him to lunch. They spoke about the events in Poland. It transpired that Wojtyła had not been aware of Ratzinger's discreet presence there during his papal visit. At the end of the lunch Wojtyła came to the point. Yes, he wanted Ratzinger in Rome. Indeed he wanted him as prefect of the Roman Congregation for Catholic Education, which was vacant. Ratzinger hesitated, then flatly refused. He had only been in office as a bishop for two years and could not leave his flock so quickly. Moreover, he knew the German higher education establishments and Catholic faculties well, but these were very different from those in other countries, for which he would then also be responsible. No, sorry, it wouldn't do.

It was Wojtyła's first attempt to get Ratzinger onto his team. Both of them were well aware that it would not be the last.

12

The Küng Case

Gradually a routine had been established in the bishop's working day. Every morning began with Mass at 7.30. In the mornings Ratzinger liked a very short and simple celebration without prayers of intercession. After lunch he spent a brief time with his sister. People saw the light go out in his flat at 10 p.m. 'He was ideal as a superior', secretary Bruno Fink reported; 'he made notes about everything. He was humorous and said how we ought to proceed.'[1] He was very patient about everything. At most there was a deep breath when he had a problem to deal with.

Exercises in Scheyern Abbey were an established part of his yearly programme. He wanted to stay there alone. 'There were the broad open spaces, the great forests and the calm silence,' he enthused, and also 'the simple life of the abbey with its constant rhythm'.[2] When the bishop travelled overland, observers thought his 'Bavarian soul' bloomed. Part of the area in the centre of the diocese was known as *terra Benedictina*. It was cultivated by Benedictine monks and also blessed. Ratzinger loved the generous, tolerant country people, their deep feelings, their art of living, which preferred the inclusive 'both/ and' to the harsh 'either/or'. *Gott mit dir, du Land der Bayern* ('God Be with You, Land of Bavarians') is still the region's official anthem today. Here they didn't like pushiness or affectation, but they did like unconventional thinkers. 'So this region has always been inward-looking but also insistent,' Ratzinger once said, 'because it was open to cultural exchange. And perhaps Bavaria has been inconvenient in German history precisely because it never allowed itself to be forced into becoming a purely national culture, but always remained open to a wide culture and intellectual exchange.'[3]

A great church event in November 1979 was the ecumenical youth meeting of the Taizé community. Munich Cathedral was packed with bright young people. To the surprise of all, Brother Roger Schutz, the founder of the community, spoke on the subject of confession. When, the next morning, Schutz appeared with two young brothers at the service in the bishop's house chapel, Ratzinger faced a moral dilemma. Could he give Holy Communion to the non-Catholics? Brother Roger reassured him. The question of inter-denominational communion had long been decided affirmatively in agreement with the pope. During the Second Vatican Council, he said at the final breakfast, the Vatican had offered to accept the community into the Catholic Church. But his fellow members of the community had decided that they wanted to continue being a special impetus to the unity of all Christians. He himself had found his Christian identity by reconciling his Protestant tradition with the mystery of Catholic faith.

Ratzinger paid special attention to the revival of the mission work in his diocese. 'The church gets her light from Christ. If she does not pick up this light and pass it on, then she is just a dull lump of earth.'[4] 'How often we have preferred success to the truth and our reputation to justice,' he said elsewhere.[5] Episcopal committees should not just make resolutions and produce papers: 'they should be geared to making consciences become clear and free in the light of the truth'.' So it was not right for bishops to become 'stifled by their often heavy bureaucratic structures'.[6] When priests kept feeling overworked, tired and frustrated, the cause was often 'a tense straining for performance'. So a clergyman should be 'above all, a man of prayer, a really "spiritual" man. Without a strong spiritual substance he can't last out in his job for the long term.'[7]

Ratzinger never tired of insisting that a priest should

lead people towards reconciliation, forgiving and forgetting, tolerance and generosity. He should help people to accept others in their otherness, be patient with one another, judiciously trusting and wise, discreet and open, and a lot more. Above all, he should support people in pain, bodily suffering as well as all the disappointments, humiliations and fears, from which no one is spared.[8]

The priest could learn from Christ 'that his life was not about self-realization or success'. And when the bishop came to the end of his sermon, he sounded like a revolutionary of the old school: 'Only if we have the courage to go up to the fire and catch fire ourselves can we kindle his fire on this Earth, the fire of life, hope and love.'[9]

In the late autumn of 1979 Ratzinger faced his first acid test. No one could say that he came out unscathed. It was about who should occupy the vacant chair of fundamental theology at Munich University. The Bavarian culture minister Hans Maier was responsible for the appointment. According to the concordat, the bishop also had a say. Unfortunately, the university senate had unanimously decided to put Johann Baptist Metz from Münster first on the list for the job. Metz was the founder of 'political theology'. Everyone involved must have realized that Ratzinger would not be enthusiastic about the appointment. 'Maier spoke to me about it,' said the future pope, 'he said he was against it. I agreed with him. Metz was so madly political, and yet so clueless. And he did not have a good reputation regarding nominations and doctorates.'[10] 'If someone is left-wing I am for them,' is how the Münster theologian Herbert Vorgrimler described Metz's nomination policy. Of course, Ratzinger admitted, he and Maier had been aware that the matter would 'clearly cause a big fuss'.

Metz was rejected, and there was a fuss. Ratzinger did not dispute that Metz had very good academic qualities. For him the problem was Metz's linking Christ's message with political activism. Metz's aggressive line had been one reason why he had left Münster. Metz himself later conceded: 'I made mistakes. I underestimated the influence that the name "political theology"' had. What I wanted was something quite different.'[11] At any rate, Ratzinger 'never questioned my orthodoxy'. Metz had been pleased to note that Ratzinger had cited with approval his term 'God crisis' in his lectures, as the underlying reason for the church crisis.

When it became known that the culture minister Maier preferred the second name on the university list, Karl Rahner also raised his voice. 'I protest, I protest that the archbishop of Munich, Cardinal Ratzinger, and the Bavarian minister of state for Education and Culture, Prof. Hans Maier, have prevented the appointment of Dr Johann Baptist Metz,'[12] Rahner raged in the left-wing Catholic

Publik-Forum on 16 November 1979. Metz had been Rahner's star student. Before appearing in the journal, Rahner's furious protest had been published on 14 November with a two-page spread in the *Süddeutsche Zeitung*. It made his objection sound like Émile Zola's famous '*J'accuse*'. 'I can understand that Ratzinger does not like Metz's theology and thinks he has, and can formulate, substantial grounds for opposing it', declared the grand old man of German theology, 'but I dispute whether those grounds are sufficient for the bishop actually to prevent Metz's appointment and to regard that as a service to the church and theology.'[13] It was an attack on academic freedom.

But the decision stood. 'Now *you* must defend it,' Maier told the bishop. 'What disappointed me,' Ratzinger said in our conversation, 'was that Maier suddenly wanted nothing more to do with it.' In fact, Maier had told Metz that Ratzinger had almost forced him to take the step. 'Mr Metz, believe me, I would definitely have appointed you,' Maier had told him, according to Metz.[14] In his detailed memoirs *Böse Jahre, gute Jahre* ('Good Years, Bad Years') Maier, who was the president of the Central Committee of German Catholics, did not mention the affair.[15]

Later Ratzinger and Metz were reconciled. Things were also sorted out with Rahner. The story in a 'critical biography' of the future pope that Rahner 'avoided his former Council colleague Ratzinger until his death in 1984' is a myth. Secretary Fink reported on a meeting between them in the archbishop's house, at which he had 'the firm impression' that the two theologians had reached a 'deep understanding' in their conversation, which concluded with supper together.[16] Ratzinger himself confirmed: 'We remained in contact. He just said: Now there must be an end to the quarrel.'[17]

In a public answer to Rahner's 'objections' Ratzinger made clear that the faculty council had not voted unanimously for Metz, as Rahner had maintained. There had been some 'important critical voices against the appointment of Metz'. The dean of the faculty had assured him 'that any of the three listed candidates [...] without exception would be welcome as a successor to the post'. So there could be 'no question' of a 'gross affront to the faculty's decision'. Indeed, the bishop had a formal right not only by the concordat but also 'because of the fact' that he 'was ultimately responsible; to the theologians, and to the community where the teachers would work, who had been taught by those professors'. In addition, he regarded 'a fundamentally ecumenical education of theologians as imperative'. For his own teacher, Gottlieb Söhngen, 'ecumenism had been at the heart of his whole theological work'. Because of the nature of his chair in Münster, that had not been ensured with Metz.[18]

The Metz affair gained so much weight because it overlapped with another conflict. Once again, this was with Hans Küng. Ratzinger's quarrel with the prominent Tübingen theologian was of great importance in church politics because it showed the two opposing camps that are still in dispute today over the Catholic Church's programme and strategy. It also clearly showed the line that Ratzinger would follow as prefect of the Congregation for the Doctrine of the Faith.

The 'Küng case' had begun in 1957, when Küng's book on 'justification' was put on the Index of prohibited books by the Holy Office, as it was then called, with file reference 399/57/i. Ten years later, in May 1968, Küng was invited to Rome for a 'colloquium', to speak about his work on *Die Kirche* (*The Church*). Then Küng's book *Unfehlbar? Eine Aufrage* (*Infallible? An Inquiry*), published in 1970, resulted in a year-long correspondence between the author and the Vatican. Rome continually reminded the professor of his status as the holder of a chair answerable to the church, and insisted that he should keep to the correct doctrine.

Twenty years after the first warning, the so-called Stuttgart colloquium in 1977 sought to reach agreement with Küng on his theology. Besides Küng, those attending the colloquium were Cardinals Höffner and Volk as well as Professors Lehmann and Semmelroth. At Küng's express request, Ratzinger was not invited to be present. Küng's biographer Freddy Derwahl saw this as a sign of how strongly the church leadership 'were still concerned to smooth a path for Küng's return through spectacular personal-political concessions'.

The four-hour conversation in Stuttgart came to an 'informal arrangement' with the German Bishops' Conference, by which Küng agreed to hold back on new statements on sensitive issues. Shortly afterwards, in the spring of 1979, Küng returned with a devastating criticism of John Paul II's papacy, in an introduction to the book entitled *How the Pope Became Infallible,* by the Swiss theologian and historian August Hasler. So the German bishops felt they had been simply 'taken for a ride', as Derwahl remarked. The clear provocation brought things to the boil and made a reaction inevitable. The dismissal of Küng from his professorship gained huge publicity. It was regarded as punishing a critic and aroused worldwide protests. It is still romanticized today. A reconstruction of the events may help to clear up the myths surrounding the case.

11 November 1979: An event in Freising Cathedral set the ball rolling. On the annual feast of St Corbinian, Ratzinger summoned young people to a stronger confession of their Christian faith. (The title of his sermon was 'Time to rise again'.) A student asked him whether it was right that Professor Küng should have had his authorization to teach Catholic theology cancelled. By then Ratzinger knew that the 'Küng file' in the Roman Congregation for the Doctrine of the Faith was as good as closed. In the course of a plenary meeting of the College of Cardinals at the beginning of November the German cardinals were invited to a private audience with John Paul II and informed that the removal of Küng's authorization to teach was to be expected. Ratzinger answered the student's question by saying that Küng, with whom he personally had always got on well, was actively disputing essential doctrines of the Catholic Church. So it was only right 'that he can no longer speak in its name'. Of course, Küng was quite at liberty to speak in his own name or anyone else's name. Literally Ratzinger meant: 'I think there is no bishop in the whole world, except the pope, who has so many chances to express his thoughts to humanity.' Küng's criticism of the pope was published in the *Frankfurter Allgemeine Zeitung, Le Monde* and in Italy and America. So probably nothing would change in the future.

14 November: Unfortunately, Ratzinger's answer in Freising was given by his press officer to the Catholic News Agency without discussion or authorization. The off-the-cuff statement, which linked Ratzinger to Küng's case, immediately provoked public protests. Within a few days more than 500 letters had reached the archbishop's house, alleging that he clearly wanted to force the downfall of his former colleague. Küng used Ratzinger's statement as a good opportunity. In a press conference of his own he accused Ratzinger of 'falling back on pre-conciliar customs of heresy-hunting, insinuation and defamation'. The valid questions of countless Catholics could not be settled by damning theologians. He regarded Ratzinger's statement as a 'frontal attack on my Catholicity and my intellectual and moral integrity'.

16 November. Küng's local bishop, who had remained loyal to Küng, told journalists that Küng had a habit of provoking and occasionally overdid it. But 'No one, certainly not Cardinal Ratzinger, will want to deny Küng's faith.'[19]

15 December. Küng persisted. Ratzinger's statements were an 'outrageous procedure', he stressed in an article in the daily paper *Die Welt*. He had been brutally hit by the denial that he 'was a Catholic' and by a public campaign of defamation. He insisted on his *missio canonica*, his church authorization to teach.

18 December. At 10 a.m., on behalf of the apostolic nuncio, a Jesuit delivered a letter in Latin to Küng's house in Tübingen. Küng himself was not present so the Jesuit got a receipt for the letter from the household staff. The withdrawal of Küng's *missio canonica*, dated 15 December 1979, was signed by 'FRANJO *Cardinal* ŠEPER, *Prefect*; JÉRÔME HAMER, O.P., Titular bishop *Secretary*'. The German Bishops' Conference called a press meeting to communicate the decision of the Roman Congregation and also the reasons given for it in a *Statement on Some Main Points of the Theological Doctrine of Prof. Hans Küng.* An extract from it read as follows:

> The Church of Christ has received the commission from God to preserve and protect the deposit of faith so that [it ...] inalienably safeguards the faith once given to the faithful. [...] When it happens that a teacher of theological disciplines presents and disseminates his own judgement and not the faith of the church as the standard of truth and perseveres in this undertaking [...] the honour and dignity of the church demands that such behaviour should be revealed. [...]
>
> With that in view, the Congregation for the Doctrine of the Faith [...] declared in a public document on 15 February 1975 that, to varying degrees, some of the doctrinal opinions of Professor Hans Küng were contrary to the teaching of the church. The Congregation warned Professor Küng at the time not to

continue teaching such ideas. It expected him to bring his own doctrinal opinions into line with the authentic official doctrine of the church. However, Professor Küng has not changed his above-mentioned doctrinal opinions at all up to this day.

In 1975 the Congregation took no further action on condition that Professor Küng renounced those opinions. As that condition has not been fulfilled, the Congregation sees itself as duty-bound from now on to state the following: Professor Hans Küng deviates in his writings from the full truth of the Catholic faith. Therefore he can neither be called a Catholic theologian nor teach as one.[20]

Surprised by the news of the removal of his *missio canonica*, which reached him while he was away on a skiing trip, Küng immediately hurried back to Tübingen. When he arrived that evening he went to the microphone to speak to the journalists, who were already waiting for him. 'I am ashamed of my church, that in the twentieth century secret inquisition procedures are still taking place. It is a scandal for many people, that in a church which invokes Jesus Christ […] its own theologians are defamed and discredited by such methods.'[21]

20 December. The *Frankfurter Allgemeine Zeitung* called it a 'landmark case for the papacy of John Paul II'. In Tübingen 1,000 students marched in a torch-lit procession to the ancient collegiate church. Prominent Catholics founded a 'Committee to Defend the Rights of Christians in the Church'. Countless German theology professors threatened to hand in their authorizations to teach. French, Spanish, American and Canadian theologians also expressed their solidarity. On the other hand, Karl Lehmann said that Küng had undoubtedly 'infuriated' the church authorities. Hans Urs von Balthasar wrote in the *Frankfurter Allgemeine Zeitung* reminding readers of the nearly 200 pages of documentation that the German Bishops' Conference published as an appendix to the statement of the Congregation for the Doctrine of the Faith. He was amazed 'at the Roman and German officials' lamb-like patience' with Küng.

21 December. Küng appeared clearly ready to relent. At his request, Bishop Georg Moser travelled to Rome to deliver a statement in which the professor stressed he had always thought of himself as a Catholic theologian and wanted to continue to be one. He had not intended to provoke a new dispute about infallibility by his Introduction.

28 December. At Moser's urgent request, a meeting took place in the Vatican with John Paul II. Those present were Cardinal Franjo Šeper (the head of the Congregation for the Doctrine of the Faith), the German Cardinals Höffner, Volk and Ratzinger, as well as Bishops Moser and Saier. In our interview Ratzinger recalled the passionate discussion:

> Cardinal Šeper was very angry. He said: 'I have now been here for 15 years and the church is being destroyed and we are doing nothing. If this carries on, then I will give up the job.' He had really reached the point where he could no longer stand it or reconcile it with his conscience that nothing should happen. The decision had already been made. And we said – with the bishop of Rottenburg abstaining – that he [the pope] could no longer alter it, he had to stand by it.

The die was cast. However, Rome conceded that a re-granting of the authorization to teach had not been ruled out. Küng was to consider his position 'very seriously'. According to Ratzinger, he himself had never been a party to the removal of Küng's authorization. 'I never advised that measures should be taken against him,' he stressed in our interview. 'Ratzinger stood up strongly for Küng,' the dogmatic theologian Ludwig Hödl confirmed.[22] 'When Küng's *missio canonica* was withdrawn, they could also have taken away his basic authorization to teach in a German university, the *venia legendi*. But that did not happen.' Of course, indirectly Ratzinger's voice carried great weight. He had already described parts of Küng's book *Christ sein* (*On Being a Christian*) as no longer covered by Catholic doctrine. But he had not called for a condemnation of Küng's views.

After the turbulence of the past few weeks, Ratzinger's New Year sermon in the Munich Cathedral of Our Lady was tensely awaited. Once again he began his speech with a quotation. This time it was from Alexander Solzhenitsyn. The Russian critic of the Soviet regime spoke of 'worldwide absolute evil'. The reason for its triumph was 'most effectively [...] facilitated in the world by the mixture of truth with untruth'.

That indicated the thrust of the sermon: the adulteration of the truth. Everyone knew what he was talking about as he went on to say that the church was currently being disparaged as 'an intolerable relic of the darkest Middle Ages in which, instead of democratic reason, powerful Ayatollahs furiously hold forth'. But a campaign alleging that the church was trying to muzzle an unwelcome critical spirit gave a completely false picture. In fact, the magisterium protected 'the faith of the simple people, those who do not write books, or speak on television, or write leading articles in the newspaper. That is its democratic task. It is to give a voice to the voiceless.' Anyone today who 'has authority in the church does not have power. On the contrary, they stand against the dominant power, the power of opinion, whereby faith in the truth is an annoying disruption of randomly ascribing certainty to anything.'²³ But the norm for theology was the Catholic baptismal confession and not the other way round. 'It is not the intellectuals who are the standard for the simple people, but the simple people who are the standard for the intellectuals.'²⁴

On 11 January 1980 Ratzinger admitted in an interview with the *Frankfurter Allgemeine Zeitung* that there was clearly an 'inner tension between the church and a world shaped by the Enlightenment'. The public constantly showed more sympathy for the church's critics. But the church owed it to herself and also to the world to preserve her identity. So she had to give 'evidence of maintaining that identity' as in a court of law. That would not cut off dispute between theologians but merely clarify it. Küng's views boiled down to all dogmas being subject to revision. He had spoken negatively about the doctrine of the Trinity, questioned the doctrine of the sacraments and cast aside the mariological dogmas. Of course, Küng had the right to express his opinion freely. However, the church also had the right 'not to regard him as an exponent of its views, and to draw the consequences from that'. In conciliatory words Ratzinger said that Küng was a man who had done a great deal to reach out to people who could usually no longer be reached by the church. Therefore 'the doors were not shut' against him for ever.²⁵

After the removal of his church authorization to teach, the University of Tübingen created an independent chair of his own for Küng. Ratzinger said in a conversation in 1982 that Küng 'had told him he did not want to resume his previous post and that his present position suited him much better'. For now he was free from duty lectures and exams for theology students and could devote himself wholly to his own work. 'I respect his way, which he follows according to his conscience, but then he should not still seek the church's approval for it. He should admit that now in vital questions he has come to different, wholly personal decisions.'[26]

13

The Legacy of Munich

In September 1980 Ratzinger travelled to Poland as a member of a delegation of German bishops. They were returning the visit of the Polish bishops the previous year. The meetings to promote the reconciliation between the two peoples began in Częstochowa. Ratzinger laid a wreath at the death wall in Auschwitz and visited the death cell of the Franciscan friar Maximilian Maria Kolbe, who was murdered by the Nazis.

In the same month, at the pope's urgent request, Ratzinger acted as *relator general* of the World Synod of Bishops at a meeting on the subject of marriage and the family. He provided a comprehensive outline of the synod's theme at the beginning of the meeting and over five weeks he summarized the bishops' contributions. He returned to Munich exhausted, and there he produced a brochure for his parish priests on the findings of the synod (including on the question of remarried Catholics receiving communion). Then he threw himself into preparing for the next great event, the Polish pope's first visit to Germany.

John Paul II's tour passed through Cologne, Osnabrück, Mainz, Fulda, Altötting and Munich. It was a mammoth programme, with two church services a day and about 20 speeches. In Altötting, Ratzinger accompanied the pope into the Chapel of Grace. He was an unassuming host, who kept in the background. But it was unmistakable how close the relationship between the German cardinal and the Polish pope had become. They were not like princes of the church but friends, two mates who were having a good time together, and exuded good humour and vitality. 'I'll be able to rest in heaven,' said Wojtyła when his friend offered him a rest room for a siesta in the bishop's house. The pope was in high spirits and cracked jokes whenever the opportunity arose. They both knew he still had something in mind for Ratzinger. But it was not spoken about.

Despite the bad weather, when the closing ceremony took place in the Theresienwiese in Munich on 19 November, the crowd was about half a million people, greater than ever seen before for a Mass in Germany. To give a sign, Ratzinger ordered that a girl, rather than a boy, should act as server to hold the papal crosier. A young woman caused a 'scandal' when she criticized the church's moral and social teaching in her greeting speech to the pope. Journalists gathered that she had spoken quite spontaneously to defy the pope. In fact, the text had been shown to the cardinal beforehand. He had had no objections. When he was asked about the excitement caused by the critical speech, he declined to comment. He did not understand all the fuss. Such questions were often heard these days.

One of the unpleasant things that occurred during Ratzinger's time as bishop was a scandal about the diocese's financial dealings. The events in question went back to the 1960s and 1970s but only now came to trial in the Munich regional court. The accused were the estate agent Karl Heinz Bald and the Olympic athlete Armin Hary. The two of them had defrauded the archdiocese of 3 million marks in property transactions. It quickly became clear that the church administrators' weak management had enabled the fraud to take place. The judge ordered an inquiry into the archiepiscopal finance offices and called Ratzinger to the witness box on 13 March 1981. Secretary Fink was immediately instructed: 'Fetch Dr Marianne Thora. She is a woman who knows what's what.'[1]

Dr Thora, an experienced lawyer, trained Ratzinger in three sessions for the upcoming hearing. 'The Cardinal took note of which arguments are appropriate and which are not,' Fink observed.[2] After his testimony the accused were sentenced to prison, but the damage to the Munich church's image was enormous. Ratzinger learned a lesson from it. He appointed a new finance director and set in place stringent control mechanisms, so that such things could not happen again.

In Regensburg, Ratzinger had already taken an interest in the Integrated Community (later the Catholic Integrated Community [*Katholische Integrierte Gemeinde* or KIG]), whose leading figures had courted him. His long-standing connection with this group became one of the most remarkable relationships in the future pope's biography. He saw it as one of those new initiatives that could bring fresh impetus to a people's church, beyond its institutionalized structures. Undoubtedly, this was one of the reasons for his openness. And he must have been excited by the idea that here was a Catholic project that was striving for better relations with Judaism.

The community, founded by Traudl and Herbert Wallbrecher, took as its starting point the experience of the Holocaust, from which they wanted to draw the right lessons. In the 1960s and 1970s church renewal was understood as deliberate secularization and colourful alternatives. For example, as the historian Franz Walter concluded, the 'Catholics' Conferences from below', which began in the 1980s, conformed to the 'ecological-pacifist mainstream'. 'They were not innovatory or original,' he said. The scene was dominated by 'Nicaraguan coffee and organic fruit, disarmament slogans, Third World problems and liberation theologies'. Instead of the pope, the alternative Catholics had 'little anti-popes, whom they idolized: for a time it was Hans Küng, later it was Eugen Drewermann'. On the other hand, the Integrated Community strove to 'regain the strength of the early church's faith' and live as 'a differentiated community', as a June 1969 programme put it. Ultimately, the 'the mission to the world can only be carried out by the church if it is a contrasting community, the salt of the world, not conformed to the world'. One sentence of this programme must have resonated particularly with Ratzinger: 'At the beginning there wasn't theology, just the community with its experience of God acting upon it.'

The community, which had arisen in the enthusiasm of the 1968 revolt, soon attracted more than a thousand adults and young people – laity and priests, single people and families – who lived, worked and prayed together. They also wanted to celebrate the Eucharist together in a modern form, aesthetically polished and stylistically choreographed. Strengthened by well-known theologians such as Gerhard Lohfink and Rudolf Pesch, the community focused on modern exegesis, the Jewish roots of Christianity and the philosophy of French existentialists. In the summer of 1976 they became known beyond regional boundaries through sit-ins in the episcopal churches of Munich, Münster, Paderborn and Rottenburg.

The church occupations were a reaction to smear campaigns and the ignorance of the church leadership. A few days later an irritated Cardinal Döpfner, who until then had ignored all requests for a meeting and left letters unanswered, announced that the Integrated Community was a 'free group within the church', not a sect. In 1978 the community was legitimized as an apostolic community by Cardinals Johannes Degenhardt and Joseph Ratzinger, in accordance with the decree *Apostolicam actuositatem* no. 18/19 of the Second Vatican Council. Ratzinger as bishop of Munich proclaimed: 'By this step, the lifestyle of the Integrated Community is recognized as a possible way of realizing the faith in the Catholic Church. It is part of the church's catholicity, incorporated into the whole church, without any *exclusive claim*. We also recognize other ways of realizing the faith, both old and new.'[3]

There were many good sides to the Integrated Community, but also quite a few bad ones. Most of the members kept seriously and honestly to their faith, but the leadership ran the risk of slipping into sectarianism. They set up companies, schools, medical practices, academies and publishing houses. Local bishops recognized branches in Austria, Italy and Tanzania. Ratzinger was impressed that they organized meetings with Jewish scholars, celebrated Mass with great simplicity and cared about his sister Maria and brother Georg. However, within the Integrated Community strict obedience was demanded, there were autocratic hierarchies, trials of members and demonization of renegades who asked critical questions. Rather as in the Nazi past of Traudl Wallbrecher, whose maiden name was Weiss. Contrary to what she said, she had not been in the resistance but a leading member of the League of German Girls (Bund Deutscher Mädel, or BDM), as was noted in a document of 8 September 2001 addressed to Cardinals Degenhardt and Ratzinger. The community used Ratzinger, the bishop and future prefect, as a figurehead and protective shield. A memoir entitled *Dreizig Jahre Wegbegleitung – Joseph Ratzinger/Papst Benedikt XVI. und die Katholische Integrierte Gemeinde (30 Years' Association – Joseph Ratzinger/Pope Benedict XVI and the Catholic Integrated Community)* was published in 2006, at a time when Ratzinger had long since distanced himself from it and the Catholic Integrated Community was showing clear signs of dissolving.

It was no secret in Munich that the pope had his eye on Ratzinger. John Paul II had made an excellent start. The Polish pope went up three steps at a time when he was hurrying upstairs. Nothing was fast enough for him. Many feared for him but many were also afraid of him, regarding him as determined and stubborn. Whereas part of the church apparatus had developed into a ponderous bureaucracy of officialdom, Wojtyła still burned like tinder. Sometimes his air of combined energy and reflection made him also seem like a being from another world. An Italian boy wrote to him saying: 'I saw you on television yesterday. But are you actually real?'

Until then Ratzinger had been able to hold off the advances from Rome. Wojtyła's second attempt began on 6 January 1981. Ratzinger had decided at short notice to take part in the episcopal ordination of the parish priest of his titular church in Rome. He said to his secretary that 'dear Don Ennio' had deserved it. But when he landed at the airport he was unexpectedly met by Erwin Ender, the head of the German section of the secretariat of state. The Holy Father wanted to speak to him urgently, in fact immediately, Ender told him. 'It would be fine for Your Eminence to go wearing your suit.' It quickly became clear that Wojtyła wanted to renew his pressure. But the meeting came to nothing. Ratzinger had 'made a condition which I thought could not be fulfilled. I said that I could only accept if I was still allowed to publish.'[4] Visibly surprised, the pope said he would think it over and have the matter clarified.

Two months later del Mestri invited Ratzinger to another conversation with the pope. Urgently, as ever. Ratzinger was at a meeting in Freising and took the next flight from Basel to Rome. 'Isn't setting conditions an affront to the pope?' I had asked him in our interview. The pope emeritus laughed. 'Perhaps, but I thought it was my duty to say that. Because I felt an inner conviction that I was able to say something to humanity.' Meanwhile Wojtyła's colleagues had established that Cardinal Gabriel-Marie Garrone had also been active as a writer while he had been prefect of the Congregation for Catholic Education. 'You can publish,' Wojtyła beamed as he welcomed his guest. He was only obliged to give up tasks such as editing the journal *Communio*. Checkmate. 'Then I really could not say no any longer.'

At first the appointment was to be kept strictly secret. In fact, considerable turbulence in world affairs prevented him taking it up for some time. In Wojtyła's Poland in the spring of 1981 the conflict between the regime and the Solidarność trade union, which was widely supported by the population, had escalated. At the same time units from the Warsaw Pact states were posted to the Baltic Sea coast for extensive 'manoeuvres'. More than 150,000 soldiers from several Soviet bloc states took up positions along the Polish frontiers. The US minister of defence, Caspar Weinberger, responded with a declaration that, if the Soviet troops invaded, the deployment of military force by the US was not ruled out.

On 30 March 1981 radio and television broadcasts announced that at 2.27 p.m. local time the US President Ronald Regan had been shot at in front of the Hilton Hotel in Washington DC. Reagan and three other people survived the attack. The 26-year-old assailant, John Hinckley, was declared psychologically unfit and of unsound mind by a court judgement. The motive he gave was that he had wanted to go down in history for his deed and, above all, to impress the actress Jodie Foster, whom he idolized. Twenty-four days later the world not only held its breath but its heart stopped.

It was 13 May 1981, a wonderful spring day, when John Paul II left the Apostolic Palace at 5 p.m. to make his way to the weekly general audience in St Peter's Square. On that day his lunchtime conversations had lasted longer than usual. One of his guests had been the French geneticist Professor Jérôme Lejeune, the discoverer of the chromosome anomaly that causes Down's Syndrome. On the morning of the same day the Turk Ali Ağca prayed on his knees to Allah for ten minutes in his boarding house near the Piazza Cavour. Finally, he shaved his body hair to prepare himself for a hero's death. For three days Ağca had only eaten fruit and vegetables. The diet was intended to help him feel light and carefree. He left his boarding house at 9 a.m. 'I realized that the name of the boarding house could also mean Jesus in Arabic writing', he explained later to the journalist Anna Maria Turi. 'I smile and it seems predestined that I go from the Jesus boarding house to kill the head of the Catholic Church.'[5]

It was 5.19 p.m. when the pope drove in his open 'pope-mobile' along the route that had been kept free into St Peter's Square, packed with 20,000 people. Among the public, there were many Polish

Catholics and a 450-strong delegation from Solidarność, which had only got permission to travel abroad after long negotiations with the communist regime. Wojtyła lifted a small girl who had been held up to him. He made the sign of blessing. But he had only just given the child back when there was an ear-splitting bang. Pigeons flew up in fright, and the joyful crowd became rigid with horror.

What millions of his devotees had feared had suddenly come true. An attack on the pope! The assailant, Ali Ağca, had managed to fire several shots from only seven metres away. The first shot hit Karol Wojtyła on the elbow, the second slashed his left index finger and the third went into his stomach area below the navel. Those nearest to him saw the pope slump. The arms of his secretary, Stanisław Dziwisz, and Swiss Guardsman Angelo Gugel only just managed to catch him. Seconds later, his white cassock was stained with blood. There were still nine bullets in the attacker's pistol. But the 9mm calibre Browning Hi-Power weapon jammed, and Ağca was overpowered. Wojtyła was barely conscious. An emergency ambulance took him to the Gemelli Clinic, six kilometres away. It covered the distance, which usually took half an hour, in just eight minutes. During the journey the pope lost three litres of blood.

On that 13 May, the feast day of Our Lady of Fátima, Ratzinger was in Bavaria going to a meeting. When he returned to the archbishop's palace with his driver at about 6 p.m., his secretary greeted him asking whether he had heard the news during his journey. At that point it was unclear whether the pope was still alive. 'The news struck the cardinal like a bolt of lightning,' said Fink. His appointment in Rome was still secret. Suddenly everything was up in the air. Would the chalice pass from him without anyone knowing about it?

The pope survived. But he took over 100 days to recover. Ali Ağca was sentenced and after 19 years in prison was extradited to Turkey. It remained unclear whether it was a lone attack or one directed by an organization such as the Bulgarian secret service, as was at first suspected. John Paul II forgave his attacker, who repented of the action and kissed the pope's ring at a private meeting with him. Wojtyła attributed his survival to a miracle by Our Lady of Fátima. 'A hand fired the shot,' he said later, 'and another hand directed the shot.' In May 1982 he laid his bloodstained cassock at the feet of Our Lady of Fátima. In 1991 he had the bullet that had been removed during his operation inserted into the crown she wore on her statue. He regarded the attack as the fulfilment of the prophecy in the third secret of Fátima, which spoke of a shot at a white-clad priest.

At the end of July 1981 Ratzinger travelled to Lourdes to the Eucharistic World Congress and then on to Toulouse, to the International Heart of Jesus Congress. The appointment of the bishop of Munich as prefect of the Roman Congregation for the Doctrine of the Faith was made public at a Vatican press conference on the morning of 25 November 1981. On the same day, at 3 p.m., Ratzinger stood before 60 journalists at a rapidly convened press conference in Munich. As well as Ratzinger's appointment, the appointments of the president of the International Committee of Theologians and the Papal Biblical Committee had also been announced. When the question was asked how long the cardinal would continue as archbishop of Munich, the diocesan canon lawyer shrugged his shoulders. Neither could Ratzinger answer the question. As a rule, when a bishop was transferred to another diocese his former office immediately became vacant. Even a phone call to the nuncio in Bonn only half-clarified the matter. The cardinal remained as reigning archbishop of Munich until his retirement was ordered by the Holy See, but he was to take up the office of prefect immediately. 'How would it feel to be the papal "watchdog" in future?' one of the journalists wanted to know. The cardinal grinned. A watchdog wasn't just something negative. A dog was a lovable creature. A dog could give a warning and then bite the right person!

On 28 February 1982 the day of departure came and perhaps in the history of the Catholic Church no dignitary on the way to Rome ever had a send-off like that of the bishop of Munich. Radio and television reported live. The Bavarian government also took part on behalf of the region. There had never been a ceremony like it. It displayed the recognition, popularity and respect the former professor had won.

Ratzinger himself sat at his desk all day. He wanted to find the right words to commit the flock he was leaving behind to their Christian Catholic faith. Many things in the letters he wrote sounded like the bequest of a man who was about to be banished for ever. 'Now I am exchanging a pulpit for a chancery,' he complained to the philosopher Richard Schaeffler.[6] But nothing sounds so wistful as the words he attached to Mary's column: *Etiam Romae, semper civis bavaricus ero* – 'I will always remain a Bavarian citizen even when I am in Rome.'

His five years as a bishop had turned the theologian into a pastor close to his people. 'We say it openly: we are not happy to let you go off to Rome,' said the minister-president Franz Josef Strauss at the ceremony in the Hercules Hall of the Munich Residence. He said goodbye to the cardinal 'beyond all denominational differences in the name of all the people of Bavaria, who have learned to value and love you'.[7]

Strauss could not resist going into fundamentals: 'So many fixed matters of faith and devotional life have become weaker and are increasingly questioned,' said the Christian Social Union (CSU) politician. A new generation had 'grown up in our country without any understanding of their parents' way of life, problems, questions and answers'. So 'the church and Christian faith' were facing 'an unprecedented test to defend the core of the Christian message and the roots of Christian existence'. Strauss also expressed a hope: 'So we trust the valour and fortitude, deep piety and wisdom of our Old Bavarian cardinal to play their part in his new job of steering the ship of the church through the storms of our time into the next millennium.' Previously the bishop, 'with a clarity for which we should be grateful', had 'repeatedly fended off any attempts to reduce the gospel to a political social programme'. The whole of Bavaria wished their departing bishop 'strength and success for this good fight in the service of truth, for the genuine freedom of the children of God against the ideological falsification of the gospel, the bewilderment of minds and enticement of souls'.

Then the bishop of the Evangelical-Lutheran church in Bavaria added his thanks for Ratzinger's 'admirable friendly spiritual partnership'. Aware of 'the urgent need for a joint Christian witness against the threat of atheism, the materialism of our society, the constant criticism of the church as an institution', Bishop Johannes Hanselmann continued, he was delighted 'by that new impetus from you even if – indeed because – it now comes from Rome'.

It was a particularly emotional moment when Ratzinger gave his farewell sermon in Freising Cathedral to more than a thousand priests. During his time as bishop he had introduced a number of reforms. They included the restructuring of the church's finance system, the creation of Catholic 'school work', the promotion of pastoral work for women, the reorganization of first confession, as well as reforming parish councils, the Catholic council, with the inclusion of laity, and the pastoral department. A particular concern had been the promotion of future priests and vital contact with the faithful. 'The bishop's job today is burdened with all kinds of conferences, meetings and papers.' So he had been especially glad 'when you can get out to the communities, experience and see the living church, how strong the church's presence still is there today, and how happy it still makes people, how much it still provides their living space'.[8]

Priesthood was a service, he reminded the assembled clergy, 'that can only be carried out together as "we". So let's go to one another. Speak with one another. Bear one another. Let's help each other [...] and don't let's quarrel with one another in factions!' The bishop begged them, 'Don't let's invent our own Jesus, as better than the real one who meets us in his body the church! Don't let's invent a better gospel, that we set against the troubles and failures of the church!' The harvest was great. It could 'bewilder young people if in conversation with them', who were seeking an answer, you pointed to 'a better life, an alternative, a new meaning'. Particularly 'if you see what kind of birds also prey on this harvest in order to reap it for themselves'.

No one guessed that this would be goodbye for ever. Ratzinger used the city squares as platforms where the meetings, ceremonies, sermons and speeches mounted to a climax. It was the city of *his* church. It was its Catholicism that had made it beautiful, delightful and successful. 'Let us always keep talking with God, then we will keep talking with each other,' he preached at the pontifical Mass on 28 February to a packed Cathedral of our Lady. The world was 'not saved by being perfectly looked after and insured. On the contrary, it is only really looked after if the powers of the heart are active, which make people open to one another and help them to deal rightly with this world's goods.' The pervasive general helplessness, despite material wealth, was because 'we have completely forgotten the deeper hunger'. As bishop he appealed to his community: 'Let us not just call upon God, but also listen to him. Let him call upon us. Let us relearn to love God's word. Let us learn to have time for that word again.' Finally, 'nowhere was it said that faith comes from reading – it comes from listening'. 'Let us be not sceptical but trusting,' he concluded: 'Trusting in Christ, which leads to faith and so to knowledge of truth and to life. That is the real heart of the matter.'

Emotionally he recalled Bavaria's vital, almost unbroken, tradition:

The sign of the cross, God's new rainbow, stands over our land. It greets us on our journey in wayside crosses. It speaks to us from our church towers. It always still has a place of honour in our homes. Let the cross remain the centre of our land, the centre of our life, the centre of our homes.[9]

Elsewhere when he had changed jobs he had mentioned some of his health problems, but this time he did not do so at all. But in one of his farewell sermons he chose an image that also suggested something about his own state of mind. It was the example of a man who felt 'the heavy burden of loneliness': 'It had become dark around him. He just wanted to be a human being like all the rest; but still himself.' In his time as a student and the first years of his priesthood that man had 'been an enthusiast, who had discovered the joy of God's word and calling. He had gone further and further into that word and in conversations, lectures, meetings and by the witness of his own life he became a leader and a signpost for many.' But then he had realized 'that after he had sown the word, it was as if it had trickled away into emptiness'. So 'the weight of futility had weighed more and more heavily upon his heart'. But eventually he had pulled himself together 'to recognize again the precious value of a service that offers people not just this or that but the very stuff of life'.

In his parting letter to priests, deacons and pastoral colleagues Ratzinger reiterated the key points to what gives the Christian Catholic life its unchanging identity. His advice was a kind of master plan for the new evangelization. First came the *Eucharist*. The Council had called it the 'peak and source'. The celebration also brought 'deeper familiarity with the *Missal*'. The more you went into the liturgical book of the Latin church 'the more you discovered its riches'. They should also practise Eucharistic *devotion*, spending time in adoration before the Blessed Sacrament. Only thus could the Eucharist 'become a source from which we always drink fresh water. Only thus can *receiving communion* remain fruitful in the long term.'

As for the *sacrament of confession*, of course it was not about 'building up a sense of guilt' but about 'the experience of grace, the experience of being forgiven', so that 'the past has really passed away': 'People can only bear to acknowledge guilt when they have experienced forgiveness; they can only confront the truth about themselves when it is overtaken by the new and greater truth of divine kindness.' And vice versa: 'being unable to acknowledge guilt' was 'the most dangerous form of spiritual blunting imaginable, because it makes people unable to improve and get rid of what is wrong'. He himself 'from his time as a student had used the ancient prayer *Ab occultis meis munda me* – Lord, cleanse me from my hidden faults'. So then he had learned to see 'that nothing is more fatal than self-righteousness, which only finds other people in the wrong. Self-satisfaction which can no longer acknowledge any guilt is a dangerous kind of hardening.' If you examined the 'cruelties of this century', it was clear that 'they nearly always come from a deadening of the heart, which is no longer able to acknowledge guilt'.

Ratzinger's Munich legacy concluded with a pastoral letter to the communities. For five years as archbishop he had 'been permitted to serve in our homeland and thereby received far more than I was able to give'. He asked for 'forbearance for all that was unsatisfactory in my service'. Being a Christian meant 'first of all that we give God the glory. Giving him the glory simply means: believing in him.' Believing in the Christian sense was 'accepting God as a reality, not just as any reality, but as the vital and fundamental reality'. At first it might seem 'to change very little if you leave God out of your life. Indeed it even seems as if everything becomes easier and more comfortable. But the more godlessness spreads through a whole community, the more it is as if the ship has been torn from its anchorage.'

His last words were for the young: 'You have realized what is unsatisfactory about our materialistic society more sharply than the older generation. That's why you protest and call for alternatives.' But they should take care. 'All possible ideologies' sought to exploit the longings of the young: 'I beg you, be critical of them too. What masquerades as social criticism is often just party-political talk. Get to the bottom of things! Seek the heart of the matter, dare to go for the real alternative!' And then he gave the motto that would become the key to his papacy:

> Let us dare to live like Jesus Christ. Let us have the courage to live the faith. Don't be talked into calling that old-fashioned or out-of-date! What is out-of-date and a failure is a materialistic lifestyle, all attempts to live a life without God. But Christ is not just yesterday and today, he is also tomorrow, because eternity belongs to him.

The bishop brought the ceremony to an end with a prayer at Mary's column: 'Be our teacher of faith, hope and love,' he prayed to God's mother, 'protect this diocese, this whole region, which has so often been entrusted to your protection and which we are again commending to you.' There was still a final chord to come. It came from the Company of Bavarian Mountain Riflemen. As the cardinal blessed the thousands of people, the men in their grey costumes fired a triple salute: 'Glory to God!'

The correspondent for the newspaper *Die Welt*, the future *Stern* writer Rudolf Lambrecht, summed up the departing bishop. He had 'the uncanny knack of uttering simple, obvious truths outright in a surprising way'. Not that Ratzinger had consciously polarized people in the past. 'He understood his job was to be a bastion against the *Zeitgeist* and saw himself as a teacher and protector of the truth of Jesus, whose inconvenient demands always divide people.' Ratzinger, who had once been a 'progressive thinker', had not changed his character but corrected his course, 'when he saw developments emerging that could lead to dismay and dissolution'. As archbishop and cardinal, he had 'not been a prince of the church. He saw his stringent thinking and behaviour as service. And you have to accept that about him.'[10]

PART TWO

Prefect

14

The Prefect

With an area of 44 hectares (109 acres), the smallest state in the world is hardly any bigger than a medium-sized farm in South America. Nevertheless, the Vatican has diplomatic relations with 150 countries on Earth. Its main post office dispatches 4 million letters and 15 million postcards per year. And in relation to its approximately 4,000 inhabitants, its army of about 100 Swiss Guards is the largest in the world.

It has a heliport, a station, a supermarket, petrol stations and the Hospitaller Brothers of St John of God's day-and-night pharmacy, which sells medicines and supplies the pope. The first 35 popes were martyred. Their bones are mostly laid in the catacombs on the Via Appia, together with 200,000 other Christian martyrs from the early days of the new religion. In the labyrinth of the Vatican administration, which contains 12 papal councils, 25 commissions and committees, three law courts, and nine congregations, the Congregation for the Doctrine of the Faith is especially prominent. It is the first-named and most important, but also the one with the worst image.

To this day, people connect the 'Holy Inquisition' with interrogations, torture and burnings. The institution was established to combat heresies, which kept causing existential crises for the faith. The gospels themselves were sabotaged by apocryphal writings by anonymous authors, which gave their own version of the life and words of Christ. Apollinarianism, Arianism, Docetism, Donatism, Gnosticism, Nestorianism, Pelagianism, Jansenism and still more heresies all had their own interpretations. For a long time the Christian principle prevailed that the weeds had to grow side by side with the wheat. It was not up to human beings but left to

Christ himself to separate the good from the bad when he returned. However, in the eleventh century the sect of the Cathars – *katharoi* in Greek, meaning 'pure', from which the German term *Ketzer* ('heretic') derives – gained countless bishops and noble houses. For Pope Innocent III the situation was serious enough to deploy Franciscans and, in particular, the Dominican Order founded by the Spaniard Domingo de Guzmán Garcés, to expose the new doctrine as dangerous fundamentalism.

The theologian and psychotherapist Manfred Lütz compared the Cathars to organizations of our own time such as Scientology.[1] The Cathars claimed to be finally practising the true form of Christianity. But they had a sombre ideology. They carried self-mortification to the point of dying of hunger; they forbade marriage and procreation; they had a pathological faith in the devil and banned private property. This presented a real danger to social peace. Whereas in the early church deviation was punished, at most, by exclusion from the community, in the early Middle Ages that shifted towards delivering religious offenders over to the secular authorities. From 1231 Pope Gregory IX set up the papal Inquisition, which meant something like 'searching' or 'smelling out'.[2] But the sentences could only be carried out by non-ecclesiastical authorities.

From the beginning, persecution of heretics was interwoven with political and economic motives. From 1478 in Spain an Inquisition under a state Grand Inquisitor, independent of the church, was guilty of persecuting whole ethnic groups. In many countries there were witch trials, which were quite often spurred on by furious, gawping crowds. On 21 July 1542 Pope Paul III created a high court for heretics and schismatics, as a Counter-Reformation measure. It consisted of six cardinals and was called the Congregatio Romanae et Universalis Inquisitionis: in short, Sanctum Officium.

Among those sentenced by the Roman Inquisition, Giordano Bruno was burned at the stake in the Campo de' Fiori in Rome on 17 February 1600. However, following his trial in 1633, Galileo Galilei was not tortured or forbidden to do his work. He spent his imprisonment together with servants in the luxurious apartments of a high Inquisition official. The abuses perpetrated by the Inquisition should not be glossed over, says the church historian Walter Brandmüller, but he says that they should not be judged 'by the standards of today'.[3] We should not ignore the fact that, in the melting-pot of the West, Christian culture was the basis of European identity. At a time when State-Christianity-Church formed an indispensable unity, denying the fundamentals of the faith was also seen as an attack on the social order. Brandmüller points out: 'The civil power, not the church's authority, was the first to proceed against heretics.' For example, it was not the reigning bishop but King Robert the Pious of France who had at least 12 heretical learned canons burned in 1022 in Orléans. In Milan members of the city aristocracy single-handedly dragged their allegedly heretical fellow aristocrats to the stake. When a council in Beauvais, in northern France, was discussing the fate of heretics, the chronicle of Hermann of Reichenau raged that accused prisoners were burned outside the city from fear that 'the mildness of the clergy' would let the delinquents escape.

Unlike the Spanish Inquisition, which acted as a political instrument of the king, the 'Holy Office' in Rome maintained strict legal procedures. They were often more restrained than many inquisitors in the modern world of the media, who are not afraid of making harsh pre-judgements and do not hesitate to put someone in the pillory who is suspected of offending against political correctness. Historians today point out that the introduction of the Inquisition, despite all its errors and abuses, was an advance on so-called 'divine judgements', by which suspects had to grasp red-hot iron in order to prove their innocence by being unhurt. Now the accused at least had the opportunity to defend themselves in the course of an orderly investigation. Most of those indicted received punishments such as carrying penitential crosses or going on pilgrimage. And it should be said that, following Luther, reformers declared that the persecution of those with deviant views was an absolutely legitimate means of guarding their faith against infiltration.

Ratzinger had always been the youngest. He was a lecturer at 25, a professor at 31, a bishop and cardinal at 50. In the spring of 1982, at the age of 54, he became the youngest head of the most important congregation of the Roman Curia. Thereby, besides the pope, he became the leading teacher of the faith of the largest church in the world. John Paul II was clear that the appointment of the clever bishop of Munich would be the most important of his whole term of office. It not only determined a direction but was also crucial to the success or failure of his whole mission. Things had changed for the church. It had to meet the challenges of the time wisely with good arguments. It had to be prepared for dialogue and behave in a spirit of fellowship. Meanwhile it also had to show unshaken firmness. Only with one of the best theologians at his side could he win the battle for the achievements of the Council. He needed a defence against the attacks on the faith's traditions, with powerful arguments that held fast.

Perhaps it would have made sense completely to dissolve the 'Holy Office' immediately after the Council. But then who would test whether Catholic theologians, bishops and priests really spoke in the name of the Church or were proclaiming obscure theories as the 'true' doctrine? Who would have the authority to determine what was Catholic and what was not? Even immediately after the introduction of printing, the archbishop of Mainz had warned in 1485 that many writers misused Gutenberg's invention 'out of lust for fame or greed for money, so that they corrupt humanity rather than enlightening them'. In particular, many of the free translations of the Bible distorted the meaning so that 'even scholars were led astray into serious misunderstandings'.[4]

On the other hand, wasn't it Ratzinger himself who had attacked the Holy Office most fiercely in his preparatory texts for Cardinal Frings? (On the Council's last day in session on 7 December 1965 Pope Paul VI proclaimed the reform of the Sant'Uffizio and changed its name to the Congregation for the Doctrine of the Faith.) Ratzinger had made his bed then at the Vatican Council; now he had to lie in it. The funny thing about it was that hardly anyone fitted the figure of an inquisitor less than the former professor from Bavaria. There was his reserve, which could be understood as coldness, and his profound intellectuality, which might appear suspect. There was something frail about him and at the same time a determination, which many felt was ruthless. In his new job the motto he had chosen as bishop – *co-operatores veritatis*: 'fellow-workers for the truth' – could be read quite differently. A 'guardian of the faith' as a 'fellow-worker for the truth'? And to top it all, the new 'pope's policeman' was really a police officer's son. Hans Küng knew that his counterpart would soon be finished as a theologian to be taken seriously.

People were aware that for years Ratzinger had used every possible means to resist the call to Rome. It was hard to communicate his refusal without damaging the authority of the pope and of the job itself. 'Had no one warned you against this unpopular job?' I asked him at our first meeting in November 1992. 'I didn't need any warning. It was perfectly clear that I was getting into a bed of nettles there,' he replied. He had found himself 'in a great dilemma'. In the end he had had no choice. 'I had to take it on.'

On 18 January 1982 Ratzinger had already spent a week in Rome on the recommendation of the secretary to the Congregation for the Doctrine of the Faith, Archbishop Jérôme Hamer, to take a look at his new place of work in the Piazza Sant'Uffizio. The palazzo, with its massive gate beside the colonnades of St Peter's Square, looked like a fortress. It was dark and secretive – an 'uncomfortable place', he felt. The mood was tense as he was led into his work room, attentively followed by the expectant glances of his future fellow workers. It was a roomy office with a noble desk, at which his predecessors had also worked. Various Baroque paintings hung on the walls; the ceiling was still in the Renaissance style. The view was not overwhelming but had its charm. Michelangelo's mighty dome of St Peter's was quite near by, and in the distance there were the loggias of the Apostolic Palace. The pope lived in the top right-hand corner of the palace with his household of Polish nuns. His faithful secretary Dziwisz had his lodgings in the attic above.

Meanwhile, Bruno Fink inspected his own office, which was right next to the prefect's. He found a simple filing cabinet, a 1950s desk, a side-table and an old typewriter with an Italian keyboard. Whereas in his Munich office he had been supported by two colleagues, now he had to do all the work on his own, including typing letters, lectures and comments. Soon he was hammering away at his typewriter late into the night in his single-room lodgings in the Casa Internazionale del Clero, a house for priests on the Piazza Navona.[5]

As a secretary ranked as '*adetto tecnico di 2a classe e di 2a categoria*', the usual initial job classification for Vatican employees without a doctorate, Fink soon had to pre-sort all the incoming post, transfer inquiries on marriage issues and laicizations to the right in-tray and look after the cardinal's extensive personal correspondence. He also had to welcome visitors: for example, monks who reported dramatic conflicts with their superiors, or bishops who told him, almost in tears, that they could see no way out.

The Congregation had at its disposal an elegant 1960s Mercedes, a gift from Daimler-Benz to Cardinal Ottaviani. The chauffeur was the indispensable Alfredo Monzo, an amiable, reliable and silent Italian who also acted as porter, messenger and caretaker. Ratzinger was offered a choice between two flats in the church-owned house at 1 Piazza della Città Leonina, outside Vatican territory. He chose flat number 8, on the fourth floor. It was 300 square metres and had two studies, living accommodation and, as was usual for cardinals, a house chapel. Administrative staff working for the Amministrazione del Patrimonio della Santa Sede (APSA) promised that the flat would be 'rapidly' renovated, which meant in about three months. It did not mean that the gas, telephone, electric sockets and shower would also be working properly. 'During my lifetime I have often moved house,' the new tenant was later heard to sigh, 'but it was never as bad as this time!'

As a cardinal member of the Curia, Ratzinger received a Vatican passport, which gave him an indefinite right to live in Italy. (This was in addition to his German passport, which he also kept when he became pope.) Like all other EU citizens, secretary Fink received a licence to stay for three months, then for a year and after that indefinitely. He was given an 'alla Vaticana' pass for his private car, a light blue Opel Kadett, which he brought with him from Munich. As the re-registration was beset with endless bureaucratic obstacles, 'I took good advice from friends and "donated" my car to Cardinal Ratzinger. I then got signed permission in both Italian and German giving me full authority to drive the car. In that way I received a Vatican vehicle registration number with the prefix SCV [Status Civitatis Vaticanae, or Vatican City State]'. That also gave him tax exemption and cheap petrol at Vatican garages.

Ratzinger's sister, Maria, was still in Bavaria. She was learning Italian and studying a map of Rome to find where the weekly markets were held. In the only interview she ever gave, a statement of less than 100 lines, she told the Süddeutsche Zeitung that she had already been to Rome five times and found the city 'beautiful'. Looking after her brother was not a sacrifice. She knew from experience that for the three siblings the feminine role 'had its own special importance'.[6]

Until his flat was ready, in February Ratzinger was given the 'Munich' room on the third floor of the German seminary, the Collegio Teutonico di Santa Maria dell'Anima, on the Campo Santo. (Other rooms were called 'Danzig' and 'Limburg'.) His room had a view of the palms in the German cemetery and the dome of St Peter's. However, for the first fortnight the heating broke down. Not only was it bitterly cold, but there was also no hot water. There was also a lack of liturgical books. His monthly salary in Munich had been 10,000 marks. He became stoically aware that it had now fallen to less than half that, at around 4,300 marks. The archdiocese then sent him a top-up (we had to 'enable our archbishop to live decently', declared the finance director, Friedrich Fahr). However, Ratzinger never touched this special account.

By the middle of April the flat in the 'Leonina' was ready at last. A big removal van from Munich parked outside the house. It was loaded with Ratzinger's old desk, piano, shelves and books, books, books. His sister, Maria, had announced she was coming in May. In the meantime, Ratzinger looked after himself in the Trattoria Tiroler Keller in the Via Crescenzio. He got on very well with his closest colleagues – the already mentioned secretary of the Congregation for the Doctrine of the Faith, Archbishop Jérôme Hamer, an exceedingly diligent Dominican from Belgium who spoke numerous languages, and Monsignor Alberto Bovone, an expert in church law, who managed the whole set-up. Both men later became cardinals.

As the senior management team, the trio discussed the Congregation's agenda and sought suitable solutions to problems as they arose. Besides the three *capi* there was a *promotor iustitiae*, who dealt with matters of church law. The advisory panel, the *consulta*, consisted of about ten bishops of the Roman Curia as well as ten professors from various Roman universities and religious communities. The decision-making body was the *sessio ordinaria*. The assembly, to which eight to ten cardinals belonged, generally sat every two weeks, on a Wednesday. These sessions were prepared for by meetings of the *consulta*. The documentation, together with analyses of the problems, was given to the pope a week before the session so that the Holy Father was kept abreast of the proceedings.

As a rule the *plenaria*, the Congregation's general meeting, met once a year. Fifteen to 20 cardinals and bishops from all over the world took part in it. The International Committee of Theologians and the Papal Biblical Committee usually also met at the same time. These committees dealt respectively with fundamental theological questions and matters of biblical scholarship. The new Prefect of the Congregation for the Doctrine of the Faith wrote to his former student Viktor Hahn on 18 July 1982: 'For weeks now the heat has become oppressive, at 35 degrees! But I like the work and also the people – although my own theological work has still been largely laid aside …'

According to the Apostolic Constitution, Ratzinger's *Sacra Congregatio pro Doctrina Fidei* had the task of 'promoting and safeguarding the doctrine on faith and morals for the whole Catholic Church'. With the 1965 reform Paul VI had given it the role of positively promoting the faith instead of its former repressive role. Nevertheless, now as before it was to 'correct errors'. It was like a ministry and divided into four departments:

- The doctrinal department tested the theological correctness of all the ordinances of the Roman Curia and the statements of theologians, priests and bishops made in the name of the church. It also dealt with ethical questions, arising from technological and medical progress, that were important for the future of humanity.
- The disciplinary section dealt with questions of church discipline – for example, the handling of the Eucharistic bread and wine, the secret of the confessional – and also with misconduct by priests.
- The third section dealt with the dissolution of marriages in accordance with Petrine and Pauline privileges and had about 2,000 applications to consider every year.
- The fourth section dealt with priests' requests for laicization. A special area of responsibility was miracles. Reported events were investigated by the Congregation to discover whether the event was a natural anomaly, due to hysteria, or actually a supernatural phenomenon.

As prefect, Ratzinger was also *ex officio* president of the Biblical as well as the Theology Committee. Since each head of a congregation also belonged to other congregations, Ratzinger's remit also included working with the Congregation of Bishops, the Propaganda Congregation and the Catechism Committee, as well as the Council for Unity and the Secretariat for Non-Believers.

At first he had 30, later about 40, mostly young colleagues, selected by a complicated proportional system. They came from all over the world and were usually appointed for five or ten years. The Congregation's primary information source was local bishops. When these were making their five-yearly duty visit to the pope, they also reported to the prefect of the Congregation for the Doctrine of the Faith on the situation in their diocese. About 90 per cent of cases handled were to do with some professor or bishop having expressed views that were not in accordance with Catholic doctrine. At the beginning Ratzinger remarked that the small wages paid to his colleagues, which 'would be near the breadline' in Germany, were hard to understand, when it was said that the Holy See 'was swimming in gold'. In fact, he 'was barely able to afford his staff's expenses'.[7]

When he took up his post, there was no meeting with the pope to discuss the direction and difficulties of his work. 'I had my weekly audience with him. That was enough time to discuss things.' And indeed it was 'actually clear what a prefect had to do'.[8] But his colleagues were astonished when their new boss began his first meeting in Latin. 'I still spoke no Italian. I had only learned it in conversation. But everyone really knew Latin then, so it was no problem.'[9]

Soon the Romans became accustomed to seeing an unassuming *signore* scurrying across St Peter's Square shortly before nine in the mornings. From the beret and shabby briefcase they realized it was the prefect of the Congregation for the Doctrine of the Faith. In his free time Ratzinger went for walks along the Borgo Pio, chatted with the fruit sellers, played the piano – or sat as his desk writing lectures or sermons that priests from home had asked him for. And if needed in Traunstein or elsewhere in the Chiemgau area, he also undertook confirmations.

On the way to his office he greeted a cat, which waited for him on the Campo Santo. He chatted with Clelia, the concierge, with whom he usually had breakfast. Clelia worked for 40 years at the entrance to the Congregation for the Doctrine of the Faith. When the Vatican administration gave her notice to quit her flat, Ratzinger's colleagues heard their boss strongly protesting about it on the telephone. Clelia stayed put. Once Ratzinger arranged an appointment for her with John Paul II. He said: 'The pope can receive you tomorrow from this to that time.' Clelia thought it over briefly but then answered definitively: 'I can't do that.'

He celebrated Mass one morning a week in the Campo Santo Teutonico. 'That Thursday was always something special,' said his former colleague Helmut Moll. 'Over a hundred people came. It was always full. It included people who spoke briefly to him, wanted to hand him something or had a request.'[10] At his office the prefect turned first to the press report. It was his only source of information besides the news programme *Telegiornale*, broadcast by RAI (Radiotelevisione Italiana, the Italian national public broadcasting company) and the *Mittelbayerische Zeitung* from Regensburg (which often arrived a fortnight late). The first part of the morning was devoted to examining the files. On days without formal meetings visitors were received at 11 a.m. At 1.15. p.m. he went home with a briefcase full of documents, dossiers and draft reports, which had to be worked on by colleagues on the following day. On Sundays they ate in the dining room but on work days in the kitchen. It was three by four metres square and barely had room for two people. And while Maria served the lunch, her brother sat on his little bench in the corner, almost as if they were still in Hufschlag, in the old farmhouse on the edge of the wood.

His work at the *Curia Romana* stimulated Ratzinger, said his secretary Fink. The work was 'clearly more of a theological-academic nature' than the onerous financial and structural matters he had had to deal with in Munich. He also began to appreciate the flexibility of the Italians. He praised them saying that you could learn from them always to make something good out of a difficult situation. Whereas Germans often abandoned a problem because 'it won't work', the Italians reacted by saying 'let's give it a go'. And when Germans said: 'That's enough!' Italians would say, 'No, let's try it once more.'

Ratzinger was the first theologian, rather than a specialist in church law, to head the Congregation for the Doctrine of the

Faith. Within a short time it began to look different. 'It was extremely unusual for a prefect of the Congregation to get mixed up in theological disputes,' remarked Wolfgang Seibel, the editor-in-chief of the Jesuit journal *Stimmen der Zeit*.[11] Ratzinger looked forward to meeting bishops and undertook to 'travel to all five continents to speak with the faith committees there'.[12] 'We are happy about what the bishops themselves are doing,' he said and added with a smile: 'You can't keep watch over the whole of Christendom with just 30 or 40 people.' The task of the magisterium was not 'to oppose thinking but to pronounce on the authority of the response we are given'. It was important 'to keep room for others to speak'.[13]

At first he had been 'rather afraid' of his new influence, the prefect admitted, 'because when you advance your own opinions it is easy to bring too much of your own into the job'.[14] He was also aware 'that the job carries the temptation to become absorbed in negations, for these are what strike you first. There is a great danger of only being reactive and getting stuck in refuting things.' So it had been important for him 'to prioritize the positive measures as well as to strengthen and transmit the new pioneering departures'.[15] 'Rather than relying on his own decision', he had 'wanted to stress the collegial way of working and the importance of various committees as strongly as possible'.[16] Above all, he had been clear that he was actually responsible not to the world but to God. And if he could answer to God, then it was all right, and it was also all right for the world.

In fact, the first documents dealt with under his leadership did stress positive, forward-leading aspects. The documents were on the relations between Catholics and Anglicans (1982), freemasonry and the Eucharist (both 1983). According to Professor Réal Tremblay, from the beginning of his leadership Ratzinger had 'reacted with great clarity and helped when things became complicated'.[17] Hermann Geissler, who was only 28 when he began the job, was impressed that 'the great Ratzinger always asked for our opinion. He took to heart what St Benedict recommends in his Rule, that in many things the young may be more right than their elders.' In December 1982 even the *Süddeutsche Zeitung* was impressed by the new prefect: 'He does not fit into any cliché, either conservative or progressive. Joseph Ratzinger is simply Catholic, body and soul, a kind of navigator in purple.'[18]

Since the Council, Ratzinger had got to know Rome well – the city's romantic back streets, amazing buildings and its people, the simple, uninhibited Catholicity of their art of living. He had brought with him the ring that Maria and Georg had given him for his ordination as a bishop. They had bought it from a Regensburg antique shop. It showed a phoenix, symbol of the power to rise again from the ashes. Would he ever rise again to be able to do the work that he actually felt called to do? Wojtyła stood there with his broad shoulders and would have liked to gather everybody round him like a hen with her chicks. What about himself? Didn't he always make himself thin and little, as if he were afraid of being crushed? Even when a group of friendly priests gathered round him, he just stood with hunched shoulders, both hands firmly gripping his briefcase, which he held in front of him like a shield. Now he would be a Roman for the next five years, perhaps even ten. But certainly not for any longer.

15

Ratzinger's Report

Was there ever a pope who travelled so much and drew such great crowds? A pope who proclaimed the *Kerygma* in such a fresh and unconventional way, the good news on which Christian faith was based: 'You are the Messiah, the Son of the living God'?

John Paul II directed his staff 'on the run'. He often had *polpettone* – meatloaf – for lunch so as not to delay discussion of the day's agenda by unnecessary chewing. Many were impressed by his wit, his poetry and sturdy piety. For him being a Christian meant bringing the faith into the world anew. Whereas Paul VI had said to bishops, 'Help me to do my job', his successor said, 'I have come to help you with your pastoral office.'

His greatest joy was to listen inwardly in silence to the mysteries of the faith, deep down where heart and soul found the way to God. You must become like little children, he said. And think about things in terms of their end. Critics pulled him to pieces, and perhaps he could be charged with trying to do too much too soon in the hurry of this world's time, whose end he sensed was coming. Like Moses, he struck the ground with his staff, convinced that the Christian religion had the right answers for modern people's loneliness. Standing apart himself, he impressed by speaking out about the arms race, corruption, racism, exploitation. People no longer thought it impossible that a pope could ever be right.

Wojtyła and Ratzinger were as different as chalk and cheese. One was big and strong, the other small and slight. One extrovert, the other introvert. One emotional, the other rational. One sporty, the other unsporty. One Marian, the other Jesuan. No one would have thought of them as blood brothers. One was a passionate character who enthused God-seekers through his charm and theatrical talent. The other was thin, sensitive, a disciplined, brilliant thinker, rock-solid, reliable, but without ambitions, except perhaps to write a great Christology one day.

Yet from month to month it became clearer that a congenial pair had come together at the top of the Catholic Church, with the ability to steer the ship even through stormy waters. For, although their differences were great, so were their similarities. They both had personal experience of racial hatred, of terror and of the millions of victims of the atheist experiments of the twentieth century. Both had an eye for which modern tendencies offered hope and which were dangerous. Wojtyła was 'thankful to the Holy Spirit for the great gift of the Second Vatican Council', as he confirmed in his testament. And although both church leaders defended the Second Vatican Council, they were united in rejecting anything that they regarded as dilution or error.

'I came here as a cardinal,' Ratzinger said proclaiming his loyalty to Wojtyła. 'So I don't need to play power games or seek a career.' He saw himself as the moderator of a great working community. However, he would 'never venture to impose my own ideas of Christianity on the decisions of the Congregation'.[1] Ratzinger's appointment had been necessary, said the philosopher Robert Spaemann, because with the complexity of modern theology 'an average intelligence could no longer judge correctly between the range of possible opinions'.

In a very short time Ratzinger had reorganized the Sant'Uffizio and increased the staff. He introduced rotas, strengthened authors' rights and gave theologians accused of dogmatic errors the right to defend themselves. The professor had become a prefect 'who could not be theologically bamboozled' by those outside the Congregation or by the team of consultants. As a *peritus* he had denounced the imperious style of the *Officium*. After he took office bishops, theologians or priests who were subject to complaints were not chastised, but in important cases they were invited to Rome to discuss differing views in person.

Ratzinger had a clear idea of what the church was facing in the coming decades. There was hardly any progress in ecumenical affairs. The Protestants could not agree on sharing communion, the Orthodox prohibited the Catholics from preaching the gospel in Russia. There was the complacency of the bishops in Western European countries. Anti-Roman opposition groups threatened to undermine the faith in Catholic countries. There was also the notorious hostility of the liberal media, which saw the Vatican as the bastion against any progress in civilization, which had to be attacked. The psychoanalyst Manfred Lütz spoke of a 'Holy Father complex', which was especially prevalent in the German press. In no other country in the world 'was so much said in connection with the pope, at such a low intellectual level, about pills, condoms, pre-marital, extra-marital, post-marital sex and even women and celibacy treated as genital issues'. The 'constant chatter about sex' was 'classically pubertal' – and yet here 'it was among otherwise adult contemporaries'.[2]

In 1970 there were 448,508 Catholic priests worldwide. Twenty-five years later, despite a considerable increase in Catholics, the number of priests had sunk to 404,750. Almost 46,00 priests had given up their office.[3] Hundreds, perhaps thousands, of Catholic theologians turned away from fundamental doctrines. They denied the divine sonship of Christ, the resurrection or the primacy of the pope. Applications to the seminary to become priests had decreased sharply. Discipline slackened among the clergy; secularization grew. How widely the cancer of sexual abuse had spread was shown decades later by the countless misdeeds of deacons, priests and even bishops.

Ratzinger was convinced that previously unassailable dogmas risked being lost. And after the secession of Lefebvre's supporters, there was now the threat of a wider split in the church, this time from the left. The divisions in the faith community could no longer be overlooked. In 1984 he wrote in an article in the *Frankfurter Allgemeine Zeitung*:

My impression is that the damage the church has suffered over the last 20 years has been caused by the unleashing within it of latent, aggressive, polemical, centrifugal, perhaps irresponsible forces. And – outside [the church] by its confrontation with cultural change: the rise of the upper middle class in the West, the new third-sector bourgeoisie, with its liberal-radical ideology, which is individualistic, rationalistic and hedonistic.[4]

The church's main task at this time was to seek a new 'balance of tendencies and values within Catholicism as a whole'. The upheaval in the church also corresponded to the mental earthquake shaking the whole world. Especially in unstable times, Ratzinger preached, the church must be mindful of its own mission, given to it by Jesus: to teach, help and heal. Only by a determined ethics could it become a true adviser and partner in the difficult questions of modern civilization. Instead of a church from above or a church from below, he recommended a 'church from within'.

Ratzinger understood that Wojtyła had different ideas about strategy. However, on the whole, the agreement between pope and cardinal was almost complete. 'You can never tell what is the pope's aim or what is an idea of Ratzinger's,' sighed Wolfgang Seibel, editor-in-chief of the Jesuit journal *Stimmen der Zeit.*[5] The Spanish writer Juan Arias remarked: 'Often when you hear John Paul II speaking you get the impression that Ratzinger wrote it. And vice versa, if you read an article by the prefect of the Holy Office, you think it was inspired by Pope Wojtyła himself.'[6]

Juan Arias said that someone who often dined with the Holy Father had told him that 'except for some aspects of social and pastoral work, where Wojtyła felt more sure of himself, the pope relied on the solid views of the German cardinal-theologian in the whole area of theology and in doctrine'.[7] Ratzinger was also better informed. On their *ad limina* visits, bishops poured out their hearts to him without being asked. They had complaints and worries which they did not dare to speak about higher up, or which those higher up would not want to listen to. According to Arias, it could not be said that Ratzinger and Wojtyła were 'people who do not live in our world or that they are antediluvian in theology. They are intelligent reformers who feel that they are right as progressive and conciliar people.' For good measure, they were 'both highly educated, sensitive, young, polemical and want to introduce real reform into the church'.[8]

Ratzinger not only reorganized his Congregation. He wanted also to give it a voice. His media offensive began on 9 May 1983 with a widely noticed interview in the news magazine *Der Spiegel*. He discussed France's nuclear weapons policy under President François Mitterrand, as well as the 'weakness of the church at this time', which he saw as caused by a 'weakness in morals': 'The wretched thing in the world is that only brute facts count and moral principles are mainly set aside as unreal.' Perhaps the church should adopt 'the prophetic role of the critic' more strongly, 'which necessarily also leads to confrontation'. It was important 'to have the courage to stand up against society if the moral position required it'. However, the church should 'not overstretch its authority. Then it can very easily exert a false moral compulsion.'

On the growing influence of the new liberation theology, Ratzinger said: 'I think it is right and necessary that the church in Latin America is aware of its social responsibility, that it seeks to restrict dictators through its moral protest and that it struggles to establish justice, without which there can be no peace.' But it was different when 'with many theologians what was Christian was dissipated and dissolved into Marxism'. In that way 'the moral power of the gospel was annulled again'.[9]

Ratzinger's *Spiegel* interview was an attempt to come off the defensive and break out of the narrow area, which outsiders thought his Congregation was confined to. When the *Spiegel* interviewer confronted him about his personal change from progressive to conservative, he replied that he had 'asked himself that question a few years ago'. You could not 'stand still in life, you have to develop'. But with him it had been a 'straight development that did not swing into opposites'. He had recently 're-read the volumes of the Council speeches that I had prepared' and confirmed that to this day he had 'not abandoned anything that I advocated then'. But what had changed was 'the situation in which we are living and, of course, in some things my degree of reflexion has changed with it'.

Ratzinger's first period as prefect was largely taken up with an argument about the church's promulgation of doctrine. In the spring of 1983 he was invited by the French cardinal Jean-Marie Lustiger to speak in Notre-Dame Cathedral in Paris and in Lyon Cathedral on 'The Crisis of Catechesis and How To Overcome It'. His speech sparked a storm of outrage. He was accused of wanting to turn back the clock. 'French catechist groups reacted strongly and even bishops protested,' noted secretary Fink. Ratzinger had lamented that the new religious instruction manuals offered a fragmentary catechesis with constantly changing experiments. It had been a serious error to dismiss the term 'catechism' as obsolete. Pope Wojtyła was also outraged. But for different reasons from the critics in France. As a reaction to the abuses, that same year, he gave a new committee the task of creating a worldwide catechism of the Catholic Church. Of course, it was understood who would lead the project, which eventually became one of the most important achievements of John Paul II's papacy.

One year later Ratzinger's next coup hit like a bombshell. Journalists from all over the world queued at his office for an exclusive interview. The list of applicants ranged from the *New York Times* to the Moscow *Pravda*. The one accepted was the Italian journalist Vittorio Messori, who was offered a long conversation with the prefect during his summer holidays. This took place from 15 to 18 August, in Bressanone in South Tyrol. Shortly afterwards, it appeared as a book in Italian with the title *Rapporto sulla fede*. The target audience for the 'Ratzinger Report' was primarily the new generation of candidates for the priesthood, who had had enough of the 'candy floss theology' in the Catholic faculties. The interview contained Ratzinger's known positions, especially his criticism of the post-conciliar developments. But now he was no longer just any theologian speaking but the pope's closest collaborator. And in plain language.

On his holiday Ratzinger stayed in a seminary that let rooms cheaply, mainly to elderly clergy. He loved the long corridors, the spiritual atmosphere and even the smell in the old Baroque building. In the refectory he and the retired priests shared meals, prepared by Tirolese nuns. Occasionally, from old habit, he visited the Hotel-Gasthaus Grüner Baum, which did wonderful pancakes. Messori had prepared well. He knew that, apart from the pope, no one could answer his questions on the situation of the church and the faith 'with greater authority'. Schematic categories such as 'conservative' or 'progressive, 'right' or left' were as inapplicable to the head of the Congregation for the Doctrine of the Faith and made as little sense as other rough epithets such as 'optimist' or 'pessimist'.

Messori was born in Turin in 1941 and grew up in an atheist family. He had been baptized as an adult. He not only shared a birthday (16 April) with his conversation partner but also a passion for an intensive, open exchange of views.[10] At the very beginning of the interview Ratzinger said he would 'never have been prepared to take up this church post if my job had been mainly monitoring'. Of course, now as before, there was still the disciplinary side to the Congregation, but that too was associated with 'a positive task'. The prerequisite for the right understanding of his institution was 'a religious perspective', which took for granted that 'truth is a fundamental element in human life'. Otherwise the Congregation's 'concern' about the denial of the truths of the faith would falsely be interpreted as 'intolerance'. It should never be forgotten that 'for the church the faith is a "common treasury", wealth that belongs to all, beginning with the poor, who at least are protected from perversions of it'.

Ratzinger stressed that it was 'indisputable that the last ten years had been extremely negative for the Catholic Church'. This 'genuine crisis that had to be treated and cured' required a 'return to the documents' of the Council: 'they offer us the right tools to get to grips with the problems of today. We are called to rebuild the Church not *despite* but *thanks to* the true Council.' There was no '*pre*- or *post*-conciliar church: there is only one single church, which is on the way to the Lord.' Christians must realize again they 'belong to a minority', which often stood in contrast to those ways of thinking and behaving that the New Testament called the 'spirit of the world' – and 'certainly not in a positive sense'. They needed to 'rediscover the courage not to conform, and the ability to oppose'.

Ratzinger rejected any attempts to 'cancel' the Second Vatican Council with a 'Restoration'. The ultras linked to the renegade Archbishop Lefebvre would not revitalize the faith but fossilize it. 'If by "Restoration" what is meant is a return to the past, then that is impossible. The church goes forward towards the fulfilment of history.' However, there was also a sense of 'restoration' that meant 'a search for a new balance' to correct 'all the exaggeration of an indiscriminate openness to the world'. In that sense, 'restoration' as 'a new-found balance of tendencies and values within Catholicism as a whole' was 'thoroughly to be desired'.

There are things that are better not said. Or said differently. And there are things that others are just waiting to kick the speaker for saying. After the publication of the interview it was only a matter of hours before critics would hit upon the term 'restoration'. Ratzinger tried to quell the storm of outrage by making clear in a statement in an Italian newspaper that, semantically, the term 'restoration' should be taken to mean 'regaining lost values'. Even though for modern people the term had been 'linguistically taken over' in such a way 'that it is difficult to give it that meaning, in fact it literally meant the same as the word "reform"'.

As an example, he cited the works of St Charles Borromeo, for whom 'the classic expression of true reform' was 'a renewal that leads forward even as it promotes permanent values in a new way; it maintains the whole of Christianity and the whole of humanity'. In Milan, Borromeo had 'rebuilt – *restored*' the church, which had nearly been destroyed, 'without thereby returning to the Middle Ages'. On the contrary, he had created a modern kind of church. That could be clearly seen when 'Charles abolished a religious order that was already going under, and assigned its property to new, active communities'. Provocatively, Ratzinger said of much-criticized rigidities in the church: 'Who today has the courage to consign to oblivion what is inwardly dead (and only outwardly still alive)?' Indeed, often 'new Christian awakenings are combatted by so-called reformers'.

This later explanation was not a retreat. On the contrary. We can read from it what the prefect saw as the only possible way to proceed in those difficult years. Basically, he showed he was being more radical and reform-minded that many of his critics, who, as he remarked, 'convulsively defend institutions that only continue to exist in self-contradiction'. Charles Borromeo showed

> the essential prerequisite for [genuine] renewal: Charles could convince others because he was convinced himself. He could continue with his conviction amid the antagonisms of his time, because he experienced them himself. He could do so because he was a Christian in the deepest sense, that is, he was completely focused on Christ. Regaining that focus on Christ is what really counts.

Ratzinger saw one of the causes of the crisis in faith as a misunderstanding of what the church actually was.

> My impression is that that by and large the genuinely Catholic meaning of 'church' is silently disappearing, without it being expressly dismissed. Many no longer believe that it is about a

reality intended by the Lord himself. Even some theologians see the church as a human creation, something we created ourselves and can freely rearrange according to the demands of the moment.

But in truth 'behind the human externals' there was 'the mystery of a super-human reality, which reformers, sociologists and organizers have no authority to interfere with'. If the church was just 'seen as our fabrication, then the contents of the faith would also be optional'. The consequence would be that 'The gospel becomes a *Jesus project*, a project of social liberation or some other merely historical, immanent project, which might pretend still to be religious but is substantially atheist.'[11]

Contrary to the progressives, Ratzinger was set on the original, the classic, and insisted on the hardware, that could not be changed without also losing the source-code – and with it the core competence for which the church existed at all. He could not say often enough: the heart of what Christ gave us was not a business plan but the mystery of his divine origin. So it was necessary to 'rediscover the meaning of the church as the Lord's church, as the setting for God's real presence in the world'.

There could hardly be a greater contrast than that between the guardian of the faith and a mainstream designer church, which seemed to him neither cold nor hot but lukewarm and colourless. He liked to refer to the decisive and divisive question that Jesus asked his disciples: 'Who do you say that I am?' According to the evangelists, those who had expected a political leader, a powerful king or at least a miraculous healer soon parted from him, first inwardly and then outwardly. So it was all the more astonishing that the rest, those simple fishermen and country people, who had neither a plan nor a political vision, braved an empire and enabled the new doctrine to survive, which was faith in God's activity alone. Of course, the church in its human structures was *semper reformanda*, always needing to be reformed, the prefect stressed. But we also had to 'be clear how and how far'. For what humans could do was always 'infinitely smaller' than the contribution of the one 'it is finally all about'. 'True reform' was not erecting 'new façades' but 'as far as possible letting what is ours disappear so that what is his, what belongs to Christ, becomes more visible'.

To give an example, Ratzinger cited the Munich ordinariate, which had about 400 officials and employees during his time as bishop (it now has about 1,000). As it was in the nature of organizations to justify their existence by more and more documents, meetings and structural plans, that kind of support often became a burden for pastors. Ratzinger warned about further 'rationalistic shallows, endless talking and pastoral immaturity'. You felt a 'chill' about a post-conciliar liturgy that was often lacklustre and 'boring with its desire for the banal and low artistic quality'. 'New movements, which no one had planned and no one had called for but which had simply arisen themselves from the inner vitality of the faith, these were hopeful.' Unlike 'old forms, which have become bogged down in self-contradiction and desire for negation', these new initiatives 'hardly had a voice in the great conversation of ruling ideas'. So the task 'of clergy and theologians' was 'to open the door and make room' for these new developments.[12]

Ratzinger had always leaned a long way out of the window. 'Anyone who remembers the proverbial silence of previous prefects of the Holy Office is amazed,' Juan Arias commented. The German edition of his conversation with Messori, *Rapporto sulla fede*, had not yet been published. The translator, Gisela Zöhrer, an Evangelical student of Ratzinger's who converted to Catholicism in 1976, had problems with his still rather clumsy Italian. 'The wording and construction were unclear, many things were ambiguously expressed', she recalled.[13] There was also illness to contend with. The publisher pressed, but Ratzinger reassured them: 'Give it time. Family and health come first.'

It was as certain as thunder following lightning that Hans Küng would attack. On 4 October 1985 he crashed in with a sweeping blow in the Hamburg weekly *Die Zeit*. 'The old Inquisition is dead, long live the new,' Küng jeered in the headline. For a long time he had 'held back, old wounds still hurt', but because he 'felt daily how much men and women, and fellow clergy, suffered under the present course', he could 'no longer remain silent'. 'With regard to a recently published work by the second man in the Vatican', he wanted to speak 'a clear word with Christian candour, and wholly without fear of prelates on their thrones'. Then he struck: the 'prefect of the faith', who 'daily receives top secret information from every continent', would 'react daily to all this information in a top secret way'. It was enough 'that he should be displeased by a church broadcast – accidentally heard on his car radio – for the relevant speaker's bishop to be reprimanded'. In 'very important cases' Ratzinger would travel 'with a whole troop to the country in question' in order to 'make clear unequivocally' to the bishops' conferences 'what the "Catholic truth" is'. It was not surprising that 'in view of this worldwide activity of the German Curia cardinal, who outwardly projects his fears, that many people in Germany are saying this man has betrayed the reforming legacy of the German Council cardinal Frings'.

Küng did not fail to bring up all the cases that could be mentioned in a litany of complaints: the 'case of Galileo', the 'Chinese rites controversy', 'putting all the most important European thinkers on the Index (Descartes, Kant, Sartre etc.)', '9 million victims of witch trials'. Even today, 'in his recently acquired Roman job' a church leader could 'act as the incarnate standard of Catholic orthodoxy in the world'. The article came to a climax with the words: 'Joseph Ratzinger is afraid. And like Dostoyevsky's Grand Inquisitor, he is afraid of the truth more than anything else.' Oh yes, one more thing: 'No one is burned at the stake any longer', but 'whenever necessary, they are psychically and professionally destroyed'.

The article was momentous. To this day it has provided the media image of the prefect, which countless journalists reproduced. Labels such as 'Grand Inquisitor' and 'hardliner' hung like millstones round Ratzinger's neck, and he could never get rid of them. The 'fear-ridden psychopath, who projects his obsessions onto the whole world and hates everything that smells of openness and freedom', also became a much-used cliché. The list of complaints was long: boycotting ecumenism, persecuting modern theologians, reviving medieval church doctrines, repressing women's emancipation, betraying the Council, fighting against 'democratic societies' and' 'modern freedoms'. Literally, Küng said: 'According to Ratzinger, the church today only functions properly in the Eastern bloc totalitarian states, where at least pornography, drugs and other things are banned.'[14]

The Ratzinger 'Report' presented in unmistakable terms the guidelines for the Catholic Church on the problems of the time, nothing more. Perhaps he had not always found the right tone, so that what he said may have sounded rather harsh. But nowhere did he speak of severe counter-measures, authoritarian control or procedures against opponents of the Curia now to be constantly imposed. Nevertheless, Ratzinger stood with Karol Wojtyła at the head of the church, allegedly ruling with centralizing power, as critics kept saying. In a certain way, his book could even be regarded as a confession of failure, or at least a cry for help. The admission of the crisis was also an admission that the resources of the pope and the Vatican were not enough to make significant advances. He also described how difficult it was to defend the correct faith, whereas, simply by repeating their demands, critics could expect maximum approval. Küng's polemic had little to do with integrity or historical accuracy. It was more like an incendiary bomb. The 'Panzer Cardinal' was born. The label was given to Ratzinger by the English tabloid press, but it had been suggested by the wording and the alarming 'WANTED' description that Hans Küng was posting on any wall he could find.

To give an example, the *Süddeutsche Zeitung*'s church politics editor, who constantly used the stereotype, declared that once again the Catholic Church's top theologian had confirmed

> his reputation of being the unfriendly face of the church, a 'Panzer Cardinal' or a 'Grand Inquisitor' [...] Many things that the gaunt policeman's son [...] has done have enraged church people: the withdrawal of Hans Küng's permission to teach, the silencing of the liberation theologian Leonardo Boff [see below], the condemnation of abortion as murder, the rejection of women priests.

And finally: 'It is difficult to approach this distant and enigmatic man.'[15]

Who cared that Ratzinger had not 'ordered' the withdrawal of Küng's permission to teach and was not 'difficult to approach'? When the end justified the means, all journalistic ethics were sacrificed. Ratzinger was awkward. He interfered with business. But in fact no other churchman ran so vehemently against the bureaucratized Catholic administrative system and way of thinking as the prefect of the Congregation for the Doctrine of the Faith. Whereas those bishops who claimed to be particularly progressive harassed their parish priests, drove big cars and managed the faith in a rough and ready way, Ratzinger was basically calling for a grassroots revolution. He blamed 'the structure of the church in Germany' for 'putting the brakes on anything new'. Instead of a 'dynamic of faith' there was 'a sense of apathy and boredom'. 'Fewer structures and more life − that's what's wanted.' The church 'should not primarily be concerned with itself'.[16] 'God's revolution', which he spoke of, was about a revolt against a world that 'corrupted people for the sake of money and made a profit out of people's weakness, by tempting and winning them over'.

In a way Ratzinger's attempt to create a different public by his interview book took its cue from the time of the Nazi dictatorship. Bishops then founded their own diocesan newsletters, because the conformist media treated the Catholic Church as contemptible, told lies or simply kept silence about it. His strategy worked. Ratzinger 'unplugged', uncensored and unabbreviated was so much in demand that the original Italian edition of 70,000 copies sold out in a few weeks. The French edition consisted of 100,000 copies, and in Spain the 13th edition was soon going to press. The book was a world sensation and reached millions of readers, who wanted to learn about Ratzinger's thinking at first hand.

16

The Fight over Liberation Theology

Meanwhile, secretary Bruno Fink had acquired a typewriter with a German keyboard. He was able to replace the tiny filing cabinet in his office with a larger one, thanks to the help of the archbishop of Munich. The 'Grand Inquisitor', however, still did not have his own typist. Later the Curia bishop Augustin Mayer managed to get him the Schönstatter nun Birgit Wansing for the job. She remained faithful to Ratzinger long after his papacy and served him with great discretion. She also had the advantage of being able to read his tiny handwriting.

Fink struggled with the 'different foreign languages, especially with Italian', because he could not manage 'to write simple letters without mistakes or give clear and appropriate statements and answers at critical moments'. However, his boss never grumbled but always gave his colleague the feeling 'of being understood, accepted and respected by him'.[1] Nevertheless Fink had soon had enough of the Vatican. He longed to go home. He wanted to be back 'with people' as a simple priest. Even when a friendly Roman lawyer said to him: 'Are you mad? Now you have such an important job right at the centre of the Catholic Church, a boss admired by half the world and then you go off to be a priest somewhere in Munich?'

The stresses of the daily grind were interrupted when Fink went with Ratzinger and his sister to concerts. In the splendid Sala Regia in the Apostolic Palace they enjoyed a concert by the New York Philharmonic, conducted by Leonard Bernstein playing Beethoven's Third Symphony. They celebrated Christmas in Ratzinger's flat. It only became a proper Christmas Eve when Maria and Joseph set up their childhood crib and decorated the Christmas tree in the Bavarian way. Fink played *Alpenländische Weisen* on the guitar.

The Munich Cathedral chapter sent the ageing painter Bruno Lenz to Rome to paint a portrait of their former archbishop for the diocesan gallery. By profession Lenz was a violinist with the Munich Philharmonic. Obediently, Ratzinger sat for him, first in his office and then in private. The painter asked to see all kinds of clothes and chose a scarlet cassock for his subject to wear. 'He was so enthusiastic,' Fink reported, 'that in the end he painted eight portraits.' All the paintings showed 'an amiable man with a clear, friendly expression'. They radiated 'a calm and composed attitude', which Fink said was 'quite typical of the then prefect of the Roman Congregation for the Doctrine of the Faith'.

Others may have seen it differently. The Küng case had already been settled before Ratzinger took office. The 'Drewermann case' was at first not handled in Rome, even though the prefect was convinced that the dispute about the German theologian 'went far beyond problems of exegesis'. As he wrote to his Regensburg colleague Professor Franz Mussner, it was about a 'quarrel with a new form of gnosis, which sought to set itself up as a syncretic religion of humanity instead of Christianity'.[2]

At that time the prefect had fallen foul of the communist regimes, which accused him of slandering them. The reason was an 'Instruction of September 1984'. In it Ratzinger said it was 'a disgrace of our time' and a 'deception' that 'whole nations are kept in slavery under conditions unfit for human beings, while it was claimed that they are being given freedom'.[3] In October 1986 he made a first statement about homosexuality. In a letter to bishops about the 'pastoral care of homosexual persons' he wrote that their sexual orientation was 'not sinful in itself' but that 'the use of the sexual faculty' was 'only good in marriage'. There were shouts of 'Rat', 'Nazi' and 'Devil' at a demonstration called by pro-gay groups when Ratzinger spoke in the Lutheran St Peter's Church in New York. The event had to be guarded by 40 police and security officers.[4]

On the other hand, Ratzinger spoke out for the strengthening of women in society. In an interview with *Die Welt* he said: 'I believe that women largely pay the price for our technical culture, which is an essentially masculine culture. It is a culture of doing, success, performance and self-promotion, that is, it has typically masculine features.' As for the church, it needed 'a feminine culture, which ranks highly and is valued as least as much as what men do'.[5]

The statement *Donum vitae* of 22 February 1987 was an 'Instruction on Respect for the beginning of human life and the dignity of procreation'. In it the Congregation for the Doctrine of the Faith dealt with the Catholic Church's position on the protection of life, abortion, artificial insemination and ante-natal diagnosis. According to *Donum vitae*, the child was defined as a person at the moment the egg and the sperm cell fused, so that the embryo had the same human rights as a new-born baby and people of any age. Their right to life should be respected and protected. That was a fundamental moral value. The Instruction rejected surrogate motherhood and artificial insemination.

From month to month a storm had been brewing in Latin America, which threatened to develop into a fight to change direction for the whole world church. The southern part of the continent had fallen into the hands of tyrants and exploiters. The cities were becoming slums; the population was sinking into poverty. Military regimes reigned with terror and persecution. Between 1968 and 1979 alone at least 1,500 priests, nuns, catechists and Christian trade unionists were arrested, tortured or killed. The big landowners' death squads stuck up posters saying: 'Do something for your country, kill a priest!' On 24 March 1980 the archbishop of San Salvador, Óscar Arnulfo Romero, was shot dead at the altar, because during Mass he had dared to denounce violations of human rights and to read out the names of those who had been murdered or disappeared. Rome was looking at a complicated problem. In Eastern Europe the church was on the side of the rebel movement which was trying to fight for freedom from the communist regime. But while the population in Poland and other countries wanted to shake off the yoke of Marxism, now priests and bishops in Latin American were using communist language.

The conflict had a long prehistory within the church. At their second general assembly at Medellín in Colombia in 1968, the Latin American bishops called for action on the dramatically worsening situation of the population and supported 'a preferential option for the poor'. Three years later the Peruvian Dominican Gustavo Gutiérrez published his book *A Theology of Liberation*, which gave its name to the movement. The movement saw itself as impelled by the gospel to be the 'voice of the poor' for liberation from exploitation and oppression. Many of the young Latin American theologians had studied in Europe. They were inspired by the student rebellion and the teaching of professors such as Johann Baptist Metz and took home ideas of political theology. Western Marxist theorists now became enthusiastic about realizing those dreams of social revolution, which the 'events' of 1968 in Europe had failed to do.

In the same year as Gutiérrez's *Theology of Liberation* came out, 80 Chilean priests founded the 'Christians for Socialism' group. They called for a 'strategic alliance between revolutionary Christians and Marxists for the common realization of the historical project of liberation'. When Salvador Allende's socialist Popular Unity Party was elected to power in Chile, Cuba's revolutionary leader Fidel Castro, a former Jesuit student, travelled there to assure 140 assembled priest of his solidarity. Following the meeting, those who had attended it issued an appeal declaring that it was the duty of all Christians to work with Marxists to establish socialism in Latin America. In Peru the priest Camilo Torres, a friend of Gustavo Gutiérrez, joined the Maoist 'Shining Path' underground movement and announced, with a weapon in his hand, that priests as well as other Christians should engage in the revolutionary struggle.

In Argentina, Brazil, Chile and Nicaragua thousands of Christian base communities sprang up, small local groups seeking a Christian socialist society. In their struggle for the poor and dispossessed they also contemplated the use of force. Priests who joined the new movement included the brothers Clodovis and Leonardo Boff, both members of the Franciscan order. Leonardo Boff had studied with Karl Rahner and gained his doctorate in Munich, supervised by the dogmatic theologian Leo Scheffczyk, a friend of Ratzinger's. 'At that time Boff was still completely Catholic,' Ratzinger told me in our conversation. Clearly he was congenial enough for his professor to be prepared to pay the printing costs of Leonardo's doctoral thesis out of his own pocket. Boff first came to the notice of the Congregation for the Doctrine of the Faith in 1975. The problem was the increasingly aggressive rhetoric of individual leaders of liberation theology, and co-operation with communist-leaning groups. Ratzinger, who was then a member of the papal International Theological Committee, was understanding. The base communities would only react to the wrongs in their own countries. At the same time the Theological Committee's statement warned that religion could neither 'baptize Marxism' nor support class struggle. Otherwise the danger might arise of being drawn into violent conflicts.[6]

Ratzinger was already well informed about the developments in Latin America when he was a professor in Regensburg. His informant was Maximino Arias Reyero, one of his doctoral students. Reyero, a Spanish priest and theologian, had followed his teacher from Bonn to Tübingen and in 1969 from Tübingen to Regensburg. Since 1971 he had been teaching dogmatics at the Santiago de Chile Catholic University and he was the director of the Seminario Latinoamericano de Documentación. When he was bishop of Munich, Ratzinger used the opportunity of his visit to Ecuador in 1978 to see for himself. After that he praised the Latin American church in several articles because 'it gives a good example with a substantial contribution from its so-called base communities'. In 1982 he wrote in his *Theologische Prinzipienlehre* ('Principles of Catholic Theology') that in the present situation it was necessary 'to form vital cells that deliberately withdraw from the pressure of the modern environment and live together according to the gospel "alternative", to create an environment of faith. In these cells, through a culture of prayer and Christian service, a new church can grow that is governed by the double commandment to love God and neighbour.'[7]

Ratzinger was 'very sympathetic to the deep problems of Latin America', said Hansjürgen Verweyen, and saw the formation of base communities as 'fundamentally positive'.[8] But more and more, Reyero was reporting great tensions within his faculty, which broke out between the traditional theology and the supporters of Christian socialism. According to Verweyen, this inside information had a considerable influence on Ratzinger's increasingly critical attitude. As a prefect, he also kept in touch personally with the situation, for example during a ten-day lecture and sermon tour in Chile and Colombia.

John Paul II wanted peace in this area. The pope had sympathy with the poor and oppressed, but none at all with people who wanted to establish a system that his fellow citizens in Poland were trying to get rid of. He was urgent. Ratzinger admitted that the quarrel with liberation theology had been 'the first great subject' that the pope had assigned to him on his appointment as prefect.[9] Salvation in a future life or salvation in this life was a subject tailor-made for Ratzinger. It engaged him as a student in his doctoral work, then as a doctor in his *habilitation* work, and again as a *peritus* when it was about formulating the decree on Divine Revelation. He taught that human beings could improve their situation, but they could not rid the world of the disorder in creation, the fact of sin and the fact of evil, which were the ultimate causes of temptation, oppression and misery. Humans should never presume to try to bring about a peaceful end-state of history. For 'when the impossible becomes the guideline of reality, then violence, destruction of nature, and humanity with it, is an inner necessity'.[10]

As a child, Ratzinger had heard it said that Christianity and National Socialism belonged together. In his study of St Bonaventure he had researched the quarrel of the Franciscan superior with a Catholic revolutionary movement that lost all restraint in its impassioned commitment and its criticism of the church. It dreamed of a 'third age' and a paradise of the free and equal, which was worth fighting for. Had Bonaventure not followed a course based on Catholic doctrine, the quarrel would not only have split the Franciscans but the whole church. That was precisely the quarrel Ratzinger had with liberation theology: as a Christian socialist movement it propagated a society of peace and freedom within this world.

His Tübingen experiences also played a part in Ratzinger's thought process, not as a 'trauma' but as an experience. He could see what it looked like when religion was politicized from the socialist expectations of salvation of many students and quite a few of his academic colleagues. At that time the ringleaders did not represent a broad movement. 'It was actually a small group who drove the development in that direction. But this group determined the climate.'[11]

In the spring of 1983, ten years after the publication of *A Theology of Liberation*, the Congregation for the Doctrine of the Faith began an investigation into the theology of Gustavo Gutiérrez. In the same year prefect Ratzinger met Gutiérrez in Rome. Both set out their positions in a 'long, very friendly conversation'. Ratzinger said, 'I take it that the various dialogues we had with Gustavo Gutiérrez helped him develop his thinking positively.'[12] In 1984 Ratzinger warned that in liberation theology the people of God were played off against the hierarchy, thus inciting class struggle within the church. In the same year he met representatives of the Latin American Bishops' Conference (CELAM) without achieving any practical result. Hans Küng then intervened. After a visit to Bogotá he could report that the progressive wing of the Bishops' Conference had openly broken with Cardinal Ratzinger. The report was immediately denied by the general secretary of CELAM.

On 6 August 1984 the prefect of the Congregation for the Doctrine of the Faith signed the *Instruction on Some Aspects of Liberation Theology*. It immediately led to violent protests. The *Instruction* said that revolt against 'injustices crying to heaven' between rich and poor must, of course, raise a 'strong and fraternal echo' in the hearts of Christians. However, 'uncritical borrowings from Marxist ideology' and a rationalist interpretation of the Bible threatened 'to ruin what the initially generous commitment to the poor authentically possessed'. The *Instruction* opposed the 'politicization of the tenets of the faith' and the misrepresentation of the figure of Jesus as a political rebel. Class struggle had proved to be a myth that only increased misery. Revolutionary violence did not automatically bring a more just society, let alone the coming of the reign of God. Unusually, the *Instruction* was prefaced by a personal introductory statement by the prefect, which showed what a powerful potential for conflict Ratzinger saw in this challenge. He constantly found it 'painful', he confessed in an interview with Messori, 'to converse with theologians who adhere to that illusory myth', namely 'the myth of class struggle as an instrument to create a classless society'. He had been dismayed by reading their writing: 'There is a constant refrain: "We must liberate people from the chains of political and economic oppression."' Reforms only distracted from the fact that 'what is needed is revolution'. At the same time he had found that 'those who keep repeating all this' seemed 'to have no concrete, practical ideas about how a society should be organized after the revolution'.

In his 'Report' Ratzinger had already made clear that in those parts of liberation theology that referred to Marxist ideas what he saw was 'in no way a grassroots, indigenous product of Latin America or other underdeveloped countries' which had sprouted and grown from among the people. 'Parts of liberation theology were a creation by intellectuals – indeed by intellectuals who were born or educated in the rich West. The theologians who started it were Europeans. The theologians who are promoting it in South America are Europeans or educated in European universities.' So in a sense the political myths and utopias in that theology were an export and 'a form of cultural imperialism, if [that theology] is also presented as a spontaneous creation by the dispossessed masses'.

Ratzinger was convinced: 'What is theologically unacceptable and socially dangerous here is this mixture of Bible, Christology, politics, sociology and economics. You can't misuse Scripture and theology in that way, by sacralizing a theory about the socio-political order and turning it into an absolute.' For if you 'sacralize the revolution – by mixing up God, Christ and ideology – you generate a rapturous fanaticism, which can lead to even worse injustices and oppression. Then what was conceived in theory is overturned in practice.' Indeed it was a completely 'unchristian illusion, that you could create a new human being and a new world, not by converting individuals but just by altering the social and economic structures'.[13]

Critics saw the *Instruction* as an attack on all efforts to bring about social justice in Third World countries as well as a betrayal of Latin American Catholics, who would be left alone in their struggle against dictators. Meanwhile, the priest brothers Ernesto and Fernando Cardenal, sons of a well-to-do family, had become members of the Sandinista government in Nicaragua, which had overthrown the despotic Somoza dictatorship. Fernando was education minister and Ernesto was minister of culture. In May 1985 Leonardo Boff travelled to Rome again to speak with Ratzinger about his newly published book *Church, Charism and Power*. They already knew each other from Munich. The Brazilian bishops Aloísio Lorscheider and Paolo Evaristo Arns travelled with him to give him support. In his work Boff maintained that the church 'as an institution did not belong to the thought of the historical Jesus'. At their meeting Ratzinger asked Boff to take a year quietly to think over their conversation and questions about liberation theology, which had by then become a hotly contested controversy in the media. During that time he should not publish or express any views about it. Boff was relieved. He could have been penalized by the withdrawal of his authorization to teach. As the Brazilians left the Congregation, Arns raised his arm to the waiting cameras in a sign of victory.

Boff promised to keep to the condition of a sabbatical (and used the time to reinforce his line in further books). The verdict against him was far from draconian. Ratzinger made clear that the decisions of his Congregation were taken with the greatest care: 'We are always blamed for being rigorous, but generally our patience is very great.'[14] The decision acquired its dramatic resonance because journalists were seeking a powerful catchword fitting the image of the 'Panzer Cardinal'. They had trapped him before by fixing on the catchword 'restoration', which he had used in his interview book. (And now the responsibility for the disciplining of Küng was also foisted onto him.) In the Boff case the term 'penitential silencing', an expression not found in church law, conjured up the image of a persecuting Inquisition and caused outrage. Boff himself suddenly spoke out about it, saying that his meeting with Ratzinger had been like an interrogation, at which he was put through the mangle. Ratzinger later felt humanly so disappointed by Boff that he would no longer reply to questions about him.

The core of Ratzinger's criticism of Boff had less to do with liberation theology than with his views which questioned the priesthood. That was wholly ignored in the loud protests aroused by the announcement of the 'penitential silencing'. In fact, it had not been Ratzinger who had pressed for sanctions but the Belgian Curia cardinal Jérôme Hamer, who as prefect of the Congregation for Religious Orders was immediately responsible for the case. Ratzinger had stood aside. In the Boff case, he explained, Marxism was not the crux of the dispute but questions about the church model, revelation and dogma. As for liberation theology, he made clear to journalists in Rome that there were completely different sides to it. He distinguished between the 'fully legitimate, indeed necessary', the 'dubious' and finally the 'unacceptable'.[15] Gerhard Müller, who later became prefect of the Congregation for the Doctrine of the Faith, confirmed: 'Boff was certainly not disciplined for liberation theology but he posed as a guiltless victim of persecution.'[16]

The Vatican took the crisis very seriously. That was shown by the fact that on 22 March 1986 the Congregation for the Doctrine of the Faith followed up with a second clarification, the *Instruction on Christian Freedom and Liberation*. In it the base communities were expressly commended as a 'reason for great hope'. On 19 July 1986

Ratzinger went to Peru to present the paper personally at the Catholic University of Lima. He made it clear that the church was on the side of the poor, for whom it had a special care. The struggle for liberation was part of the Christian heritage. At the same time he warned against the violent course and against particular aspects of liberation theology, which aroused hopes that could not be fulfilled. Anyone promising people a utopia led them into a new slavery, as the experience of history showed.

The quarrel dragged on for many more years. In 1992 Leonardo Boff left his order and started a family. On Pope John Paul II's visit to Nicaragua in 1983, when Ernesto Cardenal, minister of culture in the Sandinista government, greeted him at the airport, the pope wagged his finger at him. In 1987 the Ministry of Culture was dissolved for economic reasons. During the Contra War the people became even poorer and the country was wrecked. In Europe Ernesto Cardenal was showered with honours. He made it clear that he was still a 'Sandinista, Marxist and Christian'. Clodovis Boff, whose church authorization to teach had been withdrawn in March 1984, changed his stance. He stated in the Brazilian newspaper *Folha de São Paulo* that Ratzinger had done no more than defend 'the original core of liberation theology, the faith's commitment to the poor'. He concluded self-critically with the words: 'In fact the church was irrelevant for us. And not only the church but Christ himself.'[17]

In retrospect Ratzinger's gaining control in the conflict over liberation theology can be seen as one of the triumphs of his time as prefect. If the theories of political theology had prevailed, a new schism would have been inevitable. 'Ratzinger saved the continent for the Catholic Church,' said a fellow campaigner in the Congregation for the Doctrine of the Faith. This was not just plucked out of the air. It was the poorest people in the country who abandoned liberation theology. The Marxist interpretation of the gospel meant little to them, and they turned in great numbers to the Pentecostalists and other Evangelical groups. In Brazil alone more than 35,000 free churches arose. Once the population of Latin America was about 100 per cent Catholic, but today almost 30 per cent have become members of sects.[18]

In an interview in 2014 with the Polish journalist Wlodzimierz Redzioch, Ratzinger said his aim had been to counteract a concept of liberation inspired by Marxism, while calling for a commitment to freedom inspired by the Christian faith. In 1988 Gustavo Gutiérrez published a revised edition of his book, which was the bible of liberation theologians. When he became pope, Ratzinger appointed Bishop Gerhard Müller, a declared disciple of Gutiérrez, as prefect of the Congregation for the Doctrine of the Faith. Ratzinger also advanced the beatification process of the murdered Salvadorean archbishop Óscar Romero. In March 2012 he met Fidel Castro in Cuba. Castro had drawn back closer to Catholicism and offered Ratzinger some of his works. His long-term partner did not hide the fact that, shortly before his death on 25 November 2016, Fidel had asked for the sacrament of extreme unction. A year later, Good Friday was made a public holiday on the communist Caribbean island.

In November 2016 the Latin America correspondent of the *Süddeutsche Zeitung* described what had become of Nicaragua, the country once praised by many liberation theologians. 'The former model country of left-wing idealists is now once again ruled in the "lord of the manor" style. [President Daniel] Ortega incorporates nearly everything that he had once fought against with the Sandinista Front. There is no longer any recognizable distinction between state, party and family.' In 'the second-poorest country in Latin America' Daniel Ortega ruled with an 'autocratic family dynasty'. They controlled 'the most important businesses, trade unions and media outlets and also the laws'. The opposition was 'got out of the way by juridical means'. The report concluded: 'All that remains of socialism are the old hollow clichés.'

Two years later the correspondent updated his report saying that 'in a new level of ruthlessness' now 'priests, curates, cardinals and churches are targeted'. The writer concluded:

The church in Nicaragua has a long tradition. In 1979 left-wing liberation theologians were among the intellectual leaders of the revolution against the dictatorship of the Somoza clan. The poet and former Trappist monk Ernesto Cardenal, who founded a contemplative base community on the Solentiname archipelago, gained worldwide fame. Here the unshakeable spirit of Sandinismo was nurtured. 'Revolutionary thinking began with Christ,' Cardenal preached to the guerrilleros. One of them was Daniel Ortega.[19]

17

Teamwork

As well as giving his guardian of the faith the question of liberation theology to deal with, early on Wojtyła also gave him the task of leading the conversation with the dissident archbishop Marcel Lefebvre. The French archbishop, who rejected the Council's reforms, had founded a fraternity of priests, the Society of St Pius X, and had attracted thousands of followers. In 1976, on his own initiative, he ordained priests who wanted to hold on to the traditional rites of the Catholic Church. Any attempt made by John Paul II to come to an understanding was rebuffed.

Lefebvre had always been polite, but also 'thick-headed as a reinforced concrete wall', reported the Swiss cardinal Henri Schwery, who had met him repeatedly on orders from Rome. Schwery 'panicked somewhat' when he realized that Lefebvre intended shortly to ordain his own bishops as well as priests. He requested an urgent meeting with the pope: 'Then we met at the end of January 1988 at 9 o'clock in the morning in Rome: Pope John Paul II, Cardinal Joseph Ratzinger, Cardinal Édouard Gagnon and I. The pope wanted advice on the danger of a schism.'[1] The discussion was resumed after lunch. In the end it was decided to set up a committee with Ratzinger as chairman, to make an offer to the Society of St Pius X in order to prevent its final separation from the Catholic Church.

Ratzinger had no personal connection with the Lefebvre circle. 'I think he also saw that there was a lot of obstinacy, egoism and bitterness there,' his later secretary Georg Gänswein reported.[2] But he was concerned about the unity of the church. 'A Christian can never be happy about a split', he believed. Even when the blame for the rupture in Lefebvre's case 'certainly can't be laid on the Holy See', the question had to be asked: 'What are we doing wrong?' It was part of 'the basic awareness of ecumenical theology that splits only become possible if certain truths and values of the Christian faith are no longer well enough lived and loved'. So the conflict with the Society of St Pius X 'should be regarded as a moment to examine our consciences and seriously ask about the shortcomings in our pastoral work,' he said. Nevertheless: 'Defending the Second Vatican Council as a valid and binding council of the church against Monsignor Lefebvre remains a necessity.'[3]

By Archbishop Lefebvre's wish, the conversations took place in Ratzinger's flat. Lefebvre looked depressed. Ratzinger assured him that his community would be allowed to celebrate Mass according to the rite of Pope Pius V. Their differences on ecumenical matters, dialogue with non-Christians and various matters of church discipline remained almost unalterable.[4]

At the beginning of May 1988 Schwery received a telephone call from the prefect. He was to come to Rome immediately. The pope had agreed to a proposal by the Congregation for the Doctrine of the Faith. Lefebvre had already signed the document. On 5 May Lefebvre had accepted a 'Protocol on an Agreement', which gave the Society of St Pius X limited autonomy within the framework of church law. In return Lefebvre signed a far-reaching submission on behalf of his community. Among other things it contained the duty to be faithful 'to the Catholic Church and the pope in Rome', as well as to recognize the 'validity of the rites of the *Editiones Typicae*, which had been promulgated by Paul VI and John Paul II'. He also promised to 'respect the general discipline of the church and the church's laws, particularly those that are contained in the *Codex Iuris Canonici* of 1983'.[5] However the document's ink was not yet dry when the agreement became obsolete.

Cardinal Schwery had warned about this. He told the prefect on the telephone: 'Each time when Lefebvre promised me something, next day he was not of the same opinion, after he had consulted his colleagues, especially Father Franz Schmidberger.' Schwery reported that Ratzinger had practically 'jumped down his throat' and said: 'Don't be so pessimistic. Come tomorrow. It is signed.' Next day at 10 a.m. Schwery knocked on the door of the Congregation for the Doctrine of the Faith:'Ratzinger scowled. He explained to me that Lefebvre had phoned him in the evening to say that he was withdrawing his signature. What a shame!'[6]

A break could no longer be prevented. When Lefebvre ordained four bishops without authorization on 30 June 1988, according to church law he was automatically excommunicated. Nevertheless, henceforth the fraternity was not considered to be schismatic but merely 'irregular'. The task the prefect had undertaken was once formulated thus by the apostle Paul:

Proclaim the message and, welcome or unwelcome, insist on it. Refute falsehood, correct error, encourage – with the utmost patience in teaching. The time will come when people will not tolerate sound teaching, but with itching ears, according to their own tastes will accumulate teachers for themselves. They will turn from listening to the truth and become involved in myths.[7]

Paul added:'But you must remain sober in everything, put up with suffering, do the work of proclaiming the gospel, fulfil the service asked of you.'' I don't want to be presumptuous,' Ratzinger said in 1996, 'but I would say that those words really express what I saw as my standard at that time.'[8] It was important for him 'to be able to say something that is not unimportant for tomorrow'. His task was 'to struggle to shape the time, to defend a certain legacy' – and thus 'present the essentials of the Christian faith to a new time'. It was far from being just a 'private battle'.[9]

However, Ratzinger felt he was in a continual dilemma. 'The professor and the prefect are the same person,' he wrote in a letter to his former student Damaskinos Papandreou, but they had different jobs:

The professor (which I still am) labours for knowledge and presents his findings in his books and lectures. The prefect, on the other hand, is not supposed to present his personal views [...] he must take care that the institutions of the teaching church do their work very responsibly, so that a text is cleansed of anything merely private and truly expresses the doctrine of the church.[10]

On the question of reform, Ratzinger made no secret of the fact that he had little use for many of the populist efforts. Since 1968 increasingly there had grown a church as *concilium*, a kind of 'church consisting of councils' instead of the church as *communio*, a genuine community of faith and fate. But he showed that he had his own mind, for example, on the question of laicization. From the beginning of his papacy John Paul II had handled priests who requested to be released very strictly. But Ratzinger pleaded that these priests should be let go, because otherwise too many would remain in the job who were unfit for it and that would lead to trouble. Further disagreement arose when Wojtyła invited 60 delegations from Christian churches and non-Christian religions to Assisi for common prayer on 27 October 1986. Critics saw it as a form of syncretisim when Buddhist monks set up a statue of the Buddha over the tabernacle. It would encourage the idea that religious freedom meant religious parity, whereas the Catholic Church had to hold fast to the uniqueness of Jesus Christ as the universal saviour. The prefect of the Congregation for the Doctrine of the Faith pointedly avoided the event.

In the run-up to the meeting Ratzinger had deplored the fact that since the Council there had sometimes been an 'overemphasis on the value of non-Christian religions'.[11] At the same time he stressed that salvation was not confined to the Catholic Church and inter-religious dialogue was a necessity and enrichment. In our conversation Ratzinger stressed that he had not really 'quarrelled' with the pope about the Assisi idea,

> because I knew that he wanted the right thing and he knew that I had a different point of view on this. Before the second meeting in Assisi he told me that he would like it if I went to it. Then he took my objections into account and a form was found for me to take part in an acceptable way.[12]

Like Paul VI, Wojtyła had also adopted the custom of welcoming a small conversational group (usually on a Tuesday) to discuss current questions. Those at the table included representatives of the individual Curial authorities, experts in various fields or bishops who were in Rome for their *ad limina* visits. The pope introduced the meeting with a short report, then listened patiently to the statements of his individual guests, asked questions, made suggestions and summed the meeting up at the end. The participants changed. However, as well as private secretary Stanisław Dziwisz, Ratzinger was a permanent member of the group. But he always declined when the pope concluded the working lunch with coffee and a glass of vodka.

Wojtyła frequently telephoned Ratzinger and invited him to further conversations, often several times a week. The set protocol consultation between them took place every Friday at 6 p.m. It was always private and unrecorded. Ratzinger arrived punctually to the minute. They spoke German together but did not address each other with the informal 'Du' for 'you'. 'First I wait, then the pope comes. We shake hands and sit down at the table together. Then we usually have a bit of a "natter" which has nothing to do with theology,' Ratzinger said of these meetings.[13] The meetings were 'conducted in an atmosphere of warmth and trust from the beginning'. The Holy Father usually confirmed the decisions of the Congregation for the Doctrine of the Faith. Otherwise he made suggestions about 'how the subject can be followed up and agreement be sought'.[14] But Wojtyła interfered 'very little' when it was a question of legal forms. 'Then he would say, "Be generous."'[15]

Liberation theology, appointments of cardinals and bishops, bio-ethical and social ethical problems, preparation for synods and journeys, drafting encyclicals or the political situation in different regions of the Earth − none of the major themes that marked the 27-year-long papacy of John Paul II was left out of these confidential meetings. 'I have to thank Cardinal Ratzinger alone for the theological level of my papacy,' Wojtyła told his friend the Cologne Cardinal Joachim Meisner.[16] Occasionally, of course, the pope quelled the agitation of his prefect. Ratzinger once spoke critically about his compatriots in the preparation for an *ad limina* visit by the German bishops. After the meeting the pope spoke to nuncio Karl-Josef Rauber, who had been present at it, saying, 'Don't worry, I'll deal with the German bishops!' Rauber recalled this and added that John Paul II 'had a great regard for Ratzinger; he needed him but he also knew his weaknesses'.[17]

There was no doubt that the pope and the prefect valued one another highly. Ratzinger said he had learned from John Paul II 'to think broadly'. Through Wojtyła 'I became much more aware of the dimension of religious dialogue in ethical problems'.[18] In the 2,000-year history of the church there had probably been no closer relationship between a predecessor and successor to the papacy than that between the Polish pope and the German cardinal. As an occasional sharer in the conversations, Professor Réal Tremblay observed how Ratzinger 'informed the pope about everything with great precision, very intelligently and distinctly, in order to bring him up to speed with the movements in the church. He was a master at it. And John Paul II had great admiration for him. They were real friends. It was a deep, good friendship.'[19]

Their teamwork was based on an unshakeable foundation: both made it clear that faith had to do with thinking – and vice versa, that thinking without faith was always a reduction of the truth. Both practised a deep, simple piety. Both stood firmly by the gospel, in order to give Catholics a clear lead. The fact that their temperaments were different proved to be no obstacle, as Ratzinger found: 'He was a person who needed conviviality, life and movement. Unlike me. I prefer more peace and quiet. Precisely because we were different we complemented each other very well.' It was not just the good chemistry between them. They also knew 'that we want the same thing'. At the altar, when he concelebrated Mass with Wojtyła, he got to know the pope even better. 'Then you feel his inner closeness to the Lord, how deep his faith goes there. You really experience him as a believing, praying, spiritual human being. More so than when you read the books, which do give a good picture of him but do not reveal the whole personality.'[20]

John Paul II did not rule over Ratzinger's work, nor did he ever leave him out. A top member of the Curia even reported that 'the pope always had proposals from Cardinal Secretary of State Angelo Sodano checked by Ratzinger before he made a decision. Plainly his confidence in Sodano was distinctly less than his faith in Cardinal Ratzinger.'

Sodano was regarded as a *possibilista*, one of those pragmatic people whose maxim was to do what could be done under the given conditions. He was born in Piedmont in 1927, in the same year as Ratzinger. He was the picture of an old-style prince of the church. In 1959 he had entered the Vatican diplomatic service and only returned to Rome in 1988. At first he served as Agostino Casaroli's right-hand man. From 1 December 1990 he succeeded

Casaroli in one of the most important positions in the Curia. His power-conscious behaviour and his habit of promulgating his own statements which had not been agreed were clearly not likely to endear him to John Paul II, and even less to his influential secretary Dziwisz, who got on better with Ratzinger. The Legionaries of Christ, and especially their founder, Marcial Maciel, helped Sodano open a European University at the walls of Rome. Shortly before his election as pope, Cardinal Ratzinger once again left the Maciel file open, which resulted in the uncovering and condemnation of Maciel's double life. According to the Vatican expert Guido Horst, this may have set Sodano against Ratzinger.[21]

The trust between John Paul II and his close colleague also grew, said Georg Gänswein, 'because the pope saw that Ratzinger stayed the course'. And Ratzinger saw that Pope John Paul 'holds his hand over me and covers my back'.[22] And conversely, the prefect received the arrows that were really directed at the pope and the Catholic Church. The whole arsenal of criticism – celibacy, ordination of women, abortion, papal dogma, homosexuality – each of them now became a personal attack on the guardian of the faith. Outwardly he seemed to bear the hostility stoically. 'I have never seen him quarrelling, angry or losing his temper. He was always self-controlled even when he unmistakably contradicted something and expressed his displeasure,' his secretary Fink reported. 'He knew that Italians despised the so-called *furore teutonico*. So he tried to convince by the force of his arguments.' His leadership style was very paternal, very gentle in practice,' said Gänswein. 'He never ordered something but always said clearly what he wanted. Because he was theologically supreme, the team drew round him. He was the leader, and the others followed him.'[23]

Ratzinger was definitely never someone signing death warrants at his desk. He engaged verbally, entered the fray, often enough on hostile territory. 'Despite unavoidable hostilities,' said the philosopher Robert Spaemann in November 1986, 'Cardinal Ratzinger has raised the reputation of the office of "Grand Inquisitor" to a level never known before in its fairly long history.'[24] However, a curious contradictory situation arose. On the one hand, the prefect was regarded as a 'persecutor'; on the other hand, he himself became a sort of scapegoat, comparable to the Old Testament sacrificial animal, upon whom the Israelites loaded all their sins once a year before sending it out into the wilderness. Herbert Riehl-Heyse, the Munich-based writer for the *Süddeutsche Zeitung*, was not wrong when he said that you only had to mention the name of Ratzinger for everyone to tremble with indignation.

Many newspapers were happy to celebrate Fidel Castro, even though they knew that the Cuban regime persecuted its opponents mercilessly. But among journalists it was almost impossible to find anything good to say about Ratzinger. And whereas the 'rebels' who criticized the church went from talk show to talk show and filled whole pages of newspapers with their guest contributions, Ratzinger became a synonym for what you could not like: the nasty German, a fundamentalist, a remote theoretician who sat at his books, refused to explain and signed condemnations that destroyed people. In short a hard man, dry and cold.

At best, for the media, Ratzinger functioned as the mysterious *éminence grise*, whose intentions no one knew for certain. The *Bild* journalist Andreas Englisch is a particularly striking example of the type of deliberate manipulation that other 'experts' also employed. In order to ingratiate himself with Benedict XVI after his election as pope, Englisch admitted that in his previous reporting he had 'celebrated a hero: Karol Wojtyła; and criticized someone else too strongly: Joseph Ratzinger'. Englisch claimed to be remorseful: 'In order to let Karol Wojtyła's light shine more brightly, I needed an enemy to make the story more dramatic.'[25] However, Englisch had no scruples about later applying his business model to books about Pope Francis, whom he raised almost to heaven, in order finally to shove the retired Benedict XVI down to hell.

Nevertheless, the prefect was not completely without fault in the tense relationship with the media. He often did not communicate well. His arguments had something coercive about them, and that was not just their logic. He often operated out of a corner, into which he felt he had been driven, and with a 'now more than ever' attitude that made him sound unnecessarily harsh. He insisted that a real understanding of the church was only possible through faith, certainly not just by a sociological or psychoanalytic approach. Anyone who proclaimed the gospel 'the truth that is worth suffering for' had also to be a witness to the faith, and so 'a martyr in the deepest sense of the word'. He once rebuked 34 Christian Social

Union (CSU) local councillors who had applied to the pope with a critical inquiry about the Vatican's attitude to marriage and the family. Ratzinger had censured them for becoming involved in an anti-Roman campaign. He asked for an apology from them for having taken 'a public step' through 'lack of information'. In the course of the correspondence it had been 'shown that neither their tone nor their behaviour was what I expect from representatives of the people'. Angrily, he added that it had become clear to him 'that people neither listen to arguments nor want to think at all'.[26]

In an interview in 1992 Ratzinger himself admitted 'that in personal polemic I sometimes react too harshly'. In retrospect, now he would 'do many things differently, because when you get older you see things from a different perspective'. It was to be expected that Hans Küng would carry on tackling him. Now he commented: 'How greatly being in office changes a person. Even when it is not a high office.' Speaking for himself, Küng said: 'How easy it would have been for me, yes, how easy it would have been for me to push myself forward in the direction of the hierarchy, like my colleague. But how glad I am that I have remained true to theology and proceeded independently.' The Swiss Küng painted the usual picture for the cameras: himself as a William Tell and persecuted reformer, Ratzinger as the 'Grand Inquisitor' and 'Panzer Cardinal'.

Küng's relentlessly repeated complaint sounded as if it was like dealing with a dictator. 'You must either sign some rubbish about original sin or guardian angels or whatever, or you lose your authorization to teach,' he said in a conversation published in the *Süddeutsche Zeitung* magazine.

> It's like with the Stasi, the system is exactly the same. For example, he keeps all the important things in the Tübingen local paper. There are countless victims. The whole younger generation of theologians in Germany must live in fear. This regime is really totalitarian. It is the Inquisition, even when people are now only burned psychologically.

His snap judgement of the prefect was: 'He has become a man with a mission. Even bishops who previously had reasonable views, like Karl Lehmann, must now mindlessly parrot everything.'[27]

However, the theologian Siegfried Wiedenhofer was convinced 'that "Inquisitor" is a fantasy his opponent projects onto him'. In fact, Ratzinger had been more of a servant. Everything rigid during his time as prefect was 'due to the responsibility of the office and out of care for the church'.[28] Unlike his critics, Ratzinger had never denigrated other people. Karl Lehmann confirmed this: 'The head of the Congregation for the Doctrine of the Faith, dismissed as a bogeyman and aggressor', had 'in quite a few cases protected the free speech of theologians, prevented restrictive measures and promoted a balance of interests'.[29] 'He was intolerant of stupidity. Then he kept an icy silence when he had to listen to it,' said Heinz Joachim Fischer, the Vatican correspondent for the *Frankfurter Allgemeine Zeitung*. Finally, all the theologians in Rome agreed: 'Since Martin Luther no German figure has made such an impact on the Catholic Church as Joseph Ratzinger.'[30]

It was not only theologians in Rome who came to that conclusion. The Munich fundamental theologian and philosopher of religion Eugen Biser, Karl Rahner's successor to the Romano Guardini chair, stressed that Ratzinger had achieved 'what no one believed possible, namely the rediscovery of the church'. He had managed to do so 'because he consistently referred the church and Christianity back to the figure of Jesus Christ'. Unlike other theologians, 'who had rejected stone upon stone of the old structure, because it did not fit into their new building', Ratzinger remained 'faithful to the original'. He had given a particularly strong sign by 'revitalizing the structures in accordance with the principle of dialogue called for by Vatican II'. Of course, the prefect sometimes had to speak a word of authority. 'But I think that is more by way of serving the office he has undertaken.'[31]

Biser described Ratzinger's personality in these words: 'Prudent and accomplished, critical acumen and perspicacity are linked with empathy and insight into the way others are thinking.' The prefect was 'a personality far superior to the other members of the Curia. I don't know anyone who is of higher quality than him.' This was also 'because he has never tried to identify wholly with his office but always sought to remain himself. I regard that as humanly great, for there is nothing I fear more than those who identify with their office.' Biser himself was seen as a liberal theologian with a thoroughly critical spirit. He summed the prefect up thus: 'Ratzinger is basically a very modern person and shares the concerns of people today. In the final analysis it will be seen that he prevented many things and mitigated others. And he sacrificed more than we realize of his feeling for life and happiness to his office.'[32]

Of course, the prefect was not deserted by all his fans and friends. Every Christmas he received about 1,700 cards and letters from all over the world. When he could not write a personal reply, at least he always thanked the sender with a brief remark and his signature. In May 1987 he received countless goodwill messages for his 60th birthday. The 'signs of friendship and attention' had reached a number 'that went far beyond my expectations', he noted in his letter of thanks. 'Friends and companions from all stages of my life, people I know and don't know have remembered me.' He had been 'richly gifted with words and signs of goodwill, whose personal character and cordiality have deeply moved me and still do'.[33]

Simple believers, the American theologian William May noted, had a sixth sense about whether someone was telling the truth or not. That was why Ratzinger's success among the 'Catholic people' was so great – in contrast to the broadcasts and what was written in the newspapers about him. The Austrian theologian Christoph Schönborn, the future cardinal and archbishop of Vienna, was certain: 'We are regaining the stature of the great bishops who have occurred in the history of the church.' Ratzinger 'gave back its credibility to the church magisterium'.[34]

Above all, his fellow Bavarians remained faithful to him. On his anniversary a delegation, headed by Minister-President Franz Josef Strauss, consisting of 450 performers in traditional costume, companies of mountain riflemen and musical bands, travelled to Rome to honour 'Bavaria's greatest son' (as the future Minister-President Edmund Stoiber called him). They gave him a present of a shepherd's horn so that their compatriot could blow it 'in duet' with the pope. Pope John Paul II, who was looking on, was amused and joined in lustily with the Bavarian anthem. The riflemen did not fire their guns. They refrained of their own accord when they realized that on that day the Romans celebrated the liberation of their city from the German Wehrmacht.

18

The Collapse

Mikhail Gorbachev's rise to power in the Kremlin not only changed the political relations between East and West but also the relationship of the Catholic Church to the countries in the Soviet bloc. Sometimes with almost grotesque results. For example, on 20 February 1988 the Red Army choir belted out an *Ave Maria* in the Vatican in the presence of the pope.

When, in June of the same year, at Gorbachev's instigation, the thousandth anniversary of the Christianization of Russia and Ukraine was celebrated, the Holy See sent a high-ranking delegation led by Cardinal Secretary of State Casaroli. A second group, the 'delegation of Catholic bishops', consisted of the cardinal archbishops of Vienna, Hanoi, Milan, Warsaw, Munich and New York, bishops from Latvia and Hungary and the chairmen of the Latin American and African Bishops' Councils. On 10 June Casaroli spoke in the Moscow Bolshoi Theatre on aspects of religious freedom and human rights. Then he had personally to deliver a confidential letter from the pope to Gorbachev.

Casaroli found himself in a dilemma. A dress code dilemma. What should he wear? His cardinal's cassock and pectoral cross? Or a normal black suit with a shirt and clerical collar? 'Your Eminence,' Joaquín Navarro-Valls, the Vatican spokesman, urged him, 'This photo will appear on the front pages of newspapers all over the world!' On a hot June day Casaroli sat in the car with a thick overcoat on, so that his red cassock and pectoral cross could not be seen before he arrived in the Kremlin. There Gorbachev reassured him. There was no need to take precautions. His foreign minister, Eduard Shevardnadze, and he himself had been secretly baptized as children. Furthermore, in his parents' house a holy picture had always been hidden beside the portrait of Lenin.[1]

The pope's message, dated 7 June 1988, was written on private writing paper and began 'To his Excellency Mr Mikhail Gorbachev'. The general secretary of the Communist Party of the Soviet Union (CPSU) immediately opened the envelope. He read: 'The Catholic church looks with great respect and affection upon the magnificent spiritual legacy of the Eastern Slavonic peoples.' They had observed the peace initiatives and the 'promising developments which have occurred in recent months through the meetings and agreements between the Soviet Union and the United States of America – particularly with regard to disarmament'. They had followed with great interest 'what you have declared about the link between the life of the religious community and civil society', and about 'the right of believers to free expression of their religious convictions and their contribution to society'. In conclusion the message said: 'Mr General Secretary, please accept this expression of my deep respect!'[2]

Until then there had been no official contacts between the Holy See and the Soviet Union. And because of the opposition of the Protestant churches the United States had only set up official diplomatic relations with the Vatican State in January 1984. Gorbachev answered the pope's historic message 14 months later with a letter written in Russian: 'The time has come for a new world solidarity. For us that means a new attitude to religion and the church, to the ecumenical movement and to the part that the great world religions play.' Then he praised 'the attitude and personal activities' of the pope and the 'positive contribution of the Vatican State to international life'. He regarded this as particularly important 'in the sphere of ethics' in order 'to heal the international situation'.[3]

In 1985 Gorbachev had still been praising the 'rightness of the great Lenin doctrine', which was 'confirmed throughout all of life and the whole course of history'.[4] Four years later, on his symbolic visit to the Vatican, he renounced the Marxist dogma of religion as the 'opium of the people' and paid tribute to religion's 'valuable contribution to society'. On 6 October 1989, the 40th anniversary of the founding of the GDR, on a visit to East Berlin as the guest of honour, Gorbachev uttered a saying that soon became widely quoted: 'Whoever comes too late is punished by life.' (However, Gorbachev never said those actual words. When he warned Erich Honecker against opposing a renewal of the GDR, he said: 'I think dangers await those who do not react to life.' This was polished to become 'whoever comes too late is punished by life', which fitted Gorbachev's image better.[5]) A month later the opening up of the wall between East and West Berlin was the most visible expression of the beginning of a new era, a change of epoch which made clear that the world was pointing that way. On the night of 9/10 November, 10,000 East Berliners streamed joyfully into the Western part of the city, where they were enthusiastically welcomed.

During the years of the great change the communist bloc states toppled like dominoes. The Iron Curtain had fallen, the Cold War which had divided the continent now belonged to the past. Communism had shown itself to be a utopia that, instead of being a society of the free and equal, was a murderous system of fear, terror, lies and despotism, to which countless millions of people were sacrificed. Without the brave people fighting for freedom and democracy the year 1989 would not have become a beacon. Nor would it have done so without the active politicians who had recognized the signs of the times. Or without John Paul II, who like Gorbachev, was someone who supported the historic change.

Under Pope Paul VI the policy had been to annoy the communist leaders as little as possible, so as not to make the situation even worse for the faithful. Wojtyła radically changed the Holy See's foreign policy. Even his first words as the new successor of Peter had alerted the people in the East: 'Don't be afraid,' he called, 'open, yes, fling open the gates for Christ!' And further: 'Open the borders of states, the economic and political systems to his saving power.' The members of the red politburos reassured themselves that the customs of his office would have a moderating effect on the priest from Wadowice in Poland. However, Wojtyła's church 'would not be a church that kept mum', as the Italian historian Andrea Riccardi put it, 'but a church of persistent religious resistance': 'Wojtyła believed in the power of the people, even when they were oppressed and degraded. He was sure that the system behind the Iron Curtain would not stand for ever.'[6]

Gerd Stricker, the historian of Eastern Europe and the Eastern church, saw it in the same way: Wojtyła's visit to his homeland 'was the initial spark for the rise of Solidarność, which destabilized the Communist regime in Poland and in the long term led to its collapse. That had caused a chain reaction which finally brought about the fall of the Soviet Union.'[7]

Mikhail Gorbachev was also convinced that 'all that has happened in East Europe over the last few years would not have been possible without the presence of this pope, without the great part he played politically on the world stage.'[8] Hans-Dietrich Genscher, the former German Federal Minister of Foreign Affairs, pointed out that Karol Wojtyła 'recognized the spiritual dimension of that revolution much more clearly than most of those taking part in the discussion on globalization'.'As pope he had had an effect that went far beyond the Catholic Church', Genscher wrote. In retrospect it could be seen 'that the Solidarity movement, strengthened by the pope and protected by his responsible and clear attitude, had an enormous effect on the whole Soviet area'.[9] Lech Wałęsa confirmed: 'Without the support of the Holy Father Solidarność would have been shattered. Without him there would have been no end to Communism or at least not until much later, and the end would have been bloody.'[10]

Their agreement about policy with the Eastern bloc brought John Paul II and his guardian of the faith even closer together. The collapse of Communism in Eastern Europe confirmed the two church leaders in their attitude towards Marxist-leaning liberation theologians. Ratzinger stated in an interview in May 1988 that the changes in the Soviet Union would 'perhaps unwittingly create wide-ranging repercussions'. There was 'a strong expectation of a broad new direction'. It could be said: 'Just as with us in the West people have grown tired of religion and faith, over there in their third generation they have grown tired of atheism.'[11]

Although Wojtyła played such a great part in the liberation of Eastern Europe from the yoke of Communism, for the main Western media he embodied the relapse into a pre-conciliar, reactionary past for Catholicism. Catholic reformers agreed. 'Basically the reformers want a church that is wholly secular,' said the historian Franz Walter, adding rather maliciously, 'a church that suits the changing needs of the middle class in middle Europe, an easy-care church that is undemanding and no bother to live with'. It was quite astonishing that 'the strength of Catholicism in modern society has been that it has been able to oppose something persistently its own to the ramblings and wrong turnings of those secular trends'.[12]

The anti-Rome complex did not weaken. That was shown in the year of the change by the so-called Cologne Declaration. Under the title *Wider die Entmündigung – für eine offene Katholizität* (*Against Disempowerment – For an Open Catholicity*) – 14 German theology professors formulated their criticism of the pope's leadership style. A further 163 theologians from Germany, Austria, Switzerland and the Netherlands added their names to the protest note. The point of contention that split Catholic opinions in Ratzinger's home country, as almost never before, was the dispute about pregnancy.

Meanwhile Karl Lehmann, representing a wing of the church, had become the chairman of the German bishops. As the 'Lehmann church' demanding 'scope for experiments', it soon became synonymous with a deal between church and *Zeitgeist*. The revision of the abortion paragraphs permitted abortions within the first 12 weeks of pregnancy. The prerequisite was a certificate of counselling by an authorized establishment. These included the Catholic Church's counselling centres. According to Volker Resing, editor-in-chief of *Herder Korrespondenz*, Lehmann had 'worked out' the compromise together with Chancellor Helmut Kohl. The argument was: church counselling centres could not only help women in their difficult situations, but in the event of doubt they could also prevent an abortion. However, the pope stressed that a certificate permitting abortion obscured the witness of the Catholic Church to the unconditional value of human life. Ratzinger agreed that it was about 'the dignity of the human person as such, of keeping that right'. For 'The right to life is the precondition for all other rights. Anyone not living cannot exercise any other rights.'[13]

The dispute continued for four long years until Wojtyła categorically insisted on Catholic withdrawal from the state counselling system. Lehmann suffered his worst defeat in church politics with composure and even defended Ratzinger. During these years, 'if somewhat primitive criticisms were directed at the prefect of the Congregation for the Doctrine of the Faith', he had always argued against them and answered: 'My God, don't bark like that. You need to know his work and really bring everything into the conversation.' He had had to comply with Ratzinger, and it could not be said, 'It wasn't him, it was the pope himself. It was the two of them together.' However, he had

> found that I could often talk about everything with Joseph Ratzinger and also with John Paul II. The fairness with which I was listened to actually reconciled me somewhat. I was clear from the beginning that we cannot decide on our own. And the fact that I sometimes had to defer was part of the job of being a Catholic bishop and theologian.[14]

In the eyes of faithful Catholics who regarded Ratzinger as *fidei defensor*, the defender of Christian fundamental values, the prefect had won respect. His firmness of principle and intellectual brilliance also impressed people outside the church. For example, the dramatist and Büchner prize-winner Botho Strauss celebrated Ratzinger as the 'Nietzsche of the outgoing twentieth century'.[15] *Time* magazine in the USA included him among the 100 most influential people in the world. On 6 November 1992 he was accepted into the Académie Française as the successor to the Russian regime critic and human rights activist Andrei Sakharov (in the 'moral and political sciences' section). This was an honour that only one churchman had been awarded before him, Cardinal Richelieu. He was even awarded a carnival medal: Narrhalla, the Munich carnival society, distinguished the alleged 'Grand Inquisitor' for his humour. Ratzinger countered the expected criticism of giving the medal to a guardian of the faith by saying: 'I think that it fits perfectly. For it is well known that it is the privilege of a fool [*Narr*] to be allowed tell the truth.' Since it was 'part of his job to tell the truth' he was delighted at the honour. For 'Anyone who tells the truth and does not look a bit like a clown would all too easily become self-important.'[16]

Ratzinger was not afraid of giving the church hierarchy a telling off. That was seen at an event in Rimini in September 1990. The liberal left newspaper *La Repubblica* reported that at the annual meeting of the Communione e Liberazione movement, attended by tens of thousands of people, the prefect – 'celebrated as a star' – had resumed his now familiar 'provocations'. The cardinal mocked the idea of a 'bustling church'. There were ever more panels, jobs, events. 'Somehow people think there must always be church activity, always talk about the church or something going on in it. But a mirror that only shows itself is no longer a mirror. A window that does not look out onto the world but stands in the way of it has lost its purpose.' He called for a renewed spirituality with a 'relentless examination of conscience', to begin 'everywhere in the church'. That also included the Roman Curia. It could happen 'that someone is continually involved in church activities but is still not a Christian'. And vice versa, it was possible for 'someone simply to live by the word and the sacrament and the love coming from faith, without ever belonging to a church committee or having anything to do with church politics, without belonging to synods or voting in them – and still be a true Christian'.[17]

In the Curia the prefect was respected but was also a loner, who did not play games. Ratzinger had direct access to the pope. That made him almost invulnerable. At the same time his distance from the Curia machine did not help him make friends. The fact that he did not seek the limelight curbed the envy and jealousy of the others a bit, especially power-conscious princes of the church such as Angelo Sodano. 'But his superiority was so obvious', an insider observed, 'that in the long term it is not easy for someone of equal rank to have to live with such an intellectually and theologically outstanding man as Ratzinger.' In his privileged position Ratzinger neither formed networks nor was influenced by them. He did not do politics, especially not personal politics, Unlike the Italians, who relentlessly pushed their own people forward for jobs, Ratzinger did not get involved in intrigues or dance attendance on anyone. 'He kept out of the Curia's cliques altogether,' said the former nuncio Karl-Josef Rauber. 'Although he was in Rome for 23 years, I got the impression that he did not know the Curia particularly well.'[18]

When Bruno Fink left, on his recommendation Josef Clemens took over the job of private secretary. Born in 1947, Clemens was a priest and moral theologian from the archdiocese of Paderborn. With great skill he shielded the prefect for 19 years and served his boss with great devotion. That included happy outings in his Volkswagen Golf. As prefect, Ratzinger also had a confidential relationship with his chief colleague, the Salesian Tarcisio Bertone, who took over administrative tasks from him. Outside his congregation in his inner circle there were only Bernardin Gantin from Benin, the first black Curia cardinal (prefect of the Congregation for Bishops and also president of the papal committee for Latin America) and the Slovak Jozef Tomko (cardinal prefect of the Congregation for the Evangelization of Peoples). Ratzinger's social life was limited to parties on his name day when he invited a few dignitaries from the College of Cardinals to the Hotel Columbus for a little drink. He hardly ever accepted invitations. 'In the evenings, with few exceptions, it was not his thing to go to receptions,' a colleague reported: 'I think (a) he regarded that as a waste of time and (b) it was not in his nature. He was a man who used the time that he had for his own theological work.'[19]

During these years Ratzinger was often alone. He spent the weekends by himself, and on Sunday afternoons he went for a walk through St Anne's Gate up to the Vatican gardens, to potter round them in peace. He regularly travelled to his house in Pentling, always for a fortnight after Whitsun and usually for five weeks in the summer. He spent the days between Christmas and New Year with his brother in the seminary house in Traunstein, 'traditionally', as he put it in his Christmas card to Esther Betz. In another card he told her: 'As has now become a tradition, I spent the week before Whitsun for the first couple of days meditating in Scheyern Abbey, and then in the familiar little house at Pentling.'[20] He celebrated daily Mass in the Paulusheim in Regensburg city centre, usually with Father Martin Bialas, one of his former students. When they breakfasted together after Mass, he refused to talk about spiritual or church matters. He preferred to converse about things that happened in people's daily lives.

His holiday arrangements followed a three-yearly cycle. He went and stayed with his brother almost exclusively in seminaries, monasteries and presbyteries. One year they went to Bressanone, in South Tyrol; in the following year they went to Bad Hofgastein in Austria; and in the third year they went to different places, either to Längsee in Carinthia or to Linz to stay with the musical brothers Josef and Hermann Kronsteiner, or to the Convent of the Poor Clares in Mallersdorf in Lower Bavaria. Even on holiday he spent the mornings hard at work. In the afternoons they went on long trips. When they visited Adelholzen in Upper Bavaria as guests of the Sisters of Charity in the Villa Auli, they sometimes gave a joint piano concert, usually playing pieces by Mozart.

At home in the Piazza della Città Leonina it was a firm custom for him to celebrate Mass at 7 a.m. with his sister. Maria acted as a sort of combined sacristan, who helped the priest into his vestments, server and 'congregation'. Before the service Ratzinger sorted out hymns and wrote the numbers in the right order on a piece of paper. On Sundays and feast days there was a 'procession'. They stood in the corridor by the kitchen and proceeded solemnly into the house chapel. 'A church feast was celebrated as in a cathedral, as far as that was possible, for two or three people in a flat,' reported Christine Felder from the Familia Spiritualis Opus Catholic community. On Sundays work was taboo. In the evening they read a book. 'Sometimes he read to her and sometimes she read to him,' said Felder, 'that was a sacred moment for them.'[21]

For Maria Ratzinger, whom everyone just called 'Fräulein Maria', Rome was not a prison, but neither was it a city in which she felt at home. Her personal friendships were limited to 'Fräulein Mayer', the sister of Cardinal Augustin Mayer, who lived in the same house. 'Joseph needs me,' she said now. That was the constant expression for the life of sacrifice that became her life's work. You could have taken Maria 'for a servant', Klaus Dick, the auxiliary bishop of Cologne commented. But she was not just the 'cricket on the hearth'. She reliably took care of her brother's correspondence, saw to it that he did not forget his scarf or cap. On the other hand, she was 'like a shadow', always two steps behind her brother, almost invisible, said Dick: It was 'not easy for Maria to be a cardinal's sister, because that continually brought her to public notice, which she did not at all want'.[22]

His life together with his sister in their shared home was both a series of rituals and a scholar's den, in which even the dining room was half full of books. 'His friends are his books. Or if it is not a book then a great figure from church history,' said his secretary Gänswein. 'For him literary or intellectual contact through books is just as fulfilling, just as real and important, as contact with living people around him.'[23]

Christine Felder had got to know Ratzinger through the Cardinal Newman Foundation. In 1988 she had said she was prepared to help his sister twice a week with the housekeeping. She admired Ratzinger 'for being able to enjoy the smallest things'. Also for his discipline, 'which keeps him going. For him there is always his work time and also time to rest.' For example, when he lay on the sofa and listened for an hour to classical music. 'He became absorbed in it, because it had been planned. During that hour he could switch off completely, and had no worries.'

However, practical life was 'a huge challenge' for him: 'Everything always had to be regulated precisely, otherwise he would have become unsettled and mentally unfree.' Regularity protected him against surprises. 'He suffers from anxiety, for example, he worries that his suitcase won't arrive.' So he always took a small 'security suitcase', which he did not let out of his hand. Everything was kept strictly in order at his desk, in the hall and in the bathroom. Everything had its place. 'Once he said to me agitatedly: "Sister Christine, have you been dusting the books? The Kafka is upside down."' Ratzinger had never been 'angry or bad-tempered' with her, but he could also be 'strict and peremptory', she said: 'You noticed that a point had been reached where there was no more to be said. You felt an inner authority. He did not have to put it into words. His decisive tone of voice made everything clear.' Josef Clemens, his private secretary for many years in the Congregation for the Doctrine of the Faith, reported that with his boss it was 'how you say something. You needed a certain technique. For example, I developed a way of approaching him: "Today you will hear something that you won't want to hear." He would say: "So what's up now?" "Herr Cardinal, are you feeling strong or weak today?" "Middling." "But I must tell you …"'

Ratzinger had doled out plenty of criticism. Now he had to take some. Until then his books had been best-sellers in the church and politics departments. But increasingly his publications were relegated to a remote corner in bookshops (whereas the products of Küng and Drewermann prominently filled whole shelves). In Catholic theological colleges in Germany students were reprimanded if they did not keep in line. 'Throughout my time as a student I had to listen to diatribes against Ratzinger of the meanest and nastiest kind,' said Petra Haslbeck, a former theology student, 'because these ladies and gentlemen were not up to him intellectually.'[24] Anyone in Germany who had written a doctoral or *habilitation* thesis on Joseph Ratzinger or John Paul II had hardly any chance of 'getting a professorship', Gerhard Müller, the future prefect of the Congregation for the

Doctrine of the Faith, recalled: 'They were not even invited to the "audition", even when they were far superior to their competitors.'[25]

There was also derision. In 1992, at the height of his own popularity, Eugen Drewermann said of him: 'I don't know of anyone who was particularly excited by Ratzinger's thinking.'[26] The Regensburg philosophy professor Ulrich Hommes received a rebuff when he proposed his former colleague Ratzinger for the Guardini prize of the Bavarian Catholic Academy. Franz Henrich, the director, told him to his face, said Hommes, that 'the reputation of the Academy would suffer if it distinguished that Panzer Cardinal'.[27]

Ratzinger did not complain. 'I think he took it as the price he paid for his job,' said his secretary Gänswein, 'and that price has to be paid without complaining.'[28] But the prefect was astonished: 'Many of them even want a sort of "Order of the Blood" [a Nazi medal] for having been persecuted,' he marvelled at his critics' attacks. 'There are professors who are unhappy, because they have not yet been censured, and would love to enjoy the prestige of having been persecuted by Rome.'[29] He even bore with silent composure the humiliation when the red-green council of Munich, where he had been bishop, rejected the proposal to give him the freedom of the city. Then his birthplace, Marktl am Inn, immediately sprang into the breach and conferred its honorary citizenship on him. He was visibly happy with his own people, simple folk whose piety he trusted more than the scholarship of many of his colleagues. 'Insofar as we have come safely through the crisis of recent decades,' he said, it was 'not down to the theology professors but to those simple village people.'

He had never wanted the office of prefect. Sometimes he thought back to his time as a student, such as when he had embarked on Aloys Wenzl's *Philosophy of Freedom*. Or to his carefree beginnings in Bonn and the enthusiastic young people who had found a new way into the church's dogmas thanks to his fresh approach. In Rome he confessed to his first secretary, Fink, while they were sorting books on the shelves in his flat, that he wanted to serve as prefect at most for two five-year periods. After that he would ask the Holy Father to allow him to retire. He still had important works to write: 'After ten years I'll go back to Pentling and that will be my last move.'[30]

It was not just the attacks on the church but above all the evils in the church itself that sapped his energy. The extent of clerical abuse was not yet known, but the reports of abuse that he received on his desk as head of the Congregation for the Doctrine of the Faith (including the cases of liturgical abuse) were enough of a burden. 'It pains me deeply, when I think that is how they behave with our Lord,' he said.[31] He was also aware of the danger that his office itself brought him: 'If you regard life as a whole as hostile and take on the role of prosecutor, then you become increasingly identified with what you are denouncing. Life can only succeed if you have the will to be positive.'[32]

The Swiss cardinal Kurt Koch was convinced that as prefect Ratzinger had 'struggled very hard with the condemnations, which went quite against his nature'.[33] Once Ratzinger spoke about the prophet Jeremiah in a sermon – as if he felt they shared a common fate. Jeremiah passionately desired to be freed from his office. Ratzinger commented: 'He would have loved to shake off his prophetic role, which had made him become a lonely fool, a marked man, whom no one wanted anything to do with. But he had to bear the burden of the word.'[34] 'For me the price to pay was that I could not do what I had planned to do,' he said elsewhere, 'I had to descend into the nitty gritty of actual conflicts and events.'[35]

He had already stated that he did not regard his physical strength as particularly great when he was appointed bishop of Munich. His students recalled that after journeys their professor was exhausted for days. Indeed, an examination had diagnosed a heart defect in him, as his brother Georg reported.[36] 'He is not actually a fighter by nature,' said Georg. 'He had to force himself to be hard. But if a fight was called for, then he did not shirk it; he stood firm in accordance with his conscience.'[37] But the office took its toll, and however hard the cardinal's outer shell seemed to be, he remained soft inside. 'It cost him enormous energy to do the job,' observed Siegfried Wiedenhofer; 'he took it personally. It really got to him.'[38] The Munich theologian Eugen Biser even feared that with Ratzinger 'the difference between the person and the office is very painful and destructive'.[39]

With the last ounce of his strength the prefect worked on the *Catechism of the Catholic Church*, the task given to him by the pope in 1986. The project was regarded with great scepticism by critics. It was condemned to fail. The US theology professor David Tracy thought 'the proposal to create a universal catechism is hubristic'.[40]

In a way he was right. Indeed, it was a monumental task. By the autumn of 1990, 16 Roman congregations, 28 bishops' conferences, 23 out of a total of 295 groups of bishops and 797 individual bishops had replied to the draft sent to them by Ratzinger's congregation. As well as the 24,000 comments received, there were the suggestions from 12 theological institutes and 62 experts who had also been asked for their opinion.

According to his secretary Josef Clemens, Ratzinger had not written a single line of the mammoth work. But as chairman of the Catechism Committee, for years he led the worldwide co-ordination of the texts. The final editorial proofing was almost done when, in September 1991, the prefect suffered a stroke at a student meeting in Germany. At first the cerebral haemorrhage was barely noticed. 'There was so much to do. I did not have a free moment,' Ratzinger reported, 'I have always slept badly. Then there was an ordination service for priests.' Someone finally told him that in his sermon he had repeated several sentences without noticing it. In Rome the chauffeur Alfredo met him at the airport. 'In the car something ran out of my eye', said Ratzinger, 'it was really strange. When I arrived home I didn't know whether I lived on the third or the fourth floor. My sister opened the door and saw that my face was chalk white. She gave me something to eat and then sent me straight to bed.'[41]

For Maria the cerebral haemorrhage was an alarm signal. 'I thought Brother Death was moving in with my brother', she told Sister Christine. As one of the few people close to him, she knew that her brother had suffered from almost permanent headaches since 1946/7 – sometimes so severe that work was impossible. Pills did not help. There was some relief from physiotherapy, which her brother regularly underwent. The cerebral haemorrhage affected his left visual field. Ratzinger was treated for two weeks in the Pius XI Hospital in Rome. He slowly regained his sight but he suffered from the physical and psychological after-effects, including constant tiredness, until 1992.

Barely two months later he suffered another stroke, which was more severe than the first one. As usual at the feast of All Saints, Maria wanted to go to Pentling to take care of their parents' grave. She booked a return ticket with Lufthansa. She begged her brother in her absence not to stay at the usual nuns' institute. She had read that there had been burglars. Joseph offered no resistance and stayed in a retreat house on a hill, belonging to the community of the Figlie della Chiesa (Daughters of the Church) in La Storta, a suburb of Rome. It was lucky. Because it was near the airport, Ratzinger was able to get on a flight immediately after an alarming phone call from his brother saying that Maria had suffered a heart attack. But when he reached the hospital of the Barmherzige Brüder (Merciful Brothers) in Regensburg, Maria was no longer conscious. 'She lay there sleeping peacefully.'[42] A few hours later she was dead. Maria Ratzinger was a member of the Third Order of St Francis. On 2 November 1991, All Souls' Day, she succumbed to a heart attack followed by a cerebral haemorrhage.

His sister's death wounded him deeply. After the requiem in Regensburg Cathedral the cardinal was seen standing alone under its huge Gothic portal with tears in his eyes. The Regensburg Domspatzen ('Cathedral Sparrows': the cathedral choir) accompanied Maria on her final journey through the sleet to lay her in her parents' grave in Pentling. There were bishops, nuncios and high church dignitaries in numbers probably never seen before at a secretary's funeral. Her obituary said that Maria Ratzinger had served her brother Joseph for 34 years 'on all the stages of his journey with tireless devotion and great goodness and humility. She had always been a sisterly help and support to both her brothers.'

When he was asked how much his sister had influenced his life and work, Benedict XVI answered: 'I would say not the content of my theological work, of course, but through her being, her faith and her humility.' An existential bond grew between them 'in our common faith, the atmosphere in which we grew up, that faith which grew up with us and stood firm through the new currents of the time, that faith which took a great deal from what the Council renewed but still remained steadfast. Yes, I'd say our basic atmosphere of thinking and being was co-determined by her.'[43]

Joseph was shaken deeply. It would soon become clear how deeply. Work went on. On 16 November 1992 the *Catechism of the Catholic Church*, which had originally been drawn up in French, was presented to the public for the first time in Paris. All the reservations about it turned out to have been doom-mongering. Unlike all the national catechisms, whose sales figures only amounted to a few thousands, within three weeks more than 500,000 copies of the new catechism were sold. In total it reached a worldwide figure of more than 8 million copies. That was reason enough for John Paul II to call it one of the 'most important events in recent church history'.[44]

However, Ratzinger's stroke and his sister's death had lasting effects. He tired more quickly and evinced a previously unknown listlessness if there was extra work. In 1986, after his first five-year period, he had already said to John Paul II 'my time is up. But he told me that would not do.' On 25 September 1991, 23 days after his sister's death, his second five-year period came to an end. After ten years in office the so-called power-seeker begged his pope again to let him retire, this time more urgently. 'After my cerebral haemorrhage I was very outspoken and told him I can't do it any more. But he said "No, no, no, that won't do".'[45]

On that 25 September Sister Christine put a greetings card on his side-table with a gold-framed number '10' on it. She wanted to wish him joy on the tenth anniversary of his appointment as prefect of the Congregation for the Doctrine of the Faith. But his reaction was the opposite of joyful. 'That's no cause to celebrate,' he answered shortly. 'I never did it again,' said Sister Christine. 'That was the first time I became aware of how heavy the burden on him lies.'[46]

A year after his stroke Ratzinger suffered another blow. The *Süddeutsche Zeitung* reported on 17 August 1992: 'Joseph Ratzinger, the Curia Cardinal, who injured himself by a fall on holiday in Bressanone in South Tyrol, has been able to leave hospital. He suffered a head wound when he fell over in the bathroom and needed ten stitches.' That was not quite what had happened. According to his own account, when he was in the seminary Ratzinger had rolled his office chair across the floor from his desk, to reach the ringing telephone. Unfortunately, he fell over a heater and hit his head. He lay unconscious on the floor in a pool of blood until his brother found him.

When I visited him in Rome in November 1992 to interview him, I did not know about his health problems and he did not say a word about them. He was weak and rather melancholy. He answered one of my questions saying, of course, there were demands made by Jesus, which 'quite certainly' not even a cardinal could fulfil, 'because he is just as weak as other people'. And yes, he knew the feeling of being helpless and overstretched. 'In my job now my powers are far below what I actually should be doing. And the older you become, the more you find that your strength is just not enough to do what you should. You are too weak, too helpless or unable to deal with situations.' At such moments he turned to his God and besought him: 'Now you must help. I can't do any more.'

We spoke about his parents' house, his experiences of the war and the Nazi era. When we spoke about his work as the top guardian of the Catholic faith, this man, whom his opponents presented as a relentless persecutor, told me he felt terribly tired. He was old and exhausted. It sounded like a cry for help. Yes, he was burned out, he said. 'I am old now, at my limit. I feel myself more and more unfit physically to do the job. I feel worn out.' It was simply time for other, fresher minds to take over. For him, at least by 1996, after three periods of office, that should be an end to it. Finally.

19

The Long Suffering of Karol Wojtyła

For a long time it looked as though John Paul II had survived the May 1981 attack on him without any after-effects. He went skiing and hiking in the mountains. He had a pool dug at his summer residence, Castel Gandolfo, to keep fit by swimming. Shortly afterwards the first paparazzi photos appeared: the pope in swimming trunks.

It was hard to classify him. Was he now a reactionary or a progressive, a hardliner or a prime example of empathy? 'Everything has become different with Wojtyła,' the Italian Cardinal Achille Silvestrini had declared immediately after Wojtyła's enthronement. 'They have crossed the Alps. Now everything is possible.'

The Polish pope visited the poor districts of Latin America, and in Senegal he asked Africans for forgiveness for the enslavement of their ancestors. He warned against greed for profit and consumerism, the arms race and corruption. He castigated the social sins of capitalism and globalization. In his *Theologie des Leibes* (*Theology of the Body*) he wrote about the dignity of the human body, the beauty of being a woman or a man and the vocation to love. He appealed for the preservation of life at all its stages. Life was not created by humans, and it was not at their disposal.

His first encyclical, *Redemptor hominis* (*The Redeemer of Humanity*), laid out his programme: human beings, the world and the political system had 'departed from the demands of morality and justice'. The church had to speak out against that with clear teaching. Not as an administrator but as a saviour of life.

He was someone who not only thought that God existed but also lived by that thought throughout his life. He believed Catholics were different. Sometimes they seemed a bit mad, but even that marked them out as God's jesters, who had kept something by their unconventionality that others never had.

Wojtyła believed not only that he himself had survived through the help of Our Lady of Fátima but also that the fall of the Iron Curtain, which had tumbled like the walls of Jericho, was due to her. In 1984 he had appealed directly to her, he later confessed, to bring about the collapse of Communism. Indeed, the change in the East had followed a Marian Year, which he had proclaimed. Portentously, he asserted that we could 'recognize the ways of the Lord in the signs of the time'. He spoke more and more often of an 'end time' It was advisable to 'purify ourselves by repenting of our errors, faithlessness, inconsistencies and delays'.

Despite the pope's agility, the truth was his regime had become more fragile since the attack on him. In 1994 speculation began about his retirement. 'His shepherd's crook has become a crutch', the *New York Times Magazine* announced. It was not difficult to 'predict his departure'. It was as good as certain that he would not go on any more trips, the German illustrated paper *Der Stern* told its readers. The reports were sensationalist. Each wanted to be the first to forecast the news of the end of the reign of the 264th servant of the servants of God. But when the pope had to return to the Gemelli Clinic, he joked to reporters that now he read the papers to find out how he was getting on. He called the clinic the 'third Vatican', besides the Apostolic Palace and the Castel Gandolfo residence. However, a French journalist's remark seemed to be proving truer by the day: 'This is not a pope from Poland, this is a pope from Golgotha.'

One of the keys to understanding his papacy could be found in what happened during the difficult 100 days after the attack as he lay, pale and exhausted, on a white sheet. 'Over the last few months God has let me endure suffering,' he would say. 'I had to feel the danger of losing my life.' Then he said something that explained the power, endurance and trust in God that distinguished his final period of office: 'At the same time I realized, clearly and deeply, that this was a special grace for me as a person and – with regard to my service as bishop of Rome and successor to St Peter – also a grace for the church.'[1]

On the question of retirement he had it checked whether a pope, like bishops, could give up his office when he reached a certain age. The experts among his closest colleagues advising him included Cardinal Ratzinger. The contents of this report were never made public. After the pope himself had studied the texts that Paul VI had left on the question of retirement, according to his secretary Stanisław Dziwisz, he came 'to the conclusion that he must submit to God's will. That meant staying at his post as long as God wanted. "God has called me, and God will call me again in the way he pleases."'[2] However, he set up a procedure for his retirement in case his strength did not last to carry on serving to the end.

Perhaps Wojtyła also remembered a letter that Pope Pius V wrote to a frail archbishop of Goa in India, who was requesting to be discharged: 'We feel brotherly sympathy for you because you feel tired. But remember that suffering is the normal way that leads to heaven, and we may not leave the post that Providence has assigned to us. Don't you realize that we also sometimes feel tired of life? And that we also wish to return to our original status as simple priests?'

On 10 September 1571, a few days before the Battle of Lepanto, St Pius V wrote a moving letter to the Grand Master of the Knights of Malta, Pietro del Monte, to encourage the old military commander:

> You know without doubt that my cross is heavier than yours, that my powers are failing and how many there are who want me to succumb. I would have already given up and renounced my office (and thought of doing so more than once) if I had not preferred to give myself completely into the hands of the Master, who said: Those who want to follow me must deny themselves.[3]

In connection with his own experiences, on 11 February 1984 Wojtyła had published the Apostolic Letter *Salvifici doloris* (*Redemptive Suffering*) on the 'salvific power' of Christian suffering. The deep meaning of suffering, he wrote, came in the light of faith if it was borne with Christ, who died on the cross and rose again. It thereby also became a spiritual good for the church and the world. Wherever Wojtyła went, he asked for the sick and the handicapped to be given a special place in the front rows. In San Francisco he took a child in his arms who was suffering from AIDS. In a Korean home he kissed a man who had leprosy. 'In this way the pope wanted to show sufferers and also our selfish world the value that suffering together with Christ had in the eyes of God,' said his secretary. 'He wanted to remind people that suffering could be accepted without losing your dignity.'[4]

Wojtyła bore his own disabilities with patience and composure. No one near him could later remember him ever letting his bodily complaints become a burden to others. However, he had no problem with speaking openly about his health. In 1992 he told the faithful in St Peter's Square that he had colon cancer and needed an operation. A year later, after a fall, he had to have an operation on his shoulder. In 1994 he stumbled in the bathroom, which resulted in a femoral neck fracture. In 1996 he had another colon operation. In addition, osteoarthritis in the knee made walking permanently difficult for him. When reporters noticed a trembling in the fingers of the left hand and a partial stiffening of his face muscles, speculation arose over whether he had Parkinson's disease. In fact, his doctor, Renato Buzzonetti, had already connected his fall in the bathroom with a defective sense of balance, caused by a neurological extrapyramidal syndrome: Parkinson's. That did 'not particularly worry' the Holy Father, his secretary recalled: 'He asked for some things to be explained and told Buzzonetti that he was ready to be treated.'[5]

The pope's increasing disability did not lead to the attacks on him becoming milder. Quite the contrary. The fiercest attacks came from Luther's country. The Hamburg magazine *Der Spiegel* had taken upon itself to accompany the Christian festivals with anti-Christian title stories. Punctually on feast days – Christmas, Easter and Whitsun – long-winded cover stories appeared, which sought to 'debunk' the biblical message in constantly new ways. The stories had little to do with 'news' or even with facts, although the paper boasted of their accuracy. They had more to do with speculation and the famous 'Spiegel sauce', which gave each article the necessary pinch of cynicism and malice. For example, on Christmas Eve 2018 the paper gave readers discoveries about 'Mary Magdalene, the first pope' and revived a favourite question: 'Did Jesus have a wife?' This time it declared that one of *Der Spiegel's* top reporters had discovered large parts of his story over many years without it attracting attention in house. People wanted to believe what they were told.

In November 1980 the magazine had already found a catchy nickname for John Paul II: 'Ayatollah Wojtyła'. It said his charisma was merely to breathe 'a kind of fake media life into the apparatus he was standing in front of'. He gave a 'Christmas performance' broadcasting 'the benevolent illusion that the church could really still move the masses'.[6] When it was about Wojtyła, the editor, Rudolf Augstein, who claimed that his paper was the 'assault rifle of democracy', liked to take up arms himself. Augstein attacked Wojtyła for his authoritarian rule. He said the pope propagated a 'doctrine of sexual inhibition' and followed a 'despotic course'. He called Wojtyła an 'enemy of humanity', 'sickly old man', a 'backwoodsman', a 'pig-headed Pole' and an 'autocrat' who 'plays the despot'.

In January 1995 the pope covered 33,000 kilometres in 11 days on a tour of Asia. He held 30 conversations with different people, and in Manila he celebrated Mass with 5 million people, the largest Mass congregation of all time. *Der Spiegel* had to respond. 'I am against Pope Wojtyła,' Augstein blasted defiantly a week after the Manila event, 'because he does not allow any other opinion to be valid except his own, even though his own is drawn from the pool of "Ratzingerism".' The Wojtyła church was going into 'a future without hope'. To illustrate the article there was a photo showing the pope yawning and leaning on his crosier. The caption read: 'Graveyard of a past history'.[7]

After a cutting lead story on 26 January 1998, Augstein struck out again on 20 September 1999: 'The Pole Wojtyła wants to keep bullying women,' he commented on the Roman decision to opt out of pregnancy counselling. In a sweeping attack, he castigated the church for complicity with Hitler: 'He [Hitler] needed the church's blessing to begin and win his war.' Augstein's fury reached its peak in the accusation that 'the torture and appalling torments resulting in death inflicted by the Roman church' were 'comparable to the crimes of Hitler and Stalin'.[8]

However, it was an open secret that after the end of the war quite a few Nazis were taken on by *Der Spiegel*, including Rudolf Diels, the former SS Oberführer (senior group leader), who became the first head of the Gestapo. At the beginning of 1934 Diels had passed a report to Hitler through Herman Göring, which was a list of 'particularly outstanding cases of political excesses by Catholic clergy against the state and the National Socialist movement'. For *Der Spiegel* he wrote the articles 'The Night of the Long Knives ...

Did Not Happen' and 'Lucifer *ante portas*'. According to research by his biographer Klaus Wallbaum, Rudolf Diels was 'one of the most important actors in the Nazi regime, with direct access to Adolf Hitler'.[9]

In a review of Augstein's book *Jesus Menschensohn* (*Jesus Son of Man*) Karl Rahner attributed Augstein's attacks on the papacy and the church to his attempt to break free from the fears of his Catholic childhood. About Christ, Augstein had come to the conclusion that Jesus was very probably 'a synthetically composed figure from several personages and tendencies, who had been 'consciously or unconsciously invented by imaginative, hellenistically educated Jews as a personified expectation of salvation of the Jewish people'. It was a 'fact' that 'religion, as it is understood by believers and unbelievers, has no future – with any God at all. There is no God whom we could know or speak about, no Almighty. That a God acted once and for all, two thousand years ago, is a myth and magic from the childhood of humanity.'[10]

Only four months after Augstein's death on 7 November 2002, *Spiegel* editors were suddenly writing about John Paul II as the 'God's marathon man' and the 'millennium pope'. 'The Romans Loved Him' was one front-page story. The pope fought against 'the misanthropic ideology of communism as decisively as against the secularization, cynicism and ruthlessness in high-powered capitalism'. And 'Everywhere in the world they seem to be keen for his message [...] especially the young.'[11]

The end of the Cold War, globalization and the new electronic media catapulted the world into a new age – with challenges to which there were as yet no answers. Ratzinger had bounced back again after his exhaustion and regained his old strength. As the Vatican's acknowledged chief thinker, he gave lectures to Europe's new leading politicians and lawyers. He was invited to Cambridge and New York, and received nine honorary doctorates. He visited the USA five times and South America six times. His commitment to the revoking of Galileo's condemnation earned him such respect among scientists that in the year 2000 a minor planet was named after him. Hans Urs von Balthasar's Johannes Verlag also celebrated him, praising Ratzinger as 'the fearless diagnostician of the church today: no iron is too hot for him to touch, no theological jungle is too tangled and thick for him to penetrate'.[12] All his works were distinguished for their courage, wisdom and an outspoken sense of moderation and fairness.

Ratzinger was the most interviewed bishop in the media worldwide. He was also unsurpassed in analysing the situation within the church. 'I had been given the subject,' he reported on his preparation for an assembly of bishops from all over Europe at the beginning of the 1990s. 'They expected me to outline the problems with which theology had to deal in Europe's present situation.' He was also asked to go into 'the deeper reasons for today's battle *over* and *against* the church' and 'invite further thought about it'.

Ratzinger's analysis in the year 1992 is noteworthy, because it is still not out of date. He said that the faith situation in Europe not only suffered from people being tired of the church. 'In order to understand the real trouble for the faith in our time' we had to 'look deeper'. The 'reduction of the world to what was provable and the reduction of our life to what was perceptible' had led to a 'fading of the image of God': 'Superstition seems to be better substantiated than faith, and the gods to be more believable than God.' People were less and less able to imagine a God 'who cares about individual people or who acts in the world at all. If he actually existed, God might have set off the Big Bang but had nothing else to do with the enlightened world.' And the reverse was also the case: the idea 'that a human action could offend God' was no longer comprehensible to many people: 'so there is no longer any reason for redemption in the classical Christian sense, because it occurs to hardly anyone that the cause of misery in the world and individuals is sin.'[13]

The idea that the world bore a divine message within it and thereby gave us 'valid standards for our behaviour' was no longer regarded as tenable. In that way God became at most a 'guiding framework' but 'without content; what morality means has to be determined purely within this world'. This meant that Catholic catechesis should not 'avoid the great questions of the faith because of the deafness of many people today to divine matters, or try to justify the church's existence by its social usefulness. Even though the church's social work is very important, it withers away if the heart of the church, the mystery, disappears'.

The prefect also had some encouraging words for the bishops. Despite all the losses, they should not 'overlook a counter-movement, which is becoming increasingly apparent in the younger generation'. Young people, in particular, were seeing through 'the banality and childish rationalism of home-made liturgies with their feeble, arty theatricality'. Ratzinger concluded with the words: 'Ultimately, everything depends on the God question. Faith is faith in God or it is nothing.'[14]

Many of his talks arose from matters dealt with in his office: questions of social change, bioethics or genetic research. One of his main themes was the loss of identity. As a German, he had a special sensitivity in that area. Ratzinger came from a country that had inflicted the greatest wound on Christianity, a gaping split, as his student Vincent Twomey said, 'that over the centuries had spread over the whole world. It was a country whose population and identity still today were inwardly torn apart by that split.' And, Twomey said, it was not only the split between Catholics and Protestants that had started from Germany, but also the great atheistic currents of modern times, 'including the philosophical movements of the Enlightenment with Kant and Hegel, the political movement of Marx and Engels and the would-be finale in the rebellion against God, the Fascist attempt at world domination'.[15] Ratzinger insisted in his speeches that the soul of Europe was based on common human and Christian values. Only a Europe that rediscovered its roots would be able to meet the challenges of the third millennium.

Ratzinger reacted to a new paganism that was about to conquer the public space. The biblical message was giving way to all sorts of substitute religions; celebrities took on the role of saints; barbaric rites and obscene cults were regarded as viable. The prefect warned that the loss of identity, direction and truth led to a concentration on self in an egoistic society and thus to brutal isolation. There was a connection between the loss of faith and the decline of values. Anyone could see that the loss of a higher dimension led to the sinking of the culture's groundwater table. People had to realize again 'that humanity's great moral insights were just as reasonable and true' as the knowledge gained by the natural sciences or technology. For 'in fact natural law is a moral law. Many attitudes are really always false because they contradict the nature of being. Modernity's problem is that it no longer realizes that this is self-evident.'

Ratzinger produced an impressive number of spiritual books, such as:

- *Auf Christus schauen: Einübung in Glaube, Hoffnung, Liebe* (*To Look on Christ: Exercises in Faith, Hope, and Love*);
- *Diener eurer Freude: Meditationen über die priesterliche Spiritualität* (*Ministers of Your Joy: Scriptural Meditations on Priestly Spirituality*);
- *Wesen und Auftrag der Theologie: Versuche zu ihrer Ortsbestimmung im Disput der Gegenwart* (*The Nature and Mission of Theology: Essays to Orient Theology in Today's Debates*).

He produced collections of essays on politics and society, such as:

- *Ökumene und Politik. Neue Versuche zur Ekklesiologie* (*Church, Ecumenism and Politics: New Endeavours in Ecclesiology*);
- *Abbruch und Aufbruch. Die Antwort des Glaubens auf die Krise der Werte* (*Deconstruction and Awakening. The Answer of Faith to the Crisis of Values*).

He also published:

- *Wendezeit für Europa? Diagnosen und Prognosen zur Lage von Kirche und Welt* (*A Turning Point for Europe? The Church in the Modern World*);
- *Wahrheit, Werte, Macht: Prüfsteine der pluralistischen Gesellschaft* (*Truth, Values, Power: The Cornerstones of a Pluralistic Society*).

Ratzinger's diagnoses of the time combined criticism of the present with the attempt to show Christianity's contribution to a humane, democratic society. His works often recalled the prophetic insight of George Orwell. 'The reduction of reason to the world of "facts" and "use" results in the abolition of morality,' he said plainly 'and thus to the abolition of humanity.' Such a development could 'lead to the exercise of naked power without any moral obligation – and so to the control of the many by the few'.[16] The 'Christian alternative' was only hesitatingly brought into the public debate 'because Christians have no confidence in their own vision of reality. In their private devotion they hold on to their faith, but they dare not assume that this faith has anything to say to people in general, any vision of their future and their history.'[17]

When the interview book *Salz der Erde* was published in September 1996, even the bourgeois media for once had to agree with the prefect. Whereas the 'Ratzinger Report' published just ten years earlier had strengthened the horror image of the 'Panzer Cardinal', now that image was beginning to crack. 'No top member of the Curia before has been so open and communicative', declared *Der Spiegel*.[18] The *Süddeutsche Zeitung* considered: 'This man reads the riot act to his church as no one has done since Martin Luther.' *Die Zeit* said the book would 'perhaps be taken as a sign of a remarkable change of tendency'. For now it could be seen that Ratzinger's 'conservatism was not complicity with the dominant culture but nonconformism in the face of a current view that believed in progress'. Now the cardinal was not 'maladjusted' or 'critical' of modernity, which had long become the mainstream, 'but swimming against the tide of the *Zeitgeist*'.

At first there was a further health set-back to the book project. After his cerebral haemorrhage in 1991 the cardinal had regained his sight completely. But in the spring of 1995 he suffered a thrombosis during a student meeting for the 50th anniversary of his *Abitur* class. His left eye was affected again. 'In the Regensburg University clinic I was thoroughly harassed by three days of investigations,' Ratzinger wrote to his friend Esther Betz. 'The result was that nothing was to be done for the present, my sight would return after a couple of weeks.' However, that optimism met with disappointment. Further treatment could bring no improvement. When he later developed macular degeneration, an age-related condition of the retina, the last hope vanished of ever being able to see out of his left eye again.

Eventually, as the interviewer commissioned by the publisher, I sat with the cardinal at the back of the Congregation to the Doctrine of the Faith's old Mercedes. Alfredo drove us to a house at Frascati belonging to the Integrated Community, to hold the interviews for the book. On the Via Appia the car slowly slid past a chapel. It was the *Quo vadis* spot. According to the legend, here Peter had met Christ. Jesus had raised his hand, like a policeman. 'Where are you going?' he asked. Then he sent Peter back. Back to Rome to do his job. Small black wreaths lay in front of the little church. It was a picture of sadness.

A few people were standing about, looking rather awkward, with their eyes on the ground. They gave the impression that they had suddenly realized they had valued much too little what they had lost.

The days at Frascati began with Mass. Then 'Ratzinger tea' was brought – fruit tea with lemon and lots of sugar. We began punctually and stopped punctually. In the intervals the prefect went to his room. Yes, he meditated then, he said. He asked the Holy Spirit for help, because he did not presume to do it all on his own. That was self-evident for a believer.

Later our meeting reminded me of a story by Paulo Coelho, in which a simple old man makes chairs and tables alone in a village. He makes nothing of the fact that he is the world's leading archery master. Ratzinger also taught without any jovial or attention-seeking ploys. He was often silent with a kind of monkish attitude that needed no words. Coelho had prefaced his book with a prayer as a motto: 'Mary, conceived without sin, pray for us, who turn to you. Amen.' He also added a quotation from the US poet and visionary Ella Wheeler Wilcox: 'A prayer without a purpose is like an arrow without a bow. A purpose without a prayer is like a bow without an arrow.'[19]

Ratzinger had long since stopped being regarded as a 'stern German' in Italy. His way of listening and pondering, before he poured something out in words when he was sure of the truth of what he wanted to communicate, reminded the Italians of classical philosophers like Plato and Aristotle. His great strength was being able not only to analyse but also to structure, to offer possibilities that could help individuals or the whole of society. He could recognize what was wrong and use what was good to make better progress. My questions for the interview book were about things such as 'Why can't many people believe any more?', 'Why is there so much evil in the world?' and 'Does it make any sense to board this leaky ship of the church?' Sometimes Ratzinger happily threw his leg over the armrest of his chair, like a student getting into a discussion and feeling at ease. If he did not know something, he freely admitted it. It was important for him to be in line with the great saints and teachers of the faith, whose instructions had proved true in life. At one point I asked him how many ways there were to God. The cardinal did not take long to reflect. There were precisely as many ways to God as there were people, he said, for each person had their own way.

In our interview he said that he regarded celibacy not as a dogma but as 'a way of life that developed very early in the church on good biblical grounds'. However, we should not 'define such a deeply anchored and well-founded way of life as an absolute'. With regard to sex, of course, a cardinal had to 'speak about everything that is human. And sex should not just be dismissed with the label sin.' About his compatriots he said that the Germans were 'on the one hand, a people who value discipline, performance, work and punctuality. But that easily leads to a certain self-conceit and to a one-sided view that values only performance, work, production, discipline, what is self-made, and neglects many other aspects of human life.'

In our time, Ratzinger continued, 'Christianity has suffered an enormous loss of importance'. In more and more areas of life it now took courage 'to confess to being a Christian'. There was even 'the danger of an anti-Christian dictatorship'. On the other hand, in many places the church was 'suffocated by its institutional power'. Perhaps we should 'say goodbye to the idea of national churches. Possibly a different age of the church is coming, in which Christianity is seen again as seed corn, in apparently unimportant small groups, who resist evil and bring good into the world, who let God in.' Finally, and that was the point at which I thought I had misheard, the cardinal swung into an emotional declaration: 'The church needs a revolution of faith. It must not associate itself with the *Zeitgeist*. It must not give up its values in order to preserve its property.'

He was not really afraid of the future. Those who had 'survived through the experience of the modern' were precisely the ones able to recognize that in the apparently sclerotic Catholic Church there was 'something fresh and also bold and generous awaiting, that offers a way out of our stagnant way of life'. Faith meant seeking understanding. 'As creation comes from reason and is reasonable, faith is the fulfilment of creation and so a door to understanding.' To the question of whether it was right that Christianity was an event rather than a theory, his lightning reply was: 'And that is very important. The essential thing about Christ himself is not that he proclaimed particular ideas – which he did – but that I become a Christian by believing in this event. God came into the world and he acted. So it is an action, a reality, not just an idea.'[20]

The recording of our conversation took two days and produced a tape that took 12 hours to play. That became a book, which was translated into 30 languages all over the world. A Vietnamese man who had come to Germany as one of the boat people translated it into Vietnamese. A professor from Beirut translated it into Arabic. Probably it was also Ratzinger's musical way of speaking that caused the worldwide success of the recording. 'You can still hear in his theological language today how important music is for him, especially Mozart's music,' said Max-Eugen Kemper, a member of the St Peter's Cathedral chapter in Rome. It was the 'remarkable polyphony' that linked Ratzinger to Mozart. 'That polyphony confronts us in an ordered, harmonically controlled way: it is comforting and encouraging, conciliatory and exhilarating.' There was also something in it that the violinist Yehudi Menuhin once called *la part de Dieu*, God's part, which did not come from all the notes, instructions and instruments but simply required a certain openness. 'That is where any good music gets its radiant power from,' said Kemper; 'it is only then that we get an inkling that another "player" is also at work.'[21]

Despite the book's success, for the prefect the year 1996 did not end with the event he wished for. Ten years earlier he had reminded the pope that with his first quinquennium his task was done. When he officially asked for his retirement after his stroke in 1991, his request was again refused. Now again, at the end of his third five-year period, John Paul II still showed no mercy. No, he was not allowed to leave his post. And yet another thing dismayed him, his coming 70th birthday. 'I try to keep birthday celebrations, which unfortunately cannot be altogether avoided, within bounds as much as possible,' he wrote to Esther Betz on 12 February 1997. However, his desk 'to my dismay is piled with so many papers, which overflow all over the place. I sometimes think how lovely it would be if I could be a professor emeritus and had the freedom to read and ramble as I pleased.'

Six months later, when the anniversary celebrations were over, he wrote in a letter to Betz: 'Now I am trying to recover a bit from all of that. I feel my strength becoming weaker and the demand for all the hectic preparations for the year 2000 is growing. I am not planning (I never have) but let myself be led by Providence, even if everything were to turn out quite differently from how I had imagined it.'[22]

20

Millennium

In the early summer of 1997 Ratzinger had to go into a clinic in Rome for a few days of heart treatment. On 7 January 1998 he underwent a preventive operation on his healthy right eye, 'which Professor Gabel from the clinic regarded as urgent. Hopefully, everything will go all right,' he wrote to Esther Betz.

By the end of the month he was off again. First to Pamplona, to receive an honorary doctorate from the Opus Dei University, together with a Jewish economist from the USA and a Reformed pharmacologist from the Netherlands. There was no time to visit the Guggenheim Museum in nearby Bilbao, which his friend Esther had strongly recommended him to do. From Pamplona he went to Hamburg, 'where first we were to celebrate the ecumenical St Ansgar Vespers together', Ratzinger noted, 'then a lecture to the Overseas Club in the great hall of the stock exchange with an audience of about 1,500 – an unforgettable evening'.

It was not only the preparations for the millennium that made the prefect's work harder. He continued to feel tired and old. 'With the passage of years you feel the burden of such days more and more,' he told Esther in February 1998, 'I will have to limit such adventures in the future.'[1] At the beginning of August 1999 he went on holiday with his brother Georg to the Mallersdorf Convent. 'The atmosphere of silence was wonderful after the noise and busy schedule in Rome,' he told Esther. Effusively he praised the 'wonderful hospitality' and especially the 'broad, fertile country, whose gentle hills and valleys have something peaceful and relaxing about them in comparison with the massive Alpine mountains'.

On 31 October there was the signature of the 'joint declaration on the doctrine of justification' by the Lutheran World Federation, the World Council of Methodist Churches and the Catholic Church. It was regarded as a milestone in the ecumenical dialogue; despite all remaining differences, the Catholic Church expressed its understanding of the Protestant doctrine of justification 'by grace alone'. The theologian Theodor Dieter, head of the Lutheran World Federation's Institute for Ecumenical Research in Strasbourg, stressed that without the intervention of the prefect, 'this declaration would not have happened'.[2] When the talks on the declaration had come to a dead end, Ratzinger entrenched himself with the Evangelical local bishop Johannes Hanselmann, at first in the Hotel Münchner Hof in Regensburg and the following day in his brother's private flat, to overcome the final, apparently insuperable theological stumbling blocks. At last, an amendment was found, which was hastily faxed to the Lutheran World Federation in Geneva. The historic agreement was saved.

'This autumn was extraordinarily heavy-going', Ratzinger wrote in his Christmas greeting to Esther that year: 'Symposium on Bible interpretation, Europe Synod, Theological Committee, *ad limina* visits, lectures – particularly in the Sorbonne in Paris, where a cardinal was speaking again for the first time since time immemorial, and many other engagements. So I am pretty exhausted and shall be glad if I can go to Germany for a week at the end of the year.'[3]

At least by the mid-1990s nearly all the Vatican preparations were in train for the millennium. John Paul II seemed to be almost obsessed with this date. In the fifth century the monk Dionysius Exiguus miscalculated when the pope gave him the task of creating an exact calendar. Dionysius (who was born in Ukraine) set the Bethlehem event at the year 754 *ab urbe condita* – i.e., since the foundation of Rome. However, more recent research has dated the actual year of Jesus' birth five to seven years earlier. But Dionysius' date stood and since then the Western world has counted every month, every week, every hour from the birth of Christ, good days and bad.

Jesus' final words delivered a mission: 'Go into all the world and proclaim the good news to the whole of creation. Whoever believes and is baptized will be saved', it says in Mark. In Matthew it says, 'Teach them to obey whatever I have commanded you.'[4]

Two thousand years later the New Testament has been translated into 6,700 languages and dialects, and there are about 1.7 billion (1.7 thousand million) printed Bibles spread throughout the whole world. Not that people, as Christians, all became united and better. Or that their church did not support any wars. Schism developed in their community, and schisms from schisms, so that there were now about 41,000 Christian communities. The Catholics were the only community to remain one and universal. It harked back to the primacy of Peter and claimed to have been directly founded by Jesus with an unbroken apostolic succession, so that it was not only a national but *the* world church. At the millennium the Catholic Church was spread over 200 countries with 1.2 billion members from among more than 1,500 ethnic groups. The Catholic Church had universities and schools with about 60 million students. It ran about 5,000 hospitals, 18,000 health clinics, 10,000 orphanages, 17,000 care homes and homes for the disabled.

John Paul II saw the millennium as an incomparable opportunity. The significance of the year 2000, he declared, was to give an answer to 'the meaning of humanity', not only to Christians but to the whole world. 'We must put out to sea,' he declared. He had prepared his flock for the great event with the Apostolic Letter *Tertio millennio adveniente* of 10 November 1994. From 1997 the mega-event was to be approached in three steps, beginning with the 'Year of Jesus Christ', followed by the 'Year of the Holy Spirit' and the 'Year of God the Father'. The pope had proclaimed the millennium year itself to be a 'Holy Year'. Its starting signal was to be on Christmas Eve 1999, when he would knock on the usually locked Holy Door of St Peter's Basilica with a golden hammer. He would be accompanied by the verse of the psalm *Aperite mihi portas iustitiae* ('Open to me the gates of justice'). According to the plan, as soon as a mechanism set the ton-weight of the side-door in motion, an unprecedented stream of pilgrims, estimated at 20 million, would transform the Eternal City into a kind of heavenly Jerusalem.

Ratzinger did not deny the symbolic power of the millennium. But he was much too sober-minded to share John Paul II's expectations for the date. He was clear that there would not be a mass new beginning. Whereas the pope wanted to counter the decline of Christianity with huge events, well publicized in the media, his guardian of the faith preached that the church must think of its message, which probably could only really be sustained by a small but vital and authentic circle of believers.

His scepticism about the millennium spectacle also found expression in his letters to Esther Betz.[5] On 18 February 2000 he wrote: 'On 16.2. I had to go to Madrid to give a lecture. To my surprise there was an audience of more than 2000. After further meetings on 17 Feb I only got home to Rome at nearly midnight. […] Here we are feeling the surge of the Holy Year very strongly. There is something special happening nearly every day.' On 7 June 2000 he noted:

> The Holy Year is bringing a lot of hullabaloo. I can hardly take my usual walk to work across St Peter's Square. The Square is either shut for an event or it is packed with so many people that it is impossible to get through. The pope loves continual new happenings and keeps us all on the go. The multitude of activities seem to enliven him – whereas I would prefer something quieter.

Either way non-Christians and especially anti-Christians were bound to take the Catholic agenda for the millennium as pure provocation. *Der Spiegel* proclaimed: 'The pope's planned millennium hoo-ha has a single purpose', namely, 'to demonstrate his church's power claim to be the custodian of the truth that alone saves, and the world's supreme moral authority.' What it offered was 'the programme of the Middle Ages'.[6] It was no surprise that Rudolf Augstein also did not keep silent. 'It will become a mock-holy year,' declared the *Spiegel* editor, for basically it was 'not even clear today whether this Jesus actually existed'. Nobody understood 'how the Christian churches managed to fill people with feelings of guilt and anxiety'.[7]

Der Spiegel had earned great credit from its coverage of political and economic scandals. However, on the question of the founder of Christianity the *Spiegel* editor persistently ignored all the findings of more recent research. The historical existence of Jesus and the veneration of him as the expected Messiah were not only attested by the gospel writers but also by many extra-biblical texts: for example, the Syrian historian Mara bar Serapion (about AD 73),

the Roman historian Tacitus (56–117) and the Jewish historian
Flavius Josephus (about 37–100). It had long been recognized that
the synoptic gospels were written 10 to 30 years after the death of
Christ, earlier than accounts of any other person in antiquity. For
example, the first writings about Alexander the Great were written
400 years after his death – which did not give anyone the idea
of doubting their credibility. Moreover, with umpteen thousand
transcripts no other manuscript of antiquity has been passed
down in so many copies as the New Testament. The text historian
Ulrich Victor believed that, apart from uncertainties about the
translation of single words or phrases and stylistic questions, anyone
reading it today would be reading it exactly as it was written
2,000 years ago.

Notwithstanding *Der Spiegel*'s predictions, John Paul II's Holy Year
was not a flop, although the expected number of visitors proved over-
optimistic. However, the World Youth Day for the millennium year
at the Tor Vergata University in Rome was attended by more than
a million Catholics and guests. On his millennial pilgrimage to the
Holy Land the pope visited the Yad Vashem memorial, to say a prayer
to commemorate the 6 million people killed simply for being Jews.
At the Wailing Wall in Jerusalem he read out in a low voice a plea for
forgiveness. After that he inserted the paper into a crack in the wall.
Cardinal Ratzinger had publicly made the millennial confession of
guilt beforehand in St Peter's Basilica. He said in conversation that
his often reported initial refusal to do so was not in accordance with
the facts. Indeed, he had questioned 'whether the many confessions
of guilt are really meaningful. But following the model of the psalms
and the book of Baruch, I have always thought it quite right that the
church should confess its guilt over the centuries.'[8]

Ratzinger was proved right in his expectations of the aftermath
of the millennium. The Holy Year was followed not by golden times
or a renaissance of faith but by dramatic events full of suffering and
distress. It began with the BSE outbreak of mad cow disease. There
were reports of glaciers melting and other warning signs of a climate
apocalypse. Then there was the global financial crisis triggered by
the Lehman Brothers bankruptcy, which threatened to drag whole
national economies into the abyss. When, on 11 September 2001, the
al-Qaeda terror planes crashed into the twin towers of the World

Trade Center in New York and into the Pentagon, the apparent security of the world collapsed.

The Catholic Church was regarded as stable, but its influence on political and social life continued to decrease. It could not gain ground anywhere for its teaching. Its positions on abortion, gene technology and celibacy were heavily criticized and even more frequently ignored. Despite its determined effort, the church failed to get a reference to God into the European Union constitution (whereas the German constitution speaks of responsibility 'to God and humanity'). For the first time in a number of Spanish and Italian schools nativity plays and Christmas celebrations were dropped. They were no longer appropriate today, especially in the light of Islam, the only religion in Europe whose numbers were growing. Within the church the gap between the progressives and traditionals was not getting any smaller. In many countries Catholics were obliged to set up their own networks of 'priests and laity faithful to Rome'. On the other hand there were protests within the church – for example, over controversial bishops such as Kurt Krenn in Austria who, like his fellow bishop Hans Hermann Groër, had to resign because of a sexual abuse scandal.

Ratzinger had tried to give the millennium his own impulse. His most important spiritual work from this period was published in the year 2000: *Der Geist der Liturgie (The Spirit of the Liturgy)*. The book was presented as a practical manual on the connections between liturgy and cosmos, holy places and the correct conduct of divine services. In a way it was a contemporary reworking of the book by Romano Guardini, with the same title, published in 1918. As he said in the foreword, Ratzinger had consciously followed Guardini's example in order 'to offer help in understanding the faith and the right conduct of its central forms of expression in the liturgy'.[9] Like Guardini, he hoped his book would 'encourage the "liturgical movement" to become a "movement towards the liturgy" in a new way'. That hope proved to be naïve.

Another contribution to the Holy Year was the disclosure of the 'third secret of Fátima', which three shepherd children said they had received from appearances of Our Lady in Cova da Iria in Fátima in Portugal in 1917. The 'child seers' had also announced a 'sun miracle' in connection with the appearances. In fact, 7,000 people camping in the fields saw an unprecedented spectacle in the sky at the appointed time. They included reporters, academics and government officials. By order of the authorities and the church, at first the three Fátima secrets could not be made public. Her confessor ordered the child seer Lucia dos Santos to burn her record. On 31 August 1941 Lucia wrote down the 'secrets' again. The first secret gave a look into Hell. The second secret said that another war would follow the First World War, if people continued to offend God and Russia was not converted.

Both secrets were finally released on 13 May 1942. But the popes hesitated to reveal the third secret. From then on speculation grew about the content of the document. Was it about the future of the church itself? Might it be about a third world war, an atomic war? Or even the end of the world? John XXIII read the message in 1959. After reading it he decided, 'Let us wait.'[10] Six years later Paul VI also decided it was better not to publish the contents of the document. The sealed envelope from Portugal remained one of the Vatican's best-guarded secrets. Only three to five people had access to it, including Ratzinger. Something happened only after the attack on John Paul II. 'Ağca knew how to shoot. He definitely shot intending to hit. But it was as if "someone" had directed and diverted that bullet,' the pope said in a memoir.[11] Wojtyła connected the Fátima secret with the attack on him. He saw its prophecy fulfilled in that attack, also because it had taken place precisely on the anniversary of the first Fátima appearance.

However, Wojtyła also hesitated. It was only in the year 2000 that he thought the time had come to publish the text of the document's four A5 pages. What was so explosive in it? In the pope's view it was above all this passage: 'And we saw in a great light, which is God: something that looked like people in a mirror, walking by, one a bishop dressed in white. We guessed it was the Holy Father.' The bishop in white was 'trembling and walking with staggering steps', through a half-destroyed city, said Sister Lucia. As he knelt before a great cross, a group of soldiers killed him with firearms and arrows.

As head of the Congregation for the Doctrine of the Faith, it fell to Ratzinger to classify the prophecy. 'What does the secret of Fátima mean? What does it tell us?' the prefect asked in his text accompanying the publication. His answer was: 'Anyone who expected exciting apocalyptic revelations about the end of the world or the future course of history, will be disappointed.' The message of Fátima for the present and future remained 'encouraging prayer as a way to save souls'. But was that really all it had been? Conspiracy theorists nurtured the suspicion that the Vatican had only published the 'third secret' incompletely. The rumour lingered so persistently that the Vatican press office was obliged to make a statement about it in 2016. Pope emeritus Benedict XVI stated personally: 'The publication of the third secret of Fátima is complete.'

The millennium was still not over. On the Catholic side a finale was still lacking, as at the end of a fireworks display. However, no one in the Vatican had expected the bang to have such reverberations. Perhaps that was due to a certain naïvety about the mechanisms of the modern media. It was a 32-page document from the house of Ratzinger. Its title was *Dominus Iesus*, a statement 'on the uniqueness and salvific universality of Jesus Christ and the church'. A forerunner to this paper, the papal *motu proprio* titled *Ad tuendam fidem* (*On the Defence of the Faith*), of 18 May 1998, had already caused a considerable stir. Because Catholic professors were falling away, in this instruction John Paul II obliged them to take an oath of loyalty to the doctrine of their church. Hans Küng compared the vow to the loyal addresses 'made to Hitler'. Referring to the pope, who was suffering from Parkinson's disease, he spoke of 'fossilized figures' who could not let go of power. Ratzinger's Congregation was also targeted: it was a 'faith police authority'.[12]

Dominus Iesus suited the millennium perfectly, but it was not a rush job. Before the text could be passed unanimously, it had to go through the whole machinery of Roman Catholic checking. There were long internal deliberations and countless working sessions in the Congregation for the Doctrine of the Faith, and also with the Council for Inter-Religious Dialogue and the Council for Christian Unity. Its content dealt with the danger to the church of relativist theories. In theological discussions the truths of the faith were either regarded as out of date or relativized. That included Christ himself, who was increasingly regarded as a particular, limited historical figure. Against that *Dominus Iesus* stressed that Catholics 'must firmly believe that in Jesus Christ the whole fullness of God really dwelt'. On the definition of 'church' the document followed the Second Vatican Council dogmatic constitution *Lumen gentium*, saying that, despite the many divisions in Christianity, the church of Christ still existed fully in the Catholic Church alone. Nevertheless, 'in churches and church communities not in full communion with the Catholic Church many saving elements and truths' were to be found. Indeed, those church communities which had not kept the valid episcopate and Eucharist were not 'churches in the true sense'. But their members were 'incorporated in Christ through baptism and are in a certain – though imperfect – communion with the church'. With regard to the world religions the paper repeated the doctrine of the Second Vatican Council, according to which they also received God's grace 'in ways that he knows'.[13]

The declaration was confirmed by the Holy Father 'with certain knowledge and by virtue of his apostolic authority', as the language of the Vatican record put it. Its central concern, the clarification of the figure of Christ for the church, received little attention. Press reports homed in on the Holy See declaring itself to be the only legitimate trustee of Christ, which aroused a storm of outrage. In Germany the chairman of the Evangelical Church Council, Manfred Kock, protested that the Vatican wanted 'evidently to turn back the clock'. 'We won't let the church in Rome deny our existence as a church,' exclaimed Bishop Margot Kässmann. Hans Küng saw it as a 'combination of medieval backwardness and Vatican megalomania'.[14] Journalists spoke of a new low to which the Ratzinger era had sunk. After the media furore it was no surprise that Catholic fellow clergy stabbed the prefect in the back. Walter Kasper complained that the language of the text had lacked the 'necessary sensitivity'. Bishop Lehmann spoke of an 'operational accident'. Johannes Friedrich, the local Evangelical bishop in Bavaria, kept his cool, saying that *Dominus Iesus* was a declaration by the Congregation of the Doctrine of the Faith and no surprise.[15]

It was to Ratzinger's credit that he did not hide behind the pope or any other colleagues but took on the full responsibility himself. However, it was not his greatest asset to communicate well in a conflict rapidly becoming heated. *Dominus Iesus* in no way presented a 'new doctrine', he said at a press conference in the press room (Sala Stampa) in Rome. The aim of the document was merely to point out certain 'errors and misunderstandings' about the doctrines of the Catholic Church, which had also been emphasized by the Second Vatican Council. *Dominus Iesus* was intended to combat the indifference that saw all churches as equal. The declaration was of an internal Roman Catholic nature. As for 'our Lutheran friends', the prefect added in a typically Ratzingerish way, he could not understand the excitement. It seemed 'completely absurd' to him if 'fortuitous historical formations' wanted to be seen as churches in the same sense as 'we believe the Catholic Church depends on the apostolic succession of bishops'. None of those other communities claimed that for itself, as Rome did. In that sense no one should be offended.[16]

Even today people still wonder whether Ratzinger wrote the disputed document himself. No, he did not, he made clear in our interview. 'Of course I co-operated on it and critically modified it and so on. But I did not write any of the documents myself, and that included *Dominus Iesus*.' He had quite consciously 'never written the Holy Office documents myself, so as not to give the impression I wanted to publicize and promote my own private theology'. He also denied speculation that there had been a quarrel about the document with John Paul II. 'The pope stood by me with incredible loyalty and kindness. In the turbulence that arose around *Dominus Iesus* he told me he wanted to defend the document unambiguously during an *Angelus*.' Wojtyła had asked Ratzinger to write the text himself. It had to be made clear and 'watertight' that he 'unreservedly approved the document'. Ratzinger went on to say that he had then 'written a short speech', 'but once again I did not want to be so harsh and I tried to write the text clearly but without harshness. After the pope read it, he asked me again: "Is that really clear enough, what I said?"'[17]

Ratzinger had made a mistake. In February 2001 John Paul II stood in St Peter's Square under a cloudless blue sky creating new cardinals. After the pope had cautiously distanced himself from *Dominus Iesus*, the media began fostering the speculation that Ratzinger was due for the sack. 'This was not only the first consistory, the first creation of new cardinals in the new third millennium,' noted Robert Leicht from *Die Zeit*, 'it was also the farewell to an era. That era bore the name of Ratzinger.' That became clear with the appointment of bishops Lehmann and Kasper, opponents of Ratzinger, as cardinals. For the 'eminently capable and eminently controversial guardian of Roman Catholic orthodoxy' this day marked 'a departure if not from power as such, then at least from the monopoly of spiritual power under the primacy of the pope'. By his recent appointment of cardinals the pope had 'clearly distanced himself both from Ratzinger's Roman centralism and from Ratzinger's central importance in the Vatican'.[18]

A short time later it became apparent how wrong the *Zeit* correspondent's analysis was. On 30 November 2002, the feast of Andrew the apostle, John Paul II officially confirmed the appointment of Ratzinger as dean of the College of Cardinals. That made Ratzinger the only cardinal with constant immediate access to the pope.[19] On the appointment of Lehmann and Kasper as cardinals, the former prefect revealed in a passage from our conversation published here for the first time:

> John Paul II had discussed the two appointments with me. Of course, he would not have appointed anyone from Germany or elsewhere as cardinal if I had spoken against it. Indeed, there were friends who told the pope I would behave in too gentlemanly a fashion in such cases and not appreciate the situation realistically enough. But it seemed to me that temperaments and views different from my own ought to have a place in the College of Cardinals, in so far as they remained within the bounds of the Catholic faith.[20]

It went completely unnoticed that the scope of Ratzinger's congregation was broadened in 2001, when the cardinal took on responsibility for cases of abuse. It had become clear to the prefect that offences, in the USA or elsewhere, were often covered up or at least not investigated with due attention. Possibly the pope himself had underestimated the problem or even acted to keep things under wraps. With the document *De delictis gravioribus* (*On Serious Crimes*), of 18 May 2001, which the prefect had sent to all officiating bishops, ordinaries, hierarchs and superiors, the world church was informed of new standards for dealing with crimes against the faith, the holiness of the sacraments and morals. The new instruction removed a paragraph in *Crimen sollicitationis* from the year 1962, which demanded that the secrecy of the confessional be kept. The jurisdiction in abuse cases was also made the responsibility of the Congregation for the Doctrine of the Faith, which could now prosecute cases independently of national or local concerns, and no longer just suspend priests but also laicize them. 'I developed the penal law,' Ratzinger said in our conversation, 'because it was very weak.' It was to prioritize victim protection and create possibilities to 'act more quickly'.

When he became pope, the former prefect also followed the zero-tolerance line against any abusers. That was confirmed by the Italian investigative journalist Gianluigi Nuzzi, who caused a stir with several insider reports from the Vatican: 'Pope Benedict XVI's battle against abuse was more decisive and severe than that of his successor,' said Nuzzi: 'Benedict removed the cloak of silence and forced his church to look to the victims. Meanwhile it has all become a "Stop and Go" process. Pope Francis has missed the decisive next step.'[21]

The prefect once again showed himself to be a historically and politically thoughtful church leader at the end of his time in office. In 2002 his congregation published a note on the place and conduct of Catholics in political life. It said: 'The present democratic societies demand new and more extensive participation of citizens – Christians and non-Christians – in public life.' Society was undergoing 'a complex cultural process, which marks the end of a period and uncertainty about the coming era'. Because of these changes, it was necessary to 'review the way humanity has progressed and gained more human living conditions'. For example, there was 'the growing responsibility towards developing countries', but there were also certain dangers caused by 'some attitudes of mind'. In particular, 'there were legal attempts to destroy the sanctity of human life'. In 'that difficult situation Catholics have the right and the duty to intervene in order to recall the meaning of life in the deepest sense and the responsibility that everyone has for it'.

Just as 'the rights of the human embryo were to be respected and defended', so must 'protection and support for the family be guaranteed, the family founded on monogamous marriage between persons of different sexes'. The 'social protection of minors' must be ensured in order to 'develop an economic order which serves the person and the common good, respects social justice and the principles of human solidarity and subsidiarity [devolution]'.[22] The prefect had no illusions about the future. 'We have to realize that the situation of national churches in Europe has changed,' he said in April 2002: 'As a result of Europe's dwindling identification with Christianity, we find a minority situation.' As this process cannot be stopped, 'the church as a minority must do everything to keep its major values effectively present. We certainly must not retreat into a cosy ghetto and say: now we are among ourselves'.[23]

Ratzinger led the way by personal example for Christians entering into public debates. He aroused international attention by his disputes with contrary intellectuals: for example, on 21 February 2000, with Paolo Flores d'Arcais, an Italian social democrat, and in May 2004 with the Italian senate president and philosopher Marcello Pera. Four months before that, his legendary debate had taken place with the formerly neo-Marxist sociologist Jürgen Habermas, which was about the 'pre-political moral foundations of a liberal state'. Thanks to Hans Küng, the discussion was attended only by a select circle of about 30 listeners, including the editors of the big German daily and weekly papers and representatives from *La Repubblica* and *Le Monde*.

The organizers still remembered that in 1998 Küng had sent furious protest letters trying to sabotage a similar conference, for Johann Baptist Metz's 70th birthday, to which Metz had also invited Ratzinger. Küng protested that it was a 'great scandal' to offer such a platform to the 'Grand Inquisitor'. It was 'like having a general conversation on human rights with the head of the KGB'. However, when Ratzinger was elected as Pope Benedict XVI, that did not prevent Küng immediately requesting a confidential conversation. After it he solemnly affirmed to the waiting journalists that there had been no need for a reconciliation: 'During all this time neither of us has ever spoken ill of the other; on the contrary.'[24]

The starting point for the disputation with Habermas was a statement by the former German constitutional court judge Ernst-Wolfgang Böckenförde, a brother of Ratzinger's former assistant Werner Böckenförde. The statement declared: 'The liberal secularized state depends on assumptions it cannot itself guarantee.'[25] The argument was about whether religion was really needed as a pre-political authority or whether the democratic state succeeded in basing its standards on secular reason alone.

The position taken by Ratzinger was not particularly surprising. Perhaps the sophistication of his arguments was impressive. But the debate really became exciting when Habermas, a last representative of the left-wing Frankfurt School, proved to be in complete agreement with Ratzinger in rejecting an anti-religious society.[26] The pugnacious spokesman for the Enlightenment declared that religion could set values for fulfilling the human task of preserving the creation. Otherwise everything was only measured by money. Habermas had already stressed in a conversation with Eduardo Mendieta that he thought Christianity was particularly fitted for this role: 'The egalitarian universalism from which the ideas of freedom and living together in solidarity sprang, is a direct legacy of Jewish justice and the Christian ethic of love.' There was 'no alternative' to that.[27] Unfortunately, this awareness was getting lost and giving way to a 'narrow-minded Enlightenment', which rejected faith and religion as 'irrational'. For an open, rational discussion the contributions 'of religious as well us non-religious citizens' were needed, Habermas told the *Neue Zürcher Zeitung*. That also went for morally complex questions such as abortion, euthanasia or pre-natal genetic modification.[28]

Shortly after the millennium Ratzinger was sure he would finally be released from his yoke. That he was firmly set on departure was shown by his provision for his long-standing *segretario particolare del prefetto*, Josef Clemens. Clemens was appointed as sub-secretary to the Congregation for the Institutes of Consecrated Life and Societies of Apostolic Life. He was also ordained as a bishop by Ratzinger personally in St Peter's. Later Clemens organized the International World Youth Days, set up by John Paul II in Cologne, Sydney, Madrid and Rio de Janeiro, which were attended by about 6.4 million participants. On 1 March 2003 Georg Gänswein began work as a new private secretary. He was a theologian from a small village in the Black Forest and had studied in Munich. In the Congregation for the Doctrine of the Faith he at first worked on the laicization of priests and applications to annul marriages.

John Paul II had gradually accepted slowing down his rhythm and planning fewer dates. However a hip replacement had been followed by dizzy spells, leading to thoughts that the strength of the 79-year-old pope would not last out much longer. At least by his 80th birthday in May 2000 he would retire. At the time *La Repubblica* was also reporting that the prefect might 'lay down his office and withdraw to meditate in his German home'.[29] The speculation flared up again when there was a major staff reshuffle in the Congregation for the Doctrine of the Faith. Tarcisio Bertone was appointed archbishop of Genoa. The sub-secretary had to be replaced because he was moved to the Apostolic Penitentiary. The *capo-ufficio* of the *sezione dottrinale* returned to being a professor, and the position of *promotor iustitiae* also had to be refilled.

Ratzinger wrote to his penfriend Esther Betz on 16 February 2003: 'No wonder rumours are gathering that my end is also in sight.' The pope did not seem 'to be thinking in that direction for the time being', he continued regretfully, 'even though I would be glad if more peaceful times were also in store for me'.

21

Agony

On the way into the third millennium the head of the largest institution in the world was a man who would not have got a job or a flat anywhere else. He was a man with trembling hands, bent and tired, with sunken head. If he stuttered into speech in his wheelchair, spit dribbled from his mouth.

The scars of the century could be read from the biography of Karol Wojtyła, from his time under the Nazis, when he rescued Jews from the ghetto, to the moment when he asked his compatriots what they had made of their chances since their liberation from atheism.

He was the first pope to visit Islamic and Buddhist countries. He was the first to pray in Assisi with representatives of the world religions. He was the first to announce consistent resistance to the Mafia. He had rehabilitated Hus, Copernicus and Galileo and acknowledged the church's historical guilt. He had organized international congresses for the rights of migrants and children. 'Don't let hope die! Don't be afraid!' he called to his public. He regarded the change in the Soviet bloc, in which he had played a part, as one of the greatest revolutions in history. Interpreted from the viewpoint of faith, it was a grace, a divine intervention, which he had no doubt was connected to the Fátima revelation.[1]

In the evenings when his wheelchair was rolled to the window to look out on St Peter's Square, his memories stirred. Of a girl he had loved. Poems he had written. How soon death had entered his life. There was his sister, who died straight after her birth, his young mother, who died of myocarditis when he was just eight years old, and his only brother, Edmund, a doctor, who had died four years later of scarlet fever. When he was 15, for the first time, death nearly hit Wojtyła personally. A playmate had found a pistol and shot at him for fun. The bullet passed over his head by a hair's breadth.

His friends called him Lolek. He was a football goalkeeper and an enthusiastic amateur player, a 'proper man', as was said. But he was also someone who spent many hours a day on his knees praying, even when he was a forced labourer in the German chemical plant Solvay. Then one day, when he returned after a ten-hour shift to their small two-bed flat in Kraków, his father had also died. He found him dead in the kitchen – of a heart attack. A few years later, when he was 23, he himself stood on the threshold of death again when a German Wehrmacht lorry ran into him. An unknown woman found him injured and unconscious in the gutter. How could it not be God's mother herself who had saved his life? He was convinced it was.

Below him in St Peter's Square a few clerics were hurrying over the pavement. Gaunt priests in long cassocks and fat bishops with red sashes, who had just left their desks in their congregations, secretariats, courts and committees. It was late. Also late in the pope's life. Once he had stood before young people together with Bob Dylan. He had travelled tirelessly all over the globe. He had set new saints in the firmament, shining stars in the darkness of a godforsaken world. He was the first pope with a global mission. Many had the impression that he was also someone who put out the light. 'After Paul VI two popes will come before the end of this time,' the Spanish child seer Conchita had proclaimed in the 1960s, like Malachy's Prophecy in the past, which had counted 112 popes until the end of time.

'You are young and the pope is old and rather tired,' he had called out to young people a few years before. 'And I tell you it makes a difference if you are 82 or 28.' Certainly, he was an old, sick man. But his frailty was not the problem. How many heads of government had praised him as 'the world's conscience'? But who among the powerful really wanted to follow him – except for meeting him in audiences? Hadn't his church as good as lost the battle to influence the future of civilization on nearly every question? On abortion, cloning of embryos, the unique character of marriage or the ban on euthanasia?

His time in office had also witnessed the abuse scandals, which had driven whole dioceses in the USA into both moral and financial ruin. Communities had developed with a kind of mishmash religion, where it was questionable whether they could still be called Catholic at all in the traditional sense. Had he really done enough to prevent his church degenerating even more, because bishops were afraid of scaring off sensitive modern people by all too stringent demands?

No, he had not abdicated, even though he had been urged to do so. Every drop of sweat on his forehead had been counted and every tremble in his right arm had been noted. If he came anywhere near his home country on his travels, they said that he had come to be buried in Poland. But in a world set on youth and practicality, in which life threatened to become increasingly valueless, he held up his suffering like a golden monstrance, *Ecce homo*: behold the man! No one could look away. As a 'witness to Christ and servant of the gospel', he declared he remained 'a man of joy and hope, a man who completely confirms the value of existence, the value of creation and the hope of a future life'. He had originally thought he would do his work by prayer, preaching and exhortation, but then he had 'grasped', as he once put it, 'that I must do it by suffering'.[2]

He had not made it easy for anyone with his countless exhortations, admonitions and pleas for repentance and conversion. He felt called to a cosmic mission, for which he believed he had received light, to see the ways of the Lord in the signs of the time. Had he been too severe? Since he had taken up office, millions of people in the West had left the Catholic Church. But was it any better for others? Despite having women priests and not having celibacy or a Roman pope, hadn't the Protestants suffered even greater losses? In the Netherlands, hitherto a hotbed of Catholic modernizers, the number of Catholics was not increasing but the number of those with no religion was – and already stood at 62 per cent. That was predicted to become 72 per cent by the year 2020.

What would have happened if the Church had liberalized itself more, just at a time of constant challenge, external and internal attacks and confrontation with a lifestyle strongly opposed to the faith? Ultimately, it would have meant a lack of authenticity, or real Christianity. 'With his uncompromising insistence and unconditional obedience, this smiling, joking, grim, thundering and often obstinate pope does not make it particularly easy for committed Catholics in his church', he read in a comment. But was numerical or political success really a measure of God? Yes, he had shuddered before the abyss of all those who called themselves church and betrayed the message of Jesus without batting an eyelid.

What really mattered was having kept and consolidated the faith, pointed a clear direction to Christ's message, without any ifs and buts. Even about things that it was difficult to make a secularized world understand. After the turbulence of the Council discussions and new definitions, hadn't the church successfully found its way back to itself? The dams had been weakened, but they had not failed.

The old pope was wheeled back from the window into his room, the *appartamento*, as it was generally called. The word had become a synonym for the small management circle round the pope, who now pulled the strings. First of all, there was his faithful secretary for 40 years. 'Pope Stanisław', as he was called behind his back, decided who could access the pope and who could not, which documents to present to the pope and which not. Dziwisz had gathered reinforcements, such as the priest Mieczysaw Mokrzycki, another Pole. Cardinals Camillo Ruini and Giovanni Battista Re had joined the staff. Others had also gained key positions. They included the plump Angelo Sodano, the most experienced of all – and the most power-conscious – and the Argentine archbishop Leonardo Sandri, his assistant.

Then there were the secret circles: for example, the 'St Gallen Mafia', with cardinals such as Carlo Maria Martini, Godfried Danneels and the German Walter Kasper, who had their own plans, soon to become apparent. 'From week to week the importance of the German Ratzinger is also growing', *Der Spiegel* reported. That year the prefect celebrated the most important service of the year in St Peter's Basilica, the Easter vigil celebrating the resurrection of Christ – actually the pope's own most special task. Ratzinger had been the first cardinal to whom Wojtyła was allowed to speak when he was in the Gemelli Clinic. Dziwisz and the doctors only allowed the others into the outer room, where they signed a visitors' book – in order to be able to tell waiting journalists that the pope was doing well.

Wojtyła was convinced the church had to re-equip itself. In the short or long term many of its buildings and structures would no longer be financially and organizationally viable. The chair of Peter is not a hereditary dynasty. And as popes usually do not have sons or daughters, there is no family tradition. According to Vatican custom, it was not even allowed to speculate during a pope's lifetime about who would succeed him. But there was only one person who could really ensure his legacy. Someone who had helped shape his papacy, as if it were his own. Someone who would keep carrying the cross and suffer in silence. And Wojtyła knew what it meant to carry your cross.

The winter was not yet over when, at the beginning of 2005, the health reports on the pope began to mount up. He kept collapsing in full view of millions of watchers, for example in September 2003 in Slovakia, on his 102nd foreign trip, where cameras sent pictures all over the world of the decline of this man who had once been so fit and sporty. 'He is about to die,' lamented the then cardinal of Vienna, Christoph Schönborn. A year later, in August 2004 (this was to be his last trip), his frail body slumped during a sermon to 300,000 people in Lourdes, the French pilgrimage site. 'Pomóz mi,' he whispered, 'help me!' A glass of water helped. 'I must finish,' he gasped, and went on preaching. Showing signs of pain, he knelt down in the grotto and laid a golden rose in honour of Mary on the floor. He confessed ambiguously: 'My pilgrimage is over. I am at the end of the road.'

Now he could only move forward in a special chair. His arm shook, his head lolled to one side, as if it was hanging on a silk thread. On 1 February 2005 he was admitted to the Gemelli Clinic with acute breathing problems. When he left the hospital, he was a sorry sight. Carefully, his body was heaved into the car: a pale, swollen figure with eyes alert in a stony face. On 24 February he returned to the clinic with flu symptoms, this time for three weeks. A trachea operation would make his breathing easier. It was 'just a small thing', the doctor said. 'A small thing?' Wojtyła whispered to the surgeon, 'I wonder for whom?'

The discussions about the pope's possible retirement ceased. Now it was more a question of how long he would last. Every day millions of Catholics prayed for his recovery. Even anti-Catholic media now paid respect to 'God's marathon man': the 'Pole on the chair of Peter' was 'the most political but also probably the most morally rigid pope there has ever been', said Der Spiegel. After 26 years in office his public life and sufferings had also made him 'the greatest media star of all time' – 'and his friends dread the day when this era comes to an end'.[3]

Christ's representative on the chair of Peter was better known than the Rolling Stones. Not even Michael Jackson had been able to mobilize 5 million people, as the pope had for the World Youth Day Mass in Manila. Although his words fell on deaf ears among the Establishment in Europe, he found a hearing among those who had long lost faith in politics. Young people streamed together wherever he summoned them. There were over a million at the 1997 World Youth Day in Paris, 2 million for the 2002 World Youth Day in Rome. Observers spoke of a rock concert without drugs. It had become a love story between the young people and the old pope, in whom no one else had confidence. 'The teenagers find him "honest" and "clear"; they are astonished at his certainty,' one newspaper noted. 'He simply knows what is right and what is wrong,' the fans answered; 'he doesn't say one thing today and another tomorrow.'[4]

The shortest papacy in church history lasted just four days, that of Stephen II in 752. The longest papacy after that of St Peter was that of Pius IX, which lasted 32 years. Once there were three competing popes at the same time. Once someone was pope three times, Benedict IX deposed and re-elected. John Paul II, whose papacy lasted a quarter of a century, was the third-longest-serving pope after St Peter and Pius IX. He became 'the first world leader', the 'global moral authority', as the British sociologist and agnostic Timothy Garton Ash called him. According to Garton Ash, all other leaders were local chiefs, occasionally with global significance. Only the pope had an overriding programme, a universal message.

The 'hurrying father' kissed the ground in 129 countries. He gave a total of 2,415 speeches in 697 cities outside Italy. He also produced an incredible amount of doctrine, with 14 encyclicals, 44 apostolic letters and hundreds of discourses. He covered about 1.2 million kilometres on 104 international journeys. That amounted to 29 round-the-world trips, three times the distance to the moon. He was proclaiming the idea of the Catholic as the all-embracing, the inner unity of I and You and We.

Karol Wojtyła mixed with the 'Little Flowers' girl dancers in Taiwan, pinched noses, waved and embraced. Or he appeared between wrecked tanks and bomb craters in Angola to demonstrate for peace. In his general audiences in Rome he received 16.8 million pilgrims and visitors. It is estimated that 250 million people worldwide experienced his live presence. As for the road to heaven,

Wojtyła was also superlative: he declared 1,338 Catholics blessed and canonized 482 saints, more than all the previous popes put together. They included the Capuchin monk Padre Pio, who was said to have predicted to the student Wojtyła in 1947: 'You will be pope, but I see blood and violence coming upon you.'[5]

On Sunday, 13 March, the pope returned once more to the Vatican from the Gemelli Clinic at 6.40 p.m. He went to the chapel to join in the lamentations, which recalled the sufferings of Christ in the Polish language. They had learned from the mistakes of the past when John Paul I, suffering from severe heart trouble, was all alone at the hour of his death. A multi-disciplinary Vatican team included ten emergency doctors. They were specialists in cardiology, infection, ear, nose and throat, internal medicine, radiology and clinical pathology, and were supported by professional nurses, a physiotherapist and a speech therapist. The cannula with a speech valve, inserted into his neck after the tracheotomy, required intensive attention, and his arthritic knee needed movement exercises. The medical task force was co-ordinated by the Polish nun and trained nurse, Tobiana, and the papal doctor Renato Buzzonetti, who was himself 81. 'He was never afraid of death, not even now when he saw the gate in the distance, behind which his meeting with God was to take place,' secretary Stanisław Dziwisz said later: 'He often had himself taken into the chapel, where he spent a long time in conversation with the Lord.'[6]

CNN and other broadcasters had rented rooms and roof terraces round St Peter's Square. Bayerischer Rundfunk acquired new mobile broadcasting units. A super-fast transmission line was reserved and could not be used to broadcast anything else, in order not to lose a single minute at the hour of the pope's death. On Palm Sunday, 20 March 2005, for the first time during his papacy, the pope was unable to celebrate Mass at the beginning of Holy Week. Ten thousand faithful in St Peter's Square waved their palm branches towards his apartment. *Giovanni Paolo*, as the young people were now calling to him, only stood for a few minutes at the window, to wave back with an olive branch. He made no attempt to smile and looked tired – and sad that he could not pronounce the blessing himself. Then he put his hand on his forehead, covered his eyes and let his fist drop to the lectern in front of him, powerless and disappointed that the words would not come out of his mouth.

Every day in his room Karol Wojtyła practised voice exercises, in order at least to be able to pronounce the *Urbi et orbi* Easter blessing to the city and the world, which he had previously given in 62 languages. Cardinal Ratzinger had to preside over the Easter Vigil on the Saturday, the liturgical celebration recalling the wait for Christ's resurrection. At the pope's wish Ratzinger had also written the text for the Stations of the Cross at the Colosseum. On the Wednesday of Holy Week Wojtyła appeared again at the open window for a few minutes to bless the faithful. But once again no sound came from his mouth. On the following day at 11 a.m. he had a shivering fit in the chapel, followed by a high temperature. A severe septic shock, resulting from a urinary tract infection, also caused cardiovascular failure. In the late afternoon Mass was celebrated at the foot of his bed. The pope concelebrated with half-closed eyes. At the consecration he feebly raised his right hand twice over the bread and wine. At 7.17 p.m. Cardinal Marian Jaworski administered extreme unction. At the end of the Mass the nuns also kissed the pope's hand after the secretaries. He said their names and added: 'for the last time'. The doctors and nurses also drew near him with great emotion. Doctor Buzzonetti pressed his hand firmly and said, 'Your Holiness, we love you and we are with you with all our heart.'

On 25 March 2005, Good Friday, a picture became an icon. On that day in St Peter's Basilica, with an imploring look John Paul II laid a plain, dark brown wooden cross, about one metre tall, into the hands of his faithful companion in battle. Here, you take it, said the intimate-seeming gesture. Now you must carry it. I no longer can.

Seen in retrospect, it was handing on the baton, which made a single papacy become a double one, the millennium papacy. And in an almost mystical way it seemed to fulfil the sign of Joseph Ratzinger's birthday, whose date he had seen early on as a special pointer for his whole life: 'At the door of Easter, but not yet in.' Now (Good Friday that year fell on the same day as the feast of the Annunciation) he began to go through the door. Liturgically, it was the hour of God's agony, that mysterious time span after his crucifixion during which Christ went into hiding, into the darkness of death. A terrible desolation, as his disciples felt. But through it the transformation to resurrection occurred, which proclaimed both to individuals and to all humanity the victory of the lord of the universe, which Christians believed saved and transformed creation into another dimension.

The grain of wheat must die in order to sprout again, as the Bible says.[7] It was a turning point. During John Paul II's long suffering the church had to understand the change of papacy as a test, a purging, in order to rethink the situation of the faith and the tasks for the future. As Ratzinger read out the text for the Stations of the Cross in the Colosseum, he delivered a shock. 'What can Jesus' third fall under the cross mean?' he began his reflection at the ninth station. 'We have thought about the fall of humanity as a whole,' he continued after a brief hesitation, 'the falling away of so many from Christ into godless secularism.' And then he beat his own breast:

> Mustn't we also think about how much Christ suffers in his church? How often the holy sacrament of his presence is abused, how often he encounters emptiness and wickedness of heart? How often we only celebrate ourselves and take no notice of him? How often his word is distorted and misused? How little faith there is in so many theories and how much empty talk there is?

Nobody guessed how true these words would prove. They anticipated the tremendous scandal in the church, which came wholly to light during the papacy of Pope Francis. In his quiet, trembling voice, both reproachful and remorseful, Ratzinger uttered statements that would later be quoted a thousand times: 'What a lot of filth there is in the church, and especially among those in the priesthood who should be most loyal to Christ! What arrogance and self-importance! How little we respect the sacrament of atonement, in which he awaits us to pick us up from our fall!'

His prayer was not yet over: 'Lord, your church often looks to us like a sinking ship that is already full of water and leaking everywhere. In your cornfield we see more weeds than wheat. Your church's dirty dress and face appal us. But it is we ourselves who soil it. We ourselves keep betraying you in word and deed.'

He pressed the point further:

> We drag you to the ground by our fall, and Satan laughs, because he hopes you won't be able to stand up again from this fall. That

In 1978 Archbishop Joseph Ratzinger greeted Roger Schutz, the founder of the Taizé community, at the ecumenical prayer night in the Cathedral of Our Lady in Munich. He gave him communion as a 'fully Catholic Christian at heart' and developed a deep friendship with him.

Together with German and Polish bishops, Joseph Ratzinger (*right of picture*) prays at the Auschwitz concentration camp on 13 September 1980.

Munich was an important stage on John Paul II's visit to Germany in November 1980. The Polish pope had twice invited the German archbishop in vain to come to Rome. The third time he asked it was an order. The two church leaders formed a perfect team: 'There was the humour and then the piety, which you felt had nothing artificial about it.'

Full of compassion, the prefect of the Congregation for the Doctrine of the Faith gives communion to the severely ill John Paul II. Joseph Ratzinger stood firmly beside Karol Wojtyła for a quarter of a century to keep the ship of Peter on course through stormy times.

As dean of the College of Cardinals it was Joseph Ratzinger's task to celebrate John Paul II's funeral mass on 8 April 2005. Five million people gathered in Rome to pay their last respects to the dead 'millennium pope', who was buried in a plain wooden coffin.

A sensation. In one of the shortest conclaves in history, Joseph Ratzinger was elected as the first German pope for nearly 500 years. On 19 April 2009 he stepped out onto the balcony of St Peter's as Pope Benedict XVI to present himself as a 'simple labourer in the Lord's vineyard'.

The pope and his private secretary Georg Gänswein presented a *bella figura*, which led to 'Benedetto mania' during the first years of his papacy.

At his summer residence in Castel Gandolfo, Benedict XVI worked on his Jesus trilogy. He was the first pope to write a Christology, his comprehensive theological work earning him the title of modern doctor of the church.

Hundred of thousands of young people exuberantly welcomed Benedict XVI to the Cologne World Youth Day on 18 August 2005.

One of the most significant changes of Benedict XVI's papacy was the *motu proprio 'Summorum pontificum'*, which reintroduced the 'Old Mass' as the extraordinary form of the Latin rite. Ratzinger was convinced that the fate of the faith and the church depended on the liturgy.

The mass celebrated on 20 August 2005 in Marienfeld near Cologne on the twentieth World Youth Day had over a million participants and was the biggest religious ceremony ever held in Germany. Benedict celebrated Jesus as the 'pole star of human freedom'.

Benedict XVI meets with former concentration camp prisoners at Auschwitz-Birkenau, 28 May 2005.

On his 2009 trip to Israel the German pope visited the Wailing Wall in Jerusalem. After the troubles caused by the Williamson affair, the relationship between Judaism and the Catholic Church became better than ever.

Benedict XVI prays at Ground Zero in New York with relatives of the victims of the 2001 9/11 attacks.

After his 2009 visit to Cameroon and Angola, Benedict XVI visited Benin on his second trip to Africa. A girl with a drum greeted him in the parish of Saint Rita in Cotonou.

An action which changed the papacy forever. To the shock of the cardinals assembled in the Sala del Concistoro, Benedict XVI announced his resignation on 11 February 2013. It was the first resignation of a reigning pope in the history of the Catholic Church. Benedict gave his declining energy as the reason for his retirement.

Rome, 28 February 2013: pilgrims waved sadly to Benedict XVI as his helicopter flew over the dome of St Peter's on his way to Castel Gandolfo. It was the last day of his eight year papacy.

There had never been a picture like this one: two popes in a friendly meeting. On 30 June 2015, Pope Francis visited his predecessor in the Mater Ecclesiae convent in the Vatican garden. 'Benedict covers my shoulders and back with his prayers,' he said, Benedict's wisdom was 'God's gift'.

you yourself will be dragged down by your church's fall and lie on the ground defeated. And yet you will stand up again. You have stood up again, risen again, and you can pick us up again with you. Heal your church and make it holy. Heal us and make us holy.[8]

On Easter Sunday, 27 March 2005, John Paul II appeared at his window again. He stood for 13 minutes, holding the paper with his text in his hand. About 150,000 people had gathered in St Peter's Square to receive the *Urbi et orbi* blessing. John Paul II wanted to speak; he struggled with his words. It was a shattering scene. He raised his arms in despair and became a dumb witness. Silently he made a big sign of the cross with his right hand – over the church and the world. 'Perhaps it would be better,' he finally whispered to his secretary, 'for me to die, if I can no longer do the job I have been entrusted with.' Then he added, 'Your will be done ... *Totus tuus.*'[9]

Since Wojtyła was no longer able to arrange his diary himself, he left it completely to his staff. 'It was the time when various newspapers were criticizing the so-called flaunting of his suffering,' Dziwisz recalled. 'To tell the truth those criticisms hit me and others in the Holy Father's immediate circle far more than him. He took little notice of them.'[10] But whereas others criticized the publicity surrounding Wojtyła's illness as almost obscene, Ratzinger withheld any comments at all. 'He is a man who does not speak about others if he is distressed about something or finds it hard,' his secretary Gänswein said.[11] Nevertheless, he said he was convinced that during the years of his suffering the sick pope had given his papacy a depth that it did not have before.

On 1 April 2005, a Friday devoted to the Sacred Heart of Jesus, events came to a head. In retrospect, for Ratzinger their complexity could only be explained by divine providence. They were full of extraordinary symbolism. At 6 a.m a fully conscious Wojtyła celebrated Mass. In the late morning 'his body was shaken from inside', Dziwisz recalled. His temperature rose to nearly 40 degrees. The doctors diagnosed a severe septic shock with cardiovascular failure. On that day Ratzinger had been invited to give an evening lecture and stay overnight in Subiaco, about 70 kilometres east of Rome. The following morning he was due to celebrate a pontifical Mass. Subiaco had been a sanctuary for St Benedict. Around the year

500 he meditated for three years there in a cave before he founded his monasteries and became the father of Western monasticism.

The reason for the prefect's visit was the presentation of the 'St Benedict Prize for the promotion of life and the family in Europe', awarded to him by the Vita e Famiglia (Life and Family) association. His talk was advertised with the title 'Europe in the Crisis of Cultures'. But that morning when he got an alarming telephone call from Dziwisz, Ratzinger hurried to the pope's sickbed. He did not know that this would be their last meeting. There was a deep spiritual friendship between him and Karol Wojtyła. It was based on mutual affection, respect for each other's abilities and the will to steer the apparently decrepit ship of the church through the storms of the time. It needed captains who knew the course and could keep to it. The meeting was short. John Paul could no longer speak. Ratzinger asked the pope to bless him once more. When Wojtyła raised his hand in blessing, Ratzinger bent over the sickbed and whispered: 'Holy Father, thank you for everything you have done.'[12]

After the prefect other members of the Curia came to say goodbye to the pope. Ratzinger considered cancelling Subiaco, but Cardinal Secretary of State Sodano advised him not to. No one knew how things would go with Wojtyła. Ratzinger was undecided. 'But as so often, if Sodano said go, he went,' Gänswein reported. The two cardinals agreed that Sodano's secretary, Monsignor Pioppo, would telephone as soon as the situation got any worse.

The journey to Subiaco took about an hour. Alfredo the chauffeur was at the wheel, and Don Giorgio was in the seat beside the driver. 'Take your mobile phone into the lecture, you can set it to silent,' Ratzinger said to his secretary, Georg Gänswein. In the packed Subiaco church Gänswein sat on a side-seat in the front row, so that he could intervene at once. Ratzinger had reached the third and final part of his talk, which he had constructed very precisely like an academic lecture. 'Christianity must also remember,' he said, 'that it is the religion of the Logos. It is faith in the *creator spiritus*, the creator spirit, from whom all reality proceeds.' Catholics had to take care to live by a faith that 'stems from the creative reason and is therefore open to everything that is really reasonable'. However, today it was no longer as it once was, 'when the great fundamental convictions established by Christianity for the most part stood firm and appeared indisputable'.

When Gänswein's mobile vibrated, it was Sodano's secretary saying, 'It's coming to the end for the pope.' 'We'll leave immediately', Ratzinger decided. When they arrived in night-time Rome, he saw that St Peter's Square was full of people praying for *Giovanni Paolo* with candles in their hands. They kept looking up at the dimly lit window on the third floor of the Apostolic Palace. The pope was still alive.

No one knew what legacy Ratzinger had received from John Paul II. He himself did not guess that with his Subiaco lecture he had written the draft for the sermon that he would give 16 days later at the Mass to elect a pope. Or that the sermon would acquire a special significance, like his Genoa speech, with which he had pointed the direction of the Second Vatican Council. His Subiaco talk's key statement was that in the modern world God would be excluded 'from public consciousness in a way humanity had never known before, either by complete denial or by deciding his existence was unprovable and uncertain and therefore relegating it to the subjective area, an area not relevant to public life'.

In answer to the argument that led to the omission of God from the preamble to the new European constitution, Ratzinger said:

> The assertion that a reference to the Christian roots of Europe hurts the feelings of the many non-Christians in Europe is not convincing, because it is above all about a historical fact, which no one can seriously deny. Who would be hurt? Whose identity will be threatened? Muslims, who are often invoked here, do not feel threatened by the fundamentals of our Christian ethics but by the cynicism of a secularized culture that denies their own fundamental values. Neither will our Jewish fellow citizens be hurt by a reference to the Christian roots of Europe, because these reach back to Mount Sinai [...] Mentioning God does not hurt those belonging to different religions; what hurts them is the attempt to create a human society wholly without God.

His lecture continued by saying the true opposition 'characterizing the world today' was 'not between the various religious cultures but between humanity's radical emancipation from God, from the roots of life, on the one hand, and the great religious cultures, on the other'. Relativism had become such a 'dogmatism believing it has the ultimate rational knowledge and that it is right to regard everything else as merely an obsolete stage of humanity, which it is appropriate to dismiss as relative'.

At the end of his speech, quivering with fierce emotion, Ratzinger called for courage and loyalty to the faith:

> What we need above all at this moment of history are people who make God believable in this world by an enlightened and active faith. We need people who look straight towards God and thus grasp what true humanity is. We need people whose understanding is lit by God's light and whose hearts God has opened, so that their understanding speaks to other people's understanding and their hearts can open other people's hearts. God can only return to humanity through people who have been touched by God.[13]

The pope had survived the night, but on Saturday morning 2 April, he was beginning to lose consciousness. Later on in the morning there was another sharp temperature rise. It was hopeless. Any new treatment was useless now. At 3.30 p.m. the Holy Father whispered in a weak, barely audible voice to Sister Tobiana with a final request: 'Let me go to the Lord now.' With difficulty he asked for John's gospel to be read to him. A picture of the shackled, suffering Christ hung on the wall. Beside it there was a picture of Our Lady of Częstochowa. There was a photo of his parents on the small table. Below in St Peter's Square many thousands of people had gathered again. They were hoping and fearing. It was the vigil of the feast of the Divine Mercy, a special day that John Paul II had introduced into the church's liturgical year to commemorate the vision of the Polish nun and mystic Faustyna Kowalska, who had died in 1938. It had become a central theme of his mission. 'Proclaim my great, fathomless mercy to the world,' Jesus had told Faustyna in her vision, 'prepare the world for my second coming. Before I come as judge I still open wide the gates of my mercy.'[14]

According to Polish tradition a small candle lit the semi-darkness of the room when, shortly before 7 p.m., the pope fell into a coma. When the monitor also recorded the decrease in vital functions, there was a sense of certainty. At 8 p.m. Stanisław Dziwisz, together with Cardinal Marian Jaworski, Archbishop Stanisław Ryłko and two Polish priests, began the Mass for the feast of the Divine Mercy at the foot of the pope's bed. The house nuns, a few priests and friends, the doctors and nursing staff gathered round the altar and sang Polish hymns. At exactly 9.31 p.m. it pleased the Lord of the universe to call home to himself his servant on Earth Karol Jósef Wojtyła of Wadowice, the 263rd successor to the apostle Peter, and head of the holy Roman Catholic Church for 26 years. When Dr Renato Buzzonetti confirmed the pope's death, all those present spontaneously broke into one of the most majestic and moving Christian hymns, the *Te Deum*:

We praise thee, O God: we acknowledge Thee to be the Lord.
All the earth doth worship Thee, the Father everlasting.
To Thee all Angels cry aloud: the Heavens and all the powers
therein.
To Thee Cherubim and Seraphim continually do cry,
Holy, Holy, Holy: Lord God of Hosts.[15]

At the end of the hymn the words

O Lord, save Thy people: and bless Thine heritage.
Govern them and lift them up for ever

mingled with the unanimous prayer rising from the Christian people in St Peter's Square to the pope's room. As the light became brighter in the *appartamento*, they all knew that they had lost a great pope.

The representative of the secretariat of state, the Argentine archbishop Leonardo Sandri, announced the death of John Paul II through a megaphone from the *palco*, the small roofed balcony in front of St Peter's Basilica. He was greeted by a breathless silence below among the hundreds of thousands who had come to the square and surrounding streets to be near the pope in his final hours. For a moment it was as though, not only in the city of Rome but in the wider world, the heart had stopped beating. The *Frankfurter Allgemeine Zeitung* wrote later: 'Never was seen a ruler, a mighty one, who was so little, so lowly, so helpless, so ill and so pitiful, but also never one who was so great in his weakness, so eloquent in his dumbness.'[16]

When the crowd's pulse began beating again, thunderous applause broke out. Nearly everyone had tears in their eyes. A choir struck up an emotional *Ave Maria*. People bowed in gratitude for the good shepherd on the chair of Peter, who had accompanied them for half his life and given them something that they could not do without.

The pope's death interrupted daily life all over the world. It ousted all the other news, as if that was just sound and fury. Politics was no longer of interest or even politicians. The Italian government announced three days of national mourning. President Carlo Azeglio Ciampi declared that the whole of Italy was weeping for the Holy Father: 'We loved him, we admired him for his strength, his ideas, his courage, his passion and his ability to give us values and hope.' All sporting events in Italy were cancelled, including football matches. Even the broadcasting of Formula 1 was cancelled. The newspaper headlines announcing the death of John Paul II showed how deeply attached Italy was to this pope and how much they respected him. *Il Manifesto*: 'There will never be anyone like him again.' *L'Avvenire*: 'The Deepest Void.' *La Stampa*: 'The whole world mourns for the pope.' *Corriere della Sera*: 'The pope who changed the world.' *La Repubblica*: 'Addio Wojtyła.' *Il Tempo*: 'Ciao Karol.'

Ratzinger heard of John Paul II's death by telephone from Cardinal Secretary of State Angelo Sodano. Together with the *camerlengo* or chamberlain (Cardinal Eduardo Martínez Somalo), Ratzinger as dean of the College of Cardinals had the task of confirming the pope's death. According to the prescribed ritual, the chamberlain called to the pope twice by his name in order to establish ' *Vere Papa mortuus est*' – the pope is really dead. Then he covered the Holy Father's face with a white cloth before the corpse was washed, dressed and brought into the private chapel. The next day it was laid out in an open coffin in the Sala Clementina and after that in St Peter's Basilica. Part of the ritual was for the chancellor of the Camera Apostolica to hand over to the *camerlengo* the fisherman's ring with which the pope sealed official documents, in order to make it unusable.

Together with the pope, all the heads of the Vatican dicasteries became 'dead' and immediately no longer operative, even the cardinal secretary of state and the prefect of the Congregation for the Doctrine of the Faith. But as dean of the College of Cardinals, it fell to Ratzinger to lead John Paul II's funeral celebrations. 'If he was even more silent than ever, it was during those days,' Gänswein noted. 'We only spoke about official business.' There was an extraordinary mood in St Peter' s Square. It was clear that the death of the pope of the century would trigger a mighty tremor. When pictures were shown of the young people filing past to bow to the pope for the last time, it was clear: this was not a farewell, it was a resurrection.

They all came. There were people like Mia Fiumara, a lawyer from Messina, who stood for ten hours in the sun in order to be the first to be allowed into St Peter's. Or the pizza baker Raul Mazzanti, who had taken the early morning train from Pesaro with his daughter. Or church groups – Franciscan friars with white cord girdles, and behind them young girls from the Italian provinces, with rucksacks, flags and banners. And many, many Poles. It was probably the largest pilgrimage in the history of Christianity – a happening at which rosaries were recited, ancient litanies muttered, as if it were the most obvious thing in the world to give the Blessed Virgin her rightful place even in an age of Google and Microsoft. As the longest funeral procession humanity had ever seen – with up to 2 million taking part – made its way through the streets of Rome, it was as if a capsized ship was righted again by a mighty heave given it by a new generation of uninhibited and devout young Catholics who wanted to re-experience the faith in all its wealth and vitality.

Joseph Ratzinger's pain at the loss of his friend could clearly be seen as he introduced the ceremony at the altar in St Peter's Square. Blue rings round his eyes spoke of wakeful nights; his snow-white hair showed his advanced age. The wind kept ruffling the 165 cardinals' vestments as they stood in front of St Peter's to concelebrate the Mass. Opposite them, on the right beside the steps, world leaders had gathered, filling 300 square metres. Chancellors and monarchs, heads of state and heads of churches, revolutionaries grown old, ayatollahs and modern global players like Kofi Annan. There was a total of 70 heads of state and government, as well as 2,500 invited civil and religious authorities. Never before had a US president bowed to a dead pope. Bill Clinton, together with George Bush senior and junior, all three came to pause before the pope laid out in his coffin.

The sun shone from an almost cloudless pale blue sky, but the wind blew where it would. 'Follow me!' Ratzinger proclaimed, copying that scene which the spring breeze, whipping over the pages, blew open in the red book of the gospel lying on the plain wooden coffin: 'Follow me! Those succinct words of Christ served as a key to understanding the message of the life of our beloved pope John Paul II. Today we bury his mortal remains in the ground as a seed of immortality, while our hearts are full of sadness but also full of joyful hope and deep gratitude.'

Three thousand five hundred journalists had been accredited to cover John Paul II's funeral. Apart from China, television broadcasters sent pictures to every country in the world. More than a billion people followed the event live on screen. Other estimates put it at 2 billion, which would make it the biggest audience in the history of television. For them the Mass would have been an opportunity to put themselves in the picture. But Ratzinger himself spoke only of Wojtyła, who had learned from God's mother 'to be like Christ'. Visibly moved, with a sweeping gesture of his left arm, he concluded:

> We can be sure that our beloved pope is standing now at the window of the Father's house, and sees us and is blessing us. Yes, bless us Holy Father. We entrust your dear soul to God's mother, your mother, who guided you every day and will lead you now into the eternal glory of her Son, Jesus Christ our Lord.[17]

The man from Poland dreamed of a 'civilization of life and love'. So it seemed as if it was preordained that this pope should be called to eternity on the vigil of the feast of the Divine Mercy. A more loving legacy than this pointer to the kindness of Jesus could scarcely be imagined. And hadn't Wojtyła always spoken enigmatically of a 'new spring for the human spirit'? Now it actually was springtime in Rome, as the mourning procession, spurred on by young people sustained by the power of an uninhibited love of Jesus, was transformed into an unforgettable demonstration of faith. It gave an idea of how the church might look if it headed towards Jesus again.

22

Conclave

Sede vacante, the leaderless phase between two popes, is a strange time. No light burned any longer in the Apostolic Palace, and it almost seemed as if the darkness and emptiness of these weeks spread over the whole Christian world.

During the nine days following the solemn funeral of a pope (called *novendiali*, from the Latin *novem dies*, 'nine days'), the cardinals pray for the repose of his soul, in accordance with the *Ordo exsequiarum romani pontificis*). They also gather in the synod hall for the *congregationes generales*, a kind of pre-conclave in which individual speakers give a brief analysis of how they see the situation and current priorities for the church. A special congregation consisting of the *camerlengo* and three cardinals runs the church business. They can take practical decisions but no important ones.

The previous conclave had taken place 26 years, 5 months and 16 days ago. In October 1978 the Iron Curtain was still up. Since then a whole generation had not experienced how it felt when millions of people worldwide became excited to see black or white smoke rising out of a slender chimney. Nevertheless, the head of the Catholic Church represented not just a country but, so to speak, a single great nation spread over all the continents. And this time it was not seeking a Pius XIII or XIV, following on from before, but the first pope of the third millennium.

International attendance at the old pope's funeral had been strong. Interest in the choice of the new pope went beyond anything that had ever been seen at a conclave. Seven thousand special correspondents descended upon Rome. Television broadcasters positioned themselves in the Via della Conciliazione. Great telephoto lenses were directed at St Peter's Square and the Apostolic Palace from a hundred roof terraces. The state of the Sistine Chapel chimney was reported day and night, as were the speculations of the *Vaticanistas*, who claimed inside information 'from the long corridors behind the closed Vatican walls'.

Many regarded Ratzinger as a 'popemaker', because of his position, his reputation and his influence. But he was barely mentioned as a possible candidate. A 'Grand Inquisitor' as Christ's representative? An unsociable intellectual on the chair of the 'fisher of people'? And a German to boot! 'Pope Ratzinger would be a shock' was a headline in the *Süddeutsche Zeitung*. The German CDU (Christian Democratic Union) politician Heiner Geissler declared that, instead of making Ratzinger pope, they should make him a village priest.

Ratzinger himself had said often enough that he was looking forward to retirement. After the conclave he wanted to go on retreat at Scheyern Abbey and then on holiday with his brother Georg to Mallersdorf Abbey. He had booked the flight from Rome to Munich for 4 May.

Even though he was nearly 78, there was still something boyish about him. But the rings round his eyes also showed the strain his job had caused him. His heart was weak, and he was blind in his left eye. 'Dear Brother Karl,' he had written a few weeks before to the Bamberg archbishop, Karl Braun: 'I had a second heart pacemaker inserted a little while ago. May the Lord pace the heart better than a machine can.'[1]

Even as a prefect he had asked to be discharged three times and been forced to continue in the job. But was it so extraordinary that, once he came out of the shadow, one who had until then been the second-in-command should display a quality that no one had expected? 'My life has not been coincidental,' Ratzinger once stressed, 'but someone foresees and thinks ahead of me and arranges my life.'[2] When he was asked if he was ever afraid of God, in the spring of 2000 his answer was: 'I wouldn't call it afraid. We know from Christ what God is like, that he loves us.' Then he added: 'However, I always have this burning feeling about my vocation. The idea that God has of me, of what I could and should give.'[3]

Ratzinger cannot have been unaware that his colleagues' desires were growing. To general astonishment, on Monday, 4 April 2005 the

Corriere della Sera's list of the *papabili*, the promising candidates for the papacy, had Joseph Ratzinger at the top. The Munich *Abendzeitung* observed: 'They no longer call him *il Tedesco*, the German. His image in the Vatican City has no nationality. He is regarded as a man of the world, with a brilliant intellect.'[4] Even *Time* magazine in New York regarded him as the appropriate 'transitional pope'. British and Irish bookmakers put him in top place as Wojtyła's 'natural successor', above Jean-Marie Lustiger from Paris and Carlo Maria Martini from Milan. The odds on Ratzinger were 3 to 1.

No candidates stand for election to the chair of Peter. Public canvassing is not allowed. Oral agreements or plots to promote a particular candidate are completely forbidden. The world's most secret and fascinating election is a mixture of divine service and conscientious inquiry, oracle and debate, both a religious act with meditation and prayer – and a straightforward assessment with speeches and replies. According to the Catholic faith, it is ultimately for the action of the Holy Spirit to decide who, to the best of the electors' knowledge and belief, should become head of Christ's church.

Nevertheless: popes do not fall from heaven. Who is both the most suitable and the most worthy? With whom can the church remain true to the gospel and preach it truly in a changed world? Who is capable of guarding and carrying on the rich legacy of great predecessors? The new pope should have a cultured education, knowledge of the modern world and be mobile. At the same time he should lean quietly on Christ's breast. He should have a heart for the poor – but also have an eye for economic matters. He should have tireless energy for thousands of meetings and at the same time have a feeling for the yearnings of the masses. Lies and deceit, an incontinent life or lectures with million-dollar fees would not be tolerated. He should be rational and pragmatic and also be a radical follower of Christ with matchless devotion. He should be kind and warm and, as an absolute monarch, also rigorous and incorruptible. His statements should be clear and unambiguous but also conciliatory, so as not to divide the flock. And yes: fluent Latin and Italian are required. He should also have a pleasing appearance. At least, he should not be too ugly. However, he does not have to be *infallible*. That dogma only relates to doctrinal statements that are seen as definitive and proclaimed by the pope.

The shoes of the fisherman are not ballet shoes. But after a giant like Wojtyła wouldn't any successor seem too small for them? With John Paul II, Jesus' message had been embedded in a certain folklore and events that could be televised. The pope himself was very popular. For continuity in change, the new pope had to carry on what his predecessor had done well. But if possible, he should also improve on what had been less successful. Now that the emotions of mourning the old pope's death were over, all the remaining problematic things from his papacy had to be soberly assessed.

The church had been lucky with the popes of the last three to four hundred years. That cannot be said about all the popes in its long history. For example, Alexander VI, the famous Borgia pope, ended his life of spectacular luxury with foam spewing out of his mouth. His tongue was monstrous, gases hissed out of every orifice. His whole body was so swollen that the undertakers apparently had to jump on his belly in order to be able to close the coffin lid. However, it is remarkable that, even with popes who were far from holy, after their death none of their documents was allowed to be rewritten or thrown away.

Ratzinger was prepared. During the previous summer he had read to his now blind brother a standard work on the history of the popes by the Munich church historian Georg Schwaiger. In a letter to his previous fellow student on 15 February 2005 he praised Schwaiger for his 'strict objectivity and the accuracy of his information [...] This historical truth appears in all its aspects and the negative ones are not suppressed.' For 'thus it also appears how the papacy fulfils a task given to it by the Lord, as another power operates through human weakness'.[5]

As dean of the College of Cardinals, Ratzinger not only had to lead the funeral service for John Paul but was also in charge of the arrangements for the election of his successor. The general congregations had to put together the various presentations by the cardinals, from which to draw a synthesis of the main points to be considered. As a former college lecturer, Ratzinger did not seem to find his new role disagreeable. Now his walk became 'a bit more energetic than before, as if he were hosting the show', a reporter remarked: 'He went from one person to another informally, greeting here and chatting there, with his shiny golden cardinal's ring glittering.'[6]

As prescribed for all cardinals in the apostolic constitution *Universi Dominici Gregis* of 1996, during the *novendiali* Ratzinger wore the black cassock with red piping and sash, together with skull-cap and pectoral cross. At the first sitting of the general congregation, which took place daily between 9 a.m. and noon, he confidently took the chair and opened the meeting with a prayer. Then he summoned the cardinals to be sworn in. Each cardinal had to swear 'to make no use of transmitting or receiving devices of any sort during the conclave' or use any photographic apparatus – 'so help me God and the holy gospels, which I touch with my hand'. He also instructed his colleagues neither to give any interviews nor hold any private talks in the corridors. The first to come to the microphone was Cardinal Martini, the archbishop emeritus of Milan. The Jesuit Martini was regarded as the figurehead of the progressive wing and a constant opponent of the Wojtyła–Ratzinger line. Self-mockingly, he described himself as the 'ante-pope', which could sound like 'anti-' as well as 'pre'- pope. He overran the prescribed time of seven minutes and went on for twice as long as he jumped round an obstacle course, confronting collegiality between bishops and Curia, bioethics and family policy. At the end he spoke of the sick Wojtyła. That recent experience made it necessary in future to have more precise rules to introduce and order a pope's retirement. Within a few minutes Martini's speech caused enough excitement for the list of speakers for the remaining sessions to be abandoned.[7]

The term 'conclave' – from the Latin *con clave*, 'with key'– relates both to the keys to the kingdom of heaven, which would be given to Peter's successor, and to the strictly locked room in which the voting took place. Until the papal election of 1978 the electors still had to spend three days in the rooms around the Sistine Chapel. Their accommodation consisted of an iron bedstead and a wash-basin. The windows were bricked up, and the doors were sealed with silk ribbons. John Paul II changed this to allow the electors to stay in St Martha's guesthouse, the Casa Santa Marta. But here too they were forbidden to communicate in any way until the public announcement. The window shutters were sealed, the televisions removed and the telephone lines disconnected. The strict secrecy was to ensure the vote's independence. Only the room service telephones worked. Of course, the cardinals did not have either their own mobile phones or computers.

The Vatican security service checked the Sistine Chapel, where the voting took place, with particular care. Millions of visitors came to marvel at it every year. Unlike in previous conclaves laser microphones could pick up conversations via vibrations in the window-panes. Even the smallest bugging devices in the furniture, ceiling or walls could carry information outside. Now jammers under a specially constructed false floor were introduced to prevent any mobile phone communications, and as a defence against bugging an electronic jamming screen was installed. Lift attendants, housekeepers, cooks, cleaners and technicians were sworn to secrecy. Anyone who dared pass on even the most unimportant information to a third party was threatened with excommunication and loss of their job. According to papal decree, the staff were not permitted even to 'have a conversation' with the cardinal electors if they met them by chance.

Essentially, any male Catholic can become pope. He does not even have to be a priest (though that has not happened since 627). Until the ninth century the bishop of Rome was chosen by the people of Rome. Because the choice became a contest between the interests of Roman feudal cliques, the German emperor Heinrich III decided unceremoniously to choose the popes himself. At the Third Lateran Council, in 1179, Alexander III from Siena (Roland Bandinelli in civil life) changed that to requiring the vote to have a two-thirds majority of the cardinals.[8] That did not get rid of the mixture of politics, corruption and nepotism. In his memoirs Pope Pius II (Enea Silvio Piccolomini) recalled with disgust the stitch-up by which he himself became pope in 1458. The strings were pulled while on the privy, he wrote, 'the right place for a vote of that kind'.[9]

Some conclaves made a decision in a few hours, such as the election of Julius II on 31 October 1503. Others were long-drawn-out affairs, often for weeks, or even months. They were sometimes held in the church of St John Lateran (the actual papal church), sometimes in Avignon or Constance and, with political turmoil, also in Venice.[10] The longest papal election, in the palace of the bishop of Viterbo, lasted nearly three years, although only 18 cardinals took part in it. They only managed to agree on a compromise candidate on 1 September 1271. That was because angry Catholics at first locked in the procrastinating assembly, then rationed their food and finally took the roof off.

Only a pope has the legal authority to make new rules for a conclave. Like Pius X, Pius XI, Pius XII, John XXIII and Paul VI before him, John Paul II had also introduced a reform. In the Constitution on the Vacancy of the Apostolic See in 1996 he changed the voting process, as well as making new provisions for secrecy and the cardinals' accommodation. As Paul VI had already laid down, only cardinals who had not completed their 80th year of life before the beginning of the *sede vacante* had the right to vote. Voting was to take place in two voting periods, in the morning and afternoon. The names on the ballot papers were read out loud, and a voting officer punctured the papers with a needle and threaded them onto a string. They were then burned every day in the stove, which was used for the first time in 1939. If black smoke rose, the conclave continued. If after three days the required two-thirds majority of the votes had not been achieved, there was a day off for prayer and 'relaxed conversation between the electors'. There followed a maximum of seven more rounds of voting, then a pause, then seven more rounds and so on. If after 30 rounds there was still no decision, then the result could be decided by a simple majority.

John Paul's admonition was particularly important:

With the same insistence shown by my predecessors, I earnestly exhort the Cardinal electors not to allow themselves to be guided, in choosing the pope, by friendship or aversion, or to be influenced by favour or personal relationships towards anyone, or to be constrained by the interference of persons in authority or by pressure groups, by the suggestions of the mass media, or by force, fear or the pursuit of popularity. Rather, having before their eyes solely the glory of God and the good of the church, and having prayed for divine assistance, they shall give their vote to the person, even outside the College of Cardinals, who in their judgement is most suited to govern the universal Church in a fruitful and beneficial way.

In Chapter VI, Wojtyła stated that after the pope's death 'in all cities and other places, at least the more important ones [...] humble and persevering prayers are to be offered to the Lord that he may enlighten the electors and make them so like-minded in their task that a speedy, harmonious and fruitful election may take place, as the salvation of souls and the good of the whole people of God demand'.[11]

On the 'Vaticanistas' Stock Market', as a column in the Corriere della Sera was called, Ratzinger was quoted high a week before the beginning of the conclave. During his years in Rome he had earned high esteem among bishops worldwide. He was respected not only as a vigilant guardian of the Catholic faith but also for his theology, rooted in a deep piety. It was too soon for the Brazilian Cláudio Hummes. The Nigerian Francis Arinze was an outsider. The German Bild newspaper's expert, Andreas Englisch, knew that the conclave would last 'a very long time' and would probably end up with a South American. Or it might come up with 'Cardinal Puljic of Sarajevo. He is familiar with Muslims, knows the Qur'an from start to finish. He was a hero because during the war he stuck it out in Sarajevo.'[12]

It was the stage of mutterings, machinations, calculated friendships and malicious jibes. 'You meet, eat together, drink sambuca.' Cardinal Kasper enthused about his 'informal meetings in the afternoon and evening', which were 'not to be underestimated'.[13] Meanwhile Cardinal Lehmann used every conversation to describe the qualities required by the new pope. All ones that apparently Ratzinger did not have. The Welt correspondent Paul Badde reported on a confidential meeting three days after Wojtyła's funeral, at which Cardinals Achille Silvestrini, Karl Lehmann and Walter Kasper, as well as cardinals from England, Belgium, Lithuania and Italy, had attempted 'to develop a strategy for the election of one of their desired candidates'.[14] One of the groups had come out strongly for Carlo Maria Martini, not that they thought Martini was right for the job. He was 78 years old, spent most of his time in the Holy Land and suffered from Parkinson's disease. But when it became clear that Ratzinger was in fact a candidate to be taken seriously, the voting for Martini reached a stalemate. It could only be solved by seeking a completely new name.

One who regarded himself as papabile was Cardinal Godfried Danneels, archbishop of Brussels and primate of Belgium. Before his arrival in Rome he released a 'ten-point programme' to the international press on the future of the church. He thought well enough of his chances to consider the name John XXIV, if he were to be elected. Later on, at the launch of his memoirs, he confessed that he had been a member of 'a sort of mafia club' that strove to prevent the election of a Pope Ratzinger at all costs. The group was founded by Cardinal Martini in 1996 and called St Gallen (after the place where they met). It aimed to torpedo the policy of John Paul II and to make the church 'much more modern' by things that were thought of as 'reforms'. Ratzinger did not know of the existence of the St Gallen group.[15] As well as Danneels and Martini, its members included the Italian Cardinal Achille Silvestrini, the Germans Lehmann and Kasper, Audrys Bačkis from Lithuania and the Dutch Adrianus Simonis. The group's clear favourite for the current election was Jorge Bergoglio. Danneels hit the headlines in 2010, because when he was in office as archbishop he had covered up child abuse by priests and then also kept secret about a bishop who abused his own nephew. That did not prevent Pope Francis from appointing him to the Synod on the Family in 2014.

Cardinal Meisner, archbishop of Cologne, was also active. He reported on the general congregations: 'If two of us met, the question arose: "Do you know whom we should go for?" Then I said: "Only one name comes to mind for me, Joseph Ratzinger" And most of them agreed: "Yes, for me too."'[16] A week before the beginning of the conclave, on Sunday, 10 April, Meisner made his way to the Piazza della Città Leonina. Ratzinger was sitting at his desk in his flat 'behind a huge mountain of documents, which he had to sign', Meisner recalled. As dean of the College of Cardinals, during the *sede vacante* he had to sign off all the decisions and countless letters. Gänswein was constantly arriving with a new stack of papers, to be collected on the following day. It was Meisner's first papal election, Ratzinger's third. According to Meisner, the following conversation took place between them:

'Watch out, Joseph, now you'll say I am mad,' Meisner began, 'but I don't care. For we are talking about the good of the church.'

Ratzinger looked up briefly from his desk, but said nothing. After a brief pause, Meisner plucked up courage to say: 'You must be pope.'

Ratzinger went on signing his papers and merely said: 'You really are mad.'

'There is no one else suitable for the church in this situation.'

No answer.

'Joseph, I beg you not to refuse, if it depends on you.'

'I am not that healthy. Please pray that the cup will pass from me.'

'But not my will be done ...', Meisner continued with the allusion to Jesus' prayer in the Garden of Gethsemane.

'Now, scram!'

There the poor man sat, so small and pale. Meisner thought to himself: 'Have I done something wrong? No, for the sake of the church, I had to do it to him.'[17]

On 16 April Ratzinger celebrated his 78th birthday. At the final general congregation before the conclave, the *camerlengo*, Cardinal Eduardo Martínez Somalo, congratulated him in the name of his fellow members. Later his colleagues in the Congregation for the Doctrine of the Faith surprised him with a bunch of orchids and a softly rendered Marian canon. The speaker said: 'May help come from above in these difficult days.' When Ratzinger's great-nephew Alois Messerer congratulated him on the telephone and asked whether next week he should still address his uncle as '*Du*, Joseph' or 'Holy Father', Ratzinger replied: 'I'll be glad when it is all over. I want to retire and write books.'[18]

While the workmen opened up the Sistine Chapel roof and pushed out the two-metre-tall metal chimney, the former prefect made his way home. He wanted peace and quiet to sit down with his well-worn Greek New Testament and work on his sermon for the eagerly awaited opening Mass. A bit further on, St Peter's Square had been transformed into an army camp. Whole caravans and individual pilgrims from all parts of the Earth were standing, camping, walking about on the pavement that had been trodden for so many centuries. Many had come carrying Bibles. Others were praying the rosary or studying the English *Sunday Times*, which had a whole-page article on how the future pope might well be someone who had served the Nazis in the Hitler Youth.

Ratzinger's former private secretary Josef Clemens was standing in the middle of the crowd. No, he couldn't imagine that the 'Chief' had a chance, he said. 'He is not a man for administration but that's what we need now.' At the end of Wojtyła's time as pope quite a few things had been left undone.[19]

Georg Gänswein thought the same: 'A German from Joseph Ratzinger's generation has no chance, even though he was so close and important to John Paul II and his papacy.'[20] At the same time Georg Ratzinger gave the Munich *Abendzeitung* an interview in Regensburg, saying that in his last telephone call his brother had sounded 'very tired'. Speculations about him – a German – being *papabile* were completely absurd: 'My brother will definitely not become pope.'

Wojtyła was a mystic, a devotee of Mary, a man of prayer. Ratzinger was also all those things. But not in the same way. Yet the mood had changed. 'What will the next pope be like?' Jan Ross asked on 14 April in *Die Zeit*. The 'massive concern and condolence displayed when Karol Wojtyła died' had 'defied all platitudes'. 'Is it perhaps the uncompromising, unfashionable nonconformity of the conservatives that impresses the young and earns respect for the church?' Ross continued. 'What liberal critics object to – celibacy, no joint communion with Protestants and so on – are problems for the church in Europe, where it is shrinking. It has different worries where it is growing, such as Africa and parts of Asia, or where it is strong, as in Latin America.'[21]

In fact, the composition of the worldwide church had clearly altered. Well over half of the 1.2 billion Catholics now lived in Africa or Latin America.[22] However, European cardinals, with 55 out of the 117 eligible to vote, comprised the largest group in the conclave. The Italians came top with 20 cardinals, followed by the USA with 11, Germany and Spain with 6 each, France with 5. Twenty-one cardinals came from South America. Africa and Asia had 11 each, Oceania had 2. 'People think that we vote as in an election,' Óscar Andrés Rodríguez Maradiaga, archbishop of Tegucigalpa, in Honduras, commented, 'but it is quite different. We will listen to God and the Holy Spirit.'[23]

Two days before the election, the Roman paper *La Repubblica* reported that the College of Cardinals had split into two camps: one would vote for Ratzinger and the other for Martini. Meanwhile, Ratzinger was now favoured so highly that Martini's election could be discounted. 'He might well receive a respectable number of votes in the conclave,' *Spiegel Online* reported, 'but certainly not the necessary two-thirds for a papal election.'[24]

On Saturday, 16 April the 115 cardinal electors (Jaime Sin from the Philippines and Adolfo Suárez Rivera from Mexico had reported sick) took up their lodgings in St Martha's guesthouse. The rooms were allocated by drawing lots. Georg Gänswein landed up in a cell on the fifth floor. His presence was due to the rule that the dean was the only person allowed to bring an assistant. On Sunday morning there was breathless tension among the 60,000 faithful and guests in St Peter's Basilica, as the cardinal dean, followed in solemn procession by scarlet-robed dignitaries, approached the high altar to open the conclave with a pontifical Mass. The spellbound spectators in St Peter's Square watched the centuries-old tradition on the screens set up by the Vatican broadcaster CTV. They heard the Gregorian chant and the reading delivered in Greek – the *Missa pro eligendo Romano Pontifice* (its long title was 'Mass for the election of a new pope who is pleasing to God on account of the holiness of his life'). The service had a sacred solemnity and epic weight, which no one could resist.

Ratzinger looked exhausted. His face was tense, almost mask-like. As at the funeral Mass for John Paul II, he was the celebrant and carried the thurible. This time he incensed not just a simple coffin but the altar under Bernini's magnificent baldachin. Those attending the Mass were reminded of the farewell to John Paul II. The fine voices of the Sistine Chapel choirboys, the surprising gesture when Ratzinger offered communion to the Protestant Brother Roger from Taizé in his wheelchair, the red leatherbound book of the gospels on the plain cypresswood coffin, whose pages were blown over by the wind until a particularly strong gust blew the cover shut. Christiane Kohl from the *Süddeutsche Zeitung* remarked: 'It was almost as if the pope wanted to take leave of the faithful in that wind, which in his lifetime he had kept stirring up all over the world.'[25]

The church's influence had decreased during Wojtyła's time. The bond of many Catholics to the church had become frayed, like a worn rope that might break at any moment. The term 'loyal to the pope' had become synonymous with very small conservative groups. However, millions of young people had joined the procession. What a demonstration for Wojtyła's cause! *Santo subito!* Thousands of young voices had shouted in the streets of Rome. And wasn't the decline in the spiritually exhausted regions of the formerly Christian West countered by the rise elsewhere? The Catholic Church was growing. More than 30,000 new Catholics were baptized every day, with a pastoral care service at least 4 million strong. It included more than 400,000 diocesan priests and monks, about 30,000 deacons, more than 780,000 nuns, as well as 2.8 million catechists.[26]

Couldn't Cardinal Giovanni Battista Re state in one of the general congregations that the administration functioned well on the whole – with the 2,600 patriarchal, metropolitan, archiepiscopal and episcopal sees, together with 2,038 titular sees, their 110 bishops' conferences and 19 regional synods? The mighty papal machine, with its secretariat of state, congregations and commissions, tribunals, courts, offices, committees and institutes. Just to keep the global episcopate going, between 140 and 170 new bishops had to be appointed every year.

The question was: which pope was needed in such times?

Ratzinger summoned his remaining strength for his sermon. He meant it as a final service, the last act in a strenuous career. Among the simple white bishops' mitres he stood out with his mitre decorated with a big golden cross. Later it was said that his sermon was a candidate's speech. Others referred to the astonishing parallel with the previous conclave. Then a cardinal from Poland had convinced people by a sweeping analysis of the challenges of Marxism to the church. But Ratzinger's homily was not that. In retrospect he said, 'I mean I had to give the sermon as the cardinal dean. I simply expounded the Letter to the Ephesians, so that's what came out.'[27] He began, '*Cari fratelli e sorelle* ...'. His voice was weak, but, as the daily newspaper *Il Tempo* proclaimed in its next edition in big letters on its first page, it was 'Ratzinger's Day'. Ratzinger himself barely dreamed what a colossal impact his speech would have.

In his life history there are three decisive speeches. The first was his presentation for Cardinal Frings in Genoa, which gave the Council its direction. The third was his resignation speech on 11 February 2013, by which he took the papacy into a new era. Now with his second speech he looked at the apostle Paul's Letter to the Ephesians to talk about of his own mission.

Meeting Jesus Christ meant 'meeting God's mercy', he began, but Christ's mercy was 'not a cheaply available grace'. Paul spoke of growing to maturity 'in the knowledge of the Son of God', not 'tossed to and fro and blown about by every wind of doctrine' (Eph. 4.14). Up to this point the sermon was rather stiff and academic, but now the congregation at the Mass caught on. 'How many opinions about the faith have we heard about in these last few decades?' Ratzinger recalled. 'How may ideological currents, how many ways of thinking? Many Christians' little mental boat is often rocked by these waves from one extreme to another: from Marxism to liberalism, even to libertinism, from collectivism to radical individualism, from atheism to a vague religious mysticism, from agnosticism to syncretism and so on.' In these times 'having a clear faith in accordance with the church's creed is often branded as fundamentalism, whereas relativism that is "tossed to and fro and blown by every wind of doctrine" is presented as the only appropriate attitude today.' Furthermore, 'A dictatorship of relativism has arisen, which acknowledges nothing as final and takes its own self and desires as the ultimate standard.'

Ratzinger spoke falteringly and kept clearing his throat. But again and again loud applause broke out in the basilica. We Christians, he continued,

> have a different standard: the Son of God, the true human being. He is the measure of true humanism. To be 'mature' does not mean having a faith that is driven by the waves of fashion and the latest novelty. A mature, adult faith is one that is deep-rooted in friendship with Christ. That friendship opens us up to everything good and gives us the criterion to distinguish between true and false, truth and lies.

The church must proclaim the truth of the faith with a new offensive. And like a football coach sending his team out for the second half of a match, Ratzinger urged his listeners: 'We must be inspired by a holy anxiety: the anxiety to bring everyone the gift of faith and friendship with Christ.'

To conclude his sermon he launched once more into the big picture, into eternity:

> All of us want to leave behind us something that remains. But what remains? Not money. Neither do buildings remain; books

even less so. After a certain time – longer or shorter – all these things disappear. The only thing that remains is the human soul, the human being created by God for eternity. The fruit that remains is what we have sown in human souls – love, knowledge, actions that touch the heart; the word that opens the soul to the joy of the Lord. So let us open up and ask the Lord to help us bear fruit, a fruit that remains. Only thus will the Earth be transformed from a vale of tears into God's garden.[28]

At the end of the Mass, Ratzinger clasped his hands together in prayer: 'At this time, above all, let us earnestly pray to the Lord that, after the great gift of John Paul II, he will again give us a shepherd after his own heart.' And indeed, 'a shepherd who leads us to the knowledge of Christ, to his love, to true joy'.[29]

In his analysis of the trends of the time, he wanted to make clear to his church the tasks that a new pope should be prepared for. But it could be seen from the cardinals' faces that they were not just thinking about the speech but about the speaker. The more Ratzinger belittled himself, the more strongly his charisma shone out. His snow-white hair, the seemingly unquenchable fire of his devotion, the dignity with which he celebrated the Mass. And when he faltered now and again during the ceremony, it gave him a special note of humanity and authenticity. His reflection in the cardinals' eyes became increasingly irresistible. It was easy to imagine how they were already picturing him wearing the white cassock, to see how he would look in it.

23

Habemus Papam

Cardinals are usually honest men. They have undertaken to abide by the highest ideals. But despite the confidentiality agreement, solemn oaths and security controls, it is almost impossible to keep all the details of the conclave secret. Some are natural chatterboxes, and others want to make themselves important. Others still can't keep their mouths shut out of annoyance, or their hearts are so bursting with joy that they just *have* to speak.

Of course, the *Vaticanistas* among the journalists are importunate enough to grill the cardinals known to them and to reconstruct the secret procedure in a way that can be read. And despite the considerable security, somehow some information or other is leaked from the conclave, as happened in this case. It could not be verified from whom or why it was leaked. Or how trustworthy it was. But the information sounded so plausible (and matched other reports), that in 2005 the Italian television broadcaster RAI had no problem quoting from the 'forbidden diary' of an anonymous elector. The magazine *Limes* published the whole text, which in its way gave an insight into the dynamics of the conclave. In particular, it went into the strategic procedures of the St Gallen group, mentioned above, and their aim to prevent a Pope Ratzinger.[1]

After Ratzinger's speech, as the 115 cardinal electors walked from St Peter's to the Sistine Chapel, in a dignified procession that looked as if it was in slow motion, the tension among them had risen to almost unbearable levels. To the sound of Johann Sebastian Bach's *Jesu meine Freude* ('Jesus My Joy') the venerable crocodile reached its goal. Meanwhile, workers from the Edilizia dell Stato Vaticano, the Vatican State construction team, had set up two rows of benches and tables along the side-walls of the Sistine Chapel. A Bible was placed on every seat. The story was told of Karol Wojtyła that he had brought a Marxist newspaper into the conclave, to read it quietly during the long meetings. Before the altar stood the silver urn, into which the voting papers were thrown in a solemn procedure. At the back by the entrance, beyond the marble screen dividing the chapel, there was the rather shabby-looking, grey-green cast-iron stove, where the used voting papers would go up in smoke. As they went to the polls the cardinals could look up at Michelangelo's *Last Judgement*, which was meant to remind them of their heavy responsibility. There were Satan and other horrors of the descent into hell.

As they entered the double row of benches, Father Giuseppe Liberto, a small rather plump priest, launched into the hymn *Veni Creator Spiritus* with his Capella Musicale Pontificia (in Vatican language called just the Sistine Chapel Choir). Thirty-five boys' and 20 men's voices intoned: 'Come Creator Spirit, visit us.' Then those watching the Vatican Television's live coverage in St Peter's Square saw how the papal electors went up to the altar one by one to swear on the Bible: 'O Lord, let us choose a worthy candidate. Lead our deliberations so that the conclave may be neither long nor divisive, but an image of the unity of our church. Amen.'[2]

Cardinal Tomáš Špidlík, who was over 80 and not entitled to vote, led his colleagues in a short meditation. At 3.30 p.m. the master of ceremonies, the Italian archbishop Piero Marini, gave the signal to begin. With the shout '*Extra omnes*' ('everybody out'), the television lights were switched off, the officers, the choir, the cameramen, the security staff, the official photographer and the commander of the Swiss Guards with his white-feathered helmet left the chapel. Apart from the cardinals, the only people left were a confessor – and a doctor.

First, the master of ceremonies gave out the voting papers, then three scrutineers passed among the cardinals, as well as three *infirmarii*, who could collect the voting papers of the disabled voters. In his painstaking directions for the conclave John Paul II had laid down that the voting slips for the urn should be 'rectangular' and printed at the top with the words '*Eligo in Summum Pontificem*' ('I am voting for the supreme pontiff'). On the empty bottom half of the sheet the name of the chosen candidate was to be filled in. Each cardinal was called upon to write his choice secretly and with disguised but legible handwriting. After that the voters had to walk up to the voting table, lay their paper on the paten above the urn and make the following oath: 'I call upon Christ, who will be my judge, to witness that I have voted for the one whom I believe should be elected in accordance with God's will.'

Cardinal Meisner had quickly bought a small Madonna statue, Mary with the three hands, in a Borgo Pio souvenir shop, which he gave to Ratzinger in the conclave. 'I said to him: "Stick her in your left pocket, and take an example from your mother, who was also an all-rounder. Don't run away from what is going to happen in the next few days."'[3] But Ratzinger was still confident that the cup would pass from him. 'Of course, many had said they would bet on me. But I really could not take it seriously,' he reported in our conversation. 'I thought to myself, if the rule is that a bishop retires at 75, then they can't let the bishop of Rome begin at the age of 78.' At least he had been able to stop the canvassing by a Ratzinger lobby headed by Jorge Medina Estévez from Chile and the Colombian Cardinal Alfonso López Trujillo. He had told them both that he was prepared to be a candidate if there was a swift consensus for it. But he was against the way it was being canvassed: 'No, it is true that I knew Cardinal López wanted to push for me, but I begged him to desist. However, I was afraid that he went on doing so. But there were no further conversations about it.'

When the cardinals returned to their seats after the voting, which took half an hour, the voting slips were mixed up, counted, checked and the result was written on a separate sheet. Then the papers were punched and strung onto a scarlet cord, to be burned together with the ones left over. An attendant opened the oven door, pushed in the cord threaded through the voting papers, added a firelighter and set it all alight. In the past they had used damp or dry straw to make the smoke come out white or black. Now a cartridge with chemicals (a mixture of potassium perchlorate, anthracene and sulphur) was put into a second stove to create the required signal.

Anything can happen at a conclave. Nothing is impossible. But the rule holds that anyone who goes into a conclave as pope comes out again as a cardinal. The faithful in St Peter's Square had waited hours for a first signal. At last, on Monday, 18 April, shortly after 8 p.m., the first clouds of smoke rose from the Sistine chimney. The waiting seemed to have come to an end. Like a flock of doves flying up after a shot is fired, the crowd ran from all directions into the middle of St Peter's Square. 'Papa, papa,' shouted the first-comers. Others gazed at the chimney or the giant TV screens showing the smokestack enlarged. 'Black or white?' cried a nun as she ran past. Those she had asked shrugged their shoulders. Now the first smoke signal was rising clearly into the Roman sky. But it was black. Definitely. Rather abashed, as after a football match when the home team has lost, people trudged back to their places, home or into one of the bars to recover from the day's excitement.

According to various media reports, there had been two favourites in this first round of voting. As well as Ratzinger, there was Cardinal Martini. Apparently, the Italian Martini had got a few more votes than the German Ratzinger. However, the 'forbidden diary' of the anonymous elector reported a somewhat different result. It said that Ratzinger had 47 votes (40.9 per cent). Second came the Argentine Jorge Bergoglio, with 10 votes. Martini got nine, Camillo Ruini the episcopal vicar of Rome got six and Cardinal Secretary of State Angelo Sodano got four. Then followed Óscar Rodríguez Maradiaga, archbishop of Tegucigalpa in Honduras, with three, and Dionigi Tettamanzi, archbishop of Milan, with two votes. More than 30 votes went to other cardinals. The most striking result was the bad performance of the 'progressive' wing in the College of Cardinals. The 'forbidden diary' also mentioned the attempt by the St Gallen group, led by Martini, Danneels, Lehmann and Kasper, to come up with an opposition candidate. The plan to block Ratzinger had led to the search for a 'compromise candidate'. The procedure had worked in 1978. Then the Florentine Benelli blocked the Genoese Siri and gave a Pole the chance to come out ahead of both of them.

After the result of the vote no one, except for the cardinals, was allowed to stay in St Martha's guesthouse after midnight. The nuns were sent back to their quarters. The security staff kept watch in their cars in front of the guesthouse or patrolled the Vatican gardens. In the Palazzo San Carlo, 50 metres away, two doctors were on stand-by. For the second and third rounds of voting, which had been set for Tuesday morning at 9.30, the cardinals were bussed to the Courtyard of St Damasus in front of the Apostolic Palace. Then they went up in the lift to the first floor, in order to reach the Sistine Chapel on foot.

It was Tuesday, 19 April, the feast day of Leo IX, who reigned from 1049 until 1054 and was the only one of the seven German popes to date to be canonized. The voting on the previous day had been exploratory. Now, in the second round, it was a matter of pulling in the scattered votes. This time Ratzinger got 65 votes (56.5 per cent) and Bergoglio got 35.[4] The previous votes for Ruini went to Ratzinger; those for Martini went to Bergoglio. Sodano kept his four votes and Tattamanzi kept his two votes. When the third voting round began at 11 a.m., it was clear that the conclave had become a contest between two favourites: Joseph Ratzinger and Jorge Mario Bergoglio.

At that point, apparently, Martini had spread the word that Ratzinger was not capable of getting a sufficient consensus. If his result did not improve, surely the former prefect of the Congregation for the Doctrine of the Faith would withdraw, in order not to block the conclave. That would leave the way clear for the desired compromise candidate. In fact, in the third round Ratzinger increased his vote to 72, thereby coming close to the necessary two-thirds majority. Bergoglio's vote also increased to 40, enough for a blocking minority. So the race was back on. The anonymous diary writer noted at this point: 'Martini is among those who predict a complete change of candidates for the morning of the next day.'

Ratzinger did not retire, as Martini had hoped. It was Bergoglio who did. He had intimated, said the 'anonymous diary', that he was no longer available to stand. In retrospect, Bergoglio stated in an interview with the Argentine newspaper *La Voz del Pueblo* that he had not really been an opposition candidate to Ratzinger.[5] He told the British newspaper the *Catholic Herald* that he had called upon his supporters to vote for the candidate Joseph Ratzinger. In his interview book *Latinoamérica*, published in October 2017, he explained that he had felt then the time was not yet ripe for a Latin American pope. As he put it in his book: 'At that moment of history Ratzinger was the only man with the stature, the wisdom and the necessary experience to be elected.'[6]

Because the voting papers for both the second and the third round were burned together, smoke only rose again from the Sistine chimney at about 11.50 a.m. But what colour? The same question was called out among the crowd: '*Nero*' or '*bianco*'? For a few minutes it was uncertain. For a while it looked dark. Then an apparently paler-looking smoke cloud rose from the chimney. The *Agence France Presse* correspondent shook his head; 'They really should think about getting a different system.' A German radio correspondent shouted into his mobile: 'It looks as if Ratzinger, who was seen as the favourite, has been blocked. Now the race is on again.'

That was not true. In fact, during the midday break the only question for the electors was whether Ratzinger would really accept the job. Like the others, Ratzinger sat at the round table in the guesthouse dining room. There was no order of seating. 'As the voting process slowly made me realize that – as it were – the guillotine would fall on me,' he said later, 'I felt quite dizzy. I believed that I had done my life's work.' Then he had 'said with deep conviction to the Lord: Don't do this to me! You have younger and better people who can take up this great work with much more energy and strength.'[7] At the same time, however, 'a little note' had come into his mind ('it came into my heart,' he said literally) that in the run-up to the election the 93-year-old Cardinal Mayer had said to him: 'If the Lord were to say to you now, "Follow Me", then remember what you have preached. Don't refuse! Be obedient, as you have said about the great departed pope.'

At 4 p.m. the cardinals returned to the Sistine Chapel. They all knew that this was the decisive moment of the conclave. This time Ratzinger did not go by bus with the others. He wanted to walk. Secretary Gänswein accompanied him. They did not speak. What should he do? Could he really refuse? Hadn't John XXIII also been 78 when his colleagues had elected him pope? Sophocles had finished his *Oedipus at Colonus* at the age of 89. Titian had been an old man when he created one of his most impressive works, *The Crowning with Thorns*. In paragraph 86 of John Paul II's direction it read: 'So I ask the one who is elected not to refuse to accept the office to which he has been called through fear of its burden, but humbly to comply with the plan of God's will. For God, who lays the burden upon him will also support him with his hand, so that he is able to bear it.'

For the count of the 115 voting papers the cardinals had sheets of white A4 paper in front of them with the names of the candidates written on them. It was the fourth round of voting, and the name of Ratzinger kept coming up. Most cardinals did their own counting and added their marks to their own paper. Ten marks, 20, 50. At 70 it became tense, Nobody spoke. But at 5.30 p.m. they knew from their list that the quorum for a two-thirds majority had been reached with the mystical number 77. Two sevens – 77. Seven was a sacred number. It stood for the conclusion of a series, for fulfilment. There are 77 names in the genealogy of Jesus in Luke's gospel, going back to Adam. And in Genesis 7.7 it is written: 'And Noah with his sons and his wife and his sons' wives went into the ark to escape the waters of the flood.'

As always at that moment the cardinals stood up, one after another, and the whole auditorium began to clap. Softly, and then louder and louder. 'I covered my face,' said Meisner, 'I cried with emotion. And I wasn't the only one.' A day later, at his first sermon as Pope Benedict XVI, the newly elected Ratzinger revealed how nervous he was. 'I feel as if his [John Paul II's] strong hand is holding mine. I feel as if I can see his smiling eyes and hear his words, which at this moment are for me in particular: Don't be afraid.'

In my research for this book I asked the *papa emeritus* whether he had been aware early on that the conclave might go for him. 'Of course, I realized that,' he answered. 'But I did not want consciously to do anything for or against it.'

Wasn't it discussed among the cardinals?

Not in itself. To tell the truth I did speak with Martini about it. I said to him 'I don't want it, and if you tell your friends that I don't, I will be grateful.' But anyway, of course, he was not for me, so it was not so important.

Was there a moment in which you still considered whether you should really accept being elected?

Yes. The whole time. But somehow I realized that I simply was not allowed to say 'No'.

When did you think of the name?

During the course of the voting. Even on the first day it appeared that it might possibly be me. I still hoped that it would not be. But then it came into my mind that Pope Benedict XV and before him St Benedict himself was the right reference.

Why didn't you call yourself John Paul III?

I thought that was inappropriate. Because he set a standard I could not match. I could not be a John Paul III. I was a different figure, a different nature, a different kind of talent.

According to the information of the 'forbidden diary', the former prefect finally received 84 votes (73 per cent) in the fourth round. Votes for Bergoglio fell to 26. Five votes were still cast for others. The Catholic *Tagespost* reported about a hundred votes for Ratzinger: 'Some say 98, others 107 votes.' *La Repubblica* asserted the total had fallen from 115 to 110 votes. There was no one who could confirm or deny the numbers. Nevertheless, the Munich cardinal Friedrich Wetter declared that Ratzinger's election as pope had been 'almost unanimous'. What is certain is that the election took only 26 hours, so the conclave to elect the first pope of the new millennium was one of the shortest in history. It was a decisive and united conclave. By it the Bavarian Ratzinger became the first German pope for 480 years. Or rather, 900 years, for in the strict sense, the previous one, Hadrian VI, had been Dutch. Holland at that time was merely within the jurisdiction of the Holy Roman Empire of the German nation.

The conclave had produced a pope, the Spirit had spoken – and Ratzinger submitted once more. He had already suffered so many disruptions in his life. He had only just managed to present his *habilitation* when an examiner marked it down. He had just become a professor in Bonn when he received a beating. He had just enjoyed the triumph of being able to help shape the Council as a *peritus* when he was suddenly maligned as an enemy of the Council. He had just built himself a house in Regensburg and believed he would be able to build up his body of writing when he was torn away. He was just proving himself as a bishop in Munich when he was called to Rome. He had just thought that after 23 years of strenuous service he would be able to retire when he was pushed up – onto the chair of St Peter. Cardinals described his appearance as 'fervent, calm and very solemn' at the moment when he became 'servant of the servants of God', their fellow bishop and also their supreme teacher. 'Do you accept your canonical election as pope?' Angelo Sodano, as the now competent cardinal, asked him. Ratzinger replied: 'In obedience to the Holy Spirit I say yes to the vote by the cardinals.' In accordance with the conclave directive that made him 'immediate bishop of the church of Rome, true pope and head of the college of bishops'. He had ' full and supreme power over the universal church and can exercise it forthwith'.

By 4 p.m. the conclave camp followers had spread over the huge St Peter's Square to its furthest corners. The sky was a pale blue, and a mild spring sunshine bathed the scene in a warm, sparkling light. The people in the square did not yet know that the decision had been made. Even Carlo de Lucia, the deputy editor-in-chief of *Osservatore Romano*, still had no idea, even though it had been announced that a special edition of the newspaper would come out within 15 minutes of the result of the election. He had got his sub-editors to prepare 57 short biographies in advance. One of them would serve.

At 5.48 p.m. there was a shout from the front corner where the young people were sitting. Then everything took off. For ten minutes the big television screens had been showing nothing but the smokestack in close up. Now there really was a fire under the roof. And just as they had at the morning signal, the crowd swirled in seconds to the middle of the square. But what smoke signal would there be this time? Black? Or white? It was black. (The cardinals explained later they had had trouble with the stove: 'All at once the whole chapel was filled with smoke.') But the chimney relentlessly went on puffing out more smoke into the hazy blue Roman sky. Clouds of it, bigger and smaller, lighter and darker. Yes or no? It was not possible to be sure of the smoke's colour, but it was definitely beginning to get lighter. So what was happening?

The Sistine chimney kept puffing. Not smoke rings but proper clouds of smoke. White clouds. Were they really white? A hundred thousand people gestured, called wildly to each other, waved their hands, began to tremble and shriek. Hysterical outbreaks. Hands covering stunned faces. Gaping mouths. At 5.54 p.m. the smoke was white. It could not be any whiter. More and more people began clapping. The mobile phone network had long since collapsed. The people threw their arms into the air. There were still several long minutes of fraught waiting until the *proclamatio cura popolo*. Yes, there was a pope. No, no one knew who it was. Or what name he would take. The name gave a first hint of the direction in which the new pope would steer the ship of the church. There have been a total of 82 different papal names. John easily comes at the top of the list (23), followed by Gregory (16), Benedict (15), Clement (14), Innocent (13), Leo (13) and Pius (12). There has only been one Peter – at the beginning. Out of respect for the first pope, two of his successors even shed their baptismal name of Peter. The second of them, Bishop Peter of Albano, had been known until then by the nickname 'Pig's Snout'. Not the worst reason to take the name Sergius IV as pope.

For the new pope there was a small dressing room furnished with a red sofa directly behind the Sistine Chapel. Three sets of vestments were laid ready in it. The room was called the *camera delle lacrime*, the 'weeping room', a reference to the emotional state of many of those who had just been elected. Some were said to have broken down through fear of the responsibility. The papal tailors, the Gammarelli family, had done the whole job. They were known to be punctual, discreet and reliable. The three vestments of different sizes had to be prepared for any of the possible candidates. But oddly enough, for Ratzinger, who seemed so slight, the vestments were not too big but too small. The cassock was much too short, the red slippers did not fit, and the white skull-cap was so badly ironed that he looked as if he was wearing a Bavarian hiking cap. His old, worn black pullover could be seen poking out from under the half-length sleeves. Clearly, a little joke by the divine director, reminding people in the new pope's first official portrait that the church of Christ is a church of the poor.

After various formalities prescribed by the *ordo rituum conclavis*, the cardinals went up to the new pope – now in papal dress– to swear loyalty and obedience to him. Ratzinger sat on a huge chair in front of the Sistine Chapel altar. 'I came in at the moment when the cardinals knelt before the pope, one after another,' said Georg Gänswein. As secretary he went up last. The former prefect's face was 'almost as white as his new white cassock and the *pileolus* [skull-cap] on his head. I wouldn't say he was suffering from shock but he looked very haggard.' Gänswein himself felt an inner 'whirlwind', he recalled. 'It was quite impossible to think clearly. The days that followed were also rather like a tsunami. Everything turned upside down and one impression followed another.'[8] He also knelt down. It was the minute that changed his life. The blacksmith's son from a village of 450 people in the Black Forest became private secretary to the pope. 'Holy Father, I promise you my obedience, my loyalty, my service in everything you ask from me,' he said at that moment. 'I am at your disposal with all my powers without restriction.' The new pope was so exhausted that he could only give a tired smile. 'He looked at me, nodded and said "Thank you. I accept."'

The election result was still not publicly known. Some who were informed were the viewers of the German broadcasting company Phoenix. Its presenter Stephan Kulle had succeeded in getting the news from a telephone contact in the Vatican (which he trumpeted on air at 6.39 p.m.).[9] At 6.04 p.m. the bells of St Peter's began to ring. First the great heavy bell in the belfry, then also the smaller bells in the basilica. Eventually, the bells of all the churches in Rome joined in, together with hundreds of thousands all over the world. In the Italian capital people were streaming in from all directions to reach St Peter's Square. A hundred thousand or more. Millions followed the live broadcast event on their own television sets. '*Viva il papa!*' the crowd kept shouting. When at 6.43 p.m. the heavy red velvet curtains behind the windows of the central loggia of St Peter's Basilica began to move, for a moment there was a breathless silence.

It was the longest-serving cardinal deacon, the Chilean Jorge Arturo Medina Estévez, who appeared first from behind the curtain. From the left he was passed a large briefcase containing the election deed. From the right he received a microphone. 'Brothers and Sisters,' he began in Italian. Pause. Then in English, French and German. Another pause. The tension grew. '*Annuntio vobis gaudium magnum* – I announce a great joy to you.' The first wave of applause broke out in the square. And with all the force his voice could muster he called out: '*Habemus papam!* – we have a pope!' At the crowd's jubilation he again paused for effect. Then he raised his voice to a dramatic staccato: '*Eminentissimum ac Reverendissimum Dominum* ... the most eminent and reverend gentleman ... *Dominum Josephum, Sanctae*

Romanae Ecclesiae Cardinalem … Joseph, cardinal of the Holy Roman church …'. But in the storm of enthusiasm, after he said '*Josephum*', the rest of the name was almost unheard. '*Josephum … Cardinalem … Ratttzingerrrrr … qui sibi nomen imposuit Benedictum XVI* … Joseph Cardinal Ratzinger, who has taken the name Benedict XVI.'

St Peter's Square shook. Clapping and cheering broke out like a tornado. People hugged each other. Later rock legend Patti Smith added to the record: 'Even from a great distance you could feel the humanity of this man. I cried. I know he is not to everyone's taste, but I think he is a good choice. I like him very much.'[10]

During these minutes in the vibration of all the feelings and thoughts, while trillions of nerve cells fluttered simultaneously, a consistent rhythm developed, like a harmony of souls. It was not grand opera that was being experienced here in the collective consciousness of the faithful but something like a moment of full clarity. As if heaven had opened and a heavenly choir of cherubim and seraphim struck up a Gloria never heard before. At that moment, at last, the new pope, happy and smiling, stepped onto the balcony of St Peter's to greet the faithful. The rejoicing knew no bounds. A hundred thousand people leaped into the air and clapped like mad, enthralled by the magic of the moment. Happy and excited like children. A *frisson* of warmth flooded their bodies, waves of joy, such as are very seldom experienced.

Many people knew Ratzinger as questioning, always on guard. Sometimes his lips were pushed out in a cautious, concentrated expression. Now, when he stepped up to the balustrade, people thought they could still see traces of an inner battle. Like the biblical forefather Jacob, who wrestled with God at the River Jabbok. Perhaps he would have liked to cry in his emotion at the great God's preference, who had entrusted this whole flock to him at the end of his life – to him, little Joseph, son of Maria from the little village of Marktl am Inn. In his self-image he was such a frail person. Then he threw up his arms, happy, relieved, though rather stiff, with the palms of his hands pointing vertically upwards. For a moment the former prefect came out of his shell and displayed a glimpse of a man with great facility. An impression confirmed by the correspondent for the *Süddeutsche Zeitung*: 'At ease and unconstrained, Benedict XVI now smiled at the people, he raised his arms and greeted them warmly.

Joseph Ratzinger has won the battle, and even the mitre looks a bit less heavy on his head than it did before.'[11]

In the metamorphosis of the conclave Joseph Ratzinger had become Benedict XVI. It almost seemed as if a new aura had immediately gathered round him, a nimbus that was beginning to weave itself like an invisible second body round the figure in his papal regalia. It was his slender frailty that fascinated, rather than an imposing stature. And from that minute Ratzinger-mania could be seen, a changeover accompanied by enthusiastic fans. The spark of sympathy for the former pope sprang over to the new pope. Cries of 'Ben-e-det-to!, Ben-e-det-to!' were already resounding up towards the balcony. With a slightly shaky voice Benedict – the blessed – began to speak:

Dear sisters and brothers, after a great Pope John Paul II, the cardinals have chosen me, a simple, humble worker in the Lord's vineyard. I am comforted by the fact that the Lord knows how to work even with inadequate tools. Above all I commend myself to your prayers. Let us go ahead in the joy of the risen Lord and trusting in his perpetual help. The Lord will help us and Mary, his blessed mother, is standing beside us. Thank you.[12]

There had been weeks of mourning. Weeks of emptiness. Waiting. Trepidation. The pope was dead, but the hopes and fears were followed by rejoicing: *Habemus papam!* The new pope was about to assume a great and heavy legacy. But he could profit from the work of his predecessor. From his predecessor's steadfastness, the power with which he drove the plough, pushed obstacles aside, tilled the field. Now came the nurturing, the weeding, the cutting back. Quite in accordance with St Benedict's motto: *Cut back and it always sprouts green again.*

PART THREE

Pope

24

The First Pope of the Third Millennium

After the homage on the St Peter's loggia, Ratzinger invited the cardinals to celebrate a little in the dining room of the Casa Santa Marta. Bean soup, cold meat, salad and fruit were served and, as it was a special occasion, also ice cream and champagne. As he was entering the room, the cardinals thundered an '*Oremus pro pontifice nostro Benedicto*' ('Let us pray for our Pope Benedict'), the powerful voice of Salvatore De Giorgi, archbishop of Palermo, loudest of all. The new pope sat at a table with vice-dean Sodano, the chamberlain Eduardo Martínez Somalo and the proto-deacon Medina Estévez. 'There was a short greeting,' a participant reported, 'then the pope also said a few words and that was it.'

With the *habemus papam* the mobile phone network on St Peter's Square had already broken down. On the same evening books by Joseph Ratzinger reached the first four places on the Amazon ranking of top-selling titles. Editors worldwide worked feverishly on the headlines for the front pages of the morning editions of their newspapers. A German as pope? A man from the country of the Reformation that split the church, and of the Holocaust, on the chair of the fisher of people? A 'Grand Inquisitor' as vicar of Christ? What could be more provocative?

In England the result of the conclave was an opportunity to voice old grievances. 'God's Rottweiler is the new pope' was the *Daily Telegraph* headline. The *Sun* had 'From Hitler Youth to Pope Ratzi'. The *Daily Mirror* resorted to the 'Panzer Cardinal' and spoke of 'the journey of the enforcer, which had now reached its goal'. The *Independent* showed not the rejoicing crowd in St Peter's

Square but a picture from 1943 of Ratzinger the flak auxiliary, in uniform, of course.

There were also well-considered voices. Charles Moore, the *Spectator* columnist and long-term editor of the *Daily Telegraph*, commented that the worldwide church's election of a German as pope recognized that Germany had made its atonement and that its respect among the nations was now restored. It was important for Moore to add a personal remark. He said that when he met the cardinal he had been struck by three things. 'First, his politeness, which put me to shame.' Second: 'his curiosity. Far from living remotely in the past, he was keenly interested in the new thinking.' Third: 'a friendly, even chatty, openness with which he went into every question. The cardinal seemed to me to be happy in himself but also with a sadness about the state of the world.'[1]

The bishop of Paris, Jean-Marie Lustiger, also interpreted Ratzinger's election as a kind of rehabilitation. It had to be seen as a 'sign of Providence for Germany and the church in Germany,' said Cardinal Lustiger, who had converted from Judaism. 'Only from the church' that had lost a large number of its members in concentration camps could such a signal go out to the conscience of the world. Jean-Pierre Ricard, archbishop of Bordeaux and president of the French Bishops' Conference, thanked 'Germany with his whole heart that it has given one of its sons to Rome and the whole world'. Benedict XVI could be seen as a friend of France. It was well known how well he spoke 'the language of Molière'.

The left-wing *Libération* saw it differently. Under the headline 'A backward-looking pope', like the British press it went for the German word 'Panzer Cardinal'. But *Le Figaro* said: 'The accusation of conservatism cannot be understood, though many observers are now already making it, just as they did against John Paul II. What is criticized in Western Europe is praised in the rest of the world. The Catholic faith is a world religion, so premature speculations about this new papacy should be avoided.'[2]

Lacking in originality, the Belgian *Standaard*'s headline was 'Panzer Cardinal becomes pope'. On the other hand, *Trouw* in the Netherlands believed: 'Many will be pleased that at this time of gloom and doubt the keys of Peter are in firm hands again.' In Switzerland the liberal daily paper *Südostschweiz* commented that, as pope, the Grand Inquisitor would 'concrete over the Second Vatican Council for all time'. On the other hand, the *Neue Zürcher Zeitung* was convinced that a large majority of Third World bishops had wanted a pope who had 'a clear doctrinal profile'. The *Washington Post* saw the result of the vote as a last chance to strengthen the Christian roots of Europe. Many prejudices about Germans would have to be corrected by it.[3]

It was no surprise that Ratzinger's election aroused an ambivalent response in his homeland. As expected, Hans Küng spoke of a 'massive disappointment'. Church critic Eugen Drewermann said that Benedict XVI's election reflected the power of Opus Dei. The Vatican should finally learn from the Reformation and also from Buddhism and promote the 'integration of the unconscious'. Likewise, the church politics editor of the *Süddeutsche Zeitung* said the new pope had 'a pessimistic programme'. He should urgently stand for a church 'that is prepared to question itself'.[4]

But in Berlin the *Bild* newspaper was pleased: 'We are pope' was its legendary headline. The left-wing *Tageszeitung* printed three words on a deep black front page: 'Oh my God!' The other Berlin newspapers took the same tone. For the *Tagesspiegel* Ratzinger was 'a man of the old system – indeed with outstanding capabilities but without charisma or enjoyment of life'. The new pope would 'load his flock with instructions, admonitions and encyclicals on his distrustful-conservative lines'. The *Berliner Zeitung* saw Benedict XVI as a 'wolf among sheep'. He was the 'shrewdest courtier at the oldest court in the world. If anyone is cunning as a serpent, it's him.'

Critics saw the Benedict model as antediluvian and his election as a gaffe, an embarrassing mistake. At least he was no longer that young. Overload and the law of ageing would surely soon put an end to his reign. If not, ways would be found to thwart this pope. The news magazine *Der Spiegel* began its coverage of the German pope with the cover title 'The Unworldly One'. Rather cryptically it continued: 'Throughout his life Joseph Ratzinger has tried to ignore real life.' Clearly 'real life' did not include being harassed by the Nazis as a gymnasium student, or that as a soldier, Council adviser, bishop and prefect he had not always had to deal with pleasant things. Ratzinger was a crusader, 'shy in his actions but iron in his attitude'. His voice sounded like someone who wanted 'to tell a funny story', more like a puppet than the voice of the Lord'. His gestures were 'mechanical, his body stiff and he had to get used to smiling'.[5]

The article published on 25 April 2005 had been written cold at a desk. Observant readers could read something quite different in the magazine's online edition, which appeared on the same day. It was by a *Spiegel* reporter who had seen the person and events *in situ*. 'Benedict XVI, who before he became pope was often described as stiff and almost unapproachable walked smiling through the crowds, shaking hands and greeting people. Ratzinger seemed to enjoy the applause that kept interrupting his inaugural speech.'[6]

Der Spiegel's cover story was not to be its last attack on Ratzinger. 'The Unworldly One' was followed by 'The Remote One' (2009), 'The Infallible One' (2010), 'The Incorrigible One' (2011) and finally 'The Exhausted One' (2012), as if it was a matter of killing off a dangerous wild beast. One of the writers who had opened the sequence, Alexander Smoltczyk, later changed his mind. At first all he had known of Joseph Ratzinger was that 'he always defended with utter certainty precisely that social-political position which we enlightened people regarded as completely out of the question'. Then he had read Ratzinger's *Introduction to Christianity* and not only that. 'I read *Deus caritas est* [...] and downloaded the conclave speeches again from the Vatican home page. I listened to Ratzinger's speeches in Cologne, Regensburg, Izmir and Istanbul and gradually began to listen less with annoyance than with interest.' His conclusion: 'This pope has got something. He can't be simply dismissed with the usual suspicions.'[7]

Markus Reder of the German *Tagespost* commented effusively on the election. Here was a man 'who is far ahead of his time because he has never run after it'. Benedict XVI embodied 'that intellectual depth which is urgently needed in the superficiality of our times'. Jan Ross from the weekly *Die Zeit* came to a similar conclusion:

He does not dream of a theocracy but he fights for Christianity as the historic force for forming consciences, an ethical-cultural memory, without which there is the threat of falling back into barbarism. If we asked why the cardinals wanted Ratzinger as pope, more important than all church politics could have been his ability to explain the faith and make it luminous and enlightening.[8]

The Italian media were unreservedly in agreement. 'He will be a loved and respected pope, an intellectual with the characteristics of a shepherd', the *Corriere della Sera* wrote. *La Repubblica* said: 'This will be both a political and a spiritual papacy, one that is also full of surprises.'[9] *La Stampa* of Turin wrote:

> He won't be the dark guardian of the faith, as some wrongly see him. According to his temperament, upbringing and culture Ratzinger is a complex personality, together with a sometimes disarming simplicity. He will surprise us. Behind the outwardly distanced scholar with the reputation of a rugged defender of the faith, we may yet discover the real Benedict XVI.[10]

The only voices to emerge from the Curia were those that celebrated the election result, even though the whispering was not all positive. According to Giovanni Battista Re, prefect of the Congregation for Bishops, Ratzinger had long proved that he was 'a great witness to the truth about God and humanity, without ever going along with the changing fashions'. Cardinal Alfonso López Trujillo said into a microphone that for the last 20 years he himself had had the opportunity 'to admire the human and spiritual gifts of the new pope. His simple, humble, balanced manner, his ability to listen, his patient open-mindedness in dialogue.' His reputation as the 'Grand Inquisitor' had caused 'a certain hilarity' among those who knew him.

On the night after his election Ratzinger sat at the desk in his small room in the Casa Santa Marta. Work could not be postponed. Tomorrow morning, he would have to give a speech at his first Mass as pope in the Sistine Chapel. Only the members of the conclave would be present, but the Mass would be broadcast live by Vatican TV and hundreds of journalists in the press office would pore over every word to interpret it. He decided to give his speech in Latin. He felt more secure in Latin than in Italian, and he found it more appropriate. He could also have spoken off the cuff. There is a magic in every beginning, he remembered from Hermann Hesse.

But he did not want to leave this beginning to the inspiration of the moment.

When on the morning of 20 April he entered the Sistine Chapel with his crosier and mitre, his tiredness could be seen. 'At this moment I have two conflicting feelings,' he confessed to his cardinals.

On the one hand, I feel a sense of inadequacy and human confusion about the responsibility that was laid upon me yesterday to be bishop of Rome as the successor to the apostle Peter. On the other hand, I feel deep gratitude towards God, who does not abandon his flock but leads it through the times under the guidance of those whom he himself has chosen as representatives of his Son and as shepherds.[11]

He mentioned his predecessor several times: 'It seems to me as if I feel his firm hand pressing my hand. It seems as if I see his smiling eyes and hear his words, which he is saying to me at this special moment: "Don't be afraid!"' At this moment when – 'to my great surprise' – 'divine Providence' had called him to become the successor to a great pope, he was thinking about what happened 2,000 years ago in the Holy Land. 'I believe I can hear Peter's words: "You are the Messiah, the Son of the living God" and the Lord's solemn confirmation: "You are Peter and upon this rock I will build my church [...] I will give you the keys to the kingdom of heaven."'

He continued:

If the burden of responsibility resting on my shoulders is heavy, the divine strength upon which I can rely is limitless [...] As he has elected me as his representative, the Lord has wanted me to be a 'rock', upon which everyone can lean for support. I pray he will help my weakness, so that I may be a brave and faithful shepherd of his flock and always quick to listen to the inspiration of his Spirit.[12]

Then the new pope became pragmatic: every Christian must give an account one day of what he has done for ecumenism. He himself wanted to work tirelessly 'for the restoration of full and visible unity' between Christians. He wanted 'with all the strength of my will to support the task of implementing the Second Vatican Council, following the course of my predecessors and in faithful continuity with the church's 2,000-year-old tradition'. In conclusion he said:

> I appeal to all, including those who follow a different religion or who are merely seeking an answer to the fundamental questions of existence and have not yet found it. I appeal to all with simplicity and affection to assure them that the church wants to hold an open and honest dialogue with them on the quest for the true welfare of humanity and society.[13]

After Mass in the Sistine Chapel, Benedict's first action as pope, together with a group of close colleagues, was to take possession of his future residence on the third floor of the Apostolic Palace. Carefully, the seal was broken that had closed up the residence after John Paul II's death. The rooms looked in a terrible state. They had not been renovated for years. The electric wiring was critical. The water taps didn't work. The carpets were worn out, and after Wojtyła's long illness it all stank of a hospital. There was not even a guest toilet. Without further ado, Ratzinger decided that makeshift repairs should be done immediately to the *appartamento* and that in summer, when he was at Castel Gandolfo, a thorough renovation should take place. At least the carpets should be removed, 'I don't like that. A floor is a floor and a carpet is a carpet.' He declined the use of the guest tower, Torre San Giovanni, an awkward medieval building, which Wojtyła had used for the transition period. 'First, I don't like that, when rooms are semicircular. I prefer normal, rectangular, human rooms. There was also such a terrible wind. So I said no, I'd rather stay a bit longer in the Casa Santa Marta.'[14]

On the same day he went back to his old flat directly behind the colonnades of St Peter's Square. Immediately the streets filled up. It was Benedict's first 'crowd bath'. '*Sono emozionatissimo*' – 'I am deeply moved' – he kept calling out. He hugged children, shook hands whenever they were held out to him and could not stop waving at the enthusiastic crowd. A few days later the Romans could see how their new pope's move took place before the Vatican gates. A few bits of furniture were loaded onto two ancient-looking lorries, an old filing cabinet, small chests of drawers, bookshelves and, above all, boxes of books. 'Very spartan', the spectators thought. Other Eminences had been given very different verdicts.

Meanwhile, in the Vatican the greetings from governments, politicians, bishops and presidents of global organizations were being received. As the representative of the German state, the federal president, Horst Köhler, expressed 'great expectations' of Benedict: 'And I am sure that he will fulfil these expectations in a very special way with wisdom and firmness of faith.' In Ratzinger's former diocese of Munich the auxiliary bishop Engelbert Siebler spoke of a 'millennial event'. 'We rejoice that now Pope Benedict will lead the church into a new time,' Siebler proclaimed in the Cathedral of Our Lady to the enthusiastic faithful. Then he read from the book of Ezekiel: 'So take care of your sheep and fetch them back from where they have strayed.'[15]

In the USA President George W. Bush praised Benedict XVI as a man 'who serves God': 'We still remember his sermon at the pope's funeral in Rome; how his words touched our hearts and the hearts of millions of others.'[16] Kofi Annan, the Secretary-General of the United Nations, paid tribute to the broad experience of the new pope and wished him strength and courage. José Manuel Barroso, the president of the European Commission, expressed his conviction that Benedict XVI would continue the work of his predecessor and work for understanding between nations and peace in the world. In his letter of congratulation, Vladimir Putin, the only great European head of government not to attend John Paul II's funeral, offered Benedict XVI a 'constructive political dialogue'. China's first message to the new pope had the same theme that had already caused a stir at his predecessor's funeral: the Vatican should break off its 'so-called diplomatic relations' with the island republic of Taiwan. Its appointment of bishops in China was regarded as the unlawful interference of a foreign power in China's internal affairs.

The reactions in Africa were different. Bishop Felix Ajakaye, the speaker for the Nigerian Bishops' Conference, repudiated the criticism that Benedict XVI was too conservative. On the contrary, he was exactly the right man: 'We have things to maintain, we must protect the Catholic heritage from damage and promote the value of life.' President Thabo Mbeki of South Africa mentioned Ratzinger's time in the Hitler Youth and the Second World War, but this time positively. The 'experience of racist evil' would help the pope to fight against racism in Africa. The news from Rome reached the Philippines shortly after midnight local time. Within seconds the rejoicing spread by SMS all over the island state. 'He is brilliant, brilliant, brilliant', said Archbishop Oscar Cruz. State president Gloria Macapagal-Arroyo was certain that, just like his predecessor, Benedict XVI would act as an 'enduring beacon' to show the faithful the way through the trials of life.

The news unleashed a wave of enthusiasm in Poland. They did not understand the coolness with which the election result had been met by their neighbours. A reporter from the news broadcaster TVN24 reported live from the German embassy in Warsaw: 'Here nothing is being done. Everything is dark.' The staff had gone home at the end of their shift. The ambassador could not be prevailed upon to express an opinion. In the studio the presenter declared: 'Let us hope that one day the Germans will love their pope as much as we are already beginning to love him.'

No one celebrated the new pope more enthusiastically than representatives of Jewish organizations. On 18 April the *Jerusalem Post* had already rejected accusations against the prefect of the Congregation for the Doctrine of the Faith. 'Ratzinger a Nazi?' was the headline of the leading article. 'Don't believe it!'[17] Israel trusted him, it said, precisely because he was a German, precisely because, as a German, he had a particular sensitivity to the Jewish people. The president of the Central Council of Jews in Germany, Paul Spiegel, expressly paid tribute to Ratzinger's contributions to reconciliation between the Catholic Church and Judaism. In New York, Edgar M. Bronfman, president of the World Jewish Congress, declared: 'We look forward to the continuation of the relations we had with the then Cardinal Joseph Ratzinger during the papacy of John Paul II.' The Israeli newspaper *Haaretz* cited Israel Singer, secretary-general of the World Jewish Congress: 'he it was who provided the theological underpinning for John Paul II's decision to establish diplomatic relations with Israel [...] He it was who had the key to open this castle. In the last 20 years he has changed the two-thousand year history of the relations between Judaism and Christianity.'

All that was still missing was what the stars said. The astrology magazine *Meridian* said that, according to his birth data (Pisces

Ascendant with the sun in the first house), Ratzinger was 'a determined fighter who set his own will at the service of a great task'. Sagittarius Saturn in the 9th house pointed to someone who 'guards what has been preserved and carries out determined reforms where changes are necessary'. As for the state of Joseph Ratzinger's soul, he had 'come to himself out of the seclusion of the 12th house and radiates a mellow, glowing joy'. However, from 2007/8 there would be a 'dramatic change'. The church was facing 'difficult days ahead'.

It was day three after the conclave, the day of the ceremonial enthronement of the new pope. For the third time in three weeks St Peter's Square was full to bursting with pilgrims and visitors to Rome. Between 350,000 and 500,000 faithful and others filled the wide area, as well as the adjacent Pius XII Square and the Via della Conciliazione. Once again thousands of journalist had been accredited. The official delegations with heads of state and heads of government came from 140 nations. Ratzinger needed a lot of sleep, seven to eight hours as a rule, but on the night before his enthronement it was not granted to him. 'I woke up at 2 a.m. and thought it will go wrong if I don't fall asleep again.' Finally at 4 a.m. he slept again. But then, when he was getting dressed, he had to battle with cuff links, which he had never worn before, 'so that I thought to myself that their inventor should go deep into Purgatory'.[18]

Wearing a golden vestment, first he went into the crypt in St Peter's Basilica and bowed before the tomb of the apostle Peter. Then the new head of the Catholic Church was seen by millions on television screens all over the world. Benedict's opening speech on the steps of St Peter's on 24 April 2005 was programmatic, and then again not. As he said, he did not want 'to present a kind of regime programme'. The actual programme was 'not to do my own will but to listen, together with the whole church, to the words and the will of the Lord, so that the Lord himself should lead the church at this moment of our history'.[19] Benedict XVI expressly referred to 'our brothers among the Jewish people, with whom we are bound together by a great common spiritual heritage'. Today too it was the task of the church and the apostles' successors 'to set out into the high seas of history and cast our nets'. He added: 'We humans live an alienated life, in the salt waters of suffering and death;

in a sea of darkness without light.' But 'we are not the accidental and meaningless products of evolution. Each of us is the fruit of a thought by God. Each one of us is wanted, loved and needed.'

The inauguration ceremony took place under a shining blue sky, befitting the hundreds of blue and white Bavarian flags, local costumes, *Lederhosen* and, last but not least, the Company of Mountain Riflemen from Tegernsee, of which Ratzinger was an honorary member. 'Even during this first speech of his papacy', *Die Zeit's* reporter noted, 'distance from the new pope and scepticism about him could be felt. But Ratzinger was increasingly able to make points.' At the end it was clear: 'With Benedict XVI a completely new style had entered the church procession. Less pomp, more intelligence and dignity.' One person who was there, the film director Franco Zeffirelli, applauded and acknowledged: 'A quite extraordinary production. I was speechless.' Another prominent person, Nichi Vendola, the governor of Puglia, an out homosexual known as 'the colourful bird', also broke a lance for the pope in St Peter's Square. 'It is completely wrong to attack Ratzinger. I can only advise all gays to read his writings with their clear, firm thoughts. The world needs someone like him as pope now.'

When he took possession of the church of St John Lateran, the actual papal church, Benedict declared two weeks later, the power of a pope 'does not stand above the word of God, but in its service. The pope has the responsibility to keep that word in all its greatness and purity, so that it is not torn apart by constantly changing fashions.' He may not 'proclaim his own ideas, but must commit himself and the church always to obey God's word – against any attempt to adapt it or water it down or any form of opportunism'. At the end of the ceremony he turned to the Roman people and thanked them for their sympathy and patience. 'As Catholics we are all Romans,' he added. 'As Catholics, in a certain sense, we were all born in Rome.' Being a Catholic meant being part of 'God's great family', 'in which there are no strangers'.

In his first sermon Benedict stressed the 'inviolability of human life from conception to natural death' and referred to the world's problems. 'There is the wilderness of poverty, the wilderness of hunger and thirst. There is the wilderness of desolation, loneliness and love destroyed. There is the desert of God's darkness, the emptying of souls, who no longer know about dignity or the way of humanity.' 'It is not violence that saves,' he cried, 'but love.' Once again he confirmed his will to implement the Second Vatican Council. Over the course of years the Council documents had 'lost nothing of their topicality; their teachings are proving to be particularly enduring in the light of the new needs of the church and today's global society'.

At the same time he stressed his will to 'restore the full and visible unity of all Christ's disciples'. There was no alternative to ecumenism. He wished to assure all nations 'that the church wants to hold an open and honest dialogue in search of the true good of humanity'. In particular, he would like to deepen the conversation with non-Christian religions, 'so that the conditions arise for a better future for all through mutual understanding'. He called upon the young: 'Don't be afraid of Christ! He takes nothing and gives everything! Those who give themselves to him receive everything back a hundredfold.' The pope was convinced: 'The church is alive. And the church is young. She carries the future of the world and shows each individual the way into the future.'

However, perhaps the most moving speech was the one he gave on 25 April in the Audience Hall to his compatriots, when he spoke of the 'guillotine' that he saw dropping on him as a result of the conclave vote. At that moment he had become 'quite dizzy'. And he had begged the Lord: 'Don't do this to me!' But his thinking had changed and he had realized: 'The Lord's ways are not comfortable, but we are not created to be comfortable but to do great and good things.'

At John Paul II's death it had 'become clear that the church is a force for unity, a sign for humanity'. She was 'not closed off and only there for herself' but 'a light for humanity'. Passionately, Benedict spoke of his predecessor:

> The church is not old and static. No, she is young. And when we look at the young people who flocked to the great Polish pope's funeral and finally to Christ, for whom he stood, then it was a comfort to see: young people don't think mainly about consumption and pleasure. The opposite is true: young people want great things. They want to put an end to inequality. They

want inequality to be overcome and everyone to be given a share of this world's goods. The want the oppressed to be set free. They want great things. They want good things. And therefore young people – you – are open again to Christ. Christ did not promise us a comfortable life. Anyone just seeking comfort and ease has come to the wrong address.

Then he concluded with words that it was not hard to see came from deep within his heart:

With grateful joy I see the delegations from my Bavarian home. I have already had opportunities to tell you how much your faithful attachment means to me. It has persisted since those days in which I had left my beloved archdiocese of Munich and Freising for the Vatican [...] Dear friends, let us not be dissuaded from this pilgrimage to Christ [...] Let us go together, let us hold on together [...] I beg your forbearance if I make mistakes, as everyone does, or if many things remain difficult to understand in what the pope must say and do, following his conscience and the conscience of the church. I beg you will trust me. And let us pray to Mary, the mother of the Lord, that she will let us feel her womanly and motherly kindness, which can lead us into the depths of the mystery of Christ.[20]

Thousands of Catholics came to Benedict XVI's reception for his compatriots, but only two German bishops, Cardinals Meisner and Wetter. On the first election of a German pope for 500 years, the secretary of the German Bishops' Conference, Hans Langendörfer, had not deemed it necessary to cancel a routine meeting of the German bishops.

25

In the Shoes of the Fisherman

From his work room it was only a couple of steps to the private chapel to read the breviary or simply say a prayer. Perhaps in the evenings he would take a short walk in the roof garden. Then his two private secretaries would retire to their rooms on the floor above him, to answer emails until late into the night or to listen to rock music. They were the young German Georg Gänswein and the young Pole whom everyone called just Mietek, because his full name, Mieczysław Mokrzycki, was so difficult to pronounce. Possibly the valet Angelo Gugel and the nuns from the lay Catholic organization Memores Domini would still be working on the papal wardrobe in the back rooms, but he had to get used to that.

Had there really been no question that he should accept the vote? Indeed, there had been a 'very serious' one. But he had been struck that even in the pre-conclave so many cardinals had urged him to accept, even if he did not want to, or believed he was not up to the job. It was simply an inner duty. 'That had been stressed so strongly and earnestly that I believed if the majority of the cardinals really do vote for it, it is a vote by the Lord and so I have to accept it.'[1]

The beginning had cost a lot of energy. His back had become a bit more hunched, his handshake weaker than before and his smile less broad. 'Pray for me,' he had asked, 'that I do not flee in terror from the wolves.' Why did he say that? Didn't the glow of the office also give each pope an aura of holiness? Of invincibility?

He could still laugh at himself. For example, at the small misfortune when at the World Bishops' Conference he forgot to turn off the microphone. 'At 4 o'clock unfortunately I have an appointment with the dentist', his high voice rang out round the room. Straight after his election he sent a surprise parcel to an Irish journalist who had been firmly convinced that Ratzinger would one day become pope. In the letter accompanying a bottle of Old Bushmills Irish whiskey, the recipient read: 'His Holiness remembers his bet.'

'Bishop of Rome, vicar of Jesus Christ, Successor to the Prince of Apostles, *Summus Pontifex* of the whole Church' was his full title, and further: 'Patriarch of the West, Primate of Italy, Archbishop and Metropolitan of the Roman church province, Sovereign of the Vatican City State'. 'By virtue of his office the pope possesses the highest, full, immediate and general ordinary power in the church, which he can always freely employ' was how Canon Law described his authority. He was the leader of the largest religious community on Earth, with 1.2 billion members. Was he now the most powerful man in the world? No, he had never felt 'power', he said in retrospect. He had regarded the responsibility that went with the office chiefly as 'something heavy and burdensome', something about which 'you have to ask yourself every day: am I right for it?' Even when the crowds were rejoicing he had always known: people don't mean this poor little man; they mean what I represent.'[2]

Perhaps the feeling of being confined was the greatest pain of all during the early weeks. He could no longer even go for a walk whenever he wanted. No longer travel to his beloved house in Bavaria. Never before had he telephoned his brother in Regensburg so often. He wrote to his schoolmate Franz Weiss in Traunstein that in future the class reunions would have to take place without him. His friend and fellow professor Franz Mussner had thought 'the time for calling each other "*Du*" [the familiar German form for 'you'] is over' and called Ratzinger 'Your Holiness' in his letter of congratulation. Fourteen days after his enthronement Ratzinger replied: 'Dear Franz, everything remains the same as ever between us. So much of my former life has been taken away from me, so I need even more urgently for our friendship to remain the same and the old ways between friends not to change. So I beg you [*Dich*] to let us go on calling each other "*Du*".'[3]

The blue rings under his eyes showed the great effort it cost him to find his way into his new job. There was the interminable study of documents. Then the dossiers that his staff put together on each of the presidents he was about to meet in an audience 20 or 30 minutes later. Every day he had to take a position on a new case of terror, natural disaster or hostilities in the Near East. He posed with first ladies, met Muslims from the USA, rabbis from Ukraine or representatives of the Senegal-Mauritania-Cap Verde-Guinea Bissau Bishops' Conference. Each evening the last post brought to him in the great briefcase from his 200-strong secretariat of state contained a pile of lecture requests, proposals and applications, which he was asked kindly to consider.

Every day was different. Sometimes there was communion instruction for Italian children, or he visited the sick in hospital or, as bishop of Rome, he baptized new-born babies in the Sistine Chapel. On Wednesdays he held a general audience; on Sundays at the Angelus blessing he pointed out where humanitarian aid was needed on Earth, because of some epidemic or natural disaster. On World Migrants and Refugees Day he called for more understanding of the needs of asylum seekers and those who had lost their homes. They should be treated with respect; we should stand up for their rights and inquire into the reasons for their flight.[4] When he received the chief rabbi of Rome, he condemned the revival of anti-Semitism: 'Because of our common ancestry, we cannot do anything else but love you. For us you are our beloved and chosen brothers.' He also had the case against the French priest Léon Dehon (1843–1925) looked into. Dehon was the founder of the Congregation of the Sacred Heart of Jesus, whose beatification, in accordance with the will of John Paul II, was to take place on 24 April 2005. After the change of popes, the beatification process was halted, on Pope Benedict's instructions, because Dehon was accused of anti-Semitic statements.

When Karol Wojtyła became pope, at the age of 58, he did not really know how a pope ought to be. As he said, he came 'from a far country'. The Iron Curtain had closed if off from the developments in the Western world. On the other hand, Ratzinger at 78 had long since become an honorary Roman. Whereas Wojtyła excused himself for his bad Italian and asked to be corrected when he made mistakes in speaking, it was joked about his successor that the Italians should not be embarrassed – he would correct them if they said anything wrong.

In Ratzinger's life everything pressed forward, whether with or against his own will. He had stressed that you were not thrown into the world accidentally. An idea and love preceded you. Later he added he had 'always had this burning feeling' of falling short of his vocation, 'short of the idea that God has of me of what I could and ought to give'.[5]

A pope was not a politician. There was no further election for him – only the Last Judgement. Political categories of right and left did not fit here, as Wojtyła had shown in his papacy, which had combated both communism and the devastation caused by capitalism. Ratzinger had a different charisma and different abilities from his predecessor. He was emotionally cautious, and his start was careful. He was gentler and less dominating, which was helpful for outsiders and those belonging to other denominations. For him the church was not a one-man show but a community of faith and values working on behalf of the generations to come against the decline of society. He wanted to reawaken a tired Christianity from its lethargy. Whereas John Paul II's main concern was to hold on to the church at all costs, his successor was set on an inner renewal – even at the risk of losing power.

For the first time there was a leading theoretician of modernity in the chair of St Peter. He had the experience of an atheist dictatorship behind him, as well as the rise and problems of postmodernism. His ability to deliver apposite analyses was more than ever in demand. The hope was that the comeback of religion would also benefit the national churches. Exhausted by the exertions of seeking after luxury and fashions, an increasing sector of society longed for new support for 'values, faith and behaviour', as Die Zeit said. After the collapse of communism and seeing the excesses of uncontrolled capitalism in the globalized world, Christianity seemed to many to be the final remaining vision of a just and peaceful world. In future, progress could mean spirituality as the source of strength and well-being, and as the foundation for responsible action. With an intellectual as pope, his followers dreamed, the Vatican would become a new 'Club of Rome', the leader of a new movement critical of society. It would offer not only criticism but also the idea of salvation for a society that was destroying itself.

The question was: did the Catholic Church's lack of adaptability damage the church? Was it against the modern way of life? Was the world looking at the end of the church? Or at the end of modernity, which had run into a blind alley by stultification and financial chaos, climate disaster and war, the destruction of civilization and the decline of the political class?

Certainly Ratzinger embodied a new intelligence in the unfolding of the mysteries of the faith. On the other hand, it could not be overlooked that Catholicism was without influence externally, and internally it was more split and undermined than ever before. The loss of Christian awareness was too far advanced. Lifestyle and culture had changed too much to make a mass conversion likely. Still, something else had changed: during the Cold War the Western political powers were intent on having the Catholic Church on their side in the fight against communism. That was over. Now the church was seen as an opponent of progress, against a wholly secularized society. No one knew the church as well as Ratzinger, who was loaded with detailed information from every corner of the Earth. But after a giant like Wojtyła, weren't the shoes of the fisherman a bit too big for the former prefect? Wouldn't he trip up in them? There were fears in the Curia that possibly he lacked the talent to translate his intellectual creativity into deeds and decisions. In this he was like another German, Albert Einstein, who had grown up in Munich. The discoverer of the theory of relativity and Nobel prize-winner also avoided complications, wherever he could, so as not to be thrown off course by the petty things in life. He seemed to be immune from emotions such as vanity, jealousy, anger or bitterness. He was untouched by most of the things that affected other people, in order to follow the revelation of an inner mental world which he believed showed him the way. For Ratzinger that meant not doing what was spectacular but what was essential. Calmly and confidently. The church's real problems in the West were not celibacy or the ordination of women, he stressed, but over-institutionalization, loss of the life of faith and lack of social-political commitment. A feel-good church failed to recognize the drama of Christianity. Jesus was not just a healer but also an agitator.

The new pope began work very cautiously. It was almost as if he was not only the vicar of Christ but also the vicar of Wojtyła, and as if he was afraid that 'the little pope', as he described himself, would detract from his great predecessor. However, in Rome it was felt that the pope was there again. A pope no longer sitting in a wheelchair, a pope not struggling for air and whose hand does not tremble if he wants to say something.

Soon a routine was established in the most famous *appartamento* in the world, the papal apartment on the third floor on the right in the Apostolic Palace. It was quite different from a real palace or grand ceremonial court. Indeed, at 300 square metres, the flat was not particularly small. However, the largest part of it was the chapel. Wojtyła had only had a work room and a sleeping room. Ratzinger also got a living room, and he had the flat renovated, exchanging dark carpets for lighter ones. The old bookshelves were brought from his former home, with each book put back in its place. Dr Buzzonetti, the pope's 82-year-old personal doctor, who had not only served Wojtyła but also Albino Luciani (Pope John Paul I), installed an exercise bike with an extra tough setting (although it was never used).

In the Palazzo, besides the pope, the 'papal family' consisted of four Italian women from the Communione e Liberazione community, as well as the German and the Polish secretaries. The valet Angelo Gugel, who like Dr Buzzonetti had also served John Paul I and John Paul II, lived out and frequently drove off secretly to a Roman beach. Ingrid Stampa, Ratzinger's former housekeeper, who wanted to join the household, was turned down. (More about that below.) Everyday conversation was in Italian. At first it was necessary to find the right *modus vivendi* in the household, the happy medium for the 'the time to speak, the time to be quiet, the time to give and the time to take', as Gänswein put it. Also how they celebrated name days (with Asti Spumante or a sweet wine from southern Italy), what films they watched together (among the Top Ten were the whole series of *Don Camillo and Peppone*). At 8 p.m. the two secretaries watched the evening news together with the Holy Father.

Benedict usually got up at 5.30 a.m. Before that he said a first prayer in bed, then celebrated early Mass in the private chapel, had breakfast and went to his work rooms on the second floor of the Apostolic Palace. Shortly after he arrived, his secretary was at the door with the first post and the programme for the morning. The pope had to be informed of which audiences were set for him and how things were in his own diocese, which he had to lead as bishop of Rome. 'Because he simply did not have time for them', the less important things usually landed up in the secretariat of state. For his morning briefing the secretary had 30 to a maximum of 45 minutes. Ratzinger needed the next 45 to 60 minutes to prepare for the morning tasks. There was a second briefing in the afternoon.

At 10 a.m. there was the international press review, put together by a department of the secretariat of state. The time between 11 a.m. and 1 p.m. was spent in the *seconda loggia*, the storey of the palazzo for the pope's work with its audience rooms, smaller rooms and the offices of the Vatican diplomatic service. These were reserved for the select few who had the honour of being received in audience by Christ's representative. As under John Paul II, Tuesday was kept free. Ratzinger wanted to devote at least one day in the week to his own writing. The biblical scholar Thomas Söding marvelled that anyone who as pope added 'regular times for study to his diary' must be 'filled with unbounded curiosity to learn, assimilate and think through what others have thought, said and written'. Since Pius II in the fifteenth century, there had 'never been such an educated humanist on the chair of Peter' as Benedict XVI.[6]

It was almost symbolic that right at the beginning of his time as pope, in addition to Gammarelli, the traditional firm in charge of the pope's wardrobe, Benedict appointed another tailor, Euroclero, the specialist supplier of church requirements in Rome. Another change was that, unlike his predecessor, he seldom or never had visitors to his morning Mass or lunch. Of course, in a way that was a deficiency, he said in our conversation 'but I could not do otherwise. I need silence and composure there, so that I can celebrate Mass without a lot of people and pray quietly. I am not capable of plunging straight into the day with meetings, which are always in different languages. It would have been too much for me. And I also need quiet at mealtimes'.

Whereas Wojtyła had often waited until the audience itself to be brought up to speed with the subject, Ratzinger had already made an extensive study of the files and often knew the problems in the different areas of the Roman Catholic world better than many local bishops. His excellent memory helped him cope with the details of a problem. As for dogmatic questions, he was regarded as a super-pope. The formerly so authoritative Congregation for the Doctrine of the Faith hardly got a look in. Theology was the pope's concern.

At 6 p.m. he withdrew upstairs into his apartment to spend an hour at the so-called table audiences with his most important colleagues, particularly the cardinal secretary of state, to discuss situations in private. From 8.45 p.m. the pope was alone. The table in his bedroom was not for stacks of papers or the often mediocre reports and unappealing case records heaped on his desk. This bedroom table was for his *Schott* missal from childhood and other liturgical books, with which he prepared for the Masses and meditations of the morrow.

At his enthronement Joseph Ratzinger was formally regarded as the most powerful pope of all time. Never had the Catholic Church been so widespread. But its composition had changed radically. During Benedict's papacy the majority of Catholics were no longer white. They spoke mainly Spanish and belonged to countries with poorer, or the poorest, populations. Sixty-seven per cent of the faithful lived in Africa, Asia and Latin America.[7] In 2004 there were more Catholic baptisms in the Philippines than in France, Spain, Italy and Poland put together. More than ever before, a pope had to deal with a church whose members lived mainly in the global South. During the previous 25 years the number of priests in Europe had dropped by 18 per cent, and the number of nuns by 36 per cent. In 1978, 85 per cent of the population in Ireland still went to Mass on Sundays, now it was only 44 per cent. And the proportion of Catholics from the South was forecast to increase further to 75 per cent by the year 2025.

The British historian and scholar of religion Philip Jenkins, professor at Pennsylvania State University from 1980 until 2011, pointed out that Western commentators had often portrayed John Paul II as a reactionary titan 'who fought against the overwhelming current of history, against modernization, secularism and feminism'. But if his time in office was looked at in a broader context, John Paul II could be seen 'as a figure who swims not against but with the current of history'. Then Wojtyła was not a throwback to the thirteenth century but 'a foretaste of the twenty-first century' – in which all those tendencies he promoted and embodied would become a new reality.

Seen from outside Europe, Jenkins continued, the pope's apparently bizarre obsessions appeared completely appropriate.

Extra-European nations would increasingly bring their culture, their influence and their attitude to bear on the world church. For example, there were dioceses in Africa that found it incomprehensible when secularized societies relativized the institution of marriage. 'The Roman Catholic Church is now the church of the young and of the faithful from the global South,' said Jenkins 'and it will become still more so in the course of the century.' In short: 'What seems important in a secularized Western society, suffocating in its riches and alleged democratic order, will be nowhere near as important for a Christian in India, Africa or China.' From the viewpoint of the South, the pressing concerns were less about questions of sexuality than about poverty and oppression. 'In the pope's mind Nigeria and the Philippines count in a way that the Netherlands or even Germany have no longer counted for decades. The United States still count – but increasingly because of its Latinos and Asians, rather than the vociferous white Americans.'[8]

The first writings of the new pope that illustrate the style of his papacy were not to his bishops or colleagues in the Curia, but to the Jewish community in Rome. 'I trust in the supreme Lord,' he wrote in a letter to Chief Rabbi Riccardo Di Segni, 'to continue and strengthen the dialogue with the sons and daughters of the Jewish people.'[9] A short time later, at his first inter-religious meeting, he announced the escalation of Christian–Muslim dialogue.[10] Things went on cheerfully. He quietly abolished the 'hand kissing', when at the end of every general audience dozens of people stood in a queue before the pope's throne. 'Let's stay normal,' he said to a former assistant who wanted to kiss his ring at a meeting in Castel Gandolfo of the Ratzinger student circle. As for beatifications and canonizations, he wanted to lead only the most recent ones himself. Beatifications ought to be decentralized and take place in the appropriate diocese. However, he spent a lot of time in meetings with the priests of the diocese of Rome, listening to their worries for hours.

His first appointment of a bishop also attracted attention. It was the liberation theologian Severino Clasen, a student of Leonardo Boff's, whom he appointed as bishop of the Brazilian diocese of Araçuaí. With the appointment of Cardinal William Levada from San Francisco, for the first time a US American became leader of the Congregation for the Doctrine of the Faith. There was similar surprise at the announcement of the resumption of official conversations with the Orthodox Church, which had been initiated in the year 2000. Authentic unity, he declared, would be 'neither absorption nor fusion' but should respect the 'manifold richness of the churches'.[11] The Christian presence in Europe could only be effective if the Christian churches pursued the path of unity.

It caused a sensation when, from among his many titles, Ratzinger dropped the title 'Patriarch of the West', which popes had borne for one and a half millennia. Curia officials mocked that the new pope was beginning to dismantle the papacy. Observers saw the action as a friendly gesture towards Orthodoxy. On the other hand, dropping the title 'Patriarch of the West' stressed the primacy of the bishop of Rome, who was not just one of the patriarchs, as he was thought of in the Orthodox Church and the Near East.

The Benedict style was taking shape. 'We are not working, as many say we are, to defend our power,' he said at the first meeting with colleagues in his secretariat of state. 'We have no worldly, secular power. We are not working for prestige, or to expand a business, or some such thing. Really, we are working so that the roads of the world are open for Christ.'[12] The basis of his authority was not just being professional, as could be demanded from any functioning administration, but also love for Christ, his church and human souls. He also mentioned the papal nuncios in 176 countries, through whom the Vatican engaged in diplomatic relations. The nuncios should not be driven by careerism and power-seeking but strive tirelessly to be model priests with an intensive life of prayer. Only thus could they do their job successfully and fruitfully. The church's mission was not to dismiss other religious and cultural traditions but to behave wisely and respectfully towards them.

By his choice of name, coat of arms and insignia this German pope had already given an indication of the style of his papacy. 'Benedict' comes from the Latin word *Benedictus* and means 'blessed' or also 'well said'. In the light of the years of slanders and insults against the former prefect, it amounted to a message. Ratzinger was also referring to two great names in the church: Benedict XV, the 'peace pope', and St Benedict of Nursia, the patron saint of Europe. 'I wanted to be called Benedict XVI,' he explained, 'because I wanted to link myself spiritually to the venerable Pope

Benedict XV, who led the church during the stormy period of the First World War.' He wanted to carry out his papacy 'in the service of reconciliation and harmony between people and nations,[...] convinced that the great good of peace is a gift from God, a fragile and valuable gift that had to be sought, protected and strengthened day by day through the efforts of all'.[13]

Benedict XV, whose name in civil life was Giacomo Paolo Giovanni Battista della Chiesa, reigned from 1914 until 1922. He went down in history as a peacemaker although, despite countless appeals and initiatives, he failed to prevent the First World War. He condemned that war as the 'suicide of the nations of Europe'. He rejected the Treaty of Versailles as a vindictive dictatorial imposition. The pope supported the League of Nations (the predecessor to the United Nations). In his apostolic letter *Maximum illud* he denounced all European nationalistic ideas. He called for the canonization of women, such as Margaret Mary Alacoque and Joan of Arc. He declared the 'Octave of Prayer for Christian Unity' initiated, among others, by the Anglican convert Paul Wattson, to be obligatory. He confirmed that 'the church is not Latin, Greek or Slavic but Catholic'. There was no difference between its children, regardless of which grouping they belonged to.

Ratzinger's reference to Benedict of Nursia, the father of Western monasticism, was also important. Benedict's motto, *ora et labora*, 'pray and work', and his Rule (the *Regula Benedicti*), founded in Montecassino, was the basis of a new departure for Europe in the sixth century. Hundreds of thousands of his monks cultivated the West with agriculture, knowledge and education. In his explanation of what linked him to the great saint, Benedict said he 'represented a landmark for the unity of Europe and a reminder of the essential Christian roots of its culture and civilization'.[14]

For his papal coat of arms Benedict took over his former shield with the mysterious 'Moor of Freising', the bear with a pack saddle as 'God's burden-bearer' and the scallop shell as a symbol of human pilgrimage, as well as a reference to his great teacher Augustine. The motto also remained the same: 'Co-operators for the truth'. As the first pope of the new era, he rejected the tiara on his coat of arms, and also the triple crown, which could be seen as a sign of worldly power. Instead, he put a simple mitre with three golden horizontal stripes, standing for the pope's three offices: ordained ministry, jurisdiction and teaching.

It was also new that he brought the pallium image into his coat of arms. The pallium was a kind of stole made of white lamb's-wool, woven by nuns from the Convent of St Cecilia in the Rome district of Trastevere. It stood for the shepherd, who carries the lost lamb on his shoulder and brings it to the water of life. The five crosses embroidered on it symbolized Christ's five wounds. Three of them were pierced by nails, recalling the three nails on the cross. At his enthronement as pope, for the first time in a thousand years, Benedict XVI again wore a pallium with red, instead of the formerly customary black, crosses on it. The last time red had been used – when the church was not yet split – it had been worn by the German pope Leo IX, on whose feast day, 19 April, Joseph Ratzinger had slipped into the shoes of the fisherman.

With John Paul II everything had reached top figures: the number of audiences, journeys, documents, liturgical feasts, canonizations. Benedict wanted to reduce things. Less is more, was his motto. Vatican colleagues confirmed that many things soon became tighter, more efficient and more transparent. He reduced private audiences, avoided long speeches, published less, and what he did publish was shorter – and he went to bed earlier. On the other hand, he restored regular conversations with all the heads of dicasteries, which he had taken over as they were from the previous papacy. But whereas John Paul II and his *alter ego*, Stanisław Dziwisz, introduced Polish confidants into all sorts of positions, Benedict did not resort to that, so missed out on building possibilities of influence. 'Certainly, I was a German pope,' Benedict said. 'I did not want to disown what was German, but neither did I want to accentuate it. It was to be a papacy for all, facing the problems of today.'[15]

John Paul II had often had speeches written for him months before the due date. Benedict sometimes stood up in an auditorium and excused himself, saying that unfortunately he had not had time to draft a speech. But perhaps, he said at an *ad limina* visit of the Swiss bishops, it was appropriate 'for a pope at this moment in church history also to be poor in this respect'. Of course, he had 'thought about it a bit' – and went on to present an analysis of the tasks that currently needed to be done in Switzerland.

At the beginning of his time as pope, Benedict's meetings with contemporaries in opposition were particularly striking. On 20 August 2005 he received Bernard Fellay, the excommunicated leader of the Society of St Pius X. 'The conversation must have been very thin' was how newspapers interpreted the dry communiqué that the Vatican subsequently published. He also invited the combative atheist journalist Oriana Fallaci, and then his sharpest critic, Hans Küng. Secretary Gänswein arranged the room, had Küng met at the airport and accompanied the two former colleagues in their walk through the Castel Gandolfo park. After lunch Ratzinger and Küng had a private two-hour conversation. After it Küng told the waiting reporters that they had agreed on a statement, in which he spoke of a 'personal reconciliation'. Archbishop Rino Fisichella said of the meeting: 'The signal was that the pope does not shy away from anyone. In the Vatican's press statement the meeting with Küng was presented positively. That did for Küng as the figurehead of protest. He had become a sacrifice to his own vanity.'[16]

Ratzinger's active secretary kept on working positively for Ratzinger's image. Gänswein came from the Black Forest. His father was a seventh-generation blacksmith and had a smallholding. Later he also ran an agricultural machinery business. However, it did not bring in much money. ('Sometimes we had to eke things out very carefully.') His mother came from an innkeeper's family, and as a housewife she brought up five children on her own. 'Compliance is not exactly my forte,' Gänswein recorded, so there were frictions with his father. His hair became longer and longer, and Pink Floyd and other rock music blared from the adolescent boy's room.

The young man was non-political; his passions were music, football and skiing. In his later school years and as a student he earned money as a post-boy on his bicycle. As the first-born, he was expected to take over the father's agricultural machinery business, but he wanted to become a stockbroker. 'Suddenly existential questions cropped up. So I began to search, and in that way I was unintentionally pushed towards philosophy and theology.' He approached the priesthood step by step. He was ordained in 1984 and spent his first years as a curate in the Black Forest. After that he was sent to Munich for further studies. 'I had always enjoyed studying and found it easy, but I found the study of canon law as dry as working in a dusty quarry,

where there was no beer. After six months I had had enough.' Help
came from his doctoral supervisor, the church lawyer Winfried
Aymans, who was able to show him new perspectives. 'That really
helped me not to throw everything away.'

The press images of an ageing church leader with snow-white
hair and a good-looking young monsignor standing beside him
brought a new note into the presentation of a pope. Critics accused
Gänswein of being too outspoken. A papal secretary should stay in
the background. However, colourful illustrated magazines happily
pounced on the 'sunny boy in the soutane', who was soon gracing
front covers as the 'Vatican George Clooney'. According to the Swiss
Weltwoche, he was 'decidedly the most handsome man in a cassock
ever to be seen in the Vatican'. The designer Donatella Versace even
dedicated one of her fashion lines to him. His mail often included
letters from yearning admirers. 'Don Giorgio' did his own thing, and
on trips to the mountains or walks in Castel Gandolfo he put a chic
white baseball cap on his boss's head, which made the pope look
young and cool. However, the *camauro* (the winter cap traditionally
worn by the pope, made of red wool or velvet with white ermine
trim), last worn by John XXIII, swiftly made a comeback. No one
had interpreted the baseball cap as the signal that the pope wanted
reform, but the press trumpeted that the *camauro* meant that he was
definitely for restoration. Actually there was a simple reason for the
use of the historic cap. 'I had become frozen, and my head is sensitive.
And I said, if we've got a *camauro* then let's put it on. It was really just
to resist the cold. But after that I did not put it on again. To prevent
superfluous interpretations arising.'[17]

Benedict was also sensitive about something else, which had
far-reaching effects on his time in office. It was his constant worry
about his health, which he believed to be weak. Ratzinger assumed
that his time in office would not last long, at most three or four
years. In retrospect, that could be interpreted as a design fault of his
papacy. 'I knew it would not be a long papacy,' he told me in our
conversation,

> that I could not carry out any great long-term projects. For
> example, I could not summon a new council or undertake great
> reorganizations. I knew that organizational things were not my

forte but also were not necessary. John Paul II's reform of the Curia, *Pastor bonus*, had just come into force and I did not think it right to overturn that immediately.

But, I asked him, didn't that attitude affect the whole programme of your papacy?

Clearly, it did. I realized that, above all, I had to do things to reinstate the centrality of faith in God, give people the courage to believe, and courage to live that faith in this world. Faith, reason, those were things that I recognized as my mission and for which it was not important whether my papacy lasted long or not.[18]

One of the pope's central concerns was his worry about what Johannes B. Metz called the 'God crisis': the estrangement of people from faith. If God was left out, a God who knew us and spoke to us, he warned, then society lost the foundations of a civilized existence. He illustrated the church's task with a sentence ascribed to Teresa of Ávila: 'We are the eyes with which his pity looks at sufferers, we are the hands that he stretches out to bless and to heal; we are the feet he uses to walk with and to do good; we are the lips that proclaim his gospel.' Ratzinger added in his own words: 'We are called to overcome our differences, to bring peace and reconciliation in conflict situations and to give the world a message of hope. We are called to be open to people in need and share our earthly goods generously with all who have less than us.'

He was not an ideologist, and as a Christian he did not dream of Paradise on Earth, but like the apostle Paul, whom he often quoted, he had a vision of a better world: 'Let us build a community of love according to the Creator's plan, which was made known to us by his Son.' 'The vital power of his light,' he said at Christmas 2005 in his first *Urbi et orbi* address, 'gives us courage, to work for the creation of a new world order, founded on just ethical and economic relationships.'

26

Benedetto Mania

There is no apprenticeship for the papacy, not even any training for a new head of the Catholic Church and his closest colleagues. No briefing or instructions. 'Everything had to go on quickly,' said Georg Gänswein, 'the general audiences, the bishops' *ad limina* visits, which had already been arranged, parish visits, inquiries from cardinals and requests from heads of governments and state presidents.' As well as that, Easter was coming. The secretariat of state had prepared eight pages of greetings in 60 languages in phonetic script and provided a demo tape so that the pope could practise them in time.

'The only thing I got was a private conversation with my predecessor,' said Gänswein. 'He pressed an envelope into my hand, containing some papers and a key to a safe. A very old safe of German make.' In the safe there were account numbers and a jumble of valuable rings that John Paul II had been given, and also pectoral crosses and jewellery from the time of Pius XII and John XXIII. The envelope contained personal data of the Curia, which was passed on from one papal secretary to the next. 'Monsignor Stanisław Dziwisz only said: "Now you have a very important, very beautiful but also very, very difficult job. It is important that the pope should not be crushed. He must be able to breathe. You have to see that he has a buffer zone. That is the only thing that I advise you. As for the rest, you will have to deal with it yourself, as it comes."'[1]

The new pope could not imagine how heavy the demands on the head of the Catholic Church were, even though he had observed the papacy of his predecessor for a quarter of a century as his closest colleague. 'I did not feel too bad,' Benedict reported, 'but it is true that at the beginning you are almost crushed by this burden.'[2] He was only able to cope with the almost overwhelming programme of the first few months through his disciplined use of time and his lightning-quick mastery of the documents. However, when 'things lay on his desk which he knew must have already been worked on, in time he became restless', his secretary reported. 'He could not bear it. The work had to be taken off the table.'[3] After a start at full speed Gänswein himself observed that 'the pace I had set myself was too fast'. To begin in a position of advantage was one thing but 'to get through and come to the end is another'. Now they had to 'find the right pace'.

It was tricky to cope with the countless requests for private audiences, 'which were all for good reasons'. The 'endless inquiries' – with footnotes such as 'just for a minute' or 'an exception for once' or 'the pope has known me for a long time'. It became urgently necessary 'to introduce a stronger filter, which again led to the criticism that it was impossible to get to the Holy Father; he was isolated in a golden cage'.

Ratzinger made his first journey as pope on 29 May 2005 to the 24th National Eucharistic Congress in Bari in the south of Italy, the city of St Nicholas. On the way he asked the helicopter pilot to land in his Puglian home village and chatted casually with the inhabitants who flocked to meet him. In Bari as the helicopter circled over the coastland and the sea, a wave of enthusiasm broke out. Four hundred – mainly young – people had gathered to greet him, twice as many as expected. The pope spoke about Sundays and the essential food of the Eucharist. It was as silent as a monastery. But as soon as the elderly man with his shaky voice intoned the *Sanctus*, loud rejoicing broke out. At that moment Ratzinger was confirmed as pope by acclamation of his Italian people. 'The church is certainly not old and static,' he had proclaimed before his enthronement, 'no, it is young.' The pictures of Benedict's first appearance to his young public gave the impression that, after John Paul II, someone had given Catholicism a fresh lick of paint, made it a kind of pop culture, which people had thought came only with sex, drugs and rock and roll.

Something had changed. When the public saw the man and his impact directly, unfiltered by ideological distortions, even *Der Spiegel* had to admit 'the public goodwill for Pope Benedict, alias Joseph Ratzinger, did not dwindle'. 'If I am honest, I could not bear him,' a 59-year-old housewife, Teresa La Peruta, told a *New York Times* reporter, but now Ratzinger was beginning to convince her: 'I hope he goes on being like that.' A pilgrim from Bavaria reported that during a papal Mass she had 'suddenly clicked'. She had felt: 'There is nothing artificial about him, his smile is not switched on, but suddenly there is a man whose soul is in his eyes.'

Even before Benedict's election a certain 'Ratzinger fashion' had grown among intellectuals in Germany. The sharpness of his arguments, his voluminous education and the accuracy of his analyses aroused a desire, even in agnostics, to come to terms with his philosophical work in particular. The weekly paper *Die Zeit* noted that many people had grasped 'that Ratzinger is not a power-seeker, that his conservatism does not mean allying himself with the prevailing circumstances; he is nonconformist because he does not conform with the current belief in progress.'

'This is something new', said Antonio Tedesco, the director of the German-speaking pilgrim centre in Rome. 'I have never seen so many people. In the midst of the summer heat, in the midst of the winter cold. And many of them do not just come along passively but want to show that they belong together.'[4] Wojtyła was a man of images; his successor was a man of words. People came to the former to see him; they came to the latter to hear him. As a first assessment, *L' Osservatore Romano* put it: 'If during the 27 years of his papacy we learned to see Pope Wojtyła as a zealous and tireless "shepherd of the world", in the first two months of Ratzinger's papacy we have begun to see him as a sensitive and attentive "spiritual leader" of the people of God, thirsting for truth and hope.'

The wind had changed first in Italy. From the former 'Cardinal No', the strict guardian of the faith, overnight in the media he had become a sensitive old man, a man with an aristocratic attitude, brilliant rhetoric and exemplary humility. The magazine *Panorama* said he had a 'blessed power'. Journalists kept reporting that Ratzinger was a cordial soul, who went for walks in the streets round St Peter's Square, got on well with cats, asked fruit sellers which were the best apples for apple turnovers and was a close friend of the football manager Giovanni Trapattoni. (Trapattoni himself said the new pope was a man 'who knew how to score goals'.) Philosophers boasted they were on good terms with the ex-prefect. The commentator Pietroangelo Buttafuco said: 'The former "priest-eaters" [*mangiapreti*, an Italian word for anticlericals] are no longer there, because this time the priest is one of the finest and deepest.'

At public demand Italian television broadcast Benedict's Sunday and Wednesday messages live from St Peter's Square. Suddenly Catholicism was being hyped in the media with the pope as its star. Publishers competed for the rights to publish his catecheses and speeches. Prominent people such as the German actor Mario Adorf now found the former grand inquisitor 'very experienced, very intelligent'. Benedict was 'reserved, competent and friendly'. 'We spoke about my mother's death,' said the actress Veronica Ferres. 'What he said moved me deeply.' This pope reached 'even those for whom the church had long since had nothing to offer'. Football's 'Kaiser' Franz Beckenbauer said his 48-second audience with Benedict was 'the high point of my life'. The pope had inspired him: 'I have seldom seen a man with such radiance, such kindness and such friendliness in his face. Humanity needs him,' he said of the new pope, 'I believe he is more necessary than ever.'

The view of him changed, and Ratzinger was surprised because he himself was no different. The writer Martin Walser said about Ratzinger that in the past he had only heard 'short news reports without seeing him in person'. Now that he had become aware of Ratzinger's 'essence', he was 'tremendously impressed that he is so credible'. There was a 'difference between opinion and essence', according to Walser. 'You can be right or wrong about opinions. But the essence appears and is then credible or not.'[5]

Seldom did a pope stand in such a light at the beginning of his time in office. The change of millennium, the sufferings of John Paul II and a new younger generation of passionate Christians created a situation in which Benedict XVI could carry forward the harvest of his great predecessor and stop the downward trend. Since Ratzinger had become pope, the numbers leaving the church had declined. Places to rejoin the church such as the 'St Michael's Faith Information' in central Munich were now in demand in a way previously unimaginable. In Berlin Cardinal Georg Sterzinsky received more applicants for adult baptism than ever before. After years of decline the Catholic Theological Faculty Days in Germany reported a 'significant growth' in new applicants for all theological courses of study in the winter semester of 2005/6. In Bavarian seminaries 50 per cent more applicants for the priesthood enrolled than in the previous year. 'We need not be embarrassed by living authentically, lovingly and faithfully to God's word,' the Bamberg auxiliary bishop Werner Radspieler proclaimed. There was also a climate change among the Catholic youth. One activist said about the new feeling of self-worth: 'Where there was once shame and reserve about matters of faith', now there was an awareness that 'we have a message that makes us free, that is something wonderful, which we want to tell others about'.

As prefect of the Congregation for the Doctrine of the Faith, Ratzinger had sometimes failed to communicate well. People thought he often seemed depressed. But now 'the face of a blooming, liberated man' was to be seen, the theologian Eugen Biser told the *Süddeutsche Zeitung*. 'In fact, it is a paradox. Manifestly Benedict XVI is liberated from his previous job.' Moreover, he was 'a pope who has the greatest theological competence since Leo the Great'. Biser confirmed: 'He is a pope who puts the idea of being a representative at the heart of his papacy. He is not the head of the church, not the cult object of the church. He stands for another, who alone must be loved and believed in.' That was the beginning of 'a church in which faith does not consist merely in the acceptance of dogma, but is understood as an invitation to experience God'. The new pope was already one of the 'most important popes in history'. The former Bavarian culture minister Hans Maier added that after 'the larger than life-size, almost Renaissance figure' of the Polish pope, now they had a head of the church 'who has a sense of order and regularity, who does not stand out by an impatient zeal for reform, who does not want to do everything himself, who can also wait for time to do something for him'.[6]

The unexpected qualities of the new pope also made former critics thoughtful. The *New York Times* commented: 'Whereas any other new pope would soon have been contrasted with the powerful, magnetic and charismatic John Paul II, Benedict has his own reserved, modest attraction.' His appearance was 'gentle, even shy, his voice was quiet and his thinking clear'. Joaquín Navarro-Valls, director of the Vatican press office, said: 'Benedict XVI is a media phenomenon – despite or because of the fact that he is challenging. People listen to him.' The secret of his communication clearly lay in the fact that at a time of ambiguity he spoke clearly and fascinated people by the richness and simplicity of his expression.

Indeed, never before were a pope's words heard by so many people at once all round the globe. The pope's speeches appeared on the front pages of the world's press. Everywhere the pope's books stormed the best-seller lists and provided the largest crash course in the faith of all time. It was not a flash in the pan. For the first time in history a papal encyclical could be sold to millions of people, something previously inconceivable. In Italy even the Latin edition of Benedict's first encyclical had to be reprinted – following a first edition of 450,000 copies. He did not appeal only to a restricted audience, but was able to reach both intellectuals and simple believers. Up to 60,000 people awaited him on Sundays and Wednesdays in St Peter's Square. At the beginning of May, 100,000 people gathered for the *Regina coeli* prayer, and for many of them the meeting was a magic moment. '*Corragio ti vogliamo bene*' was displayed on young people's banners held high, as they waved at the pope: 'Courage, we like you.' There was a 'constant attitude of expectation', the German *Tagespost* reported, 'as if in the pope's every action, every gesture, every word there was something to be found that would show the way forward'.[7]

Even in his first year of office Benedict gathered almost 4 million people round him – more than any of his predecessors in a similar time span. 'You have conquered many people's hearts,' Franca Ciampi, the Italian president's wife, enthused about the new pope. 'And that was not easy after the glittering papacy of John Paul II.' The country's leaders had realized that this project also offered the chance for a regeneration of the nation. Catholicism was almost unthinkable without Italy, and Italy without Catholicism. State president Ciampi declared that the 'Italian model', with its separation of church and state, combined with a respect for Christian values, would soon set a precedent elsewhere.

There were signs of this. 'Germany is not a land of God-fearers, and there is only a rush to church at Easter and Christmas', the journalist Hans Leyendecker wrote in the *Süddeutsche Zeitung.* However, 'even the members of the consumer society' felt that 'there was something greater than Mammon and wealth. And who embodies modesty more than the Catholic intellectual with the scurrying walk?' Benedict XVI was 'someone who finds a foothold on unstable ground'.[8]

Rolf Hill, chairman of the Working Group for Evangelical Theology, was convinced that 'the enthusiasm for Catholicism expressed by many Protestants was probably because with the pope Catholics have someone who says things simply and clearly'. The culture critic and historian Gustav Seibt saw it thus: the 'astonishing attraction' of 'a Catholicism once again representing itself in its ritual strength' derived 'less from renewed piety than from the contrast with the couldn't-care-less attitude of the liberal present with its wealth of ideologies on offer, and the non-committal feel-good factor of modern religiosity. If there is to be any religion, then let it be Catholic.' But the bishop of the Evangelical-Lutheran regional church of Hanover, Margot Kässmann, was unconvinced. She could not go along with 'unrestrained pope euphoria'.

It had been said of Ratzinger that he could not get on with people, especially not large crowds. He had a fear of touching and could not embrace anyone. The former Franciscan Leonardo Boff prophesied: 'It will be difficult to love this pope.' But all at once a great number of the public saw how Ratzinger, who was regarded as shy, withdrawn and hard-hearted, hugged children and warmly shook hands. 'He looks at everyone he has to do with, sometimes searchingly, sometimes genially. He likes to grasp both hands when he is talking to someone', the author Christian Feldmann observed. 'He goes slowly from one person to another, takes time for a couple of sentences, stays a while with an old lady or a child and keeps bishops waiting who want to speak to him.'[9]

'If you don't how you should pray, then ask God to teach you,' he said to teenagers from the Netherlands. He was decidedly sober on questions of the future: 'I think there is no system for a rapid change,' he told priests in the Aosta Valley. 'We must keep going along this passage, through this tunnel, with patience and the certainty that Christ is the answer and at the end his light will shine again.' When he gave his *Urbi et orbi* blessing at Christmas, he made an appeal: 'You modern people, who are grown up and yet weak in thinking and willing, let the child of Bethlehem take you by the hand. Don't be afraid, trust him!'

At the beginning he was a bit embarrassed when someone addressed him as 'Holy Father' or 'Your Holiness'. Or he flinched when someone tried to kiss his hand. Then he abolished hand-kissing. Sometimes, quite against protocol, he sprang from his chair, as if he were not worthy to remain sitting. His emotions were still kept in check, his gestures sometimes uncertain. He looked interested but also shy. However, he did not want to go for effects that would impress the public or the media. 'That was his style,' said Gänswein. 'None of us tried to foist anything upon him. Of course we made certain suggestions, but he did not take them up.'[10]

Not even when, with his lack of rhetoric, Benedict gazed into space as if to read a text from an imaginary page within him. 'I have to admit that my voice was often not powerful enough and I was not yet familiar enough with the text really to be able to offer it ad lib,' Ratzinger said in our conversation. 'That was certainly a weakness. And my voice is naturally weak. But I think that when you have to speak as much and as often as a pope must, then you are sometimes over-taxed.'[11]

Evidently, many professional observers underestimated two things. First was the aura of the office. Being pope is not just any job. It lends a powerful mystique. Second was Ratzinger's ability to grow very quickly into a new role. There was also a new lightness, the power of his poetry and a gleam in his eyes, which had not been seen for a long while. Benedict was writing with new ink. He was writing with his heart's blood. It was the transformation of a man, who with the light of life could again be the person he actually was. After the decades of attacks in the Congregation for the Doctrine of the Faith his defensive position gave way to an aura of gentle kindness. Above all, without any hectic agitation Ratzinger had done something that no one had thought possible: a transition without any break, the seamless fusion of two papacies. And whereas at the beginning he described his election as a 'guillotine', now he corrected that with an emotion in his voice that could not be missed: 'I thank God [...] who has called me to be a successor to the apostle Peter in the service of the church and has given me his vital help.'

His appearance in Bari gave a foretaste of what was to come, but after the 20th World Youth Day in Cologne in August 2005 there could no longer be any doubt about the potential of the new papacy. In the run-up to it, critics like Eugen Drewermann dismissed the event as 'cheap entertainment'. But in fact it was perhaps the most beautiful manifestation of Christian faith that had ever occurred on German soil. People from 200 countries came to meet the pope, to spend the night praying and singing and to celebrate the Eucharist in Marienfeld, an enormous open air space in the Cologne district.

After the death of a pope and new pope's election, the Catholic Year 2005 in Cologne reached a new climax. Eight hundred bishops gave the blessing, 10,000 priests distributed Holy Communion and with 1.2 million participants the World Youth Day was the biggest religious event ever in Germany. 'The volcano erupted there,' secretary Gänswein recalled. 'The enthusiasm for Benedict XVI knew no bounds. That did him good and also encouraged him. From that moment, with that wind in his sails, many things that had looked difficult to him before became easier.' Benedict himself confessed that he would 'not have dared to arrange it' himself. So it had been God's act of providence that had taken him to Germany so soon, on his first foreign trip as pope to the long-planned World Youth Day. Even on his arrival he had told journalists: 'I am very moved, that I can come back to my own country.' Then he called out: 'God bless my dear fatherland.'

Many thousands flocked the streets, millions sat at home watching television, as the federal president, Horst Köhler, met his important guest at the airport saying, 'Welcome home, welcome to Germany'. The schedule and security arrangements were at the highest level. Ingeborg Arians, head of protocol for the city of Cologne, said: 'Like the protocol for the English queen, our protocol is one of the strictest. Not just minutes were planned but even seconds.'[12]

When the first 179,000 young people crowded onto the banks of the Rhine to wave to the pope on his boat, many of them up to their hips in water, the scene recalled Jesus' disciples at the Sea of Galilee. 'I want to show the young people of the world that it is beautiful to be a Christian,' Benedict XVI called to his audience. 'Being borne along by a great love and knowledge is not a burden but wings.' The

Cologne archbishop Joachim Meisner had placed his three-room flat at his friend's disposal. He observed: 'At first Ratzinger only spoke to the young people from the steamboat. […] I said to him: "You must also turn to the left." Then he said: "You can always find fault with me." Later he said: "I must really thank you."'[13]

The pope did not spare himself. Over four days he kept 21 appointments and made 12 speeches. He made Angela Merkel, then a candidate for the chancellorship, promise to uphold Christian policy. When he met the German bishops, he said: 'The young people are not seeking a church that artificially pretends to be young, but a church that is young in spirit, a church that allows Christ, the new human being, to shine through.' He set up an ecumenical meeting (which he allowed to overrun by 70 minutes), insisted on a meeting with Muslims and was the first pope to visit a synagogue in Germany. 'Shalom alechem!' he called in the Jewish house of prayer. He wanted vigorously to pursue 'the way of improving relationships and friendship with the Jewish people'. Benedict insisted that in the sight of God 'all people have the same worth, regardless of what nation, what culture or religion they belong to'. Today again 'signs of anti-Semitism and forms of xenophobia are emerging'. This was cause for concern and vigilance. 'The Catholic Church,' he said, 'is for tolerance, respect, friendship and peace between nations, cultures and religions.'

His spontaneous gestures continued. He fought back the tears when he shook hands with Holocaust survivors. When he was saying goodbye on the steps of the synagogue and the synagogue leader, Abraham Lehrer, was standing on the step below him, he pulled him up to stand beside himself. Neither did he forget to recall Frère Roger Schutz, who three days earlier had been stabbed to death with a knife by a mentally disturbed woman. Brother Roger, the founder of Taizé, had just written him a final letter in which he thanked him for his friendship.

The Cologne World Youth Day had an 'overwhelming feeling of togetherness and peace', was the verdict of *Spiegel Online*. In particular, the pope impressed 'by his modest bearing without any vanity or pomposity'. The pope had no problem with being close to people. At one point he went hand in hand with a gigantic young man from Africa; at another he met 12 teenagers from different continents for lunch, without cameras or journalists. He was especially concerned to meet seminarians. Klaus Langenstuck, who was present, reported: 'When the Holy Father arrived, there was an enthralled silence in the room.' After grace in Latin, the pope spoke briefly about his visit to the synagogue. 'Then he talked with individual seminarians. Where do you come from? How do you live?' Langenstuck said he only realized in retrospect 'how normally' he had spoken with the pope, without any strain, almost as if 'I was talking to my "real" father'. When the meal was brought in, there was omelette for everyone but fish was planned for the Holy Father. But not for Benedict. 'The fish was sent back and another omelette was brought in – for the pope.'[14]

Joseph Ratzinger was never a friend to liturgy that tended to become a show. As Benedict XVI, he changed the international youth meeting into a giant catechesis. His starting point was the story of the Three Kings. Their shrine in Cologne is one of the most precious reliquaries of the Christian world. The pope began like a grandfather telling an exciting story: the wise men were looking for the star of life. Finally, they found it. However, after they had found it, they had to go through a whole process, a process of inner change:

> They had to change their idea of power, of God and of humanity, and so change themselves. Now they saw God's power was different from the power of the powerful in the world. The way God worked was different from the way we thought he did and would like to think he did. [...] God was different – now they realized that. That meant that now they themselves would become different; they had to learn God's way.

He summed up: 'You must become people of truth, of justice, kindness, forgiveness and mercy.'

In Cologne the term 'revolution' had become a catchword. But the pope adjusted it: 'Real revolution – the fundamental changing of the world – comes only from the saints, only from God,' he stressed. It came from the creator as guarantor of freedom, the creator of what was good and true. Ideologies would not save the world: 'Real revolution means a radical turning towards God, who is the standard of justice and also eternal love. And what can save us, if not love?'

Pre-marital sex, contraception, celibacy? Benedict said nothing about any of these. He was not a preacher of morality. Clearly, he wanted to defer these questions. For too long they had distracted attention from what Christianity was really about. Remaining youthful in the radicalism of his persistent faith, he spoke to young people about the search for what was great and for wholeness: practise worship, he urged them. That is the way to union with God. Keep Sundays. Tell other people about Jesus. Don't just make up your own religion: it does not work when it really comes down to it. Read the Bible, to become familiar with God's word. Understand how the world works and also how God is. Discover the Eucharist. You can only draw on its strength and help when you approach its mystery and learn to love Christ. Believe it: life is unique, life is beautiful, life is holy.

Like a spiritual master who leads his pupils step by step into an inmost dazzling treasure chamber, the pope led the way to his goal through Holy Communion and the message Jesus gave on the cross and at the Last Supper: 'That is like a nuclear fission in your inmost being – the victory of love over hatred, the victory of love over death,' he solemnly declared. 'Only that inner explosion of the good which conquers evil can bring about the other changes that are necessary to change the world.'

It was a tailor-made opening. The *Corriere della Sera* reported: 'At his first test before the people the German pope showed his way of communicating, his symbolism and his style'. He had 'his own intellectual charisma', with moderation and self-restraint. 'Here on the Rhine', said the left-liberal *La Repubblica*, 'Ratzinger's second baptism has taken place.' The image of the hard cardinal disappeared and the face of the pope shone out, who was sensitive and addressed everyone 'with love'. The armour of the guardian of the faith was shattered in the sight of his mistrustful compatriots. Here was a head of the church who spoke of a loving and merciful God and described the church as a 'place of kindness'.

The pope did not try to appear any younger than he was, or to ingratiate himself with the youth cult or youthful language. He simply opened his school of faith. But, like John Paul II, he also hit another note. After the 'Open the windows for Jesus' message came 'Open your hearts'. And following Wojtyła's 'Don't be afraid', he said: 'Anyone who believes is not alone.'

Looking back on his days in Cologne, Benedict XVI 'thanked God from the depths of his heart for the gift of this pilgrimage'. His predecessor had set up the World Youth Day with 'prophetic intuition'. He thought of individual moments with young people, such as the prayer vigil on the Saturday night or the 'unique meeting' with the seminarians, who 'are called to a more radical discipleship of Christ'. Encountering representatives 'of other churches and church communities' had given him the hope that ecumenism would not remain just words. With his 'Jewish brothers' he had commemorated the Shoah and the 60th anniversary of their liberation from the concentration camps. Young people had met 'Emmanuel, "God with us" in the mystery of the Eucharist'.

What made the World Youth Day really great was not its size. It was the pope's modesty. The new pope's style nipped any hint of triumphalism in the bud. For Ratzinger it was not about the backlog of so-called reforms. He declared that every real reform of the Catholic Church always aimed at strengthening faith, rather than weakening it. Unfortunately, in large areas of the church there was a kind of Babylonian confusion, an existentially threatening evaporation of the fundamental elements of the faith. The church should no longer be allowed to stand on its head: it should be set back up on its feet so that its heart would start beating again.

In Cologne there was a young, dynamic generation of cheerful devotees who wanted to rediscover the faith, in all its vitality and fullness. The Catholic Church was attractive to them *because of* its firm principles, not despite them. In their eyes the fact that it stood by the truth made it not ridiculous but spot-on. In this the pope played a vital part. 'If Mum wants me,' it said on one of the huge banners, 'I am with the pope.' One of the young people confessed: 'The pope is like my granny, she always says the same thing. And even when I don't go along with it, I know that basically she is right.'

27

The Regensburg Speech

Meanwhile the flat in the Apostolic Palace had been renovated and the tenant for life thanked the workmen for their 'commitment' and 'competence'. Smiling, he called them 'colleagues of the Lord', who began as a carpenter in Nazareth.

Since he had become pope, things had not gone worse for Ratzinger but better. 'His strength is sensational, you don't feel anything of the difficulty of the job,' his secretary reported. It was a mystery how he managed still to work at writing his books, as well as doing his demanding daily job. His first personal decisions brought him tributes: for example, the appointment of Pietro Sambi as nuncio in the USA. Sambi had worked for a long time in the Near East and negotiated the basic agreement with the Palestinians. Cardinal Zen Ze-kiun, whom Benedict appointed as bishop of Hong Kong, could also be seen as a 'political' candidate. Zen had previously been a leading figure in the Chinese underground church. He had taken part in civil rights demonstrations and fearlessly denounced corruption. Later, during Pope Francis's papacy, he stood vehemently against a course that he saw as subjection to the Communist Party. Zen even spoke of a 'Murder of China's Catholic Church'.

Benedict's line also showed in the appointment of cardinals. The German pope did not make the archbishops of Paris and Dublin cardinals, as had been expected, since their positions had traditionally been associated with this honour. Instead, for example, Benedict appointed the US archbishop Patrick O'Malley of Boston, who had sold his residence to compensate victims of paedophile priests. He also appointed Jean-Pierre Richard, who was a peacemaker in riots in the French suburbs, and Archbishop Peter Poreku Dery of Ghana, a campaigner for the Third World.

The World Bishops' Synod on the Eucharist in October 2005 also displayed the new style. The plenary meeting was shortened from four to three weeks. Benedict also introduced a free discussion, which gave the 'synod's work more immediacy and freshness', as the church lawyer Stephan Haering said.[1] Benedict also published the recommendations of the approximately 256 participants from five continents immediately after the end of the conference. His predecessor had kept these sealed and always formulated his own 'post-synodal statement'. These meetings had been taking place for 40 years, said a cardinal, but it was only under Benedict that debate could be really controversial and unreserved.

Because there were repeated outbreaks of xenophobia in Italian football stadiums, on 1 March 2006 Benedict had a message against racism and violence read out in Florence before the match between Italy and Germany. At one of his Angelus speeches he reminded his public that 'works of neighbourly love' were 'obligatory' for a Christian. The Catholic Church was a land in which there were no foreigners.[2] He also told the Austrian bishops in an *ad limina* visit: 'Don't fool yourselves. Catholic instruction that is given in a mutilated way is a contradiction in itself and cannot be fruitful in the long term.'[3] Elsewhere he stressed, 'The only pitfall the church should fear is the sins of its members.'

John Paul II's successor had already made clear in his opening speech that he was pressing for a renewal of the church. He quoted Revelation: 'I will come to you and remove your lampstand from its place unless you repent' (Rev. 2.5). These words, originally addressed to the church in Ephesus, 'also concerned us, Europe and the West in general', he warned. 'Our light can also be taken away from us. We do well to take this warning to heart in all its seriousness and call upon the Lord: "Help us to repent! Give us all the grace of true renewal! Don't put out your light in our midst!"'[4]

No modern pope was so little set on power. This pope even demanded powerlessness, giving up church privileges. In the eyes of many observers Ratzinger seemed to be not just a pope pressing for a renaissance of Christian origins but a pope who saw his role as one of dialogue, in the collegiality of bishops, in his humility, which signalled to the Eastern churches that their connection with Rome was not subordination but community in communion. What the young Ratzinger had begun at the Second Vatican Council the old Ratzinger as pope was clearly trying to put into practice: the opening of horizons, reflection on the sources, authentic proclamation, rediscovery of a liturgy that communicated the joy of God's word. It almost seemed as if a twenty-first-century sower was abundantly strewing seeds with both hands over the fields that John Paul II had so closely guarded. Benedict declared that his plan was 'to put the subject of God, faith and the wealth of Scripture at the centre. I was a man who came from theology, and I knew that my strength, if I have one, is that I proclaim the faith positively.'[5] Within the Curia the shock over the 'horrible surprise', as many in the secretariat of state called the election of the German pope, had changed, as far as could be seen, said Georg Gänswein, 'into favourable agreement with how he does his job as pope and how he gets on with people'.[6]

However, there was resentment about the replacement of the cardinal secretary of state in September 2006, a job that Sodano did not want to give up. In particular, the resentment was because Ratzinger appointed Tarcisio Bertone, archbishop of Vercelli and cardinal of Genoa, to this office. (The August 2019 report is untrue that Benedict XVI originally wanted to appoint Jorge Bergoglio, the future Pope Francis, to the post but Bergoglio refused it.) The ascetic-looking Bertone, a Don Bosco Salesian and professor of church law, had been a long-term colleague of Ratzinger's in the Congregation for the Doctrine of the Faith. However, he had no experience of Vatican diplomacy, which was regarded as essential for a cardinal secretary of state. The appointment was made because the pope wanted the second man in the Vatican not to be someone unknown to him. But, as would be seen, it also went with Ratzinger's insufficient grasp in matters of personnel. Benedict justified the change by saying that Sodano had quite simply reached the age limit. In any case, as dean of the College of Cardinals, which he was to be, he kept his place at the centre of the Curia. Sodano had 'seen all that for himself'.[7] Clearly not entirely. Sodano took revenge by refusing to give up either the flat that went with the job or the office where he worked. Bertone, his successor, had to be content with provisional accommodation for a whole year.

Another personnel dispute occurred with the dismissal of Joaquín Navarro-Valls, the long-serving Vatican press spokesman. The Spaniard, a member of Opus Dei, was loved and respected for his professionalism and readiness to help colleagues in the international press. His direct access to John Paul II had helped him to communicate the pope's message without distortion or bureaucratic jargon and react quickly in tricky situations. At first Benedict XVI had left Navarro-Valls in post, but when he reached the age limit he replaced him with the Italian Jesuit Federico Lombardi, whom Sodano had recommended. Journalists valued Lombardi for his stylishness, but as he was the head of the Vatican television service CTV, head of Radio Vatican, director of the press office and one of the Jesuit general's delegates, the new job must have been too much for him. He was able to ignore the request to give up some of his functions, because his boss allowed it.

At first there was talk of cut-backs in the Curia administration. In fact, the new pope merged four of the Vatican departments into two, partly to save costs. But there it stopped. The pope did give Bertone the task of considering further reforms, but these were soon overtaken by the daily workload. There was no more talk of further changes in the administration. The replacement of the former master of ceremonies, Piero Marini, was interpreted by critics as a reversal in liturgical practice. Benedict himself also justified this change by Marini's length of service: 'He was and is a very good man. Certainly, he is more liturgically progressive than I am, but that does not matter. He himself was also of the opinion that it was time for him to go, to leave the job after 20 years.'[8] Critics saw the appointment of his successor Guido Marini ('Marini II' in Vatican jargon) as a return to traditional forms, particularly in liturgical vestments. In fact, Guido Marini had sometimes advised the pope to wear Mass vestments that had been worn by Paul VI or even earlier popes (in each case with a written justification). But Wojtyła had also done that. The only difference was that, as his friend Robert Spaemann had also urged him, instead of the *pastorale* (pastoral staff/crosier with curved top) with the body of the crucified Christ, first used by Paul VI, he used a simple *ferula* (staff/stick with straight top), a processional cross without the body of Christ. First, it was to express the joy rather than the pain of the Christian faith. Second, it was simply lighter to carry. Gänswein regarded the accusation that 'the pope had been wrongly "vested" to be unjustified'. Benedict XVI usually wore the same mitre he had worn as a cardinal or the one used by John Paul II.[9]

The pope made his first foreign trip in May 2006 to Poland, with the watchword 'Stand firm in the faith'. Some 4,100 journalist had been accredited to accompany him, a new record. On his arrival at Warsaw airport Benedict announced that the visit was to give special thanks to the Polish people for the gift they had made to the world church of their greatest son.[10] Before that, Benedict had said on a television programme – the first TV interview of a pope – that he himself did not want 'to publish many documents', but to work at implementing the countless directives left by John Paul II, 'because they are a rich treasury, the authentic interpretation of the Second Vatican Council'.

Benedict had learned a bit of Polish and encountered an enthusiasm that almost disconcerted him, as the photographer Christoph Hurnas observed. The young people were particularly enthusiastic. They went to great lengths to meet him, in Błonia Park in Kraków (with about 1.5 million faithful), or at the Polish national shrine Jasna Góra in Częstochowa, or in Wojtyła's birthplace, Wadowice, or in Warsaw. He had deliberately set the visit to Auschwitz for the end of his trip, as a silent finale. Alone, wordless, with hands folded and a stony face, he walked through the gate of the extermination camp and to the death block, to speak to each of the 32 Auschwitz survivors who were waiting for him there. He stroked the face of an old woman who could hardly hold back her tears. Softly on both cheeks he kissed the ageing Henryk Mandelbaum, who had worked in the crematorium burning the corpses.

The pope spent time in silence reading the commemorative plaques of the murdered Jews, Russians, Poles, Roma and Germans. With unsteady steps he descended to the underground hunger cell, where a camp doctor had ended the life of the Franciscan Maximilian Kolbe, who had offered himself to die instead of a young father of a family condemned to death. Jews and Christians were together at the memorial service with prayers. Benedict quoted Psalm 44, the lament of the suffering people of Israel: 'You have broken us in the haunt of jackals, and covered us with deep darkness. [...] Because of you, we are being killed all day long, and accounted as sheep for the slaughter. Rouse yourself! Why do you sleep O Lord?'[11] It had been raining heavily, but suddenly the sun shone through the clouds and a bright rainbow curved over the scene. 'It was a great comfort to me,' Benedict said later 'when a rainbow appeared in the sky, while, like Job, I was calling on God about the horror of this place, afraid of God's apparent absence and also certain that even in his silence he does not cease to be with us and stay with us.'[12]

He gave his speech after the laments and the prayers of clergy from different denominations were over. He began: 'In this place words fail, there can only be an appalled silence.' Then he continued:

> It was impossible for me not to come here. I had to come. It was and is a duty to truth and justice, to those who suffered, my duty to God as the successor of John Paul II and as a child of the German people. [...] So I am here today to beg for the grace of reconciliation – first from God, who alone can open our hearts and purify them; and from the people who suffered here and finally the grace of reconciliation for everybody who at our moment of history is suffering from the power of hatred and from violence fuelled by hatred.[13]

Benedict never questioned the uniqueness of the Shoah. In Auschwitz he said: 'The place where we are standing is a place of commemoration, it is the place of the Shoah. The past is never just past. It has something to tell us and shows us the paths not to take and the paths to take.' He was standing there as a son of the German people, 'who were overpowered by a multitude of crimes with lying promises, by terror and intimidation, so that our people were used and abused as instruments of that destructive fury and domination'. Those could have been the words of his father, who had warned against the Nazis early on. By the destruction of Israel, said Ratzinger, 'the roots of the Christian faith were also torn up, to be replaced by human rule, the rule of the strong'.[14]

According to the cultural journalist Arnold Kissler, more plainly than any pope before him 'Benedict acknowledged the single covenant that will bind the one God and his Jewish-Christian chosen people to the end of days'. That went with his doctrine of the unity of the Old and New Testaments. They combined to form 'a single history of God with humanity'. Until then the German media had paid little attention to the pope's historic visit to Poland. The big final Mass in Warsaw, with a congregation of 1.1 million, was not broadcast on German television. However, the reaction was quite different when the first voices criticized his speech in Auschwitz. Journalists were saying that once again Ratzinger had failed to make a clear confession of guilt. He had presented the Germans, the people responsible, as victims of a small clique. The president of the Italian Federation of Rabbis, Giuseppe Laras, saw it differently. He praised Benedict for his 'words of hope and comfort for all who have suffered'. In London the *Daily Telegraph* agreed. Benedict's visit to Auschwitz was 'the crowning moment in a long process of reconciliation between his own country Germany and its eastern neighbour. It was a moment of great historical significance.'[15]

Clearly some had not understood him – or did not want to understand him– with his quiet, reflective tone, so difficult to communicate in the media. The pope's visit to Auschwitz was not about a ritual, certainly not about a German 'coming to terms with the past'. He was not doing politics. In this place, he declared, where 'all words fail', he as St Peter's successor wanted nothing but to ask for 'forgiveness and reconciliation'. 'We humans cannot solve the mystery of history,' he stressed. The Lord 'conquered on the cross', nowhere else. It was God's way to confront violence with its opposite: love right to the end. That was 'a way of conquering, which we only grasp very slowly. Yet it is the true way to overcome evil, overcome violence.' And perhaps here he was thinking of that moving aphorism from a book by Elie Wiesel. It was about a young man who was hanged. 'Where is God?' someone in the crowd murmured. The narrator heard 'a voice answering inside him: "Where is he? There. He is hanging there on the gallows …"'[16]

Benedict had begun cautiously as pope. Then he had got going, spurred by people's enormous enthusiasm, which he had not expected. There were not only the 1.2 million visitors to the World Youth Day in Cologne. At the World Family Day in Valencia in Spain he had drawn 2.2 million to a single Mass. The new pope's charisma was most plainly apparent on his trip to his Bavarian home. Frankly he admitted the reason for his visit was that he wanted 'once again to see the places and the people where I grew up, who formed me and my life, and to thank those people'.

Alitalia flight AZ 4000 from Rome-Ciampino to Munich on airbus A321 set off on 9 September 2006.There were 60 international media journalists on the plane, together with a 30-strong Vatican entourage. Those wishing to accompany the Holy Father as a reporter had to pay for an expensive ticket themselves, go through a months-long Vatican press office selection procedure and clear the security services of the countries to be visited. With hundreds of applicants it was like winning the lottery actually to be allowed on board. 'He is a cheerful, relaxed, really cordial pope,' noted the journalist Beate Kruger, editor-in-chief of the Deutsche Welle TV Berlin studio. 'Suddenly he is standing among us in the back of the plane and manifestly rejoicing at the day before him: "I find it wonderful that I will be seeing my home again, returning to places where I used to be! I grew up and was educated here – my heartbeat is Bavarian!"'[17]

A convoy of 50 vehicles drove from Franz-Josef-Strauss airport into the inner city of Munich. Thousands of police covered every metre of the journey. It was timed in 15-minute intervals, but the pope kept interrupting the arrangements to talk to people and thank them for the trouble they had taken over his visit.The official welcome took place in the Marienplatz, where Ratzinger as bishop had said farewell to his archdiocese in 1982. An overwhelming number of people were there to cheer.At his arrival the pope spoke about the importance of religion in a secular society. 'These days we are suffering from a deafness to God,' he said. 'But that loss of awareness means that the breadth of our relationship to reality is drastically and dangerously curtailed. Our sphere of life is perilously reduced.' At the Sunday Mass with 250,000 faithful on a huge open space in Munich-Riem airport he pointed out: 'The people of Africa and Asia admire the West's technical achievements and our science, but they are alarmed at a kind of rationality that shuts God out altogether and regards this as the supreme contribution of reason to their culture.'

Benedict's other stops on his trip were to be Altötting, Marktl, Regensburg and Freising. It had been raining when his flight set out from Rome. Now the fine summer weather showed the pope the beauty of the landscape, towns and villages, as well as the beauty of the faith that had stamped this landscape and these towns. A 'visibly relaxed and emotional pope enjoys the meetings', Beate Kruger noted. He recognized 'people from the past, spoke to police, medics, volunteers'. In Marktl he carefully held on to his visually impaired brother Georg to lead him into St Oswald's parish church and show him the font where he had been baptized.

Every step the pope took seemed symbolic. For example, he stayed longer than anywhere else at the Marian pilgrim shrine in Altötting chapel. After his lecture in Regensburg University he marched straight to the cathedral, as if to say: 'Look, the way between scholarship and faith is a short one and it is not a one-way street.' At the end of the day, when he reached the Gothic cathedral of Regensburg (a former imperial free city), he brought together Old and New Testaments, West and East, in an ecumenical service of Vespers: Catholics and Jews, Orthodox and Protestants. 'I haven't seen the pope in such emotional and intellectual harmony with himself on any other occasion on this trip as here in these strongly positive moments of ecumenism,' Kruger wrote.[18]

His last stop was Freising, where he had begun as a theologian, priest and bishop. 'In the biography of my heart,' he said later, that city played 'a very special part. Here I received the training which determined my life.' In particular, his entry into the seminary shortly after the end of the war had been of decisive importance: 'We knew that Christ was stronger than tyranny, stronger than the power of Nazi ideology and its mechanisms of oppression.'[19] Now as pope he told the thousand or so priests and religious who had gathered in the cathedral about 'a great speech' he had brought with him. Of course, this was one of Ratzinger's typical ironies. For he would never describe a text of his own as a 'great speech'. The speech planned for Freising was the only one on his Bavarian trip that he had not written himself. During the night he had pored over the document. In the end it was so scrawled over with pencil jottings that it could hardly be deciphered. In the cathedral the pope laid the speech aside. Anyone who wanted to could read it later, he said shortly. Then he produced a riveting, print-ready but impromptu speech on pastoral work. Of course, he had no patent recipe to prevent 'burnout' from the ever greater burdens that were laid upon priests today. It was important, on the one hand, 'to maintain the attitude of Jesus Christ' and, on the other, to know one's own limits:

> There is so much to be done – I see I can't do it – that is also true of the pope who is supposed to do so much! I just haven't got the strength to do it all. I must learn to do what I can and leave the rest to God and my colleagues, to say: 'In the end you have got to do it, for the church is your church. And you only give me the energy I have.'

As professor it had been Ratzinger's speciality to include inspiring quotations or historical cameos in his text to make a subject more gripping. Then he would draw theses, antitheses and syntheses from them. On his Bavarian journey it was that habit that nearly led to his downfall. His lecture in the Aula Magna of the University of Regensburg, his place of work for many years, was a central point. Originally, Benedict wanted just to give personal recollections. But the university management insisted on a 'lesson'. And that was what they were going to get.

'It is a moving moment for me to be back in the university giving a lecture again,' he said. A university was a place where different experiences were communicated, a place where the different disciplines inter-reacted through the use of reason. The speech itself – a classic lecture with the title 'Faith, Reason and University. Recollections and Reflections' – criticized the idea that faith and reason were two incompatible worlds. Without reason faith threatened to become fanatical, and without faith reason chained itself up and lost its strength. A society that was deaf to the divine and relegated religion to a subculture became 'incapable of cultural dialogue'.

In his lecture Benedict referred to a book by the Lebanese Islamic scholar and Melkite Catholic priest Adel Theodor Khoury, whom he knew. The previous week he had meditated on the book as his *lectio spiritualis* in his house chapel. He quoted from a conversation about Christianity and Islam, held in about the year 1400, between the Byzantine emperor Manuel II Palaeologus and an educated Persian. The conversation ranged 'over the whole area of the belief system described in the Bible and the Qur'an and centred on God and humanity'. Benedict's speech continued on the concept of reason and its relationship with religion. The quintessence of the 'lesson' was that it was against God's nature not to act rationally. That also meant that in matters of faith it was not right to exercise compulsion, let alone brute force. The lecture was over. The public applauded, and nobody saw any reason not to resume the timetable for the day. 'The pope was there and ...' was *Spiegel Online*'s bored comment. In Regensburg he had spoken out 'for dialogue with Islam, but without saying anything particularly startling'. Conclusion: 'It could hardly have been more run-of-the-mill.' For the *Süddeutsche Zeitung* reporter the pope's Bavarian visit was a trip down memory lane. The old man from Marktl was indulging in 'a bit of anticipated dying'. On the Regensburg lecture it wrote: 'It is one of the best summaries of what the scholar Joseph Ratzinger has said on the relationship between faith and reason.'

Even in Freising, the final stop on the pope's visit, there was no sign that a storm was brewing. The world had heard with amazement how the man from Marktl fascinated people, the power he had, how he was able to address his hearers and listeners with both reason and soul. Bayerische Fernsehen (Bavarian Television), which broadcast nearly all his movements live and even employed a helicopter to be able to film his arrival in Regensburg, achieved dream ratings with its millions of viewers. Notorious critics of the pope grumbled they could not get a word in. But the papal plane no sooner left sunny Munich and landed in rainy Rome than it was not only the weather that had changed.

Without anyone realizing, in various media the Regensburg speech had been shortened to just one quotation, which was bound to lead to international protests. There was a rush to put the pope in the pillory. For example, the spiritual leader of Iran, Ayatollah Ali Khamenei, described the speech as 'the last link in a plot to mount a crusade'. A vice-president of the Turkish ruling party AKP said Benedict would go down in history 'with Hitler and Mussolini'. Ali Bardakoğlu, president of the Turkish office for religious affairs, declared that what the pope had said was 'provocative, hostile and prejudiced'. However, he admitted that he only knew the text from 'uncertain reports' in the Turkish press. Action ensued. Four days after Regensburg, an organized protest movement in Islamic countries brought many thousands of furious people out onto the streets. They set fire not only to flags but also to churches. The Italian nun Leonella Sgorbati lost her life in riots in Mogadishu. A group associated with the terror network al-Qaeda threatened: 'We will destroy the cross.' God would help Muslims to conquer Rome.

Suddenly German commentators also became furious – not about the extreme reaction or the media manipulation but because a man like Ratzinger could make such a mistake in his choice of texts. 'The theologian is getting in the pope's way', the *Süddeutsche Zeitung* now thundered, having previously praised the lecture. 'The clever thinker has behaved like a naïve, not to say thoughtless, holder of office.' It was 'wrong and politically stupid'. *Der Spiegel*, which a few days earlier had reported on the Regensburg speech saying the pope had spoken out 'for dialogue with Islam', was now outraged that Benedict had almost 'caused a global crisis [...] by his Regensburg speech'.

What had happened? Had the pope been playing with fire, without realizing it? Or even deliberately? The protests had arisen because people believed the pope had scandalously insulted Islam and all Muslims. But what exactly was in the speech? The extract being blamed was about the dialogue between the Byzantine Palaeologus and the educated Persian. It said verbatim:

The emperor must have known that surah 2, 256 reads: 'There is no compulsion in religion.' According to some of the experts, this is probably one of the suras of the early period, when Mohammed was still powerless and under threat. But naturally the emperor also knew the instructions, developed later and recorded in the Qur'an, concerning holy war. Without descending to details, such as the difference in treatment accorded to those who have the 'Book' and the 'infidels', he addresses his interlocutor with a startling brusqueness, a brusqueness that we find unacceptable, on the central question about the relationship between religion and violence in general, saying: 'Show me just what Mohammed brought that was new, and there you will only find things evil and inhuman, such as his command to spread by the sword the faith he preached.'

The emperor, after having expressed himself so forcefully, goes on to explain in detail the reasons why spreading the faith through violence is something unreasonable. Violence is incompatible with the nature of God and the nature of the soul. 'God', he says, 'is not pleased by blood – and not acting reasonably (σὺν λόγω) is contrary to God's nature. Faith is born of the soul, not the body. Whoever would lead someone to faith needs the ability to speak well and to reason properly, without violence and threats.'[20]

In the Vatican no one had objected to the text. There had also been no objection beforehand from Cardinal Secretary of State Sodano (as the Italian journalist Marco Politi claimed, also claiming that Ratzinger had ignored it). 'No one said anything about it,' Benedict confirmed in our conversation. Which did not mean that no one had seen the text beforehand. Every speech by the pope went to the secretariat of state in advance, in order to prepare the translations for the international media. Usually these were then proofread both by Secretary of State Sodano and his deputy, Leonardo Sandri. 'I don't know whether Sodano read it,' Gänswein stated, 'probably he did. He knows German.' Clearly, if Pope Benedict had written, 'a great speech, there was little inclination to say I don't find this or that convincing'. Actually in the translation some clumsy passages were noted. In such cases, said Gänswein, 'the pope would have been the last person not to accept a valid suggestion or criticism.' It had to be said about the Regensburg speech: 'None of us had seen any kind of explosive material in it.'

However, in the Regensburg case a certain carelessness or even naïvety on the part of the Vatican personnel responsible cannot be denied. It had needed at least an explanatory statement from the Vatican press office, whose director the media professional Navarro-Valls had just been replaced by the inexperienced Federico Lombardi. It could have been expected that certain agencies and editors would swoop on the quotation from Manuel II Palaeologus. It was ideal for the classic trick. For not only would the quotation be taken out of context. What was originally meant as a question asked in a discussion now became a statement, and was ascribed not to the medieval Manuel II but to Pope Benedict XVI: 'Show me just what Mohammed brought that was new, and there you will only find things evil and inhuman, such as his command to spread by the sword the faith he preached.' The message was clear: for the pope Islam was a violent religion, committed to holy war. In Italy, Marco Politi commented in *La Repubblica*, 'With his speech Benedict XVI had plunged the Holy See into a veritable Waterloo and put an end to peaceful relations between Christians and Muslims.'[21]

Shocked by the outrage in Muslim countries and parts of the Western press, the Vatican published an official statement on the evening of 14 September. It said that with his speech the pope had given 'a clear and radical rejection of religious violence'. That was clear 'from a careful reading of the text. It was certainly not the Holy Father's intention to analyse jihad or Islamic thinking on it – and certainly not to offend Islamic believers.'[22] On 16 September Cardinal Bertone added: 'The Holy Father deeply regrets that some sections of his speech could have sounded offensive to the feelings of Muslim believers and had been interpreted in a way that was absolutely not his intention.'

On 17 September, before his Angelus prayer in Castel Gandolfo, the pope himself stated that 'I deeply regret the reactions that a short extract from my speech at the University of Regensburg has provoked, which was interpreted as offensive to the feelings of Muslim believers. It was a quotation from a medieval text, which in no way corresponded to my personal opinion.' Actually his speech had been 'an invitation to open and honest dialogue with great mutual respect'.[23]

In fact, the Regensburg speech had not been about Islam but about the problem of the relationship between reason, faith and violence. The riots after the speech had essentially confirmed what Benedict had said. The pope stressed: 'Unfortunately, this quotation could give rise to misunderstandings. But for a careful reader of my text it is clear that I in no way wanted to make my own the negative words spoken by the medieval emperor in this dialogue; their polemical content does not express my personal opinion.' On 25 September Benedict welcomed 22 ambassadors from countries with Muslim majorities, as well as 19 representatives of Muslim communities in Italy. Again he stressed: 'From the beginning of my papacy [I've had] the opportunity to express my wish to build bridges of friendship with those belonging to all religions. In particular, I declared the value I set on dialogue between Muslims and Christians.'[24] In our conversation Benedict said:

> I had read the Palaeologus' dialogue simply because I was interested in Islamic-Christian dialogue. I also wanted to learn the pre-history. It was interesting because the emperor was under the supreme power of the Muslim authorities, which nevertheless gave him enough freedom to say things we could no longer say today. I simply found it interesting to bring this 500-year-old dialogue into the conversation. However, I misjudged its political significance.

Only the chairman of the Central Muslim Council in Germany, Aiman Mazyek, had seen 'no attack on Islam' in the speech. Mazyek recalled the beginning of the pope's Bavarian trip, when the federal president, Horst Köhler, welcomed him at the airport. The pope had urged him that Germany should integrate Muslims better into society. 'Now Muslims in Germany can also say: We are pope,' enthused Lale Akgün, the Islamic representative of the Social Democratic Party.

In fact, no other heads of the church had been so friendly towards Islam as Wojtyła and Ratzinger. Critics found a certain naïvety in this about the intentions of Islamic leaders. 'In the whole Islamic area from Morocco to Malaysia Christians are living in a drastic minority situation,' said Ludwig Ring-Eifel of the Katholische Nachrichtagentur (Catholic News Agency). 'They lack effective legal and police protection.' Often a small spark was enough 'to kindle uncontrollable pogroms against Christians in Egypt or Indonesia'. But whereas Christians were persecuted in Islamic countries if they merely met to pray, John Paul II had given a friendly welcome to the building of the biggest mosque in Europe in his diocese of Rome. A few months before the Regensburg speech Der Spiegel, which was now accusing the pope of risking world conflagration by his thoughtless words, had actually published an article on Islam saying that it was the Muslim claim not to separate religion and worldly power that 'made their faith so dangerous in the eyes of many Westerners [...] Because the Prophet established his desert realm with a bloody sword, many passages in the Qur'an, the revelation to Mohammed, could be read as calls to battle.' 'Jihad' had long since become 'a synonym for sheer terror'.[25]

After the 'Benedetto' hype, the Regensburg speech was an opportunity to resume the attacks on Ratzinger. It was a new offensive against the pope who had suddenly become universally popular. Its success encouraged the phalanx of critics to strike again at the next opportunity. However, even though the Regensburg speech has remained on the list of the German pope's 'scandals' ever since, the hubbub about it actually died down in six weeks. 'The pope's clarifications are more than sufficient,' stated the Sunni Grand Mufti of Syria, Sheik Ahmad Badreddin Hassoun. The alleged 'mistake' had even proved helpful. The moderate Islamic newspaper *Zaman* commented that dialogue between the religions had finally got going. 'Muslims celebrate Benedict,' *Spiegel Online* reported now. The weekly *Die Zeit* honoured Ratzinger as the 'wise man in the East', who 'has become the most important Western authority in the Islamic world'.

Later the lecture was classed as a star moment in the German university's history. The pope had succeeded in showing the inner relationship between faith and reason better than anyone else. He had made clear that each area could be preserved from dangerous pathologies by mutual scrutiny. The Israeli president Shimon Peres also threw himself into the breach for Benedict XVI. 'No other Holy Father before him in the church's history has met the immense and burning challenge of putting an end to bloodshed in the name of God.' In his Regensburg speech the pope had made clear that 'the uncoupling of terror and religion is the most pressing task of our time for any religion'. Ratzinger's 'profound knowledge of history – the history of all faiths – and his high estimate of reason and hope give him the power to see the promised land from the wilderness'.[26]

A month after Regensburg 18 Muslims from different countries and schools of thought wrote an open letter to the pope saying what they agreed with him on. The text confirmed the limits that Islamic doctrine sets to the use of violence. A year later there were 138 signatories to the letter from 43 countries. They published a second letter, which was now addressed not only to the pope but to 'all leaders of Christian churches'. The letter stated that Christians and

Muslims had in common their faith in the one God, and love of God and neighbours. It concluded: 'So our differences should not lead to hatred and strife between us. Let us rather compete in uprightness and good works.'[27]

Then the Catholic Muslim forum was founded, to meet every three years and oppose violence in the name of religion. Representatives of both religions spoke in Jordan in 2011 on faith, reason and humanity. They met in Rome in 2014 and spoke about co-operation and service. In 2017 they met in Berkeley, California, to talk about holistic human development.[28] The Jesuit and Islamic scholar Samir Khalil Samir wrote:

> Benedict XVI's *lectio* in Regensburg is seen as a gaffe by the pope, a banal error, something we should put behind us and forget, if we don't want to incite war between the religions. In fact, this pope, who thinks in a balanced and certainly not a banal way, laid the foundations in Regensburg for real dialogue between Christians and Muslims, by giving a voice to many reformist Muslims and suggesting steps forward both for Islam and for Christians.[29]

28

Deus caritas est

In liturgical and diplomatic affairs the Roman Curia functioned like a well-oiled machine. About a thousand staff took care that the 'humming clockwork of the most experienced organization in human history' continued as such.[1] Indeed, the Curia is Catholic, the saying went, but it is also two-thirds Italian. Ultimately, the staff don't care who among them leads the church.

The head of the Curia is the powerful secretariat of state in the *terza loggia*. In the long corridors there are huge maps of the world, on which former popes mapped the progress of the missions. Frescos of wild animals on the ceiling depict humanity's eternal battle against forces such as lust and betrayal. Catholicism is its state religion *de facto*, but the Vatican is not a theocracy. The 1929 citizenship law required only cardinals to be Roman Catholics.[2] There is a distinction between the Vatican City State (comprising the area of the state, the state citizens and state authority) and the Holy See (*Santa Sede*), that is, the pope plus the Curia, who form a sovereign entity in international law. During Ratzinger's papacy, 16 per cent of the employees were women. They worked as consultants, theologians, archivists or presidents of papal academies. However, only men could be cleaners, at least in St Peter's Basilica.[3]

Benedict seemed relaxed. He had not only become accustomed to being pope. He also enjoyed it. In general audiences he put on fireman's helmets or the mountain riflemen's extraordinary hats, or accepted football shirts with his name and number 16 on them. His modesty remained but his shyness seemed to have gone. The public were amazed when he skipped over the floor wearing the traditional red slippers (which came not from Prada but from a

Borgo Pio cobbler). Many of his gestures were still a bit stiff. This was not due to insecurity but because of his limited acting talent. When in fine weather he rode through St Peter's Square in his pope-mobile, he looked like an excited schoolboy, thoroughly enjoying being with friends.

He was soon to be 80 but seemed to have new, boundless energy. Without showing any visible exhaustion, he conducted the Good Friday and Easter ceremonies, which demanded enormous exertion even from a young celebrant. He visited soup kitchens, as well as hearing confessions in one of the ancient confessionals in St Peter's. When he visited a Roman prison, he insisted that, despite their offences, prisoners should be treated with respect. 'Anyone can fall', and everyone then needed help to get up again. 'I think it is important that people think well of you,' he told the prisoners, 'that they feel for your suffering.' He also gave encouragement: 'We must put up with other people speaking ill of us; people also speak very disparagingly about the pope, and yet we keep going.'

Benedict inaugurated Lent. As bishop of Rome he answered the questions of his parish priests and met relatives of Israeli soldiers who had been kidnapped. He also celebrated thanksgiving Masses, attended a Mozart concert with his friend the Italian president Carlo Ciampi, ordained priests, met a thousand members of spiritual communities, received an organ for the Cappella Paolina and shook a leg with a group of Chinese ballerinas. Again and again there were audiences: with state presidents, minister presidents, court presidents, as well as queens, ambassadors, bishops, metropolitans. There were also the prefects of his congregations, who had to make regular appointments to see him, like all other visitors. He never forgot to recall his beloved John Paul II, 'the zealous shepherd and valiant prophet of hope', as he called him.

He still kept a notebook in which he entered the events of the day. But for many of his speeches, for example to general audiences, he restricted himself to correcting the text that had been presented to him. For the first time in church history a Catholic pope appointed a Protestant as chairman of the Pontifical Academy of Sciences, and a Muslim as a professor at the papal university. For the first time a pope took part in a Protestant religious service. For him representing Christ meant trying to show what Christ was like. Above all, it meant steadfastness. 'If a pope received only applause,' he said, 'he should ask himself if he is doing something wrong.'

Early on he had been called the 'theologian pope'. 'Actually he is only interested in research and writing,' said the former nuncio Karl-Josef Rauber. But that description was inadequate. For one thing, Ratzinger was not one of those scholars who wrote weighty tomes with millions of footnotes, accurate in every detail. During his holidays in Castel Gandolfo he discussed with ethicists, natural scientists, theologians and philosophers, but mainly to theorize. 'That would not work in practice,' Benedict said. 'Visiting parishes, talking to people, holding catecheses and all kinds of meetings' were an essential part of his work. 'Perhaps I have thought and written too much, that may well be. But a priest can't just be a professor. A priest's job always includes pastoral work, liturgy and conversations.'[4]

Nobody could write a biography of Napoleon, Stalin or Mao with the title 'History of a Servant'. But that fitted Ratzinger. And when he said he felt he was being sustained by someone greater, it was not a cliché. His spiritual exercises were a set part of his day. For example, his preparation for Mass and the Mass itself. After audiences he read the breviary in the house chapel, in the afternoon he said the rosary and after supper there was compline. He took care of his bodily health with a full medical check-up every six months. He telephoned his brother Georg in Regensburg almost daily. On Sundays it was usually at five o'clock in the afternoon and during the week at nine in the evening, after he had watched the news on TV, walked on the terrace and said compline.

Had he changed? Yes and no. From very early on, for Ratzinger, everything had been centred – not in the sense of middling but related to the centre, having found its place. And yet everything had become different. On the one hand, he said he felt the unique grace of his office. On the other, he profited from the fact that in a world that had become so loud, the qualities of introverted people such as sensitivity, seriousness and shyness had attained a higher value (whereas extroverted people were regarded as careless and unthoughtful). But there was still more. Joaquín Navarro-Valls found 'the institution of the papacy enabled the man Ratzinger to express himself fully'. The psychotherapist Brigitte Pfnür observed that he was 'more spontaneous than before, not so anxious'. As pope, the 'mass oscillations had changed him'.[5] Cardinal Kurt Koch, whom Ratzinger had appointed president of the Pontifical Council for Promoting Christian Unity, summarized his impressions thus: 'First, there is the simplicity and unpretentiousness of the person, who does not draw attention to himself. Second, there is his deep faith. And finally, his exceptional intelligence.' These qualities were 'seldom so united in a single person as they are in Pope Benedict'.[6]

In the charged atmosphere of the autumn of 2006, there was great anxiety in the Vatican about Benedict's visit to Turkey. The Turkish security services had advised the pope to wear a bulletproof vest (which he refused to do). In fact, his visit to the Bosporus was 'the most difficult' of all Benedict's 24 international and 24 Italian journeys, as he himself found. 'The whole cloud of the Regensburg speech was still in the air.'

Ratzinger went at the invitation of the patriarch of Constantinople, Bartholomew I, to a country where Christians, both Orthodox and Catholic, were subjected to severe restrictions. When it began, nowhere else had Christianity grown so fast as here and in Egypt, but hardly anywhere else had it been so brutally persecuted. Eighty years earlier, Christians had still represented 20 per cent of the population. That had since dropped to 0.5 per cent. Even the pope's arrival at the airport was frosty. No cheering crowds. No long speeches. President Recep Tayyip Erdoğan had ostentatiously refused officially to welcome the head of the Catholic Church. He deemed a brief handshake on the runway a sufficient mark of respect. 'I have come as a friend and as an apostle of dialogue and peace,' Benedict declared at his first scheduled meeting with members of the diplomatic corps. He celebrated Mass in Ephesus, where traditionally Mary the mother of Jesus had lived and a church council had taken place in 431. Instead of the usual hundreds of thousands of pilgrims, there were only 500.

The breakthrough occurred when he visited the Blue Mosque in Istanbul. Accompanied by the grand mufti Mustafa Çağrici, the pope removed his shoes and continued wearing just his white stockings during a meditation, a gesture appreciated by the Muslims. Somehow 'our hearts went out to each other,' said Benedict, for which he was 'very thankful to the dear God'. At the end of his trip he celebrated the 'divine liturgy' with the grey-bearded Bartholomew I on the feast of St Andrew in the church of the Holy Spirit. The pope called it a new Pentecost. He spoke a bit of Turkish, then French, Italian and Latin. The choirs interwove Aramaic, Armenian, Syrian and German, and the patriarch added Greek. The meeting came to a climax in the joint invocation of the Holy Spirit by the two leaders, praying that he would help them prepare for the day when full unity was restored. On Europe, they promised 'to strive for unity', 'in all openness towards other religions', in order 'to maintain its Christian roots, traditions and values'.[7]

The initially hostile mood did not prevent the pope from speaking out clearly in Ankara. 'The Turkish constitution recognizes the right of every citizen to freedom of conscience and freedom to practise their religion, but these freedoms must also be respected.' This means 'that, for their part, religions must not seek directly to exercise political power, because they are not called to do so. In particular, it means that religions must absolutely refuse to justify the use of violence as a legitimate expression of religious practice.'[8]

The successful course of his Turkish trip cheered the pope. 'Part of my heart remains in Istanbul,' he exclaimed when he was saying goodbye. At least the event was not likely to daunt his confidence that with God's help he could manage difficult things. Turning a negative situation into a positive one had always been his strength, especially as a professor. He could cut through deadlocked discussions like a Gordian knot, to reach a good agreement. However, in his immediate environment, with people he dealt with every day, that gift did not always seem to work.

Ratzinger wanted to fulfil his office as someone who washed other people's feet. For him the church was a community that should strive to bring Christ's maxim to life. 'You know that those whom they recognize as their rulers lord it over them and their great ones are tyrants over them,' Jesus said. 'It should not be so among you, but whoever wishes to become great among you must be your servant, and whoever wishes to become first among you must be the slave of all' (Mk 10.42–4). The pope was convinced that the model he set, his books and catecheses, ought to be effective. The paradox of being head of the church was that it involved a fullness of power but at the same time was subject to the primacy of love and mercy. Being St Peter's successor meant keeping Christ's power present as a counterweight to worldly power, Ratzinger had said as prefect.

It meant carrying a superhuman burden on human shoulders. The place for the vicar of Christ was the cross.

One of the many pains he had to suffer was among those closest to him. In the Vatican it was an open secret that Ratzinger's former and current secretaries, Josef Clemens and Georg Gänswein, who had once been friends, had become hostile to one another. After the papal election Josef Clemens had pleaded in vain with his former boss to appoint him as his personal secretary. Now he was unashamed to speak about that refusal with anybody. He not only accused Gänswein of a lack of professionalism but also of wrongly advising the pope and pushing himself into the foreground at every opportunity. Cardinal Meisner strongly advised that Clemens should be sent away from Rome. However, the pope did not want to snub his long-term colleague. He worried about Clemens's health and accepted invitations to have supper with him at his flat in the palazzo of the Congregation of the Doctrine of the Faith.

His relationship to Ingrid Stampa was also a disturbing situation. Many in the Curia were already calling her the 'popess' (or 'Mrs Pope'). She was born in 1950 in the Lower Rhine region. As she told an interview with the magazine *Bunte*, she had given up her work as a music teacher because the Lord had come into her life. 'He asked me to choose whether I wanted to keep on with my career and just live for myself or whether I was ready to put myself entirely in God's hands and only serve him in future.'[9] She abandoned a first attempt to live in a convent as a Carmelite nun. Her second attempt was ended by the prioress. Later she went to Rome to care for Archbishop Cesare Zacchi, who had cancer. After his death, she was recommended by Dr Buzzonetti, John Paul II's personal doctor, to become Cardinal Ratzinger's housekeeper in his flat. Ratzinger had just lost his sister.

After he was elected pope, Stampa had self-confidently declared that she was moving into the Apostolic Palace 'with my husband'. In previous years Stampa had done translations for the Capuchin friar Raniero Cantalamessa, the preacher to the papal household, and for the last 15 years she had been a close friend of the papal speech-writer Paolo Sardi. She had often travelled for weeks away with both of them to support them when they gave lectures. Stampa took it for granted that, like the two secretaries and the four women members of the Memores Domini community, she would be living in the inner circle of the pope's household. She got a key to the papal *appartamento*, as well as to the lift leading directly to the pope's flat, so that she could enter it at any time. It caused a public sensation when pictures in the press showed her before the Angelus prayers always opening the big shutters to the Apostolic Palace, from which the pope made his speeches and waved to the people in St Peter's Square. It was only when secretary Mieczysław Mokrzycki insisted that only the pope, his secretaries and the Memores could live in the *familia pontifica*, as had also been the case with John Paul II, that after two and a half months Stampa was obliged to move out.

The pope breathed a sigh of relief, but the problem had not gone away. Stampa had kept the key to the *appartamento* and quite often stood without notice in Benedict's work room. Some in the Vatican compared her with the energetic housekeeper and close friend of Pius XII, Pasqualina Lehner, a nun from Altötting whom Pacelli had brought to Rome with him after his time as a nuncio in Germany. *La papessa* (the 'popess'), as Stampa was called, kept Ratzinger's diary, edited official speeches and even decided who could meet the Holy Father and who could not (which sometimes led to violent quarrels with cardinals).

Clearly, his former housekeeper was aware of Ratzinger's Achilles' heel. If it was a public dispute, he was fearless. But as soon as someone was shameless enough to become personal, he seemed paralysed. The scenes that Stampa could make included hysterical fits, bitter reproaches and floods of tears. Cardinals cursed at 'these endless outbursts of crying, by which she manipulated the Holy Father', said the Rome correspondent Alexander Smoltczyk: the pope was much too soft with her.[10] Stampa had succeeded in obtaining responsibility for translating the pope's texts from German into Italian, even though she was not a native Italian-speaker. As a priest from the Congregation for the Doctrine of the Faith was to become the director of the German section of the secretariat of state, Stampa and Sardi intervened. So the man from Ratzinger's previous Congregation was blocked. Ratzinger justified himself that in the circumstances he could not deliver his former colleague into Sardi's hands. Stampa was forced to give up her key to the papal *appartamento* in the course of the 'Vatileaks affair'. But she managed to have her close associate Sardi made a cardinal.

After the end of her service in the secretariat of state, Stampa gave lectures on 'My life in the Vatican under three popes'. However, the pope could draw on experiences from his close circle when he declared on the occasion of the 50th anniversary of Vatican II that in recent years he had 'learned and experienced [...] that bad fishes were also to be found in Peter's net. We have seen that human weakness is also present in the church [...] and have sometimes thought: "The Lord is asleep and has forgotten us."'[II]

Benedict's first encyclical was eagerly awaited. A pope's first encyclical has always been seen as a kind of keynote to a papacy. The question was, would Ratzinger again take 'the dictatorship of relativism' for his subject, as he had in the conclave. Or would he broach virulent issues of church politics and social matters? His predecessor Wojtyła had published his first encyclical, *Redemptor hominis* ('The Redeemer of Humanity'), when he had only been in office for 136 days. It was a strongly political piece, which addressed the problems of the globalized world. But Benedict XVI took his time. Perhaps it was to do with the subject, about which wonderful things could be written but which in everyday life almost always ran into obstacles.

It was 25 January 2006 when the pope's first encyclical was finally launched in the Vatican press office in the Via della Conciliazione, 270 days after Ratzinger's election as pope. The date kept getting put back. That made the subject that Benedict had chosen and the encyclical's content even more surprising. It was about love, with a gently persuasive, partly poetic text, which the author described not as 'doctrinal' but as 'an invitation'. The title was taken from its Latin first words: *Deus caritas est*, 'God is love'.

Encyclicals (from the Greek word *kyklos*, 'circle') are papal documents on questions of faith and morals, philosophy, social, state or economic matters and church politics. From the fourth century they were presented as simple church circulars. Then in the eighteenth century Benedict XIV had made them a means of leading the church. At his enthronement the new pope had already made known what one of his main focuses would be. 'There is the wilderness of poverty, the wilderness of hunger and thirst,' he preached then, and there was also 'the wilderness of desolation, loneliness and love destroyed'. Love was the core word of his theological master, Augustine. Love was also a theme of the theologian and anti-fascist August Adam, whose work Ratzinger counted among 'the key reading of my youth'. Adam wrote that the sexual drive was to be regarded not as 'unclean' but as a 'gift', which was sanctified by *caritas*, love of neighbour. Ratzinger's philosopher friend Josef Pieper's book *On Love*, with chapters such as 'What *caritas* and erotic love have in common', were pre-formulations of Ratzinger's positions. His very first piece, written when he was a student, had also been about love. It was a translation of a work by Thomas Aquinas, which he called *Eröffnung über die Liebe* ('On Love'). So it corresponded with a certain inner logic that his first publication as pope exactly 60 years later should be an encyclical on love.

The project had already begun under his predecessor, who had wanted to publish his 15th encyclical with the same title, as a plea to care for our neighbours. The initiator had been the German Curia cardinal Paul Josef Cordes. As president of the pontifical council Cor Unum, responsible for the Holy See's humanitarian aid, Cordes had already produced a draft. The plan collapsed through opposition from the Curia, but after the election of his compatriot as pope, Cordes took the idea up again. It must have seemed to Benedict like a nod from Providence. Because the text as it stood did not satisfy him, the new pope sat down at his desk. The result was that the first part of the encyclical was all written by him. The appropriate Vatican departments contributed to the second part. At the end, the whole text was checked for accuracy by the Congregation for the Doctrine of the Faith and standardized by the secretariat of state.

It seemed like a miracle. After the trouble over the Regensburg speech, suddenly now there was talk of 'the poetic pope' and 'exciting pope'. *Der Spiegel* praised it saying: 'Love, love, love. It is a love song of songs, which could not be simpler or more radical, dogmatic but not hostile to the body.'[12] 'Never before', the *Frankfurter Allgemeine Zeitung* enthused, 'had a pope written so feelingly and poetically, as well as theologically expertly, as Benedict XVI about human love, about "sinking into an intoxication of happiness".'[13] The not especially Rome-friendly weekly *Christ in der Gegenwart* wrote: 'For a Roman document it is a revolution.'

The international media response was consistent: *Deus caritas est* was the work of a loving person. The strict dogmatist had amazed his public and confounded all negative expectations. 'Since the beginning of the church this encyclical is the first doctrinal foundation and inspiration of the church's charitable mission,' said Heinrich Pompey, Freiburg professor of *caritas* studies and Christian social work. It had brought into view a dimension of the church's activity that had been neglected by theologians, popes and councils. 'If it was implemented in communities, the church could become the charitable-communal core of faith, hope and love in our societies.'[14]

Ratzinger's first encyclical began with a quotation from his favourite evangelist, John: 'God is love and those who abide in love abide in God and God abides in them.' These words, said the author, contained 'the heart of Christian faith, the Christian view of God and also its view of humanity and the way we should go'. In the same chapter John also gave 'a formula for Christian life: "We have known and believe the love God has for us".'[15]

In the church's history the relationship between body and spirit, pleasure and asceticism, had always been the subject of intense debate. However, in his encyclical the pope had not raised individual questions of morals or doctrine but expressed fundamental trust in love's victory over injustice. At the beginning he quoted Friedrich Nietzsche's words that Christianity had given Eros poison to drink; Eros had not died of it but had degenerated into a vice. 'Here the German philosopher was expressing a widespread feeling,' said Benedict, that with its commandments and prohibitions the church spoilt the most beautiful thing in life, the erotic. But was it really true 'that Christianity had destroyed Eros?' the pope asked. Immediately, he gave the answer: 'For faith, humanity means saying "yes" to our human bodies, which were created by God.' However, today 'love' had often become a dirty word; it needed to be 'taken up and restored to its original splendour', so that it could light up life again. Then love between two people 'in an indissoluble marriage between a man and a woman' would rediscover 'its form rooted in creation'. Here love for another did not seek itself but was transformed into care for the other and open to the gift of new human life.

Benedict XVI was not shy of the subject of sex. The creator's gift of Eros allowed people 'to feel something of the taste of the divine'. Yes, love was ecstasy, not just for the moment 'but ecstasy as a constant way out of the closed-in ego towards free self-giving, to self-forgetfulness and thus to self-discovery, and also the discovery of God'. In his philosophical and lyrical text Benedict sprang from Virgil to Augustine, from Dante to Nietzsche and Marx. There was no finger-pointing, even when the author was warning against an over-sexualized society that made love a commodity, failing to respect the personality of the other. 'Purification and maturing are necessary, and also involve self-denial. That is not a rejection of Eros, or "poisoning" it, but healing and restoring it to its real greatness.'

The first part of the encyclical dealt with the inner connection between the love of God and the different aspects of human love. The second part was devoted to the transformation of Eros into Agape, loving activity that knows no bounds, as the task of all Christians. Referring to the social dimension, neighbourly love, the pope also warned against the abysmal nature of unbridled capitalism: everyone should have 'their share of worldly goods'. Economic globalization had put the world in a difficult situation. Here the church should offer social leadership. 'Love thy neighbour' meant that

> I should also love fellow human beings whom I do not like or do not even know, as God does [...] If there is no contact with God in my life, then I will just see the other person as someone else and fail to recognize the divine image in them. But if I leave out love of neighbour completely from my life and just want to be 'devout' or fulfil my 'religious duties', then my relationship to God would also wither. It would merely be 'correct' but without love.

Love of God and of our fellow human beings belonged inseparably together, as did service to God and service to society. So for the church, loving 'is not just a sort of welfare work, which could be left to others, but it belongs to the church's nature and is a vital expression of itself'.

On 22 April 2007 Benedict XVI travelled to Pavia, to lay a copy of his love encyclical in person at the tomb of St Augustine in the basilica of San Pietro in Ciel d'Oro. The symbolic gesture was also a thank-you to his African master, the church father of the heart and of love. As it had to, *Deus caritas est* came to a climax in a poetic core statement: Love 'is the light – ultimately the only light – that lights up a dark world and gives us the courage to live and to act. Love is possible and we can do it, because we are created in God's image.'

29

Salt of the Earth, Light of the World

In the first decade of the new millennium it could no longer be denied that globalization and the digital revolution had catapulted the world into a new age. Never before had human life changed so dramatically in such a short time.

Mobile telephones now had more processing power than the NASA computer used for the moon landing. Navigation systems drove cars and switched on the heating. Whole new industries were invented and offered services that in the past had been reserved for emperors and kings. Through genome engineering, genes could be manipulated and it was possible to intervene in the genetic pattern of life, which had not changed since the beginning of human history. New techniques and 'artificial intelligence' also offered previously unimaginable possibilities for surveillance. Algorithms directed who read what news when, and what products they should buy.

There were other new occurrences too. For the first time in history, with Barack Obama the USA had an African American president. Romania and Bulgaria celebrated their entry into the European Union, giving it a population of half a billion people in 27 member states. In La Silla in Chile a team of astronomers from the European Southern Observatory discovered the first habitable planet outside our solar system, 20.5 light years distant from Earth. The US computer company Apple decided to enter the mobile phone market with a compact multi-functional mobile. 'We will rediscover the telephone,' said the Apple CEO, Steve Jobs. But it was more than that. The smartphone was a revolution for the information society and the gateway to social media, a completely new form of personal communication.

At the same time the UNO report on climate change hit the headlines in April 2007. The researchers' diagnosis was that the Earth's warming could no longer be halted. If the average temperature rose by 2.5° C, there was the threat of a rise in sea levels, droughts, the extinction of from 20 to 30 per cent of all animal and plant species. In North America more hurricanes, floods, heatwaves and fires could be expected. Island countries in the Pacific and densely populated river mouths in Asia threatened to sink. But also in Europe, it was thought then, by 2018 up to 2.5 million people in coastal regions might be flooded. The global discharge of greenhouse gases had be stabilized by 2015 at the latest and decreased by at least half by 2050.

Another problem was that people's personal resources were pushed to the limit under pressure from modern trends and constant stress from time-consuming activities. Thirty-year-olds felt overburdened and exhausted. Burn-out and heart problems became common. There would be no going back. For, as the French philosopher René Girard said, the mark of technical advance was always 'to keep going further'.[1]

In relation to this increasingly turbulent lifestyle Christian traditions looked to many like relics of the past. It seemed as if especially the Catholic Church, which once promoted learning, founded universities and renewed itself at the Second Vatican Council, had wholly lost any connection with the modern world. Indeed, the Vatican press department displayed the pope with an electronic tablet and set up a live link to the astronauts in the NASA international space station, but that did not work as a symbol for having entered the twenty-first century.

Didn't the Catholic Church's headquarters, with its men in weird clothes and its medieval-looking guards with helmets and halberds, look like something from another era? People came from everywhere to marvel at this extraordinary little empire with the same disbelief as they watched the fantasy world of Peter Jackson's film trilogy *Lord of the Rings*. But that was just one side of it. For with *L'Osservatore Romano* the Vatican had a state newspaper which was published in 20 different national languages, and its Radio Vatican broadcast in 47 languages. Some 298 functionaries of the Holy See had diplomatic status, and in nearly every big city on Earth there was a representative of the Catholic Church, who was the region's highest church dignitary. And although many things seemed anachronistic in the Catholic Church's traditions, by its message and its resistance it sought to offer answers to the problems and dangers of the turbulent new reality. Benedict XVI stressed that the transmission of the faith could not be confined to the private sphere. The pope's annual report *L'attivatà della Santa Sede* gave information about every single day in the Holy Father's life – every audience, every speech, every meeting. It covered 1,500 pages and showed the extent of the pope's leadership functions. In addition, the Vatican could claim to be the first state to be completely carbon-neutral.

Benedict made his first trip outside Europe in May 2007, to Brazil, which with 140 million faithful was the country with the largest population of Catholics in the world. When he arrived, in answer to a journalist's question the pope said that the change in the political situation confirmed that the position his Congregation for the Doctrine of the Faith had taken towards liberation theology had been right. It had simply been essential to distinguish between politics and the church's mission. Two days later, on 13 May, the pope was in Aparecida in the state of São Paulo as a guest of the fifth general meeting of the bishops of Latin America and the Caribbean. He visited Fazenda da Esperança in Guaratinguetá, a church institution for the rehabilitation of drug addicts. 'I love Latin America very much,' he had said on his flight. He had 'often visited the continent and I have many friends there. I know how great the problems are.'[2]

Benedict defended the evangelization of South America, saying that despite many shortcomings the Latin American church had managed to pass on the love of Christ and at the same time preserve the essential characteristics of the indigenous people. Possibly, he was also thinking of St Peter Claver, whose passionate opposition to slavery earned him the hatred of the slave traders. However, in Western Europe the pope was criticized for playing down the crimes of the conquistadors. Instead of the expected 2,000 journalists, in Brazil he was accompanied by more than 3,000. Millions lined his route in São Paulo and streamed onto the Campo de Marte to celebrate with him the canonization of the Franciscan Friar Galvão, who had died in 1822. 'His reputation for deep neighbourly love knew no bounds,' Benedict said in his speech; 'poor people and those sick in soul and body [...] asked him for help.' He had 'cared for them all as a father'.

The third year of his pontificate, the most productive of all, confirmed the impression that Benedict saw his main task as renewal through proclaiming the church's message. Whereas in a sense John Paul II had physically brought the papacy back onto the world stage, his successor wanted to attempt the most difficult thing of all, an inner purification of the church and the faith. For Ratzinger the great crisis threatening to undermine Christianity in the Western hemisphere was caused by an unprecedented loss of knowledge and awareness of the faith. It was necessary to tell the world again what the gospel was about. Proclaiming the faith was 'the most valuable gift the church can give to humanity'. Christianity did not begin with preaching duties and rules, he repeated, but with the discovery of grace. He quoted Pope Gregory I: 'How is it possible that people say "No" to the greatest thing, and close themselves off from it?' Gregory's answer was: 'They have never experienced God, they have never tasted God; they have never felt how precious it is to be touched by God.'

Ratzinger gave an example by his simplicity and by denying himself any personal luxury. He demanded the same of his church, his priests and the faithful, in accordance with the gospel. In comparison with him, many theologians and bishops who called themselves progressive sounded like politicians or journalists. They aimed at a church that adapted to worldly fashions. Ratzinger's ideal was not a priest who enthused about being able to have a bourgeois job with a wife and children in a comfortable vicarage but one who stimulated his parishioners to question what was regarded as normal. 'Above all, we must prevent people losing sight of God,' he declared, 'failing to recognize the treasure they have. Then, convinced of their faith, they should engage with secularism and be able to practise the discernment of spirits.' Becoming the 'salt of the Earth' and 'light of the world' again, as the gospel demanded, was 'today's great task'.

Returning to the sources accorded with Ratzinger's earlier vision of a church of the little people, who lived by the faith undefiled. Of course the church 'also needed intellectuals', he said. 'It needs people to put the power of their minds at its disposal. It also needs generous rich people who use their wealth to do good. But its main base is always those people who are humble believers, those who need love and give love: simple people, who are open to the truth because they have remained children, as the Lord says. They have kept their eyes on what is essential throughout the changes of history and kept the spirit of humility and love in the church.'[3]

The chair of Peter lifts a person to a dizzy height. As mediator between Christ and the world the pope is an absolute sovereign. He does not have to give an account to his people or to a senate of cardinals, but only to the one whom he represents on Earth. On the other hand, his power is extremely limited. He can't abolish things that belong to the core doctrine and tradition. Or those that were 'set by the diachronic and synchronic common creed of the apostles' successors', as the Bonn dogmatic theologian Karl-Heinz Menke put it. That is to say, decisions that were proclaimed as irreversible by his predecessors. For example, the principle that in the Catholic Church only men are admitted to the priesthood. Above all, the pope is bound to the principles linking him to the first bishop of all, the key figure: the Jewish Simon bar-Jonah, called Peter, the rock.

In choosing his apostles Jesus went for fishermen, tax collectors and even a political hothead. He criticized the religious elite for claiming the first places, for their double standards, their unwillingness to repent and be converted and for their pomp, displayed by their splendid clothes and enormous hats. What angered him most was that these religious teachers withheld God from people. Their rules and attitudes were merely a formal confession; they were phoney. He castigated the scribes: 'Woe to you, you shut people out of the kingdom of heaven. You yourselves do not enter, nor will you let in those who wish to enter.'

Simon Peter was neither a decisive leader nor an organized manager. The evangelists describe him as rough and coarse, occasionally hot-tempered, but also sympathetic and sometimes a bit slow-witted. He throws himself into the waves when his master calls and sinks into the sea because of his lack of faith. He shows fatal weakness, which he then bitterly repents. Peter's name, *Schimeon* or *Schemel* in Hebrew, means 'Yahweh has heard'. *Schemel* also refers to *Sch'ma Israel*, 'Hear O Israel', the chief prayer of the Jews. There is a third association with God's *Schemel* (the German word for 'footstool'): God's footstool in front of his heavenly throne.

Reading about Peter in the New Testament tells us what is meant by 'church'. It is a church of the holy, but not of godlike, heroic figures who never fail. If it lacks success, it should not adapt more to the world. It can sometimes be great and sometimes small, and it can't be said exactly when great is small and small is great. Nevertheless, the fishermen from the Sea of Galilee and their successors not only bequeathed a religious heritage from Judaism. They also took over from the Roman emperors and built bridges between Jews and Gentiles, races and peoples.

Jesus' words to Peter were: 'Tend my sheep, tend my lambs.' He was the shepherd, the instructor, the guardian of the mysteries. 'Do not build on sand,' the master had said, 'build on rock.' That security required someone whose authority extended over time and space: 'But I say to you: you are Peter, and on this rock I will build my church, and the gates of Hell will not prevail against it.'

The foundation of Christ's church was accompanied by a sombre warning. Peter had received the keys to the kingdom of heaven, but when Jesus went on to say that the Messiah had to suffer the passion, it is not hard to understand why Peter protested violently: that cannot be! He imagined a God and a church for Jesus that functioned in accordance with human rather than divine norms. His attitude resembled the revolt against God described in Genesis.

Peter had retreated into thinking in worldly terms and become a dependent shadow. For Jesus' answer was addressed to the eternal adversary: 'Get behind me Satan! You are thinking not as God thinks but as humans do' (Mt 16.23). That shadow accompanied the foundation of the church and, despite its holiness, would never leave it. Here was the crux: Christ's messengers should not listen to 'human thinking' but to God's word, 'power from on high'. The success of an apostle's work depended on self-denial. Only thus could Christ's words come true: 'Whoever listens to you listens to me; whoever rejects you rejects me; and whoever rejects me rejects the one who sent me.' That knowledge is important in order to understand Benedict's constant reminder: humans could not make the church and the faith themselves, shackling Jesus' foundation to the purely worldly, instead of looking to those heights from which light came into the world.

Benedict's course could be seen particularly clearly in his meeting with the Swiss bishops for their *ad limina* visit on 7 November 2006. 'We know about churches becoming empty, seminaries becoming empty, religious houses becoming empty,' he said at their Mass together. As at the time of the exodus, people were withdrawing from God. Today many Christians lived just like other people. They were occupied with material things, with what could be done or planned to be successful. So their 'God faculty' withered. That could have dramatic consequences. The pope did not confine himself to lofty abstractions. He became practical and advised the bishops not to keep jumping through every hoop held out to them by journalists. 'Whenever I went to Germany in the 1980s or 1990s,' he said, 'I always knew the questions in advance. They were about the ordination of women, contraception, abortion and similar problems, which kept coming back. If we let ourselves be caught up in these discussions, then the church becomes fixed on just a small number of rules or prohibitions. We stand there like moralists with a few old-fashioned views, and the real greatness of the faith does not appear at all.' Current society was not immoral in principle, but today morality came under the headlines of 'peace', 'non-violence', 'justice for all', 'care for the poor' or 'respect for creation'. Instead of religion, 'the great moral imperatives' had become 'what actually gives human beings dignity and also demands it for them'. However 'the morality of life' should not be abandoned when it was a matter of abortion, active help to die or the marginalization of marriage.[4]

As the rumours spread that the pope wanted to permit the use of the St Pius V missal again, the church's first internal conflict during Benedict's papacy loomed. The Tridentine or 'old' Mass, which was the customary rite in the Catholic Church until 1970, had more or less been withdrawn. Even when he was a theology professor in Regensburg, Ratzinger had been dismayed by the ban on the old missal, for 'nothing like that had ever happened in the whole history of the liturgy'.[5] As a result, liturgy was no longer seen as the fruit of a living process but as the product of scholarly erudition, which could be altered according to the point of view. With his document *Quattuor ab hinc annos* (1984) John Paul II had indeed allowed the use of the Tridentine rite again, but anyone wanting to celebrate it had to have permission from his local bishop, who often refused.

Even the possibility that the pope might change the ruling unleashed strong protests. Some warned that it was going too far in accommodating traditionalists of the Society of St Pius X. Others accused Benedict of discrediting the Second Vatican Council. Bishops from France, including Cardinal Jean-Marie Lustiger, the former archbishop of Paris, hurried to Rome to urge Ratzinger not to slacken the current rules.

Benedict reacted. The text for his coming announcement had been checked in countless consultations, 'but the pope also definitely wanted to involve the bishops', secretary Gänswein reported. 'That rather delayed things.' After the pope had explained his plan to about 30 chairmen of national bishops' conferences in the Sala Bologna of the Apostolic Palace, 'the mood became very positive'. As a precaution, Benedict also wrote a personal letter to all the bishops, in which he gave the reasons for his decision and spoke of the 'fruit of long consideration, many discussions and of prayer'.

Benedict's *motu proprio* on the subject, '*Summorum pontificum*', was published on 7 July 2007 and came into force from 14 September, the feast of the elevation of the holy cross. Briefly, it permitted the Tridentine *Missale Romanum*, in its latest form, overseen by John XXIII in 1962, to be celebrated again without having to ask for permission from Rome or the local bishop. The document also made clear that the missal created by the post-conciliar liturgical reform 'was and remained the normal form'. After the Council 'a new rite had not replaced the old rite', but the old rite and the new were 'two forms of the single Latin rite', one the ordinary and the other the extraordinary form.

In his letter accompanying the *motu proprio* Benedict explained that many Catholics had longed for the old liturgy, because 'in many places the new missal's order is not followed strictly but interpreted as an authorization or even as a duty for "creativity", which often leads to unbearable distortions of the liturgy'. He was speaking from personal experience here, because 'he had gone through that phase with all its expectations and confusion'. By a clear ruling he also wanted to relieve the bishops of the burden of 'having to keep weighing up how to answer in each different situation'. Ratzinger rejected as 'absolutely false' the claim that allowing the old missal again was a surrender to the Society of St Pius X. 'It was important for me that the church is at one with its own past,' he said in our conversation. It could not be right that 'what was once the holiest thing in the church suddenly becomes completely forbidden'.

Reform had been 'indicated. But the church's identity must not be broken. As I said, the thing touched me personally.'

Benedict's reform was not well received everywhere, not even in the Curia. Harsh condemnations 'made without full knowledge', the pope felt, came particularly from Jewish associations. They remembered the Good Friday liturgy in the old missal: '*Oremus pro perfidis Judaeis*' –'Let us pray for the treacherous Jews'. In fact, John XXIII had already changed this text and removed the term 'treacherous' in 1962. However, the result was still not acceptable. It now read: 'Almighty, eternal God, who does not exclude even the Jews from your mercy, hear our prayer that we offer you for the blindness of this people.'

Benedict himself had objected to these words and eventually personally changed them: 'I wanted to create a form of prayer that suits the spiritual style of the old liturgy, but accords with our modern knowledge about Judaism and Christianity.'[6] So he had 'phrased the new prayer exclusively using words of Scripture'. He was still 'happy that I succeeded in making a positive change on this point – with the following formula: "Almighty, eternal God, you want everyone to be saved and come to the knowledge of truth. Graciously grant that with the fullness of peoples entering your church, all Israel may be saved. Through Christ our Lord. Amen."' He could not at all understand why the criticism spread in advance saw this as an anti-Jewish text. The misrepresentation had been 'put about by my non-friends in Germany, the theologians. But these people have always tried to shoot me down and knew that it was easiest to do so about Israel. I must say I find that monstrous.'[7]

On his trip to France in September 2008, Benedict returned to *Summorum pontificum*. All his fears proved groundless. His decision was 'simply an act of tolerance on pastoral grounds for people who grew up with this liturgy, love it, know it and want to live with this liturgy'. There was 'no opposition between the liturgy, as renewed by Vatican II, and this liturgy. The Council fathers had celebrated daily Mass according to the old rite, and at the same time they had drafted a natural development of the liturgy for this century. The liturgy is a living reality, that develops and yet keeps its identity in its development.'[8]

No great changes in the church's liturgical structure resulted from *Summorum pontificum*. Certainly no mass movement developed.

Benedict's re-approval of the 'old Mass' followed the trend to return to the 'classic' and 'traditional' instead of adulterated wine and fast food. The protests against the pope's decree for the sake of the faithful who loved the old liturgy appeared odd because elsewhere the defence of minorities was regarded as most important in a civilized society. Three years after the *motu proprio*, in Ratzinger's former Munich diocese, as well as the current Oktoberfest, a 'historical Oktoberfest' was introduced called the 'Oide Wiesn'. It soon became a popular part of the festival. *Summorum pontificum* had created a new awareness of the beauty and holiness of the classic Catholic liturgy. Cardinal Kurt Koch even thought the reform was the most important decision of this papacy. 'Something permanent' had come about, which the 80-year-old pope had pushed through against all opposition, simply because he had believed for decades that this amendment was right and necessary.[9]

In 2007 the German pope not only caused excitement by re-approving the Tridentine rite. An equally long-cherished project of his was to finish his book on Christology, which he had 'long been inwardly mulling over'. It almost seemed like a personal affair between the author and his protagonist. He did not want it to interfere with his job as pope. He had begun his book on Jesus in the summer of 2003, two years before his election. Now he worked on it exclusively on his audience-free days – Tuesdays – in the Apostolic Palace and during his holidays at Castel Gandolfo. In his summer residence breakfast took a maximum of 15 minutes so that he could sit at his desk as soon as possible. 'For him that work was an inner necessity,' said Sister Christine; 'we felt it was a difficult and mentally demanding task and we were always happy when he had finished a chapter. He was not grumpy but mentally absent. When he finished work he seemed to recover.'[10]

He did not get anyone to help him with his book, not even to incorporate the extensive quotations. Burkhardt Menke, Ratzinger's long-term editor at Herder publishers, who took care of 80 books by the theologian, was struck by 'how set this author is on the Bible as the primary source of the faith and mistrusts everything that people want to create of their own accord'. Ratzinger worked like 'a Catholic Lutheran'. When he had first met him as pope, Benedict had said to him, 'I've got a book on Jesus.' When Benedict pressed the finished work into his hand on a memory stick, Menke was fascinated by how clearly the pope explained 'why God's incarnation and the resurrection from the dead are not myths but historically locatable facts'. He concluded: 'This author reminds us that the Bible is the word of God and Jesus is God's Son. Like Luther, he put the reality of God's relationship at the centre.'[11]

The pope was helped in his writing by his gift of being able to put down his pencil, then pick it up again after a week and continue exactly where he had left off. 'Something that concerned me so deeply,' he explained, was so present 'that when I pick it up again it carries straight on.' The completed first part of the Jesus trilogy appeared in print in September 2006. In order to make clear that it was not a doctrinal statement it appeared under the author's name, Joseph Ratzinger, Benedict XVI, and not with the papal seal. Even the foreword aroused attention. Disagreement was welcome, he wrote. He asked 'readers only for that advance of sympathy without which there is no understanding'.

The motive for the work lay in Ratzinger's unease at developments in theology. 'From the apparent findings of scholarly exegesis', he wrote, 'terrible books have been concocted, destroying the figure of Jesus, and dismantling the faith.' For many scholars the Christian mystery was just an academic project that had nothing to do with their lives, he told the international papal committee of theologians. Word for word he said:

> They fish in the water of Holy Scripture with a net that can only catch fish of a certain size and any fish that are too big do not fit into it. So they say: those don't exist. It's the same with the great mystery of Jesus: the Son of God become human is reduced to a 'historical Jesus', a really tragic figure, a phantom without flesh and bones. Why is that? Is Christianity the religion of the stupid? Does faith vanish when reason awakes?[12]

The pope's book on Jesus was the quintessence of a man who, as schoolboy and student, as a priest, theologian, bishop, cardinal and head of the Catholic Church, pursued the figure and message of Jesus, not only with scholarship but also spiritually. He had 'tested' in his own life in order to come as close to him as it was possible for anyone to do. With his book the pope wanted to use new historical and theological findings to open readers' eyes to the essential coherence of the gospel. Volume I covered Jesus' baptism, his temptation in the wilderness, the proclamation of the kingdom of God and the Sermon on the Mount. He discussed the 'Our Father', various parables and some of Jesus' sayings about himself. In his work Ratzinger dealt with controversies in research and did not overlook open questions, even when these occasionally tailed off into theological subtleties. He also related the gospel to current ethical problems and to the poverty in Third World countries.

Ratzinger believed that Jesus understood himself to be the Son of God, God himself, who had full authority over the law and was Lord of the universe. Jesus was the only person in history who completely fulfilled the Old Testament. Every word in the Bible had 'awaited' him – 'Christ, the Son of the living God'. 'Our main point will be that Jesus always speaks as the Son, that the relationship between Father and Son is always in the background of his message.' Precisely 'because Jesus is himself God – the Son – his whole message proclaims his own mystery, God's presence in his activity and his being.' Among other things, what was absolutely new about Jesus was that his claim to be the Lord was defined in terms of the cross: 'This king rules by faith and love, by nothing else.' That previously unthinkable 'idea' of God could not have come from any cultural group or community. It was completely 'senseless', not connected with power or the interests of a people, or of a ruler. The inner coherence of Jesus' message showed that this could only have been said by God himself: every word and every action went with the 'inner unity of his course from the first moment of his life to the cross and resurrection'.

According to the New Testament scholar Franz Mussner, in his work Ratzinger 'did not deny historical-critical exegesis its authority'. However, he tried 'with the help of canonical exegesis to get beyond it, in order to show the face of the historically real Jesus'.[13] And in his book the pope connected with the essential Jewish roots of Christianity. Seldom before had Jesus' rootedness in the Old Testament been shown more plainly. He was not afraid to point out the limits of early Christian church teachers, for example, when they compared the parable of the rich man and poor Lazarus to the relationship between Israel (the rich one) and the church (the poor Lazarus). According to Ratzinger's exegesis, here 'a completely different typology in the parable was lacking'. For in fact the parable was about Christ himself, the man who came from beyond: 'This true Lazarus rose from the dead – he came to tell us so.' The parable is inviting us to believe and follow' him, the great sign from God. 'It is more than a parable. It speaks of reality, the most vital reality in history.'

Everything that Jesus said was not only about the past but always about the present and the future too. In particular, the words about judgement and Jesus' farewell speech needed to be applied to the situation of today. For, as Ratzinger said elsewhere, the question of 'whether God exists – the God of Jesus Christ – and is recognized or whether he disappears will decide the fate of the world today'. Colleagues in the Curia kept criticizing the pope for withdrawing too much to concentrate on his beloved writing. I asked the pope emeritus: had he considered whether it was permissible for a pope to write books. Yes, he had considered it, he answered, 'but I simply knew I had to write it. And I have never doubted that it was permissible for me to write it.'

So how did you find time to do this work?

I ask myself that too. But somehow the dear God gave me special help there. The book was very close to my heart. For just as the liturgy is central as the church's self-experience and nothing works if the liturgy is no longer itself, so the church is also at an end if we no longer know Jesus. The danger is overwhelming that he will simply be talked to pieces and destroyed by certain types of exegesis. So I had to join in the jungle warfare of details. It's not enough for dogma to be interpreted only in a spiritual sense.

How does it feel when an experienced theologian and church leader ventures on such a huge task at the age of 80?

It feels completely new. You have to read everything again, think again. Both the texts and in conversation with the most important exegetical works. It was also a spiritual progress for me to go back to basics. Especially finding a way through Jesus's eschatological speech or the question of atonement, these are the most difficult points. And where I believed I had basic insights, I think I was given some new ideas.

Could it be said that this work reinvigorated your papacy?

Yes, for me it was like constantly drawing water from the depths of the sources.

Jesus of Nazareth was published in German in an edition of 150,000 copies, the largest ever first edition of a religious book. Six weeks after publication in April 2007 the work had an international print-run of 1.5 million copies. In the end more than 3 million copies of the book in 30 languages were sold. Benedict's book on Jesus, said the theologian Thomas Söding, gave the papacy a completely new style. Here Christ's representative was not formulating dogma but offering his observations for discussion as a theologian. That was revolutionary. But perhaps it needed a situation in which the basic truths of the faith were gradually being lost to require a restatement of Christianity. So it was lucky for the church that in an era like the present there was a man at the head of the church who could do this.

In 2007 there was no stopping the pope's eagerness to work. Seven months after *Jesus of Nazareth* Benedict XVI issued his second encyclical: *Spe salvi*. It was about Christian hope. The encyclical began with a quotation from Paul's letter to the Romans: '*Spe salvi facti sumus*' – 'In hope we were saved.' As we said, Ratzinger expected his papacy to be short. So he arranged the things he wanted to communicate and inspire in order of urgency. After *Deus caritas est*, on Christian love, in his second encyclical he dealt with Christ's great promise, his revelations about death, the end of the world and eternal life. Many theologians and priests handled the so-called last things, such as God's judgement, Hell and Christ's return very tentatively. Almost as if they were embarrassed by the prophecies about humanity's future, with their reek of fire and punishment. Ratzinger did not see fear and anguish but the true goal of human hope in indestructible eternal life. For him it showed God's mercy: the assurance that there was an afterlife for every soul in an unknown dimension, that went beyond all earthly imaginings of beauty, harmony and well-being.

For the author *Spe salvi* arose from the impulse to look beyond the horizon of purely worldly thinking. In his encyclical he engaged with Augustine, Kant, Marx, Horkheimer, Adorno and Dostoyevsky and grappled with scepticism about the promise of life after death. 'Do we actually want it – to live for ever?' he asked. 'Continuing to live eternally – endlessly – seems more like a doom than a gift.' But didn't everyone also long for a life that is purely happy? 'There are moments when we suddenly feel: yes, that would be it – real "life" – so should it be.' Benedict invited readers to imagine 'eternity not as an endless succession of calendar days, but something like the moment of fulfilment. [...] It would be the moment of plunging into the ocean of endless love, in which there is no more time, no more before and after.' For it was only in that dimension that life appeared in its 'full sense', the 'constant immersion in the breadth of being, where we become simply overwhelmed with joy'.[14]

The idea of Paradise, known to all world cultures for millennia, was not an empty promise of an imaginary tomorrow or a denial of social commitment. If Christian faith was seen as life-bringing, world-changing hope, the pope argued, then 'the dark gate to the future' sprang open, and the present became liveable in a new way. The hope that the world and society could really change came from the experience of unconditional love. It was an encounter with a God who loved everyone to the end. 'His love alone gives us the possibility to stand fast in an essentially imperfect world, without losing the zest of hope.' Everyone could be certain of this: 'I am definitely loved, and whatever happens to me – this love awaits me. And so my life is good.'

Benedict said the appearance of Jesus had brought 'a meeting with the living God' into the world. Henceforth people could know how life was ordered and what awaited them after their hearts stopped beating. Thus Christian hope was 'not only a personal grasping for what was to come', but in a way it also drew 'the future into the present'. Why? Because long before the final fulfilment it transformed life. 'The fact that there is this future changes the present,' said Benedict. In other words, the kingdom of heaven proclaimed by Christ was already present, and always there when its light shone on things and thus created a new dimension of reality. Rather like a sunbeam which was only realized when it fell on a firm object. Unfortunately, 'contemporary Christianity' had 'narrowed its radius of hope', said the pope, and thus also 'failed to realize the greatness of its mission'. That made it all the more important to speak about eternity and eternal life. Humanity should again become aware that ultimately it is 'not the elements of the cosmos or the laws of matter that govern the world and human beings, but a personal God. [...] The laws of matter and evolution are not the final arbiter but understanding, will, love – a person.'[15]

Three years after the beginning of Benedict's papacy many things had happened that previously no one had dared to expect. For example, the declaration of intent to restore 'full and visible unity' with the Orthodox churches, the offer to Anglican groups of a personal ordinariate, a kind of diocese of their own. Old traditions in the papal insignia and papal language usage were also curtailed. Never had the words of a pope been so widespread, with a record number of visits to the most varied places and books in editions of millions of copies. There was a new culture of discussion within the Curia and in bishops' synods. The link between Judaism and Christianity was being strengthened. After the initial irritations by the manipulation of the Regensburg speech, dialogue with Islam was as intensive as ever. There were also speeches and initiatives on the environmental crisis, which led to Benedict being called 'the first green pope'. There were public discussions about the burning questions of society. The pope warned more clearly than any of his predecessors not only against the consequences of destroying the environment, but also against the retreat into barbarism which would occur if Christianity disappeared, together with its values, its ethics, its hope, its linking of faith and reason and also its pedagogy, which helped society to bring up children and respect standards.

The great catechism which he had begun proved to be spiritually strong, impressive in its language and with an unprecedented intellectual acumen. Millions of young people recognized in this old man with his white skull-cap not a hardliner but a heartbreaker in the biblical sense, who brought the sun, moon and stars down from the sky to tell people about the reality of God. The pope had written history with his *motu proprio* '*Summorum pontificum*', which added an extraordinary rite to the ordinary rite and brought home the meaning of the liturgy. In addition, he was the first pope in history to begin a scholarly Christology, in order to make an urgent correction in theology. 'He is the great thinker,' said the Austrian Jesuit theologian Franz Xaver Brandmayr, who was very close to the Vatican and rector of the Anima in Rome: 'In an era beset by irrationalism and loss of truth, he answers rationally, without being confined to rationalism.'[16]

Benedict did not think changes were necessary in foreign policy, such as those Wojtyła had set up with his new Eastern policy. In general, he only wanted to make very slight changes to his predecessor's course. He was keen to preserve the continuity of the office, apart from his priority of setting right matters of faith that had run into difficulties. Not everything he did was successful. His failures of judgement showed in many bishops' appointments. Changing the cardinal secretary of state was also unfortunate. However, Ratzinger had replaced the smooth operator Angelo Sodano with Tarcisio Bertone, because he wanted a man close to him who he could assume was not playing his own game. He lacked anyone in the Curia able and willing to guard the pope's flanks professionally as, when he was a prefect, he himself had done for the previous pope. His papacy was still fragile. The next attack on Ratzinger showed what shaky legs it stood on. It was to be an all-out attack on the pope's whole time in office.

30

The Rupture

What Pope Benedict liked least were many political visits. 'I mean, to keep having to talk to heads of state. They were mostly people with real spiritual interest. But somehow for me the political side was the most wearisome.'[1] There were exceptions. He was friendly with Giorgio Napolitano, Italian president from 2006 until 2015, who came from the ranks of the Communist Party. 'Napolitano is a man who cares about right and justice, wants the good rather than party success. We understand each other very well.'

Another of his favourite conversation partners was the Czech writer, freedom fighter and president Václav Havel. 'I had read some of his work, what he had written about the relationship between politics and truth. I simply found it moving and beautiful to talk with Václav Havel, the human being.' He also valued Michelle Bachelet, the president of Chile: 'She is an atheist Marxist. So in many things we do not agree. But I found an ethical goodwill in her that comes close to the Christian.'

He had a special relationship with the Israeli president Shimon Peres, 'someone I admire'. Ratzinger and Peres had met on 8 September 2001 at a symposium in Cernobbio on Lake Como. 'Although my English is very inadequate, we immediately understood each other very well. Peres was a man of intellectual and human distinction. At home in White Russia he had to endure his close family being locked in a church. The story was so gruesome that it haunted me for a long time.' Despite that horror, Peres had remained 'kind, open and humane' under Nazi rule. He did not allow himself 'to be led into hatred, but the memory caused him to become a great peacemaker'. The Israeli president praised

Ratzinger's papacy effusively. He said later that under the German pope the relations between the church and Israel were 'the best since the birth of Christ'.

Benedict found Barack Obama to be a 'thoughtful person' and 'great politician, who knows how to be successful'. Of course, Obama had 'certain ideas which we cannot share, but he was not just a tactician with me. I felt that he wanted a real meeting and that he listened.' With Vladimir Putin he spoke German in the Vatican: 'We did not go very deep but I believe that he – though, of course, a man of power – somehow felt the necessity of faith. He is a realist. He sees how Russia is suffering from a loss of morality. People need God, he sees that quite clearly.'

Ratzinger regularly went to concerts, and he himself sat down at the piano in the evenings. In his speeches he often spoke of the interrelation between beauty and truth, even though in the Curia they tended to smile at the pope's love of art and music. What was beautiful was true and what was true was beautiful. We know God's beauty in the beauty of creation and in the harmony of the cosmos. The liturgy derived from that and was part of the mystery. So its beauty was not something extra but a fundamental element of the celebration. Just as there was a rationality of faith, so there was an aesthetics of faith, which in a way became proofs of faith, such as marvelling at the great cathedrals or the music of masters such as Palestrina, Bach or Mozart. Benedict asked the Pontifical Council for Culture to reconsider 'the creativity of artists and the fruitful but problematic dialogue between them and Christian faith'. That resulted in a spectacular meeting with international artists in the Sistine Chapel.

He was also increasingly concerned by sickness and mortality. Many of his schoolfellows and other friends and acquaintances had become ill or were no longer alive. When anyone's death was announced – for example, that of the wife of his war comrade Martl – he sat down and wrote a letter, to comfort those left behind. 'At our age we think about health above all', he said in his greeting card to Esther Betz. It was to be hoped that 'this last part of the journey will go well and then finally we can arrive safely where we are awaited by many'. A year later, on 17 February 2008, he wrote in a letter to Esther: 'If we have passed the threshold of 80, then our steps become slower. At least I feel the burden of the years and try, as far as I can, to make my abilities match my duties.'[2]

In 2008 Benedict had to cope with three important journeys. His trip to the USA was booked from 15 until 20 April. From 12 to 21 July the World Youth Day in Sydney was on his programme, and from 12 to 15 September he was expected in France for the 150th anniversary of the Lourdes appearances. As well as this, he had 42 general audiences and four pastoral visits within Italy. Visiting the USA caused him the most anxiety. For he had 'actually decided ten years before', as he told Betz, 'not to cross the oceans again'. However, he 'had not realized what might come up'.

The pope's trip to the USA was overshadowed by shocking reports of abuse scandals, which had now become public. These were just the tip of the iceberg, of what would appear in all its monstrosity ten years later. On the flight Benedict said to the journalists travelling with him: 'We are deeply ashamed about what has happened and we will do our best to ensure it does not happen again in future.'[3] On the day after his arrival, 16 April, his birthday, President George W. Bush, gave him a splendid reception in the White House. He also spoke to 300 bishops in Baltimore about sexual abuse: 'In many cases' it had been dealt with 'in the worst possible way'. It grieved him sorely that clergy had betrayed their priestly duties by serious moral crimes. He demanded the strict application to the perpetrators of the zero-tolerance strategy he had set up. It was a duty towards the victims to treat their wounds and heal them as far as possible. Benedict insisted that he himself should meet the victims of abuse. He saw this as a duty and henceforth made it a firm commitment on every journey.

The pope met 200 Muslims, Hindus and Jews in a cultural centre called 'John Paul II', to engage in religious dialogue, which had to depend on mutual respect. At a celebratory and emotional Mass in the Washington Nationals' stadium in Washington, DC, he won the hearts of the American faithful. Deeply moved, those present and those watching on television also followed the pope's prayer at Ground Zero in New York, where he remembered the victims of the 9/11 terror attack. The high point of his visit was on 18 April, when he spoke before the United Nations. After Paul VI and John Paul II, he was the third pope to visit the USA. But Benedict XVI introduced 'a new element into Vatican foreign policy', said Elio Guerriero, namely the principle of responsibility for every member of the human family. 'What a hit, what a trip, what a triumph!' the *New York Post* commented on the speech, which received a standing ovation. 'Anyone who is not moved is not alive.' The London *Times* summed up that on his visit to the USA Benedict XVI had unquestionably come out of the shadow of his charismatic predecessor, John Paul II – both by the content of his speeches and by the way he delivered them. And he had shown all those who doubted him that he was certainly a warmer and more feeling person than the doctrinaire academic that so many headlines proclaimed him to be when he was elected pope.[4]

The pope seemed rather embarrassed by the enthusiasm his UN appearance had aroused. He was not 'going to get stage fright there'. But he had taken advice about this important speech. He spoke about the situation in some African counties. He also warned about the environment, resources and need to prevent climate change. If individual states were not able to guarantee the rights of their own citizens, then the international community should not just look on. On the 60th anniversary of the Universal Declaration of Human Rights he stressed that these rights were founded on natural law, which was written in the hearts of all people and existed in all cultures and civilizations. The foundation of the UN had been 'the result of an agreement between different religious and cultural traditions'. Releasing human rights from that context would mean limiting their scope and making them relative to the social and political standards currently in force.[5]

Three months later Benedict travelled to Australia to the World Youth Day. The length of the journey was a record distance for him. Of Australia's 21 million inhabitants, 6 million were Catholics. The youth meeting began on 17 July, when the pope sailed into Sydney harbour. He spoke urgently against a world 'of greed, exploitation and divisions, the wasteland of false idols and half answers – and the plague of false promises'. He called on the 500,000 young people in the closing Mass, the biggest religious service ever on Australian soil, to be 'prophets of this new time' so that hope would free them 'from the superficiality, apathy and self-centredness that wither our souls and poison the network of human relationships'.[6] 'Dear friends,' said the ageing pope,

> life is not governed by chance; it is not arbitrary. Your personal self is willed by God; he has blessed it and given it a meaning! Life is not just a succession of events or experiences, even though many of them can be helpful. It is a search for truth, the good and the beautiful. [...] Don't be deceived by those who see you just as consumers in a market of indiscriminate possibilities, where choice itself becomes a good, novelty is regarded as beauty and subjective experience supplants the truth.[7]

The Australian reported afterwards that the week with the pope 'will go down as one of the most exuberant in Sydney's history'. The *Sydney Morning Herald* even spoke of a 'tsunami of joy and faith' and called Benedict 'a people's pope'.

Ratzinger's trip to France in September was almost a homecoming, although advocates of a secular state aroused protests, even before the pope had set foot in the country of 'the oldest daughter of the Catholic Church'. Yes, he had felt particularly well, said the pope: 'I love French culture and feel at home in it.'[8] Despite all the gloomy predictions, the visit was a great success. Benedict had taken the wind out of the sails of his critics when he made clear at the beginning that secularity was not a contradiction of faith. No one had thought it possible that the Mass with the pope in front of the Dôme des Invalides in Paris would be attended by at least 250,000 people. A further high point was the meeting with representatives of the world of culture in the Collège des Bernadins in the Latin Quarter. In the former Cistercian monastery 'where we were simply just together as friends', he gave what Henri de Lubac described as one of the most famous speeches of his papacy, a lecture on the birth of Europe 'from the spirit of the search for God'.

He began by saying that 'in the cultural upheaval of migrations and the formation of new states' it had been especially the monasteries in which 'the treasures of the old culture survived and at the same time a new culture slowly formed'. Monasteries had 'libraries, which showed the way to learning'. And from that schools arose. But reading on its own was not enough to pray God's word: 'it requires music.' Christian worship meant accepting the invitation 'to sing with the angels [...] to pray and to sing in a way that joins with the music of the blessed spirits, who were said to be the originators of the harmony of the cosmos, the music of the spheres'. From this inner urge 'to sing of God in words he himself has given [...] the great music of the West arose.'

The pope then went on to give a short lesson on the character of the Bible, which 'regarded in a purely literary or historical way is not a single book but a collection of literature written over more than a millennium. But its individual books are not self-contained; they are clearly linked to one another.' The tension between connection and freedom determined the monks' way of thinking and working and plainly left its mark on Western culture. There was a second component that really made monasticism the bearer of European history. According to the Benedictine motto, *ora et labora* ('pray and work'), Christian monasticism had 'a culture of work side by side with its culture of the word; together they shaped Europe's ethos and world'. Benedict's speech was received with overwhelming applause. He concluded it with the words: 'That foundation of Europe's culture, the search for God and the readiness to listen to him, remains the basis of true culture today. *Merci*.'[9]

To end off the tour, a day later the pope stood with sick people and pilgrims at the foot of the Pyrenees in south-west France, in a candlelit procession that was a river of light. According to the belief of the Catholic Church, 150 years earlier the mother of God appeared to the miller's daughter Bernadette Soubirous. Ratzinger was familiar with the place from his childhood reading of Franz Werfel. After being saved from the Nazis, Werfel had fulfilled his vow and written the moving story of Mary's appearances in his novel *The Song of Bernadette*. Ratzinger's birthday was also on St Bernadette's feast day. Since 1858 millions of people had been coming to Lourdes on pilgrimage. Thousands were healed of serious illnesses; countless people regained their faith there. 'Lourdes is one of the places God has chosen to shine a special beam of his beauty on,' the pope preached in a hoarse voice. Lourdes was 'a place of light, because it is a place of community, hope and conversion'. People needed light and were called to become light. At this place of pilgrimage all were invited to discover the simplicity of their calling, 'For it is enough to love: *il suffit d'aimer.*'

The year 2008 had ended well. But it had begun with a scandal, which in retrospect seemed like a precursor of the events that would throw the papacy off its tracks. What had happened? The rector of Rome's La Sapienza University, one of the largest universities in Europe, with 170,000 students, founded in the fourteenth century as the pontifical university by Boniface VIII, had invited Ratzinger to give a *lectio magistralis* for the opening of the academic year on 17 January. The lecture was to be on the concepts of truth and reason and would defend the university as 'the voice of humanity's moral reason'.[10] However, many of the professors and students wanted to be neither the voice of morality nor defenders of reason. Their flyer described Benedict XVI as a reactionary. As cardinal, he had not sufficiently distanced himself from the proceedings against Galileo Galilei. He was also an enemy of gay people. Left-wing student representatives occupied the rector's office. The storm of protest was strong enough for Ratzinger to cancel his lecture. He was even banned from giving a word of greeting. The theologian Armin Schwibach, who lectured in Rome, shook his head: 'If these events are an expression of "emancipated" and "enlightened" secular culture, that is to be deplored. Good night, Enlightenment. Your ignorant great-grandchildren are bearing you to your grave.'[11]

In his ungiven lecture, which *L'Osservatore Romano* published later, the pope warned of the danger that in the modern university 'cost-benefit thinking' was marginalizing the humanities. In view of the questionable developments of modernity, he called for a renewal of ideas and a civilization of love. Knowledge alone made you sad. Augustine had realized that; truth meant more than knowing. The purpose of knowing the truth was to know the good. That was also the meaning of the Socratic question: what is the good that makes us true? A university that no longer questioned whether its knowledge contributed to the good in the world did not deserve the name of university.

The events at the La Sapienza did encounter opposition. Some 200,000 people gathered in St Peter's Square to express their solidarity with the pope in protest against what they regarded as a blind academic elite. Banners proclaimed, 'Benedict, you are not alone.' It was as though the demonstrators wanted to translate words from the banned speech into action. What had Benedict urged in his lecture? In our time it depended on the 'guardians of sensitivity to the truth' not growing tired. A society that could not bear to look beyond its own time and ask what was good and true became sterile and wasted away. Perhaps the most dangerous tendency of the present was the daily growing 'pressure of power and interests'. It was important to oppose it in order to avoid 'the danger of collapse into inhumanity'.

For four years Pope Ratzinger had been carried on a wave of sympathy. He had held a dialogue with Judaism and Islam and had succeeded in making the church's teaching exciting again with his catechism and his book on Jesus. Even the trouble over his Regensburg speech had not harmed him. However, in January 2009 his papacy reached a breaking point. It began to show signs of exhaustion that ultimately led to his historic decision to resign.

The trigger was a measure by the pope, which was pressing on grounds of canon law and demanded for Christian reasons. It was the withdrawal of the excommunication of bishops belonging to the schismatic Society of St Pius X, founded by Archbishop Marcel Lefebvre. The excommunication had been imposed for a violation of papal authority in 1988. The effects of this case have persisted to this day. Together with 'Vatileaks' it is regarded as the major 'scandal' of Benedict's papacy. However, an exact reconstruction of the events makes clear there was a campaign of disinformation, reminiscent of the Dreyfus affair in nineteenth-century France. But it also throws light on the Vatican's catastrophic crisis management and the lack of support from bishops and cardinals, which left the pope out in the cold.

August 2005: Bernard Fellay, the superior of the Society of St Pius X, arrived in Castel Gandolfo to ask the pope to lift the excommunication of the four bishops unlawfully ordained by Archbishop Marcel Lefebvre. When he was prefect of the Congregation for the Doctrine of the Faith, Ratzinger had secured an agreement with Lefebvre recognizing the Second Vatican Council in full. However, Lefebvre had then withdrawn his signature. On that occasion the conversation was also broken off. The reason was that one of the bishops, the English Richard Williamson, had made the confidential meeting public. For Williamson, an Anglican convert, Benedict XVI was a heretic, worse than Luther. The Brotherhood could be 'thankful for his involuntary support' through the excommunication, he declared. It had saved them from contamination.

Saturday, 1 November 2008: The journalist Ali Fegan interviewed Williamson at the Brotherhood's seminary at Zaitzkofen, near Regensburg, for a Swedish television programme entitled *Uppdrag Granskning* ('Investigation Assignment'). In the course of the recording the reporter confronted Williamson with a remark about the Holocaust that he had made 20 years earlier. Williamson replied that he was of the opinion 'that there were no gas chambers. I have studied the proofs that there weren't any.' Indeed, 'two to three thousand Jews had died in the Nazi camps', but none of them had been gassed.[12] The 68-year-old Brotherhood bishop, a literature lecturer with a Cambridge degree, had lived in Argentina since 1972. In 1989 he had been threatened with a court case in Canada, because he had praised books by a writer who denied the Holocaust. According to information from the German daily newspaper *Die Welt*, Williamson's father had died in the Sonnenburg concentration camp in 1944, after he had helped some Jews escape.

Sunday, 9 November 2008: On the 70th anniversary of *Kristallnacht*, the Nazi attack on Jewish establishments in Germany, Benedict called for 'deep solidarity with the Jewish world' and prayer for the victims. The night of 9/10 November had been the beginning of the systematic persecution of the German Jews, which had ended in the Shoah. It was everyone's duty to oppose anti-Semitism at all levels.[13]

Monday, 15 December 2008: In a letter to Benedict XVI, Bishop Bernard Fellay of the Society of St Pius X assured him that he wanted to submit to the terms for lifting the excommunication. That also went for his three bishop colleagues. Word for word the letter said: 'We always want and are firmly decided to remain Catholic and to place all our powers at the service of the church of our Lord Jesus Christ, which is the Roman Catholic Church. We accept her teaching in filial obedience. We firmly believe in the primacy of Peter and his prerogatives. We are therefore suffering greatly in the present situation.' According to the canon lawyer Günter Assenmacher, since the point of excommunication was to move those excommunicated to repent, they 'had a right to have it lifted if they recognizably and lastingly [...] confessed allegiance to the Catholic Church'. Then a pope had no other option but to lift the church's penalty.

Saturday, 17 January 2009: After Benedict agreed with the suggestion of his prefects concerned to lift the excommunication, the decree to lift it, dated 21 January and signed by Cardinal Giovanni Battista Re (the prefect of the Congregation for Bishops), was handed to Bernard Fellay in Rome by Cardinal Darío Castrillón Hoyos. On the same day the Spanish lawyer Francisco José Fernández de la Cigoña, who clearly had good contacts with the Congregation for Bishops, announced the 'explosive news' on his blog. He had already announced on 3 November 2008 that such a decree was in preparation in the Vatican.

Monday, 19 January 2009: An article appeared in *Der Spiegel* headed 'Problem for the Pope'. It quoted statements by Williamson from the interview that had not yet been broadcast. Dieter Graumann, vice-president of the Central Council of Jews in Germany, had been 'informed of the statements in advance', as *Der Spiegel* reported. In the article he was quoted as saying with reference to the pope's planned visit to Israel: 'Anyone who cannot or will not distance themselves becomes complicit.' The article mentioned that the television interview would be broadcast the following Wednesday on the *Uppdrag Granskning* programme and could also be seen on the internet.[14] The journalist Fiammetta Venner had also been interviewed for the article. She was a gay rights activist. Together with her partner Caroline Fourest, she had published a book in France in September 2008, immediately before Benedict's visit. The book's title was *Les nouveaux soldats du pape: Légion du Christ, Opus Dei, traditionalistes* (*The Pope's New Soldiers: Legion of Christ, Opus Dei, Traditionalists*).

Tuesday, 20 January 2009: In response to the *Spiegel* article the regent of the German district of the Society of St Pius X, Father Franz Schmidberger, immediately distanced himself from Williamson's statements. It was not followed by any statement from the Vatican. According to the Swedish public television broadcaster SVT, Rome had known about Williamson's position for a long time. It said that the Catholic bishop of Stockholm, Anders Arborelius, had informed the apostolic nuncio for the Nordic lands, Archbishop Emil Paul Tscherrig, about Williamson's statements. The Vatican press spokesman Federico Lombardi later emailed the following clarification to the Swedish television broadcaster: 'I did not know that information about Williamson had been sent to the Vatican, and I do not know who received it and read it. No one has said a word to me about it.' The cardinal in charge, Cardinal Castrillón Hoyos, gave an interview describing Bishop Arborelius's statement as 'untrustworthy': 'We file all the documents that we receive in digital form. So Bishop Arborelius should say how, to whom and when he sent this information and whether it was in writing or by word of mouth.' At any rate, it was not to be found in the archives of his pontifical committee, Ecclesia Dei.[15] Perhaps the communication had gone to colleagues in the secretariat of state.

Wednesday, 21 January 2009: In the evening, as announced, Swedish television broadcast the interview with Williamson conducted during the previous November. On the same day the lifting of the excommunication came into force, although it was not yet made public.

Thursday, 22 January 2009: The Italian daily newspapers *Il Giornale* and *Il Reformista,* as well as the Catholic news agency ASCA, quoted Williamson's statements. There was still no reaction from the Vatican secretariat of state, press office or any other Vatican authority. Georg Gänswein, Benedict XVI's secretary, was in bed with flu. He was not reading any emails or going to his office so as not to infect the pope. Cardinal Secretary of State Bertone had invited a group of bishops and cardinals to meet in the Prima Loggia of the Palazzo Apostolico at 5.30 p.m. As well as Bertone, those attending the meeting were Cardinal Darío Castrillón Hoyos (president of the Ecclesia Dei pontifical committee), Cardinal William J. Levada (prefect of the Congregation for the Doctrine of the Faith), Cardinal Giovanni Battista Re (prefect of the Congregation for Bishops), Cardinal Cláudio Hummes (prefect of the Congregation for the Clergy), Archbishop Francesco Coccopalmerio (president of the Pontifical Council for the Interpretation of Legal Texts) and Bishop Fernando Filoni (substitute for General Affairs in the Secretariat of State). In the four-page minutes of the meeting it read:

After the prayer the Cardinal Secretary of State, who was leading the meeting, introduced the subject of the future and directed the attention of those present to the situation that had arisen when on Saturday 24 January at 12 noon, Rome time, the decree was published lifting the excommunication of the four bishops.

The first question was whether this benevolent action by the pope concerned priests, religious and the faithful laity or not. The second question was whether an explanatory statement had accompanied the decree.

According to the minutes, none of those at the meeting mentioned Bishop Williamson. An explanatory statement for the better understanding of the decree, 'which seems clear enough in itself', was not regarded as necessary. It would only complicate the matter. Instead, Archbishop Coccopalmerio would compose an article commenting on it, which would be published in *L'Osservatore Romano* in the next few days. According to the minutes, the meeting ended 'at 7.30 p.m. with a prayer'.[16]

Saturday, 24 January: According to a report in *Die Welt*, an email came from England to the Vatican in the early morning saying: 'If the pope wants to lift the excommunication after Williamson has denied the Holocaust, the pope's enemies will try to destroy him. We are on the brink of a catastrophe. Doesn't Mgr Gänswein know about it?' *Die Welt*'s correspondent Paul Badde reported an anonymous statement by 'a high prelate in the secretariat of state': 'There was a conflict of authority. We had information about Bishop Williamson in front of us from 22 January. We tried everything to prevent the document being published on the 24th. It had already been signed on 21 January. Nevertheless, it would have been possible to postpone it.'[17]

In the Vatican press office the communiqué on the lifting of the excommunication of the four Society of St Pius X bishops was released at 12 noon. It said that after a dialogue process the Holy Father had accepted the renewed request and had lifted the excommunication imposed 20 years earlier. That was done 'through the decree of the Congregation for Bishops of 21 January 2009, with benevolence, pastoral zeal and paternal mercy'. Together with the communiqué, the decree signed by Cardinal Re was also published. In the document it says:

His Holiness Benedict XVI in his paternal concern for the spiritual distress which the parties concerned have voiced as a result of the excommunication, and trusting in their commitment, expressed in the aforementioned letter, to spare no effort in exploring as yet unresolved questions through requisite discussions with the authorities of the Holy See in order to reach a prompt, full and satisfactory solution to the original problem has decided to *reconsider* [author's italics] the canonical situation of Bishops Bernard Fellay, Bernard Tissier de Mallerais, Richard Williamson and Alfonso de Galarreta, resulting from their episcopal consecration [...] This gift of peace, coming at the end of the Christmas celebrations, is also meant to be a sign which promotes the Universal Church's unity in charity, and removes the scandal of division.[18]

Italian newspapers such as *Il Giornale* described the lifting of the excommunication as an 'act of extraordinary magnanimity'. By these 'truly generous gestures' the Society had been compelled to recognize the authority of the pope and the Second Vatican Council.

Monday, 26 January 2009: The *Süddeutsche Zeitung* took a very different attitude in its reporting. The article set the tone for the sharpness of the discussion that followed about the Williamson case. The title page headlines read: 'Pope brings back Holocaust Denier into the Church.' The newspaper's Rome correspondent stressed in his commentary: 'Benedict XVI allows a Holocaust denier to be a bishop again.'[19]

But nothing in that sentence fitted the facts. First: the pope did not let the Holocaust denier 'be a bishop again'. He *was a* bishop, but not in the Catholic Church. As an Anglican, Williamson had joined the Lefebvre community in 1970 without ever getting to know the Catholic Church .The decree did not bring the bishops 'back into the Church'. The Society remained a community separate from the Catholic Church. The article assumed the pope had known about Williamson's statements about the Holocaust and nevertheless 'rehabilitated' him, which was completely untrue.

In his commentary the *Süddeutsche Zeitung* correspondent wrote:

Even clergy who remain loyal to their pope speak of disillusionment, unease and disappointment [...] They are puzzled why Benedict XVI has accepted four reactionary bishops, who have long been excommunicated, back into the church community – including a man who denies the Holocaust. As before after his Regensburg speech in 2006 with its anti-Islam quotation, the world is asking:

what drives this pope? Where is he taking his church? Indeed, '[...] now all those who, despite misgivings, greeted Benedict XVI's election as pope with joy four years ago must feel uneasy.

The *Süddeutsche Zeitung* pointed out that Benedict had published his reconciliation with the enemies of the Second Vatican Council on exactly the same weekend that John XXIII had announced it 50 years earlier. That meant there was 'doubt about the pope's faithfulness to the Council'. The article came to a climax saying: 'One of the bishops has been a Holocaust denier for years. The pope and his advisers must have known that. Benedict lifted the excommunication, although it was clear what a bad sign he was giving by doing so.' Therefore, 'harmony with an arch-conservative splinter group was more important than the relationship with Judaism and with the moderate, modern-leaning forces in his own church.'

According to research by the media expert Hans Mathias Kepplinger, long-term director of the Institute for Journalism at the University of Mainz, 72 per cent of German journalists approved of manipulative presentation methods if they believed that this would serve to combat abuse. Of course, it would figure large if a German pope freed a bishop from excommunication who denied the Holocaust. But even cursory research would have shown that the lifting of the excommunication did not mean re-inclusion in the Catholic Church. By canon law the four bishops were still suspended. They were forbidden to exercise their office. They were unlawful as long as the Society was not structured in accordance with valid church law. In practice, the lifting of the excommunication meant that from then on the Society's bishops could go to confession, receive Holy Communion and have a church burial. However the *Süddeutsche Zeitung* had not made those facts clear.

The Society of St Pius X tried again to smooth things over and stated in a communiqué: 'Jesus was a Jew, Mary was a Jew, the apostles were Jews and therefore no true Christian can be anti-Semitic.' Bishop Williamson's statements were 'not the views of the Society of St Pius X'. But the storm of protest could no longer be stopped. Representatives of Jewish organizations were the most furious. David Rosen, president of the Jewish Committee for Inter-Religious Relationships, stated: 'By accepting a clearly anti-Semitic Holocaust denier into the church, without any retraction from him, the Vatican has mocked the moving and impressive condemnation of anti-Semitism by John Paul II.' Salomon Korn, vice-president of the Central Council of Jews in Germany, went as far as to say that the pope had 'wanted to make a Holocaust denier socially acceptable'. The president of the Central Council of Jews in Germany, Charlotte Knobloch, declared that dialogue with the Catholic Church was at an end.

In Rome, Chief Rabbi Riccardo Di Segni, who had just invited Pope Benedict XVI to visit his synagogue, said: 'It looks as though storm clouds are gathering over Jewish–Christian dialogue.' But the Vatican still kept its head in the sand. None of the three press conferences that took place that week dealt with the lifting of the excommunication. Benedict only spoke about the matter at the end of a general audience on 28 January: 'I performed this act of paternal mercy because these bishops repeatedly told me of their deep distress about the situation they were in.' He hoped that as a result of his 'gesture', the 'necessary steps' would follow 'to attest their true faithfulness and true recognition of the magisterium and authority of the pope and the Second Vatican Council'.[20]

In view of the forthcoming Shoah memorial day, the pope then went on to speak indirectly about Holocaust denial. During these days he would be remembering 'the images of my repeated visits to Auschwitz', which was

one of those camps in which millions of Jews were brutally murdered, innocent victims of blind racial and religious hatred. With all my heart I again express my total and unquestionable solidarity with our brothers, the recipients of the first covenant. I hope the Shoah will move people to reflect on the incalculable power of evil which can take hold of the human heart. The Shoah was a reminder for all not to forget or deny or play it down.

Cardinal Castrillón Hoyos, the cardinal in charge of the dealings with the Society of St Pius X, also spoke. On 30 January he stated in an interview: 'When I handed over the decree signed by Cardinal Re to Monsignor Fellay, we did not know about that interview. By the time it was broadcast the decree was already in the hands of those concerned.' Meanwhile it became known that Cardinal Re had declared in a fit of fury that Castrillón Hoyos had dealt with the matter much too quickly and had not properly informed the pope. At the same time a dossier was doing the rounds in the Apostolic Palace. The paper asserted that the pope had been led into a carefully timed trap by particular circles, which he had fallen into unawares. The responsibility for the catastrophe lay with 'ignorant carelessness and poor communication in the Curia', especially in the Ecclesia Dei pontifical committee.

Neither Benedict's statement for the Shoah memorial day nor his declaration of solidarity had any effect. Many reports suggested that the lifting of the excommunication meant a retreat from the Council declaration *Nostra aetate*, about the church's relationship with Judaism. The acting chairwoman of the German Greens, Claudia Roth, said that the pope had 'destroyed' dialogue between Catholics and Jews and had endangered 'life in multi-religious societies'. Federal Chancellor Angela Merkel took the opportunity of a press conference on 3 February with the Kazakh president Nursultan Nazarbayev, who reigned autocratically over his country, rich in raw materials. She said the pope must clearly state 'that here there can be no denial and of course there must be positive relations with Judaism'. These clarifications 'have not yet been forthcoming in my opinion'. The former SPD leader Kurt Beck sharply criticized the chancellor for hitting on Benedict XVI in 2009, an election year. Never before had a head of state in Germany interfered in Vatican politics in such an undiplomatic and offensive way. 'I should have liked to see what would have happened if a Social Democrat chancellor had given the pope public advice,' said Beck. He had been 'infuriated that the chancellor only did this because she had an eye to the *vox populi*'.

It was only on 4 February that the Vatican secretariat of state first published a note in answer to the protests. It said that by his gesture the pope had wanted to overcome an obstacle to dialogue. Of course, 'Bishop Williamson's statements on the Shoah were absolutely unacceptable.' They had been 'rejected by the Holy Father'. Williamson's statements 'were unknown to the Holy Father at the time of the lifting of the excommunication'.

Meanwhile Rabbi David Rosen softened his tone and said the Jewish–Catholic relationship was not in danger. He had never believed that Benedict XVI regarded dialogue as unimportant: 'Anyone who knows his writings and his previous statements will not take that idea seriously.'[21] However, such calm words had no chance of being heard in the loaded atmosphere of those weeks. Mathias Döpfner, the chairman of Axel Springer publishing company, announced in *Bild* that the pope had done great damage to Germany in the world. He had inflicted a 'fearful stain' on his office. The *Financial Times* reported: 'Benedict XVI is stuck in the most serious crisis of his four-year period of office. [...] Cardinals and bishops are planning a revolt.' The *Frankfurter Rundschau* declared: 'The pope was once a respected German [...] But anyone who whitewashes a Holocaust denier with bland speeches' must face the question 'how long can his organization still enjoy state support in Germany'. A Munich tabloid called the pope a 'self-righteous old man', a 'reactionary with the intolerable hubris that all non-Catholics are worthless as human beings'.

In the *Süddeutsche Zeitung* the acting editor-in-chief, Kurt Kister, declared: 'We don't want to be pope any longer.' Chancellor Merkel had 'acted correctly in her admonition to the Vatican. A pope coming from Germany who inflames the Jewish communities against him and indulgently helps a Holocaust denier to prominence has failed to understand something fundamental.' Benedict had 'brought the Lefebvre bishops, including their radical right-wing fellow bishop, back into the lap of the church'. He had thereby 'sinned against religion', namely against 'the civil religion operating in this land'.

The Munich-based newspaper started a kind of propaganda campaign. One of its headlines read: 'The Catholic crisis: Pope Benedict XVI has compromised the Catholic Church's relationship to the world.' The church politics editor declared: 'A storm is brewing in Catholicism, especially in German-speaking countries [...] A tide of people leaving the church is sweeping the country.' (This was incorrect. Only 2,700 more people left the church than in the previous year.) The article continued: 'Benedict XVI has rehabilitated a Holocaust denier. Bishops are distancing themselves.' And 'Should a Holocaust denier be rehabilitated just to safeguard church unity? Benedict XVI's decision is causing increasing discontent – particularly among Catholics.' And finally: 'Dialogue with Jews has been set back 100 years. Theologians and church representatives are furious about the Holocaust denier Richard Williamson being reaccepted into the church.'

Naturally, Hans Küng re-entered the fray with a prominent article in the paper. Headline: "'Reconciliation" with four arch-reactionaries means more to the pope than the confidence of Catholics.' Then he let rip: Benedict XVI was suffering from 'an increasing loss of trust. Many Catholics no longer expected anything from him. Even worse: by the lifting of the excommunication from four illegally ordained traditionalist bishops, including a notorious Holocaust denier, all the fears expressed when Ratzinger was elected pope have been confirmed.' 'Apologies after the event' could not 'mend matters' now. Whereas President Obama 'radiates hope [...] Pope Benedict XVI is locked in a state of fear and wants to limit people's freedom as much as possible, in order to enforce an "era of restoration".'

Very few readers would remember that, in the conflict with Lefebvre and the Society of St Pius X, Küng himself had been in favour of 'speaking with each other again'.[22] The position he took on Lefebvre in 1979 had been that he had never understood why the Tridentine Mass had been forbidden.[23] In his 2007 autobiography he wrote: 'Conservative people, whether individuals or groups, must also have a home in the Catholic Church. Being Christians together is more important than being traditional or progressive. With this conviction I am now also putting in a good word for Bishop emeritus Mgr Marcel Lefebvre's traditionalists of the "Fraternité internationale de Saint-Pie X".' He was against 'any split in the church', Küng insisted: 'I demand justice even for traditionalists and am arguing for the overcoming of polarizations in the Catholic Church and mutual tolerance.'[24]

The headline of a hastily cobbled title story in Der Spiegel on 2 February looked cynical: 'Lost in abstraction. A German pope disgraces the Catholic Church.' As if the Hamburg magazine had a problem with the Catholic Church making itself unpopular. 'So bitter. So sad', said the headline inside.[25] On 11 pages Benedict was described as a technocrat, enveloped in a 'distant coolness'. He was governed by an 'abstract truth bigotry' and was leading the church 'back into the ivory tower of theological dogma'. Gleefully, the magazine quoted an anonymous 'committed Christian': 'What will happen if Williamson lets off a bomb in a synagogue? Will the pope then make him a cardinal?' A year later Der Spiegel's editorship decided the time had come for further coverage of the pope and declared that Ratzinger's papacy was finally done for. After 'Lost in

Abstraction' now the epithet was 'The ~~Infallible~~ One'. Underneath that: 'Joseph Ratzinger's Failed Mission'.

German-speaking theologians also wanted to contribute to the general outcry. It began on 27 January 2009 with the 'Münster Declaration'. Soon colleagues in Frankfurt, Bonn, Freiburg, Tübingen, Bamberg, Würzburg and also in Graz, Lucerne, Vienna and other universities followed suit. The four Society of St Pius X bishops rejected many of the principles adopted by the Second Vatican Council, said the protest note. So their 'rehabilitation' seriously damaged the 'credibility of the church and thereby repudiates our efforts to implement the Council in our theological work'. Colleagues in Frankfurt declared that the lifting of the excommunication might create the impression that central doctrines were at the pope's own strategic disposition. Fifteen Tübingen theologians wrote to the pope that they were 'very worried about the unity of the church on the basis of the Second Vatican Council'. They did not mention that there were decided gaps in their own loyalty to the Council. The Council confirmed the primacy of the pope, defended celibacy as 'a precious divine gift of grace' and stressed that ordination as a priest was for men only. It also forbade communion in divine service if there was no church communion.

It did not fit the picture to remember that Benedict never tired of denouncing any form of anti-Semitism. The subject of Jewish–Christian relations was a constant in Ratzinger's life and work. It was no accident that his election had been so strongly applauded from the Jewish side. 'In the last 20 years,' said Israel Singer, chairman of the Jewish World Congress, Ratzinger had 'changed the two-thousand-year old history of the relationship between Judaism and Christianity'. He had provided the theological support for the rapprochement between the two world religions. It was also forgotten that at the beginning of his papacy Ratzinger had stopped the beatification of a French priest who was charged with anti-Semitic speeches.

Meanwhile, the attacks on him had reached a level that caused the *Neue Zürcher Zeitung* to speak of the 'aggressive ignorance' of journalists' who conducted a media campaign without reference to the facts ('The Pope travestied by the media'). 'The excessive outrage' depended on a 'minimum of information'.[26] The French-Jewish philosopher Bernard-Henri Lévy remarked that, as soon as the talk was about Benedict, then 'prejudices, falsehood and even plain disinformation' dominated every discussion. The German federal president, Horst Köhler, no longer hesitated to take his fellow countryman in Rome under his protection: 'There could never have been any [...] doubt about the pope's attitude to the Holocaust It is unambiguous.' That was a clear reprimand for Angela Merkel, but also a sideswipe at officials of Jewish organizations, such as the journalist Michel Friedmann, who accused the pope of being a 'hypocrite' who rehabilitated 'active haters of Jews'. The president of the German Parliament (the Bundestag), Norbert Lammert, commented: 'Much of what is implied about the pope now is malicious.' Werner Münch, former minister president of the Saxony-Anhalt region, left the CDU: 'The last straw was the way in which the party leader had publicly discredited the head of our Catholic Church, the German Pope Benedict XVI, although there was no reason for it.'[27]

In the USA Yehuda Levin, chairman of an association of 800 orthodox rabbis, spoke out. He supported the attempt at a reconciliation with the members of the Society of St Pius X, he said, 'because I understand the whole context'. Many gestures of reconciliation over the last three decades had been directly instigated by Cardinal Ratzinger: 'This man, Pope Benedict XVI, has a decades-long record of anti-Nazism and sympathy for Jews.'[28]

There was now occasional support from within the church, for example from Cardinal Walter Kasper, well known for not being an unconditional member of the Ratzinger party: 'When people denigrate the pope completely unjustly, then it is directed not only against the pope but also against the Catholic Church. That will not do. We can't let it happen.' Kasper made clear: 'We are for church unity. So also for unity with this brotherhood.' In a letter to the faithful in his diocese Kurt Koch, the bishop of Basel, who later became the Vatican chief ecumenist, asked the question 'how do we as a church want to present ourselves in the future to outsiders? [...] Hasn't the pope just given us an example, that we should first practise in the church what we expect and demand from society?'

Was the unsavoury development of the Williamson case actually due to a conspiracy, as the secret Vatican document claimed? Or was it caused by the naïvety and dilettantism constantly to be found in the Curia, despite all its professionalism? Possibly linked to an accumulation of unfortunate circumstances that made the pope an easy prey?

It is clear that the pardon was preceded by a long decision process. By the end of 2007 the overwhelming majority of cardinals had agreed with the step, if the requirements were met. Four cardinals were involved in the preparation of the decree itself: the old Castrillón Hoyos, Tarcisio Bertone, Giovanni Battista Re and Walter Kasper. As president of the papal committee Ecclesia Dei, Castrillón Hoyos had dealt with the traditionalists on behalf of the pope. 'Until the last moment of that dialogue we knew absolutely nothing about this Williamson,' he passionately insisted. He had 'never, I repeat never, received documents, information, letters or reports, or heard any talk about Holocaust denial from the Society of St Pius X or their members'. In the conversations Fellay had fully recognized the Second Vatican Council. So it was meant to be symbolic that the decree was published on the 50th anniversary of the announcement of the Council, precisely as a confirmation of the Council. However, Castrillón Hoyos admitted that on 20 January he had 'heard on the internet of declarations by Father Schmidberger', in which he distanced himself from Williamson's statements. So that was at a point in time when it would still have been possible to take appropriate measures.

The Vatican management model was what made it possible to make a scandal of the case with fake news for weeks on end, and to discredit the pope as anti-Semitic. With the pope's trip to Israel planned for May, the campaign was bound to strain relations badly between the Catholic Church and Judaism. A disinformation campaign had already converted Ratzinger's Regensburg speech into the opposite of what it actually contained. Dialogue between religions had become hatred of other religions. His decision to allow the Tridentine Mass again, by which Benedict sought a reconciliation, was interpreted as this pope returning to the past and undermining the Council.

The philosopher Robert Spaemann called the uproar an 'unparalleled media campaign'. The writer Martin Mosebach asked:

> Why didn't the general public notice that Bishop Williamson is still not permitted to exercise his office, because the lifting of the excommunication did not affect his suspension from the episcopate? Instead of that, people were surmising whether this

pope was secretly inclined towards anti-Semitism. But this was a pope who, in his theology, could be said to be the first pope since Peter who had tried to read and understand the whole gospel as a work of Judaism.

The condemnation in advance of Benedict XVI was made possible by the decades-long incitement against him. The religious scholar Rudi Thiessen called it astonishing 'how resolutely this partly offensive, partly embarrassing affair was used as an opportunity to turn Benedict's whole papacy into a succession of scandals'. Seen from the viewpoint of the Williamson case, everything now became hateful. Benedict XVI was stamped as a sinister reactionary who systematically provoked Jews, Muslims and Protestants against him. But critics overlooked the fact that Benedict's so-called irrational behaviour towards the Society of St Pius X was theologically very rational.

Benedict shared John Paul II's concern to preserve church unity. Moreover Ratzinger's successor also continued the policy of change through rapprochement. Pope Francis even said that the Society of St Pius X could retain certain individual characteristics. And certain statements by the Council had 'less authority and were less obligatory'. It was enough to subscribe to the 'doctrinal statements' and rely on a 'personal ordinariate'.[29] Francis said he trusted 'that in the near future solutions can be found to restore full unity with the priests and superiors of the Brotherhood'.[30] Francis even helped them buy a church and a centre in Rome, recognized marriage ceremonies by the Society and gave them permission to ordain priests. No journalist objected to that. I asked the pope emeritus in our conversation:

Do you know when exactly you were informed about the Williamson problem?

Only after it had already happened. I don't understand why, if it was so well known, no one among us had realized. That is incredible to me, incomprehensible.

Cardinal Secretary of State Bertone could have asked you to suspend the decree.

Yes, clearly.

That would have been no problem?

Of course not. However I don't believe that he knew about it. I can't imagine that.

The Williamson case can be seen as a turning point in your papacy. Do you see it like that?

There was a huge propaganda campaign against me then. The people who were against me ended up saying I was unfit. It was a dark and difficult time.

Is it true that there were no staff changes?

No it isn't. I completely reorganized the Ecclesia Dei committee, who were responsible here. Because I had gathered from the case that it was not functioning properly.

Was there a moment when you prayed to God, 'I can't go on. I don't want to go on'?

No. Not that. I mean that, thinking of the Williamson case, I did pray to God to get me out of it and help me. That yes. But not like that. I knew he had put me in the position, so he would not let me fall.

Richard Williamson was excluded from the Society of St Pius X in 2012. Even years after his resignation Benedict XVI was condemned for trying to make a Holocaust denier socially acceptable. In their 2010 book *Der Papst im Gegenwind* (*The Pope in the Headwind*) Andrea Tornielli and Paolo Rodari made a detailed study of the attacks on Ratzinger. They concluded that attacks on him would always break out 'if negative prejudices about what the pope says or does can be harnessed'. In this way 'they went from one storm of indignation to another and from one row to the next'. The result was 'that Benedict XVI's message could be "packed away". It disappeared under the clichés of a "backward" pope and was lost. Thus crucial subjects which Joseph Ratzinger had addressed in the first five years of his papacy, such as poverty, care of the creation, globalization became forgotten.'[31]

The storm over the Vatican had not yet passed. There was still a pitter-patter of steps in the corridors of the Apostolic Palace.

Otherwise heavenly peace reigned. The traditional week of spiritual exercises for the pope and the Curia began, as usual, on the first Sunday in Lent, which fell that year on 1 March 2009. For a whole week the pope had no public appearances or other big appointments. The Lent exercise leader was the Nigerian Cardinal Francis Arinze, whose subject was 'The priest meets Jesus and follows him'. He said Jesus invited sinners to go into themselves and offered them a place at his table. He told the Pharisees who criticized him for sitting at table with sinners: 'I have not come to call the righteous but to call sinners.' Arinze urged that priests should follow Jesus and also seek the lost sheep. They should invite sinners to repent and proclaim the message of the Father's mercy.

Like the others taking part in the exercises, Pope Benedict devoted himself intensely to meditation, silence and prayer. Exactly ten days later, on 10 March 2009, he signed a letter to the bishops of the world, in which he set out the reasons for the lifting of the excommunication, clarified individual aspects of the case again and took responsibility for the blunders, which he 'truly regretted'. There had never yet been such a personal, humble and emotional message from a pope. Ratzinger had always borne the countless attacks on him without much complaint. However, the lifting of the excommunication affair openly showed his vulnerability.

The pope's letter to the 4,000 bishops was delivered personally by the nuncios. He began by saying that he wanted to give 'a word in clarification'. He hoped 'in this way to contribute to peace in the church'. The debate had been conducted with 'a violence' that 'we have not experienced for a long time'. Various groups had openly accused him of 'wanting to go back on the Council'. The affair had unleashed an 'avalanche of protests' whose 'bitterness revealed damage that goes beyond the moment'. When it published the measures taken, the Vatican had not made their 'limits and scope' clear enough. A further 'unforeseen pitfall for me' was that 'the lifting of the excommunication was overlaid by the Williamson case'. Thus the 'quiet act of mercy towards four validly but uncanonically ordained bishops' had suddenly been understood 'as a rejection of Christian–Jewish reconciliation, a retreat from what the Council stated about this matter for the church'. He could only 'deeply regret' that through the Williamson case the 'peace between Jews and Christians and also peace in the church had been upset', even if it was 'only for the moment'.[32]

In the style of the Apostolic Fathers the pope described the step he had taken as in the spirit of the gospel. Christ had told us that it was only gestures of mercy and love that could positively change people and society as a whole. He explicitly recalled his encyclical *Deus caritas est*, which had been hailed by critics. It was clear that 'anyone who proclaimed God as love to the last' had also 'to give testimony of love' himself. The lifting of the excommunication had the same aim as the penalty itself, namely 'to invite the four bishops to return'. The gesture had become possible 'after those concerned had expressed their fundamental recognition of the pope and his pastoral authority, although with reservations'. Benedict stressed: 'As long as the doctrinal questions are not clarified, the Society [of St Pius X] has no canonical status in the church. Even though they are now free from the church penalty, the office holders in the Society do not exercise these offices canonically in the church.'

The pope devoted most of his letter to the motives for lifting the excommunication. There remained 'the question: was that necessary?' Of course, there were more important and pressing matters, he admitted. However, for Peter's successor the first priority was what Jesus had said to Peter at the Last Supper: 'But you, strengthen your brothers' (Lk 22.32). St Peter had formulated that priority thus: 'Always be ready to make your defence to anyone who demands from you an account of the hope that is in you' (1 Pet. 3.15). Especially at a time 'when in wide parts of the world the faith threatens to die like a flame that has run out of fuel', it was important 'that all who believe in God should seek peace with each other'. Thus despite 'the differences in their image of God' they can go together 'to the source of light'.

Civil society should also try to 'forestall radicalizations' and re-socialize people by seeking to 'reconnect them with the great shaping power of social life'. Thus isolation could be avoided and 'tensions and constrictions' resolved. Defiantly, the pope asked the question: 'Was it really wrong to approach a brother "who has something against you" and seek reconciliation?' Even at the risk of 'the gentle gesture of a hand held out causing a great uproar and thus the opposite of reconciliation'?

As for the Society of St Pius X, they had heard many 'discordant notes' from the representatives of that community. The pope criticized their 'arrogance and know-all manner'. But it was not just about four bishops. There were something like 600,000 faithful, '491 priests, 215 seminarians, 6 seminaries, 88 schools, 2 university institutes, 117 monks and 164 nuns'. The question was: 'Should we really just let them be driven away from the church?' Or shouldn't the church also be generous, knowing her own staying power and aware of the promise she has been given? Shouldn't we behave like a good teacher here and 'be able to overlook many misdeeds and calmly call the perpetrator out of the corner'?

Furthermore, there had not only been 'discordant notes' from the Society: 'Sometimes we get the impression that our society needs at least one group which does not need to be tolerated', one group towards which hate can be freely directed. And anyone who dared to tolerate them – in this case the pope – lost their own right to be tolerated and could likewise be treated with unreserved hatred.' He had been particularly upset 'that even Catholics, who could have known better, thought they ought to attack me with outright hostility'. So he was all the more grateful 'to the Jewish friends who helped quickly to clear up the misunderstanding and restore the atmosphere of friendship and trust'. In his letter the pope could not refrain from referring to a quotation from Paul's letters to his bishops. He had always been inclined to think of this statement by the apostle as 'one of the rhetorical exaggerations occasionally to be found in Paul'. Now he had realized that it was timeless. 'If you go snapping at one another and devouring one another, take care that you are not eaten up by one another' (Gal. 5.15). Unfortunately, Benedict said, there was that 'snapping and devouring' in the church today.

31

The Condom Crisis

Even though the waves had calmed down, the Williamson affair did not pass without trace in the Curia. The numerous management failures had given rise to insecurity and mutual blame. It was said that under John Paul II the leadership of the church had not been more competent, but it had simply had more support. Curia bishop Rino Fisichella felt: 'Ratzinger was the right man at the right time. But perhaps the pope should have more people to help him.'[1] Benedict's reserved nature did not exactly give his leadership punch, grumbled Benny Lai, a long-serving *Vaticanista*. 'He needs perfect machinery, which runs like clockwork and is a real support.'

Most of the criticism was directed at Cardinal Secretary of State Tarcisio Bertone. Bertone's appointment was regarded as problematic from the start. He was felt to be rigid and authoritarian at work. The cardinal was always in a hurry and not conciliatory. By his mixing in Italian internal politics he had also made political enemies. Above all, he was accused of not being present if there was trouble, either mentally or physically. Instead of protecting the pope he was constantly away on trips. The Williamson affair would not have broken out under a professional secretary of state.

Bertone's frequent absence left a vacuum. Because of failure in the Vatican administration there was a gap which, according to Cardinal Gerhard Ludwig Müller, 'the traditional cliques would exploit' and 'immediately fill'.[2] Curia personnel recalled a quarrel between the pope's secretary Gänswein and Bertone, in which Gänswein argued with Bertone for a whole hour about his new travel plans at the height of the crisis over the lifting of the excommunication of the Society of St Pius X. 'Just listen,' Gänswein had thundered,

> the pope has spoken with you, and I tell you in confidence: you have a load of opponents who accuse you of being incompetent. You are travelling to Spain to explain Benedict XVI's policy and theology to the bishops. That is laughable. It does not have to be explained to the Spanish bishops and certainly not by the cardinal secretary of state. You have work to do at home and what you have to do here is your job.[3]

In April 2009 the pope's office received a letter from Curia bishop Paolo Sardi of the secretariat of state. Sardi informed the pope of his opinion of various abuses that had arisen in some departments of the Curia. He also mentioned the secretary of state's trips away. These frequent absences meant that the secretary of state was missing to co-ordinate the work, which led to confusion and loss of confidence among colleagues. But it was not only Sardi who had complained. Cardinals close to Benedict – such as the patriarch of Venice, Angelo Scola, and the archbishop of Cologne, Joachim Meisner – also intervened and asked the pope to dismiss his secretary of state. In our conversation the *papa emeritus* did not confirm that Cardinal Schönborn had also asked for Bertone's removal: 'No, that did not happen.' However, Meisner had suggested a staff change not only orally but also in writing. But the pope was not convinced. His word was: 'Bertone stays. There is no more to be said about it.'

Observers saw Bertone as the reason why the rich potential in Benedict's papacy could not be anywhere near fulfilled. The hope was that when Bertone reached the age limit at his 75th birthday Benedict would dismiss him. However, the pope decided in January 2010 to confirm Bertone in office. Secretary Gänswein protested: 'Bertone has already inflicted a few hammer blows. This is simply too much.' The pope would not be diverted. 'You don't know all that Sodano did,' he replied. 'He made his blunders, just as Bertone has made his blunders and if it was anyone else they might blunder too.'

Ratzinger had always been loyal to Bertone. When he had been prefect of the Congregation for the Doctrine of the Faith, Ratzinger had got on well with Bertone both at work and at a human level. In answer to the question why he had not dismissed the controversial secretary of state, Benedict explained in our conversation:

> Because I had no reason to. It's true Bertone was no diplomat. He was a shepherd, bishop and theologian, professor and canon lawyer. As a canon lawyer he had also taught international law and thoroughly understood the legal aspects of the job. There was a strong prejudice against him from many sides. Yes, perhaps he made mistakes, with too many trips, too many speeches. Now he was being criticized and I think a lot of criticism directed at him was basically aimed at me. We trusted one another, understood one another, and that's why I stood by him.[4]

It accorded with Ratzinger's principles not to select friends and colleagues and then simply to drop them. If God was prepared to write straight with crooked lines, then that could also be expected of his servants. Those around the pope regarded that characteristic as a weakness. His boss had 'kept far too many people far too long', Gänswein judged. Cardinal Kurt Koch was convinced: 'He can't expose anyone, he would never withdraw his trust from people to whom he had given it.' Sister Christine Felder said: 'If he gets into the personal and into other people's lives, he finds it difficult to draw the line. He remains bound to that person.' She added a remarkable statement: 'He does not end a friendship even when he suffers from it.'[5]

As pope emeritus, Ratzinger also remained faithful to his close colleague when Bertone came under suspicion of misusing donations to renovate his retirement home (a penthouse in the city centre of Rome for himself and some nuns). The sum involved was about 400,000 euros. As long as the suspicion of embezzlement was not proved in court, said Benedict, he saw no reason to condemn Bertone. It did not come to court. In March 2016 Bertone (a Salesian) freely paid back 150,000 euros. In the course of the inquiry into abuses in the Vatican financial management Pope Benedict had finally restricted Bertone's remit and withdrawn him from taking part in international investigations. In December 2012 that was regarded as the first step in Bertone's downfall from power.

Benedict also showed incomprehensible blind loyalty in his relation to the Catholic Integrated Community. When the group was accused of repressing its members, Ratzinger distanced himself a little, but did not break off the relationship. As pope he congratulated Traudl Wallbrecher, the founder of the Integrated Community, on her 85th birthday in May 2008. But he added an admonition: 'May your community's quiet flame always be fuelled by the great flame of the church's faith and so become one of the tongues of fire with which the Holy Spirit speaks in this world.'⁶ However, he advised a son of Wallbrecher's and his wife to leave the Community. The Integrated Community project had once been so promising. But in 2019 a report on the visitation of it by the Munich diocesan authorities confirmed that it had failed. The group had shrunk to 15 members. Among other things, the report criticized that through their assembly resolutions marriages were 'arranged or broken up' or decisions were made about 'whether and when a couple could have children'. Contacts with the home family were 'made difficult or wholly prevented', job training was controlled and community members were used as 'cheap labour'. 'Collective liability' was partly enforced; 'income, legacies or gifts' had to be handed over to the Community. Those who retired were intimidated and outlawed. There was also 'disrespectful treatment of the Eucharistic gifts'.⁷

Within the Vatican it was not only Bertone and leading members of the Curia, such as Cardinals Castrillón Hoyos and Levada, who were criticized for failures. So were the pope's own weaknesses. Jean-Marie Guénois, the Vatican correspondent for Le Figaro, found 'that this papacy has a problem with leadership'. The basic problem was that 'from the beginning of his papacy the pope decided to leave the day-to-day running of the Vatican government to someone else'. Bertone did what he could. The question was: 'Would another secretary of state, a diplomat, do it better, if at the head of the hierarchy the opinion reigns that the conduct of government, including what results from it, is not particularly important or decisive?'⁸

Benedict liked to let decisions mature. If compelling circumstances forced a quick decision to be made, that was a problem for him. It was difficult then, said Gänswein, 'to gather from him what he actually wants, or whether he wants something or not'. As his secretary he had expected the pope 'to say without being asked, I want this so and that so'. Unfortunately, the way 'to a clear decision about simple things had sometimes been 'very long and wearisome'.

Cardinal Koch thought Ratzinger's weakness in decision-making derived from his character: 'He was too gentle with opponents and did not clearly go against them.' Father Norbert Johannes Hofmann, secretary of the Papal Committee for Religious Relations with Judaism, observed that during those years Pope Benedict had been 'simply too kind and too nice'. 'But he is not someone who actively tackles things.' Cardinal Müller saw it likewise: 'He does not believe in the evil in people. He can't imagine it because he is not like that.' Thomas Frauenlob, who had worked for seven years in the Congregation for Catholic Education, thought 'the pope is unwilling to get mixed up in questions that are not concerned with doctrine'. Perhaps he was hindered by a certain 'lone wolf quality, which he already displayed as a schoolboy. He retained a certain awkwardness.'[9]

For his former assistant Peter Kuhn, a professor of Jewish Studies, 'the pope's weakness lay simply in his choice of colleagues. It was always like that.' Benedict himself admitted that, for one thing, a good knowledge of people was not exactly his thing and, for another, as pope he had sometimes failed to give 'clear, purposeful leadership': 'In retrospect I am actually more of a professor, someone who considers and reflects on spiritual things. Practical government is not my strong point.'[10]

During the conclave Ratzinger had imagined seeing a guillotine dropping on him. Now he was experiencing how the guillotine did its work. A week after the turbulence over the Society of St Pius X, the next scandal arrived: the so-called condom crisis.

On 17 March 2009 the Holy Father went on a one-week journey to Cameroon and Angola. He wanted personally to hand over the *Instrumentum laboris* to the African bishops assembled in Yaoundé. No pope had ever done that before. The *Instrumentum laboris* was the working plan for the debate at the second special assembly of African bishops, which he had summoned for the autumn in Rome. It was the first time he had visited the enormous continent as pope. In Angola, Catholics had endured the war and persecution by the ruling socialist party, the MPLA. In order to welcome the pope the streets in the capital, Luanda, were freshly tarmacked and the lighting was repaired. 'We need the pope very much,' said Sister Maria Salome in the run-up to the visit. As a result of rapid economic growth the people craved money 'and material things are blocking us. I hope he will refresh the faith again.' And what about AIDS? 'The pope has his opinion,' Salome commented, 'but basically everyone must decide for themselves.'[11]

In 2009 about 60 per cent of the 15.5 million inhabitants of Angola were Catholics. On Sundays the churches were full to overflowing, and there were so many priests that quite a few were ordered to Europe, to support the dying communities there. From 2006 to 2007 the number of priests in Africa and Asia rose by over 20 per cent, while in Europe it decreased by 7 per cent. Benedict had barely set foot on African soil when he reaffirmed that the church was always on the side of the poorest. He called for creation to be preserved and enthused about the people's vital joy in the faith. In Luanda he said the international community must 'get to grips with climate change' and give 'full and honest attention to its duties to implement development'. The industrialized countries' frequent promise to give 0.7 per cent of their gross national product for official development aid was still awaiting fulfilment. He was thinking of his dead friend Cardinal Bernardin Gantin from Benin, who had encouraged a 'theology of fellowship' to combat tribal feuds, family killings and other acts of violence. Cameroon was 'a land of hope', the pope declared, because it ensured the protection of unborn children and had accepted thousands of refugees from Central Africa.

In Angola, his second stop in Africa, Benedict demanded more rights for women. The equal dignity of men and women had to be 'recognized, affirmed and defended'. The oppressive yoke of discrimination that weighed on women and girls had to be rejected. But also to be rejected was the bitter irony of those 'who promote abortion as "maternal" healthcare'. He warned those politically responsible against a soulless 'progress', as propagated by the big international oil companies. That sort of development only enriched an oligarchy of privileged persons and led to new forms of exploitation and colonialism. In order to liberate a country it was not enough only to strive for material well-being. Strong moral powers and constant educational work were also needed to bring about reconciliation between tribes and ethnic groups and develop the country.

On his return journey to Rome the pope looked calm and relaxed. His African mission had been a great success. 'We are grateful for the message of hope that the Holy Father gave us in Cameroon and Angola,' said the regional West African Bishops' Conference in farewell. 'And we thank him that he has again told us all the church's teaching on pastoral care of those with AIDS in a clear and understandable way.' However, beyond Africa the situation was presented quite differently. People in Europe had hardly taken in anything about all the pope's meetings and speeches during his visit. And the pope had not realized that a new storm was brewing over his head. The *Figaro* reporter Jean-Marie Guénois said he had been surprised that Benedict wanted to meet journalists again on his return flight to Italy. 'In a few minutes he gave a marvellous summary of his trip that had just come to an end, and reported that he had been particularly impressed by the extraordinarily warm welcome he had received from the people he had visited.'

What had happened in the meantime? As usual, the pope had held an on-board meeting with journalists on his flight. Benedict had received the questions in advance in order to be aware of them. Question 5 came from Philippe Visseyrias, a journalist with France 2: 'Your Holiness, among the many ills that beset Africa, in particular, there is the spread of AIDS. The Catholic Church's position on the ways and means to combat it is often regarded as unrealistic and ineffective.' It seemed as though the Holy Father had been waiting for this question in order to clear up some misunderstandings. 'I would say the opposite,' he replied. 'I think that the most effective and most active presence in the battle against AIDS is precisely the Catholic Church with its movements and various structures.' He recalled the many church institutions that cared for people with AIDS. In fact, the Catholic Church looked after 25 per cent of all the AIDS sufferers in the world. More than anyone else. Then he continued: 'I'd say that the AIDS problem can't be solved just with money, although money is necessary. But if the soul is not involved, if the Africans do not co-operate and take some responsibility themselves', then the problem could not be overcome 'by giving out condoms. On the contrary, they increase the problem. The solution can only be found in the twofold effort: first, to humanize sexuality, which creates a new way of relating to one another; and secondly, in real friendship, especially with the sufferers.'[12]

Benedict's statement had barely reached the news agencies when it appeared online and in print with hostile headlines. The

Corriere della Sera had: 'Pope in Africa: AIDS – condoms useless.' *La Stampa* reported: 'Condoms don't help against AIDS. Benedict XVI: "Condoms increase the problem."' Taken out of context, the news had considerable explosive power. *Il Manifesto* wrote: 'Benedict XVI began his trip with a strong attack against the use of condoms.' The *New York Times* commented: 'Sadly the pope has set himself on the wrong side.' Other papers went even further, for example with the headline 'Pope condemns Africans to death'.[13]

The pope's picked-out words ignited a milieu ready for battle. The European Union Humanitarian Aid Office, the Paris foreign ministry and the German ministries of health and development aid all reacted with fury. In Belgium the parliament sent an official protest note to the Holy See. The health minister, Laurette Onkelinx, said she was convinced that the pope's words could destroy years of preventive care and put countless lives in danger. The socialist government in Spain under José Luis Zapatero declared it would immediately send a million condoms to Africa.

The excitement was not yet over when critical journalists began to ask wasn't it strange that, despite commitments given, countries that had just drastically reduced their aid to Africa were criticizing the church, whereas priests, religious and lay volunteers were looking after the sufferers, often at the risk of their own lives. Riccardo Bonacina, editor of the Italian weekly *Vita*, which was concerned with non-profit issues, wrote: 'It is fashionable to attack the pope. But what is intolerable is that now the attacks are coming from representatives of governments which don't even blush at the fact they reported that, up till the year 2006, they had failed to give the 0.33 per cent of gross national product for international aid agreed at the Barcelona conference in 2002.' It was 'all too true that the promotion of condoms, both in big cities and rural areas has often caused more problems than help, and has been of more use to the consciences and the budget of Western agencies than the population.' In order to combat AIDS 'as the pope rightly said, three things' were necessary: 'a) free treatment; b) humanization of sexuality, especially to protect women; c) true friendship with the sufferers, which is even prepared for self-sacrifice. So a challenge that is a bit more complex than just giving out condoms.'[14]

The Italian editor Bonacina was not the only one to support the pope from his own practical experience. Edward C. Green, a medical anthropologist from the University of Harvard, had served for 35 years in 34 different countries in social marketing programmes dealing with the distribution of contraceptives. He stated in the Italian weekly *Tempi*: 'The facts are as follows. There are no proofs that condoms can be seen as a successful means for public health authorities to reduce HIV infection in the population. The *British Medical Journal* and even *Studies in Family Planning* published that information in 2004.' In his 1988 book *Aids in Africa*, Green had said: 'For the prevention of AIDS it is more effective to promote faithful partnership than the use of condoms. Condoms fail because people do not use them properly – or because they create a feeling of false security, so that people take more risks, which they would not have taken if they had not had any condoms available.'[15]

In Africa, Benedict XVI had said that the Vatican's attitude to AIDS was neither unrealistic nor ineffective. Merely relying on condoms meant trivializing sexuality. In a later statement he said: 'They may be justified in individual cases', for example, 'to decrease the danger of infection' or if prostitutes used a condom, 'where this can be a first step towards behaving morally, a first sign of responsibility, to realize that not everything is permitted and people can't do anything they want. But it is not the actual way to cope with the evil of AIDS infection.'[16] A much more important approach was the 'ABC theory' – Abstinence, Be faithful, Condom.

The British journal *The Lancet* had also published a study in January 2000, showing the limited effect of condoms as a barrier against AIDS. There was still a 15 per cent risk of being infected with the HIV virus even when condoms were used. It was no accident that in Africa, the countries where condoms were most widely distributed (Zimbabwe, Botswana, South Africa and Kenya) were also the countries with the highest AIDS rates. The Italian oncologist Umberto Tirelli said:

The pope is right. The problem can't be solved with condoms in Africa. The thing is: in Washington, the capital of the most progressive country in the world, where people are extensively informed about the HIV virus and the Vatican has no power, 3 per cent of the population over the age of 12 are infected with the virus. So it is right that we ask how credible the promotion of the use of condoms in Africa is.[17]

The pope's trip to the Holy Land was planned for May 2009. After the turmoil of the Williamson affair it was not an easy tour. Benedict began his pilgrimage in Jordan to look at the Holy Land from Mount Nebo. On his arrival in Amman, Prince Ghazi bin Muhammad, professor of Islamic philosophy, expressly came to the defence of his papal guest against critics of the Regensburg speech. In fact, the lecture had been a great catalyst of Christian–Muslim dialogue. When he landed in Tel Aviv, the pope spoke of the 'ugly face of anti-Semitism', which was still showing itself in 'many parts of the world'. He recalled the '6 million Jews who were victims of the Shoah' and insisted 'that humanity must never again witness a crime of this magnitude'.

His visit to Yad Vashem was observed very closely. Visibly nervous, Benedict stood awkwardly before the eternal flame at the memorial. He did not want to utter any clichés. Mere lip-service would reduce the memory of the horror to a formality. Benedict said a prayer: 'May the names of these victims never die! May their suffering never be denied, belittled or forgotten!' But here the pope was seen first and foremost as a German. Critics complained he should have spoken out more unequivocally and louder. It had been 'half-hearted', said the president of the Central Council of Jews in Germany, Charlotte Knobloch. The pope had not said 'sorry' for the Holocaust.

The trip was also physically strenuous, if only because for the flights to the different places the Israelis had provided old military helicopters. Benedict did not bat an eyelid but his travelling companions found the transport uncomfortable, noisy and dusty. In no other country had the pope's team been offered such shabby planes. In Jerusalem the pope's prayer for peace at the Wailing Wall acknowledged 'the common spiritual inheritance of Christians and Jews' to the chief rabbinate. At the grand mufti's visit to the Dome of the Rock, Benedict stressed 'the gifts of reason and freedom' which, according to the Christian view, God had given to all human beings. In his speech in Bethlehem he insisted on the right of the Palestinian people 'to an autonomous Palestinian home in the land of their ancestors'. Walls had never lasted for ever: 'they can be torn down.

However, it is necessary first to pull down the walls that we build in our own hearts and the barriers we set up against our neighbours.'

In Nazareth, Benedict was able to do what John Paul II had still been forbidden to do on his visit in March 2000: celebrate Mass. The Mass was held on the hill from which Jesus' angry fellow townspeople had wanted to throw him down. Benedict spoke for a culture of peace between the different religions and appealed to Christians not to leave the country. He concluded his trip with a passionate plea for peace: 'No more bloodshed! No more battles! No more terrorism! No more war! Instead let's break through the vicious circle of violence! Let there be lasting peace, founded on justice. Let there be true reconciliation and healing.'[18]

The visit to Israel was celebrated as a success on all sides. 'Overall the hospitality was great', the pope summed up. He had been especially moved by the 'warmth with which President [Shimon] Peres welcomed me. He came to me with great frankness, knowing that we had common values. We agreed on peace, on shaping the future and that the question of Israel's existence played an important part in it.' At least, the tensions with representatives of Judaism had not been as severe 'as they were in Germany'. There had been 'mutual trust' and 'the knowledge that the Vatican was for Israel and for Judaism in the world, and that we recognized Jews as our fathers and brothers'.[19] The Israeli ambassador to the Holy See, Mordechai Lewy, praised Benedict's visit. Relations had clearly improved under the German pope. In allusion to the Williamson affair, Lewy quoted from the biblical book of Judges: 'From the bitter came something sweet.'

For Pope Benedict 2009 was a very intensive year in office. After the Williamson affair there was the 'condom crisis' and his trip to the Holy Land. He published another encyclical and completed the Pauline Year. It seemed as if the pope wanted to bequeath spiritual nourishment for the faithful to draw on in difficult times. He also continued his work on *Jesus*, volume 2, *Holy Week*, the second part of his trilogy on the life of Jesus. Ratzinger's inmost conviction was that a pope's practical work of government might be important but it was more important for a successor of St Peter to save what was in danger of being lost by safeguarding the fundamentals of the faith.

Benedict's third encyclical was launched on 29 June 2009, the feast of Sts Peter and Paul. It was revolutionary and had impressive visionary power. After *Deus caritas est* and *Spe salvi* the social encyclical *Caritas in veritate* (*Love in Truth*) dealt with the nations' threatening social and economic problems. For example: the increasing gap between rich and poor, dependence on new global economic powers such as Google, Amazon and Facebook and dangers from the still almost uncontrollable financial markets. Just a year beforehand, the collapse of the Lehman Brothers bank with losses of $613 billion had been the greatest crash in the history of Wall Street and had provoked a worldwide financial crisis.

Benedict's encyclical 'on integral human development in love and truth', as the subtitle put it, wanted 'to call to mind the great principles that are indispensable for human development in the coming years'. Its core message was that a happier 'future for all' was possible, if 'it is based on the rediscovery of fundamental ethical values'. During his flight to Prague on 26 September 2009 Benedict spoke about his text, saying it was time to find 'new models for a responsible economy, both for individual countries and humanity as a whole. It seems obvious to me that ethics is not something outside economics [...] but an inner principle of economics, which does not function if it disregards the human values of solidarity and mutual responsibility.'[20]

Following Paul VI's social encyclical *Populorum progressio*, published in 1967, the basic message of *Caritas in veritate* was that a society could only develop humanly if it put 'the whole human being and each human being' at its heart. For Paul VI the main aim had been the 'overcoming of hunger, hardship, endemic diseases and illiteracy'. In the twenty-first century hunger was still one of the main evils. It should be dealt with by the removal of tariff barriers and better access to water and food. However, there had been increasing dependence on international financial systems, which had acquired a greater influence on the distribution of goods: 'The exclusive concentration on profit, if this is wrongly gained and its aim is not the general good, risks destroying livelihoods and creating poverty.' Companies should not only serve 'the interests of their owners' but all those people 'who contribute to the life of the business'. Solidarity meant 'that all feel responsible for all'.

Benedict's encyclical castigated the 'irresponsibility' of political power holders who created crisis in order for a 'cosmopolitan class of managers and financial brokers' to 'cheat savers'. Often social systems had been established which made the needy become dependants. Practical contrary measures were to be found in the double strategy of solidarity and subsidiarity (decentralization), as recommended in Catholic social teaching. *Caritas in veritate* demanded a reform of the United Nations and also of the 'international economic and financial system', to take more account of the poorer countries. The encyclical proposed 'redistribution systems' so as not to let the financial markets, which were already almost uncontrollable, escalate further. The non-profit organizations – such as co-operatives, foundations and microfinance institutions – should work as a leavening in economic life and keep a sense of justice alive.

There was worldwide praise for his encyclical. Another success for Benedict was his model for Anglicans wanting to convert to Roman Catholicism, which did not stop dialogue with the Anglican Church as a whole. The Traditional Anglican Communion (TAC) had already approached Rome in 2007 with the request to join the sacramental community of the Roman Catholic Church. The TAC was a wing of the Anglican Church in England, the USA and Australia with about 400,00 members, who did not want to tolerate changes to their belief in the biblical foundations of their faith. After the General Synod of the Church of England voted in 1992 for the ordination of women, 440 priests turned their back on their church. The conversations with Rome lasted two years. On 20 October 2000 the Apostolic Constitution on joining the Catholic Church was announced to simultaneous press conferences in London and Rome; it was published on 4 November.

The terms for the union were fully in accord with Benedict's line, which required neither unconditional acceptance of the Catholic cult nor capitulation but respect for the spiritual legacy of a different denomination. The incorporated community was not to be regarded as an appendage but as a particular church, to be treated as a kind of special diocese with its own personal ordinariate. Thus, besides the united Byzantine rite churches, there was a new group of married Catholic priests within the Catholic Church. Through Benedict's new type of ecumenism, for the first time a legal structure was created that also made reunion possible for other communities in future.

Another special event was the celebration of the Pauline Year, inspired by Benedict for the 2000th anniversary of the apostle's birth. The Pauline Year was solemnly opened in 2008, together with the ecumenical patriarch Bartholomew I. One reason for it was to draw attention to the worsening situation of Christians in countries where confessing the Catholic faith was increasingly met with social ostracism.

According to assessments by human rights groups, at the beginning of the new millennium about 200 million Christians worldwide were disadvantaged or oppressed on account of their faith, more than any before. According to *Märtyrer 2009*, the (German) Evangelical news agency *idea*'s yearbook on the persecution of Christians, Christians made up 75–80 per cent of those subject to religious persecution and were thus the religious community suffering most severely from discrimination.[21] The Western media ignored the subject and there was little awareness of this alarming development, even within national churches. Christians were prevented from practising their religion in all Islamic-governed countries. In Pakistan Muslims were incited by their imams to trash Christian homes. In northern Nigeria Islamic terror groups conducted violent attacks and burned down churches. In India barricades were set up to prevent Christians from voting. In Uruguay, Christians were marginalized by legal and social restrictions and Catholic buildings were torn down without warning. Other countries followed the same example – especially those governed by neo-socialist regimes, such as Venezuela or Bolivia. In North Korea tens of thousands of Christians starved in concentration camps. In the People's Republic of China members of the underground church, including many bishops, were in prison or work camps, because they refused to join the state church, loyal to the regime.

The pope had accompanied the Pauline Year with a series of catecheses 'to learn the faith from St Paul, learn about Christ and how to live right'. 'Our whole way of thinking must become fundamentally different,' he proclaimed in his final sermon for the year on 28 June 2009. The new way of thinking did not mean thinking in accordance with the masses, to be certain of public applause. Instead, we should bravely stick by the church's faith, even when it was against the *Zeitgeist*. 'The apostle Paul demands that we should be nonconformist.' He called this 'mature faith'. 'In his letter to the Romans, Paul says: "Do not be conformed to this world, but be transformed by the renewal of your mind, that by testing you may discern what is the will of God.'" In conclusion Benedict warned Christians to be watchful and beware of ravening wolves and false prophets.

The pope was in a hurry. Even before the Pauline Year was over, he announced a Year of the Priest. The Pauline Year had been mainly devoted to the office of bishop and commitment to the mission. The motto for the Year of the Priest was 'Faithfulness of Christ, faithfulness of the priest'. As the model of a Catholic pastor, Benedict had chosen the 'curé d'Ars', Jean-Baptiste-Marie Vianney, who had not proved particularly gifted during his studies. Vianney was also quite unlike the conventional friendly village priest. He had abandoned his unruly parishioners several times, sometimes fleeing in the middle of the night. But he was always brought back by his repentant community. 'Punish them until they give up their sins,' Vianney begged Christ, when he saw that the souls entrusted to him avoided confession. But he preached much more positively: for example, on God's amazing kindness, the beauty of the soul in a state of grace or the salvation that Christ's cross had brought to humanity.[22]

At the official beginning of the Year of the Priest on 19 June 2009, the feast of the Sacred Heart of Jesus, Benedict told priests always to be aware of their dignity but they should also undergo purification and do penance, if necessary, in order to recover joy in their service. The Year of the Priest was to be a year of prayer, with days of study and contemplation and spiritual exercises. A circular letter to those concerned expressly mentioned clergy who were involved in criminal offences. They had to be investigated, condemned and punished accordingly. No one could imagine how important that statement, mentioned almost in passing, would become and what a serious crisis would occur. It was almost as if 'the devil could not bear the Year of the Priest and so had thrown dirt in our faces', said Benedict XVI in the summer of 2010.[23] It was their own unbelievable dirt, swept under the carpet in presbyteries, abbeys and Catholic boarding-schools for so many years, that would now shake the church to its foundations.

32

The Abuse Scandal

Benedict's meditation on the Stations of the Cross was a denunciation, as never before: 'How much dirt there is in the church and precisely among those who as priests should be most loyal!' he cried. He was speaking like someone in a confessional with Jesus as his confessor: 'By our fall we drag you to the ground and Satan laughs because he hopes that you will not be able to get up again from that fall.' As prefect of the Congregation for the Doctrine of the Faith, Ratzinger had seen enough wrongdoing not to be surprised at the dark side of the church. But what came now was worse than anything, like one of the biblical plagues, a flood. Yes, a flood.

As prefect, Ratzinger had seen to it that the responsibility for dealing with clerical sexual abuse went to his Congregation. He accused the previously responsible Congregation for Clergy of 'not pursuing a strong enough line' to clear matters up quickly and efficiently. He set up his own jurisdiction with extensive powers so that crimes would actually be punished.

The change was intended to make clear that the prosecution of abuse had very high priority for the church. In 1988 Ratzinger had already pointed out weaknesses in the church's legal code, which put responsibility for dealing with this crime at diocesan level. After countless cases of sexual abuse in Catholic dioceses in the USA became known, he pressed for the strengthening of the church's penal law, 'above all to be able to deal with matters more quickly' and increase support for victims.[1] The 2001 *motu proprio*, '*Sacramentorum sanctitatis tutela*', and the note *De delictis gravioribus* (*On Serious Crimes*), resulted from his initiative. It was a long-nurtured plan of his that he had been unable to implement until then. In 2002 Ratzinger summoned all US bishops to draw up a survey of abuse in the USA.

The provisions of the *motu proprio*, which were reinforced again in 2003, assigned responsibility for prosecuting these offences to the Congregation of the Doctrine of the Faith. It also ordered that local dioceses should investigate every charge of sexual abuse of a minor by a cleric. The local bishop would then pass on all the necessary information to the Congregation of the Doctrine of the Faith. They should always keep the civil laws prescribing notification of the charge. Before the case was resolved, the bishop could impose precautionary measures. The strategy was: accompaniment and understanding for the victims, sanctions against bishops who neglected their duties, reform of seminaries, co-operation with the civil jurisdiction, the need for purification and repentance, and, above all, zero tolerance for the guilty. The statute of limitations was extended from five years to ten.

According to Cardinal Christoph Schönborn, when the past sexual offences of the Austrian Cardinal Hans Hermann Groër became public, it had been Ratzinger who had tried to set up an investigation committee, unfortunately in vain. In 1995 a former pupil had accused Groër of sexual abuse when Groër was prefect of studies in a minor seminary from 1946 until 1974. At the end of 1997 monks from various monasteries also accused him of sexual offences. Groër was forced to resign as chairman of the Austrian Bishops' Conference. Schönborn, his successor, spoke later of the difficulties the prefect of the Congregation for the Doctrine of the Faith had encountered in pursing a harder line on sexual abuse. Ratzinger himself had told him that he had been curbed 'by the diplomatic party of the Roman Curia'. Schönborn recalled that it had been Sodano who had 'prevented the setting up of an investigation committee on the Groër case'.[2] Those who maintained that the former prefect had not pursued Catholic clerical abusers decisively enough, or failed to address the issue, 'don't know the facts'.[3]

Ratzinger was confronted with a particularly disgusting case in the crimes of Marcial Maciel (also known as Marcial Maciel Degollado). He was a Mexican, born in 1920, who as a seminarian had founded a group to which he later gave the name Legion of Christ. He had been supported by some influential families. His conservative community consisted of 650 priests, 2,500 theology students, 1,000 consecrated laity and 30,000 simple members in 20 countries. The community had dozens of schools and colleges, including the Pontifical Athenaneum Regina Apostolorum, founded in 1993 in Rome, and the state-recognized Università Europea di Roma, founded in 2004. In a US daily newspaper in 1997 eight of his former seminarians accused Maciel of sexually abusing them in the 1950s in the Legion's seminary in Rome. In 1978 and 1989 Juan Vaca, chairman for five years of the Legion in the USA, had sent letters to John Paul II but received no answer to any of them. On 17 October 1998 three other legionaries sent a request for criminal proceedings to Gianfranco Girotti, under-secretary of the Congregation of the Doctrine of the Faith. Maciel rejected the charges and claimed he was the victim of a smear campaign.

Under Karol Wojtyła, Maciel's relations with influential members of the Curia became increasingly close. His supporters included Cardinal Secretary of State Angelo Sodano, the Spanish cardinal Eduardo Martínez Somalo and papal secretary Stanisław Dziwisz. In April 2003 an interview book with Maciel entitled *Christ Is My Life* was published in Madrid. It was seen as a reaction to the ex-legionaries' accusations. Maciel's book spoke of 'misunderstandings' and 'slander'. The Italian edition was published a year later. Tarcisio Bertone, who had been appointed archbishop of Genoa in December 2002 and became a cardinal in October 2003, wrote the foreword to it. Questioned by a Mexican bishop during an *ad limina* visit, Ratzinger gave to understand that he could do nothing in the Maciel affair. Meanwhile, in November 2004 Maciel celebrated his 60th anniversary as a priest with a Mass in St Paul without the Walls, together with 500 priests, in the presence of Angelo Sodano and other cardinals. The celebrations culminated in a papal audience on 30 November for Maciel and thousands of legionaries in the Great Audience Hall.[4]

Pointedly, Ratzinger stayed away from the anniversary celebrations. By then, as prefect, he had instructed his colleague Charles Scicluna, the Congregation's chief prosecutor (*Promotor Iustitiae*), to go ahead with the proceedings against the founder of the Legion of Christ. On 2 April, Scicluna questioned one of the complainants in New York and contacted witnesses in Mexico, Ireland and Spain. A year later, by which time Ratzinger had become pope, Maciel was compelled to resign as head of the Legion. On 19 May 2006 the Vatican published a communiqué: after extensive examination of the findings, the new prefect of the Congregation for the Doctrine of the Faith, Cardinal William Levada, had decided not to proceed with a canonical prosecution of Maciel, in view of his precarious state of health. He had ordered the fallen priest to retire to a life of prayer and penance 'in which he should relinquish any public office'.

When Maciel died in the USA just two years later, at the age of 87, new details about his activities became known. Maciel had not only abused seminarians: he had also had a family with children of his own both in Spain and in Mexico. At weekends he often changed into civilian clothes, got a lot of money from the administrator and disappeared for two or three days, without giving any information of his address. Various women said that he had pretended to work in an oil company or that he was a CIA agent. A Spanish journalist reported that on his deathbed Maciel had renounced the faith and refused the last rites.[5]

As prefect Ratzinger had handled the investigations into the founder of the Legion of Christ. As pope he brought it to an end. He defended the fact that the investigations had begun far too late by saying 'We only got hold of these things very slowly and very late. They were very well covered up.' And they had needed 'unequivocal witnesses in order to be really certain that the accusations applied'.[6] After an Apostolic Visitation ordered by him in March 2009, Pope Benedict appointed an apostolic delegate to supervise the Legion and introduce the necessary reforms, together with a group of colleagues.

The revelations about Maciel also influenced the beatification process of John Paul II. In his machinations Maciel had depended on his immunity deriving from his status as the founder of the Legion of Christ. His influence was powerful enough and the damage that his exposure would cause was too great for him to fear arrest. It seemed unimaginable that a man respected almost as a saint could be capable of the crimes he was accused of. The question was whether Wojtyła had had any personal involvement in Maciel's secret network. Had he possibly used his personal influence to keep the accusations under cover? 'We all asked ourselves these questions,'

Georg Gänswein reported. 'I never understood why no one had noticed anything.' On the other hand, Wojtyła had given this 'hot iron' to his prefect for the Congregation of the Doctrine of the Faith, precisely because Ratzinger was the only one he trusted actually to throw light on the crimes.[7] During the beatification process, Curia Cardinal William Levada stated on behalf of the Congregation for the Doctrine of the Faith: 'There are some letters and requests sent from the complainants to John Paul II. However, there is no known personal involvement of the servant of God in the procedure against Fr Marcial Maciel.'[8] Vatican press spokesman Joaquín Navarro-Valls asserted that Wojtyła had 'never withheld or concealed anything'. He admitted that Benedict XVI invited upon himself 'the responsibility for mistakes that – as everyone knows – he himself did not make'.

Nevertheless, in the course of 2009 a tsunami arose that would shake the foundations of the Catholic Church right into the papacy of Pope Francis. Many people said it was the biggest ever crisis in church history. Gänswein called it the '9/11 for our faith', which traumatized the Catholic Church just as the terror attacks of 11 September 2001 had traumatized the USA. But actually no term was adequate to describe the extent of abuse or the accompanying enormous loss of trust in the church.

It began with Ireland, the traditionally Catholic country which, despite all the animosity over the centuries, had remained loyal, and from which missionaries had once been sent to large parts of the European mainland. On 20 May 2009 the Vatican had only just got over the turbulence of the Williamson affair and the so-called condom crisis when the Ryan Report was published, named after the judge Sean Ryan. He was the co-ordinator of a government committee of investigation following a film report on abuse in Catholic schools.

The result was devastating. The report stated that, over a period of 50 years, in Catholic Church institutions about 2,500 children and young people had been victims of attacks. (Later that figure was lowered.) Most of the cases involved corporal punishment and psychological violence, with a smaller number involving sexual abuse. It was notable that from the 1950s until the middle of the 1960s there was a low constant average of cases. But from then on the curve began to rise, reaching its peak in the 1970s and 1980s.[9]

Immediately after he became pope, Benedict XVI had suspended a number of priests, including, in May 2005, Gino Burresi, founder of the Servants of the Immaculate Heart of Mary, who was charged with the abuse of one of his students. Observers noted that with the new pope the wind had changed. In the years 2011 and 2012 Pope Ratzinger suspended 384 priests and high-ranking officials because they had been guilty of abuse of minors or covering it up.[10] They included the Irish bishop and former secretary to three popes John Magee and the Canadian bishop John Lahey – child pornography was found on his laptop. Another to be dismissed was John C. Favalora, archbishop of Miami, who was charged with covering up paedophile priests, tolerating a lobby of homosexual priests in his diocese and being involved in abuse himself. In 2008 and 2009, 171 clerics had already been suspended.[11] On 28 October 2006, even before the extent of offences was known, Benedict XVI asked the bishops of Ireland 'to bring to light the truth about what happened in the past', as well as 'to take all necessary measures to prevented such things ever happening again'. The bishops were also to ensure 'that the principles of justice are fully respected, and above all to bring healing to the victims and all those affected by these monstrous crimes'.

The Ryan Report was no sooner published than, on 26 November 2009, the Murphy Report appeared, named after the judge Yvonne Murphy. It caused a further shock. This time it focused on the archdiocese of Dublin and concerned 172 priests. Despite their offences between 1975 and 2004, they had been protected by their bishops, or at least not penalized. At most, they had been transferred to other dioceses. The report stated that those responsible 'were more concerned with concealment, avoiding scandal, protecting the church's reputation and saving their assets. All other considerations, including the welfare of children and justice to the victims, were subordinated.' The Irish priest Vincent Twomey, a student and close associate of Ratzinger's, demanded that all the bishops in Ireland should resign immediately. Twomey was convinced: 'The Catholic Church in Ireland is a wreck.'

The pope reacted. Two weeks after the publication of the report he ordered the leading Irish bishops to Rome. In February 2010 he summoned 24 more bishops. In the final communiqué of the crisis meeting he denounced the abuses 'not only as an abominable crime' but also 'a serious sin, that offends God and affronts the dignity of the human person'. Instead of dealing effectively with sexual abuses, 'the bishops had not intervened' but had covered up misdeeds and concealed the perpetrators in order to avoid public scandal.[12]

As a next step, Benedict wrote a pastoral letter, dated 19 March 2010, to the faithful in Ireland. Apostolic letters dealing with fundamental issues had always been not only for the community mentioned by name but for the worldwide church as a whole. For example, no one thought that the apostle Paul's letter to the Corinthians was not also addressed to Christians elsewhere. Or that John's Apocalypse was written only for the seven churches in Asia Minor. The pope said he could 'share the dismay and the sense of betrayal of trust that so many of you felt when you heard about these sinful and criminal deeds and how the church authorities in Ireland dealt with them'. He wanted to express his empathy and also 'suggest a way of healing, renewal and redress'.[13]

First, the letter addressed the abuse victims and their families, 'I am truly sorry', the letter began in a fatherly tone,

> you have suffered terribly. I know that nothing that you have suffered can be undone. Your trust was abused and your dignity offended. Many of you must have felt that no one listened to you, when you gathered the courage to speak out about what had happened to you. Those of you who were abused in homes and boarding-schools must have felt that there was no escape from your suffering.

In the name of the church he expressed 'the shame and remorse that we all feel'. It was difficult for the victims to forgive such a crime or 'set foot in a church after all that had happened'. However, he begged them at least not to lose their trust in Christ.

When he turned in his letter to address the priests who were responsible for the abuse, the pope was relentless: 'You have abused the trust that innocent young people and their families put in you, and you must answer before almighty God and the competent courts.' Then he enumerated the factors that had fostered the crisis, including insufficient human, moral, intellectual and spiritual education in seminaries and novitiates, the tendency to favour the clergy, as well as 'an inappropriate concern for the church's reputation and avoidance of scandals'. He appealed to those responsible urgently to address these factors, 'which have had such tragic consequences in the lives of the victims and their families'. He exhorted the bishops 'who have sometimes appallingly failed to observe the long-standing canon law rules on the sexual abuse of children [...] as well as failing to fulfil the canon law to co-operate with the state authorities in their jurisdiction'. It was absolutely necessary to have 'a decisive procedure that works with complete honesty and transparency'. Finally, he appointed four cardinals and archbishops as special investigators and announced canonical visitations of dioceses, seminaries and religious houses.

Almost at the same time as the turbulence in Ireland a new front developed, this time in Germany. On 20 January 2010 the Jesuit priest Klaus Mertes, director of the Canisius College in Berlin, sent a letter to all former alumni of the school. A few days before, students had informed him that there had been sexual abuse in the school. In reply to Mertes's request to report every offence, about a hundred cases of abuse emerged, mainly from the 1970s and 1980s. In an interview with *Tagesspiel* about a fortnight later, Mertes also mentioned his views: 'I hope that the church will become reconciled with modernity and freedom [...] whether that means a theological revaluation of homosexuality or the ordination of women.'[14] We should 'engage with the present and not react to everything defensively'. The defence strategy worked. Soon it was no longer the priests at the Canisius College who were responsible for the crimes at their school but the church's sexual teaching and its guardians in Rome.

Now everywhere in Germany former pupils were reporting what they had experienced in monastic schools, boarding-schools, novitiates or seminaries. In Ettal Abbey the monks themselves produced a report. The investigation showed that in their school violence was used as a pedagogical method. At the instigation of the archbishop of Munich, Reinhard Marx, the abbot had to resign. This turned out to be hasty and unlawful, so that the Vatican soon reinstated the abbot.

In March 2010 former choirboys from the Regensburg Domspatzen ('Cathedral Sparrows') also reported sexual attacks. Georg Ratzinger himself came into focus. From 1964 until 1994 he had been the cathedral choir master. The pope's brother solemnly affirmed that he had known nothing about sexual abuses. They had taken place in the Domspatzen elementary school, an institution outside the city, with its own leadership, independent of the music school. However, he admitted to sometimes giving his choirboys a box on the ear. A former student reported that Georg had once thrown a chair during choir practice. In his final report on 18 July 2017 Ulrich Weber, the lawyer appointed to investigate by the diocese, concluded that among the Domspatzen 547 cases of abuse were highly plausible, and that 67 of them occurring in the period between 1945 and 2015 involved sexual force. Most of these took place in the elementary school in Ettershausen and Pielenhofen. On Georg Ratzinger's role, Weber said that he had had 'no knowledge of the sexual violence'. After 1972 there had not been a single case of a sexual attack in the Domspatzen gymnasium (secondary school). However, Weber accused Georg of disregarding cases of physical violence.[15]

Meanwhile, an army of journalists went in search of abuse cases and Joseph Ratzinger was also reported to have been involved. On 12 March 2010 the *Süddeutsche Zeitung* published the news: 'Ratzinger's diocese deployed a paedophile priest.' The allegation was that in 1980, as archbishop of Munich, Cardinal Ratzinger had accepted a paedophile priest from the diocese of Essen into his diocese. *Spiegel Online* carried the headline 'Abuse Case Discovered in Ratzinger's Diocese'. On the same evening the TV news programme *Heute Journal* broadcast that with the Munich case abuse had now 'reached the Vatican'. In fact, the case had already been reported in the media in 1986, when the priest concerned had been sentenced to probation for abuse of minors. At that time Ratzinger had long been prefect in Rome. When he was bishop, in 1980, he had agreed at a session of the diocesan council to allow the priest concerned to come to Munich for psychotherapy. However, contrary to that decision, the vicar-general Gerhard Gruber had allowed the priest to serve in a parish again.

A new onslaught came from overseas. There was no doubt that countless members of the church were guilty and bishops had looked the other way or were involved in abuse themselves. Whole dioceses were threatened with bankruptcy from claims for damages. In its edition of 25 March 2010 the *New York Times* published a detailed article on the particularly vile case of the American priest Lawrence C. Murphy from the diocese of Milwaukee, which struck like a bomb. Murphy was accused of attacking 200 pupils in a school for deaf and dumb children between 1950 and 1974. In fact, the diocesan authorities had decided to laicize Murphy. However, Murphy appealed to Rome. The then first secretary of the Congregation for the Doctrine of the Faith, Tarcisio Bertone, wrote to the US bishops concerned in 1998, saying that the priest should only be laicized if it was not possible to repair the scandal, restore justice and amend the guilty one. Since there had been no accusations of abuse against Murphy over the past 20 years and he was near death, the Congregation advised them merely to restrict his public activity. Four months later Murphy died.

For the *New York Times* the thing was clear: the Congregation for the Doctrine of the Faith under Ratzinger had covered up the case. Critics of the story pointed out that Bertone's behaviour had been in accordance with the legal provisions of the time. In fact, it was not the church but the secular authorities who had 'shelved the case'. The *Osservatore Romano* commented that when Benedict XVI was prefect, he had always dealt with abuse cases 'transparently, decisively and severely'. The Hamburg weekly paper *Die Zeit* also said that the accusations against Ratzinger were unfounded. It finally became public that the evidence given in the *New York Times* was based on an Italian Vatican document, translated by a Yahoo computer programme. No one in the editorial department had realized that, at vital points, the clumsy text said exactly the opposite of what was in the original document.

Countless newspapers still vied with each other in a flood of double-page spreads to present sexual abuses exclusively as a problem for the Catholic Church. This was although the cases had mainly occurred 30 to 50 years ago and were mostly not sexual attacks but cases of undue severity. Benedict XVI was accused of keeping silence about them.

The coverage was like a commando raid, using the mechanisms of the modern media. Not all subjects were suited to a campaign, but when one had the potential to become a long-lasting exploitable scandal, then many journalists regarded it as a jackpot they could finally hit. For example, 'What did Ratzinger know?' was a headline in the *Frankfurter Rundschau*: 'Pope should take a stand on the Odenwald.' In the zeal for battle the 'enlighteners' had overlooked the fact that the Odenwald school was not a Catholic institution but a model project of left-liberal progressive education. Gerold Becker himself, head of the school and life partner of the education expert Hartmut von Hentig, was accused of abusing at least 200 students. Becker died on 7 July 2010 without being criminally prosecuted. In a summary of their study on 'Odenwald School as the Beacon of Progressive Education and a Place of Sexualized Violence' the authors described how Becker had used the *Zeitgeist* of the 1970s and its liberalization, with 'flexible relationships', to create the basis for a system of sexual abuse. The offences, occurring over decades, could have been prevented if parents and teachers had followed up indications about the paedophile rings in the school, and if journalists who had been students at the school and knew about the situation had not kept silence.

There were many attempts to lay the main responsibility for the abuse scandal on Benedict XVI. Observers thought that the pope would address the accusations during the Easter celebrations, but he kept strictly to the liturgy, without making any comment. However, the Capuchin priest Raniero Cantalamessa caused a mini-scandal with his sermon on Good Friday, 2 April 2010, which he devoted to violence against women. He also briefly mentioned the aggressive polemic against the church and the pope: 'Today I received a letter from a Jewish friend and with his permission I'd like to share part of it with you,' he began. Then he quoted from the letter:

I have been following with disgust the brutal, concentrated attack from all over the world on the church, the pope and all the faithful. The use of stereotypes, the transfer of personal responsibility and guilt to collective guilt remind me of the shameful behaviour of anti-Semitism. So I should like personally to express my solidarity with the pope and the whole church, as a Jew wanting dialogue, and also that of all those in the Jewish world (and there are many) who share this feeling of fellowship.

Clearly, Cantalamessa was insensitive to the turbulent state of affairs in those weeks. However exaggerated the reporting on the church was, the cause of the scandal was not journalists but rogue priests and religious, abetted by church superiors, who had covered up or were themselves members of homosexual paedophile networks. It was to be expected that the comparison with anti-Semitism would call forth sharp contradiction. The Vatican spokesman Lombardi tried to allay matters: 'Comparing the attacks on the pope in connection with the paedophile scandal with anti-Semitism does not correspond to the line followed by the Holy See.'

But things got worse. On a wet Easter Sunday, 4 April, the celebrations in St Peter's Square seemed to be going on as usual when Angelo Sodano, now dean of the College of Cardinals, approached the microphone. There had never been a scene like it before. 'Even when the rain pours down on this historic square,' Sodano began his eulogy of the pope, 'the sun seems to be shining in our hearts. We stand by you, the imperishable rock of the holy church.' It sounded rather like it had been in Moscow Red Square when homage was paid to the general secretary of the Soviet Communist Party:

> We are deeply thankful to you for your strength of mind and your apostolic courage. We admire your great love [...] Today the whole church would like to say to you through me: Happy Easter, dear Holy Father. The church is with you, the cardinals who are your colleagues in the Roman Curia are with you, the bishops of 3,000 dioceses are with you, and those 400,000 priests, who generously serve the people of God in parishes, schools, hospitals, and in missions.

Then Sodano added one more sentence: 'The people of God are with you, who are not impressed by idle gossip.'

The new storm of protest came at once. For the Vatican, the commentators wrote, the exposure of sexual abuse is just 'idle gossip'. The historian Alberto Melloni spread the word that Benedict himself had asked Sodano to give his speech. Once again Lombardi the spokesman had to issue a denial: 'I regard it as my duty to make clear that, even in difficult times, Benedict XVI does not seek demonstrations of support or organize them.'

What Lombardi did not know was that the one behind the action was none other than Georg Gänswein. He told the author that members of the Curia had come to him saying that the cardinals finally had to stand by the pope, for things could not go on as they were. He had then sought contact with Sodano. However, Sodano must have understood Gänswein's suggestion as if the Holy Father himself wanted the greeting.

Catholics kept silence, ashamed of the thousands of victims and also angry that the facts had been covered up. Anyone who regarded the church as the mystical body of Christ must have been shocked how that body had been abused. But by the middle of May 2010 many had had enough of the church in general being presented as a 'dark place', monasteries as playgrounds for sadists and every priest as a potential child abuser. Under the motto 'Rome for the pope' more than 200,000 people, from about 70 associations, gathered in St Peter's Square as a sign of support. The mayor of Rome, Gianni Alemanno, was among them. 'I thank you for this beautiful spontaneous demonstration of faith and solidarity,' the pope called to the demonstrators from the window of his study. Then he made clear: 'The true enemy to fear and battle against is sin and evil, which sometimes sadly contaminate members of the church.'

The media barrage lasted many weeks. Right from the beginning of the drama, academic studies had been appearing, showing that incidents within the church were a small, and dwindling, fraction of the number of widespread crimes of abuse. Philip Jenkins maintained that in the USA the proportion of priests condemned for abuse of minors swung between 0.2 and 1.7 per cent, according to geographical area. But among Protestant clergy it lay between 2 and 3 per cent. Jenkins's figures relied on a report by the Evangelical press agency Christian Ministry Resources, published in 2002. 'The Catholics get all the notice in the media but the greater problem lies in the Protestant churches.'

In Germany, Professor Christian Pfeiffer from the Lower Saxony Criminological Research Institute stated that in the last 15 years out of 29,058 men condemned for sexual abuse, 30 had been employed by the Catholic Church, which was 0.1 per cent. In other words: 99.9 per cent had come from the secular sphere. A US government report on 62,000 people known to have been involved in paedophile cases in the year 2008 stated that the number of priests was 18, which was 0.03 per cent.

The figures did not decrease the guilt of church members involved but demonstrated the huge problem of hidden abuse in other parts of society. According to information from UNICEF, in the early years of the twenty-first century, every year more than 220 million children worldwide were forced into sex. Hundreds of thousands of non-celibate men downloaded child pornography onto their computers. In Belgium the child abuse ring round the paedophile and murderer Marc Dutroux did not consist of priests and religious but of politicians, managers and even judges.

To mention a few more examples: it came to light in the USA that over decades about 12,250 children had been sexually abused in the Boy Scouts of America. Those in charge of the perpetrators had informed neither the police nor the boys' parents. According to an investigation by the US ministry of defence, in the US armed forces in the 2010s about 100,000 men and 13,000 women soldiers were victims of sexual attacks. In May the UN reported a paedophile scandal involving French soldiers: in an African refugee camp they had demanded sex from hungry children in exchange for food and drinking water. Although they had been informed of the abuse, the UN officials concerned had merely looked on for a whole year.

In Europe, according to a study by the Brussels Foundation for European Progressive Studies, six out of ten women were victims of sexism in the workplace. In Germany it was 68 per cent of those questioned. The estimated number of systematically ill-treated and sexually abused children in sports associations and state institutions, particularly in children's homes, in the DDR was high. In the spring of 2018 attacks on women were reported in the aid organizations Médecins sans Frontières, Oxfam and the German Weisser Ring. Paedophiles targeted children's aid organizations to gain access to minors. In November 2017 the British prime minister, Theresa May, summoned the House of Commons to a crisis session, after a 'sex pest list' bearing the names of about 40 Tory MPs leaked out. The list included secretaries of state and ministers, who were accused of sexual attacks even as serious as rape. In Sweden in November 2017, in answer to a phone call, on a single day 1,100 people reported sexual attacks in the country's entertainment industry.

It had taken more than a decade for the attention to turn from the pond to the ocean of scandals. The psychiatrist and court-appointed expert Reinhard Haller pointed out that in Austria, for example, 99.7 per cent of all abusers were not church people. A hypersexualized society projected its own abusive nature onto the church. For its part, the church had done everything 'to attract the blame'. The cases of film producer Harvey Weinstein and financier Jeffrey Epstein revealed a system of cover-up in the sphere of media and power. About 80 women accused Weinstein of abusing them. Weinstein had enough influence either to launch a career by a nod or to end one in the blink of an eye. Many connected with the media and politics knew about his attacks. They all kept silence about them. Such behaviour also characterized the world of prominent figures such as Kevin Spacey or Michael Jackson, whose sex attacks were a taboo subject for decades. Jeffrey Epstein was held to have sexually abused dozens of under-age girls and built a sex trafficking ring in New York and Florida. After he was arrested on 10 August 2019, he avoided court proceedings by committing suicide in prison.

When the Me Too movement triggered the question of whether other areas of society were not also infected by the cancer of abuse, the debate reached the political camps. An investigation asserted that the left-wing, alternative milieu had maintained and promoted symbiotic relations with gay and paedophile subcultures. For example, in February 1976 the Arbeitskreis Sexualität (Working Group on Sexuality), which was affiliated with the civil rights organization Humanistische Union, declared that 'sexuality should be allowed and promoted between children and with children'. Among the German Greens, from 1984 the Bundesarbeitsgemeinschaft Schwule, Transsexuelle und Päderasten (Federal Association of Gays, Transsexuals and Pederasts) vehemently campaigned for the abolition of the whole sexual criminal law. The demand to decriminalize sex with children even managed to be adopted into the programmes of eight regional associations. The future MEP Daniel Cohn-Bendit drew up the texts, together with Volker Becker, who later became the German Green Party spokesman for legal affairs, human rights and religion. According to a report in *Tagesspiel*, in the 'Alternative List', as the Berlin state branch of the Greens initially called itself, during the 1980s and 1990s hundreds of children were victims of sexual attacks by party members and officials. After the disclosure the party leadership stated that they had 'no responsibility for the crimes of individual party members'. However, the regional head Bettina Jarasch spoke of a 'general failure'.

When the Göttingen political scientist Franz Walter, of the Institute for Democracy Research, presented his 300-page study on the influence of paedophiles in the Green Party, he was amazed at 'the ignorance and irresponsibility with which many older Greens had reacted'. The silence of those concerned was flabbergasting: 'Hardly anyone said anything, few tried to explain. Quite a few battened down the hatches, or hung up the telephone or even became threatening.' Green Party leader Simone Peter apologized to the victims, who must have 'felt they were scorned in their pain and suffering' in the debates. They should have 'drawn conclusions much earlier'. The *Frankfurter Allgemeine Zeitung* wrote that it should be clear 'to the general public that the colourful world of the sunflower party had its deep abysses'. Herbert Reul, the interior minister of North Rhine-Westphalia, deplored that their 'policy had not taken abuse of children seriously'. That was an unforgivable omission. After more than 40 years in politics he had to admit: 'Sexual abuse takes place in sight of all of us, and probably everywhere.' But 'we didn't have the subject in mind. We missed it.'

At the same time as the revelations of sexual abuse in the Catholic Church, the battle began over its causes. Some saw it as a proof of active homosexuality among the priesthood. Others saw the cause as linked to Catholic sexual morality and celibacy, which was a breeding ground for abuse. Such attempts to explain broke down when the cases of systematic abuse in non-Catholic institutions such as the Odenwald school were exposed. People heard what the German criminal psychiatrist Hans Ludwig Kröber had said: 'It is easier to become pregnant from a kiss than to become a paedophile through celibacy.' The psychotherapist and senior consultant Manfred Lutz stated: 'Critics of the church and also many church representatives welcomed the opportunity to play their usual records: the church structures, its sexual morality, and celibacy are to blame. But that is just abusing the abuse, and dangerous disinformation which protects the abusers.'

Academic research's struggle to come to a single answer showed how complex the causes of the abuse of children and young people were. Benedict XVI himself related the sudden rise in offences, particularly in the 1960s and 1970s, to the social changes at that time, which had even affected church institutions. The sexual revolution had removed former inhibitions, and canon law was no longer applied consistently to guilty clergy. There was a conviction that only the law of love should operate, and canon law penalties were no longer up to date. There had been a change of consciousness, which had led to an 'obfuscation of the law and the need for penalties'. When he became pope emeritus, Ratzinger still felt obliged to speak of the sexual revolution of 1968 as a phenomenon whereby 'pre-existing standards' were frequently abandoned. 'Yes, there is sin in the church,' he stressed. A loss of standards and the departure from Catholic sexual morality had bad results for the education of priests, for academic theology and the selection of bishops.

His statement immediately provoked sharp reactions. Ratzinger's remarks were reduced to a sharp formula, though not what was meant by the author: 'For Benedict XVI the 1968 movement is responsible for church abuse.' On *katholisch.de*, the unofficial website of the German Bishops' Conference, one writer told the pope emeritus his comments 'endangered church unity'. He should 'show more restraint'. Benedict himself remarked in an afterword that his critics had completely ignored the fact that in his statement he had not been referring primarily to some event from 1968 but saw alienation from the faith as the central problem for the abuse crisis. Albert Sellner was an activist from 1968 who had campaigned then for the 'sexual liberation of the individual'. His snap judgement was: 'As far as I can see, the ex-pope is right.'

After cases of abuse by Catholic clergy were also revealed in Austria, Switzerland, Belgium, Italy and other countries, in July 2001 the pope again sharpened church procedure through a revision of the *motu proprio* '*Sacramentorum sanctitatis tutela*'. On the flight for his visit to Britain he told journalists travelling with him that the cases of abuse had been a 'shock' and a 'great sadness' for him. 'It is also sad that the church authority was not vigilant enough and did not take the necessary steps quickly and decisively enough.' Our 'first concern' had to be 'for the victims: How can we make amends?

What can we do to help these people overcome the trauma and recover their lives? Care and commitment to the victims are the first priority, with material, psychological and spiritual help and support.' The guilty must also receive 'the proper punishment'. The third point was 'prevention through education and the selection of candidates for the priesthood'.

In November 2010 the pope summoned 140 cardinals to Rome to consult on further possible measures in the battle against sexual abuse. He also determined to try and meet victims of abuse on every trip abroad, to ask their forgiveness and assure them of the church's presence, justice and solidarity with their sufferings. In Malta one of the victims said after meeting him: 'The pope wept with me, although he was not guilty of what happened to me.' Asked about tendentious media reports, Benedict answered: 'In so far as it is the truth, we must be grateful for the information. Truth, combined with love rightly understood, is value number one. Ultimately, the media would not have been able to report such things if there had not been evil in the church.'

Not all Benedict's measures were effective. Many came too late, some not often enough. On the whole, the German pope's crisis management was not so poor that it failed to prevent the Catholic Church from an even worse collapse during these stormy years. 'For anyone impartial,' said Patrick O'Malley, archbishop of Boston, it was clear: 'Cardinal Ratzinger and the later Pope Benedict devoted himself to the task of rooting out sexual abuse in the church and correcting past mistakes.' Cardinal Levada wrote: 'We owe him a debt of gratitude that he set up procedures enabling the church to take measures against the scandal of sexual abuse of minors by priests.' Armin Schwibach, a theologian in Rome and Vatican expert who produced a chronicle of the abuse scandal, summed up: 'No pope, no bishop in the world did as much as Benedict XVI in this swamp. He brought about a decisive change in the church.'

Six years after Benedict XVI's resignation a film, produced with public money by the German-British director and declared atheist Christoph Rohl, attempted to use the abuse cases as a massive indictment of the former pope. With the cynical title *Defender of the Faith* the film assembled plaintiffs, as if in a court, who described Ratzinger as a dubious, narrow-minded and unrealistic person who wanted to prevent progress in the church at all costs. According to Rohl, Benedict XVI, 'a tragically failed figure', had created a system of clinging to power and cover-ups. He was therefore chiefly responsible for the worldwide abuse and the ensuing crisis in the Catholic Church. Although the manipulative presentation and falsification of the facts were obvious, the film, which was supported by the Jesuit Klaus Mertes, thrilled critics, who praised it as 'an outspoken, serious documentary'. Headlines announced: 'Sobering View of Benedict's Papacy', 'Defender of a Sinking Church' and 'Rise and Fall of a Pope'. But even a writer as critical of Ratzinger as Christian Feldmann realized that the pope had pursued 'a hard line' on abuse in the church.[16] The Jesuit Hans Zollner, a member of the papal committee for the protection of minors under Pope Francis, concluded in an interview with the magazine *Zenit*: 'For me Benedict XVI was a hero. He fought abuse and did everything humanly possible to prevent it in future.' As prefect and as pope, he had 'brought about a revolution' by taking on responsibility in the battle against it.[17]

On the abuse Pope Francis said: 'With regard to Pope Benedict I'd like to stress that he is a man who had the courage to undertake many things against it.' Generally Benedict was 'presented as so kind-hearted; yes for he is kind-hearted, good-natured, good-hearted; he is kind! But he was also presented as weak. However, he is anything but weak! He was a strong man, a man who was consistent in things.'[18]

33

The Shepherd

Sometimes when Benedict was alone he felt a sense of gloom. It was
not despondency or fear. Certainly not an anxiety about losing his
inner freedom which God gave him. There was simply too much
trouble. Even in his church. No Catholic would ever think Christ's
community could be purely holy, all wheat and no weeds. But the
older he became, the more he doubted that human beings would
ever learn. 'But let's leave that,' he once abruptly ended a discussion,
when he was asked about hopes for the future. It was certain, he said,
that a world that had moved away from God would become not
better but worse.

As for himself, he knew that in the eyes of many observers he
would never be satisfactory. He had discussed with Habermas and
other left-wing philosophers the famous Kantian questions 'What
can we know?', 'What may we hope?', 'What is a human being?'
But a few rapidly assembled headlines were enough to reduce him
again to the old nightmare image. Wasn't it a revolutionary action
that he had accepted Anglicans as Catholic priests and bishops, even
when they were married and had children? Hadn't he been the first
to mention the filth in the Catholic Church to the whole world?
Who always stressed that it was his own people who did the greatest
damage? Instead, he was accused of making only other people
responsible for the evil.

Perhaps his greatest drawback was being a German rather than an
Italian. Or a Pole. Or a Spaniard. Or an Englishman. Or whatever.
He himself would have liked to have been French. From his youth
he had felt attracted to French culture. If he had been French, people
would have respected his intellectuality, his razor-sharp phrases. The

grande nation would have been proud of him as its son, precisely because his convictions did not arise from repeating what others said but from reflection. He would have had the backing that he urgently needed.

It was no consolation that many people in history had suffered envy, persecution and ignorance during their lifetime – or had failed simply through the narrow-mindedness of their contemporaries. Critics had lambasted Herman Melville, the author of *Moby-Dick*, for being 'soft in the head'. Melville gave up writing and became a customs inspector. At its first performance at the Paris Opéra Comique on 3 March 1875, Georges Bizet's opera *Carmen* fell flat. Three months later Bizet was dead. Van Gogh, François Villon, Friedrich Hölderlin and Socrates were all unknown or forgotten. The inventor of printing, Johannes Gutenberg (originally Henne Gensfleisch), could not pay back a loan and was regarded as no longer socially acceptable. People had even dropped Mozart. He died in poverty and was buried in a mass grave.

The pope was lonely, Ratzinger's former secretary Josef Clemens suspected. He no longer laughed. He was sad and low-spirited.[1] Benedict must have thought quite often of his predecessor Gregory the Great, who gave the world Gregorian chant. Hadn't Gregory also wrestled with the problems that were so familiar to him: the slow decay of a world in which faith appeared a matter of course, the insidious contamination of Christianity through a cold worldliness? 'But *we* are the bringers of death to the sinking people whom we should have been leading to life', Gregory wrote. 'Through our sins the people languish, because through our neglect they have not been taught how to live.' They had become 'preoccupied with outward affairs'. Gregory was deeply depressed: 'Those entrusted to us abandon God, but we keep silence.'[2]

Like Gregory, Benedict also knew the feeling of no longer being equal to a situation. He was also worried that his heart might fail. Now of all times! At a time when he knew his task was not yet done, his mission unfulfilled. At least, not until he had completed his Jesus trilogy. Then there was his strong sense of duty he'd had since childhood. The model of his father had taught him that you should not run away from life 'when the danger is great'. 'It is precisely then that you should stand firm and cope with the difficult situation,' he told me in one of our interviews in the summer of 2010. 'You can retire at a peaceful moment or when you simply can't do any more.'[3] The public barely noticed that suggestion, although it was actually sensational. Never before had a pope said publicly that he could imagine a situation in which he would retire. Benedict said it again pointedly: 'If a pope realizes clearly that he physically, psychologically and spiritually can no longer do his job, then he has the right, and under certain circumstances also the duty, to retire.'[4]

Actually, after five years of his papacy Benedict XVI's balance sheet was not that bad, despite its having been beset by genuine, less genuine and clearly engineered scandals. According to the *Annuario Pontificio 2010*, the Catholic Church's yearbook, in the previous year alone he had established eight new dioceses, an apostolic prefecture, two metropolitan sees and three apostolic vicariates. In addition in the 2,923 ecclesiastical districts he had appointed 169 new bishops. The number of priests rose from 406,411 to 409,166, and the number of Catholics rose to 1,166 billion. That was 1.7 per cent more than in the previous year, or 19 million people, as many as the populations of Switzerland, Austria and Uruguay put together. North and South Americans made up 49.8 per cent of the world Catholic population, Europeans 25 per cent.[5]

After the disaster of the sexual abuse, he appealed for a thoroughgoing renewal at the Easter vigil of 2010. He called unchastity and immorality 'old clothes in which you cannot stand before God'. Benedict referred to the early Christian baptismal rite with its renunciation of 'the world of lust' and lies. At his *Urbi et orbi* blessing, received by 100,000 people in St Peter's Square, he also recalled the 'water of baptism'. Now in our own time humanity did not need superficial improvements but a spiritual and moral transformation, to come out of a deep crisis and restore life in its original beauty, goodness and truth, at least to some extent.

In inter-denominational dialogue with church communities in the West he concentrated on the Anglicans, the Lutheran World Federation, the World Alliance of Reformed Churches and the World Methodist Council. He gave his Council for Promoting Christian Unity the task of producing a study on the existing points of agreement. In relation to the East, the Joint International Commission for Theological Dialogue between the Catholic Church and the Eastern Orthodox Church had resumed its work on 16 October 2007 and tackled a decisive subject, 'The role of the bishop of Rome in the church community of the first millennium', a time when Eastern and Western Christians were still in communion.

According to Cardinal Kasper, president of the Christian Unity Council, ecumenical dialogue had taken on a 'new dimension'. Metropolitan Hilarion, who was in charge of foreign affairs in the Russian Orthodox Church, said that the election of Benedict XVI, who commanded high respect among Orthodox Christians as a 'defender of traditional Christian values', had helped bring them closer. Hilarion said: 'We are approaching a time when it will be possible to arrange a meeting between the pope and the patriarch of Moscow.'

Under Benedict XVI the number of Catholic–Protestant meetings also rose to an unprecedented level. That was demonstrated in the celebration of the tenth anniversary of the 'Joint Statement on the Doctrine of Justification', which was essentially due to Ratzinger's commitment. Jens-Martin Kruse was the minister of the Evangelical Christuskirche (Church of Christ) in Rome. After a joint evening service held in his church on 14 March 2010 he stressed that Benedict grasped the big questions and concerns of the time. Anyone meeting the pope met a Christian who put not himself or his office first, but Christ – 'in a convincing way that also makes him a model for Lutherans'.[6]

To promote relations with Judaism, Benedict had visited three synagogues, more than any pope before him. He no longer called Jews 'our elder brothers', as Wojtyła had, but our 'fathers in faith'. On his visit to the Rome synagogue in January 2010, he called upon Jews and Christians to continue along the road of reconciliation and dialogue. The new direction taken by the Catholic Church through the Council was irrevocable. He decisively condemned any form of anti-Semitism and apologized for the bad behaviour of Catholics towards their fellow citizens. 'To a large extent Christians and Jews have a common spiritual inheritance,' he said. 'They pray to the same Lord, and have the same roots' and the basic ethical law of the Ten Commandments. They should work together to promote reverence for God in a world that often regarded the supernatural as superfluous and created new gods for itself. After the controversial Regensburg speech the Catholic–Muslim forum was set up. In November 2008 it published a first joint statement against any kind of repression, aggressive violence and terrorism.

On the positive side, there had also been the Year of the Priest, which had just ended. The pope had used it to discuss the abuse scandal. He called upon the priests to become newly aware of the meaning and right way of being a Catholic priest. The Year concluded with the biggest assembly of priests of all time. On the feast of the Sacred Heart of Jesus on 11 June 2010, 9,000 priests from 91 countries assembled in St Peter's Square. Last but not least were Benedict's speeches in the world's capital cities. According to Archbishop Rino Fisichella, the reactions of the cultural elite showed 'that they felt they had a partner in this pope'.[7]

There were problems with the Vatican Bank. In Benedict's time the Istituto per le Opere di Religione (the Institute for Works of Religion, or IOR) had 110 employees, about 25,000 customers and finances of 5 billion euros. The bank was constantly in the headlines because of its shady dealings. In the 1970s and 1980s the American archbishop Paul Marcinkus had been involved in the bank's affairs, and the Mafia had also played a part. In the end three major figures were dead, most probably murdered, and the Vatican paid almost $250 million in damages.

John Paul II had had no interest in reforming the Vatican Bank because it was able freely to transfer huge sums to Poland to support the anti-communist opposition. On the other hand, by his *motu proprio* of 30 December 2010 Benedict set up a financial supervisory authority to stop the Vatican's involvement in dubious dealings and money-laundering and make it conform to international banking standards. The Autorità di Informazione Finanziaria (Authority for Financial Information) controlled not just the Vatican Bank but all the money that went through the Roman Curia, the administration of the patrimony of the Holy See and the Vatican State. Benedict appointed the highly regarded banker Ettore Gotti Tedeschi to manage the IOR and reform financial policy. Tedeschi was the director of the Italian business of the Santander Bank and had written a book about money and ethics. Later Benedict removed Tedeschi because, according to some of his colleagues, he had not kept up with his job well enough. The 2012 annual report showed that the system set up in 2010 was beginning to function. After 33,000 accounts had been checked, only six suspicious transactions were found. The Italian investigative journalist Gianluigi Nuzzi found in November 2015: 'Until Benedict XVI took office, none of the modern popes had bothered about their state finances. Ratzinger was the first one who wanted to create order and control the Curia.'

An important step was the establishment of diplomatic relations with Russia. However, Benedict did not make progress in his dealings with China, which was still conducting unlawful ordinations of bishops. The problem was the religious authority of the huge communist state. For example, when the Dalai Lama said perhaps he did not want to be born again, the Chinese government authority answered, 'That's up to us to decide!'

Despite the pope's rather pessimistic mood, something had changed. There were the many young people who were finding new ways to the Catholic faith on World Youth Days, pilgrimages and in prayer groups. After Ratzinger's World Youth Day in Cologne, the 'night fever' initiative had spread like wildfire to many cities. Young people gathered to celebrate divine service intimately and emotionally. There were the young priests who were going back to the Catholic classics. New initiatives were starting up everywhere. People formed social networks, created their own websites, such as kath.net, for news and opinions that were suppressed in the mainstream press. They made catechism an event again with a project such as 'YouCat'. The 'Benedict Generation' and the young spiritual movements learned to combine tradition and modernity in a new way. For a long time they had been running conferences that were not only livelier but larger than the established Catholic associations. Treffpunkt Weltkirche (World Church Meeting Point), the conference 'Freude am Glauben' (Joy in Faith) and the Augsburg Gebetshaus (Prayer House) MEHR-Konferenz were three German examples. There was the usual quarrel with the progressives, but there was an awareness that where it said Catholic on the outside it had to be Catholic on the inside and that this pope was a guarantee the right direction had not been lost.

Benedict particularly enjoyed meeting bishops and priests. He took literally Jesus' injunction to Peter: 'Strengthen your brothers.' He was not so fond of going on trips. Nevertheless, during the year

2010 the 83-year-old pope made more journeys than in any other year of his papacy, to such different places as Malta, Portugal, Cyprus, Great Britain and Spain. After his visits to America and Africa these trips showed the historic and continuing importance of the Catholic Church on the continent that it had shaped and which had shaped it.

His tour of Europe began in April in Malta. The occasion was the 1950th anniversary of St Paul's landing on the coast of Malta on his way to Rome after being shipwrecked, together with his fellow prisoners. 'After we had reached safety we then learned that the island was called Malta' (Acts 28.1). The 500,000 Maltese called their patron saint 'father'. They were proud that they were personally converted to Christianity by the 'Apostle to the Gentiles'. Today 97 per cent of the inhabitants are still baptized Catholics. The island, which measures 316 square kilometres, is thus the most Catholic country in the world, and 50 per cent of its population attended the events with the pope, who also met victims of abuse.

A month later, on 11 May 2010, Benedict set out for Portugal. As always, the trip organizer Alberto Gasbarri had arranged the tour very well. Gasbarri was the father of a family, and the first layman to be appointed by Benedict to take care of his journeys abroad. Before that, it had been the job of the master of the horse to ride in front of the papal coach on a journey by the Holy Father. Now Gasbarri had arranged for a small private area at the front of the aeroplane with a bed in it for the pope on long haul flights. Altötting, Częstochowa, Lourdes, Loreto, Mariazell – Benedict had already been to all the major European Marian pilgrimage sites. In a sense Fátima, where Mary had appeared on 13 May 1917 to three shepherd children, was the climax and conclusion. Benedict had once called the message of Fátima the prophetic vision of the modern world. He interpreted the 'third Fátima secret' as summing up the way the church would go during the twentieth century – and as a still valid warning against alienation from the faith. The Peruvian Nobel prize-winner Mario Vargas Llosa was so impressed by Benedict's trip that he called him one of the most significant intellectuals of the present day. Benedict's 'new and bold' reflections gave answers to the moral, cultural and existential problems of our time.

In Lisbon 300,000 faithful gathered to celebrate Mass with the pope. In Fátima there were 500,000. When, 93 years earlier, 'heaven opened over Portugal', said Benedict on his arrival, then 'a window of hope' was opened, which God always opened 'when people shut the door on him'. Fátima was 'an act of God's loving providence', which the church did not 'bring about'. 'It was Fátima that asserted itself in the church.' Here something happened 'to remind us of gospel truths'.[8]

In Lisbon the Holy Father followed his prologue with praise for the often hard-won social and cultural achievements of Christianity. Even today it was presumed that faith was present as a matter of course, but that was 'unfortunately less and less the reality'. When he met hundreds of creative artists, he sought a dialogue that was not only inter-religious but inter-cultural in the face of the increasingly complex phenomenon of modernity. He said: 'With regard to the church's position in the world, a learning process must be energetically undertaken to help society understand that the proclamation of the truth is a service which the church offers society, by opening a new outlook on the future, with breadth and dignity.' The core of this dialogue had to be 'creating world citizenship, based on human rights and civic responsibility, independently of people's ethical and political affiliations and respectful of their religious convictions.'[9]

In Fátima, visited yearly by 5 million pilgrims, the 'theologian pope' seemed thankful to be able to show that his inmost conviction was that faith and reason belonged together, simply because there were more possibilities between heaven and Earth than limited, all too narrow, human thinking could imagine. In the 'third secret of Fátima', as Benedict had already explained on his flight to Portugal, 'the realities of the future of the church were revealed, which are gradually occurring and plain to see'. Christ had predicted 'that the church would always suffer until the end of the world'. Today in the message of Fátima we could see that happening 'in a really alarming way'. The message said:

> The greatest danger to the church does not come from external enemies, but arises from the sin in the church. So it is very necessary for the church to relearn how to repent, and be purified. [...] Let's be realistic, evil always attacks from outside and from within. But the powers of goodness are also always present, and in the end the Lord is stronger than evil. And God's mother is a

visible, motherly guarantee of God's goodness, which always has the last word in history.[10]

At the Fátima shrine on 13 May the pope made clear: 'Anyone who believes that Fátima's prophetic mission is over, is mistaken.' Then he said something that must have shocked many people: 'Humanity has succeed in unleashing a cycle of death and terror which they can no longer break out of.' It was important that the message of Fátima 'was not intended just for certain devotions but as the fundamental answer: constant conversion, repentance, prayer and the three divine virtues: faith, hope and love.'

In June the pope travelled to Cyprus to prepare with the bishops the special synod on the Near East, which was to take place in October that year. His visit to the island, divided both politically and religiously, was his first to a mainly Orthodox country. He wanted to strengthen relations with Orthodoxy but also with the various Eastern Catholic churches. (The Catholic Church consists not only of the Latin churches but also over 20 other particular churches.) Shortly beforehand the Orthodox Bishop Athanasius had described him as a heretic and his visit as 'a problem of conscience for many pious Christians'. Benedict XVI was outside the church and was never even a bishop. It had escaped the Cypriot bishop that the German pope exercised the Petrine primacy in a very ecumenical, self-effacing way. He wanted to make it easier for others to see the first of the apostles no longer as a competitor or as claiming to subject them, but as a symbol for the great task of the restoring joint communion.

At the Corpus Christi service in Nicosia on 6 June 2010, the feast of Christ's body and blood, the pope again quoted a metaphor used by Teresa of Ávila: 'We are the eyes with which his compassion looks at sufferers; we are the hands which he stretches out to bless and heal with; we are the feet he walks with to go about doing good; and we are the lips which proclaim his gospel.' Applied to the current situation that meant: 'We are called to overcome our quarrels, to bring peace and reconciliation to conflicts and give the world a message of hope. We are called to open ourselves to people in need and share our earthly goods generously with all those who are less well off than us. And we are called to keep proclaiming the Lord's death and resurrection until he returns.'[11]

The European Court of Human Rights had recently ruled that crucifixes had to be removed from Italian schools out of regard for students who were not Christians or belonged to other faiths. The symbol was not compatible with the European Convention of Human Rights. Benedict replied that the Christian cross was the most important sign against violence and oppression. It had nothing to do with forcing a faith or a philosophy on anyone. The cross was 'the most eloquent witness to hope' there had ever been. A world without the cross would be a world without hope, in which injustice, brutality and greed reigned unhindered and the poor were exploited. The cross stood for the triumph of God's love. The Cypriot Catholics asked Benedict to foster mutual trust between Christians and non-Christians. That was the foundation for lasting peace between adherents of different religions, political parties and cultural backgrounds.

Then in September 2010 came the beatification of John Henry Newman in Birmingham, a particularly moving event for Ratzinger. As a student he had discovered a spiritual bond with the British convert. Now as pope he was able to include the scholar, who had been made a Catholic cardinal, in 'the Book of the Blessed', a preliminary step towards sainthood. Catholic saints had to have lived a model Christian life of 'heroic virtue', to have died with the reputation of holiness and to have already attained the vision of God. Benedict came at the invitation of the British government. Protests had been planned, but they did not go beyond the level of hostility that had been foreseen. The English tabloid press fretted and fumed as usual. British lawyers questioned the pope's legal status and wanted to bring him to court on the charge of having covered up the abuse of minors by Catholic clergy. The British evolutionary biologist and atheist activist Richard Dawkins declared the pope should be arrested on his arrival in Britain.

On top of that, a Foreign Office document appeared in which junior civil servants listed activities that Benedict XVI should engage in during his stay, including 'blessing a gay couple', 'opening an abortion clinic' and launching a new condom brand called "Benedict"'. The Foreign Office was forced to state that the foolish note 'did not reflect the position of the British Foreign and Commonwealth Office or the British government'. The Orwell Prize-winning journalist Melanie Phillips spoke of a cultural, educational and moral collapse of public administration, with countless young civil servants who were immature, superfluous, but politically correct to the point of no return. These people had a world view in which minorities had to be respected, whereas Christians could be treated with snide contempt. She lashed out again that it was striking to see how the people who boasted of being the most liberal, best-educated and cleverest heads in the country were really the most petty-minded and also suffered from a dodgy form of illiberalism and complete lack of respect for the opinions of others, particularly those who adhered to the great religious convictions of the European tradition.[12] The manager who had approved the circulation of the Foreign Office note was dismissed.

Nonetheless, Benedict did not take it to heart. He 'avenged' himself by winning the hearts of millions of people in a few days through his modest presence and thoughtful speeches. The *Sunday Times* corrected its image of the Ratzinger pope with the words: 'Rottweiler? No he is a saintly grandfather.' For one thing was now certain: 'Britain learned to love the pope.'

On board the plane to Edinburgh, Benedict made his standpoint clear. When a journalist asked him whether the church should urgently do something to become more attractive, he answered with a plain 'No'. The church did not sell anything, least of all itself. It was not entrusted with goods but with a message, which it had to pass on in full. On 16 September he was welcomed in Holyrood House, the British monarch's official residence in Scotland, by Queen Elizabeth II, who was exactly one year older than himself. Everyone could see from their gestures and faces both their mutual sympathy and the nobility and civility of both church leaders. As queen, Elizabeth was also the head of the Anglican Church. In the United Kingdom the separation of church and state merely means that by law a Catholic cannot become the monarch.

At Holyrood House, Benedict introduced the subject that was the *leitmotif* of his British trip: the dangers for a society if the Christian world view and Christian ethics were completely outlawed from public debate. He recalled the brave resistance of the British to the tyranny of the Nazis and spoke about 'the sobering lessons' of 'atheist extremism in the twentieth-century world'. The following day he spoke in Westminster Hall about Thomas More, a saint honoured both by Catholics and Anglicans for his fortitude and loyalty to his faith. Thomas More was executed in the sixteenth century, and because of his integrity he was the patron saint of politicians. He had always kept the balance between reasons of state and being faithful to his conscience – and died for it. Without the Christian religion, the pope summed up, the state ran the risk of acting on purely ideological grounds or from power interests, as in Thomas More's time. On the other hand, religion without reason easily became sectarian and fundamentalist.

The climax of the pope's visit was Newman's beatification on 19 September. In his sermon Benedict highlighted an aspect that was particularly important to Newman and also to himself: having educated Catholic laity in the church who were able to bear witness to their faith articulately. He quoted Newman's statement: 'I want a laity, not arrogant, not rash in speech, not disputatious, but men who know their religion, who enter into it, who know just where they stand, who know what they hold and what they do not, who know their creed so well that they can give an account of it, who know so much of history that they can defend it.'[13] When the bells of Westminster Abbey rang farewell to him in the twilight, the pope let Rowan Williams, the archbishop of Canterbury, take his arm to lead him downstairs, like a good friend for whom it was an honour to take care that Peter's successor did not come to any harm.

34

Human Ecology

It was now late autumn, but the year's itinerary was not yet over. On 6 November 2010 Benedict visited Santiago de Compostela. He was enthusiastically welcomed at the airport by the heir to the Spanish throne, Prince Felipe of Asturias, with Princess Letizia and about 200,000 people.

Thick fog covered the pilgrimage site as the Alitalia Airbus 320 set out with the pope on board. The pope had caused annoyance because he had spoken on the plane about an aggressive secularism in Spain, 'as we saw before in the 1930s'. This was an allusion to the beginning of the Spanish Civil War in 1936, which was triggered by a military coup by nationalist forces. In the hate-filled anticlerical mood of the time republican troops had set fire to churches and murdered thousands of nuns and priests. The clergy were on the side of the Fascist Franco regime. The newspaper *El País* called the pope's remarks 'irresponsible ignorance'. The left-wing *Público* ran the headline 'The Pope comes intent on war'.[1]

On his arrival Benedict declared he wanted 'to join the great crowd of men and women over the centuries who had come from all corners of the Iberian peninsula, Europe and the whole world to Compostela, to honour St James and be transformed by the witness of his faith'. Full of hope, they created a way of culture, prayer, mercy and conversion, which was embodied in churches, hospitals, hostels, bridges and monasteries. Spain and Europe had developed a spiritual face 'indelibly marked by the gospel'. He felt 'deep joy at being here in Spain again, which has given the world a multitude of great saints, founders of religious orders and writers, such as Ignatius of Loyola, Teresa of Ávila, John of the Cross, Francis Xavier and many others'.

In St James's (Santiago) Cathedral he prayed at the apostle's tomb in the crypt and then embraced his statue on the altar. 'Going on pilgrimage does not mean simply visiting a site, to admire its natural beauties, art treasures and history,' he stressed in his greeting. 'Going on pilgrimage means coming out of ourselves in order to meet God at a place where he has revealed himself, where divine grace shone with particular splendour.'[2]

From Compostela, Benedict travelled to Barcelona, to consecrate the church of the Sagrada Família as a basilica. On his journey through the city he was welcomed by 250,000 people. The church had originally been designed in the Catalan Art Nouveau style by Antoni Gaudí, and building work was begun in 1882. It was still unfinished and exclusively financed by donations and entry fees. In his sermon Benedict described the cathedral as a 'wonderful synthesis of technical skill, art and faith'. Gaudí, 'an architect of genius', had managed to create a space of enchanting beauty, a space of faith and hope. The pope recalled Europe's Christian roots and confirmed the Church's attitude to abortion, which was being vigorously discussed in Spain. The issue was a new law allowing embryos to be aborted up to the 14th week of pregnancy.

Benedict visited the Iberian peninsula once more. The occasion was the World Youth Day in Madrid. During the vigil on Saturday, 20 August 2011, a mighty rainstorm hit the Spanish capital, threatening to put an end to the service. But the pope remained in his seat, rock-solid and in the best of sprits, while the drenched youthful chorus struck up. The terrible weather could not dampen the enthusiasm. On the next day almost 2 million people came to meet him. Tens of thousands received the sacrament of penance. Benedict himself heard the confession of four boys. When he said goodbye to King Juan Carlos, he merely said: 'Your majesty, the pope has felt very well in Spain.'

Immediately before his visit to Great Britain in the summer of 2010 the pope had given a long interview. It was the first book of interviews with a living pope in church history. It had become necessary to add background information which had not been reported in the media about the Williamson affair, and also to speak in detail about the causes and consequences of the abuse scandal. The recordings for the book took place in six one-hour meetings at the pope's holiday home at Castel Gandolfo. It was published in November 2010 with the title *Licht der Welt* (*Light of the World*), and had an international print run of a million copies. 'Of course, I'm not as fit as I was 20 years ago,' the pope excused himself at the beginning of the interview. Then after a bit of small talk he said, 'Pack ma's!' ('Let's get on with it' in Bavarian dialect.)

As a cardinal, Ratzinger had warned of the loss of identity, direction and truth if a new paganism took over human thought and behaviour. It was necessary to develop a new sensitivity to creation, which was now under threat, and oppose the destructive forces. Nothing had changed from that position. His papal summer message for 2010 was a dramatic appeal not to carry on as we had before. Humanity was at a crossroads. It was time to reflect and time to change. Benedict's option was an alternative to an ideology that made ecology a kind of religion and saw a human *homo climaticus* as the sole saviour of the planet. The pope declared: 'There are so many problems, which must all be solved, but which will not all be solved unless God is at the centre and newly visible in the world.'[3]

In Germany the pope's opponents were gunning vigorously. During the 'Benedetto mania' critics had complained that it had become impossible to publish anything negative about Ratzinger. Now they were using the abuse crisis to restock their arsenal. For example, Hermann Häring, an assistant and faithful follower of Hans Küng, published an indictment with the title *Im Namen des Herrn* (In the Name of the Lord). Under Ratzinger, Rome had become a 'dreaded, monocratic control authority'. Häring promised a 'ruthless look behind the scenes'. He accused the pope of repression, legal arbitrariness, lacking the will for reconciliation, loss of reality, embargo, denial, exclusion, anti-ecumenism, lack of understanding in cultural and social-political questions, a broken relationship with other religions and paternalism. Ultimately, everything that Ratzinger did was a 'débâcle'. The book read rather as if someone was making twice two equal five, or a minus from a plus, or like an out-of-tune concert. Naturally, he wrote, the pope had always 'sympathized strongly with the right'.[4] Häring shared this theory with Peter Wensierski, a writer for *Der Spiegel*. Since Ratzinger had taken office, Wensierski said, there had been a 'series of reactionary measures'. He cited his proof: 'There was a whole chain, from the reintroduction of the Latin Mass in the old ritual, including the controversial Good Friday prayer.' The chain was rather short. Even the Good Friday prayer was not an individual item but part of the 'old ritual'.

Benedict's critics argued that they would strike a chord in millions of Catholics with their accusations. In a certain sense they were right. Since the days of the Council the concerted action of reforming forces had been battling for an all-purpose church, in which autonomous church members would be the measure of all things, led by the high priests of the *Zeitgeist*. The retinue included those professors who had long lost their permission to teach, because they had constantly tried everything to make the Son of God a rebel leader. As '68-ers they had a problem with authority – as long as it was not their own. They were flanked by journalists who took every opportunity to portray Ratzinger as one of the worst enemies of modernity. For example, Hanspeter Oschwald declared that he had discovered 'how fundamentalist forces control the Vatican'. He called his book *Im Namen des heiligen Vaters* (*In the Name of the Holy Father*). According to the blurb, it was a 'relentless, highly illuminating look at the secret puppet masters in Rome'. Oschwald went on to say that 'fundamentalist movements secretly influenced the pope's decisions'. The result was: 'More and more people are leaving the church in dismay.'[5]

Other Ratzinger critics were saying much the same. But their arguments and accompanying allegations often made them lack credibility. For example, the *Welt* journalist Alan Posener produced a book with the title *Benedikts Kreuzzug* (*Benedict's Way of the Cross*) – no one knew that way of the cross and its soldiers better than him.[6] In order to feign plausibility, Posener resorted to an old trick: he asserted things that his stereotyped opponents had never actually said. (For example, 'The pope says democracy is a dictatorship of relativism.') Then contexts were fabricated, and only existed in the author's imagination.

The result was a brainchild like a homunculus, a figure without limbs or heart. In his lectures Posener, who boasted of being an atheist, promised his public 'neat quotations to enjoy'. That was no empty promise. The former Maoist declared that after Ratzinger's 'takeover of power' he had striven for a 'dictatorship of the truth, *his* truth'. The 'thinking in the Vatican' was 'Talibanesque'. The pope demanded that the state should be controlled by Christianity. This 'dictator' was against natural science, against reason. He had 'accepted the Society of St Pius X back into the church' and was 'head of a state that combats the decriminalization of homosexuality, like Iran and other rogue states'. Ratzinger was conducting a crusade 'for Europe to become Catholic again, so that the church was the ultimate authority in politics and society'. In his performances, for example, to the Bund der Atheisten (Atheists' Society), Posener liked to imitate Benedict's voice, adding: 'He says that himself.' The journalist concluded his speech, 'Welcome to clerical fascism!'

Hans Küng re-entered the fray with an open letter to the 'honourable bishops'. It was published on 15 April 2010 in the *Süddeutsche Zeitung*. It appeared simultaneously in the *Neue Zürcher Zeitung*, *La Repubblica*, *El País*, *Le Monde* and with the *New York Times* syndicate. Küng said Ratzinger's papacy was a unique accumulation of 'missed opportunities'. For example, he had wasted the opportunity for 'an approach to the Evangelical churches', 'a durable understanding with the Jews', 'a trustful dialogue with the Muslims' and 'the chance to help the African people' (a reference to the 'condom crisis'). Again and again this pope had demoted the Council texts. He had accepted 'unlawfully ordained bishops of the traditionalist Society of St Pius X [...] into the church unconditionally'. The open letter reached a climax of free improvisation of the truth with the assertion that 'the worldwide systematic cover-up of clerical sexual abuse was operated by Ratzinger's Roman Congregation for the Doctrine of the Faith'. The bishops should no longer feel obliged to keep their 'oath of obedience to the pope' and should demand a council 'to solve the now urgent problems of reform'.[7]

The main theme of Benedict's catecheses during his general audiences in the autumn and winter of 2010 was great women in church history. They included mystics such as Hildegard of Bingen, Mechtilde of Hackeborn, Teresa of Ávila, Angela of Foligno, Julian of Norwich and Veronica Giuliani. Mystical contemplation, said the pope, was the beginning of 'seeing God with eyes and heart'. He quoted the words of his favourite St Bonaventure, saying the ascent to God succeeded by relying on grace 'not doctrine; yearning not intellect; the sighing of prayer not the study of texts'. This, said Benedict, 'is not anti-intellectual or against reason. It presupposes the way of reason, but goes beyond it in love for the crucified Christ.' Bonaventure's words marked 'the beginning of a great mystical current, that purified the human spirit and raised it to a new dimension'.

Instruction in the Catholic faith was combined with Ratzinger's diagnosis of the times. If faith wasn't just a hobby horse but was meant to give answers to the signs of the times, then both went together. It was not new that the Catholic Church had always seen it as its task to give the nations a helping hand. Others called it indoctrinating them. 'Popes were successors to Peter – and the Caesars,' said the church historian Ulrich Nersinger.[8] 'They made use of the secular for the spiritual and the spiritual for the secular' to shape civilization and write history. An intellectual as pope meant there was a voice able to bring spiritual thinking and the experience of religions into the social debate.

When he had been archbishop of Munich, Ratzinger's critique of the times had usually been met with a lack of understanding. Some people called him a cultural pessimist, others an apocalyptic. Since then, over the course of time he had produced many more analyses, particularly of the imminent dangers to humanity and the basis of human life. His warnings as a bishop had become campaigns. The green movement that had arisen all over the world was a new 'grand narrative of the world community', as Christianity, the Renaissance, the Enlightenment, the battle for social progress, justice and freedom had been before. The difference between the pope and many environmentalists was that Ratzinger tried to think un-ideologically and, above all, holistically. He did not distinguish between protecting animals and the rainforest and protecting unborn life. It was just as wrong to pollute or manipulate human beings as the ozone layer or the groundwater. Otherwise the consequences would be devastating. The pope thought in terms not just of creation but also of a creator. For him not only humans but God too had a part to play. God's plan had seen to it that the world and the universe remained in order, with meaning and beauty. It made freedom possible and gave human beings the conditions to be able to live at all.

Ratzinger only had an elementary practical knowledge about technical progress. He was amazed at the intricacies of a simple dictating machine or the possibility of ordering an Uber taxi through an app. But that did not mean he failed to follow the basic advances attentively.

At least since the beginning of his papacy the debate on progress had been aired on all channels. There were discussions about the impact of artificial intelligence in robots, about cyber weapons and household appliances. About 'Industry 4.0' (the computerization of manufacturing) and its consequences for jobs. Activists argued in talk shows about CO_2 emissions, plastic waste, fine dust pollution, the massive consumption of meat and the consequences of cheap package tourism.

The sociologist Hartmut Rosa described how in an average household around the year 1900 there were about 400 things. Now the occupiers were surrounded by about 10,000 things. Then they had to decide what they would soon throw away and deal with where to dispose of them. While, on the one hand, there was stress on the limits of growth, on the other hand, people still wanted to invent new things. Starts-ups shot up like mushrooms from the ground and offered services that people had never dreamed of before. Terms like 'data storage clouds', 'streaming platforms', 'real-time transmission' and 'shit storm', which had previously only been heard at academic conferences, became expressions in everyday use. Digital technologies created 'electronic brains', which provided the strategically best solutions for all kinds of processes. And with the most recent software it had become possible to generate computer portraits and texts, which produced a kind of hyper-reality that looked more authentic than real people and real faces. This effect was not now called 'fake news' but 'deepfakes'.

The world as it had been known was definitely becoming unrecognizable. The paradigm shift was like moving on to a different stage, or to a different house or planet. The military worked on automatic weapons systems to wage algorithmic war with killer robots, and 3D printers could produce replacement body parts or even whole houses. Because 5,000 Facebook friends and 50,000 followers on Instagram could not prevent loneliness, resourceful firms in the porn industry created robots with artificial intelligence to snog and copulate with. After the merger of the messenger services Instagram, Facebook and WhatsApp, 2.7 billion people would use the same chat programme. Escape from this community, which left the previous forms of democracy behind and produced influential movements with 'Like' buttons, would become almost impossible. One hype was quickly replaced by another, following the logic of overstimulation. Politics had long been driven by Newsfeed or Timeline algorithms, 'whose originators and purposes remain completely nebulous', as the *Süddeutsche Zeitung* observed. The political agenda was increasingly determined by manipulation, set in motion in 'opaque computer rooms'.

In China the technology of personal recognition had become so advanced that with video recording of faces, ways of moving, body shape and gestures, the total surveillance of everyone at any time came within tangible reach. US presidents, with their chiefs of staff and security, followed live on screen when special navy SEAL units liquidated the leaders of Islamic terror organizations in the Hindu Kush or Syria. Scientists worked on new-generation microchips to further the integration of humans and machines. The problem was that many of them no longer understood the artificial intelligence they were developing. The Munich cultural journalist Tobias Haberl wondered whether 'we are becoming both richer and poorer, both more secure and more frightened'.[9]

Seldom before had a society been so spoon-fed, so remote-controlled, so subject to the dictatorship of fashion and opinions. Newspaper commentators said scientists and artists used to look forward optimistically to the future. Today dystopia – negative, fearful visions of the future – had become mainstream. In its annual eco-report the UNO warned of melting permafrost and gene-manipulated creatures, such as a genetically modified version of a gnat that killed off previous populations. In just a few decades, the report summed up, humanity had allowed global temperatures to rise 170 times faster than normal, altered 75 per cent of the Earth's surface and 93 per cent of its river courses, leading to drastic changes in the biosphere.[10] The various end-time scenarios included an ultimate act of destruction. This could be both extreme violence and extreme liberation. One scenario appeared in literature and was also discussed in scientific forums: at the end there was nothing left, no human beings, no world and no one left to see the Earth destroyed together with its human population.

Ratzinger was never tempted to give way to despair about the global situation. 'Christians do not pray for the end of the world but for the return of Christ', he would say. The pope looked further. He looked to the source code, which held the world at its heart, and to things in detail – human relationships with self and others. He called this 'human ecology'. The term arose from the typical Catholic 'both-and' (rather than 'either/or'). This meant humans couldn't be omitted from the question of the basis of life.

The concern for the right relation between protecting humanity and protecting the environment was a constant theme throughout his papacy. In a speech in 2006, shortly after he had taken office, he called for 'respect for nature, to take care of it as God's garden and also to make it a garden for humanity'. In July 2007 he spoke at a meeting of clergy in Treviso in Italy of 'obedience to the voice of nature'. Listening to the Earth's teaching, the voice of Being, was important 'because the Earth, and everything that is, was brought into being by a Creator, who also gave his creation a message'. In July 2008 Benedict said in Australia that 'insatiable consumerism' was behind 'erosion, deforestation, wasting of global mineral and maritime resources'. On 8 January 2009 the diplomatic corps were the recipients of his sombre warning that the future 'was more than ever at risk today, even the fate of our planet and its inhabitants'. Food crises and climate change affected the poor most. In November 2009 he urged governments to battle more vigorously against hunger: 'What we need is a change in the lifestyle of individuals and communities, in consumption habits and awareness of what is really necessary.' In December 2009 he told ambassadors newly accredited to the Holy See that continual damage to the environment was threatening human peace and survival. So consumption had to be checked and 'the unlimited accumulation of goods' had to stop.

Environment, sustainability and responsibility remained top subjects on Benedict's agenda. The motto of World Peace Day 2010 was: 'If you want to promote peace, look after the creation.' 'How can we remain indifferent,' the pope demanded 'to phenomena such as global climate change, desertification, the loss of productivity in large agricultural areas, the pollution of rivers and groundwater, the loss of biodiversity, the increase in extraordinary natural events and tropical deforestation.' That also involved 'moral crises', which made 'a lifestyle of moderation and solidarity' urgently necessary. Humanity had completely to rethink its dealings with nature. What was required was a way of life that made use of renewable energy. It had to be clear that much was at stake, and no one should be indifferent towards what was happening around us.

Benedict also gave the environment theme plenty of space in his encyclicals. For example, the second chapter of *Caritas in veritate* went into detail and demanded that the necessities of life, such as food and water, should be available to everyone. Solidarity with developing countries was necessary and, above all, solidarity with future generations, to whom we should pass on the Earth in a condition 'in which they could also live on it with dignity and continue to cultivate it'.[11] The basic insight that 'the book of nature is single and indivisible' meant that we had duties towards the environment but also towards human beings. So, according to the Catholic view, an ecology was merely half-hearted if it was concerned to protect greater spotted woodpeckers and sea turtles but denied their rights as a person to unborn or dying humans.

Benedict's human ecology relied on faith in creation and the recognition of human dignity. In the biblical tradition there was already 'a mutual influence to be seen between the human face and the "face" of the environment'. The Earth's constitution was reflected in the inner constitution of its inhabitants. 'When humans degenerate, the environment in which they live degenerates,' he said in his New Year sermon of 2010. At the reception for members of the diplomatic corps, he told them: 'Denying God disfigures human freedom, but also destroys creation.' The roots of a shattered environment were nearly always of a moral nature. That meant that an educational effort was necessary, to promote an effective change of awareness and establish new ways of living.

In countless speeches and sermons Benedict referred to natural law as the 'source' from which the binding moral commandments sprang, together with basic rights. Truth and love, which disclosed nature, had their basis not in humans but in God. No laws made by human beings could ever overturn the rule written by the Creator. Otherwise 'society will be damaged in what actually constitutes its own foundation'.[12] The state had to accept that there was a body of truth which was not subject to consensus. The book of nature is 'single and indivisible', he had said in his encyclical *Caritas in veritate*, 'even in sexual matters, marriage, family, social relationships, in short, the whole of human development'. That was the reason for the Catholic Church's position in the gender debate: 'Creatures differ from each other and can be protected or endangered in different ways. One of these attacks results from laws or projects, which in the name of anti-discrimination, attempt to tamper with the biological basis of the difference between the sexes.'

Ratzinger saw a world without God reaching its limit. Didn't the secularized world keep complaining ever louder about a lack of ethics, morality and direction? Didn't it feel more and more sick, burdened with excessive demands, arguments, discontent? Hadn't the de-Christianizing of society led to a loss of an indispensable elixir of life? Wasn't this comparable to the genetic information that had echoed for millennia in every body cell – records that were essential for life and survival, because they contained the world's moral law, transmitted in this way from generation to generation?

Seen in the light of faith, ignorance about the order of creation was the fundamental catastrophe for humanity. The pope's great concern was that, if God was eliminated, a God who knew human beings and spoke to them, who loved them and through his love also urged them to become aware and be converted, then humanity lost the basis for a civilized existence.

Benedict's target was a way of thinking and living that was out of step with how humanity was originally conceived. Therefore the church could give the world no greater gift than to keep insisting on the priority of God. Christianity had often strayed from the right path. Nevertheless, from its conception it had had to do with culture, law, the social fabric, with the right relationship between humanity and nature. It was 'from the conviction of a Creator God' that 'the idea of human rights, the idea of the equality of all human beings before the law, awareness of the inviolability of human dignity and knowledge of people's responsibility for their own actions had developed'.[13] These traditions constituted humanity's cultural memory. Ignoring them 'or regarding then as belonging to the past would be an amputation of our culture and rob it of its wholeness'. Even the scientist Richard Dawkins, an activist for the New Atheism, who had wanted to have Benedict XVI arrested on his visit to Britain, had changed his mind about the brutalization of society. In 2019 he warned in *The Times* against eliminating Christianity. People needed God in order to behave morally and see that not everything was allowed. As author of the book *The God Delusion*, in 2015 Dawkins had demanded that children should be protected against the faith being handed on to them by their parents.

35

Desecularization

It could no longer be ignored that the image of the pope created by the media had developed into the main problem of his papacy. Benedict XVI did not allow himself to be manipulated, the communications expert Friederike Glavanovics said in an academic study, but journalists had gained the prerogative of interpreting him, and that was decisive.

Furthermore, there was no active media policy in the Vatican or professional advisers who could point out traps and gaffes in advance. Marcello Foa, lecturer in journalism at the University of Lugano and an expert in media disinformation, said: 'Vatican public relations have not understood that modern wars are fought with unconventional weapons. In particular cases they also use the right "twist", that is, the technique of manipulation through the media. The Vatican has not adopted appropriate countermeasures.' So the church was an easy target: 'It is like a city that is often bombed from the air but refuses to get itself any air defence, air force or highly sensitive radar equipment.' It had become the perfect target by making the most obvious mistakes.[1]

During John Paul II's time in office the media landscape had altered dramatically. Wojtyła had used that development to create a modern media papacy with a worldwide press presence. Most experts agreed that with Ratzinger 'the church had never had such an intellectual pope, a scholar and truth-seeker', as Glavanovics said in her dissertation on 'Pope Benedict XVI and the Power of the Media'.[2] He was probably 'one of the last world thinkers or the last one altogether'. With his substantial style, which relied on content rather than slogans and effects, during the course of his papacy Benedict spoke to people who were prepared not only to look but to listen. He relied on moments of silence and communal prayer to motivate people. At the same time, according to the American theologian George Weigel, John Paul II's biographer, for his opponents Ratzinger embodied 'the last institutional obstacle to what he himself had once called the "dictatorship of relativism". So he had made enemies and quite a few of them.' As with Wojtyła, most journalists refused to deal with his contents and ideas: 'They limited themselves to deploring and denouncing what they – falsely – regarded as a reactionary theology.'[3]

The Williamson affair had clearly damaged Benedict's image. The 'media meltdown' for him and the Catholic Church, said Glavanovics, began in the spring of 2010, when the abuse cases became known worldwide. Critical observers called the discussion about paedophile priests a typical example of 'moral panic'. However important it was to report the scandal, the 'moral panic' caused it to be hyped in a way that did not help the victims but was used for other purposes. In the first three months of the year, Glavanovics established, Germany's so-called mainstream media did not publish a single article in which Pope Benedict XVI was portrayed positively. For example, there was no mention of his initiatives as prefect which had introduced a zero-tolerance policy on abuse. When on 20 March 2010 the Vatican published his pastoral letter to the church in Ireland, which 'contained a statement about the abuse debate and an apology', *Der Spiegel* declared: 'Pope silent on abuse in Germany'.[4] Matthias Matussek, who wrote for *Der Spiegel* at that time, described the magazine's policy. After he had written a positive review of the pope's interview book *Licht der Welt* (*Light of the World*), he was cautioned by the acting editor-in-chief, who said: 'Take care, we have 13 people on the frontline seeking to prove the pope's involvement in the abuse scandal. You can't just wade in and let him off!'[5]

Basically, in the modern press world it could not be assumed 'that media would describe reality', said Glavanovics. The media's function to reduce complexity was fulfilled, 'but journalists brought their own contexts and interpretations into the news'. Journalists operated politically. In subjects where there was conflict they always reported one-sidedly and thereby used the report as a means to achieve certain aims. Journalists' interpretations of reality were 'dependent both on their own focus and world view, and on the world view and political line of the medium for which they were writing'.

According to academic research, with Pope Benedict many journalists noticeably tended to embed negative news in an even more negative context. An image had been constructed 'that is related not to reality but to viability'. It was a fictional picture to serve a particular purpose. Reporters had to deliver. And if they did not find any verifiable facts, then they resorted to accusations and rumours, which were presented as facts. Articles were twisted and shortened. They presented his concerns as confined strictly to the conduct of his office. That 'strengthened the media image of Pope Benedict XVI as conservative and backward-looking'. For example, in the Regensburg speech 'one sentence was taken out of context', and with that sentence 'Pope Benedict was stigmatized'. Glavanovics: 'In that way and also through other communication failures, Pope Benedict was "framed" in a media set-up that no longer permitted serious reporting.' The result: 'Pope Benedict's papacy, which had begun so brilliantly in 2005, increasingly developed into a "serial breakdown papacy".' Every appearance by the pope promised the media new negative headlines.'

The reporting on the pope and the church also showed a trend towards 'tabloidization', a way of presenting news 'with a striking style in both design and content that does not just seek to inform, but also specifically aims at forming' opinion. There was the 'expectation of failure', a mechanism that survived by satisfying those expectations. Journalists themselves did not now 'expect to consider what the pope had said of interest about the relation between faith and reason or on the global economy, but to look out for mistakes'. That lack of ethics had had 'a decisive influence on the media images of Pope Benedict'. Now it was often just a matter of 'exposing the pope': 'That occurs through doubting his credibility and integrity or finding possible contradictions between his speeches, actions or omissions and his publicly proclaimed attitudes and intentions.' At least since his Regensburg speech, Benedict had been framed as 'a timid, misunderstood old man fixated on marginal subjects'. The media picture had led to a construct that 'did not fit the truth'. The 'power of manipulation' had become clear.[6]

However, in the late autumn of 2011 a development occurred that did not need to be exacerbated by the media in order to be called a scandal. There was talk of corruption and money-laundering, envy and resentment, 'high treason in the Vatican'. It had not yet spread very far. Only three or four people could imagine that in the Vatican flat of a lowly employee a bomb was hidden that was waiting to be let off.

At the beginning of May 2011 the first item on the pope's programme was the beatification of John Paul II. Often beatification and canonization processes of outstanding Catholic Christians had taken decades or even centuries. Sometimes it was quicker. Little Thérèse of Lisieux had been canonized 28 years after her death, but for Francis of Assisi it was less than two years. Mother Teresa was also canonized in record time. Wojtyła had waited less than two years after her death to begin the process, in which 23 cardinals, archbishops and bishops as well as 71 advisers and six associates were involved. Canonization requires the recognition of a healing that cannot be medically explained and which can be ascribed to praying to the person who is up for canonization. During the four-year process in Mother Teresa's case the dark nights which she had suffered, like so many other saints, were no hindrance. She had written about these times in her life: 'I feel that God does not want me and that God is not God and he does not really exist.'[7]

On 13 May 2005, exactly a month after his election as pope, Benedict had announced the beginning of John Paul II's canonization process, to the joy of the Roman clergy. He set aside the usual waiting time of five years. Only six popes had been canonized in the past 700 years, and Benedict missed no opportunity to express his admiration and affection for his beloved predecessor. When the committee of cardinals recognized the validity of an appropriate miracle, all the conditions were fulfilled. The date for the celebration was set for the first Sunday after Easter, which John Paul II had introduced into the church calendar as the 'Feast of the Divine Mercy'. In his beatification sermon, on 1 May 2011, Benedict stressed that Karol Wojtyła had 'spread enthusiasm for the faith and witness among the faithful 'with gigantic power'. Personally, he added: 'His exemplary prayer always moved and edified me: He was immersed in his encounter with God even in the midst of the many obligations of his office.'

After that Benedict visited Croatia, where he quoted Cardinal Newman. In Zagreb on 4 June 2011 he said that conscience must be rediscovered as 'where we listened for the truth and the good, as where we were responsible to God and our fellow humans'. It had been a mild spring and was a joyful summer for his papacy, which culminated with 2 million young people at the World Youth Day in Madrid. But that was followed by a German autumn with a trip to his home country, which Benedict had only agreed to very reluctantly. Six years before, the World Youth Day in Cologne had been an enthusiastic occasion and his Bavarian tour in 2006 had been a radiant event under a white-blue sky. However, he had few joyful expectations of his first official visit to Germany, which was to start in Berlin. 'Actually, he did not want to go,' his secretary reported. 'Basically, he disliked Berlin and everything Prussian.' He recalled his experience in 1996 when he had accompanied John Paul II on his visit to the German capital. 'That tumult, that hatred had shaken him,' said Gänswein. 'But he had been to Bavaria and to Cologne, so then he could not turn down the official invitation.'[8]

After the Easter celebrations the pope's strength had decreased so much that his secretary had to 'reduce the frequency of audiences'. But Benedict wanted to give his all to his visit to his home country. He prepared for the trip more intensively than ever before. He sat for hours over the speeches he wanted to give, in order to leave a kind of legacy to the church in Germany. His meeting with Protestant fellow Christians represented a historically important gesture. But in the days before the journey he could not sleep. The mission lay heavy on him, 'and on his stomach', Gänswein added. 'He put so much psychic pressure on himself that he said he could not make it.'

No one could expect the pope to be as welcome in his own country as John Paul II had been in his. Benedict had read the letters that Romano Guardini had written to his friend Weiger about his time in Berlin. 'It is scary when he says that the power of Protestantism is so great there. I don't know how we will manage,' Ratzinger felt. Of course, he was aware 'that it won't be the same in Berlin as in Madrid or even in London or Edinburgh. They are not Catholic cities but the public is different there. In comparison, Berlin is chilly.'[9] Wojtyła's Poland was decisively Catholic. Faith had united the nation in resistance to the communist dictatorship. In Germany since the Reformation, Catholics had been persecuted in large parts of the country. Catholic Christians lost their civil rights under Chancellor Otto von Bismarck and had been regarded as 'hostile elements' under the Nazis. First the Jews, the saying went, then the Jews' friend.

The Holy Roman Empire of the German Nation had lasted for almost a thousand years and shaped the country. German cities sprang up, grouped around cathedrals. There had been the Carolingian minuscule script, which paved the way for the literacy in Europe. There were the first universities which pioneered the academic era, and a Jewish-Christian middle class which was a crucial influence on the culture of the continent. But the great split that tore the Latin world in half had also arisen from German soil. Marxism was founded here, which resulted in dictatorial communist regimes around the world. And here an atheist power had raged which unleashed the greatest world conflagration of all time and tried to get rid of the Jewish people from the face of the Earth by mass exterminations. That historical experience was the reason why the words 'responsibility before God' were inserted into the preamble of the constitution of the Federal Republic of Germany after 1945. Sixty years after the war and Nazi madness, a new heathen culture had long since been on course to attain cultural and political dominance. 'God is dead', announced a news magazine but that was 'no reason for dismay'.

Now most of the population in Germany were no longer baptized and, except in Poland, Italy or Spain, half of those baptized were not Catholics. The Catholic Church itself was marked by constant strife, self-secularization and a massive loss of members. Leading church positions were occupied by people who challenged the fundamentals of Catholic identity. At least since the Würzburg Synod in the 1970s and what he regarded as the undesirable post-conciliar developments, Ratzinger's relationship with Germany's Catholic establishment could be described as strained. As prefect of the Congregation for the Doctrine of the Faith, his constant conflict with fellow clergy, such as Cardinals Lehmann and Kasper, had not exactly improved matters. As pope, during the Williamson affair he had to bear the disappointment of a 'substantial stratum' of German theologians, 'who are on the lookout to be able to bash the pope'.[10]

His relationship with the current chairman of the Bishops' Conference, Robert Zollitsch, was also not untroubled. Ratzinger regarded him as opportunistic because all too often he just told politicians and media people what they wanted to hear. Ratzinger lamented that often in Germany there was 'that entrenched and highly paid Catholicism, frequently with Catholic employees who confront the church with a trade union mentality'. The 'surplus unspiritual bureaucracy', as well as 'the surplus money which then becomes too little, together with the bitterness that derives from it' was 'the greatest danger for the church in Germany'.[11]

What the welcome would be like on his first official visit to his home country became clear with a 'Memorandum' signed by 311 Catholic theologians. They wanted 'to be silent no longer', they said in the paper entitled *Ein notwendiger Aufbruch* ('A Necessary Awakening'). Of course, the initiators had never kept silence. They included professors who had signed the 'Cologne Declaration' of 1989 against John Paul II, calling him the church's gravedigger. Once again it was about removing the rule of celibacy, letting women become priests, equal treatment for same sex partnerships and participation in the appointment of bishops and priests. This time the reason given was not only the lack of priests but also the abuse scandal. The paper swarmed with terms such as 'synodal structures', 'dialogue process' and 'field of action', and spoke of 'dialogue without taboos'. At the same time it lacked typical Catholic markers such as prayer, Eucharist, humility or succession. It also lacked any reference to the bishop of Rome or the recent Year of the Priest which, against the background of abuse and betrayal, had looked for a way forward in renewal, awareness and thorough purification.

The document was looking towards Protestants in Germany. No one could say that the sister church had been particularly successful. Since 1950 it had lost more faithful every year than Catholicism, and from once being the church with the most members, it now had fewer. The 'Memorandum' not only received the agreement of the Central Committee of German Catholics. The secretary of the German Bishops' Conference, the Jesuit Hans Langendörfer, was also enthusiastic. The paper showed 'academic far-sightedness' and 'intellectual acumen'. On the other hand, a broad Catholic alliance that distanced itself from the Memorandum with a *Petition pro ecclesia* found no echo in the official church or the media, which usually reported at length even on small groups, whenever they came out with 'critical' demands.

Germany was not generally anti-pope. As soon as Benedict XVI produced a new book, it leapt to the top of the best-seller lists. In his home country he even ousted Günter Grass as number I on a list of leading intellectuals. Clearly, public opinion was different from the published opinion. Friederike Glavanovics found that 'the German press is the most critical of Pope Benedict in the whole of Europe'. She recalled the Berlin *Tagesspiel*, which had commented on the result of the 2005 conclave as follows: 'The election of Joseph Ratzinger as the new pope is backward-looking. It fails to respond to the signs of the times and, because of his age, can at best be regarded as a tactical solution.'[12] The *Süddeutsche Zeitung* had said at the time: 'But nothing, absolutely nothing, up till now suggests that this awkward old man from Germany can offer more than the dust of a thoroughly fossilized religion.'[13] Seen thus, it was no surprise that in the run-up to Benedict's state visit *Die Zeit* ran as its headline 'A Guest among Enemies'. The pope could expect 'happy' but also 'indifferent and hostile Germans'. For 'Germany is a land of protest, the domain of Martin Luther and other full-time papal critics'.[14]

As usual, *Der Spiegel* led the media onslaught. As already mentioned, the magazine had run titles such as 'The Remote One. A German Pope Disgraces the Catholic Church' and 'The Infallible One: The Failed Mission of Joseph Ratzinger'. One cover showed the pope floating rapturously towards heaven, the other showed him wearing a crooked mitre as if he had been drinking not Fanta but high-proof spirits. 'In the German-language media-negative or manipulated portrayals of Pope Benedict XVI are always used,' said Glavanovics, 'if the "old image" or a generally negative picture of him is to be conveyed.' To welcome the pope, now the *Spiegel* title gracing the kiosks was 'The Incorrigible One'. The accusing subtitle, 'Pope Causes Germans to Fall away from the Faith', was odd because the magazine itself left nothing untried, even bizarre stories, in its attempt to reduce Christianity to absurdity. Another magazine, *Chrismon*, produced by the Evangelical Church of Germany, declared in relation to the pope's visit that 'enlightened Catholics' would 'despair at the dogmatic announcements from Rome'. To be Protestant was 'better than feeling like a sheep trotting behind a chief shepherd who claims to be the only one knowing the way to go'.

The same tone continued. In Berlin the mayor, Klaus Wowereit, stated that he had great sympathy for the anti-pope demos, summoned by gay and left-wing groups. Self-styled representatives of the tolerant wing of society described Benedict supporters in broadcasts as 'Hurrah Catholics' or 'blind Catholics'. Exasperated by the continual barrage, citizens of Berlin joined together at least to produce an announcement opposing the aggressive coverage. It said: 'We welcome Benedict XVI, as head of the Catholic Church and one of the globally most important intellectuals of our time in Germany.' Benedict XVI sought 'inter-church and inter-Christian dialogue, because he wants to unite us in faith, based on the Bible, and does not see the church as a power institution'. On the other hand, Green and left-wing members of the Bundestag announced that if the pope was permitted to speak in the Bundestag, they would leave the chamber. Later the film-maker Werner Herzog, an icon of German writer–directors, praised the pope as one of the 'deepest thinkers' of modern times. No one had had 'such deep thoughts as he had in the last 300 years – no one!' It was 'contemptible that when he spoke before the Bundestag many deputies left the chamber. Simply appalling!'[15]

It was nearly a thousand years since a German pope had officially visited his home country. That was Pope Victor II in 1056. So it was all the more remarkable that the German church organizers, headed by Hans Langendörfer, initially selected a venue for the event, Charlottenburg Castle in Berlin, which could only hold 20,000 people. Finally it was decided in Rome to rent the Olympic Stadium for the opening Mass, which had space for at least 70,000. Despite the 6,000 police officers who had been called in from several regions to protect him, Benedict wanted to dispense with the journey through the city that was customary on other trips. Ratzinger had become the head of a church of 1.2 billion Catholics worldwide, but on his flight to Germany on 22 September 2011 he confessed to the journalists on board that he had 'been born in Germany: the root can't be cut off and should not be cut off'. He had received his cultural formation in Germany: 'My language is German, and language is the way the mind lives and works.'[16] He was not amused when, immediately upon his arrival, the German federal president Christian Wulff confronted him with a long list of demands, which sprang recognizably from Wulff's own sensitivities as a recently divorced and newly married man. Benedict turned things round with his speech in the German Bundestag. Some deputies had left the chamber, as they had said they would. All the rest applauded enthusiastically and spoke of a great moment in the history of the German parliament.

Benedict's speech was wholly in the spirit of his twenty-first-century humanism and his doctrine of human ecology. First he spoke of the foundations of a liberal constitutional state. He stressed that success at the polls should not be the ultimate standard for a politician's work. A politician had to focus on justice, the will to do right, and understanding what was right. Germans had experienced what happened if power became separated from what was right. At a time like this, when humanity had gained previously unimaginable power to destroy the world, to manipulate itself, 'make human beings' and exclude people from being human, the task of serving what was right and combatting the domination of what was wrong was particularly urgent. King Solomon's prayer for 'a hearing heart' to distinguish good from evil remained the decisive question for politics today. A positivist and purely functional concept of nature, which was becoming more and more prevalent, could not build bridges to ethics and what was right but only give functional answers. The same went for reason, if it was understood in an exclusively positivist and therefore 'largely a purely scientific' way. That led to ethics and religion being relegated to the subjective realm and dropping out of the area of 'reason in the strict sense of the word'. But when positivist reason was regarded as the only satisfactory culture, and all other cultural realities were pushed into becoming subcultures, 'then it belittles humanity, indeed it threatens humankind'.

The importance of ecology was undisputed, the pope continued:

> We must listen to the voice of nature and answer accordingly. But I'd like to stress a point that it seems to me is generally omitted: there is also a human ecology. Humans also have a nature, which we must respect and cannot manipulate at will. Human beings are not just free self-making subjects. We do not make ourselves. We are spirit and will, but also nature and our will is right when we respect that nature, listen and accept it as what we are, which we have not made ourselves. That is the only way in which true human freedom can be achieved.[17]

The Greens were pleased with the pope's words when he described 'the appearance of the ecological movement in German politics since the 1970s' as 'a cry for fresh air which must not remain unheard'. In the end Benedict himself found it 'very moving how intense the atmosphere in the Bundestag was during my speech. There was such concentrated attention that you could have heard a pin drop.' He said in retrospect that his rather cool reception by Wulff and others had 'not surprised or dismayed me'. But it meant he had been all the more delighted by the standing ovation he received from the parliamentarians: 'You realized it wasn't just politeness but real listening.'[18]

Benedict's visit to Erfurt was tensely awaited. The region had once been a stronghold of Protestantism, but now Evangelicals in the population had sunk to under 14 per cent. For the Vatican the main thrust of inter-denominational dialogue had been with the Orthodox churches. They had less and less hope from conversation with the Lutherans. In the view of many Curia bishops some Protestant churches kept moving further away from what they had in common with Catholics in the traditional faith. The pope himself said that in the ecumenical process he was 'difficult to disappoint, because I simply know the reality and what we can actually expect or not. I mean, the situation between us and the Protestants and us and the Orthodox is very different.' With the Protestants 'the great problem was their own internal lack of unity'. There were 'forces which are very close to us and others which are very far from us'.[19]

Before the pope's visit Evangelical church officials had raised the expectation of a 'gift' that the pope would bring with him to Germany. They hinted at a request for 'intercommunion'. But the 'gift' did not come. From the Catholic viewpoint the obstacle to celebrating the Eucharist in common was a different understanding of the priesthood, the sacraments and especially Holy Communion. For the Vatican it was already a gesture that with Benedict XVI, for the first time in history, the head of the Catholic Church visited Martin Luther's spiritual home town. So there was astonishment that just the chapter room of the former Augustinian monastery was booked for Benedict's meeting and his speech would not be broadcast outside. When he spoke about Luther and praised his search for God, only the handpicked Protestant officials could hear him, and they looked disappointed because they felt robbed of their hoped-for 'gift'.

Benedict flew on by helicopter to the remote East German Marian pilgrimage site of Eichsfeld, where 90,000 pilgrims had arrived for

Marian vespers. In his speech he thanked them warmly for their faithfulness to the church. Ratzinger was hoping for a positive impact from his state and pastoral visit's farewell event, which took place in Freiburg. In fact, his Freiburg concert hall speech was counted as one of the greatest of his papacy. It set out the programme for a renewed church.

At the Mass at Freiburg airport with 100,000 faithful, first Benedict had thanked the countless 'full-time and part-time' workers without whom life in the parishes and the church would be 'quite unthinkable'. Through 'many social and charitable bodies' Christian love of neighbour was practised in 'a socially effective form to the ends of the Earth'. Regardless of sensitivities, he addressed spiritual deficiencies. 'Agnostics who are preoccupied with the God question' were today often 'nearer to the kingdom of God than routine churchgoers', who 'only see the apparatus without their hearts [...] being touched by the faith'.[20] This was the message of a deeply humanistic visionary. Christian life meant 'existing for others, humble dedication to fellow human beings and the common good'. Of course, humility was a virtue that had never been highly regarded by the world, 'but the Lord's disciples know that this virtue is the oil that makes conversation fruitful, co-operation possible and unity warm-hearted. *Humilitas*, the Latin word for humility, is related to humus, being down to Earth.'

In his speech in the Freiburg concert hall Pope Benedict threw out the question 'Shouldn't the church change?' There had been 'a decline in religious practice for decades. We see many baptized Christians distancing themselves from church life.' So shouldn't the church 'adapt its ministry and structures to the present, in order to reach the searching and doubting people of today'? The pope answered with a quotation from the Blessed Mother Teresa. She had answered a journalist who asked her what, in her opinion, was the first thing that should change in the church: 'You and me!' That small episode made two things clear: 'First, she wants to tell her interviewer that church is not just other people, not only hierarchy, pope and bishops. We are all church, we who are baptized. Second, she is saying yes, there is a reason to change. There is a need for change. All Christians and the community of the faithful are called to constant change.'

Then he went on to the subject that had concerned him since his time as a curate in the Munich district of Bogenhausen, for which he then coined the term 'desecularization' (*Entweltlichung*). Indeed, a church becoming more like Christ necessarily had 'to differ sharply from the world around it', he quoted from Pope Paul VI. It had to 'distance itself', we could say 'desecularize itself'. Jesus became human 'not just to confirm the world in its worldliness and be its companion' and then leave it as it was. No, a church that 'settles in this world, is self-satisfied and conforms to the world's standards' contravened its founder's mission, 'to be an instrument of salvation, imbued with God's word' and thus 'be not of the world'. The pope expressly made clear that necessary 'desecularization' also included the church's charitable works and its 'organization and institution'. For 'a church freed from material and political burdens and privileges can devote itself to the whole world better and in a truly Christian way. [...] It opens itself to the world, not in order to win people for an institution with its own claims to power, but to bring them to themselves.'

Benedict spoke with increasing urgency, and he had not finished yet. It was an illusion to think that if Christians behaved well enough they could become accepted in secular society:

> For people of every era and not just our own, Christian faith is always a scandal. That the eternal God should care about us and know us, that the intangible should become tangible at a particular time and place, that he who is immortal should have suffered on the cross and died, that resurrection and eternal life are promised to us mortals – believing that is a lot to expect of anyone.

The scandal 'cannot be eliminated without eliminating Christianity itself'. However, in a way the church's history could be a help, precisely in times of secularization, which contributed significantly to its purification and reform: 'Whenever societies became secularized – expropriating church goods, removing its privileges or the like – each time this led to a profound desecularization of the church; it both lost its worldly wealth and accepted its worldly poverty again.' So the point was

> not to find a new tactic to make the church relevant again. It is a matter of dropping the purely tactical and seeking total integrity, which does not exclude or repress anything about the truth of

today, but brings the faith completely into today's world. [...] It must bring the faith fully to itself by stripping it of what is merely apparent faith but in truth is just convention and custom.

The Freiburg speech was a wake-up call. Benedict himself even said it was 'revolutionary', as he put it in our conversation. But soon the pope realized that his urgency was largely ignored. Many of his audience interpreted his demand for 'desecularization' as meaning the church should stick to its own world and give up on social service to society, which of course was nonsense. Even Ratzinger's opponents must have been amazed at that idea. Actually, the pope was not talking about turning away from people, but about turning away from power, from Mammon, from collusion, from false appearances, from fraud and self-deception. By turning away from the world he meant returning to souls and safeguarding humanity's spiritual resources. His idea of 'desecularization' had nothing to do with withdrawing from social and political commitment or giving up on Christian charity. For him, what mattered was being resistant, uncomfortable, not adapting, showing that Christian faith reached far beyond everything to do with a purely worldly, materialistic world view. Christian faith included the mystery of eternal life.

In retrospect, Benedict said that naturally it was clear to him that the proposal he made on his German visit would not 'really be supported by entrenched Catholicism'. But he had still hoped that his pastoral visit would 'silently have an effect in its own way; that it awakens silent forces, inspires and encourages them to emerge'. It remained a pious wish. Eight years later, after the unsuccessful 'dialogue process', the German Catholic Church establishment set out on a 'synodal course', from which Pope Benedict's signposting was completely absent. The main points of the programme did not even include the task of new evangelization, which Benedict XVI and John Paul II had called a basic requirement for the renewal of the Christian faith.

36

The Betrayal

In the dining room the pope's valet, Paolo Gabriele, brought him and his two secretaries soup, main course and pudding as usual. There was not any particular ceremony. Not even the crockery had anything particularly elegant or courtly about it. The four Memores (members of the Memores Domini lay organization) ate in the kitchen. Paolo sometimes sat down at table with the Holy Father, but the mood in the papal household had changed. Since the indiscretions from the Apostolic Palace had burst like grenades, it was clear: one of them was a traitor.

The leak had begun to drip in the autumn of 2011, and that was just the beginning. The revelations appeared in various Italian newspapers, sometimes on successive days. They included letters, faxes, conversation notes and internal documents, which contained accusations of corruption, mismanagement and cronyism. Or an internal Vatican memorandum for a meeting of the pope with the Italian president, Giorgio Napolitano. There was even a confidential note in which Benedict XVI remarked after Federal Chancellor Angel Merkel's rude criticism in the Williamson affair: 'The nuncio's reaction to Frau Merkel's statements is too weak. Strong words of protest were necessary.'

None of the documents came from Benedict's own desk; they came from his secretary's. The media spoke of '*il corvo*', a thieving raven. There had also been a raven in the life of St Benedict of Nursia, one that had saved the man of God from poison attacks when it made the poisonous bread disappear. According to the tradition, jealous priests and monks had tried to get the saint out of the way. It was said that Benedict suffered more for his opponents who pursued him than 'for himself'. He even gave a penance to a young brother because he had dared 'to rejoice over the enemy's fall'.[1]

The question was how many more of the partly compromising revelations would still become public. Who was behind the campaign? And above all, what was their aim? Up till then no one had succeeded in decisively destabilizing Benedict's papacy. Now a weapon had emerged that was more toxic than any other: the poison of suspicion and insecurity. Who could still be trusted? Wasn't everyone in the pope's household under suspicion, because they all had access to the pope's study? And who were the attacks aimed at? Was it Cardinal Secretary of State Bertone, whom the pope had always supported, even when he was criticized for the way he was doing his job? Or could it be secretary Gänswein, whom many accused of being high-handed and arrogant? Or could the leaks, which the Vatican spokesman Lombardi had carelessly named 'Vatileaks', be aimed at the pope himself? Were they to show that the 85-year-old was no longer master of his own household? A household that obviously raised serious concerns? The *Vaticanista* Marco Politi, a critic of Ratzinger's, spoke out. The media had been completely wrong about the 'Rottweiler' or 'Panzer Cardinal', he now said. Rather, the man should be seen as 'an amiable scholar', a white-haired pope who sat alone and powerless at his desk to devote himself to his passion for writing.

That year Politi sat at his computer writing a book with the title *Joseph Ratzinger: crisi di un papato* (*Joseph Ratzinger: Crisis of a Papacy*).[2] The blurb on the cover read: 'Since Joseph Ratzinger was elected pope, there have been more crises than almost ever before in the history of the Catholic Church.' Historians might shake their heads in amazement. Politi added that Benedict was 'a great intellectual but unfit for the office of pope'. The pope was not a giant, but he was heavy enough to tread hard on some people's toes. He followed a determined course and that irked people. Benedict himself said to his household: 'We are a small team. If we distrust one another, we can't live together.' There had been a traitor among the Lord's companions, so that was 'nothing new. But of course, it is very, very painful.'[3]

After his visit to Germany the pope travelled to Benin on a three-day visit for the publication of the Final Document of the Africa

Synod. With its stable democratic structures he praised Benin as 'a religious and political model' for Africa. A month before that, on 27 October, he had invited the leaders of other Christian churches and religions to Assisi. Exactly 25 years after the first meeting organized by Pope John Paul II, he had modified the approach for this meeting, which was intended as a day of reflection, dialogue and prayer for peace. This time there would be no misleading religious or para-religious gestures. Three hundred representatives of 12 religions from more than 50 countries had enrolled. The Buddhists were the largest group of non-Christians, with 67 representatives. From Asia came 17 Shintoists, 5 Hindus, 5 Sikhs, 3 Taoists, 3 Jainists, 3 Confucians as well as 1 Zoroastrian and 1 member of the Bahai religion. Fifty representatives came from Islam. Delegations from the Israeli Chief Rabbinate and the International Committee on Inter-Religious Consultation came as representatives of Judaism. The traditional religions of Africa, America and India sent four delegates. The so-called new religions of Japan sent 13. For the first time atheists took part in the meeting, including the former chairman of the Austrian Communist Party.

The trip to Mexico and Cuba was set for March, which was to be a decisive turning point. 'Dear Josef,' Benedict wrote to his former fellow student Josef Strehhuber before it, 'my mobility has recently decreased a lot. I can only try to carry on doing my duty with my feebler powers.' Of the Latin American trip he said: 'The people's joy will doubtless outweigh the trouble it costs.'[4] But that was only half the truth. In fact, he was afraid of this new exertion, afraid of no longer being able to cope with such a huge, exhausting workload. On the other hand, it was an opportunity to escape the upset of Vatileaks, at least for a few days.

Secret betrayal was not invented by the Vatican. Since countless whistle-blowers had started anonymously uploading quantities of internal information from banks, secret conferences and classified government documents onto the Wikileaks website, breach of confidence had almost become a popular sport. For example, even secret US government documents about the conduct of the war in Afghanistan were published. They were called 'Obamaleaks'. Vatileaks began with the publication of documents about the private life of the journalist Dino Boffo, the editor-in-chief of the church newspaper *Avvenire* and the Catholic broadcasting network TV2000. This was followed by Cardinal Paolo Sardi's letter to Benedict XVI, listing various problems in the Curia. As a next step, on 25 January 2012 the investigative journalist Gianluigi Nuzzi held two documents in front of the camera on the Italian television channel La7, which showed confidential letters to the pope from the year 2011. The sender, Archbishop Carlo Maria Viganò, former general secretary of the governorate, the government of the Vatican state, complained of 'countless practices of corruption and abuse of office'. Investments had been put into the hands of bankers to serve personal interests. This had resulted, he said, in a deficit of nearly 8 million euros.

Internal documents from a pope's desk had never been published before, and certainly not documents like these. On 27 January 2012, two days after Nuzzi's television broadcast, the newspaper *Il Fatto Quotidiano* also published Viganò's confidential letters. On 8 February readers of the communist newspaper *L'Unità* saw letters accusing the Vatican Bank IOR of money-laundering. On 10 February *Il Fatto Quotidiano* returned to the fray. It published a document written in German, dated 30 December 2011. It quoted the bishop of Palermo, Cardinal Paolo Romeo, as saying the pope would not survive the next 12 months. The archbishop of Milan, Cardinal Angelo Scola, would succeed him. Romeo denied it categorically. The words, which he was supposed to have said on his trip to China in November 2011, were entirely fictitious. But the rumour remained. At the end of June the *Frankfurter Allgemeine Zeitung* reported that the pope was the 'victim of an intrigue' because he had declared war on the clerical cover-up. Even his life was threatened.

Vatileaks had reached its first climax in January 2012, when Nuzzi not only presented letters on television but also the principal witness, albeit incognito, with face covered and disguised voice. It was said that Nuzzi had good contacts with the Italian secret service. He worked for newspapers in Berlusconi's stable. He presented his own television programme and had already been acclaimed for his 2009 best-seller, which also contained Vatican stories. He described his anonymous witness, code-named 'Maria' – allegedly a man from the Vatican inner circle – as a member of a group of about 20 people who aimed for more transparency in the

Vatican. The broadcast was a sort of preview for the next blow that Nuzzi was preparing. But not yet.

In the middle of March 2012 *L'Osservatore Romano* announced that the pope had set up comprehensive inquires into the thefts. The police and state prosecution service were searching exhaustively for the source of the leaks. At the same time Benedict set out on his journey to Mexico and Cuba. On his six-day tour from 23 to 29 March he particularly wanted to encourage people. 'Be on the side of those who are excluded by force, power or wealth that ignores people who lack nearly everything,' he urged the bishops of Mexico and Latin America at a Vespers service on 25 March in León de los Aldamas, in central Mexico. 'The church cannot separate praising God from serving humanity.' He avoided a detour to the shrine of Our Lady of Guadalupe, who meant so much to the whole of Latin America. He was begged not to ignore the greatest Catholic pilgrimage site in the world, to which John Paul II had made his first visit abroad. But Benedict told them that his doctor had insistently advised against it. The site's high altitude of 2,000 metres made it an undertaking he had to avoid for his health's sake.

On 26 March he greeted the Cuban head of state, Raúl Castro, in Havana. Before the visit, at the pope's request, 2,900 prisoners had been set free. The climax of Pope Benedict's stay in Cuba was the celebration of Mass on the Plaza de la Revolución, attended by 300,000 people. Benedict demanded freedom of religion and declared that with Jesus' message the church preached reconciliation and peace. After that a meeting took place in the nuncio's residence with the sick Fidel Castro, who had abdicated. Contrary to often repeated reports, the *comandante* had never been excommunicated. A comrade said of him: 'Fidel is a revolutionary first, a Jesuit second and only then a Marxist.'

The pope's Latin American tour had added to the strain on his health. After his return his doctor, the cardiologist Patrizio Polisca, diagnosed a state of chronic exhaustion. In view of his advanced age and the huge demands of his office, that would hardly improve. Meanwhile, Vatileaks had blown up further. In Berlin the *Tageszeitung* speculated that it was 'an attempt from outside further to destabilize a church government seen as collapsing'. In Italy a prelate did not exclude the possibility that the source of the leaks might be a bribed member of the Curia: 'Given our education and responsibilities, we are decidedly underpaid. And Rome is expensive.'

As a precaution, the pope was advised not to discuss any internal Vatican matters in telephone conversations with his brother Georg. He might be overheard. As a further measure a committee of investigation was to be set up that was independent of the secretariat of state and was to report directly to the pope, not to Bertone. Benedict agreed that was a good idea, and on 31 March 2012, two days after his return from Latin America, he assembled a group consisting of the Spanish cardinal Julián Herranz, the Slovakian cardinal Jozef Tomko and the Italian cardinal Salvatore de Giorgi. These three were supported by the Vatican interior minister, Archbishop Giovanni Angelo Becciu. Given their rank, the trio could also interrogate cardinals, who were only obliged to answer to fellow cardinals. As all three of them were over 80, they were not *papabile* at a conclave and therefore could not be influenced by personal ambition.

Naturally, the betrayal in his immediate surroundings, the devious machinations, the harassment among people who had dedicated themselves to Christ shocked the pope. But they did not really surprise him. He knew his church history and was therefore aware that the centre of Christianity had always been exposed to particular assaults. It was a naïve idea that an institution concerned with holiness would be completely holy. Hadn't the trigger for the Reformation been the corruption of the Roman Curia? 'Corruption in the truest sense of the word, both spiritual and sensual', as Wladimir d'Ormesson, the French writer and diplomat, put it: the resulting 'loss of the pope's reputation' had led Luther, Zwingli, Calvin and their students 'to hate Rome', he said. So they renounced their obedience to the chief magisterium of the church and created the doctrine of justification through faith alone and the principle of Scripture alone, which caused a split in the church.[5]

On the other hand, wasn't it in accordance with the inner logic of the purification process, which Benedict had prescribed, that now so much dirt was coming to light? Cleaning raised dust and dirt. There was no renewal without clearing away what had become fruitless. It might sound like a paradox, but the bad also had its goodness. It raised the basic question: what was false and what was right? What was a lie and what was truth? Benedict suffered with the traitors, who sat like fallen angels in the prison of their bad consciences. But he also felt that many things had to take place so that what had to happen could happen. 'I don't know what will be imposed on me,' he said to the assembled Curia on 16 April 2012, his 85th birthday, 'but I know that God's light is there. And that allows me to carry on with assurance.'

Gianluigi Nuzzi was enough of a professional to know how to make a scoop become a sales success. On 18 May 2012 the *Corriere della Sera* published an advance extract from his whistle-blowing book. A week later the work was in the bookshops. Its title was: *Sua Santità: le carte segrete di Benedetto XVI* (*His Holiness: The Secret Letters of Benedict XVI*).[6] In his introduction Nuzzi stressed that, thanks to Benedict XVI's secret documents, now anyone could 'have a look at the difficult situation the church is in day after day'. The pope himself was a light in this dark wood and a shepherd who 'knew the neuralgic points of daily life in detail and positively tries to bring about changes'. Benedict demanded 'a constant *aggiornamento*, a reform of all the things that burden the church'. His informant, said Nuzzi, the 'brave man with the code name "Maria", had been driven by love of the church'. By betraying secrets he wanted to free himself 'from the unbearable feeling of complicity with all those who keep silence, although they are in the know'. Hypocrisy reigned in the Vatican. 'Maria', Nuzzi repeated from his January TV broadcast, belonged to a Vatican 'group of people who document what is wrong and want to act'. They were frustrated 'by the prevalence of unlawful infringements, personal interests and suppressed truths'. By their indiscretions they hoped to 'speed up Benedict XVI's reforms'. They were all honest, 'good Catholics'.[7]

Sua Santità contained 25 confidential documents printed in facsimile. In his text Nuzzi wrote about relationship networks, ambition, secret agents and interference in Italy's affairs. 'There are no big secrets,' the writer Christian Feldmann summed up: 'there are a couple of dilettantish attempts at bribery, a television journalist sends 10,000 euros "for the pope's charitable work" and asks discreetly for a private audience for his family [...] a Piedmont businessman wants to give Benedict an expensive truffle tuber, because he is so enthusiastic about the pope's plea to preserve the creation (it was accepted and the delicacy was passed on to the

Caritas soup kitchen for the homeless).' There were also 'tedious thank-you letters, self-regarding complaints, the nagging and the back and forth of portentous comments, that are familiar from any office'.[8] The *Süddeutsche Zeitung* correspondent Andrea Bachstein remarked unexcitedly: 'The occurrences were mostly known about.' What many were calling 'explosive interference' could 'been seen as a normal affair'. Even the whistle-blower Gianluigi Nuzzi admitted that what was special about the documents printed in his book was simply that 'we have here unpublished documents of a pope who is still in office'.

In comparison with the news to be read week by week in the economic section of any daily newspaper, the documents in the book describing mismanagement and fraudulent bank transfers were distinctly modest in scope. What was shocking about the Vatileaks were the cockfights and the mechanisms of a system in which personal connections often counted for more than professional competence. The very language used struck the modern reader like scenes from a historical play. For example, a letter often spoke of 'sincere feelings of the deepest admiration' and was signed 'Your Holiness's most devoted son'. Or someone claimed in a letter to a cardinal to be 'afflicted above all by having to bother you, when I know how many worries you have to cope with every day. God knows, how much I wish that I could rid myself of the troubles I am suffering from.'

The criticisms of Archbishop Viganò, whom Benedict XVI had personally appointed to bring the Vatican finances into order, included the fact that the same firm was always appointed to do the work, at fantastically high prices. Viganò had swept up ruthlessly. However, in March 2011 he was informed by Cardinal Secretary of State Bertone that he had been appointed as apostolic nuncio in the United States. Viganò was convinced he was the victim of a plot. He implored the pope personally: 'Holy Father, my removal from the administration would cause deep insecurity and depression [...] among those who believed we could get rid of countless practices or corruption and abuse of office.' But in vain. In November 2011 Archbishop Viganò had to leave on his journey across the Atlantic.

In our conversation Benedict XVI rejected the accusation that Viganò's transfer was a punishment. 'The matter is very complicated,' he said. 'Viganò was the second man in the governorate. Well, he stirred things up mightily. In part, but only in part, rightly so.' As supreme head, Benedict himself had discussed the matter with Cardinal Lajolo, the leader of the governorate.

> He told me Viganò was certainly right about a lot of things, but had simply created a climate of general suspicion of all against all. They would try to sort things out, but Viganò could not stay. When our nuncio in the USA died suddenly, one of the most important posts, of high rank and real importance, we said: this is the moment, now he can leave here and begin anew out there. It was clear that he was honest and capable. So that was a sign from Providence for me. It was not a punishment, absolutely not, for at that moment he could not have been given a higher position.[9]

The publication of *Sua Santità* meant big sales for Nuzzi, but the end for his top informant, the 'raven'. As one of the readers who studied the book line by line, Georg Gänswein had found an enlightening passage. Immediately afterwards he told Pope Benedict that his impression was 'that one of us is pretending to be this person under cover. It's either me myself or it is my colleague, or it is the valet, or one of the Memores or Sister Birgit.' The facsimile of the 30 November 2011 annual balance sheet of the 'Joseph Ratzinger Foundation – Benedict XVI' put him on the right track. Without passing through anywhere else in the Vatican it led directly to the papal apartment. That meant only the pope and his secretary – or someone with access to their rooms – could have set eyes on it.

On that same Thursday morning Gänswein called the household together. He was holding some originals of the documents printed in Nuzzi's book. He spoke straight to the valet, Paolo Gabriele: 'Dear Paolo, I have a strong suspicion that these two papers, which were published in that book, came from your desk. Because only you and I knew about them. It wasn't me. So that just leaves you.' Because Gabriele vehemently denied the accusation, Gänswein told the Holy Father at lunch that he had sent him home: 'It is better, because I don't trust him any more.'

Paolo Gabriele, the father of three children, had begun his career in one of the crews that polished the marble floors of St Peter's to a high gloss. Since 2006 he had worked as His Holiness's personal attendant in the papal apartment, even though his predecessor, Angelo Gugel, found Gabriele, then aged 40, too inexperienced and would not recommend him. The position of absolute trust so close to the pope, said Gugel, required a mature character. However, Archbishop Paolo Sardi from the secretariat of state commended Gabriele to Archbishop James Harvey, the prefect of the papal household. When Gugel retired, Harvey then recommended Gabriele to Gänswein: 'I thought he was a smart, loyal and unambitious man, which is what Harvey had told me.' Gabriele was allocated a beautiful flat in a house behind St Anne's Church for himself and his family. Ingrid Stampa lived two floors below and often visited him. Paolo helped the pope get dressed, he served lunch, took care of the gifts during audiences and prepared Benedict's bedroom for when he went to bed. He packed the luggage for journeys and accompanied the pope to the most distant countries. Everyone thought the reserved valet was perhaps a bit simple but also absolutely loyal. The pope himself had 'loved Paolo like a son', said Cardinal Secretary of State Bertone.

The noose round the thief in the Apostolic Palace was still not tight. In his general audience on Wednesday, Benedict continued his reflections on the prayer of St Paul. He recalled that the apostle had often suffered severely, but never became discouraged. Then for the first time he spoke about the Vatileaks revelations: 'The events that have occurred recently concerning the Curia and my colleagues have filled my heart with sadness,' he said. However, the reports in many of the media were often exaggerated. They went 'far beyond the facts' and did not correspond 'to the reality'. 'So I'd like to express my trust and encouragement to my closest colleagues and all those who help me day by day faithfully, silently and in a spirit of sacrifice, to carry out my task.'[10]

According to the statements of the four police who searched Gabriele's flat on 24 May from 3 p.m. to 11 p.m., a shocking picture emerged. For years, like an expert raven, Gabriele, now aged 46, had snatched whatever came under his fingers. Heaps of material thrown together anyhow contained thousands of documents from the papal palace (many had the word 'Destroy! handwritten in German on them). Gabriele had hoarded not only papers but also a gold nugget from Peru, which had been given to the pope by a family in an audience. There was cheque for 100,000 euros from the University of San Antonio in Guadalupe and a precious edition of a translation of the *Aeneid* dated 1581.

In the end the police hauled 82 boxes of material from the flat. Letters from politicians, correspondence between the pope and cardinals, documents on freemasonry, various lodges and secret services. There were also researches into how .jpg and Word data could be concealed, or how to use a mobile phone secretly, two hard disks, various memory chips, a Playstation, an iPad, two leather suitcases and two yellow plastic bags full of more letters. Gabriele was arrested on the spot and locked up in a police station cell, four days after *Sua Santità* went on sale. The strange thing was that he had not used the two days since his exposure by the pope's secretary to find a safe place for his booty – almost as if he was waiting to be arrested, as though it would be a relief.

Georg Gänswein felt guilty of neglect of his duty and begged to be replaced: 'Holy Father, I am responsible for the appointment of this person. I am formally his line manager. I ask you to give me a different job.' Benedict's answer was short and conclusive: 'There is no question of that.'[11]

Actually, the head of the IOR Vatican Bank, Ettore Gotti Tedeschi, had lost his job on the same day. The supervisory board had unanimously withdrawn its confidence in him. In the record of his dismissal that was passed to the press, it said that he had failed to fulfil the most important tasks, had spread false information in 'a careless way', created division among the staff and behaved 'bizarrely'.[12] However after detailed inquiries, a short time later the Council of Europe gave the IOR a good interim report. According to Moneyval, the Council of Europe Committee to Combat Money-Laundering, the Holy See had 'achieved much in a very short time'. In many categories the Vatican Bank had performed better than many EU countries. The case remained suspect. In the IOR Tedeschi stood against the board and the general director, Paolo Cipriani. Clearly he had also made an enemy of secretary of state Bertone, who never forgave him for co-operating with the state authorities in the money-laundering scandal. A year later, on 7 February 2013, Benedict XVI again expressed his trust in Tedeschi but did not think it advisable to cancel his dismissal. He replaced Tedeschi with the

German financial adviser and lawyer Ernst von Freyberg, with the specific task of cleaning up the Vatican Bank more thoroughly and making it transparent.

The public prosecution service began Gabriele's interrogation on the morning after his arrest, Friday, 25 May 2012. 'It was important to me that the independence of the judiciary should also be maintained in the Vatican,' the pope said in our conversation, 'that the head of state should not take it in hand himself, but that in a state governed by the rule of law the judiciary should go its own way. Afterwards the head of state can exercise clemency but that is something else.'

There were plenty of questions to be answered to bring light into the darkness. Gabriele himself had set up the contact with Nuzzi. But had he really given a copy of the documents to former Cardinal Secretary of State Sodano, even before he passed them to the journalist?[13] Who were the members of the 'Maria' group, whom Nuzzi had spoken of both in his television broadcast and his book? And whom were the revelations intended to serve? Or was something completely different behind the scandal?

Shortly after Gabriele's exposure, the months-long campaign suddenly turned to blackmailing Georg Gänswein. On 2 and 3 June 2012 *La Repubblica* presented three more documents alleged to come from the Vatican. The texts were blacked out. Only the letter-heading and the signature Georg Gänswein were legible. *La Repubblica* said that an anonymous informant was threatening further revelations unless the pope quickly got rid of his 'incompetent colleagues'. According to Gänswein, the alleged 'proof documents' were 'pure inventions'. The attack was 'relatively quickly quelled. Nothing came of it.'

In the Vatican, Paolo Gabriele was known as a sociable man. On his way home from work he would pause here and there for a chat. Many people thought he was seeking reassurance but was also reserved. Yet a completely different person lay under the mask of the timid man who always observed the forms. 'He was obsessed with secret services and suchlike things,' said Gänswein. The investigation established that he had copied secret documents just a few weeks after his appointment. The question was whether his mania had become compulsive behaviour or whether there were people round him who directly or indirectly encouraged his actions. After his arrest the first person he contacted was Ingrid Stampa, who at that time was in Germany.

In the middle of August, on the pope's express instructions, the Vatican spokesman Lombardi released the 35-page indictment of Gabriele to the hundreds of journalists in the Vatican press office. According to the indictment, Gabriele had said that, as an 'agent of the Holy Spirit' in solidarity with the pope, he had wanted to reveal cases of corruption and other evils. A psychological report commissioned by the examining magistrate on the defendant's soundness of mind attested that he was easily influenced and 'displayed simple intelligence and a fragile personality with a propensity to paranoia'. 'Obsessive behaviour in thought and action (pedantry, tenacity), guilt feelings and megalomania' were also observable, 'together with the wish to act in accordance with a personal ideal of justice'.[14]

The trial in the Vatican City tribunal began on 29 September. The president was Giuseppe dalla Torre. Gabriele was accused of grand theft, not of treason. He faced up to six years' imprisonment. Claudio Sciarpelletti, a computer scientist from the papal secretariat of state, was also accused of assisting with the theft. He faced a year's imprisonment because he had kept a document-filled envelope addressed to Gabriele in his office desk drawer. On application by the defence, that case was dealt with separately. Gabriele stated before the court that he himself had given Sciarpelletti the envelope, so that he would be updated on the state of things around the pope.

Usually, the Vatican City tribunal dealt with smaller offences such as pickpocketing. There had never been a trial there like this one. Gabriele took his seat in the dock, immaculately dressed in a white shirt and grey suit. The courtroom had just 18 public seats. To observe the trial eight seats were awarded by lot to journalists from the press and two Radio Vatican representatives. Gabriele pleaded guilty. He had acted to avert damage to the pope and the church. He had been convinced that 'the pope was being manipulated'. At table he had occasionally asked questions about subjects on which he actually should have been informed. This had worried and disturbed him. At first he had only copied the documents for himself, to get a clearer picture. It was only later that he got the idea of going further. Then he had made two copies of each paper, one for himself and one for the public. At first he had given his copies to a confessor, 'Father Giovanni'. (The clergyman called 'Witness B' in the indictment placed on record that he had burned the photocopies in an A4 folder with the papal arms on it, given to him by Gabriele.) Gabriele had exchanged information with 'an enormous number' of people. However, he would not call them 'accomplices'. He had only spoken with them about the 'general atmosphere'. While he was being investigated, he had already mentioned a good many names of those who had 'influenced' him: for example, Cardinal Paolo Sardi, Cardinal Angelo Comastri, Bishop Francesco Carina and Professor Ingrid Stampa. 'I do not feel guilty of grand theft,' Gabriele pleaded, 'but I do feel guilty of having abused the trust that the Holy Father placed in me.'

The defence and prosecution followed the statement by the sole defendant. After the sessions the trial ended on 6 October. Gabriele was sentenced to 18 months' imprisonment for theft. On 25 October 2012 he began his sentence in the Vatican prison. On 22 December Pope Benedict visited him, forgave him and quashed the rest of his sentence. Gabriele was released on the same day and returned to his family. 'He was appalled at himself,' the pope reported about his meeting with his former valet: 'I can't analyse his personality. It is a remarkable mixture, what people have made of him or what he has made of himself. He has realized that it should not have happened and that he was simply on the wrong road.'[15]

Although Gabriele had spoken of people he had contacted, none of those named was summoned for questioning – not even Nuzzi, the journalist who revealed the story. Vatican insiders doubted that Gabriele had not received any money to improve on his monthly salary of 1,500 to 1,800 euros. A good two months before the beginning of the trial Paul Badde, the Italy and Vatican correspondent of *Die Welt*, had issued a possible explanation of the background to the Vatileaks affair. His article appeared on 15 July only in the online edition of the paper. Badde had good contacts in the Vatican and knew the set-up through careful research. The article only attracted notice when Marco Ansaldo, the correspondent of the left-liberal *La Repubblica* in Turkey, found *Die Welt*'s story on the internet and filled two double sides with it in the 23 July edition of *La Repubblica*. The subject then took on a new aspect, which led to international headlines.

Both the *Welt* and the *Repubblica* journalists had come to the conclusion that there had been 'whisperers' who had acted from raging jealousy. They mentioned Ingrid Stampa, Josef Clemens and Paolo Sardi by name. Their contacts had been found on Gabriele's mobile phone. Stampa had not only lived in the same house as Gabriele but had also often been a guest in his flat. 'No one in the Vatican was as close to the master thief as she was.' She had found like-minded friends: the Curia bishop Clemens, Ratzinger's former secretary, 'harboured an irrational hatred of his successor', and Paolo Sardi from the secretariat of state was a long-term acquaintance of hers. It was 'not too much to assert', Badde concluded, 'that these three persons – in varying degrees – stood by, with or behind Paolo Gabriele'.[16] Stampa and Clemens denied it. The Vatican press office felt obliged to protest as vigorously as the secretariat of state. The article rested on 'false and groundless interpretations and assertions', for which there were no objective proofs, and had inflicted a 'serious injury' on the honour of the persons concerned. Both *La Repubblica* and *Die Welt* stuck to their version.

On 17 December 2012 the pope's special committee presented him with their final report. In one chapter there was also mention of a homosexual lobby within the Curia, who had set up meeting places in a villa outside Rome, a sauna in the suburb of Quarto Miglio and a beauty salon in the historic city centre. There was no end to the speculations that it had been this report that led Benedict XVI to resign. In fact, by the time the dossier was delivered his decision to resign had long been made. The report did not have 300 pages but only 30. The rest consisted of a supplement containing other documents. Besides the three cardinals, only the pope and his secretary knew its contents. On Benedict's instruction Gänswein had put the documents in order and made a nine-page summary of them to hand over to Benedict's successor, to be appointed by the conclave. In fact, these documents were in the big box on the coffee table in Castel Gandolfo, which could be seen in the press photo showing the first meeting between the retired and the newly elected pope.

Benedict told me in our conversation that the matter had not affected him enough 'to make me fall into despair or *Weltschmerz*'. He had found his valet's behaviour 'simply incomprehensible'. Neither had Vatileaks made him feel tired of his office: 'For I think that can always happen. Above all you must not walk away in the midst of the storm but stand firm.' On the speculations that Paolo Gabriele might have had accomplices, he said: 'That may be so but I don't know that it is.' However 'nothing was discovered'. It was indeed troubling but also all too human that there were power games, jealousy and careerism in the Vatican, with its Curia staff of 3,000 and a further 2,000 in the state administration, with their different personalities from different countries and societies: 'In such a large organization it is impossible for there to be nothing but goodness.' But in the Vatican he had also met 'so many really good people, really sincere people, who work devotedly from morning till night. That outweighs the other side for me. That's just the world! We know that from the Lord. There are bad fishes in the net.'

In retrospect, Georg Gänswein thought that, on the whole, the Vatileaks crisis was 'considerably smaller' than it had been portrayed in the media. What had been really drastic was 'that the bishops had lost confidence and thought that if they wrote personally to the pope their letter would end up in the press. But everything else also happened elsewhere.'[17] Despite all good intentions and precautions, after Vatileaks 1 came Vatileaks 2, this time under Pope Francis. It was also about financial machinations and betrayal of secrets, and once again Gianluigi Nuzzi wrote a book about it. At the beginning of November 2015 leading members of COSEA, the audit committee set up by Pope Francis, were arrested and later found guilty. Francis had appointed them, even though the secretariat of state had warned that they were untrustworthy. 'I think that was a mistake,' Bergoglio said later. He referred to the efforts of his predecessor 'to fight corruption': 'He was the first one to bring accusations,' Pope Francis said: 'We elected him because he spoke out freely about such things.'[18]

Archbishop Viganò also made the news again. After his return from the USA, in August 2018 he published a dossier of accusations of hushed-up cases of abuse by members of the church hierarchy. They included Cardinal Theodore McCarrick, the archbishop of Washington, who had abused seminarians countless times. Benedict XVI had proceeded against McCarrick, but then Pope Francis *de facto* lifted the sanctions. Although Viganò had allegedly informed the pope about the crimes, McCarrick was permitted to undertake diplomatic missions for the Holy See. For example, there were the dealings with the People's Republic of China, which eventually led to a secret agreement putting the Catholic underground church, which Benedict still supported, under the state authorities. Unlike the scandals during Benedict's XVI's papacy, those under his successor created less of a stir in the media. The Dutch bishop Robertus Mutsaerts said: 'These media regarded it as a matter of course to criticize John Paul II or Benedict XVI. But all those who criticized Pope Francis were dismissed as conspiracy theorists.'[19]

Paolo Gabriele, who like St Benedict's raven apparently wanted to protect his master, had to leave the Vatican. Benedict XVI took care to find him a job. Gabriele had to sign an undertaking not to give any interviews or publish a book. However, his new job in the Catholic Bambino Gesù children's hospital would remind him of his wrongdoing every day. He worked there as a printer. And where exactly? In the photocopying room.

37

The Resignation

Rome, Monday, 11 February 2013. It was just before 6 a.m. when
the pope got up from his bed. A silent prayer, as always, but a bit
more intense than usual: 'I pray to you, my God, and I love you with
my whole heart.' Under Pius XII the Vatican timetable gave the Holy
Father an hour and a half for his morning toilet. Pius took 45 minutes.
He shaved himself with an electric razor while speaking to a goldfinch
that regularly came to his open bathroom window. He called it Gretel.

Benedict XVI trotted about here and there. He enjoyed the few
minutes of the day that were not planned. Dawdling a bit when he
got up was the only luxury he enjoyed. Then he took a bit of time
for private reading, letters and notes that had remained unattended
in his daily workload. Like Albert Einstein, he avoided complications
so as not to waste energy unnecessarily, which might affect his
intellectual activity. Today everything was different.

It was the most difficult day of his eight-year term of office. Perhaps
even the most difficult in his life. After it the papacy would never be
seen again as it had been before. He had not slept particularly well,
'but not altogether badly', he said later, 'because he had already made
up his mind', which gave him peace and assurance. His secretary
wanted him to change his mind, but he replied sharply: 'I have
wrestled with the Lord.' The decision was final, so 'That's that!'[1]

The pope stood at his window. His gaze wandered from the obelisk
in the middle of St Peter's Square to the façade of the cathedral. Early
in the morning, when the saints were still asleep, the incomparable
square lay in mist as if it was weeping. Soon the Swiss Guards would
march up. The taxi drivers, the homeless in ragged coats, the Sicilian
schoolgirls with sleepy eyes looking out from Madonna-like faces.

At 7 a.m. the biggest church in the world opened its doors to the huge crowds of people who streamed in every day. Benedict himself had set a record. Within a day the Twitter account newly set up in his name had attracted over 500,000 fans. No one else had ever gained so many followers so quickly.

It was still quiet in the basilica's mighty oval. How Michelangelo had complained to his pope while he was working on the great project! 'I am your workhorse,' he grumbled to him, 'and the more I struggle the less you pity me.' Wasn't Benedict, the German pope, also an uncommonly diligent worker? Hadn't he also toiled harder than anyone without evoking notable pity?

Two days ago he had welcomed 4,500 Knights of Malta into St Peter's, and in the evening he had given the Rome seminarians an impromptu brief summary of his theology. On Sunday he had prayed the Angelus as usual at his window with the faithful in St Peter's Square. 'Failures and difficulties' should 'not lead to discouragement', he had glossed the gospel of the day, for 'it is our task to cast the net in faith and the Lord does the rest'.

No candidate since 1730 had been older than him at his election. And now he was one of the oldest popes ever. John Paul II had died six weeks before he became 85. Benedict had had a new heart pacemaker inserted two months ago when he had reached 86. But he had not missed a single one of his almost 3,000 days in office. 'Joseph, be careful,' Cardinal Meisner, his Cologne friend, had urged him, 'you'll say I'm mad, but I don't care.' Benedict's sceptical look had not discouraged Meisner. 'You must become pope! In the church's present situation we haven't got anyone better for the job than you.'

Should he have refused when he was offered the chair of Peter? Hadn't he already then been a sick, exhausted old man, who longed for peace? For an intellectual life in privacy? In his retirement he would happily have taken over the management of the Vatican Library. That was his dream. And, incidentally, still written a couple more books. He had never wanted to be a public person, always in the limelight. So many people, the endless meetings, the thousand duties, the constant overload.

Hadn't he at least been confident that his papacy would not last long? He had geared everything towards it soon coming to an end. That was why with his encyclicals on the divine virtues of faith, hope and love he had begun with the highest one, love. He did not allow his collected works to be published chronologically but published first those in the field most important to him, the liturgy. Even his Christology's first part was not on Jesus' birth and youth, which he barely still expected to be able to write, but on the central aspects of Christ.

'Do the necessary things first,' St Francis had advised, 'then the possible. And then perhaps even the impossible some time or other.' Benedict had kept to that. He was sure that 'in a papacy that begins when you are 78 years old, you should not strive for great changes, which you won't be able to see through'. 'You have to do what is possible for the moment.' So he saw his 'central task' as ensuring 'that the faith remains for today. All the other things are administrative problems that did not necessarily have to be solved in my time.'[2]

What had he actually managed to achieve? The world had entered a post-Christian age. The church had lost its power to shape society. People got spiritual stimulation, if at all, from streaming services, or from things on YouTube or Instagram which promised happiness, success and a fulfilled life. The Holy Eucharist? Always dispensable. Large numbers of the clergy had become bourgeois. Lay organizations were often filled with people who spoke endlessly about dialogue and structural change but never mentioned the word 'Christ'. Who bothered about defending life in its true humanity, which sprang from its divinity, or the battle for the good in the divine mission? Priests dropped out because they no longer found any meaning in their work. Baptisms were dramatically decreasing. Marriages were contracted, if at all, in registry offices. People coming to Mass wanted music by Helene Fischer and other pop stars. Then there were the horrifying abuse cases. Weren't they also signs of dissolution, of de-Christianization among the clergy themselves? Nevertheless, was it right ever to give up believing in a reawakening of the spirit, even if you could not make it happen? 'The church awakes in souls,' the great Romano Guardini had written.

On a historic day like this, images from his own life must have gone through Benedict's mind. The mountain wanderings with his father. Up Kampenwand. Or to the little chapel on the River Salzach where the carol 'Silent Night' was sung for the first time. Benedict had never denied his roots. He loved the simple people's piety, which was able to bring heaven down to Earth. As the child of a baker's daughter and peasant's son, he remained a supporter of the have-nots, without romanticizing poverty.

But there were also images of the skinny boy, always standing somewhat on the side-lines, the one left out when the others were picking their teams for sporting events. The memory of his oddities, which made him seem like a gifted genius but also a bit autistic. His humiliation by the Nazi thugs. It had been a life story with breathtaking turning points and quiet dramas, with triumphs and set-backs, which had led him to a position of enormous responsibility. His term in office had begun with such zest and excitement! More than 300,000 faithful and visitors had come to his enthronement. They had listened to his words as if spellbound. His books as pope stormed the best-seller lists. His speeches became headlines in the world press. During his first year in office alone, 4 million people streamed into St Peter's Square, frenetically cheering him and demanding all kinds of poses from him. Benedict with a mobile phone. Benedict wearing a fire helmet. Benedict with a lion cub.

Perhaps because of his thin body and also his experiences from the Nazi era, he had lacked effective gestures, the theatricality so beloved by the media. He fought with a pen not a battle-axe. His speeches were written for a concert hall rather than the piazza. Anything too boastful, too polished and flawless, as loved by dictators, was suspect to him. So he had learned to live with the unfinished. He did not even want a church aspiring to be a community of the pure. That ignored human nature and selected its members.

One of his talents was to give his texts the structure of a musical composition. He could have given his speeches impromptu, but that contradicted his desire for exact expression, as well as for beauty of language, so he carefully prepared important texts. 'Bear in mind that it is always the pope speaking. And a pope's every word must be worthy of his office!' Pius XII had responded to his confessor, who begged him, for health reasons, not to write out a special speech for every small group of pilgrims. So it had come to those incomparable Ratzinger sentences from the mouth of a theologian, who was also a poet and whose hard sense of duty could not diminish his artistic side. In one of his formulations he said, 'Faith is just holding God's hand in the night of the world, hearing the word and seeing the love in silence.'

The pope shuffled back from the window to his desk. Three years beforehand the *Frankfürter Allgemeine Zeitung* had announced: 'The probability that Benedict will give his critics the pleasure of his early retirement can confidently be rated at zero.'[3] Since then his left eye had gone completely blind from macular degeneration, something only those in the know were aware of. But the arthritis in his right knee was no secret since, rather stiffly like a waving puppet, he had rolled into St Peter's on an ungainly four-wheeled platform, which looked like a supermarket trolley. He had given up long pastoral journeys a good while since. Public appearances were planned with regard to his frail health, avoiding unnecessary exertions. His body was emaciated, and tailors had trouble keeping up with clothes that fitted him. He did not look really ill, but the tiredness that had overcome the whole person, body and spirit, could no longer be ignored. It bothered him that his memory was failing. Despite all his trust in God, his mind was his indispensable instrument. And he had begun to be embarrassed that this instrument no longer functioned as well as before.

It was time to dress for Mass in the house chapel. Wojtyła had nearly always invited guests in the morning. But Benedict needed the silence, time for himself. Perhaps that was a deficiency, he once confessed, but he was 'not up to plunging straight into the day with meetings. I simply need to celebrate Mass without a lot of company and pray silently afterwards.' Wordlessly, his secretary passed him the alb, cincture and stole. Vesting was also a spiritual act, a moment of silence to prepare for meeting the Lord. His secretary looked pale and very overtired. But that was no surprise. He was one of the few people to have been told what was going to happen on that day. And he was not the only one among those few who wanted to dissuade the pope from the step he was planning.

History would record 2012 as one of those years that are unspectacular and ordinary in terms of events. There were no high points or momentous world happenings or the excitement of a change of decade. Barack Obama continued to be the US president. Angela Merkel was still the German federal chancellor. The boxer Vladimir Klitschko won his 50th knock-out victory and remained world champion. The media celebrated the 84th Oscar awards in Los Angeles, the new operating system Windows 8, the 20th anniversary of SMS texting and the landing of a robot on Mars. Curiously, the

NASA rover had been named *Curiosity*. Natural events and disasters included a cold spell in February during which 6,000, mostly home-less, people in Europe died. In the Philippines at least 51 died in a 6.7 magnitude earthquake. In Italy there were two earthquakes, one magnitude 6.1 and the other 5.8, in which 24 people died. In July the USA suffered the 'drought of the century', with the highest tempera-tures ever recorded in the region: 30 per cent of the maize crop withered. Oh yes: Spain won the European football championship.

The Gregorian calendar introduced by Pope Gregory the Great was not in use everywhere. Gregory measured time from the years that had passed since the birth of Christ. However, in the Buddhist calendar the year was not 2012 but 2556. The Jewish calendar had reached the year 5772. In the Islamic calendar it was the year 1433. In the *Vikram Samvat* Hindu calendar the year was 2068, and in the Chinese calen-dar it was 4708 (or 4648). Another calendar, which caused fascination but above all fear, displayed the proverbial 5 minutes to midnight. Or rather: exactly 12 midnight, the high noon of Earth time.

This was the legendary Maya calendar, a complex dating system of astonishing precision, which after a cycle lasting about 5,125 years, allegedly ended on 21 December 2012. A flood of media reports, books and broadcasts hyped the Maya catharsis, which could be read as the end of the world, the end of time or the beginning of a new age (or perhaps nothing, as critics suggested). In fact 21/12/12 went by without conflagrations or meteorite onslaughts. The eternal calendar of the Maya astrologers had not predicted any specific events but a state of affairs based on the cosmic energy flow, caused by a supernatural system that lay behind earthly events.

According to the Maya prophecy, from 21 December humanity would enter the fourth and final phase of world time. Instead of the Earth moving, as in previous centuries, outwards from the centre of the galaxy, in the new cycle the Earth's axis would move in towards the galaxy's centre. That process, which the Maya called 'divine breath', would speed up time and change living conditions on Earth. In short, the world was on course towards a new era through a revolutionary transformation of consciousness. At least for the church the prophecy of a great transformation proved true, as 2012 was the year in which Benedict XVI took the decision to change the papacy for ever by taking an unprecedented step.

Joseph Ratzinger's whole life was concerned with the question of whether the man from Nazareth was really the Messiah, the Son of God. Hardly anyone else had engaged with it so intensively and boldly. With his final strength in the summer of 2012 he finished the last volume of his Jesus trilogy. It was a short work of just 135 pages, plus appendix: 'My last book,' as he said sadly. Then he added there was 'not much more' to expect from him: 'I am an old man, and my power is failing. I think that's enough, what I have done.' 'Are you thinking of retiring?' I asked him. His answer was: 'That depends on whether my physical strength makes it necessary.'

The truth was that at this time he had long been trying to decide when exactly he would give up his office. The decision was as good as taken, but the battle was not yet quite over. Those close to him had never seen him so exhausted, so flat and listless, almost depressive. His face looked haggard, and his whole appearance was weak and feeble. He complained of constant tiredness. He felt every new folder that landed on his desk from the secretariat of state was an attack on his life. He was still plagued by the feeling that he had given too little. At the same time he wrote to one of his doctoral students that their forthcoming meeting would probably be his last.

In the spring his doctor had told him that he was organically in a better state than two years before, apart from his chronic exhaustion. He had asked for a walking-stick, even though he did not yet need one and the number of his audiences had been reduced almost by half. But secretary Gänswein found that in theological questions or when it was about his book, he was 'still all there'. He had just written a very good foreword to the volume on the Council, which was to appear among his collected works. However, after the Angelus and the general audience the pope looked completely exhausted. In the summer of 2012 his secretary said: 'There is no dynamism, he doesn't want to go on any longer. He's done. He feels that he is on the home straight, he has done his job. Actually, he just wants to stay at home here in the Apostolic Palace and the garden.'[4] Had Vatileaks exhausted him far more than he had admitted? According to Gänswein: 'The pope himself said no. Of course it was a great disappointment. But he had experienced worse as cardinal.' With Paolo Gabriele's reprieve 'the matter had also been settled in his mind.'

Much in that summer of 2012 recalled Pope Gregory the Great's depression in old age. In the foreword to his book on St Benedict, Pope Gregory wrote that he felt nearly crushed by the many tasks and duties of his office: 'One day I was overwhelmed by the vociferous importunity of some people expecting solutions for their business problems from us, which we are not competent to give.' Gregory suffered not only from a workload that had become insupportable but also from alienation from the spiritual purpose of his office. He finally turned for help to '*memoria*'. Remembering positive experiences from childhood gave the feeling of not being impotently exposed to changes and being able to halt time a bit. In Gregory's case it was the memory of the peace and quiet in a monastery.

Benedict XVI had also remained a theological writer when he became pope. His student group wondered how he managed to keep grasping and absorbing such a quantity of new theological literature. He finished the third volume of his work on Jesus during his holidays in July 2012. That fulfilled his final wish. In his long-nurtured project he counterposed his conviction of Jesus as true God and true man to an image of God and Christ that had become unstable. '*Ecce homo*', Pilate had declared. Joseph Ratzinger replied that in the man from Nazareth 'humanity itself' appeared. 'He reflects the distress of all who have been beaten and flayed. His distress embodies the inhumanity of human power, which tramples down the powerless.' But the other is also true: 'Jesus' inner dignity cannot be taken away from him. The hidden God remains present in him. The beaten, downtrodden human being remains the image of God.'

In his reflection on Christ's birth in Bethlehem, Benedict described the shepherds as night-watchers: 'perhaps they were living not only outwardly but also inwardly closer to the event than the peacefully sleeping townsfolk'. He saw the coming of Jesus as the paradox of the Christian faith:

From the moment of his birth, he belongs outside the realm of what is important and powerful in worldly terms. Yet it is this unimportant and powerless child that proves to be the truly powerful one, the one on whom ultimately everything depends. So one aspect of becoming a Christian is having to leave behind what everyone else thinks and wants, the prevailing standards, in order to enter the light of the truth of our being, and aided by that light to find the right path.[5]

His work on Jesus was one thing the pope imperatively wanted to get on with. The other was to lay the necessary organizational foundations for the new evangelization. Benedict was convinced that the new evangelization was one of the most important and forward-looking projects of modern times. If things were not going well for faith, then they could not go well for society, even though the public debate ignored the fact that the loss of spiritual resources would have as catastrophic effects as the extinction of species or climate change. For him it was a matter of strengthening the core of the Christian faith, rather than the centrifugal forces. The task was to give the world an anchor, offer it a future that reached beyond earthly limits, towards humanity's actual purpose. Technical achievements might advance humanity and be fascinating, but without the fulfilling faith in God's greatness and mercy all remained a wasteland and desolate loneliness. On 29 June 2010 the Vatican finally announced the foundation of a Council for Promoting the New Evangelization of the Western World. 'The pope has not only founded the Council,' its president Archbishop Rino Fisichella declared; 'he has carefully worked out the questions and said these were the questions the new council should answer. But he did not impose obligatory plans or limit the freedom of our work.'[6]

Another initiative of Benedict's was to establish a 'Court of the Nations' for dialogue with atheists and agnostics. The idea linked to the tradition of the ancient Jerusalem temple. It also had a 'Court of the Gentiles' as a place of meeting between believing Jews, those of other religions and unbelievers. Benedict's 'culture minister', Cardinal Gianfranco Ravasi, found top-flight associates for the trial run of the project: the Sorbonne in Paris, the Académie Française and UNESCO. The discussion meetings of the 'Court of the Nations' took place in Paris, Bucharest, Stockholm, Lisbon and Assisi. However, the project was not a resounding success.

The Jesus trilogy was finished; the new evangelization project was on its feet. The 'Year of Faith', which he had opened on 11 October 2012, the 50th anniversary of the opening of the Second Vatican Council, was going forward. It was intended to reinforce awareness of that Council. In retrospect he said: 'Over these last months I have begged God in

prayer to enlighten me with his light, to help me make the right decision, not only for my own good but for the good of the church.'[7]

In the Apostolic Palace the Mass in the private papal chapel was
over. It was followed by praying the breviary. Then the pope had his
breakfast, with tea and jam rolls, as always. Today nearly all the Vatican
offices were empty. No one was telephoning, using a computer or
the internet. That included the Governorate, which was responsible
for maintenance work, post and residence permits, and the Ufficio
Merci, the Vatican Goods Office. But a day off was not given to the
Swiss Guards or the anti-terror unit of the Vatican police corps. They
sat at the 50 monitors in the Sala Operativa, the control centre by St
Anne's gate, amid 500 video cameras keeping an eye on nearly every
corner behind the Leonine walls to prevent any suspicious persons
causing trouble from among the nearly 19 million annual visitors to
the cathedral and museums.

It was a holiday in the Vatican, as on every 11 February, to celebrate
the conclusion of the Lateran Pacts. On that day in 1929 the new
status of the Vatican City was established after the dissolution of the
powerful Papal States. The pope recognized the city of Rome as the
seat of the Italian government. For its part the Italian state guaranteed
the political and territorial sovereignty of the Vatican. Not altogether
willingly, the Catholic Church had sent a signal to emphasize the
spiritual dimension of its mission by reducing the extent of its
territory. A symbolic gesture of desecularization – becoming less
worldly – which the reigning pope had so frequently demanded.

On this 11 February secretary Gänswein accompanied Benedict
XVI to the old-fashioned, jolting, wood-panelled lift to go down
one floor from the third floor of the Apostolic Palace, the *terza loggia*,
to the *seconda loggia*, where audiences were usually held, state guests
received and bishops from their own countries were prayed with
when they arrived for their *ad limina* visits on a five-year rota. From
the lift the two of them went through the long corridor to the Sala
del Concistoro, one of the Vatican state rooms. It was said that the
gilding of its unique panelled ceiling had been a gift from the Spanish
infanta. Christopher Columbus had brought the gold back from the
New World on the *Santa Maria*. When the pope entered the room,
those present stood up. They were the approximately 70 members
of the papal senate who were resident in Rome and had deemed

it appropriate to attend the announced consistory. Some cardinals were away travelling; others had preferred to attend to more exciting matters than listening to the now almost routine announcement of new saints from past centuries, even though this time, as well as the canonization of Laura di Santa Caterina da Siena and Maria Gaudalupe García Zavala, there was to be the collective honouring of 800 witnesses to the faith from Otranto in southern Italy who in the year 1480 had chosen to be beheaded by Muslim invaders rather than give up their Christian faith.

The consistory was set for 11 a.m. Benedict and his secretary had left the papal apartment at 10.53. At the same time, 200 to 300 metres away as the crow flies, Giovanna Chirri entered the Vatican press office, the Sala Stampa, situated at 54 Via della Conciliazione. The sky was grey, the weather unpleasant. That morning in Rome it had poured with rain, and the few tourists who were in the city at this time of year mainly kept in the dry in the Vatican museums or in one of the historic *palazzi*. Giovanna was wearing a dark grey trouser suit. She had medium-length hair and was wearing large rimless, not altogether fashionable, glasses. She could have worked in a law office with her discreet appearance, which indeed perfectly fitted her job processing mostly colourless news far from the screens and spotlights. The 54-year-old Roman was one of the most experienced Vatican experts. She had been writing for the biggest Italian news agency, ANSA, for 20 years, and she was convinced to date that during her remaining years in the job she would never again experience anything that she had not already experienced.

Besides Giovanna, on that morning only four other journalists found their way to the press office: one Mexican, one Japanese and two French. They read newspapers and considered which trattoria they would have lunch in, or perhaps they would prefer a sandwich to spare the tight budget of a *Vaticanista*. The Holy See press office, established in 1966, had originally been set up as the information source for the Second Vatican Council. The press room had about 200 sitting and standing places and simultaneous translation equipment. In the next room internet connections and an archive were available. The press spokesman Lombardi usually sat before the microphone with an unchanging expression, announcing news of the pope's activities and fielding media questions.

The press appointment for that day to announce a few canonizations did not promise much excitement. On the monitor now the picture could be seen that the Vatican broadcaster CTV (Centro Televiso Vaticano) displayed for the journalists. It came from a cameraman stationed in a window bay in the Sala del Concistoro moving his camera from the pope to the cardinals sitting comfortably on the chairs arranged along the three walls. As usual at these ceremonies, the pope sat at the front on a red-gold throne seat, wearing a red *mozzetta* cape with white fur border. He looked a bit absent. It was a long time since he had been able to maintain eye contact with his public during an address. On that day he also looked tired. Eleven days beforehand the Vatican had given out the programme for the months of February and March, again with a marathon timetable for the Easter ceremonies. However, that year the Easter Vigil had been brought forward half an hour to 8.30 p.m., to give the 86-year-old pope a longer rest before the Easter Sunday Mass.

Joseph Ratzinger was one of those people who said what he thought and did what he said. Basically, the step he was about to announce in a few minutes should not have surprised anyone, other than by its timing. He had already stated that he did not regard the office of pope as being for life when John Paul II could only appear before the public mute, with shaking hands and sitting in a wheelchair. In 2010 Ratzinger had said in the interview book *Licht der Welt* (*Light of the World*) that a pope not only had the right to retire if he 'physically, psychically and spiritually can no longer do his job, but under certain circumstances he also has the duty to retire'. However, the decision should not be forced upon anyone.

The first 35 popes in history are all counted as martyrs. They gave their lives for Christ, and at a time of Christian persecution they could be relatively certain they would die in office. It was once said that the papacy would become secularized if a pope retired. That would mean it was no longer God himself who ended it, by the pope's death, but human considerations. Then it would not be a special office but a job like any other. The church set a valuable yardstick that remained valid. If it was shortened or lengthened at will, then it would be a yo-yo and not a yardstick any longer. The papacy also stood for that. Although individual bishops operated in their own style, as the shepherd answerable only to Christ the Holy Father was the supra-national counterweight to popular parochialism. That was why he was called a rock. Over the centuries it was said that what was constantly new about and in the Catholic Church was not because it adapted or became just like other institutions. It renewed itself in its own unique way, by constant, necessary recovery of its Christian heart.

It had happened that both a pope and an anti-pope were proclaimed or that a pope was forced to leave office. For example, in the year 537 Pope Silverius was deposed by Byzantine pressure. Three weeks later he was dead. But there had only been one single instance of voluntary retirement, and that was 718 years ago. Pope Celestine V, the founder of the Celestine Order, resigned from the papacy in December 1294. More than two years before that, the Roman noble families had been haggling over the papal throne, until King Charles II of Naples begged the hermit Peter of Mount Morrone, high in the Abruzzi, to write a sharp letter to the conclave of cardinals assembled in Perugia, finally to give the divided church a head again. When the hermit himself was elected pope there and then, the 85-year-old rode on a donkey to his coronation and was welcomed by the faithful as an 'angel pope' – Celestine V. He spoke hardly a word of Latin and had as much idea of administration and church leadership as a carpenter would have of blacksmithing. He was constantly appointing new cardinals and agreed sometimes with one and sometimes another in his decisions. A contemporary remarked: 'He does not rule with the fullness of his strength but with the fullness of his naïvety.'

Celestine became a puppet in the intrigues of the powerful. Charles II compelled him to live in Naples, while chaos and confusion reigned in Rome. After five months he gave up his office and exchanged his papal vestments for his monk's cowl again. On 13 December 1274 he read out his resignation speech before the College of Cardinals: 'I Celestine hereby retire from the papacy of my own free will. I am moved to do so for legal reasons as well as reasons of conscience.' He resigned from the throne, rank and honour of the office 'from necessary humility, for moral improvement and also because of my body's weakness and my unfitness for the office, and above all because of the feebleness of my whole person'.[8] His successor, Boniface VIII, put him in the castle of Fumone, to the east of Rome, for fear the deserter might return. A year and a half after his resignation Celestine died in captivity. He was canonized in 1313.

However the poet Dante Alighieri accused him of cowardice in his *Divine Comedy* and consigned him to Hell.

The *Codex Iuris Canonici* states that every pope has the right to resign. Canon 332, paragraph 2, states: 'Should the pope resign from his office, for this to be valid it is required that the resignation occurs freely and is adequately promulgated, but not that it be accepted by anyone.' In modern times Pius XII, Paul VI and John Paul II had at least prepared in writing for their resignation. Pius XII had ordered an immediate retirement should he be kidnapped by Hitler's henchmen, an anxiety that was not unfounded. In the autumn of 1971 there was a rumour going round Rome that Pope Paul VI wanted to lay down the burden of his office when he reached his 75th birthday. In fact, Paul had commissioned a report on the pros and cons of resignation (which, however, rejected retirement). In August 2017 Cardinal Giovanni Battista Re stated that he had seen two retirement documents of Paul VI's. They were intended to prevent the church being paralysed by an incapable pope, should he lose his intellectual faculties. Ratzinger had also heard about the documents in October 2003. Don Ettore Malnati reported later that Ratzinger's reaction had been: 'That is a very wise thing, which every pope should do.'[9]

John Paul II also checked whether, like bishops, a pope could give up his office when he reached a certain age. In 1989 he wrote a letter, posthumously made public by Sławomir Oder, the postulator in his beatification process. It said that, as with his predecessor Paul VI, retirement would be an option should serious illness make the exercise of his office impossible. However, five years later he came to the conclusion that 'there was no place in the church for a pope emeritus'. According to his secretary Stanisław Dziwisz, John Paul II had been convinced that he should stay in office, as God wanted him to: 'God has called me and God will call me again, as he will.'

For Benedict XVI the greatness of God's servant lay in his powerlessness, which in the end was stronger than all the other powers put together, because it was linked to the Almighty. So that meant that someone new could always do the job that his predecessor had become unable to do. 'The grain of wheat must die, so that it rises again', was one of his favourite sentences from John's gospel: 'Truly I tell you, unless a grain of wheat falls into the earth and dies, it remains just a single grain; but if it dies it bears much fruit' (Jn

12.24). In his case that teaching applied not only to his successor but also to his own work, which could only then blossom fully.

It had caused a certain stir when in 2009 Benedict visited the city of L'Aquila, which had suffered a terrible earthquake. The pope expressed his particular wish to go into the basilica of Santa Maria di Collemaggio. He laid down the pallium he had received when he took office on the tomb of Pope Celestine V. It symbolized the authority of Peter's successor as bishop of Rome. A year later Benedict celebrated Celestine's 800th birthday. He spoke about the power of silence, the timeless charisma of holiness and humanity's question: 'Where do I come from? What am I living for?'

Meanwhile, Giovanna Chirri had settled in her place and was watching on the monitor what was happening in the Apostolic Palace. The usual atmosphere of calm routine could be felt among the cardinals. The master of ceremonies, Guido Marino, was sitting on the pope's left. He was a learned canon lawyer and communications psychologist. At major church services he handed the pope his missal and mitre and unobtrusively directed many auxiliary ceremonies to ensure the service was conducted with due dignity. But a consistory was also a liturgical act. It began with a Latin office from the Book of Hours. That was followed by various psalms until the prefect of the Congregation for the Causes of Saints introduced the new saints in Latin. On that day the Congregation's prefect, Curia Cardinal Angelo Amato, proclaimed the two women, together with Antonio Primaldo and his 799 companions from Otranto.

That should have been the end of the consistory. But soon the cardinals felt that there was something else. There was a very special atmosphere, an uncomfortable feeling like weather that affected you without your being aware of it. Years later they would recall the private secretary's stony face, the pale face of the Holy Father they thought they saw at that moment. A sense of confusion. Then many of them had stared with gaping mouths, others had tears in their eyes, dumb and dismayed. Later Cardinal Angelo Sodano put it thus: 'It was like lightning from a clear blue sky.'

Giovanna Chirri also noticed that the consistory was over. But remarkably, the pope was still sitting down. When his secretary stood up to pass a paper to him, Giovanna pricked up her ears. Why was the text that the Holy Father was now beginning to read in Latin, the church language used for important occasions and significant acts? She saw later that the *Bolletino no. 0089*, which Benedict was holding, had just 18 lines. But no one guessed how weighty the declaration was that had been typed, printed, recorded and treated like a normal official document to be kept secret. No computer data, written documents, telephone or email communication about it were permitted. It was well known that the Vatican could be a gossip shop. Moreover, indiscretions were part of the *Vaticanista* game, which was always trying here or there to recruit a monsignor as an informant. Vatileaks had shown that leaks were to be found even within the inmost circle of the church leadership. So the fact that this paper had been kept secret was almost a miracle, although there were good reasons for discretion. Benedict said in retrospect: 'The moment people knew about it, the job would crumble because then its authority would collapse. It was important for me to be able really to fulfil my office and service to the end.'[10]

Giovanna Chirri noticed on her screen how the cardinals' heads suddenly moved; many turned to their neighbours, as if they were wondering whether they had heard right. 'Dear brothers,' the pope had said, 'I summoned you to this consistory not just for the three canonizations but also to communicate to you a decision of great importance for the life of the church.' Benedict seemed stricken, his shaky voice was almost inaudible. His eyes were fixed on the document, and it was almost as if he did not dare look his cardinals in the face.

'*Conscientia mea iterum atque iterum coram Deo* ...' What? What did the pope actually say then ? '... *explorata ad cognitionem certam perveni vires meas ingravescente aetate* ...'. The pope's words fell upon the Sala del Concistoro like bread upon the water, and the cardinals snapped them up open-mouthed like fishes. '... *iterum atque iterum...*'. But what exactly did it mean? By 'examined again and again'? Giovanna delved in her memory for the Latin words, which she had once learned '... *non iam aptas esse ad munus Petrinum aeque administrandum*'. Giovanni's colleagues goggled at the screen. They knew no Latin, but what could be happening? Within ten minutes Lombardi was handing out copies of the translated text to them. For Giovanna Chirri it was the moment when she began to understand. 'I realized instinctively,' she said later, 'that something big had happened. My knees shook as I typed the news.' But she herself still could not believe what she had heard. 'It seemed simply untrue.'

38

The Beginning of a New Era

The decision began to form in the spring of 2012 after his strenuous journey to Mexico and Cuba. His doctor had told the pope that he would not withstand another transatlantic flight. That did not matter for his work in Rome, but how would he be able to take part in the World Youth Day 2013 in Rio? The festival had been brought forward a year so as not to clash with the football World Cup. Originally, Benedict had assumed that he would manage to 'hold out' until the beginning of 2014. From his own experience he knew how stimulating it had been to meet millions of young people at the beginning of a papacy. It became clear to him, he said, 'that I must retire at the right moment for the new pope to have an impetus'.[1]

The idea that a work could be completely perfect was always suspect to Ratzinger. What humans achieved was always partial. That did not mean that they should lay off work but that they should engage in it without overstretching the bow. As a young professor he had ceased work when he heard the gong that told him that it was time to stop. Everything was given, found, discovered and not the result of autonomous genius. Accepting the unfinished was part of trusting that someone greater would finish the work. Ratzinger set to work, but not at all costs. He left Bonn, Münster and Tübingen. He had also wanted to leave Rome after his first period of office as prefect. Paradoxically, a constant in his life course was a certain discontinuity. He moved on as soon as he found the circumstances would no longer allow him to do the job he thought he ought to be doing.

The resignation of Christ's representative on Earth was theoretically possible but never envisaged in practice. A pope was not a monarch like others; he had to die in office. 'Your authority is not moderate',

St Bernard of Clairvaux had written to his former student Pope Eugene in a letter of advice in 1153. 'If you have rightly considered who you are, then you won't be mistaken about your duty either.' And in order to make clear 'the part you play in God's church' Bernard spelt it out: 'Who are you? The high priest, the head of the priests. The most prestigious of bishops, the heir to the apostles, a shepherd like Abel, a helmsman like Noah, a patriarch like Abraham, a priest in the order of Melchisedech, you have the dignity of Aaron, the authority of Moses, the judgement of Samuel, the powers of Peter and anointing by Christ.' That was to say: 'The keys are given to you, the lambs are entrusted to you [...] And you are not only a shepherd of the sheep but also a shepherd of the shepherds. How do I prove that, you ask? By the words of the Lord.'[2]

Nobody guessed yet what the pope was thinking about, not even his brother Georg. Day after day Benedict weighed things up in order to throw light on every hurdle, every remote consequence of his step. But weighing the question rationally was not enough. He prayed about it. Examined his conscience. He considered whether possibly it was a temptation, because a voice was saying to him that his plan was quite simply sensible and he should now definitely throw off the yoke that had become so heavy and finally be himself, free. It was the most momentous decision of his life. By it he created a precedent that might change the papacy for ever, even if future popes were inclined to stick it out until death. Certainly, the world would applaud him. On very worldly grounds. But didn't resignation mean de-sacralizing this unique office? So wouldn't it be a 'relativizing', which he had criticized so vehemently in other areas?

The pope believed he would get an answer by listening to the word of the Lord. Was it a flight? Because he wanted so much to yield to his exhaustion? Almost always it had been 'Providence' that decided for him. Coincidences that showed him the way. But where could he look for 'Providence' now? It was God who ended a papacy. But couldn't the Almighty also recall someone, even if that apparently happened *before* time? However that might be, did trusting in God mean staying? Or did trusting in God mean going? Because even without him the ship of Peter would find its way? With any successor at the helm, it was said, the Lord would be able to correct the course that a captain followed in the years ahead. He had neither taken advice from trusted friends nor commissioned expert canon law or theological opinions. He wanted to decide on the most complex and momentous decision of his papacy alone in majestic sovereignty. He said later that it was incorrect to say he had not spoken to anyone about his retirement. 'For I spoke at length with God about it.' The question tormented him, but from week to week there grew in him 'the inner certainty that I must do it'.[3]

In May there was a pastoral visit to Arezzo in Tuscany, with a Mass at which the Italian prime minister, Mario Monti, was also present. From 1 to 3 June 2012 Pope Benedict went to Milan for the seventh World Meeting of Families. It was the longest apostolic visit in Italy to date. Daniel Barenboim conducted Beethoven's Ninth Symphony at La Scala in Benedict's honour. About 850,000 faithful took part in the farewell Mass at Milan Bresso airport. On 26 June there followed a pastoral visit to the earthquake region of Emilia Romagna, where a priest had been killed by falling debris in his church on 29 May.

Day-to-day work went on as before, including the preparations for the World Youth Day in Rio. 'A pope will be coming,' Benedict had answered curtly to his secretary's anxious question. From June 2012 Gänswein noticed that the pope 'was particularly reserved, silent and inward-looking'. In meditations in the house chapel he looked like the figures in the pictures on the walls by Old Masters, kneeling and praying for their lives. Gänswein thought the change was because he was working on the third volume of his Jesus trilogy: 'I thought he was struggling with his book.' In addition there had been some problems with choosing staff for church leadership positions. It was only later that it had become shatteringly clear 'that the man had been struggling for months with this momentous decision'.[4]

Sister Christine Felder, who looked after the papal household, also became aware only in retrospect that over those weeks and months the pope had been 'grappling with what his step meant theologically. What a watershed it would be for the church. That nothing would be the same as before any longer.' She was 'fully convinced that he had agreed it with God. When he could say before God with a good conscience that it was right, then he had always gone ahead.'

Benedict was firmly convinced that he had considered every aspect in his decision-making. 'You considered everything that would result from the step you were taking?' I asked him. 'I'd say yes,' he replied.

Did you also consider that in the future, if it was no longer a matter of course that a pope should remain in office until the end of his life, that there might be demands for him to retire?

Of course you can't submit to such demands. That is why I stressed in my speech that I was doing so freely. You can never leave if it means running away, you can never submit to pressure. You can only leave if no one is demanding it. And no one has demanded it in my time. No one. It was a complete surprise to everyone.

Did you also consider the shock that you would cause?

Yes, I had to accept that.

The struggle must have cost you a great deal.

In these matters one gets help.

Are you clear with the Lord?

Yes, I really am.

After long months of prayer and weighing things up, Benedict made his final decision in August 2012 on holiday in Castel Gandolfo. 'I had thought it over for long enough and discussed it with the Lord.' Now he was sure 'that it was *Nunc dimittis* for me. I have done my job'. According to Luke's Gospel, *Nunc dimittis* are the opening words of Simeon's hymn. They come from the biblical story of the presentation of the Lord in the Jerusalem temple. The old man Simeon recognized Jesus Christ as the awaited Messiah and felt he was now ready to die. 'Lord now let your servant depart in peace, according to your word.'

It was important to Benedict that his plan should remain secret. But, he said, there had been an unfounded report that, in a private conversation, at the height of the Vatileaks scandal, Cardinal Carlo Maria Martini had pressured him to resign. As a first step Benedict had spoken about the matter to Cardinal Secretary of State Bertone on 30 April 2012. 'I could hardly believe it that he had really come to such a decision,' Bertone recalled; he had only taken it seriously when Benedict had spoken to him again in August at Castel Gandolfo. Bertone had then given the pope 'respectful but pressing' reasons against retiring from his office.[5]

In September 2012 Benedict also informed Georg Gänswein. 'Of course I was shocked,' his secretary recalled; 'my first reaction was: "No Holy Father, you can't do that!"' In his agitation Gänswein argued that it might be possible 'simply to concentrate on the core business and let all the other duties go'. Moreover, there were medicines to keep him healthy in old age. 'But that was just my emotion. And then I realized that he was not telling me something in order to discuss a decision, he was telling me his decision.'

So far, neither the time nor the procedure for his retirement had been clarified. Originally Benedict's plan had been to announce his decision to the Curia on 21 December 2012, during his traditional Christmas speech. Then his papacy would end on the feast of the Conversion of St Paul, on 25 January 2013. Gänswein disagreed strongly: 'Holy Father, if you announce it before Christmas, then the Christmas festival will have had it. I believe that is not the right occasion. A better one would be either in a consistory or on an occasion especially arranged for it.' A glance at the calendar showed that a date for a consistory was set for 11 February 2013. It was about various canonizations. Benedict was unwilling to delay the date any longer, 'because my strength keeps on failing'. The date had the advantage that after it there came the Lenten exercises for the Curia, with prayer and silence. It was also the feast of Our Lady of Lourdes. 'The feast day of St Bernadette of Lourdes', said Benedict, was on his birthday (16 April), so 'he had a personal connection' with Our Lady of Lourdes and that date. 'It seemed to me that it was right to do it on that day.'

Meanwhile the planned visit to Lebanon drew nearer. Because of the chaos of war in Syria the trip had been uncertain until now, but the pope stood by his commitment. No, he said in the plane, while it kept plunging into turbulence, he had 'no fear'. It was work for peace. After landing in Beirut, Benedict went to the Marian pilgrimage site of Harissa to sign the final document of the Middle East Synod of Bishops. Security was very tight, with cordoned-off motorways, soldiers standing at every 100-metre post, marksmen controlling the area from rooftops. The pope met representatives of 18 Christian and Muslim communities, and on the evening of 15 September he had a discussion with some 20,000 young people. Among them there was a small delegation of young Muslims, whom he specifically welcomed. 'Together with your Christian contemporaries you are the future of this wonderful country and the whole Middle East,' he told them. 'Co-operate with one another. And when you are grown up, live harmoniously together with Christians. The beauty of Lebanon lies in that wonderful symbiosis.' The final ceremony was a Mass on the Beirut waterfront, attended by 300,000 people.

Benedict made his last trip as head of the Catholic Church on 4 October, the feast day of St Francis of Assisi. On a pastoral visit to the pilgrimage site of Loreto he prayed for Our Lady's blessing on the Bishops' Synod for New Evangelization and for the 'Year of Faith' he had convoked. Three days later he solemnly opened the synod in Rome, and on 11 October he celebrated the 50th anniversary of the opening of the Second Vatican Council by a Mass with members of the synod and bishops who, like himself, had taken part in the Council. The Mass was also attended by Patriarch Bartholomew of Constantinople and the Anglican primate, Rowan Williams. In the evening young people gathered for a torchlight procession under the pope's window, in memory of the torchlight procession in honour of John XXIII exactly 50 years earlier. Benedict called out to those in the square that he had been one of the young people then who were looking hopefully up towards the Apostolic Palace to wave to their beloved *Papa buono*.

The encyclical *Lumen fidei* ('The Light of Faith') was due in October, but its publication date was quietly deferred. The pope himself had stepped in. He did not think the text was ready. It did not yet have the feeling of an encyclical. It was clear to him that his papacy would register just three rather than four encyclicals. The revised encyclical could have been published at the end of January, but Benedict argued in a conversation with his secretary that with the excitement of his resignation it would get lost and quickly be forgotten. He didn't want that. Moreover, it might have looked as though he wanted to shove the encyclical in his successor's face. The almost complete document was finally published as the first encyclical of Pope Francis. 'In the brotherhood of Christ' he had taken over the 'valuable work' of his predecessor, said Bergoglio in the foreword, and supplemented 'the text with some further contributions'.

It was already November when Archbishop Giovanni Angelo Becciu, substitute for general affairs in the Secretariat of State, was made privy to the secret operation for Day X. Benedict had chosen to live as pope emeritus in the Mater Ecclesiae ('Mother of the Church') monastery in the Vatican Garden. Pope John Paul II had consecrated it on 13 May 1994, the feast of Our Lady of Fátima. However, the two-storey property, with a small house chapel, had to be renovated first. Personally instructed by Benedict, Becciu was in charge of the building work. On 21 December, at the Christmas reception for the Curia, Benedict recalled his trip to Mexico and Cuba, the meeting with families in Milan and his visit to Lebanon. He stressed the importance of the family and his worry about the disconnectedness of people today. 'If you cancel that connection, then the basic figures of human life disappear: father, mother, child. Essential ways of experiencing being human disappear.' In the positions it took the Catholic Church incorporated 'human memory, the memory from its beginnings over the centuries of human experiences and events'. For the Church 'humane civilization' had grown 'out of the encounter between God's revelation and human life'.[6]

Secretary Gänswein was still not allowed to speak with anyone about the coming end of Benedict's papacy. That was 'not easy – almost unendurable'. When on 6 January Gänswein was consecrated bishop by Benedict XVI in St Peter's Basilica, he experienced the ceremony 'as if I was standing on a mountain but at the same time in a pothole'. Those who knew the customs of the papal court recognized a clear sign of coming changes with Gänswein's consecration and the dismissal of Archbishop James Harvey from his post as prefect of the papal household for, by dismissing Harvey, Benedict was freeing a post that he wanted to secure for none other than his secretary.

At the fifth general audience of the year, on 30 January, Benedict resumed his catechesis on the Creed. He pointed out that many people today denied that God was almighty. However, God's almightiness was different from how humans thought of 'power'. It was not power that struck but power that was kind, gave freedom and healed, power that was able to wait and convinced people through love.

It was just two weeks before the day, when the pope sat down at his old walnut desk to work on his resignation statement. The text ought not to be too long or complicated. But precision was necessary to avoid challenges from canon law. In fact, because of ambiguous terms in the statement, many years later there was a dispute about whether it was really valid or whether Benedict was still the lawful pope. As always, Ratzinger wrote in pencil. The reason why he did not write his text in Italian was 'because something so important is written in Latin'. He was also worried he might make mistakes in a foreign language.

It was time to let more people into the plan. First, Cardinal Gianfranco Ravasi was put in the picture. He had been appointed exercise master for the Lenten exercises and might help 'to soften the blow' of the pope's retirement with appropriate meditations and metaphors. Master of Ceremonies Marini was also apprised of the plan. He had to know that the consistory on 11 February was not going to end after the announcement of the new saints but that a second part would follow. At the same time Sister Birgit Wansing was also told. She had to type Benedict's statement, written in his tiny, barely decipherable handwriting. What a drama that caused, Gänswein recalled, because 'she was flabbergasted'.

Under the papal seal of silence a member of the secretariat of state was also informed, who was to check the retirement statement for its content and its formal and linguistic correctness. (In fact he slightly changed the text in some places for stylistic reasons.). On 8 February Cardinal Angelo Sodano was told about the *papa choc*, the 'pope shock', as *Il Messagero* later called Benedict's resignation. As dean of the College of Cardinals, Sodano was asked to make a short speech after the resignation statement had been read out. The news also came as a shock to him, but he did not try to change Benedict's mind.

On the same day, at an appointment in the diocese of Rome seminary, the pope blessed about 190 young priests for their missionary work. At the event he compared the church to a tree that had sprung from a mustard seed. 'Many would think,' he declared, 'that now its time is over, now the time has come for it to die.' But that was a mistake. 'The church always renews itself, is always being reborn.' Today Christians were 'the most persecuted group in the world'. Because the church 'is not conformist, it is a thorn in the side, because it is against tendencies to selfishness, materialism, all those things'. For despite Christianity's great history and culture, Christians are always strangers and belong to a minority. But you are a Christian 'not by your own decision, or personal choice'. No, being a Christian did not mean just 'joining a group'. It concerned 'the depth of being [...] that is to say, becoming a Christian begins with an act of God, his doing above all, and I let myself be formed and changed'. Despite all hardships, young people should not be afraid of the future: 'We are "heirs" not of a particular country but of God's Earth, God's future. The inheritance is a thing of the future.' Passionately he cried out: 'The future belongs to us, the future belongs to God.'[7]

Perhaps the most difficult moments for the pope in the countdown to the resignation came on 9 February. Within the papal family, whose members honoured the pope like a saint, no one except his private secretary knew that their days of being together were numbered. 'It was a catastrophe,' Gänswein recalled. The news hit the four Memores and Don Alfredo, the second secretary, very hard. There was also the question of which of the women would stay at the side of the retired pope in the future. Two of them would be plenty, Benedict said. His secretary contradicted him: 'Holy Father, they are all growing older. Sometimes one will be ill and sometimes another. Suddenly the pressure is off and that can also become very boring and very empty.' So it was better 'if the team stuck together'. But the question was quickly decided by the women themselves: 'Holy Father, we are not leaving you, we are staying with you.'

Gradually there was movement in the Sala Stampa. Up until that moment, the correspondent Giovanna Chirri had been convinced that after 20 years in her job, she 'would not experience anything new'. But now suddenly there were words on her notepad that sounded completely strange, like news from another universe. Joseph Ratzinger had composed countless texts. Even before he was elected pope, the list of his publications had grown to about 600. During his papacy he had written 13 *motu proprio*, 116 apostolic constitutions and 64 apostolic letters. In addition there were 274 published letters to bishops, patriarchs and state presidents, and 198 dispatches. Not forgetting his encyclicals. But the words Giovanni had noted down were one of those texts marking a historic change that would go into school books. 'Dear Brothers,' the pope began, after his secretary had passed him the paper. His voice sounded as if he were giving the usual words of blessing or making an incidental remark. But it was news that would cause a worldwide sensation:

> I have convoked you to this Consistory not only for the three canonizations but also to communicate to you a decision of great importance for the life of the Church.
>
> After having examined my conscience again and again before God, I have come to the certainty that my powers, due to an advanced age, are no longer suited to an adequate exercise of the Petrine ministry.
>
> I am well aware that this ministry, due to its essential spiritual nature, must not only be carried out with words and deeds, but no less with prayer and suffering.
>
> However, in today's world, subject to so many rapid changes and shaken by questions of deep relevance for the life of faith, in order to steer the ship of St Peter and proclaim the Gospel, strength of both mind and body is necessary, strength which in the last few months has deteriorated in me to the extent that I have had to recognize my incapacity to fulfil adequately the ministry entrusted to me.
>
> For this reason, and well aware of the seriousness of this act, with full freedom I declare that I renounce the ministry of bishop of Rome, successor of St Peter, entrusted to me by the cardinals on 19 April 2005, in such a way, that as from 28 February 2013, at 20:00 hours, the See of Rome, the See of St Peter, will be vacant and a conclave to elect the new Supreme Pontiff will have to be convoked by those whose competence it is.

Even on the small monitor in the Sala Stampa it could be seen that from one second to the next an unprecedented *tohu bohu* had arisen among the assembly of cardinals. They were gaping at each other in amazement. Many plucked at their neighbours' vestments, asking what the pope had meant. 'Some of their faces were petrified, incredulous, shocked, at a loss,' said Georg Gänswein, describing the scene. Even Cardinal Kurt Koch was unsure. 'Perhaps my Latin is so bad', he thought, 'that I have misunderstood.'

Some of them had only seen the shock of their colleagues, without realizing that they were witnesses of an historic moment. At last Sodano spoke: 'Holy Father, beloved and honoured successor of St Peter,' he began, and there was a distinct tremble in his voice. This news had struck 'like lightning from a clear sky'. The cardinals had 'heard the disturbing news with bewilderment, and could hardly believe it'. But they had never felt so close to their pope as at that moment.

Sodano recalled that after the conclave on 19 April 2005 he himself had been the one who had asked Cardinal Ratzinger if he accepted his election as pope. But the sturdy doyen of cardinals was unable to say any more. He looked deeply affected as he went up to the pope with leaden steps. The pope stood up and kissed him on the cheeks, grasping him with both hands, but in the agitation of the moment he was incapable of anything but a slight smile.

It was only when Sodano had spoken that it became clear to them all that what no one had even dreamed of was true. But none of them dared to make the smallest remark to the pope or shake his hand, or even rush up to him, whether in protest or agreement. The ceremonial was strict, and indicated that after a consistory the pope, as head of the church, solemnly leaves the room, without in any way being importuned.

Giovanna Chirri now not only knew that her Latin had not let her down but also that on this most exciting day of her life she had an exclusive, a journalistic scoop, which thousands of her colleagues dreamed of all their lives. At 11.45 a.m. she finished the ticker message, even though it did not yet have any official confirmation from the Vatican press office. 'I was trying to keep my nerve, though my knees were shaking even while I was sitting down,' she said later. 'The pope went on speaking. He mentioned the convoking of a conclave, but I simply did not hear any more.' Giovanna finished her message and pressed 'Send' on her laptop. But even before her agency ANSA shot the sensational news into the ether, Giovanna's Twitter timeline reported: '*B16 si è dimesso. Lascia pontificato dal 28 febbraio*': B16 has resigned. Quits papacy from 28 February.

The news travelled round the world as if with the speed of light. The incredible story appeared on news websites all over the globe. At that moment Giovanna Chirri burst into tears. 'I was so sorry he was resigning,' she reported later. She had loved this pope, who 'was little understood by the public and the media'. Contrary to the clichés, he had 'a rich and deep personality, he could really listen to his fellow human beings'. A few tweets later she wrote: 'It pained me that #Pope #B16 is stepping down. He is a great theologian.' Finally she tweeted: '*Cari amici di twitter, meno di 140 battute bastano per le vere notizie. Grazie a tutti per affetto*': 'Dear Twitter friends. It only takes 140 characters for the real news. Thanks to all for affection.'

There are moments in world history when time seems to stand still. Earth's axis stops turning. All movement ceases. The news of the resignation of the 265th successor to St Peter came like a thief in the night into the hurly-burly of a carnival society. It caused a shock as if there had been another 9/11. The pope was still alive, but he no longer sat on the chair of St Peter. Nothing like it had ever happened before in church history. It was like a paradigm shift, marking the start of a new epoch, perhaps even a new age.

Editors hastened back from holiday. Catholics stared aghast at the live news online, like children who had lost their father. The Vatican internet site had long since gone down. Even the press office home page had collapsed. He had come so quietly, this simple labourer in the Lord's vineyard, as he had described himself after his election. Why was he leaving with such a thunderclap? 'Nobody knew anything,' said a watcher of the news site kath.net: 'At present it's mostly confusion. The situation is so extraordinary that even a 2,000-year-old institution like the *Una Sancta* has had no protocol for it.'

The incomprehensible, the impossible, the almost forbidden thing had happened. And even if you had seen it coming, it hit you like a blow. 'Colleagues, friends and relations were all shocked,' said Gänswein; 'the Curia was speechless, stunned. It seethed like a kettle. What has happened? Is he ill? Can't he do it any more? Has he been pressured? Even people whom I know well were so disappointed that they felt wounded, abandoned or betrayed.' Faxes declared you could not give up fatherhood. Someone wrote: 'John Paul II suffered much worse and held on, but *he* skedaddles.' Now a pope was no longer a mystical figure.[8]

At the time Norbert Hofmann, secretary of the Pontifical Committee for Religious Relations with Judaism, was on a trip to Siena with a colleague. When the two priests took shelter in a bar from the storm that was falling over Rome and Tuscany, they saw the Vatican spokesman on television. The sound was turned off, but both of them were convinced that if Lombardi was reading out a statement on a Vatican holiday, it could only mean that the pope had died. They hurried back to Rome and were greeted everywhere with consternation. 'The mood was catastrophic,' said Hofmann; 'everyone was shocked. Cardinals were running about like lost sheep. They were all wildly phoning about. Conferences were cancelled, people put off. Like being mutilated.'[9]

Hermann Geissler, from the Congregation for the Doctrine of the Faith, was also away when at 11.30 a.m. a colleague phoned him on his mobile. He said, 'My first reaction was that it's no use moaning about it, you have to accept it. The combination of reason, faith and humility was only possible for Benedict. He lived through John Paul II's final years, when other people made decisions for the pope. He does not want to repeat that.'[10]

Cardinal Gerhard Ludwig Müller, prefect of the Congregation for the Doctrine of the Faith, was on his way to a lunch that Cardinal Walter Brandmüller, the emeritus chief historian of the Vatican, was giving for him and the German ambassador to the Vatican. Cardinal Müller had missed the meeting in the Sala del Concistoro. He was suffering from jet lag after his return flight from the USA. In St Peter's Square he met Cardinal Koch. 'It took him a long time to convince me that the news was really true,' Müller said, 'I thought it was a Carnival Monday joke. No one could believe it, they were all upset. Everyone was saying that he was mentally fit.' Just in the last few days he had given his speech to the Roman priests. Müller, the chief defender of the faith after the pope, was convinced: 'The resignation was not handled theologically correctly. In principle the pope is the foundation of unity – a perpetual principle. A bishop steps down and is then a simple church member. But a pope is set in his post by Christ.'[11]

At 11.46 a.m. ANSA broadcast the exclusive report of the pope's resignation, which would take effect on 28 February at 8 p.m. At 11.47 Reuters also announced the news. At 12.24 there was the first official statement of the German federal government in Berlin. Chancellor Angela Merkel gave a further statement at 2.30 p.m. In it she praised Benedict XVI as 'one of the most important religious thinkers of the present day'. However, she applauded the pope for his retirement with 'my highest respect'. In an age when life was growing longer, many people could understand 'that the pope also had to cope with the burdens of old age'.

Meanwhile, other heads of state had spoken. US president Barack Obama and his wife thanked the pope for his co-operation: 'In the name of all Americans Michelle and I want to convey our esteem and our prayers for his Holiness Pope Benedict XVI,' Obama declared in his speech from the White House. The British prime minister, David Cameron, said the pope would be 'missed by millions of people as a spiritual leader'. Great Britain remembered his visit with 'great respect and affection'. The Italian prime minister, Mario Monti, was deeply moved. 'I am shocked at this unexpected news,' he said in Milan. UN Secretary-General Ban Ki-moon thanked Benedict XVI for having been strongly committed to inter-religious dialogue and for taking on global challenges such as the fight against poverty and hunger.

In Poland, state president Bronisław Komorowski said in a first statement: 'We are all distressed' because with the resignation of the head of the church 'the last fixed point, which stands firmly till the end' disappeared. At the Polish Bishops' Conference auxiliary bishop Wojciech Polak made clear: 'This resignation is not an escape into private life and personal comfort but shows far-sightedness.' Just half an hour after the resignation announcement, a Facebook post was initiated in Karol Wojtyła's home country: 'BXVI – thanks for everything!' Within a few minutes 10,000 users joined in. 'God will honour you for your love of the church', many messages said.

In Israel the Chief Rabbi Yona Metzger thanked the departing pope for his commitment to fighting anti-Semitism. Relations between Israel and the Vatican were 'better than ever before'. Aiman Mazyek, the chairman of the Central Council of Muslims in Germany, stated that Pope Benedict had made clear 'that he regarded Muslims with great respect and gave great importance to inter-religious dialogue'.

The most remarkable reactions came from Latin America. Benedict XVI's resignation was a loss for the cultural and spiritual life of the world, said the Peruvian writer Mario Vargas Llosa in Lima. In a guest article in the Spanish newspaper *El País*, Nobel prize-winner Vargas Llosa praised the spiritual and intellectual greatness of the departing head of the church. The pope's uniquely profound reflections derived from his great theological, philosophical, historical and literary knowledge. His writings encompassed 'audacious new reflections' on the moral, cultural and existential problems of our time. Because of the rapidly advancing secularization of society, Benedict's papacy had occurred at one of the most difficult stages that Christianity had been through in the 2,000 years of its life. But his resignation, and not just his resignation, showed anyone saying that this pope was a 'conservative' how nonsensical that reductionist label was.

Another statement almost got lost. When the news reached Buenos Aires, Argentinian journalists sought an opinion from the country's most important churchman. Cardinal Jorge Bergoglio placed on record that Benedict had 'shown he was very responsible'. He had tried to avoid mistakes and prevent the danger of manipulation: 'What the pope did is a revolutionary gesture. People talk about a conservative pope, but in fact Benedict's announcement has opened a new page in church history.' And, as if to confirm that this was about things that were above the ordinary and subject to a higher power than personal considerations, Bergoglio added: 'A pope is a human being whose decisions are made in the presence of God.'

Statements by politicians were one thing but how would the international press react to the sensation? With sadness? With understanding? Or perhaps with criticism? The Polish daily paper *Rzeczpospolita* was torn. 'His retirement shocks us,' said one commentary, 'for we thought that he would carry on – as his predecessor John Paul II did.' On the other hand, it was 'to the credit of the exhausted pope that he – intellectually and theologically brilliant – preferred to retire before he presented an image of weakness'. 'Pope Benedict to step down', the *Washington Post* reported matter-of-factly. In the end it had to be said: 'Benedict was a bit less conservative than the liberals feared, and a bit less conservative than the conservatives hoped.' In Paris *Le Figaro* commented: 'It can be imagined that the astuteness that characterizes this philosopher also drove him to choose a solitary and considered retirement.' The Spanish *Última Hora* said: 'The pope's retirement shakes up the church and begins a new era.'

In Madrid *El Mundo* announced: 'Benedict XVI ends the tradition whereby the pope dies on the cross.'

In Germany the pope's critics felt confirmed. 'Liberation in Rome' was the headline in *Die Zeit*. Another article was entitled: 'And Now Renewal. What Christians in Germany and the World Are Hoping For'. As if Ratzinger had not decidedly proclaimed the task of renewal as the programme from his first day in office. The pope had 'given up', *Der Spiegel* declared. His resignation speech had been 'hastily mumbled like a rosary, almost as casually as if he were giving back the key of a rented car rather than St Peter's fisherman's ring'. The *Süddeutsche Zeitung* began a series in which atheists, Muslims and Protestants were to write everything they had disliked about the German pope. The television broadcaster ZDF-History also gave its interpretation with the heading: 'The Head of the Catholic Church Jacks It In. The Memory Remains of Scandals and Intrigues.'

There were plenty more voices from his home country. According to a flash poll for the *ARD-Morgenmagazin* television programme, approval of Benedict XVI among German Catholics was 69 per cent, and 5 per cent among Protestants. In the general population just 24 per cent were not much or not at all in agreement with the pope's work.[12] Archbishop Robert Zollitsch stated: 'As chairman of our Bishops' Conference I should like to ask the Holy Father's forgiveness for all the errors about him that may have come from the church in Germany.'[13] The German Curia cardinal Walter Kasper paid tribute to the pope. Ratzinger had 'contributed a great deal to the consolidation of the church in faith and to deepening the faith. And he has performed the duties of his office in a very gentle and human way, even in difficult situations.' Kasper concluded with the words: 'It will be a long time before we have a pope again of Benedict's XVI's intellectual and spiritual calibre.'[14]

Meanwhile, the council chairman of the Evangelical Church in Germany, Nikolaus Schneider, commented on Benedict XVI's resignation that on his 2011 visit to Germany the pope had snubbed Evangelical Christians because 'he did not bring any ecumenical gifts'. But the Evangelical pastor Matthias Schreiber, commissioner for religion in the North Rhine-Westphalia local authority, observed that during Benedict's papacy the Roman Catholic Church had increased by 100 million members. In Germany the number of Catholics leaving the church was much lower than that of Protestants, and Catholic church attendance was three times higher. 'What is the long-term outlook for an institution when 96.4% of its members do not attend church?' Schreiber concluded self-critically. Rolf Schwärzel, pastor of the Northern Lower Saxony Evangelical Free Church, wrote: 'Quite a few orthodox believing Protestants, Lutherans, Evangelical Christians and representatives of confessing communities respect Benedict highly for his witness to Christ, which they themselves could subscribe to word for word.' For him personally, 'this quiet, modest pope fascinated me in a unique way. And that was although until then I had only heard the name "Ratzinger" in a negative context. I will miss him.'[15]

As the historic day of 11 February drew to a close, the rain had still not stopped in Rome. When night came, heavy storm clouds gathered over the Vatican. And when terrifyingly bright lightning struck the dome of St Peter's, the heavenly management produced a theatrical finale. Many interpreted the image, which immediately went round the world, as heaven's protest that a last fixed point had gone, through a decision that was not for humans but up to God to make. Others read the sign from heaven thus: 'You have got rid of the prophets again. But this man, whom many did not want to listen to, can become even louder by his silence!' The BBC photographer who had taken the photograph said later that on the day of the pope's resignation he had stood for three-quarters of an hour in the terrible weather waiting for the lightning to strike. His intention had been to suggest the idea of downfall, the end of the world or at least the end of an epoch.

★★★

Benedict's papacy lasted just eight years, exactly as long as the time John Paul II suffered. The German pope was convinced that he should not damage the memory of his predecessor's passion by a public passion of his own. Or if he became decrepit, a power vacuum might ensue that would be ominous for the church in the face of its current challenges. 'My predecessor had his own mission,' said Benedict. He was convinced that 'a phase of suffering belonged to that papacy. And was its own message.' However, he was also certain that 'it should not be repeated at will. And after a papacy lasting eight years one should not hang on for another eight years like that.'

In his reflections the pope had realized that his resignation would cause bewilderment. However, in retrospect he said that the wave of disappointment was stronger

> than I thought it would be. Friends and people for whom my message was important and pointed the way were really distraught for a while and felt abandoned. That hit me. But I was clear that I had to do it and that this was the right moment. Otherwise, I would just wait to die to end my papacy. Then people came to accept it. Many are grateful that now the new pope goes about it in a new style.

He had been convinced 'that my time was up and that I had given what I could give'.[16]

It was no accident that the departing pope celebrated his last major liturgy on Ash Wednesday. At the afternoon Mass in St Peter's, Benedict marked a cross of ashes on the foreheads of the faithful to signal the beginning of Lent. 'Remember, man, that thou are dust and to dust thou shalt return.' The ceremony was like a legacy: see, this is where I want to lead you. This royal way is the one I want to show you. Purification. Fasting. Repentance. Detoxify yourself. Free yourself of ballast. Don't be devoured by *Zeitgeist*s and time thieves. Less is more! Decrease in order to increase is also the church's programme. Slim down in order to gain vitality, spiritual freshness, inspiration and radiance. Also strength to cope with the programme that in many ways has become so difficult. And when the time of fasting and repentance is over, there will be a new resurrection, Easter, the time of light. The church will live on, it is indestructible, and in the thrill that comes with the beginning of every papacy it will receive a new impetus.

'I did not think about Carnival Monday,' Benedict XVI said in our conversation,

> but about Ash Wednesday. A major liturgy was to be celebrated on that day. And I found it very providential, that this final liturgy should be the beginning of Lent and also a *memento mori*

['remember you are mortal']. It embraces the seriousness of entering into Christ's passion and also the mystery of resurrection. Easter Saturday was at the beginning of my life. Having Ash Wednesday, in all its significance, at the end of my time in office was something arranged but also deliberate.

His hair shone like white gold when unliturgical applause kept breaking out in St Peter's. People had tears in their eyes, wherever you looked. Even Tarcisio Bertone battled with tears, as he addressed the pope in a personal word of thanks:

> We would not be honest, Your Holiness, if we failed to say that this evening our hearts are veiled in sadness. You were a model for us. You were truly a simple and modest labourer in the Lord's vineyard. You were a labourer who understood how to bring God to people and people to God. Your teaching was a window for the beams of truth and God's love to shine through onto the church and the world [...] Every step of your life and service can only be understood from the perspective of being with God and being in the light of God's word.[17]

On the day after Ash Wednesday Benedict once more summoned the Roman clergy, to talk for a long time impromptu about the Second Vatican Council. He recalled that there had been two different interpretations of its conclusions. The 'media Council', as he called it, had been the prevailing one, and unfortunately it had 'done a lot of harm, caused many problems, really a great deal of distress'. The 'true Council had difficulty in being implemented and realized.' However, it had proved to be the force to bring about 'real reform, real renewal for the church'.

The idea that the German pope was not loved or was alone was contradicted by the huge stream of pilgrims that poured onto St Peter's Square before the beginning of his penultimate midday Angelus on 17 February. Finally, 150,000 people gathered to show their love and respect for the departing pope. They included the mayor of Rome, Gianni Alemanno, and the members of the city council. Many of the faithful held up banners and celebrated the pope by calling out 'Benedetto!' From 17 to 23 February the

Curia were engaged in Lenten exercises. Cardinal Ravasi, who led the daily meditations, had been able to prepare and compared Benedict XVI to Moses in the biblical battle between Israel and Amalek. Just as Moses had strengthened his own troops by his prayer on the mountain, so in the future Benedict XVI's main function would be praying for his church.[18] The pope heaved a sigh of relief. It was 'moving and good' for him 'that no one could disturb me, because there were no audiences, and they all had a rest from the hustle and bustle'. They had become 'quite new inside […] because we all prayed and listened together four times a day. But each of us also stood before the Lord with his own personal responsibility.'[19]

At the end of the retreat Benedict felt confirmed in his decision and thanked them all for 'this praying and listening community, who have been with me during this week'. He thanked Cardinal Ravasi 'for this beautiful "walk" through the universe of faith, the universe of the psalms. The richness, the depth and the beauty of this universe have delighted us and we are grateful that God's word has spoken to us afresh with fresh power.' With a slight bow he said, 'In conclusion, dear friends, I'd like to thank you all […] for these eight years, during which you have borne the burden of St Peter's office together with me with great competence, devotion, love, and faith.' Even though soon now 'the "outward", "visible" community is coming to an end, the spiritual closeness remains and a deep community in prayer'.[20]

Ratzinger had already proved to be adept at farewell ceremonies in those he had organized as bishop of Munich. Then too he had quit his office on 28 February. In retrospect, he found his plan for the end of his papacy 'even better than I had realized'.[21] There were still a few personal decisions to clarify, as well as the question of whether the conclave could take place in Rome earlier than the prescribed date of 15 to 20 days after a pope's death, since the pope had not died. As there was no precedent for a pope resigning, he discussed with colleagues whether his future title should be *papa emerito*. As for the dress code, he decided to keep the white cassock but not to wear a *mozzetta* or a cincture any longer. In future he asked to be addressed not as 'Holy Father' or 'Your Holiness' but as 'Papa Benedetto'.

It was 24 February 2013 when Benedict gave the Angelus greeting from the most famous window in the world for the last time. Despite the unsettled cold weather, this time about 200,000 people had come. Ratzinger had never used the words 'providence' or 'dispensation' in connection with his retirement, although these were favourite words of his to describe certain forks along his road. But at this final Angelus the gospel of the day, which spoke about a mountain, 'acquired a very particular meaning' for him, as Benedict later confessed. 'Dear brothers and sisters,' he said. 'I feel how this word of God applies especially to me at this moment of my life. The Lord is calling me "to go up the mountain" to devote myself more to prayer and contemplation. But that does not mean I am deserting the church, on the contrary. If God asks this of me, it is so that I can continue to serve it, with the same commitment and the same love as I have tried to do until now, but in a way more suited to my age and my powers.'[22]

On Tuesday, 26 February, two days before the end of his papacy, the papal household had a farewell meal in the Apostolic Palace. It was a small group: the four Memores, the two secretaries and Sister Christine. 'It was so normal, that we could not believe it,' Sister Christine recalled. 'At the same time, of course, we all felt a certain heaviness.' When she said goodbye, she knelt on the floor to receive the apostolic blessing once more. 'That was a very dramatic moment. Everyone cried.' Only the pope kept his cool. 'Sister Christine,' he said drily as he gave the blessing, 'I see that over the years your hair has gone grey.'[23]

In the discussion about the end of his papacy it had become clear that with Ratzinger possibly it was the last time that a European sat on St Peter's chair. Since Benedict had timed his retirement to take account of the World Youth Day in Rio de Janeiro, it could be assumed that his considerations included a possible successor who did not come from the East or the West but, as did indeed happen, 'from the end of the world'. At the same time, sooner or later, whoever the next pope was, Ratzinger's successor would have to realize the greatness and importance of his teaching. If he had remained in office, become ever more frail, he would have had to fear the daily grind, instead of writing history again, as he would now, and as he had already done by his contribution to the Council.

The circle had been closed. It began when he removed the tiara – a sign of the church's worldly power – from his coat of arms. It ended when he renounced the power of a mighty office. Benedict XVI did not schedule a great farewell celebration.

> If you have a farewell party that would really be worldly. It had to be in keeping with spiritual service. In this case there was the Ash Wednesday liturgy and the later meeting with the faithful in St Peter's Square, in joy and recollection. It was absolutely right both to meet the church as a whole and also meet the people who wanted to say goodbye. Not with a worldly party but as a coming together in the word of the Lord and in faith.[24]

Benedict's resignation was not only the first resignation of an actually reigning pope. It also gave the opportunity for the first time in history to question a pope personally about his actions. It was not only the Italian media that speculated immediately after his retirement on whether the real reason for it was to be sought in the Vatileaks affair, which not only included Paolo Gabriele's leaks but also the financial problems and intrigues in the church. Perhaps the investigation report on these matters had so shocked him that he had seen no alternative but to give way to a successor as pope. 'No, that's not right,' said the pope emeritus in our conversation. 'On the contrary, the matters had been fully cleared up. I said then that you cannot retire when things are going wrong, but only if they are at peace. I was able to retire because things had become calm again. It was not the case that this was a retreat under pressure or a flight, through being unable to deal with these things.'

Asked whether failing capacity was a sufficient reason to step down from the chair of Peter, he answered:

> Of course, that might cause a misunderstanding about function. The Petrine succession is not only linked to a function, but also concerns being. So functioning is not the only criterion. On the other hand, a pope must also do particular things, must keep an eye on the whole situation, must know how to set priorities and so on. Receiving heads of state, receiving bishops, with whom you must be able really to have an intimate conversation, then all

the decisions which have to be taken every day. Even if you say that some things can be dropped, it still leaves so many that are essential, that if the work is to be done properly, it becomes clear: if you are no longer capable it is advisable – at least for me, others may see it differently – to vacate the chair.

It was from this perspective that he became convinced that 'the Lord does not want anything more from me and, so to speak, frees me from the burden'.[25]

For his final general audience, the 348th of his papacy, 350,000 faithful from all over the world came to hear and see their pope once more. They pressed against all the barriers. From the basilica down to the Tiber closely packed Benedetto fans stood holding flags of all countries and continents. It was papal weather, a light early spring day. He was '*troppo puro, troppo innocente, troppo santo!*' – 'too pure, too innocent, too holy' – a grey-haired police chief dictated to a reporter, as the old pope drove into St Peter's Square once more in his pope-mobile. Full of emotion, he wiped the tears from his eyes.

Over the last eight years the pope had met more than 18 million people in general audiences in St Peter's Square or in the Nervi Audience Hall. 'At this moment my spirit expands and embraces the whole church spread all over the world,' Benedict XVI greeted the faithful with a shaking voice,

and I thank God for the 'news' that I have gathered in these years in the Petrine service about the believers in Jesus Christ the Lord, the love that really flows through the body of the church and enables it to live in love, and the hope in which it opens us out towards fullness of life, to our heavenly home. I feel I hold them all in prayer in a presence which is the presence of God.

It was a very personal emotional speech. 'When on 19 April, almost eight years ago, I agreed to take on the papacy,' Benedict continued,

I had the firm certainty, which I have always kept, that the church lives and lives by God's word. As I have often said before, I took these words to heart: 'Lord, why do you ask this of me, and what do you ask of me? It is a great burden that you are laying on my shoulders, but if you ask me, then at your word I will throw out the nets in the certainty that you will lead me, even with all my weaknesses.' Eight years later I can say that the Lord has really led me. He has been close to me. I have been aware of his presence every day.

Often in his work he had felt 'like Peter with the apostles in the boat on the Sea of Galilee'. Yes, the Lord had given him and his companions 'many sunny days with a light breeze, days on which to get a good catch of fish'. But there had also been situations

in which the water was stormy and we had a contrary wind, as has happened throughout the whole of church history, and the Lord seemed to be asleep. But I always knew the Lord was in this boat and I always knew that the boat of the church does not listen to me, or to us, but to him. [...] And that is the reason why today my heart is full of gratitude to God, because he has never failed to give the whole church and me his comfort, his light and his love.

The departing pope's final speech sounded like a letter, a love letter:

I'd like to invite you all to renew your firm trust in the Lord, let God's arms enfold you like children, in the certainty that those arms always support us and make it possible for us to go forward day by day, even when things are difficult. I'd like each of you to feel loved by that God, who gave his Son for us and showed his boundless love. I'd like each of you to feel the joy of being a Christian.

He not only wanted to thank God, Benedict continued. He had 'never felt alone in bearing the joy and the burden of the Petrine service'. He thought of 'many people who do not appear, who remain in the shadows, but who were a firm and reliable support for me in their daily devotion, in the spirit of faith and humility'. He was attached, without exception, to each and every one of them with that pastoral love which was the heart of any shepherd, especially the bishop of Rome, St Peter's successor. 'Every day I have remembered each of you with fatherly love in my prayers.' He now realized 'more deeply in a heartfelt way' that he had so many friends. He received many letters

from the great ones of the Earth – heads of states, religious leaders, representatives of high culture and so on. But I also receive many letters from quite simple people, who write to me straight from the heart and make me feel their affection. These people do not write to me as you write to a prince or a great unknown person. They write to me as brothers and sisters or sons and daughters, in a warm, family bond.

Similar words of unconditional love were heard from some of the really great popes. But no one ever spoke them like Benedict XVI as once again, almost apologetically, he explained his historic step to the flock entrusted to him. He began this part of his farewell speech by saying that in recent months he had felt

that my powers have been failing, and I begged God in prayer to give me his light, and help me make the decision that is best not for my own welfare but for the welfare of the church. I have taken this step in full awareness of its seriousness and novelty, but with deep calmness of spirit. Loving the church also means having the courage to make difficult, considered decisions and always bearing in mind the welfare of the church rather than my own.

Then for the first time he described the status of a pope who had freely given up his office as a *papa emerito*. Benedict made clear:

There is no return to private life. My decision to give up the active exercise of my office does not affect this. I am not returning to private life – into a life without journeys, meetings, receptions, speeches and so on. I am not coming down from the cross but staying with the crucified Lord in a new way. I no longer have the official authority to lead the church, but in the service of prayer I remain, so to speak, within the inner circle of St Peter. [...] I shall still accompany the way of the church in prayer and reflection, with that devotion to the Lord and his bride which I have tried to give up till now and should always like to give.[26]

For the last time the pope greeted the people in different languages, in English, Italian, Arabic and Polish. 'My wish is that you all feel the joy, that you feel how beautiful it is to be a Christian and belong to the church.' Then he stood up and spoke the 'Our Father' in Latin. A small, white-haired man with folded hands and a quivering voice, standing upright.

As for every inland flight, the Italian government had provided the pope with the white Sikorsky Sea King helicopter, which was now waiting on the Vatican City heliport. Colonel Girolamo Iadicicco of the 31st squadron of the Italian air force was assisted by a co-pilot and a technician. The heliport was taboo for the press. So every available roof terrace around St Peter's Square was rented for the day at high rates, to serve as improvised television studios and catch the moment that had never occurred in history before. It was 28 February 2013, the last day in Benedict XVI's papacy. His term of office had lasted seven years, ten months and 17 days. During that time 3,641 journalists had been accredited in Rome. They worked for 968 media organizations, including 247 TV stations, and they came from 61 countries.

In the morning Benedict met the cardinals once more. He had brought with him a book by one of his important teachers during his youth, Romano Guardini's *Die Kirche des Herrn* (*The Lord's Church*), and showed it round. The church 'is not an invented and constructed institution,' he read from it, 'but a living being. [...] It lives on through time, it *becomes* as every living thing *becomes* [...] nevertheless, in essence it is always the same and its inmost being is Christ.' He concluded with a request: 'Dear brothers, let us remain united in this mystery, especially in the daily Eucharist, and so we serve the church and the whole of humanity.' Following a spontaneous inspiration he added: 'And among you in the College of Cardinals is the future pope, to whom today I promise my unconditional respect and my unconditional obedience.'

The promise of obedience was not in his prepared text. 'Did you have any idea who your successor might be?' I asked him in our conversation.

No, absolutely not!

No inkling, no idea?

No. No.

So how could you immediately offer absolute obedience to your successor?

The pope is the pope. It doesn't matter who it is!

Georg Gänswein confessed that he 'had not grasped anything more, because I was simply so shocked and exhausted' during his final moments as the pope's secretary. They had put out the light in the *appartamento*, taken the old lift down to the Courtyard of St Damasus. To the pope's surprise, colleagues were waiting there to say goodbye with thunderous applause. Then they drove to the heliport. At 5.05 p.m. the heavy rotor blades began slowly to lift the 'pope-copter' into the sky. As well as the crew and the pope, his two secretaries and Cardinal Harvey were on board. To enable countless millions of viewers from Cape Town to Tokyo to see the farewell live, a plane chartered by CTV immediately took off as well. The Vatican broadcaster usually documented the pope's audiences or provided other media with recording crews, or video and audio support. Now the eager CTV reporters followed the breathtaking manoeuvre of the pilot, who had decided to fly a final lap of honour round St Peter's dome.

Shortly before his departure Benedict's final tweet was released: 'Thank you for your love and support. I wish you always to feel the joy of putting Christ at the centre of your life.' As soon as the helicopter took off, the Vatican bells began ringing, and gradually all the other bells of the 400 churches in the Eternal City joined in. Santa Maria in Trastevere, St John Lateran, Santa Maria Maggiore, St Paul outside the Walls, St Sebastian at the Catacombs. 'No one in the helicopter said a word during the flight,' Gänswein said later. He himself had felt 'wretched': 'It was a farewell and an ache, and the natural expression of pain is that your tears come.' Light as a feather, carried by the bells of Rome, the papal plane hovered over the Colosseum, the Roman Forum and soon swung over the Via Appia, the ancient queen of highways following a long, straight line through the Campagna.

Never before had a pope's decision offered such a challenge to the Catholic Church from one day to the next. Never before in the 2,000 years of its history had a reigning successor to St Peter had the courage to take such a step. There had never been a pope emeritus before. But neither had there ever been such pictures before. Benedict XVI tried not to be overcome by his feelings, but in our conversation about his farewell his emotion was so strong that he could not hold back his tears. They were tears for a long battle, tears of relief, which allowed him once more to feel the whole burden that had lain on his narrow shoulders for many years. They were tears of gratitude to a loving God, who had given him the strength to fulfil a Herculean task, which he could never had trusted himself to do. 'It moved me deeply,' said the pope emeritus. 'The warmth of the farewell, that some of the staff were in tears. Then over the Pastor Bonus house there was a big poster saying "Vergelt's Gott, Heiliger Vater" ['Thank you, Holy Father']. Hovering above and hearing the bells of Rome ringing, then I knew I could be thankful, and that thankfulness is my basic feeling.'

At 5.15 p.m. the helicopter landed in the garden of the pope's summer residence. The Castel Gandolfo market-place had long been full to overflowing. Visitors who had hastened from Rome also tried to sneak a last look at the departing pope. Shortly afterwards Benedict appeared at the palace window. He was joyfully welcomed by his followers and the local inhabitants. 'From 8 p.m. I shall no longer be pope, no longer the chief shepherd of the Catholic Church, but simply a pilgrim stepping out on the final stage of his journey on Earth,' he began with a slight tremble in his voice. 'But I want to keep on working with my heart, my love, my prayers, my thoughts, with all my intellectual powers, for the good of the church and humanity.'

At 5.40 p.m. he gave those present his blessing, waved to the faithful once more from his balcony. And as the carpet with his coat of arms on it, which hung over the balcony, was rolled up, the traditional wall relief appeared over the porch: the tiara, the triple papal crown, together with St Peter's crossed keys. After his final 'Buona notte' Benedict retired to the flat one floor below. He went into his bedroom to unpack the small suitcase his sister had given him many years earlier, containing his underwear, pyjamas and slippers, which he had always looked after himself. When it was supper time, the Swiss Guards could be heard closing the great door, with its bolts at the top and bottom and crossbeam in the middle. At supper there was an unprecedented silence. Benedict did not say a word. 'We didn't know whether we should eat anything, say anything or not say anything. Just ate what was in front of us,' the secretary recalled. 'Then we went up and watched the Telegiornale, and went for a walk as usual. Then, as usual, the pope said Compline in the chapel next to his bedroom.'

As announced, the papacy ended at 8 p.m. But why not at midnight, as was customary? Quite simply because for Benedict the working day ended at 8 p.m. He watched the evening news and went to bed. At the same time the Roman church camerlengo, Cardinal Secretary of State Bertone, sealed Benedict XVI's apartment on the third floor of the Apostolic Palace in Rome and the lift leading up to it. When Benedict appeared at Mass next morning in Castel Gandolfo, the fisherman's ring was not on his finger.

It was the end of an era, one of those moments in time that mark great changes. He was the last pope to have experienced the terror of evil in the twentieth century. The last to have helped shape the Council. And the last pope to possess such an education in intellectual history and theology, a level that would not be reached again. Benedict XVI was regarded not only as the greatest theologian ever to sit on the chair of St Peter, but also as one of the most important thinkers of our time. The English historian Peter Watson included him in the list of personalities like Beethoven and Hegel, to whom the label 'German genius' applied.

That would all be missed now: his shy smile; his often rather clumsy movements when he stepped onto a stage; his clever speeches, which could cool the mind and warm the heart; the elegance with which he made difficult subjects easy, without losing their mystery or trivializing the holy; and above all, his readiness to listen, which no one could surpass. He was both a thinker and a man of prayer, for whom the mysteries of Christ were the decisive reality of the world creation and world history. He was a lover of humanity, who did not have to think long about the question of how many ways there are to God, to answer: 'As many as there are human beings.'

Joseph Ratzinger incorporated a new intelligence in recognizing and expressing the faith and at the same time defended the piety of simple people. He was a nonconformist and non-comfortable; his conversation partners were always also people who were at odds with the Establishment. He gave the papacy a new quality. He rid it of false attributes, unnecessary pomp, the lust for power, and showed Christ's representative as a symbol of Christ being in the world. Without any ifs or buts, he was wholly dedicated to what the office had to give.

'Do you see yourself as the last of an old era or the first of a new one? I asked Benedict once again. He cleared his throat and answered,' I'd say it was between the times.'

'As the bridge, the link between the worlds?'

'I no longer belong to the old one, but the new one is not yet really there.'

It was clear that never before had a pope changed the papacy as much as he did. His step symbolized the end of the old and the beginning of the new in the history of the church. That is also one of the paradoxes of this biography: that the apparently last is also the first.

'The Lord is calling me to climb the mountain,' the departing pope had called to the crowd, whose mute question he sensed. No, he was not going 'back into private life', but remained 'with the crucified Lord in a new way', with the difficulties of Christians and their church. In the end God's philosopher, the great thinker on the chair of St Peter, went where reason alone was not enough. Into mediation and prayer.

Final Questions to Benedict XVI

After the many interviews I was able to have with Benedict XVI, a few more questions arose, which I proceeded to ask him in the autumn of 2018. However, the pope emeritus failed to answer many of the questions. For 'what you are asking me there leads naturally very far into the church's present situation', he explained in an accompanying letter of 12 November 2018. Answering such questions would 'inevitably be interfering in the work of the present pope. I must avoid and want to avoid anything in that direction.'

Papa Benedetto, do you follow events in the Church?

Yes.

You didn't want to write a spiritual testament. But have you done so?

Yes.

As pope you immediately introduced the canonization process of your predecessor, without waiting for the usual five years. What drove you to that haste?

The obvious desire of the faithful and the model given by the pope, which I myself had experienced over more than two decades.

It is often said about your papacy that you came up against many blockades in the Curia.

The blockades came more from the outside than from the Curia. In the first place I wanted to promote the clean-up not just of the small world of the Curia but of the church as a whole. The pope is not primarily pope of the Curia, but he is responsible for the church at that historical moment. Events showed that the crisis of faith had also led to a crisis in Christian living. That is the dimension the pope must keep in mind.

Did Vatileaks contribute to your decision to retire?

In my *Last Testament* I made clear that my retirement had nothing to do with the Paolo Gabriele affair. If I had run away from such occurrences, then there would have been other occasions of that kind. But to withstand them and not bend to them seems to me now, as it did then, an essential job for the pope. That is why my retirement had absolutely nothing to do with all that.

There is still speculation today about your visit to the tomb of Pope Celestine V in 2009, the only pope to have resigned before you. What was behind it?

My visit to Pope Celestine V's tomb was more of a coincidence. But I realized that Celestine V's situation was unique and could not serve as an example in any way.

The US journalist Rod Dreher said: 'A friend who was close to Benedict told me that the pope had resigned, as he had realized that the corruption in the Curia went much further than he could cope with.' Was that invented?

Yes.

A sentence in your inauguration sermon remains particularly in mind: 'Pray for me that I don't flee in terror from the wolves.' Did you foresee all the things that would come upon you?

Here I must also say that the radius of what a pope may fear is taken to be much too small. Of course issues like the Vatileaks are annoying and, above all, unintelligible and very disturbing to people in the wider world. However, the actual threat to the church, and so to the papacy, does not come from these things but from the global dictatorship of ostensibly humanist ideologies. Contradicting them means being excluded from the basic social consensus. A hundred years ago anyone would have found it absurd to speak of homosexual marriage. Today anyone opposing it is socially excommunicated. The same goes for abortion and creating human beings in a laboratory. Modern society is formulating an anti-Christian creed and opposing it is punished with social excommunication. It is only natural to fear this spiritual power of Antichrist and it really needs help from the prayers of a whole diocese and the world church to resist it.

Volker Reinhardt, a church historian at the University of Fribourg in Switzerland, said: 'For me Benedict XVI's resignation is an act of extreme self-distancing from the condition of the church and an admission that he can't lead the church in the way that is needed.'

An 'extreme self-distancing from the condition of the church' was certainly not my intention. If you study papal history, you soon realize that the church has always been a net with good and bad fishes in it. It belongs to the Catholic understanding of the church and its leadership not to conceive of an ideal church but to be prepared to live and work with a church that is up against the power of evil.

John Paul II wrote in 1989 that the question of retirement in the event of serious illness came up. Five years later he reached the conclusion that there was 'no room for a pope emeritus in the church'. Have you ever asked yourself what your predecessor would have said about your retirement?

It is right that very early on both Paul VI and John Paul II signed statements declaring their retirement in the event of an illness that made the proper exercise of their office impossible. They were thinking primarily of various forms of dementia. Following their example, I also signed a similar statement relatively early on. In the end I realized that other kinds of failing capacity to do the job properly were also possible.

By your resignation have you laid the foundation stone for a new tradition in the Catholic Church? You are the first successor to St Peter to call yourself 'pope emeritus'. Church historians declare that there can't be a 'pope emeritus' because neither can there be two popes.

It is hard to understand how a church historian, who is someone who studies the church's past, should know better than others whether there can be a pope emeritus or not. From my point of view I'd like to say the following. Until the end of the Second Vatican Council bishops could not retire either. When finally, after vigorous debates, retirement for bishops was introduced, at once a practical problem arose, which no one had thought of: you can only be a bishop in connection with a particular diocese. The ordination of a bishop is always 'relative': that is to say, related to being assigned to a bishopric. That relative character of the office of bishop, inherent in the sacrament, means that for non-resident bishops (today usually called auxiliary bishops) a fictional see has to be found. More than a hundred sees from the early church are available, most of which are in present-day Islamic regions, which can no longer really be occupied by bishops. So for a retiring bishop, who was no longer the bishop of his own diocese (for example, Munich or Berlin), a titular see was found (for example, Carthage or Hippo etc.). But with the rapidly growing number of retiring bishops and other titular bishops, it could be seen that soon the titular bishoprics would run out.

What does that mean?

I believe the solution was found by the then bishop of Passau, Simon Konrad Landersdorfer, who was a very energetic and learned man. He said that after his real diocese he did not want a fictional one. He had to be satisfied with being bishop 'emeritus' of Passau.

What is an emeritus bishop or pope?

The word 'emeritus' meant that he was no longer the active holder of the bishopric, but remained in a special relationship to it as its former bishop. So the need to define his office in relation to a real diocese was met without making him a second bishop of it. The word 'emeritus' said that he had totally given up his office, but his spiritual link to his former diocese was now properly recognized. In general, a titular see was a pure legal fiction, but now there was a special relationship to a see where the retired bishop had formerly worked. This real, but hitherto legally unrecognized, relationship to a former see is the new meaning of 'emeritus' acquired after Vatican II. It does not affect the legal substance of the office of bishop but acknowledges the spiritual link as a reality. So there are not two bishops but a spiritual assignment, whose essence is to serve his former diocese by being with it and for it in prayer with all his heart and with the Lord.

But does that apply to the pope?

It is hard to understand why this legal concept should not also be applied to the bishop of Rome. In this formula both things are

implied: no actual legal authority any longer, but a spiritual relationship which remains even if it is invisible. This legal-spiritual formula
avoids any idea of there being two popes at the same time: a bishopric can only have one incumbent. But the formula also expresses
a spiritual link, which cannot ever be taken away. I am extremely
grateful to the Lord that Pope Francis's warm and generous attitude
towards me has made it possible to implement this idea in practice.

*In the past it was always held against the retirement of bishops that he is
a father, and fatherhood cannot be withdrawn.*

There is something right and something wrong about that. Of
course, someone remains a father and the human-spiritual meaning of fatherhood remains until death. But fatherhood is not only
ontological but also functional. A new generation comes to adult-
hood and the father gives up his legal position. He no longer has
potestas paterna but has to hand the helm over to his son at the
right moment. I find this beautifully expressed in the way that
was customary among the Bavarian peasants. There is a so-called
settlement [*Austrag*], physically expressed in a simple dwelling
which stands beside the big farmhouse. The father 'gives over' his
property to his son. He moves out from the big farmhouse into
the smaller house and also receives a 'settlement' in the form of
material goods (food, money etc.). So his material independence
is assured, as well as the handover of actual legal rights to the
son. This means that the spiritual side of being a father endures,
whereas the rights and duties change. It is not difficult to see that
this arrangement could also apply to a bishop emeritus.

Critics accuse you of not keeping to your self-imposed discretion.

The allegation that I regularly interfere in public debates is a malicious distortion of the reality. They are probably thinking of the
words of friendship that – at the invitation of Cardinal Woelki – I
devoted to Cardinal Meisner at his funeral. I took what I said about
the little ship of the church running into heavy storms almost
word for word from the sermons of Gregory the Great. Anyone
calling such an image of the church today, whose basic truth can
hardly be disputed, dangerous interference in the administration
of the church is participating in propaganda against me, which has

nothing to do with truth. A particularly crass and sorry case of such twisting was the reaction to my *Last Testament*.

There was particularly harsh criticism of your article on the Jewish question, which was published in the theological journal Communio *on 12 July 2018.*

I had written my 'Remarks' on the subject of Christianity and Judaism as an internal paper and sent it to Cardinal Koch, who was responsible for the matter of Judaism in the Roman Curia. I expressly said that the text was not for publication. After long consideration Cardinal Koch wrote to me saying he thought the text was so important that it ought to be published now, and asked me for permission, which I gave him. Perhaps I should have said no, for the sake of my own peace and quiet. But the spectacle of the reactions from the German theologians was so absurd and malicious that it's better not to speak about it. The actual reason for it – that people want to silence my voice – I'd rather not analyse.

Cardinal Raymond Burke, one of the four authors of the 'dubia', which formulated doubts about the Apostolic Exhortation 'Amoris laetitia', stated in November 2016 that 'Amoris laetitia' had created confusion: 'It caused a terrible split in the church and that is not the church's way.' Pope Francis has never replied to the 'dubia'. Should he have done so?

I don't want to take a position on that last question, because it goes into too much detail about the government of the church and would therefore go beyond the spiritual dimension, which alone still remains my remit. I accept that all those who constantly denounce me for my public statements would find confirmation in those answers. So I can only refer to what I said in my last public general audience on 27 February 2013. In the church among all humanity's troubles and the bewildering power of the evil spirit, the gentle power of God's goodness can still be recognized. Although the darkness of successive eras will never simply leave the joy of being a Christian unalloyed […] in the church and in the lives of individual Christians again and again there are moments in which we are deeply aware that the Lord loves us and that love means joy, is 'happiness'.

In his book The Mystery of Evil: Benedict XVI and the End of Days *the Italian philosopher Giorgio Agamben expresses the conviction that the actual reason for your retirement was a wake-up call to eschatological awareness. In the divine plan of salvation the church's function was to be both the 'church of Christ and the church of Antichrist'. Your retirement was an anticipation of the separation of 'Babylon' from 'Jerusalem' in the church. Instead of subscribing to the logic of clinging to power, through your resignation of office you stressed its spiritual authority and finally also strengthened it.*

St Augustine said of Jesus' parables about the church that, on the one hand, many people in it are only apparently so, but are really against the church. And on the other hand, many who are outside it belong – without knowing it – deeply to the Lord and thus also to his body, the church. We must always keep reminding ourselves of that mysterious overlap between inside and outside, which the Lord illustrated in various parables. Then we realize that there are times in history in which God's victory over the powers of evil is comfortingly visible, and times when the power of evil darkens everything. In conclusion I'd like to quote the Second Vatican Council, whose Constitution on the Church (I: 8) refers to Augustine when it summarizes this view: the church, 'like a stranger in a foreign land, presses forward amid the persecutions of the world and the consolations of God' (Augustine, *Civ. Dei*, XVIII, 51, 2: Patrologia Latina 41, 614), announcing the cross and death of the Lord until He comes (cf. 1 Cor. 11.26).

On 23 March 2013 the first meeting between the newly elected and the retired pope took place in Castel Gandolfo – an event unprecedented in history. What thoughts did you have at that moment?

I knew Pope Francis from his *ad limina* visit and various contacts by letter that my Congregation had had with him. I also knew that he tried to telephone me immediately after his election, even before he showed himself to the people from the balcony. So I was glad to meet my successor and gratefully aware that it would be a good meeting between brothers. Of course I had carefully considered what I should say to him, without taking up too much of his time. So that first meeting remains as a bright light in my memory. As you know, my personal friendship with Pope Francis has not just continued but grown stronger.

Notes

CHAPTER 1: TÜBINGEN

1 Interview with the author.
2 Freddy Derwahl, *Benedikt XVI. und Hans Küng: Geschichte einer Freundschaft* (Munich, 2008).
3 Ibid.
4 Hans Küng, *Erkämpfte Freiheit* (Munich, 2002).
5 Daniel Deckers, *Der Kardinal: Karl Lehmann – eine Biographie* (Munich, 2002).
6 Michael Karger, 'Walter Jens – Hans Küng und Joseph Ratzinger', in Rudolf Voderholzer, Christian Schaller and Franz-Xaver Heibl (eds), *Mitteilungen des Instituts Papst Benedikt XVI.* (Regensburg, 2009), vol. 2.
7 Interview with the author.
8 *Der Spiegel* (14 January 1980).
9 Interview with the author.
10 Ibid.
11 Derwahl, *Benedikt XVI. und Hans Küng*.
12 Interview with the author.
13 Derwahl, *Benedikt XVI. und Hans Küng*.
14 Manuel Schlögl, 'Joseph Ratzinger und die Nouvelle Théologie', in *Klerusblatt* (2017).
15 Norbert Trippen, *Josef Kardinal Frings* (Paderborn, 2005).
16 Interview with the author.
17 Joseph Ratzinger and Peter Seewald, *Salz der Erde* (Stuttgart, 1996).

CHAPTER 2: DEEPLY AFRAID

1 Gianni Valente, 'Benedikt XVI. 1966–1969: die schwierigen Jahre', in *30 Tage*, vol. 5 (2006).
2 Joseph Ratzinger, *Das neue Volk Gottes* (Düsseldorf, 1969), quoting Rom. 12.2.
3 Joseph Ratzinger, *Das Konzil auf dem Weg: Rückblick auf die zweite Sitzungsperiode des Zweiten Vatikanischen Konzils* (Cologne, 1964).
4 Joseph Ratzinger, *Aus meinem Leben* (Stuttgart, 1998).
5 *Kirche + Leben* online magazine (1966).
6 Valente, 'Benedikt XVI. 1966–1969'.
7 Joseph Ratzinger, 'Weltoffene Kirche? Überlegungen zur Struktur des Zweiten Vatikanischen Konzils', in Josef Ratzinger, *Zur Lehre des Zweiten Vatikanischen Konzils,* vol. 7/2 of *Gesammelte Schriften* (Freiburg im Breisgau, 2012).
8 Joseph Ratzinger, 'Der Katholizismus nach dem Konzil', in Zentralkomitee der Deutschen Katholiken (ed.), *Auf dein Wort hin,* 81st German Catholics' Conference (*Katholikentag*), 13–17 July 1966, in Bamberg (Paderborn, 1966); repr. in vol. 7/2 of Ratzinger, *Gesammelte Schriften.*
9 Siegfried Wiedenhofer, 'Joseph Ratzinger und die nachkonziliare Auseinandersetzung um den zukünftigen Weg katholischer Theologie', in Ulrike Irrgang and Wolfgang Baum (eds), *Die Wahrheit meiner Gewissheit suchen: Theologie vor dem Forum der Wirklichkeit. Festschrift für Albert Franz* (Würzburg, 2012).
10 Henri de Lubac, *Meine Schriften im Überblick* (Einsiedeln, 1996).
11 *Kirche + Leben* (13 February 1968).
12 *Kirche + Leben* (6 March 1968).
13 Interview in the Chilean newspaper *Comunione e Liberazione* (summer 1988).
14 Rudolf Voderholzer, *Henri de Lubac begegnen* (Augsburg, 1999).

15   Hubert Jedin, *Lebensbericht* (Mainz, 1984).
16   Alfred Lorenzer, *Das Konzil der Buchhalter* (Frankfurt am Main, 1984).
17   Manuel Schlögl, *Joseph Ratzinger in Münster, 1963–1966* (Münster, 2012).
18   *Die Tagespost* (2 February 2016).
19   Hansjürgen Verweyen, *Joseph Ratzinger – Benedikt XVI.: die Entwicklung seines Denkens* (Darmstadt, 2007).
20   Franz Walter, 'Katholizismus in der Bundesrepublik – von der Staatskirche zur Säkularisation', in *Blätter für Deutsche und Internationale Politik*, vol. 41 (1996).
21   Norbert Trippen, *Josef Kardinal Frings* (Paderborn, 2005).
22   Interview with the author.
23   Trippen, *Josef Kardinal Frings*.
24   Michael Gurtner, kath.net (11 October 2012).
25   Walter, 'Katholizismus in der Bundesrepublik'.

CHAPTER 3: 1968 AND THE MYTH OF THE CHANGE

1   *Süddeutsche Zeitung* (7/8 April 2018).
2   *Süddeutsche Zeitung* (3/4 February 2018).
3   Interview with the author.
4   Bayerischer Rundfunk interview with Martin Lohmann (28 December 1998).
5   Ratzinger, *Aus meinem Leben*.
6   *Die Tagespost* (19 December 2017).
7   Stéphane Courtois (ed.), *Das Schwarzbuch des Kommunismus: Unterdrückung, Verbrechen und Terror* (Munich, 1998).
8   Ratzinger, *Aus meinem Leben*.
9   Karl Wagner and Hermann Ruf (eds), *Kardinal Ratzinger: der Erzbischof von München und Freising in Wort und Bild* (Munich, 1977).
10   Benedikt Sepp, 'Schwenken, Schmücken und Studieren', in Anke Jaspers, Claudia Michalsk and Morten Paul, *Ein kleines rotes Buch: die Mao-Bibel und die Revolution der Sechzigerjahre* (Berlin, 2018).
11   Ibid.
12   *Die Zeit* (19 April 2012).
13   *Süddeutsche Zeitung* (14 May 2016).
14   Ibid.
15   Interview with the author.
16   Ratzinger, *Aus meinem Leben*.
17   Götz Aly, *Unser Kampf: 1968 – ein irritierter Blick zurück* (Frankfurt am Main, 2009).
18   *Lausitzer Rundschau* (29 April 2018).
19   Interview with the author.
20   Horst Herrmann, *Benedikt XVI.: der neue Papst aus Deutschland* (Berlin, 2005).
21   Hermann Häring, *Theologie und Ideologie bei Joseph Ratzinger* (Düsseldorf, 2001).
22   Christian Feldmann, *Papst Benedikt XVI.: eine kritische Biografie* (Hamburg, 2006).
23   Christian Feldmann, *Benedikt XVI.: Bilanz des deutschen Papstes* (Freiburg, 2013).
24   John L. Allen, *Kardinal Ratzinger* (Trier, 2002).
25   John L. Allen, *Worum es dem Papst geht* (Freiburg, 2008).
26   Ibid.
27   Interview with Manuel Schlögl.
28   Ibid.
29   Ibid.
30   Gianni Valente, 'Benedikt XVI. 1966–1969'.
31   Bayerischer Rundfunk interview.
32   Hansjürgen Verweyen, *Joseph Ratzinger – Benedikt XVI.*
33   Freddy Derwahl, *Benedikt XVI. und Hans Küng*.
34   Interview with the author.
35   Hubertus Halbfas, *Das Christentum* (Mannheim, 2004).

CHAPTER 4: THE CATHOLIC CRISIS

1   *Der Spiegel* (5 August 1968).
2   Interview with the author.
3   Jedin, *Lebensbericht*.

4 Ibid.
5 Ibid.
6 Joseph Ratzinger, *Einführung in das Christentum* (Munich, 1968).
7 Ibid.
8 Alexander Kissler, *Der deutsche Papst – Benedikt XVI. und seine schwierige Heimat* (Freiburg, 2005).
9 Ratzinger, *Einführung*.
10 Hansjürgen Verweyen, *Ein unbekannter Ratzinger: die Habilitationsschrift von 1955 als Schlüssel zu seiner Theologie* (Regensburg, 2010).
11 Ibid.
12 *Die Tagespost* (8 April 2016).
13 Marie-Gabrielle Lemaire, 'Joseph Ratzinger und Henri de Lubac', in *Mitteilungen des Instituts Papst Benedikt XVI.*, vol. 8 (Regensburg, 2015).
14 Derwahl, *Benedikt XVI. und Hans Küng*.
15 Interview with Manuel Schlögl.
16 Interview with the author.
17 Ratzinger and Seewald, *Salz der Erde*.
18 Bayerischer Rundfunk interview with Martin Lohmann (28 December 1998).
19 Interview with the author.
20 Quoted from George Orwell's proposed preface to *Animal Farm*, 'The Freedom of the Press', written in 1945 but not published then with the book.
21 Interview with the author.

CHAPTER 5: A FRESH START

1 Hans Küng, *Umstrittene Wahrheit: Erinnerungen* (Munich, 2007).
2 Interview with the author.
3 Karl Birkenseer, *Hier bin ich wirklich daheim: Papst Benedikt XVI. und das Bistum Regensburg* (Regensburg, 2005).
4 Benedikt XVI and Peter Seewald, *Letzte Gespräche* (Munich, 2016).
5 Letter from Benedikt XVI to Prof. Mussner of 28 January 2011.
6 Interview with the author.
7 Interview with Manuel Schlögl.
8 *Rheinische Post* (26 April 1970).
9 Feldmann, *Papst Benedikt XVI.: eine kritische Biografie*.
10 Interview with Manuel Schlögl.
11 Vincent Twomey, *Benedikt XVI.: das Gewissen unserer Zeit* (Augsburg, 2006).
12 Vincent Twomey, sermon at the solemn high Mass on the 60th anniversary of Joseph Ratzinger's ordination as a priest in the church of Sts Peter and Paul, Cork.
13 Interview with Manuel Schlögl.
14 Ibid.
15 Interview with the author.
16 Interview with Manuel Schlögl.

CHAPTER 6: TENSIONS

1 Franz Walter, 'Katholizismus in der Bundesrepublik – Von der Staatskirche zur Säkularisierung', in *Blätter für deutsche und internationale Politik*, vol. 41 (1996).
2 Rudolf Voderholzer, 'Der Geist des Konzils: ein Blick auf seine Deutungsgeschichte', in *Die Tagespost* (8 March 2014).
3 Joseph Ratzinger and Hans Maier, *Demokratie in der Kirche: Möglichkeiten, Grenzen, Gefahren* (Limburg 1970).
4 Gianni Valente, 'Ratzinger in Regensburg', in *30 Tage*, no. 8 (2006).
5 Ratzinger, *Aus meinem Leben*.
6 Karl Rahner, *Erinnerungen* (Innsbruck, 2001).
7 Marie-Gabrielle Lemaire, 'Joseph Ratzinger und Henry de Lubac', in *Mitteilungen des Instituts Papst Benedikt XVI.* vol. 8 (Regensburg, 2015).
8 Ratzinger, *Aus meinem Leben*.
9 Joseph Ratzinger, 'Éloge. Le Cardinal de Lubac', in *France Catholique* (22 May 1998). De Lubac himself was made a Knight of the Legion of Honour in 1967.
10 Ratzinger, *Aus meinem Leben*.

11 Bayerischer Rundfunk interview with Martin Lohmann (28 December 1998).

12 Ratzinger and Seewald, *Salz der Erde*.

13 Ratzinger, *Aus meinem Leben*.

14 Ratzinger, *Glaube und Zukunft*.

15 Küng, *Umstrittene Wahrheit*.

16 Wiedenhofer, 'Joseph Ratzinger und die nachkonziliare Auseinandersetzung um den zukünftigen Weg katholischer Theologie'.

17 Derwahl, *Benedikt XVI. und Hans Küng*.

18 Interview with the author.

19 Verweyen, *Joseph Ratzinger – Benedikt XVI*.

20 Interview with Manuel Schlögl.

21 Rüdiger Mai, *Benedikt XVI.: Joseph Ratzinger: sein Leben – sein Glaube – seine Ziele* (Cologne-Mühlheim, 2010).

22 Quoted from *Mitteilungen des Instituts Papst Benedikt XVI.*, vol. 1 (Regensburg, 2008).

23 Interview with the author.

24 Karl Rahner, 'Widersprüche im Buch von Hans Küng', in Rahner (ed.), *Zum Problem Unfehlbarkeit: Antworten auf die Anfrage von Hans Küng (Quaestio disputata)* (Freiburg im Breisgau, 1971).

25 katholisch.de (19 March 2018).

26 Joseph Ratzinger, 'Wer verantwortet die Aussagen der Theologie?', in Hans Urs von Balthasar et al., *Diskussion über Hans Küngs 'Christ sein'* (Mainz, 1976).

27 Ibid.

28 *Frankfurter Allgemeine Zeitung* (22 May 1976).

29 Küng, *Umstrittene Wahrheit*.

30 Ibid.

31 Ibid.

32 Ibid.

33 Ibid.

34 Ibid. Landgrave is a German aristocratic title.

CHAPTER 7: THE VISION OF THE CHURCH OF THE FUTURE

1 Joseph Ratzinger, *Die Einheit der Nationen: eine Vision der Kirchenväter* (Salzburg, 1971).

2 Joseph Ratzinger, *Zur Lehre des Zweiten Vatikanischen Konzils*, vol. 7/1 of *Gesammelte Schriften* (Freiburg im Breisgau, 2012).

3 Ibid.

4 Ibid.

5 Joseph Ratzinger, 'Zehn Jahre nach Konzilsbeginn – wo stehen wir?', in Dogma und Verkündigung (Munich, 1973).

6 Joseph Ratzinger, *Glaube und Zukunft* (Munich, 1970).

7 Interview with the author.

8 Letter to Raymund Kottje, 16 September 1971, copy in the author's archive.

9 Joseph Ratzinger: 'Zur Frage der Unauflöslichkeit der Ehe: Bemerkungen zum dogmengeschichtlichen Befund und zu seiner gegenwärtigen Bedeutung', in Franz Henrich and Volker Eid (eds), *Ehe und Ehescheidung: Diskussion unter Christen*, Münchner Akademie-Schriften 59 (Munich, 1972).

10 Joseph Ratzinger/Benedikt XVI., 'Zur Frage nach der Unauflöslichkeit der Ehe', in *Einführung in das Christentum,* vol. 4 of *Gesammelte Schriften* (Freiburg im Breisgau, 2014).

11 Joseph Ratzinger, *Tradition und Fortschritt in der Kirche*, broadcast on Bayerischer Rundfunk (9 December 1973).

12 *Hochland: Zeitschrift für alle Gebiete des Wissens und der Schönen Künste*, vol. 60 (August/September 1968).

13 Klaus Rüdiger Mai, *Benedikt XVI.: Joseph Ratzinger*.

14 Hans Urs von Balthasar and Joseph Ratzinger, *2 Plädoyers: warum ich noch ein Christ bin. Warum ich noch in der Kirche bin* (Munich, 1971).

15 Ibid.

CHAPTER 8: RECONQUEST

1 Address by Pope Benedict XVI to the College of Cardinals and members of the Roman Curia at the Christmas reception on 22 December 2005. *Verlautbarungen des Apostolischen Stuhls*, no. 172 (Bonn, 2006).

2 Alexander Kissler, 'Ich, Küng', in *The European* (9 October 2012).

3   Joseph Ratzinger, *Zur Lage des Glaubens: ein Gespräch mit Vittorio Messori* (Munich, 1985).
4   Ibid.
5   Interview with the author.
6   Address to the College of Cardinals and members of the Roman Curia, 22 December 2005.
7   Ratzinger and Seewald, *Salz der Erde*.
8   Michael Schmaus, 'Internationale Katholische Zeitschrift "Communio"', in *Wissen und Leben*, www. 2198-Artikeltext-3336-1-10-20150722-2.pdf.
9   Interview with the author.
10 Derwahl, *Benedikt XVI. und Hans Küng*.
11 Hans Urs von Balthasar, 'Communio – ein Programm', in *Communio* 1 (1972).
12 Deckers, *Der Kardinal: Karl Lehmann*.
13 Von Balthasar, 'Communio – ein Programm'.
14 Carl Bernstein and Marco Politi, *Seine Heiligkeit Johannes Paul II. – Macht und Menschlichkeit des Papstes* (Munich, 1996).
15 Ibid.
16 Kissler, *Der deutsche Papst*.
17 Gianni Valente, 'Ratzinger in Regensburg', in *30 Tage*, no. 8 (2006).
18 Karl Joseph Hummel and Christoph Kösters (eds), *Kirche, Krieg und Katholiken: Geschichte und Gedächtnis im 20. Jahrhundert* (Freiburg im Breisgau, 2014).
19 Margot Kässmann (ed.), *Gott will Taten sehen: Christlicher Widerstand gegen Hitler* (Munich, 2013), p. 192.
20 Karl Jaspers, *Der philosophische Glaube angesichts der Offenbarung* (Munich, 1962).
21 Martin Luther, 'Von den Juden und ihren Lügen, Schrift aus dem Jahr 1543', quoted by Pastor Dirk of Jutrczenka, St Remberti Community.
22 Ratzinger and Maier, *Demokratie in der Kirche*.
23 Joseph Ratzinger in a broadcast on Bayerischer Rundfunk (8 October 1972).
24 Interview with the author.
25 Katholische Nachrichten-Agentur (Catholic News Agency) (12 September 2011).
26 Interview with Manuel Schlögl.
27 Ibid.
28 Private archive of Sr Maria-Gratia Köhler.

CHAPTER 9: THE DOCTRINE OF ETERNAL LIFE

1   Ratzinger and Seewald, *Salz der Erde*.
2   Joseph Ratzinger, *Eschatologie: Tod und ewiges Leben* (Regensburg, 1977).
3   Ibid.
4   Helmut Hoping, 'Die Auferstehung der Toten bei Joseph Ratzinger', in *Auferstehung und Ewiges Leben*, vol. 10 of *Mitteilungen des Instituts Papst Benedikt XVI* (Freiburg im Breisgau, 2012).
5   Joseph Ratzinger, 'Mein Glück ist, in deiner Nähe zu sein', published under the title *Dass Gott alles in allem sei*, in *Klerusblatt* 72 (1992); Ratzinger, *Auferstehung und Ewiges Leben*.
6   Ratzinger, *Eschatologie*.
7   Ibid.
8   Ratzinger, 'Mein Glück ist, in deiner Nähe zu sein', in: *Klerusblatt* 72 (1992); Ratzinger, *Auferstehung und Ewiges Leben*.
9   Ratzinger, *Eschatologie*.
10 Ratzinger, 'Mein Glück ist, in deiner Nähe zu sein'.
11 Ibid.
12 Twomey, *Benedikt XVI.: das Gewissen unserer Zeit*.
13 Interview with the author.
14 Ibid.
15 Ratzinger and Seewald, *Salz der Erde*.
16 Ibid.
17 Interview with P. Gereon Michael Strauch, former Regensburg student.
18 Interview with Manuel Schlögl.
19 Manfred Lochbrunner, *Hans Urs von Balthasar und seine Philosophenfreunde: fünf Doppelporträts* (Würzburg, 2005).
20 Ibid.
21 Birkenseer, *Hier bin ich wirklich daheim*.
22 Interview with the author.

23 Ratzinger, *Aus meinem Leben*.
24 Ibid.
25 Ibid.
26 Interview with the author.
27 Peter Pfister (ed.), *Joseph Ratzinger und das Erzbistum München und Freising: Dokumente und Bilder aus kirchlichen Archiven, Beiträge und Erinnerungen* (Regensburg, 2006).
28 *Der Spiegel* (4 April 1977).
29 Derwahl, *Benedikt XVI. und Hans Küng*.

CHAPTER 10: ARCHBISHOP

1   Interview with Manuel Schlögl.
2   Pfister (ed.), *Joseph Ratzinger und das Erzbistum München und Freising*.
3   *Deutsche Zeitung/Christ und Welt* (1 April 1977).
4   *Süddeutsche Zeitung* (25 March 1977).
5   *Neue Zürcher Zeitung* (31 March 1977).
6   Interview with the author.
7   Joseph Ratzinger, *Der Geist der Liturgie: eine Einführung* (Freiburg im Breisgau, 2000).
8   Ratzinger, *Aus meinem Leben*.
9   Ibid.
10 Karl Wagner and Hermann Ruf (eds), *Kardinal Ratzinger: der Erzbischof von München und Freising in Wort und Bild* (Munich, 1977).
11 Ratzinger, *Aus meinem Leben*.
12 Ibid.
13 Pfister (ed.), *Joseph Ratzinger und das Erzbistum München und Freising*.
14 Ratzinger, *Aus meinem Leben*.
15 Gianni Cardinale, 'Der Herr wählt unsere Wenigkeit: fünfundzwanzig Jahre nach dem Konklave, bei dem Papst Luciani gewählt wurde', in *30 Tage,* no. 9 (2003).
16 Ibid.
17 Ratzinger and Seewald, *Salz der Erde*.
18 Interview with the author.
19 Joseph Ratzinger, 'Erster Hirtenbrief vom Juni 1977', in Wagner and Ruf (eds), *Kardinal Ratzinger*.
20 Karl Gabriel, *Die Kirchen in Westdeutschland*, www.bertelsmann-stiftung.de/fileadmin/files/.../xcms_bst_dms_28291_28292_2.pdf
21 Letter of the archbishop of Munich, 24 August 1977, concerning the Roman decision on the order of first confession and first communion.
22 From a broadcast on Bayerischer Rundfunk, 1978.
23 *Münchner Ordinariatskorrespondenz* (21 September 1977).
24 *Süddeutsche Zeitung* (7 January 1978).
25 *Süddeutsche Zeitung* (13 July 1977).
26 Interview with the author.
27 Ibid.
28 Interview with Manuel Schlögl.
29 Bruno Fink, *Zwischen Schreibmaschine und Pileolus: Erinnerungen an meine Zeit als Sekretär des Hochwürdigsten Herrn Joseph Kardinal Ratzinger* (Regensburg, 2016).
30 Interview with the author.

CHAPTER 11: THE YEAR OF THREE POPES

1   Pasquale Macchi, *Paul VI. in seinem Wort* (Rome, 2003).
2   Ulrich Nersinger in *Die Tagespost* (2 August 2018).
3   Cardinale, 'Der Herr wählt unsere Wenigkeit'.
4   kath.net, 5 March 2014.
5   Cardinale, 'Der Herr wählt unsere Wenigkeit'.
6   Ibid.
7   Ibid.
8   Bernstein and Politi, *Seine Heiligkeit Johannes Paul II.*
9   John Cornwell, *A Thief in the Night* (New York, 1989).
10 *Die Tagespost* (6 November 2017). Stefania Falasca at the launch of the book *Papa Luciani: cronaca di una morte*, with a foreword by Cardinal Parolin (Milan, 2017).

11   Kathpress, Vienna (24 August 2018).
12   Cardinale, 'Der Herr wählt unsere Wenigkeit'.
13   Ibid.
14   Carlos Widmann, in *Süddeutsche Zeitung* (10 October 1978).
15   Interview with the author.
16   Ratzinger and Seewald, *Salz der Erde*.
17   Ulrich Nersinger, in *Die Tagespost* (2 August 2018).
18   *Süddeutsche Zeitung* (18 October 1978).
19   Fink, *Zwischen Schreibmaschine und Pileolus*.
20   Bernstein and Politi, *Seine Heiligkeit Johannes Paul II.*

CHAPTER 12: THE KÜNG CASE

1   Interview with the author.
2   Ibid.
3   Winfried Römmel (ed.) and press office of the archdiocese of Munich and Freising Ordinariate, *Wir leben vom Ja: Dokumentation der Verabschiedung von Joseph Kardinal Ratzinger* (Munich, 1982).
4   Joseph Ratzinger, Foreword to Christoph Schönborn, *Leben für die Kirche: die Fastenexerzitien des Papstes* (Freiburg im Breisgau, 1999).
5   Kissler, *Der deutsche Papst*.
6   Twomey, *Benedikt XVI.: das Gewissen unserer Zeit*.
7   Ordinariats-Korrespondenz, no. 24 (19 June 1980).
8   Quoted from Anton Štrukelj, *Vertrauen: Mut zum Christsein* (St Ottilien, 2012).
9   All quotations from Štrukelj, *Vertrauen*.
10   Interview with the author.
11   Ibid.
12   *Süddeutsche Zeitung* (14 November 1979).
13   Ibid.
14   Interview with the author.
15   Hans Maier, *Böse Jahre, gute Jahre: ein Leben 1931 ff.* (Munich, 2011).
16   Fink, *Zwischen Schreibmaschine und Pileolus*.
17   Interview with the author.
18   Ordinariats-Korrespondenz, no. 37 (13 December 1997).
19   Derwahl, *Benedikt XVI. und Hans Küng*.
20   Sacred Congregation for the Doctrine of the Faith, 'Statement on Some Main Points of the Theological Doctrine of Prof. Hans Küng', www.vatican.va
21   Derwahl, *Benedikt XVI. und Hans Küng*.
22   Interview with the author.
23   *L'Osservatore Romano*, German edn (18 January 1980).
24   Joseph Ratzinger, *Zeitfragen und christlicher Glaube: acht Predigten aus den Münchner Jahren* (Würzburg, 1982).
25   *Frankfurter Allgemeine Zeitung* (11 January 1980).
26   Ratzinger and Seewald, *Salz der Erde*.

CHAPTER 13: THE LEGACY OF MUNICH

1   Interview with the author.
2   Ibid.
3   Elio Guerriero, *Benedikt XVI.: die Biografie* (Freiburg im Breisgau, 2018) [italics added].
4   Interview with the author.
5   *Chronik-Bildbiografie Papst Johannes Paul II.* (Gütersloh/Munich, 2003).
6   Interview with Manuel Schlögl.
7   Speech of the Bavarian minister president Franz Josef Strauss at the reception in the Antiquarium of the Munich Residence on 12 February 1982, in Rommel (ed.), *Wir leben vom Ja*.
8   Sermon at the Mass with priests and deacons on 28 February 1982 in Freising Cathedral, quoted in *Wir leben von Ja: Dokumentation der Verabschiedung on Joseph Kardinal Ratzinger*, ed. Pressereferat der Erzdiözese München-Freising (Munich, 1982).
9   Ibid.
10   *Die Welt* (27 October 1981).

CHAPTER 14: THE PREFECT

1 Manfred Lütz, *Der Skandal der Skandale: die geheime Geschichte des Christentums* (Freiburg im Breisgau, 2018).
2 *Meyers Große Enzyklopädie*, 9th edn (Mannheim, 1971).
3 Walter Brandmüller, *Licht und Schatten: Kirchengeschichte zwischen Glauben, Fakten und Legenden* (Augsburg, 2007).
4 Georg Blüml, 'Dichtung und Wahrheit', in *Die Tagespost* (21 July 2017).
5 Fink, *Zwischen Schreibmaschine und Pileolus*.
6 *Süddeutsche Zeitung* (5 March 1983).
7 Ratzinger, *Zur Lage des Glaubens*.
8 Interview with the author.
9 Ibid.
10 Ibid.
11 Ibid.
12 Ibid.
13 Quoted from: Štrukelj, *Vertrauen: Mut zum Christsein*.
14 Ratzinger and Seewald, *Salz der Erde*.
15 Letter of the departing archbishop of Munich to the priests deacons and colleagues in pastoral work in Rommel (ed.), *Wir leben vom Ja*.
16 Ratzinger and Seewald, *Salz der Erde*.
17 Interview with the author.
18 *Süddeutsche Zeitung* (9 December 1982).

CHAPTER 15: RATZINGER'S REPORT

1 Ratzinger and Seewald, *Salz der Erde*.
2 *Die Tagespost*, no. 45 (16 April 2005).
3 George Weigel, *Zeuge der Hoffnung: Johannes Paul II, eine Biographie* (Paderborn, 2002).
4 *Frankfurter Allgemeine Zeitung* (7 November 1984).
5 Interview with the author.
6 Juan Arias, *Das Rätsel Wojtyła: eine kritische Papst-Biographie* (Bad Sauerbrunn, 1991).
7 Ibid.
8 Ibid.
9 *Der Spiegel*, no. 19 (9 May 1983).
10 Ratzinger, *Zur Lage des Glaubens*.
11 Ibid.
12 Ibid.
13 Interview with Manuel Schlögl.
14 *Die Zeit*, no. 41 (4 October 1985).
15 *Süddeutsche Zeitung* (5 February 1998).
16 *Die Welt* (30 May 1988).

CHAPTER 16: THE FIGHT OVER LIBERATION THEOLOGY

1 Fink, *Zwischen Schreibmaschine und Pileolus*.
2 Letter of 23 February 1988, transcript in the author's archive.
3 Heinz-Joachim Fischer, *Benedikt XVI.: ein Porträt* (Freiburg im Breisgau, 2005).
4 *Süddeutsche Zeitung* (29 January 1988).
5 *Die Welt* (1 June 1988).
6 Rüdiger Mai, *Benedikt XVI*.
7 Joseph Ratzinger, *Theologische Prinzipienlehre, Bausteine zur Fundamentaltheologie* (Munich, 1982).
8 Verweyen, *Joseph Ratzinger – Benedikt XVI*.
9 kath.net (20 March 2014).
10 Joseph Ratzinger, *Eschatologie: Tod und ewiges Leben* (Regensburg, 1977).
11 Kissler, *Der deutsche Papst*.
12 Interview with the author.
13 Joseph Ratzinger and Vittorio Messori, *Rapporto sulla fede* (Milan, 1984). German edition: Joseph Ratzinger, *Zur Lage des Glaubens: ein Gespräch mit Vittorio Messori* (Munich, 1985).

14 *Die Welt* (1 June 1988).
15 Fischer, *Benedikt XVI.: ein Porträt.*
16 Interview with the author.
17 katholisches.info (21 December 2018).
18 Klaus Brunner, religion.ORF.at (7 May 2017).
19 *Süddeutsche Zeitung* (1 August 2018).

CHAPTER 17: TEAMWORK

1   kath.net (12 June 2012).
2   Interview with the author.
3   *Die Tagespost* (9 July 2013).
4   Fink, *Zwischen Schreibmaschine und Pileolus.*
5   Announcement by the Holy See of 16 June 1988, in *Der Apostolische Stuhl 1988: Ansprachen, Predigten und Botschaften des Papstes. Erklärungen der Kongregationen. Vollständige Dokumentation* (Cologne, 1989).
6   kath.net (12. June 2012).
7   2 Tim. 4.2–5.
8   Ratzinger and Seewald, *Salz der Erde.*
9   Interview with the author for an article in the *Süddeutsche Zeitung* magazine (5 March 1993).
10 *Communio*, (2001).
11 Ratzinger, *Zur Lage des Glaubens.*
12 Interview with the author.
13 Ratzinger and Seewald, *Salz der Erde.*
14 Interview in the *Deutsche Tagespost* (18 May 1995).
15 Ratzinger and Seewald, *Salz der Erde.*
16 Interview with the author.
17 Interview with Manuel Schlögl.
18 Interview with the author.
19 Ibid.
20 Benedict XVI and Peter Seewald, *Letzte Gespräche.*
21 *Die Tagespost* (22 November 2017).
22 Ibid.
23 Ibid.
24 *Deutsche Tagespost* (25 November 1986).
25 Andreas Englisch, *Benedikt XVI.: der deutsche Papst* (Munich, 2011).
26 *Süddeutsche Zeitung* (17 January 1990).
27 'Die Geschichte des Dieners', interview with the author for the *Süddeutsche Zeitung* (18 June 1993).
28 Ibid.
29 Feldmann, *Benedikt XVI.: Bilanz des deutschen Papstes.*
30 Fischer, *Benedikt XVI.: ein Porträt.*
31 Ibid.
32 Interview with the author.
33 Letter of thanks from Joseph Cardinal Ratzinger of May 1987 in the author's archive.
34 *Deutsche Tagespost* (25 November 1986).

CHAPTER 18: THE COLLAPSE

1   Weigel, *Zeuge der Hoffnung.*
2   Ibid.
3   Ibid.
4   Stephan Baier, *Die Tagespost* (23 August 2018).
5   https://www.zeit.de/wissen/geschichte/2010-03/gorbatschow-sowjetunion
6   Andrea Riccardi, *Johannes Paul II: die Biografie* (Würzburg, 2012).
7   Stricker in an interview with the aid organization Kirche in Not ('Church in Need'); kath.net (15 September 2009) (http://www.kath.net/news/23949).
8   Stanisław Dziwisz, *Mein Leben mit dem Papst* (Leipzig, 2007).
9   *Spiegel Special*, no. 3 (2005).
10 *Der Spiegel* (11 April 2005).
11 *Die Welt* (30 May 1988).

12 Franz Walter, 'Katholizismus in der Bundesrepublik – von der Staatskirche zur Säkularisation', in *Blätter für deutsche und internationale Politik*, vol. 41 (1996).
13 *Deutsche Tagespost* (18 May 1995).
14 *Deutschlandfunk Kultur* (6 October 2012).
15 *Frankfurter Allgemeine Zeitung* (27 October 1994).
16 *Münchner Merkur* (4 January 1989).
17 *Süddeutsche Zeitung* (3 September 1990).
18 Interview with Manuel Schlögl.
19 Interview with the author.
20 Greetings card of 21 May 1994.
21 Ibid.
22 Interview with the author.
23 Ibid.
24 Letter to the author.
25 *Die Tagespost* (6 December 2018).
26 Interview with the author.
27 Interview with Manuel Schlögl.
28 Interview with the author.
29 *Die Zeit* (29 November 1991).
30 Fink, *Zwischen Schreibmaschine und Pileolus*.
31 Interview with the author.
32 *Die Welt* (1 June 1988).
33 Interview with the author.
34 Ratzinger, *Dogma und Verkündigung*.
35 Ratzinger and Seewald, *Salz der Erde*.
36 Interview with the author.
37 Ibid.
38 Ibid.
39 Ibid.
40 Guerriero, *Benedikt XVI*.
41 Interview with the author.
42 Ibid.
43 Interview with the author.
44 *Süddeutsche Zeitung* (28 December 1992).
45 Interview with the author.
46 Ibid.

CHAPTER 19: THE LONG SUFFERING OF KAROL WOJTYŁA

1   Sergio Trasatti, Arturo Mari und Hendrik van Bergh, *Johannes Paul II.: Leidensweg der 100 Tage 13. Mai–16. August 1981* (St Ottilien 1982).
2   Dziwisz, *Mein Leben mit dem Papst*.
3   Quoted from Roberto de Mattei, *Catholic Family News* (4 January 2019).
4   Dziwisz.
5   Ibid.
6   *Der Spiegel* (17 November 1980).
7   *Der Spiegel* (30 January 1995).
8   *Der Spiegel* (20 September 1999).
9   Klaus Wallbaum, *Der Überläufer: Rudolf Diels (1900–1957) – der erste Gestapo-Chef des Hitler-Regimes* (Frankfurt am Main, 2010).
10 *Der Spiegel* (24 May 1999).
11 *Der Spiegel* (26 March 2005).
12 Blurb for Joseph Ratzinger, *Kirche, Ökumene und Politik: neue Versuche zur Ekklesiologie* (Einsiedeln, 1987).
13 Joseph Cardinal Ratzinger, 'Probleme von Glaubens- und Sittenlehre im europäischen Kontext', in Joseph Ratzinger, Hugo Staudinger and Heinz Schütte (eds), *Zu Grundfragen der Theologie heute* (Paderborn, 1992).
14 Ibid.
15 Twomey, *Benedikt XVI.: das Gewissen unserer Zeit*.
16 Ratzinger, *Kirche, Ökumene und Politik*.

17   Ibid.
18   *Der Spiegel* (16 December 1996).
19   Paolo Coelho, *Der Weg des Bogens* (Zürich, 2017).
20   Ratzinger and Seewald, *Salz der Erde.*
21   Matthias Kopp (ed.), *Und plötzlich Papst: Benedikt XVI. im Spiegel persönlicher Begegnungen* (Freiburg im Breisgau, 2007).
22   Letter to Esther Betz of 9 August 1997, transcript in the author's archive.

CHAPTER 20: MILLENNIUM

1   Letter to Esther Betz of 16 February 1998, transcript in the author's archive.
2   Vatican Radio (18 November 2017).
3   Transcript in the author's archive.
4   Mk 16.15. Mt. 28.20.
5   Letter from Joseph Ratzinger to Esther Betz, transcript in the author's archive.
6   *Der Spiegel* (7 December 1999).
7   *Der Spiegel* (24 May 1999).
8   Interview with the author.
9   Ratzinger, *Der Geist der Liturgie.*
10 Domradio.de (13 July 2017).
11 John Paul II., *Erinnerung und Identität: Gespräche an der Schwelle zwischen den Jahrtausenden* (Augsburg, 2005).
12 Derwahl, *Benedikt XVI. und Hans Küng.*
13 Congregation for the Doctrine of the Faith, statement 'Dominus Iesus on the Uniqueness and Salvific Universality of Jesus Christ and the Church', 6 August 2000.
14 *Die Tagespost* (15 March 2018).
15 Derwahl, *Benedikt XVI. und Hans Küng.*
16 *Frankfurter Allgemeine Zeitung* (22 September 2000).
17 Interview with the author.
18 *Die Zeit* (1 March 2001).
19 *Die Welt* (2 December 2002).
20 Interview with the author.
21 Frankfurter Rundschau (9 September 2018).
22 kath.net (16 January 2003).
23 *Die Welt* (2 April 2002).
24 *Süddeutsche Zeitung* (26 September 2005).
25 Ernst-Wolfgang Böckenförde, 'Die Entstehung des Staats als Vorgang der Säkularisierung', in *Kirche und christlicher Glaube in den Herausforderungen der Zeit* (Münster, 2004).
26 Jürgen Habermas and Joseph Ratzinger, *Dialektik der Säkularisierung: über Vernunft und Religion* (Freiburg im Breisgau, 2005).
27 From Jürgen Manemann, *Befristete Zeit: Jahrbuch politische Theologie* (Münster, 1999).
28 Quoted from *Die Tagespost* (16 June 2014).
29 *Passauer Neue Presse* (26 October 2000).

CHAPTER 21: AGONY

1   See also Dziwisz, *Mein Leben mit dem Papst.*
2   *Der Spiegel* (26 March 2005).
3   Ibid.
4   Ibid.
5   Ibid.
6   Dziwisz, *Mein Leben mit dem Papst.*
7   Jn 12.24.
8   *L'Osservatore Romano*, German edn (8 April 2005).
9   Dziwisz, *Mein Leben mit dem Papst.*
10 Ibid.
11 Interview with the author.
12 According to Georg Gänswein in an interview with the author.
13 https://www.decemsys.de/benedikt/reden/05-04-01.htm (lecture by Cardinal Joseph Ratzinger in Subiaco on 1. April 2005, translated into German by Claudie Reimüller).

14   Diary of Sister Maria Faustyna Kowalska, Hauteville, Switzerland, 2013.
15   German quotes Romano Guardini's translation. English quoted from the *Book of Common Prayer*.
16   Quoted from *Christ in der Gegenwart*, special edn on the pope's death (April 2005).
17   *L'Osservatore Romano*, German edn (15 April 2005).

CHAPTER 22: CONCLAVE

1   Copy in the author's archive.
2   Joseph Ratzinger and Peter Seewald, *Licht der Welt* (Stuttgart, 1996).
3   Joseph Ratzinger and Peter Seewald, *Gott und die Welt* (Munich, 2000).
4   *Abendzeitung* (6 April 2005).
5   Copy letter in the author's archive.
6   *Süddeutsche Zeitung* (5 April 2005).
7   *Der Spiegel* (18 April 2005).
8   https://www.wissen.de/lexikon/alexander-iii-papst
9   *Spiegel Online* (4 April 2005).
10   Ulrich Nersinger, *Tatort Konklave* (Künzell, 2013).
11   Quoted from the Apostolic Constitution 'Universi Dominici Gregis' (http:/www.vatican.va/).
12   *Pur-Magazin* (April 2005).
13   *Der Spiegel* (18 April 2005).
14   *Die Welt* (18 April 2005).
15   As he told me when he was pope emeritus.
16   Interview with the author.
17   Ibid.
18   Messerer, interview with the author.
19   Interview with the author.
20   Ibid.
21   *Die Zeit* (14 April 2005).
22   Ibid.
23   *Der Spiegel* (18 April 2005).
24   *Spiegel Online* (18 April 2005).
25   *Süddeutschen Zeitung* (19 May 2010).
26   Helmut S. Ruppert, *Benedikt XVI.: der Papst aus Deutschland* (Würzburg, 2005).
27   Interview with the author.
28   www.vatican.va/gpII/documents/homily-pro-eligendo-pontifice_20050418_ge.html
29   Ibid.

CHAPTER 23: HABEMUS PAPAM

1   *Hamburger Abendblatt* (24 September 2005).
2   Robert Harris, *Konklave* (Munich, 2016).
3   Interview with the author.
4   According to the 'forbididen diary'. From *Hamburger Abendblatt* (24 September 2005).
5   Katholische Nachrichten-Agentur (26 May 2015).
6   katholisch.de (6 November 2017).
7   Speech to German pilgrims in the audience chamber, Monday, 25 April 2005.
8   Interview with the author.
9   Stephan Kulle, *Papa Benedikt: die Welt des deutschen Papstes* (Frankfurt am Main, 2007).
10   Kissler, *Der deutsche Papst.*
11   *Süddeutsche Zeitung* (25 April 2005).
12   vatican.va (http:/www.vatican.va/holy_father/benedict_xvi.elezione/index_ge.htm)

CHAPTER 24: THE FIRST POPE OF THE THIRD MILLENNIUM

1   *Die Weltwoche*, no. 16 (2005).
2   *Die Tagespost* (21 April 2005).
3   *Die Welt* (21 April 2005).
4   *Süddeutsche Zeitung* (20 April 2005).
5   *Der Spiegel,* no. 17 (25 April 2005).
6   *Spiegel Online* (25 April 2005).

7   Kopp (ed.), *Und plötzlich Papst.*
8   *Die Zeit* (28 April 2005).
9   *Die Welt* (21 April 2005).
10   *Die Tagespost* (21 April 2005).
11   Ruppert, *Benedikt XVI.: der Papst aus Deutschland.*
12   Ibid.
13   *Die Welt* (21 April 2005).
14   Interview with the author.
15   *Süddeutsche Zeitung* (20 April 2005).
16   *Die Tagespost* (21 April 2005).
17   *Jerusalem Post* (18 April 2005).
18   Interview with the author.
19   https://w2.vatican.va/content/benedict-xvi/de/homilies/2005/documents/hf_ben -xvi_hom_2 0050424_inizio-pontificato.html
20   Speech to German pilgrims, 25 April 2005, in the Audience Hall; kath.net (25 April 2005).

CHAPTER 25: IN THE SHOES OF THE FISHERMAN

1   Interview with the author.
2   Benedikt XVI and Peter Seewald, *Letzte Gespräche.*
3   Letter to Franz Mussner in Passau of 5 Mai 2005, from the author's archive.
4   Benedikt XVI, speech of 18 October 2005 (http://w2.vatican.va/content/benedict-xvi/de/mess ages/migration/documents/hf_ben-xvi_mes_20051018_world-migrants-day.html)
5   Ratzinger and Seewald, *Gott und die Welt.*
6   Kopp (ed.), *Und plötzlich Papst.*
7   Ruppert, *Benedikt XVI.: der Papst aus Deutschland.*
8   *Süddeutsche Zeitung* (5 April 2005).
9   *Süddeutsche Zeitung* (23 April 2005).
10   *Spiegel Online* (25 April 2005).
11   kath.net (2 July 2005).
12   Katholische Nachrichten-Agentur (21 May 2005).
13   Benedict XVI, speech at a general audience on 27 April 2005 (https://w2.vatican.va/content/ benedict-xvi/de/audiences/2005/documents/hf_ben-xvi_aud_20050427.html).
14   Ibid.
15   Interview with the author.
16   Ibid.
17   Benedikt XVI and Peter Seewald, *Letzte Gespräche.*
18   Interview with the author.

CHAPTER 26: BENEDETTO MANIA

1   Interview with the author.
2   Ibid.
3   Ibid.
4   Ibid.
5   kath.net (20 May 2005).
6   *Neue Zürcher Zeitung* (21 November 2005).
7   *Die Tagespost* (14 May 2005).
8   *Süddeutsche Zeitung* (25 December 2005)
9   Feldmann, *Papst Benedikt XVI.: eine kritische Biografie.*
10   Interview with the author.
11   Ibid.
12   Domradio Köln (18 November 2019).
13   Interview with the author.
14   Kopp (ed.), *Und plötzlich Papst.*

CHAPTER 27: THE REGENSBURG SPEECH

1   Katholisch.de (2 October 2014).

2   kath.net (19 June 2005).
3   *Die Tagespost* (8 August 2005).
4   *Die Tagespost* (5 October 2005).
5   Interview with the author.
6   Ibid.
7   Ibid.
8   Ibid.
9   Ibid.
10 Christoph Hurnaus, *33 Reisen mit dem Papst: unterwegs mit Johannes Paul II. und Benedikt XVI.* (Linz, 2009).
11 *L'Osservatore Romano*, German edn (2 June 2006).
12 Alexander Kissler, *Papst im Widerspruch, Benedikt XVI. und seine Kirche, 2005–2013* (Munich, 2013).
13 http://w2.vatican.va/content/benedict-xvi/de/speeches/*2006*/may/documents/hf_ben-xvi_spe_*20060528*_auschwitz-birkenau.html
14 *L'Osservatore Romano*, German edn (2 June 2006).
15 Kissler, *Papst im Widerspruch*.
16 Elie Wiesel, *Die Nacht: Erinnerungen und Zeugnis* (Freiburg im Breisgau, 2008).
17 Kopp (ed.), *Und plötzlich Papst*.
18 Ibid.
19 Kissler, *Papst im Widerspruch*.
20 http://w2.vatican.va/content/benedict-xvi/de/speeches/2006/september/documents/hf_ben-xvi_spe_20060912_university-regensburg.html
21 Guerriero, *Benedikt XVI*.
22 Paolo Rodari and Andrea Tornielli, *Der Papst im Gegenwind: was in den dramatischen Monaten des deutschen Pontifikats wirklich geschah* (Kisslegg, 2011).
23 Angelus speech in Castel Gandolfo of 17 September 2006.
24 Rodari and Tornielli, *Der Papst im Gegenwind*.
25 *Der Spiegel* (11 April 2005).
26 Kopp (ed.), *Und plötzlich Papst*.
27 Guerriero, *Benedikt XVI*.
28 *Vatican News* (31 January 2019).
29 Rodari and Tornielli, *Der Papst im Gegenwind*.

CHAPTER 28: *DEUS CARITAS EST*

1   Alexander Smoltczyk, *Vatikanistan: eine Entdeckungsreise durch den kleinsten Staat der Welt* (Munich, 2008).
2   Ibid.
3   Gudrun Sailer, *Frauen im Vatikan: Begegnungen, Porträts, Bilder* (Leipzig, 2007).
4   Interview with the author.
5   Ibid
6   Ibid.
7   Joint statement by Pope Benedict XVI and Patriarch Bartholomew I, 30 November 2006, http://w2.vatican.va
8   Rodari and Tornielli, *Der Papst im Gegenwind*.
9   *Spiegel Online* (2 May 2005).
10 Smoltczyk, *Vatikanistan*.
11 *Die Welt* (22 February 2013).
12 *Spiegel Online* (25 January 2006).
13 *Frankfurter Allgemeine Zeitung* (20 January 2006).
14 *Rheinischer Merkur* (26 January 2006).
15 Benedict XVI, *Deus caritas est* (Vatican City, 2006).

CHAPTER 29: SALT OF THE EARTH, LIGHT OF THE WORLD

1   Peter Seewald and Jakob Seewald, *Welt auf der Kippe: zu viel, zu laut, zu hohl – macht Schluss mit dem Wahnsinn* (Munich, 2015).
2   Angela Ambrogetti (ed.), *Über den Wolken mit Papst Benedikt XVI.: Gespräche mit Journalisten* (Kisslegg, 2017).

3 Ratzinger and Seewald, *Gott und die Welt.*
4 Kissler, *Der deutsche Papst.*
5 Ratzinger, *Aus meinem Leben.*
6 Interview with the author.
7 Ibid.
8 Rodari and Tornielli, *Der Papst im Gegenwind.*
9 Interview with the author.
10 Ibid.
11 Burkhard Menke, in *Die Zeit,* no. 15/2017 (6 April 2017).
12 kath.net (1 December 2009).
13 Franz Mussner, 'Hermeneutische Überlegungen zu den Evangelien: ein Versuch im Anschluss an Joseph Ratzingers/Papst Benedikts XVI. Jesus von Nazareth', in *Mitteilungen des Instituts Papst Benedikt XVI.* vol. 2 (Regensburg, 2009).
14 Benedict XVI, *Auf Hoffnung hin sind wir gerettet: 'Spe Salvi', die Enzyklika* (Augsburg, 2008).
15 Ibid.
16 Interview with the author.

CHAPTER 30: THE RUPTURE

1 Interview with the author.
2 Letter of 16 February 2007, copy in author's archive.
3 Ambrogetti (ed.), *Über den Wolken.*
4 Kissler, *Papst im Widerspruch.*
5 Guerriero, *Benedikt XVI.*
6 Kissler, *Papst im Widerspruch.*
7 https://w2.vatican.va/content/benedict-xvi/de/speeches/2008/july/documents/hf_ben-xvi_spe_20080717_barangaroo.html
8 Interview with the author.
9 Paul Badde, *Benedikt XVI.: seine Papstjahre aus nächster Nähe* (Munich, 2017).
10 *L'Osservatore Romano,* German edn (25 January 2008).
11 Kissler, *Papst im Widerspruch.*
12 Rodari and Tornielli, *Der Papst im Gegenwind.*
13 kath.net (9 September 2008).
14 *Der Spiegel,* no. 4 (19 January 2009).
15 Rodari and Tornielli, *Der Papst im Gegenwind.*
16 Ibid.
17 Badde, *Benedikt XVI.*
18 http://ivv7srv15.uni-muenster.de/mnkg/pfnuer/Dekret-Exkommunikatio
19 *Süddeutsche Zeitung* (26 January 2009).
20 https://w2.vatican.va/content/benedict-xvi/de/audiences/2009/documents/hf_ben-xvi_aud_20090128.html
21 *Die Tagespost* (31 January 2009).
22 Kathpress (7 September 1976).
23 Vaterland [Lucerne newspaper] (16 May 1979).
24 Küng, *Umstrittene Wahrheit.*
25 *Der Spiegel* (2 February 2009).
26 *Neue Zürcher Zeitung* (12 February 2009).
27 kath.net (26 February 2009).
28 kath.net (17 February 2009).
29 kath.net (24 October 2014).
30 Katholische Nachrichten-Agentur (9 January 2015).
31 Rodari and Tornielli, *Der Papst im Gegenwind.*
32 https://w2.vatican.va/content/benedict-xvi/de/letters/2009/documents/hf_ben-xvi_let_20090310_remissione-scomunica.html

CHAPTER 31: THE CONDOM CRISIS

1 Interview with the author.
2 Ibid.
3 Private information.

4   Benedict XVI and Seewald, *Letzte Gespräche*.

5   Interview with the author.

6   Letter from Benedict XVI of 14 Mai 2008, copy in the author's archive.

7   Interim report, 1 October 2019 on the ongoing visitation of the Catholic Integrated Community in the archdiocese of Munich and Freising.

8   Rodari and Tornielli, *Der Papst im Gegenwind*.

9   From interviews with the author.

10   Ibid.

11   *Spiegel Online* (20 March 2009).

12   Interview with Benedict XVI by journalists during his flight to Africa on Tuesday, 17 March 2009 (https://w2.vatican.va/content/benedict-xvi/de/speeches/2009/march/documents/hf_ben-xvi _spe_20090317_africa-interview.html).

13   Rodari and Tornielli, *Der Papst im Gegenwind*.

14   Ibid.

15   Ibid.

16   Benedict XVI and Seewald, *Licht der Welt*.

17   Rodari and Tornielli, *Der Papst im Gegenwind*.

18   Kissler, *Papst im Widerspruch*.

19   Interview with the author.

20   Kissler, *Papst im Widerspruch*.

21   kath.net (7 December 2009).

22   René Perrin, Jean Servel and René Fourrey, *Der Pfarrer von Ars: das Leben des Heiligen auf Grund authentischer Zeugnisse*. Illustrated biography of Jean-Baptiste-Marie Vianney, the 'curé d'Ars' (Heidelberg, 1959).

23   Benedict XVI and Seewald, *Licht der Welt*.

CHAPTER 32: THE ABUSE SCANDAL

1   Interview with the author.

2   Ibid.

3   Katholische Presseagentur Kathpress (30 October 2019).

4   Rodari and Tornielli, *Der Papst im Gegenwind*.

5   kath.net (11 March 2010).

6   Benedikt XVI and Seewald, *Licht der Welt*.

7   Interview with the author.

8   Rodari and Tornielli, *Der Papst im Gegenwind*.

9   Guerriero, *Benedikt XVI*.

10   *Süddeutsche Zeitung* (20 January 2014).

11   Ibid.

12   Vatican Radio (16 February 2010).

13   Pastoral Letter of the Holy Father Benedict XVI to the Catholics in Ireland of 19 März 2010 (https://w2.vatican.va/content/benedict-xvi/de/letters/2010/documents/hf_ben-xvi_let_20100 319_church-ireland.html).

14   *Der Tagesspiegel* (7 February 2010).

15   BR24 [Bavarian radio station] (18 July 2017).

16   Feldmann, *Benedikt XVI*.

17   Zenit.org (15 July 2014).

18   Pope Francis on his return flight from the United Arab Emirates on 5 February 2019. Quoted from the official German translation on the Holy See's website (http://w2.vatican.va/content/francesco/ de/speeches /2019/february/documents/papa-francesco_20190205_emiratiarabi-voloritorno.html).

CHAPTER 33: THE SHEPHERD

1   Interview with the author.

2   Sigrid Grabner, *Im Auge des Sturms: Gregor der Große, eine Biografie* (Augsburg, 2009).

3   Benedict XVI and Seewald, *Licht der Welt*.

4   Ibid

5   https://press.vatican.va/content/salastampa/it/bollettino/pubblico/*2010/02 /20/0108/00249*.html

6   kath.net (24 April 2010).

7   Interview with the author.
8   kath.net (11 May 2010.
9   kath.net (12 May 2010).
10 https://w2.vatican.va/content/benedict-xvi/de/speeches/2010/may/documents/hf_ben-xvi
    _spe_20100511_portogallo-interview.html
11 kath.net (6 June 2010).
12 Rodari and Tornielli, *Der Papst im Gegenwind*.
13 John Henry Newman, 'Lectures on the Present Condition of Catholics in England' (1851). Quoted
    in Guerriero, *Benedikt XVI*.

CHAPTER 34: HUMAN ECOLOGY

1   *Der Tagesspiegel* (8 September 2010).
2   Greeting by Pope Benedict XVI in the cathedral of Santiago de Compostela, 6 November 2010
    (https://w2.vatican.va/content/benedict-xvi/de/speeches/2010/november/documents/hf_ben-
    xvi_spe_20101106_cattedrale-compostela.html).
3   Benedict XVI and Seewald, *Licht der Welt*.
4   Hermann Häring, *Im Namen des Herrn: wohin der Papst die Kirche führt* (Gütersloh, 2009).
5   Hanspeter Oschwald, *Im Namen des Heiligen Vaters: wie fundamentalistische Mächte den Vatikan steuern*
    (Munich, 2010).
6   Alan Posener, *Benedikts Kreuzzug: der Angriff des Vatikans auf die moderne Gesellschaft* (Berlin, 2009).
7   *Süddeutsche Zeitung* (15 April 2010).
8   Ulrich Nersinger, *Päpste* (Ditzingen, 2019).
9   Tobias Haberl, *Die große Entzauberung: vom trügerischen Glück des heutigen Menschen* (Munich, 2019).
10 *Spiegel Online* (5 March 2019).
11 Benedict XVI, *Caritas in veritate*.
12 Kissler, *Papst im Widerspruch*.
13 Ibid.

CHAPTER 35: DESECULARIZATION

1   Rodari and Tornielli, *Der Papst im Gegenwind*.
2   Friederike Glavanovics, 'Papst Benedikt XVI. und die Macht der Medien: wie Papst- und
    Kommunikationsexperten das Medienimage von Papst Benedikt XVI. Erklären', dissertation,
    University of Vienna, 2012.
3   Rodari and Tornielli, *Der Papst im Gegenwind*.
4   *Spiegel Online* (2 March 2011).
5   *Die Welt* (15 June 2011).
6   Glavanovics, 'Papst Benedikt XVI.'.
7   Leo Maasburg, *Mutter Teresa: die wunderbaren Geschichten* (Munich, 2016).
8   Interview with the author.
9   Ibid.
10 Benedict XVI and Seewald, *Licht der Welt*.
11 Benedict XVI and Seewald, *Letzte Gespräche*.
12 *Der Tagesspiegel* (20 April 2005).
13 http://www.dradio.de/dkultur/kulturpresseschau/fazit/368728/
14 *Die Zeit* (21 September 2011).
15 *Die Welt* (7 December 2019).
16 Kissler, *Papst im Widerspruch*.
17 Benedict XVI, *Die Ökologie des Menschen: die großen Reden des Papstes* (Munich, 2012).
18 Interview with the author.
19 Ibid.
20 *Badische Zeitung* (25 September 2011).

CHAPTER 36: THE BETRAYAL

1   Bernardus M. Lambert (ed.), *Gregor der Große: der hl. Benedikt, Buch II der Dialoge* (St Ottilien, 1995).
2   Marco Politi, *Joseph Ratzinger: crisi di un papato* (Rome, 2011).
3   Interview with the author.
4   Copy of letter of 15 December 2011, in the author's archive.

5   Wladimir d'Ormesson, *Der Stellvertreter Christi: Papst und Papsttum* (Würzburg, 1962).
6   Gianluigi Nuzzi, *Sua Santità: le carte segrete di Benedetto XVI.* (Milan, 2012).
7   *Spiegel Online* (28 September 2012).
8   Feldmann, *Benedikt XVI.*
9   Benedict XVI and Seewald, *Letzte Gespräche.*
10 Kissler, *Papst im Widerspruch.*
11 Interview with the author.
12 *Der Tagesspiegel* (30 May 2012).
13 Crista Kramer von Reisswitz, *Macht und Ohnmacht im Vatikan: Papst Franziskus und seine Gegner* (Zürich 2013).
14 Ibid.
15 Interview with the author.
16 *Die Welt Online* (15 July 2012).
17 Ibid.
18 katholisches.info (1 December 2015).
19 kath.net (25 October 2019).

CHAPTER 37: THE RESIGNATION

1   Interview with the author.
2   Ibid.
3   *Spiegel Online* (11 February 2013).
4   Ibid.
5   Joseph Ratzinger, *Jesus of Nazareth: The Infancy Narratives* (London, 2012), pp. 72, 67.
6   Interview with the author.
7   Benedict XVI's speech at his last general audience on 27 February 2013, kath.net (28 February 2013).
8   *Spiegel Online* (11 February 2013).
9   kath.net (31 August 2017).
10 Interview with the author.

CHAPTER 38: THE BEGINNING OF A NEW ERA

1   Interview with the author.
2   Bernard of Clairvaux, *Was ein Papst erwägen muss* (Einsiedeln, 1985).
3   Interview with the author.
4   Ibid.
5   *Vatican News* (12 March 2018).
6   w2.vatican.va, speech by Pope Benedict XVI at the Christmas reception for the College of Cardinals, members of the Roman Curia and the papal family, 21 December 2012.
7   https://w2.vatican.va/content/benedict-xvi/de/speeches/2013/february/documents/hf_ben -xvi_spe_20130208_seminario-romano-mag.html
8   Interview with the author.
9   Ibid.
10 Ibid.
11 Ibid.
12 kath.net (16 February 2013).
13 kath.net (19 February 2013).
14 Interview by Johannes Schidelko for Katholische Nachrichten-Agentur, February 2013.
15 kath.net (18 February 2013).
16 Interview with the author.
17 kath.net (18 February 2013).
18 Ibid.
19 Interview with the author.
20 kath.net (23 February 2013).
21 Interview with the author.
22 kath.net (24 February 2013).
23 Interview with the author.
24 Ibid.
25 Benedict XVI and Seewald, *Letzte Gespräche.*
26 kath.net (27 February 2013).

Index

à Kempis, Thomas 115
abortion 176, 191, 200, 236, 362
abuse scandals 163, 206–7, 230, 235–6, 241, 248, 265, 375, 413–32, 435, 446, 457, 462, 485–6, 489
Academic Freedom Association 34
Académie Française 201, 495
Adam, August 352–3
Adorf, Mario 318
Adorno, Theodor W. 4, 370
Adoukonou, Barthélemy 54–5
Africa, response to Ratzinger's election 294–5
Africa Synod 471–2
African Bishops' Council 196
Agamben, Giorgio 538
Agapita, Sister 109
Ağca, Ali 139–40, 231
Ajakaye, Bishop Felix 294
Akgün, Lale 342
Alacoque, Margaret Mary 310
Alberigo, Giuseppe 45
Albert the Great 48
Alemanno, Gianni 426, 519
Alexander the Great 229
Alexander III, Pope 262
Alexander VI, Pope 260
Allen, John 31
Allende, Salvador 177
al-Qaeda 229–30, 339
Amato, Cardinal Angelo 501
Anabaptists 14
Angela of Foligno 449
Anglicans 159, 371, 411, 433, 435, 443–4
Anhofer, Elisabeth 53
Annan, Kofi 255, 294
Ansaldo, Marco 483
anti-Semitism 26, 29, 83, 302, 324, 364, 408, 436, 516
and abuse scandals 424–5
and Williamson affair 380–98
Apollinarianism 149
Apostolic Penitentiary 239
Aquinas, Thomas 48, 54, 353
Arbeitskreis Sexualität 428
Arborelius, Bishop Anders 382–3
Arianism 149
Arians, Ingeborg 323
Arias, Juan 164, 170
Arinze, Cardinal Francis 264, 396
Aristotle 222
Arns, Cardinal Paulo Evaristo 114, 181
artificial insemination 176
Assenmacher, Günter 381
Athanasius, Bishop 441
Auer, Johann Baptist 43, 50, 53, 97
Augsburg Gebetshaus MEHR-Konferenz 438

Augstein, Rudolf 216–17, 228
Auschwitz 121, 134, 332–4, 387
Austrian Bishops' Conference 415
Autorità di Informazione Finanziaria 437
Aymans, Winfried 313

Baader, Andreas 24
Baader, Franz von 54
Bach, Johann Sebastian 272, 374
Bachelet, Michelle 373
Bachmann, Josef 23
Bachstein, Andrea 477
Bačkis, Cardinal Audrys 165
Badde, Paul 264, 384, 483–4
Bald, Karl Heinz 135
Balthasar, Hans Urs von 6, 9, 18, 22, 43, 54, 57, 60, 63, 79–81, 96, 130, 217
Bamberg Catholics' Conference 16–17
Ban Ki-moon 516
Bardakoğlu, Ali 338
Barenboim, Daniel 505
Barroso, José Manuel 294
Barth, Karl 9
Bartholomew I, Patriarch 348, 412, 508
Basil the Great, Bishop of Caesarea 67
Bavarian Bishops' Conference 111
Becciu, Archbishop Giovanni Angelo 475, 509
Beck, Kurt 388
Beckenbauer, Franz 318
Becker, Gerold 424
Becker, Volker 428
Beethoven, Ludwig van 174, 505, 531
Benedict IX, Pope 245
Benedict XV, Pope, 279 309–10
Benedict XVI, Pope (Joseph Aloisius Ratzinger)
  abolishes hand-kissing 308
  appointed cardinal 106–7
  appointed dean 235
  appointed prefect 121–2, 138–9, 141, 149–60
  Bavarian patriotism 5
  Caritas in veritate 409–11, 454
  Cologne speech (1970) 66–9
  compared with Wojtyła 161–2
  and Concilium 79–82
  confrontation with Küng 59–65
  co-operatores veritatis motto 9
  daily routine as pope 305–7, 487, 491
  denied freedom of Munich 206
  Deus caritas est 352–5, 397, 410
  disputes with intellectuals 237–8
  domestic life 204–5
  and election of John Paul I 113–15
  and election of John Paul II 117–22
  election as pope 257–84

election sermon 269–71
first appointments as pope 308
first speech as pope 291–3
first sermon as pope 297–9
Freiburg speech 467–9
German critics of 447–9
'Hans in Luck' parable 40–2
health problems 208–11, 221, 225, 258, 313, 488, 493
holidays with brother 203
and his housekeeper 350–2
humility 329–30
and Italian language 305
and John Paul II's death 247–56
and 'Küng case' 127–33, 182
and La Sapienza University protests 379–80
leadership criticized 399–403
love of animals 50
love of French culture 433–4
love of music 51, 110, 174, 203, 205, 225, 374, 378
media coverage 192–5, 218–19
'media meltdown' 456–9, 463
and Metz affair 125–7
moves to Regensburg 43, 47–55
moves to Tübingen 4–12
Munich appointment 95–103
and Munich financial scandal 135
Munich legacy 143–6
Munich lecture (1970) 84
parents' grave 52
personnel appointments 328–31
pessimism 433–5
photographic memory 88
portraits 175
Prague speech (1992) 90, 93
progressive vs. conservative tendencies 11–12, 16–18, 29, 146, 159–60, 165–6
public image as pope 312–13, 316–22
radio address (1970) 75–6
'Ratzinger Report' 166–73, 180, 221
'Ratzinger tea' 222
reception as pope 287–99
reconciliation with Küng 237
Regensburg speech 337–44, 353, 380, 385, 393, 436–7
relationship with de Lubac 57–8
relationship with John Paul II 161–2, 164, 189–91, 200–1, 234–5
resignation 269, 380, 484, 487–532
Sacramentorum sanctitatis tutela 414–15, 430
sarcasm 55
and sister's death 209–10
Spe salvi 369–71, 410
style of papacy 309–14, 345–8
Subiaco lecture (2005) 249–52
Summorum pontificum 363–5, 371
supports students 55
sympathy with youth protests 25
and technology 450–2
'Tübingen trauma' 29–34, 45
visits Australia 376–7
visits Benin 471–2
visits Brazil 358
visits Britain 442–4
visits Cameroon and Angola 403–4
visits Cyprus 441–2
visits France 377–9
visits Germany 334–7, 460–9
visits Holy Land 408–9
visits Poland 134, 332–4
visits Portugal 439–41
visits Spain 445–6

visits Turkey 348–9
visits USA 375–6
writing *Jesus of Nazareth* 365–9
Benedict XVI, *writings*:
Biblical Interpretation in Crisis 73
  Catechism of the Catholic Church 207–10
  Christian Faith and Europe 109
  The Church in the Year 2000 69–73
  Collected Works 72
  Deconstruction and Awakening 220
  Discussion on Hans Küng's 'Christ sein' 63
  Dogma and Proclamation 88
  Ecumenism and Politics 220
  'Eschatology', 88–92, 95
  Eucharist – Heart of the Church 109
  Introduction to Christianity 40–3, 62, 290
  Jesus of Nazareth trilogy 365–9, 380, 409, 493–5
  Light of the World 446–7, 457, 498, 505
  Ministers of Your Joy 220
  The Nature and Mission of Theology 220
  The New Heathens in the Church 42, 70, 108
  The New People of God 88
  Principles of Catholic Theology 109, 178
  Report on the State of the Faith 77
  Return to the Centre 109
  Salt of the Earth 59, 221–2
  The Spirit of the Liturgy 230
  Thoughts on the Crisis in Preaching 70
  To Look on Christ 220
  Truth, Values, Power 220
  A Turning Point for Europe? 220
Benedictines 123, 378
Benelli, Cardinal Giovanni 96, 106, 275
Bengsch, Cardinal Alfred 114
Benson, Robert Hugh 73
Bergoglio, Cardinal Jorge see Francis, Pope
Berlusconi, Silvio 473
Bernstein, Carl 118
Bernstein, Leonard 174
Bertone, Cardinal Tarcisio 202, 239, 330–1, 341, 372
  and abuse scandals 416, 423
  and Ratzinger's leadership 399–402
  and Ratzinger's resignation 507, 521, 531
  and Vatileaks crisis 471, 475, 477, 479–80
  and Williamson affair 383, 393–4
Betz, Esther 7, 52, 203, 221, 224–5, 228, 239, 374–5
Beuron Abbey 100
Beyerhaus, Peter 34
Bialas, Father Martin 203
Bild 24, 192, 264, 289, 389
Biser, Eugen 194, 207, 319
Bishops' Synod for New Evangelization 508
Bismarck, Otto von 460
Bizet, Georges 434
Bloch, Ernst 8, 26, 54
Blondel, Maurice 51
Böckenförde, Ernst-Wolfgang 237
Böckenförde, Werner 32, 237
Boff, Clodovis 177, 183
Boff, Leonardo 177, 181–3, 308, 321
Boffo, Dino 472
Bologna School 45
Bolshevik Revolution 26
Bolshoi Theatre 196
Bommes, Karin 53
Bonacina, Riccardo 406–7
Boniface VIII, Pope 379, 499
Bouyer, Louis 57
Bovone, Monsignor Alberto 155
Boy Scouts of America 427

Brandmayr, Franz Xaver 372
Brandmüller, Walter 61, 150–1
Brassens, Georges 18
Braun, Archbishop Karl 258
Bronfman, Edgar M. 295
Brugger, Walter 107
Bruno, Giordano 150
Brussels Foundation for European Progressive
    Studies 427
Buber-Rosenzweig medal 50
Buddhists 240, 289, 472, 492
Bultmann, Rudolf 25, 42–3
Bund der Atheisten 449
Bund Deutscher Mädel (BDM) 137
Bundesarbeitsgemeinschaft Schwule, Transsexualle und
    Päderasten 428
Burke, Cardinal Raymond 538
Burresi, Gino 419
Bush, George H. W. 255
Bush, George W. 255, 294, 375
Buttafuco, Pietroangelo 318
Buzzonetti, Dr Renato 215, 246–7, 253, 305

Çağrici, Grand Mufti Mustafa 248
Calvin, John 475
camauro 313
Cameron, David 516
Camus, Albert 54
Canisius College 421
Cantalamessa, Raniero 350, 424–5
Capella Musicale Pontificia 273
Cappella Paolina 346
Caprio, Archbishop Giuseppe 112
Cardenal, Ernesto 181, 183–4
Cardenal, Fernando 181
Cardinal Newman Foundation 204
Carina, Bishop Frencesco 483
Casaroli, Agostino 190–1, 196
Castra Regina 48
Castrillón Hoyos, Cardinal Darío 382–3, 387–8, 393,
    402
Castro, Fidel 177, 184, 192, 474
Castro, Raúl 474
catacombs 149
catechesis, crisis of 165–6
Catechism Committee 157, 208
Cathars 150
Catholic Extra-Parliamentary Opposition (Kapo) 36
Catholic News Agency 128, 342, 383
Catholic–Muslim forum 344, 437
Celestine V, Pope 499–501, 534
celibacy 71, 77, 84, 163, 191, 223, 326, 462
Central Committee of German Catholics 126, 462
Central Council of Jews in Germany 382, 387, 408
Central Council of Muslims in Germany 516
Charles II, King of Naples 499
Chenu, Marie-Dominique 11
China 3, 27–8, 412, 438, 452, 486
Chinese rites controversy 171
Chirri, Giovanna 497, 501–2, 511, 513–14
Christian Democratic Union (CDU) 258, 392
Christian Ministry Resources 426
Christian Social Union (CSU) 142, 192–3
Christian Unity Council 232, 436
Christians for Socialism 177
church attendance and membership 20, 58, 107–8,
    518–19
Ciampi, Carlo Azeglio 254, 346
Ciampi, Franca 320
Ciappi, Cardinal Mario Luigi 96, 106

Cipriani, Paolo 480
Clasen, Severino 308
Clemens, Josef 202, 205, 208, 238, 266, 350, 434, 484
climate change see environment and ecology
Clinton, Bill 255
Coccopalmerio, Archbishop Francesco 383–4
Codex Iuris Canonici 186
Coelho, Paulo 222
Cohn-Bendit, Daniel 24, 428
Cold War 198, 217, 304
College of Cardinals, Ratzinger heads 235, 254–5, 260
Collegio Teutonico 61, 155
Cologne Declaration 200, 462
Columbus, Christopher 496
Comastri, Cardinal Angelo 483
Committee to Defend the Rights of Christians in the
    Church 130
Communio 79–82, 111, 138
Communione e Liberazione 81, 86, 201, 305
Communist Party of the Soviet Union (CPSU) 197
Company of Bavarian Mounted Riflemen 146, 297
concentration camps 37, 381
Conchita (child seer) 241
Concilium 10, 18, 79–82
condom crisis 403–8, 418, 449
Confalonieri, Cardinal Carlo 113, 119
Confessio Augustana (Augsburg Confession) 54
confessional, secrecy of 235
Congar, Yves 11, 18, 22, 44, 54–5
Congregation for Catholic Education 122, 138, 403
Congregation for the Causes of Saints 501
Congregation for the Doctrine of the Faith
    and abuse scandals 206–7, 235–6, 414–18, 423, 449
    concierge (Clelia) 157–8
    and Deus caritas est 353
    Dominus Iesus 232–4
    Donum vitae 176
    'Holy Inquisition' 149–52
    'Instruction of September 1984' 175
    and 'Küng case' 127–31
    and Lefebvre schism 186–7
    and liberation theology 177–84, 358
    media offensive 164–73
    Ratzinger appointed prefect 121–2, 138–9, 141,
        149–60
    Ratzinger's birthday celebrations 266
    Ratzinger's wish for retirement 210–11, 224, 238–9,
        258
    and secrets of Fátima 230–2
Congregation for the Evangelization of Peoples 203
Congregation for the Institutes of Consecrated Life and
    Societies of Apostolic Life 238
Congregation of Bishops 202, 157, 382, 384
Congregation of the Sacred Heart of Jesus 302
Constitution on the Vacancy of the Apostolic See 263
Contra War 183
contraception 35–6, 113, 163, 326, 362
    see also condom crisis
Copernicus, Nikolaus 240
Cor Unum 353
Cordes, Cardinal Paul Josef 353
Cornwell, John 117
Corriere della Sera 254, 259, 264, 291, 326, 406, 476
COSEA 485
Council for Inter-Religious Dialogue 232
Council for Promoting the New Evangelization of the
    Western World 495
Council for Unity 157
Council of the Synod of Bishops 111
Counter-Reformation 150

'Court of the Nations' 495
Crescenti, Francesco 51
Critical Catholicism 36, 82
Cruz, Archbishop Oscar 295

Dalai Lama 438
Dalí, Salvador 18
dalla Torre, Giuseppe 482
Daniélou, Jean 11, 22
Danneels, Cardinal Godfried 243, 264–5, 275
Dante 355, 500
d'Arcais, Paolo Flores 237
Das Schwarzbuch des Kommunismus 26
Dawkins, Richard 442, 455
de Galarreta, Bishop Alfonso 385
de Giorgi, Cardinal Salvatore 287, 475
de Lubac, Henri 10–11, 17–18, 22, 43–4, 57–8, 79–80, 94, 97, 377
de Lucia, Carlo 280
de Mattei, Roberto 44
de Zotto, Cornelio 9
Deckers, Daniel 7
Degenhardt, Cardinal Johannes 137
Dehon, Léon 302
del Mestri, Guido 95–6, 98, 102, 106, 121, 138
del Monte, Pietro 214
Der Spiegel 35, 99, 164–5, 221, 228–9, 243–4, 268
    and abuse scandals 422, 457
    attacks on John Paul II 215–17
    and Ratzinger's election 289–90
    and Ratzinger papacy 316, 324, 338–9, 342–3, 353, 447, 463
    and Ratzinger's resignation 518
    and Williamson affair 382, 390
Derwahl, Freddy 33, 127–8
Dery, Archbishop Peter Poreku 329
Descartes, René 171
desecularization 15, 42, 468–9, 496
Di Segni, Chief Rabbi Riccardo 308, 387
Dick, Klaus 204
Die Welt 129, 146, 175, 264, 381, 384, 483–4
Die Zeit 28, 170, 221, 234–5, 267, 290, 297, 303, 317, 343, 423, 448, 463, 518
Diels, Rudolf 216–17
Dieter, Theodor 226
Dionysius Exiguus 226
Disciples of Christ Church 34
Dives and Lazarus 367–8
divorce and divorcees 35, 72, 84, 464
Docetism 149
Dominicans 150
Donatism 149
Döpfner, Cardinal Julius 5, 17, 37, 40, 64, 66, 82, 95, 101, 105, 107, 137
Döpfner, Mathias 389
d'Ormesson, Wladimir 475
dos Santos, Lucia 231
Dostoyevsky, Fyodor 171, 370
Down's Syndrome 139
Dreher, Rod 534
Drewermann, Eugen 136, 205–6, 289, 323
Dubček, Alexander 48
Dutroux, Marc 427
Dutschke, Rudi 23–4, 32
Dylan, Bob 3, 241
Dziwisz, Stanisław 120, 140, 153, 189, 191, 214, 243, 246, 249–50, 252, 311, 315, 500

Ecclesia Dei 383, 388, 393, 395
ecology see environment and ecology

ecumenism 8–10, 34, 37, 39, 54, 60, 84–5, 103, 124, 127, 162, 171, 186, 197, 225–6, 292, 298, 324, 327, 336, 411–12, 436, 441, 447, 466, 518
Editiones Typicae 186
Edizio dell Stato Vaticano 272
Eichsfeld 466–7
Einstein, Albert 304, 487
Elizabeth II, Queen 443
Emilia Romagna earthquakes 505
Ender, Erwin 138
Engels, Friedrich 25, 219
Englisch, Andreas 192, 264
Enlightenment 132, 219, 238, 379
environment and ecology 95, 136, 357, 371, 447, 452–4
    'human ecology' 453–4, 465
Epstein, Jeffrey 428
Erdoğan, Recep Tayyip 348
eschatology 88–92, 539
Essen Catholics' Conference 36–7, 82
Ettal Abbey 421
Eucharist 20, 72, 107–9, 136, 144–5, 156, 159, 233, 316, 323, 326–7, 329, 402, 462, 466, 489, 528
Eucharistic World Congress 141
Eugene, Pope 504
European Convention on Human Rights 442
European Court of Human Rights 442
European Union 230, 356, 406, 480
Evangelical Christuskirche 436
Evangelical Church in Germany 83, 233, 463, 518
Evangelical-Lutheran churches 142, 321
Evangelicals 6–7, 16, 23, 34, 46, 183, 449, 466, 518–19
Exaltation of the Cross 66
Existentialism 27, 136

Fahr, Friedrich 155
Fallaci, Oriana 312
Familia Spiritualis Opus 204
Faulhaber, Cardinal 105
Favalora, Archbishop John C. 419
Fazenda da Esperança 358
Fegan, Ali 381
Feiner, Johannes 57
Felasca, Stefania 117
Felder, Sister Christine 204–5, 208, 210, 365, 401, 505, 523
Feldmann, Christian 31, 321, 432, 476
Felici, Pericle 114
Fellay, Bishop Bernard 312, 380–2, 385, 387
feminism 27, 307
Fernández de la Cigoña, Francisco José 382
Ferres, Veronica 318
Feuerbach, Ludwig 51
Fichte, Johann Gottlieb 36
Figlie della Chiesa 209
Filoni, Bishop Fernando 383
Fink, Bruno 110, 120–1, 123, 126, 135, 140, 153–4, 158, 165, 174–5, 191, 202, 206
First World War 310
Fischer, Heinz Joachim 194
Fischer, Helene 489
Fisichella, Archbishop Rino 312, 399, 437, 495
Fiumara, Mia 255
Flavius Josephus 229
Foa, Marcello 456
'forbidden diary' 272, 275–6, 279
Foster, Jodie 139
Fourest, Caroline 382
Francis, Pope (Jorge Bergoglio) 113, 192, 236, 248, 265, 275–6, 279, 328, 330, 394, 418, 432, 537, 539
    and abuse scandals 485–6

Lumen fidei 508–9
  and Ratzinger's resignation 508–9, 517
Franco, General Francisco 445
Frankfurt School 3–4, 36, 238
Frankfürter Allgemeine Zeitung 63, 128, 130, 132, 163, 194, 253, 353, 429, 473, 491
Frauenlob, Thomas 403
Free University of Berlin 23
freemasons 116, 159, 480
Freiburg German Catholics' Conference 110
Freiburg Teacher Training College 36
Freude am Glauben 438
Friedbald, Brother 105
Friedmann, Michel 392
Friedrich, Bishop Johannes 233
Frings, Cardinal Joseph 4, 11, 18, 20–2, 66, 78, 113, 152, 171, 269
Frings, Klaus 24

Gabel, Professor 225
Gabriele, Paolo 470, 478–86, 493, 524, 534
Gagnon, Cardinal Édouard 185
Galen, Bishop Count von 37
Galileo Galilei 150, 171, 217, 240, 379
Galvão, Friar 358
Gammarelli firm 281, 306
Gänswein, Georg 185, 191, 204, 206, 238, 250–1, 255, 267, 277, 281–2, 300, 305, 312–13, 315–16, 322, 330, 332, 340, 350, 383–4, 460
  and abuse scandals 418, 426
  and Ratzinger's leadership 399–402
  and Ratzinger's resignation 493, 496, 505, 507, 509–12, 514, 529
  and Vatileaks crisis 471, 478–81, 484–5
Gantin, Cardinal Bernardin 106, 202, 404
Garrone, Cardinal Gabriel-Marie 138
Garton Ash, Timothy 245
Gasbarri, Alberto 439
Gaudí, Antoni 446
Geissler, Heiner 258
Geissler, Hermann 159, 515
Gemelli Clinic 140, 213, 243–4, 246
gender 454–5
General Synod of the Church of England 422
Genscher, Hans-Dietrich 199
German Bishops' Conference 36–7, 40, 51–2, 61–2, 66, 82, 84, 97, 111, 430, 461–2
  and 'Küng case' 127, 129–30
  and Ratzinger's election 299
  and Ratzinger's resignation 518
German Catholic Youth Society 82
German constitution 461
German Economic Miracle 24
Germanicum 99, 110
Ghazi bin Muhammad, Prince 408
Gijsen, Bishop Joannes 85
Giordano, Ralph 83
Girard, René 357
Girotti, Gianfranco 416
Giuliani, Veronica 449
Giussami, Don 86
Glavanovics, Friederike 456–8, 463
global financial crisis 410
Gnosticism 14, 149
Goldbrunner, Josef 50
Good Friday prayer 448
Gorbachev, Mikhail 196–9
Göring, Herman 216
Görres, Albert 79
Görres, Ida Friederike 20, 43

Göttinger Institute for Democratic Research 22
Graber, Rudolf 51–2, 102
Grass, Günter 463
Graumann, Dieter 382
Green, Edward C. 407
Green, Julien 18, 93
Green Party 388, 428–9, 464–5
Gregory I (the Great), Pope 359, 434, 492, 494
Gregory IX, Pope 150
Greiner, Franz 80
Greyberg, Ernst von 481
Groër, Cardinal Hans Hermann 230, 415
Gruber, Gerhard, 102, 107, 109, 422
Guardini, Romano 16, 68, 86–7, 94, 194, 230, 460, 489, 528
Guénois, Jean-Marie 402, 405
Guerriero, Elio 376
Guevara, Che 23
Gugel, Angelo 140, 300, 305, 479
Gustav Siewerth Academy 37, 86
Gutenberg, Johannes 152, 434
Gutiérrez, Gustavo 176–7, 179, 184
Guzmán Garcés, Domingo de 150

Haberl, Tobias 452
Habermas, Jürgen 237–8, 433
Hacker, Paul 19
Hadrian VI, Pope 279
Haering, Stephan 329
Hahn, Viktor 156
Halbfas, Hubert 34
Haller, Reinhard 428
Hamer, Archbishop Jérôme 153, 155, 182
Hanselmann, Bishop Johannes 142, 226
Häring, Hermann 10, 30, 447
Harissa 507
Hartl, Friedrich 54
Harvey, Cardinal James 479, 509, 529
Hary, Armin 135
Hasenhüttl, Gotthold 19, 32
Haslbeck, Petra 205
Hasler, August 128
Hassoun, Sheikh Ahmad Badreddin 343
Havel, Václav 373
Hegel, G. W. F. 4, 7, 36, 51, 219, 531
Heidegger, Martin 25
Heidner, Sister Eufreda 105
Heinrich III, Emperor 262
Hengsbach, Bishop Franz 16
Henrich, Franz 206
Hentig, Hartmut von 424
Herder Korrespondenz 200
heretics 149–51
Hermann of Reichenau 151
Herranz, Cardinal Julián 475
Herrmann, Horst 30
Herzog, Werner 464
Hesse, Hermann 291
Hilarion, Metropolitan 436
Hildegard of Bingen 449
Hill, Rolf 321
Hinckley, John 139
Hindus 34, 375, 472, 492
Hitler, Adolf 83, 216–17, 232, 338
Hitler Youth 266, 287
HIV/AIDS 214, 404–8
Ho Chi Minh 23
Hoagland, Hudson 35
Hochhuth, Rolf 82–4
Hochland 61, 74

Hödl, Ludwig 131
Hofbauer, Rupert 50
Höfer, Josef 7
Höffner, Cardinal Joseph 64, 66, 87, 96, 114, 127, 131
Hofmann, Father Norbert Johannes 403, 515
Hölderlin, Friedrich 7, 434
Holocaust 83, 136, 287, 324, 381, 384–7, 389–90, 392–3, 395, 408
    Williamson affair and 380–97
Holy Roman Empire 48, 279, 461
Hommes, Ulrich 51, 206
homosexuality 175, 191, 379, 449, 462, 484
    and abuse scandals 419, 421, 425
Honecker, Erich 198
Hoping, Helmut 89
Horkheimer, Max 4, 370
Horn, Stephan 53, 55, 94
Horst, Guido 191
Humanistische Union 428
Hummel, Karl-Joseph 82–3
Hummes, Cardinal Cláudio 264, 383
Hurnas, Christoph 332
Hus, Jan 240
Huxley, Aldous 73

Iadicicco, Colonel Girolamo 528
Ignatius of Antioch 54
Innocent III, Pope 150
Integrated Community 86, 135–7, 221, 401–2
International Committee of Theologians 57, 80, 141, 156, 177–8
International Heart of Jesus Congress 141
international space station 257
Iron Curtain, fall of 198, 213
Irving, David 83
Islam 240, 380, 412, 536
    and Regensburg speech 337–44, 385
Islamic calendar 492
Israeli soldiers 346
Italian Federation of Rabbis 334

Jackson, Michael 244, 428
Jackson, Peter 357
Jansenism 149
Jarasch, Bettina 429
Jaspers, Karl 51, 54
Jaworski, Cardinal Marian 247, 253
Jedin, Hubert 19, 37–40
Jenkins, Philip 307–8, 426
Jens, Walter 10
Jeremiah, prophet 207
Jewish calendar 492
Jewish Committee for Inter-Religious Relationships 386
Jewish World Congress 391
Joan of Arc 310
Jobs, Steve 356
Johann-Adam-Möhler Institute for Ecumenism 37
John XXIII, Pope 9, 76, 78, 231, 263, 277, 313, 315, 386, 508
    and Tridentine Mass 363–4
John Paul I, Pope (Albino Luciani) 113–17, 246, 305
John Paul II, Pope (Karol Wojtyła) 35, 50, 73, 81, 114, 116, 158, 160, 205, 210, 224
    and abuse scandals 417–18
    Ad tuendam fidem 232
    assassination attempt 139–41, 231
    attacked in Der Spiegel 215–17
    beatification process 417–18, 459, 500
    compared with Ratzinger 161–2, 302–4

death 253–6, 488
    and Dominus Iesus 234
    early life 240–1
    elected pope 117–22
    and fall of communism 198–9
    joins in Bavarian anthem 195
    and 'Küng case' 127–8, 130–1
    and Lefebvre schism 185–6
    and liberation theology 178, 183
    media image 192, 456–7
    and millennium 226–9
    papacy 138–9, 161–2, 166, 172, 188–9, 212–17, 238–56
    Quattuor ab hinc annos 362
    and Ratzinger's appointment as prefect 121–2, 138–9, 141, 151
    and Ratzinger's papacy 311, 313, 315, 317–20, 326–7, 329–32, 342, 346, 351, 359, 372, 375–6, 387, 394, 409, 436–7, 472, 474, 486, 491, 514–15, 517, 519
    and Ratzinger's succession 260–1, 263–5, 267–8, 271, 273, 277, 284, 288, 293–5, 298
    Redemptor hominis 212, 352
    relationship with Ratzinger 161–2, 164, 189–91, 200–1, 234–5
    and resignation process 498, 500, 535
    Salvifici doloris 214
    Tertio millennio adveniente 227
    Theologie des Leibes (Theology of the Body) 212
    visits Germany 134–5, 460
Joint International Commission for Theological Dialogue 435
Juan Carlos, King 446
Judaism 26, 50, 86, 136, 361, 371, 380, 436, 472, 538
    see also anti-Semitism
Julian of Norwich 449
Julius II, Pope 262

Kafka, Franz 205
Kant, Immanuel 171, 219, 370
Karl Albrecht, Prince-Elector 105
Käsemann, Ernst 42, 60
Kasper, Cardinal Walter 10, 42, 71, 79, 233, 392–3, 461, 518
    appointed cardinal 234–5
    and St Gallen group 264–5, 275
Kässmann, Bishop Margot 83, 233, 321
Keller, Michael 7
Kemper, Max-Eugen 224
Kepplinger, Hans Mathias 386
KGB 84
Khamenei, Ayatollah Ali 338
Khoury, Adel Theodor 337
Kirchlichkeit (loyalty to church) 94
Kissler, Alexander 41, 77
Kissler, Arnold 33
Kister, Kurt 389
Kleine Katholische Dogmatik (Short Catholic Dogmatics) 79, 88
Klitschko, Vladimir 490
Knights of Malta 488
Knobloch, Charlotte 387, 408
Koch, Cardinal Kurt 207, 348, 365, 392, 401, 403, 513, 515, 538
Kock, Manfred 233
Kohl, Christiane 268
Köhler, Horst 294, 323, 342, 392
Köhler, Maria-Gratia 87
Kolbe, Maximilian Maria 134, 332
Kolping Society 70
Komorowski, Bronisław 516
König, Cardinal Franz 114, 118–19

Königstein Declaration 36
Korn, Salomon 387
Kottje, Raymund 71
Kowalska, Faustyna 252
Kraushaar, Wolfgang 29
Krenn, Kurt 230
Kröber, Hans Ludwig 429
Kronawitter, Georg 101
Kronsteiner, Josef and Hermann 203
Kruger, Beate 335–6
Kruse, Jens-Martin 436
Kuhn, Peter 7, 9, 33, 403
Kulerski, Wiktor 121
Kulle, Stephan 282
Küng, Hans 4, 6–11, 18–20, 30–3, 41, 43–7, 49, 51, 53–5,
  136, 152, 193, 205, 210, 232
  'Answer to my Critics' 63
  The Church 8, 60–1, 127
  and Concilium 79–81
  confrontation with Ratzinger 59–65
  The Council and Reunion 7
  Infallible? An Inquiry 32, 61–2, 64–5, 127
  'Küng case' 127–33, 182
  and liberation theology 180–4
  and Munich appointment 97, 99
  On Being a Christian 62–3, 131
  and Ratzinger's papacy 289, 312, 390, 447, 449
  reaction to 'Ratzinger Report' 170–2
  reconciliation with Ratzinger 237
  Reform and Recognition of Church Offices 62
  Theological Meditation 10
Kurras, Detective Chief Inspector Karl-Heinz 24

La Peruta, Teresa 317
La Repubblica 201, 237, 239, 254, 267, 279, 291, 326, 449,
  481, 483–4
Lahey, Bishop John 419
Lai, Benny 399
laicization 153, 156, 188, 238
Lajolo, Cardinal 478
Lambrecht, Rudolf 146
Lammert, Norbert 392
Langendörfer, Hans 299, 462, 464
Langenstuck, Klaus 325
L'Aquila earthquake 501
Laras, Giuseppe 334
Lassalle, Ferdinand 26
Latin 21, 58, 259, 291, 325, 499, 501–2, 510, 513
Latin American Bishops' Conference (CELAM) 180
Latin American Bishops' Council 196
Le Guillou, Marie-Joseph 57, 80
Le Monde 128, 237, 449
League of Nations 310
Lefebvre, Archbishop Marcel 112, 163, 167, 185–7, 380,
  390
Légion d'Honneur 57–8
Legion of Christ 191, 416–17
Lehmann, Karl 7, 10, 52, 64–5, 71, 79–80, 84, 127, 130,
  193–4, 200, 461
  appointed cardinal 234–5
  'Lehmann church' 84, 200
  and St Gallen group 264–5, 275
Lehman Brothers 229, 410
Lehmann-Dronke, Johannes 36, 47
Lehner, Pasqualina 351
Lehrer, Abraham 324
Leicht, Robert 234
Leiprecht, Carl Josef 7
Lejeune, Jérôme 139
Lenin, V. I. 29, 48, 197

Lenz, Bruno 175
Leo I (the Great), Pope 319
Leo IX, Pope 276
Leo XIII, Pope 77
Lepanto, Battle of 214
Levada, Cardinal William J. 308, 383, 402, 417–18, 431
Levin, Yehuda 392
Lévy, Bernard-Henri 391
Lewy, Mordechai 409
Leyendecker, Hans 321
liberation theology 54, 56, 115, 136, 165, 176–85, 189,
  199, 358
Liberto, Father Giuseppe 273
'Little Flowers' dancers 245
Logos 42, 90, 94, 250
Lohfink, Gerhard 136
Lombardi, Federico 331, 340, 382, 425–6, 471, 482,
  497, 515
López Trujillo, Cardinal Alfonso 274, 291
Lorenzer, Alfred 19
Lorscheider, Cardinal Aloísio 114, 181
L'Osservatore Romano 280, 317, 357, 379, 384, 423, 474
Lourdes 144, 375, 378, 439, 507
Luna Tobar, Bishop Luis Alberto 115
Lustiger, Cardinal Jean-Marie 165, 259, 288, 363
Luthe, Hubert 21
Luther, Martin 14, 38, 83, 151, 194, 215, 221, 380, 466,
  475
Lutheran World Federation 226, 435
Lütz, Manfred 150, 163, 429
Luxemburg, Rosa 23

Macapagal-Arroyo, Gloria 295
McCarrick, Cardinal Theodore 485
Macchi, Pasquale 112
Maciel, Marcial 191, 415–18
Mafia 116, 240, 437
Magee, John 419
Maier, Hans 79, 125–6, 319
Malachy, prophecy of 116, 241
Mallersdorf Abbey 203, 225, 258
Malnati, Don Ettore 500
Mandelbaum, Henryk 332
Manuel II Palaeologus, Emperor 337, 339–42
Mao Zedong 3, 23, 26–9, 347
Mara bar Serapion 228
Maradiaga, Archbishop Óscar Andrés Rodríguez 267,
  275
Marcinkus, Archbishop Paul 437
Marcuse, Herbert 4
Maria Heimsuchung Abbey 87
Marini, Archbishop Piero 273, 331
Marini, Guido 331, 501
Marmann, Michael Johannes 32
marriage 72, 113, 134, 153, 156, 175, 193, 236, 238, 241,
  308, 362, 394, 402, 454, 489, 534
Mars rover 491–2
Martínez Somalo, Cardinal Eduardo 254, 287
Martini, Cardinal Carlo Maria 243, 259, 261, 264–5,
  267, 275–6, 506
Märtyrer 2009 412
Marx, Bishop Reinhard 32
Marx, Karl 4, 25–6, 48, 219, 355, 370
Marx, Reinhard 421
Marxism 22, 25–7, 29, 33, 36–7, 48, 51, 54, 165, 197,
  269–70, 273, 462
  and liberation theology 176–8, 180, 182–3
Mary, mother of Jesus 348
Mary Magdalene 215
Mater Ecclesiae 509

Matussek, Matthias 457
May, Georg 55
May, Theresa 427
May, William 195
Mayan calendar 492
Mayer, Cardinal Augustin 174, 204, 277
Mayzek, Aiman 342, 516
Mazzanti, Raul 255
Mbeki, Thabo 294
Me Too movement 428
Médecins sans Frontières 427
Medellín Bishops' Conference 56, 176
Medina Estévez, Cardinal Jorge 57, 80, 274, 282, 287
Meinhof, Ulrike 24
Meisner, Cardinal Joachim 189, 265–6, 274, 278, 299, 324, 400, 488, 537
Melanchthon, Philipp 54
Melloni, Alberto 425
Melvile, Herman 434
Memores Domini 300, 350–1, 470, 478, 511
Mendieta, Eduardo 238
Menke, Burkhardt 365–6
Menke, Karl-Heinz 360
Menuhin, Yehudi 224
Merkel, Angela 324, 388–9, 392, 470, 491, 516
Mertes, Klaus 421, 432
Messerer, Alois 266
Messori, Vittorio 166, 170, 180
Metz, Johann Baptist 5–6, 10, 55, 82, 84, 86, 88, 125–7, 177, 237, 314
    Theologie der Welt 41
Metzger, Chief Rabbi Yona 516
Michelangelo 273, 488
Middle East Synod of Bishops 507
Missale Romanum (1962) 58
Mitterrand, François 164
Mohammed, Prophet 339, 341–3
Mokrzycki, Mieczysaw 243, 300, 351
Moll, Helmut 13, 28, 32, 158
Moltmann, Jürgen 54
monasticism 377–8
Montecassino Abbey 80, 310
Monti, Mario 505, 516
Monzo, Alfredo 154, 208, 221, 250, 511
'Moor of Friesing' 103–4, 310
Moore, Charles 288
More, Thomas 444
Moro, Aldo 112
Mosebach, Martin 393
Moser, Bishop Georg 130–1
Mozart, Wolfgang Amadeus 76, 203, 224, 374
Mucha, Józef 116
Müller, Beda 34
Muller, Cardinal Gerhard Ludwig 182, 184, 205, 399, 403, 515
Münch, Werner 392
Münster Declaration 391
Murphy, Lawrence C. 423
Murphy, Yvonne 419
Muslims 34, 264, 302, 308, 346, 375, 408, 412, 437, 449, 497, 508
    and Regensburg speech 337–44
Mussner, Franz 50, 301, 367
Mussolini, Benito 338
Mutsaerts, Bishop Robertus 486

Napoleon Bonaparte 347
Napolitano, Giorgio 373, 470
Navarro-Valls, Joaquín 196, 320, 331, 340, 347, 418
Nazarbayev, Nursultan 388

Nazi period 21, 28–9, 37, 51, 82–3, 87, 173, 179, 211, 266, 333, 336, 373, 378, 443, 461, 490
    Der Spiegel and 216–17
    John Paul II and 240–1
    and Ratzinger's election 287–9, 294–5
Nersinger, Ulrich 450
Nestorianism 149
Neue Zürcher Zeitung 101, 238, 289, 391, 449
New York Philharmonic Orchestra 174
New York Times 81, 166, 213, 317, 319, 406, 423, 449
Newman, Cardinal John Henry 16, 442, 444, 459
Nicene Creed 90
Nietzsche, Friedrich 354–5
Nigerian Bishops' Conference 294
Nolte, Josef 8
Nossol, Bishop Alfons 121
Nouvelle Théologie 16
nuclear weapons 164
nuns, decline in numbers 307
Nuzzi, Gianluigi 236, 438, 473–4, 476–8, 483, 485

Obama, Barack 356, 374, 390, 491, 516
Obermaier, Monsignor Erwin 105, 110
Obermair, Gustav 48
Octave of Prayer for Christian Unity 310
Oddi, Cardinal Silvio 114
Odenwald School 424
Oder, Sławomir 500
Ohnesorg, Benno 24
O'Malley, Archbishop Patrick 328, 431
Omkelinx, Laurette, 406
Opus Dei 289, 331
Opus Dei University 225
Ortega, Daniel 184
Orthodox Church 162–3, 309, 348, 371, 436, 441
Orwell, George 45–6, 73, 220
Oschwald, Hanspeter 31, 448
Ottaviani, Cardinal Alfredo 99, 154
Our Lady of Częstochowa 252
Our Lady of Fátima 140–1, 213, 230–2, 439–41, 509
Our Lady of Guadelupe 474
Oxfam 427

P2 secret society 112, 116
Pacepa, Ion Mihai 83
Palestinian terrorists 112
Palestrina, Giovanni Pierluigi da 76, 374
Pannenberg, Wolfhart 54
Papal Biblical Committee 141, 156
Papal Committee for Religious Relations with Judaism 403
papal infallibility 13, 61, 127–8, 131, 259
papal names 281
Papandreou, Damaskinos 187
Paradise, idea of 370
Paris Commune 24
Paul III, Pope 150
Paul VI, Pope 21, 35, 57–8, 61, 64, 77, 80–1, 152, 156, 161, 186, 188, 198, 214, 231, 241, 263, 331, 375, 468
    death and succession 112–14
    Humanae vitae 35–6, 61, 113
    Populorum progressio 410
    and Ratzinger appointments 96, 98–9, 102, 106
    and resignation process 500, 535
Pauline Year 411–13
Paulus, Father 43
Pelagianism 149
Pentecostalists 183
Pera, Marcello 237
Peres, Shimon 343, 373–4, 409

Pesch, Rudolf 136
Peter, Simone 429
Peterson, Eugene 94
Pfeiffer, Christian 426
Pfnür, Brigitte 347
Pfnür, Vinzenz 44
Phillips, Melanie 443
Pieper, Josef 33, 37, 353
Pink Floyd 312
Pio, Padre 246
Pioppo, Monsignor 250
Pius II, Pope 262, 306
Pius V, Pope 186, 214, 362
Pius IX, Pope 245
Pius, X, Pope 263
Pius XI, Pope 263
Pius XII, Pope 83, 112, 263, 315, 351, 487, 490, 500
Pius XIII, Pope 257
Pius XIV, Pope 257
Plato 222
Pol Pot 29
Polak, Bishop Wojciech 516
Pole, Reginald 54
Polisca, Patrizio 474
Polish Bishops' Conference 516
Polish Communist Party 121
Politi, Marco 118, 340, 471
Pompey, Heinrich 354
Pontifical Academy of Sciences 346
Pontifical Athenaeum Regina Apostolorum 416
Pontifical Committee for Religious Relations with
    Judaism 515
Pontifical Council for Culture 55, 374
Pontifical Council for Promoting Christian Unity 348,
    435
Pope Benedict XVI Institute 50
Posener, Alan 448–9
Prague Spring 48
priests, numbers of 20, 58, 163, 307, 319, 361–2, 489
Priests for Socialism 56
Primaldo, Antonio 501
Propaganda Congregation 157
protestantization, 19, 39, 56, 60, 62
Protestants, 54, 60, 62, 124, 162, 197, 219, 226, 242,
    267, 321, 336, 346, 394, 426, 436, 460, 462–3, 466,
    518–19
Puljic, Cardinal 264
Purgatory 93, 296
Putin, Vladimir 294, 374

Quaestiones Disputatae 61
Qur'an 264, 338–9, 343

racism 26, 161, 295, 329
Radikalenerlass 29
Radio Vatican 115, 331, 357, 482
Radspieler, Bishop Werner 319
Rahner, Karl 5, 10, 37, 44, 53–4, 57, 61, 63–4, 71, 177,
    194, 217
    and Metz affair 125–6
Ratzinger, Georg (brother) 5, 47, 49, 96, 137, 160, 203,
    207, 225, 260, 336, 347, 422, 475, 504
Ratzinger, Georg (great uncle) 49
Ratzinger, Maria (sister) 5–7, 45, 47, 49, 96, 105, 137,
    154–5, 160, 174, 204
    her death 208–9, 350
Rauber, Archbishop Karl-Josef 96, 189, 202, 347
Ravasi, Cardinal Gianfranco 495, 510, 522
Re, Cardinal Giovanni Battista 243, 269, 291, 382–4,
    387, 393, 500

Reagan, Ronald 139
Red Army Faction 24
Red Brigades 112
Reder, Markus 290
Redzioch, Wlodzimierz 183
Reformation 14, 20, 38, 287, 289, 460, 475
Regensburg Domspatzen 5, 47, 49, 209, 422
Regensburg Ecumenical Symposiums 85
Reinhardt, Volker 535
religious persecution 412
Resing, Volker 200
Reul, Herbert 429
Reyero, Maximino Arias 178
Ricard, Archbishop Jean-Pierre 288
Riccardi, Andrea 198
Richard, Jean-Pierre 328
Richardi, Maria 51
Richardi, Maria Assunta 51
Richardi, Reinhardt 51–2, 105
Richelieu, Cardinal 201
Riehl–Heyse, Herbert 192
Ring-Eifel, Ludwig 342
Rinser, Luise 64
Rivera, Cardinal Adolfo Suárez 268
Robert the Pious, King 151
Rodari, Paolo 395
Rohl, Christoph 431–2
Rolduc seminary 85
Rolling Stones 3, 244
Romeo, Cardinal Paolo 473
Romero, Archbishop Óscar 176, 184
Rosa, Hartmut 451
Rosen, Rabbi David 386, 388
Ross, Jan 267, 290
Roth, Claudia 388
Rothenfels Castle 87
Rousseau, Jean-Jacques 37
Ruini, Cardinal Camillo 243, 275
Ryan, Sean 418
Ryłko, Archbishop Stanisław 253

Saier, Bishop Oskar 131
St Andrew 348
St Anna abbey 105
St Augustine 16, 76, 94, 98, 104, 310, 355, 370, 539
St Benedict 159, 249–50, 279, 284, 209–10, 470, 486,
    494
St Bernadette 378, 507
St Bernard of Clairvaux 504
St Bonaventure 16, 48, 54, 179, 449–50
St Charles Borromeo 168
St Corbinian 100, 104, 128
St Francis of Assisi 76, 459, 489, 508
St Francis Xavier 445
St Gallen group 243, 265, 272, 275
St Hedwig 119
St Ignatius of Loyola 445
St Irenaeus of Lyon 54, 86
St John of the Cross 445
St Laura di Santa Caterina da Siena 497
St Maria Gaudalupe García Zavala 497
St Nicholas 316
St Paul 14, 187, 314, 398, 411–13, 420, 439, 479
St Peter 110–11, 118, 121, 198, 213, 221, 227, 243–5,
    253–4, 259, 261, 280–1, 288, 292, 296, 303, 306, 322,
    334, 349, 352, 360–1, 381, 394, 397, 409, 438, 444, 450,
    488, 501, 504, 512–14, 518, 523–4, 526–8, 530–2, 535
St Peter Claver 358
St Teresa of Ávila 314, 445, 449
St Thérèse of Lisieux 459

Sakharov, Andrei 201
Salome, Sister Maria 403–4
Sambi, Pietro 328
Samir, Samir Khalil 344
Sandri, Archbishop Leonardo 243, 253, 340
Santiago de Compostela 445–6
Sardi, Cardinal Paolo 350–1, 400, 473, 479, 483–4
Sartre, Jean-Paul 171
Sawallisch, Wolfgang 51
Schaeffler, Richard 142
Schäfer, Gerhard 105
Scheffczyk, Leo 5, 177
Scheler, Max 94
Schelling, Friedrich Wilhelm Joseph 7
Scheyern Abbey 123, 203, 258
Schillebeeckx, Edward 32
Schlier, Heinrich 37, 86
Schlögl, Manuel 86
Schmaus, Michael 79, 100
Schmidberger, Father Franz 186, 382, 393
Schmidt-Sommer, Irmgard 25, 32
Schneider, Nikolaus 518
Schönborn, Cardinal Christoph 52, 195, 244, 400, 415
Schoonenberg, Piet 54
Schreck, Rudiger 24
Schreiber, Matthias 518–19
Schröffer, Joseph 114
Schumpeter, Joseph 19
Schutz, Frère Roger 124, 268, 324
Schwaiger, Georg 260
Schwärzel, Rolf 519
Schweitzer, Albert 43, 63
Schwery, Henri 185–6
Schwibach, Armin 379, 431
Sciarpelletti, Claudio 482
Scicluna, Charles 416
Scola, Cardinal Angelo 81, 400, 473
Sea of Galilee 323, 361, 526
Seckler, Max 44, 61, 66
Second Vatican Council 4, 7, 10–22, 29–30, 32, 37–9,
    41–5, 47, 56–60, 67, 69, 82, 85, 103, 112–14, 124, 126,
    152, 162, 194, 293, 330, 357, 497, 521, 539
    Apostolicam actuositatem 137
    and *Dominus Iesus* 233–4
    enemies of 112, 167, 186, 380, 385–7, 391
    50th anniversary 352, 393, 495, 508
    Gaudium et spes 15, 18
    Lumen gentium 54, 233
    Reconquista project 77–9
    and retirement 535–6
    and Tridentine Mass 363–4
Secretariat for Non-Believers 157
Securitate 83
Seemann, Father Michael 100
Seibel, Wolfgang 159, 164
Seibt, Gustav 321
Sellner, Albert 430
Semmelroth, Otto 71, 127
Šeper, Cardinal Franjo 131
Sepp, Benedikt 27
Sergius IV, Pope 281
Servants of the Immaculate Heart of Mary 419
sexual abuse *see* abuse scandals
Sgorbati, Leonella 339
Shah of Persia 24
Shevardnadze, Eduard 196
Silverius, Pope 499
Silvestrini, Cardinal Achille 212, 264–5
Simonis, Cardinal Adrianus 265
Sin, Cardinal Jaime 268

Singer, Israel 295, 391
Sinti people 109
Siri, Cardinal, 275
Sisters of Charity 203
Sisters of Mercy 105
Sistine Chapel 113–14, 119, 258, 261–2, 266, 268, 272–3,
    275–7, 280–1, 291–3, 302, 374
    camera delle lacrime 281
slavery 212, 358
Smith, Patti 283
Smoltczyk, Alexander 290, 351
Social Democratic Party (SPD) 342, 388
Socialist German Students' Society 3, 23, 53
Society for Faith Reform 34
Society of St Pius X 185–6, 312, 362–3, 380–98, 400,
    403, 449
Socrates 434
Sodano, Cardinal Angelo 190–1, 202, 243, 250–1, 254,
    275–6, 280, 330–1, 340, 372
    and abuse scandals 416, 425–6
    and Ratzinger's resignation 501, 510, 513
    and Vatileaks crisis 481
Söding, Thomas 369
Söhngen Gottlieb 4–5, 9, 127
Solidarność 121, 139–40, 199
Soloviev, Vladimir 73–4
Solzhenitsyn, Alexander 131
Somalo, Cardinal Eduardo Martínez 266, 416
Sophocles 277
Soviet Union, fall of 199
Spacey, Kevin 428
Spaemann, Heinrich 37
Spaemann, Robert 37, 84, 162, 191, 331, 393
Spanish Civil War 445
Spanish Inquisition 151
Špidlík, Cardinal Tomáš 273
Spiegel, Paul 295
Stahlschmidt, Father Klaus Günter 110
Stalin, Josef 26, 29, 216, 347
Stampa, Ingrid 305, 350–2, 482–4
Stangl, Bishop Josef 102
Star Wars 31
Stasi 24, 193
Stephen II, Pope 245
Sterzinsky, Cardinal Georg 318
Stimmen der Zeit 64, 159, 164
Stockhausen, Alma von 36, 86
Stoiber, Edmund 195
Strauss, Botho 201
Strauss, Franz Josef 142, 195
Strehhuber, Josef, 472
Streng, Franziskus von 7
Stricker, Gerd 198
Stuttgart Colloquium 127
Süddeutsche Zeitung 25, 28, 101, 108–9, 117, 126, 154, 159,
    172, 184, 192–3, 211, 221, 283, 289, 319, 321, 338–9,
    449, 452, 463
    and abuse scandals 422
    and Ratzinger's resignation 518
    and Vatileaks crisis 477
    and Williamson affair 385–6, 389
surrogate motherhood 176
Swedish Lutheran Church 35
Swiss Guards 114, 140, 149, 273, 487, 496, 531

Tacitus 229
Tagesspiel 421, 428, 463
Taizé community 124, 268, 324
Tantalus 92
Tedeschi, Ettore Gotti 437, 480

Tedesco, Antonio   317
Teresa, Mother   110, 459, 467
Tettamanzi, Cardinal Dionigi   275–6
Teufel, Frits   24
Tewes, Bishop Ernst   96, 102, 120
Theissing, Bishop Hermann   109
Thiessen, Rudi   394
Third Lateran Council   262
Third Order of St Francis   209
Third World   108, 136, 181, 289, 329, 367
Thomas More Academy   66
Thora, Dr Marianne   135
Three Kings shrine   325
Tirelli, Umberto   407
Tissier de Mallerais, Bishop Bernard   385
Titian   277
Tobiana, Sister   246, 252
Tomášek, Cardinal František   106
Tomko, Cardinal Jozef   475
Tornielli, Andrea   395
Torres, Camillo   177
Tracy, David   207
Traditional Anglican Communion (TAC)   411
Trapattoni, Giovanni   317
Treaty of Versailles   310
Treffpunkt Weltkirche   438
Tremblay, Réal   159, 190
Tridentine Mass   362–5, 390, 393, 447
Trimpe, Martin   32, 53–4
Trinity, doctrine of   63, 132
Trippen, Norbert   21
Tscherrig, Archbishop Emil Paul   382
Turi, Anna Maria   139
Twomey, Vincent   53, 55, 219, 419

Ulrich, Ferdinand   111
United Nations   294, 310, 357, 375–6, 411, 427, 452
UNESCO   495
UNICEF   427
Universal Declaration of Human Rights   376
Universi Dominici Gregis   261

Vaca, Juan   416
Valente, Gianni   15, 57
Van Gogh, Vincent   434
van Onna, Ben   32
Vargas Llosa, Mario   439, 517
Vatican Bank   116, 112, 437–8, 473, 480
Vatileaks   351, 380, 458–9, 470–86, 493, 502, 506, 524, 534
Vendola, Nichi   297
Venner, Fiammetta   382
Vermehren, Isa   37
Versace, Donatella   313
Verweyen, Hansjürgen   20, 61, 178
Vianney, Jean–Baptiste-Marie (the 'curé d'Ars')   413
Victor II, Pope   464
Victor, Ulrich   229
Vietnam War   3, 23, 48
Vietnamese refugees   109, 224
Viganò, Archbishop Carlo Maria   473, 477–8, 485
Villon, François   434
Villot, Jean   116
Virgil   355
viri probati   71
Visseyrias, Philippe   405
Vita e Famiglia   250
Volk, Cardinal Hermann   7, 127, 131
Voltaire   61
Voodoo   54
Vorgrimler, Herbert   125

Wailing Wall   229
Wałęsa, Lech   121, 199
Wallbaum, Klaus   217
Wallbrecher, Herbert   136
Wallbrecher, Traudl   136–7, 402
Walser, Martin   318
Walter, Franz   20, 22, 56, 136, 199, 429
Wansing, Sister Birgit   174, 478, 510
Watson, Paul   310
Watson, Peter   531
Weber, Ulrich   422
Weigel, George   457
Weinberger, Caspar   139
Weinstein, Harvey   428
Weiss, Franz   301
Weisser Ring   427
Weltenburg Monastery   51
Wensierski, Peter   447
Wenzl, Aloys   206
Werfel, Franz   378
West African Bishops' Conference   405
Wetter, Cardinal Friedrich   279, 299
Wickert, Ulrich   34
Wiedenhofer, Siegfried   8, 16, 43, 54–5, 60, 85, 94, 98, 194, 207
Wiesel, Elie   334
Wilcox, Ella Wheeler   222
Wild, Dr Heinrich   41
Williams, Archbishop Rowan   444, 508
Williamson, Bishop Richard   380–95, 399, 408–9, 418, 446, 457, 470
Winkler, Gerhard   52
Woelki, Cardinal   537
Wohlmuth, Josef   32
Wojtyla, Edmund   240
women   171, 175–6
   deacons   84
   ordination of   77, 191, 362, 462
Working Group for Evangelical Theology   321
World Alliance of Reformed Churches   435
World Bishops' Conference   300
World Council of Methodist Churches   226
World Family Day   334
World Jewish Congress   295
World Meeting of Families   505
World Migrants and Refugees Day   302
World Peace Day   453
World Synod of Bishops   134, 329
World Youth Days   229, 238, 245, 323–4, 327, 334, 375–6, 438, 446, 460, 503, 523
Wowereit, Klaus   463
Wulff, Christian   464, 466
Würzburg Synod   82, 84–5, 461
Wyszyński, Cardinal Stefan   118

Yad Vashem   229, 408
Yallop, David   116
Year of Faith   495, 508
Year of the Priest   413, 437, 462
Young Christian Workers   82

Zacchi, Archbishop Cesare   350
Zapatero, José Luis   406
Zeffirelli, Franco   297
Zen Ze-kiun, Cardinal   328
Zöhrer, Gisela   170
Zöhrer, Josef   53
Zola, Émile   126
Zollitsch, Archbishop Robert   461, 518
Zollner, Hans   432
Zwingli, Huldrych   475